Lecture Notes in Computer Science 906
Edited by G. Goos, J. Hartmanis and J. van Leeuwen

Egidio Astesiano Gianna Reggio
Andrzej Tarlecki (Eds.)

Recent Trends in Data Type Specification

10th Workshop on Specification of Abstract Data Types
Joint with the 5th COMPASS Workshop
S. Margherita, Italy, May 30 - June 3, 1994
Selected Papers

Springer

Series Editors

Gerhard Goos
Universität Karlsruhe
Vincenz-Priessnitz-Straße 3, D-76128 Karlsruhe, Germany

Juris Hartmanis
Department of Computer Science, Cornell University
4130 Upson Hall, Ithaca, NY 14853, USA

Jan van Leeuwen
Department of Computer Science, Utrecht University
Padualaan 14, 3584 CH Utrecht, The Netherlands

Volume Editors

Egidio Astesiano
Gianna Reggio
DISI – Dipartimento di Informatica e Scienze dell'Informazione
Università di Genova
Viale Benedetto XV, 3, I-16132 Genova, Italy

Andrzej Tarlecki
Institute of Informatics, Warsaw University
ul. Banacha 2, 02-097 Warsaw, Poland and
Institute of Computer Science, Polish Academy of Sciences
ul. Ordona 21, 01-237 Warsaw, Poland

CR Subject Classification (1991): D.2.1-2, D.2.4, D.2.10-m, D.3.1, F.3.1-2

ISBN 3-540-59132-X Springer-Verlag Berlin Heidelberg New York

CIP data applied for

Printed in Germany

Typesetting: Camera-ready by author
SPIN: 10485553 06/3142-543210 - Printed on acid-free paper

Preface

For more than twenty years by now algebraic specification has been an important area of research, aimed at providing foundations, methods and tools for formal development of provably-correct software. Workshops on Specification of Abstract Data Types, initiated in 1982, have become a prominent forum to present and discuss current research in the area. Since 1991 they have been held jointly with the General Workshops of the ESPRIT Basic Research Working Group COMPASS.

The 10th Workshop on Specification of Abstract Data Types was held jointly with the 5th COMPASS Workshop in Santa Margherita (about 30 km from Genova) on May 30 – June 3, 1994, and was organised by Egidio Astesiano, Gianna Reggio and Maura Cerioli.

The main topics covered by the workshop were:

- specification formalisms, languages and associated tools,
- term rewriting and theorem proving,
- algebraic specifications of concurrent systems,
- algebraic models and specifications of object systems,
- algebraic structures and their logics.

The program consisted of 63 presentations describing ongoing research and of 4 invited lectures by Catriel Beeri, Harald Ganzinger, Josè Meseguer and Martin Wirsing, mainly surveying established approaches, recent results, and directions of future work on different topics of primary importance within the area. The talks stimulated lively discussions, both directly after the presentations and during five one-hour discussion slots. The latter, chaired by Peter Mosses, Don Sannella, Manfred Broy, Hans-Dieter Ehrich and Egidio Astesiano, focused on some issues crucial for future developments within the area.

A Selection Committee, consisting of Egidio Astesiano, Marie-Claude Gaudel, Hans-Dieter Ehrich, Hartmut Ehrig, Hélène Kirchner, Gianna Reggio, Horst Reichel, Don Sannella and Andrzej Tarlecki, chose a number of presentations and invited their authors to submit a written version of their talks for possible publication in the workshop proceedings. All the submissions underwent a careful refereeing process and were extensively discussed (by e-mail) by the Selection Committee during a final acceptance/rejection round. This resulted in the selection of 23 papers that appear in this volume together with written versions of the four invited surveys.

We are extremely grateful to all the workshop participants, to the (other) members of the Selection Committee and to the following referees

M. Baldamus, M. Białasik, L. Campora, M. Cerioli, S. Conrad, F. Cornelius, G. Costa, G. Denker, E. Domenjoud, M. Gogolla, M. Grosse-Rhode, M. Hofmann, S. Kahrs, C. Kirchner, B. Konikowska, M. Korff, P. Le Gall, H.C.R. Lock, C. Lynch, E. Moggi, F. Morando, A. Pierantonio, B. Reus, L. Ribeiro, C. Ringeissen, G. Snelting, M. Srebrny, G. Taentzer, T.H. Tse, A. Wagner, U. Wolter, E. Zucca,

for their contribution to the scientific quality of the workshop and of this volume.

We also wish to thank Maura Cerioli, Ombretta Arvigo and Laura Montanari for their invaluable and friendly help with the workshop organisation.

Finally, we would like to thank Martin Gogolla, who has prepared, with some help from Maura Cerioli, a comprehensive bibliography of the talks and papers given at the ten Workshops on Specification of Abstract Data Types so far; the bibliography appears at the end of this volume.

The workshop was sponsored by DISI (Dipartimento di Informatica e Scienze dell'Informazione)-Università di Genova, and received financial support from the ESPRIT Basic Research Working Group COMPASS and CNR (Consiglio Nazionale delle Ricerche)-GNIM.

Egidio Astesiano, Genova
Gianna Reggio, Genova
Andrzej Tarlecki, Warsaw

Table of Contents

Invited Papers

Contributed Papers

Combining Algebra and Universal Algebra in First-Order Theorem Proving: The Case of Commutative Rings*

Leo Bachmair**
Harald Ganzinger***
Jürgen Stuber***

Abstract. We present a general approach for integrating certain mathematical structures in first-order equational theorem provers. More specifically, we consider theorem proving problems specified by sets of first-order clauses that contain the axioms of a commutative ring with a unit element. Associative-commutative superposition forms the deductive core of our method, while a convergent rewrite system for commutative rings provides a starting point for more specialized inferences tailored to the given class of formulas. We adopt ideas from the Gröbner basis method to show that many inferences of the superposition calculus are redundant. This result is obtained by the judicious application of the simplification techniques afforded by convergent rewriting and by a process called symmetrization that embeds inferences between single clauses and ring axioms.

1 Introduction

1.1 Motivation

Specifications of programs include both symbols with their usual mathematical meaning as well as additional function symbols that correspond to program entities. Axioms such as

$$\forall l : \texttt{sum}(\texttt{mapSquare}(l)) \geq 0$$

$$\forall x, l : \texttt{mapSquare}(x : l) = x * x : \texttt{mapSquare}(l)$$

where **mapSquare** is supposed to square the elements of a list and **sum** computes the sum of the elements of a list, involve symbols such as $+$, $*$, $\geq$ or 0 with their

* The research described in this paper was supported in part by the NSF under research grant INT-9314412, by the German Ministry for Research and Technology (Bundesministerium für Forschung und Technologie) under grant ITS 9102/ITS 9103 and by the ESPRIT Basic Research Working Group 6112 (COMPASS).
** Department of Computer Science, SUNY at Stony Brook, Stony Brook, NY 11794, U.S.A. `leo@cs.sunysb.edu`
*** Max-Planck-Institut für Informatik, Im Stadtwald, D-66123 Saarbrücken, Germany. `{hg|juergen}@mpi-sb.mpg.de`

standard mathematical meaning in addition to the functions of the program of which some behaviour is expressed.

Specifications based on standard mathematical structures, such as linear orderings, rings, or fields, require specially designed reasoning methods. A naive approach whereby one simply adds an axiomatization of a structure (e.g., the axioms of a commutative ring or the axioms of a linear order) to a specification and searches for proofs according to some universal deductive mechanism, such as resolution or paramodulation, is not very useful in practice. The axioms of the standard structure, both by themselves and in interaction with the axioms for program functions, usually create a huge search space. Consequently, in such theorem proving methods the additional knowledge provided by an embedded mathematical domain, which typically simplifies a mathematician's proof search, invariably clutters up the search space, so that many automated provers will no longer be able to find certain proofs they had been finding before.

A more promising approach appears to be the integration of decision procedures into heuristic provers and into resolution- or paramodulation-based provers, as this may allow one to more effectively cut down the proof search space. Some success has been obtained in limited scenarios. For example, replacing syntactic unification by unification modulo an equational theory allows one to effectively deal with certain classes of equational theories. Commutative semigroups have been extensively treated in approaches such as associative-commutative completion and their extensions to paramodulation-based calculi for first-order logic. This method is limited in that most nontrivial equational theories do not admit effective equation solving. But even for finitary and effectively solvable theories the number of unifiers may be excessively large, e.g., doubly exponential in the case of associativity and commutativity theories, which in fact presents a major obstacle to applying existing associative-commutative provers in practice.

Constraint-based theorem proving (Bürckert 1990, Kirchner, Kirchner and Rusinowitch 1990) is an alternative approach that is mainly applicable to hierarchic specifications, where new function symbols are defined persistently (with no junk and no confusion) over the primitive standard structures; see also (Bachmair, Ganzinger and Waldmann 1994). In requirement specifications where one may not want to define the new functions explicitly, these conditions are hardly ever met in practice. As a result, a constraint solver for the primitive theory can not be simply added as a black box, and even in cases where the new function symbols are completely defined in terms of the primitive ones, the (typically, mutually recursive) interaction between the prover and the constraint solver may present serious complications, see Boyer and Moore (1988) for a discussion of these issues in the context of their heuristic prover. The prover PVS (Owre, Rushby and Shankar 1992) is another instance where decision procedures are integrated in a heuristic manner, in this case using ideas of Nelson and Oppen (1979). In this paper we will not only be concerned with the practical aspects of such integration but also with questions of completeness of the resulting methods. Our results apply to specifications in which function symbols need not be completely defined in terms of the given primitive, mathematical symbols.

1.2 Our Approach

The deductive core of our method is a refutational, clausal-based inference system. We attempt to prove that a formula is a theorem by showing that the set consisting of its negation plus all axioms is unsatisfiable. All formulas are assumed to be in clause form. More specifically, we consider sets of clauses $N \cup R$, where R is a clausal axiomatization of the theory of commutative rings with a unit element and the clauses in N specify properties of uninterpreted function symbols.

The theorem proving method we design is *saturation-based*, like resolution and paramodulation (but unlike model elimination and other goal-oriented methods). In saturation-based methods, inferences are applied exhaustively to given clauses until either a contradiction (the empty clause) is obtained or else no further inferences are possible (and the final set is saturated). A saturation-based prover may be thought of as computing a mapping C from clause sets to clause sets, with the property that $\mathsf{C}(N)$ contains the empty clause if, and only if, N is unsatisfiable. If N is satisfiable, $\mathsf{C}(N)$ may be finite or infinite, but in either case will be closed under the given inferences. In our previous work on this subject (Bachmair and Ganzinger 1994c) we have developed a concept of *redundancy* and a refined notion of *saturation up to redundancy* so as to be able to model simplification mechanisms, such as subsumption, tautology deletion, and rewriting, that are indispensable for the efficiency of theorem provers. The refined notion of saturation does not require the application of non-redundant inferences or inferences from redundant clauses. This work is of particular relevance to the present paper as it provides the right framework for the specialized techniques we propose for dealing with certain built-in mathematical structures.

Finite, consistent sets $\mathsf{C}(N)$ often provide a basis for efficient theorem provers for the theory represented by N. An example are convergent rewrite systems, which are saturated under superposition and allow the validity of equations to be determined by (non-deterministic) rewriting. If a given clause set N can not be finitely saturated, it may still be possible to saturate some subset of N. For instance, if the given clause set is $N \cup R$, and R can be saturated, we may "partially evaluate" the saturation function and replace R by $\mathcal{R}$. The saturation of the partially evaluated set $N \cup \mathcal{R}$ then involves only inferences where at least one premise comes from N. The main inferences in our deductive calculus are binary, i.e., have two premises. Further analysis may be profitable also for "mixed" inferences with one premise from N and one from $\mathcal{R}$. If, for a clause C, one can find a set $\mathcal{S}(C)$, such that $\mathcal{S}(C) \cup \mathcal{R}$ is saturated, then no explicit inferences need to be made with C, but C may be replaced by $\mathcal{S}(C)$. This may pay off if the mapping $\mathcal{S}$ can be more efficiently computed by a special-purpose device than by off-the-shelf saturation. We will describe, for the case of commutative rings, such a function $\mathcal{S}$, called *symmetrization*, that maps any ground clause to a finite set, and design inference rules to enumerate possibly infinite sets $\mathcal{S}(C)$ for non-ground clauses. A key ingredient of the symmetrization process is the use of $\mathcal{R}$ for simplification of clauses in N. Such simplification also cuts down on the number of inferences between two clauses in N.

In sum, our approach aims at a refinement of the general saturation scheme in which the axioms of a built-in theory are replaced by more efficient special-purpose inferences that may be used for (don't-care nondeterministic) simplification.

1.3 The Case of Commutative Rings

We apply this methodology to commutative rings and present the ring structure by a convergent rewrite system. For the free commutative ring over a set of constants the word problem can be decided by applying a specialized variant of the Gröbner basis method (Buchberger 1965, Buchberger 1985, Kandri-Rody and Kapur 1988). We essentially embed this procedure in the more general context of languages with additional function symbols other than constants. Though decidability is lost for the extended languages, our goal is to adapt the techniques for the more specialized decision procedures and replace inferences with ring axioms by deterministic simplification procedures.

We do not simply use the Gröbner basis method as a black box, but achieve its integration with the general-purpose deductive mechanism of superposition on the level of the inference systems. That is, we use a rewrite-based reformulation of the Gröbner basis method to manipulate formulas in a way so as to cut down the number of general superposition inferences. More specifically, we attempt to eliminate the addition function from terms that need to be considered for superposition (and hence would require associative-commutative unification). For example, during the computation of a Gröbner basis a polynomial equation

$$xy^2z + 2xy = x + 3$$

is transformed into a rewrite rule

$$xy^2z \to -2xy + x + 3$$

with a monomial on its left-hand side. The effect is that inferences with rules, which depend only on left-hand sides, need not deal with addition. Symmetrization is the generalization of this transformation of a polynomial equation into a rule. It is the key idea in combining universal algebra and algebra "on the level of inferences." To make it work sufficiently well and to be able to obtain interesting theoretical results, such as refutational completeness, a number of technical problems need to be solved.

Most importantly, even though the elimination of occurrences of addition in the manner indicated above is readily seen to be logically sound, one needs to show that the transformation is compatible with the superposition calculus in the sense that refutational completeness is preserved. The problem looks deceptively simple, but is non-trivial. It is at this point that our concept of redundancy proves to be very useful. Refutational completeness, as we will see, is preserved if the transformation of a formula can be justified by *smaller* formulas with respect to an appropriate ordering on clauses. One of the main technical problems is to find a suitable ordering. A closely related problem is that of selecting an appropriate canonical presentation of the ring axioms.

Another problem is that we need to deal with clauses with variables, whereas polynomials, as manipulated in the Gröbner basis method, are essentially ground expressions (the indeterminates in a polynomial are constants in the logical sense). Many simplification steps on the ground level can not be replicated on the general level and need to be approximated via specially designed inference rules.

2 Preliminaries

2.1 Clauses

We consider first-order languages with equality as the only predicate symbol. Thus the only atomic formulas are equalities between terms built from variables and function symbols.[4] An important tool in our proposed theorem proving method are well-founded orderings. We typically specify such an ordering on the term level and then uniformly extend it to formulas and clauses via multiset extensions. Therefore we formally define formulas and clauses in terms of multisets.

By an *atomic formula* (or *atom*) we mean a multiset (of multisets) $\{\{s\},\{t\}\}$, called an *equality* and usually written $s \approx t$, where s and t are terms.[5] Equalities are also called *positive literals*, whereas by a *negative* literal we mean a multiset $\{\{s,t\}\}$, written $s \not\approx t$ or $\neg(s \approx t)$. A *clause* is a finite multiset of literals. We write a clause as a disjunction $\neg A_1 \vee \cdots \vee \neg A_m \vee B_1 \cdots \vee B_n$. An expression is said to be *ground* if it contains no variables.

2.2 Reduction Orderings

A (strict) *ordering* is a transitive and irreflexive binary relation; a *quasi-ordering*, a reflexive and transitive binary relation. A *rewrite relation* is a binary relation $\succ$ on terms such that $s \succ t$ implies $u[s\sigma] \succ u[t\sigma]$, for all terms s, t, $u[s\sigma]$, and $u[t\sigma]$ in the given domain.[6] An *equivalence* (*relation*) is a reflexive, transitive, and symmetric binary relation. A *congruence* (*relation*) is an equivalence such that $s \sim t$ implies $u[s] \sim u[t]$, for all terms s, t, $u[s]$, and $u[t]$ in the given domain.

The reflexive closure of a strict ordering is a quasi-ordering. On the other hand, for any quasi-ordering $\succeq$ we may define a corresponding equivalence ($s \sim t$ if $s \succeq t$ and $t \succeq s$) and strict ordering ($s \succ t$ if $s \succeq t$ but not $t \succeq s$). A quasi-ordering thus induces a strict ordering on the equivalence classes defined by its associated equivalence. Formally, we will be dealing mainly with quasi-orderings

---

[4] Non-equality atoms $P(t_1,\ldots,t_n)$ can be represented by equating them to a distinguished constant $\top$ (that is of a different sort than the ordinary terms t_i).

[5] The symmetry of equality is thus built into the notation.

[6] In our notation for terms we follow Dershowitz and Jouannaud (1990).

with associated equivalences containing a given associative-commutative equational theory. But for simplicity, we will usually specify the strict part of the ordering only.

A *rewrite ordering* is an ordering that is also a rewrite relation. A well-founded rewrite ordering is called a *reduction ordering*. (A binary relation $\succ$ is *well-founded* if there is no infinite sequence $t_1 \succ t_2 \succ \ldots$ of elements.)

Any ordering $\succ$ on a set S can be extended to an ordering on finite multisets over S (which for simplicity we also denote by $\succ$) as follows: $M \succ N$ if (i) $M \neq N$ and (ii) whenever $N(x) > M(x)$ then $M(y) > N(y)$, for some y such that $y \succ x$. (Here $>$ denotes the usual "greater-than" relation on the natural numbers.) If $\succ$ is a total (resp. well-founded) ordering, so is its multiset extension. If $\succ$ is an ordering on terms, then its twofold multiset extension is an ordering on literals, and its threefold multiset extension, an ordering on clauses. We usually use the same symbol to denote an ordering $\succ$ on terms and its corresponding extensions to literals and clauses. Note that our definition of positive and negative literals guarantees that $\neg A \succ A$, for all atoms A.

2.3 Herbrand Interpretations

A *(Herbrand) interpretation* is a set I of ground atomic formulas. We say that an atom A is *true* (and $\neg A$ *false*) *in* I if $A \in I$; and that A is *false* (and $\neg A$ *true*) in I if $A \notin I$. A ground clause is *true* in an interpretation I if at least one of its literals is true in I; and is *false* otherwise. A (non-ground) clause is said to be true in I if all its ground instances are true. The *empty clause* is false in every interpretation. We say that I is a *model* of a set of clauses N (or that N is *satisfied* by I) if all elements of N are true in I. A clause C is called a *logical consequence* of N if C is true in all models of N. A set N is *satisfiable* if it has a model, and *unsatisfiable* otherwise. For instance, any set containing the empty clause is unsatisfiable.

We denote by RA the set consisting of the reflexivity axiom $x \approx x$, by T the set consisting of the transitivity axiom $x \not\approx y \vee y \not\approx z \vee x \approx z$, and by F the set consisting of all congruence axioms $x \not\approx y \vee f(\ldots, x, \ldots) \approx f(\ldots, y, \ldots)$ where f ranges over all function symbols.

An interpretation is called an *equality interpretation* if it satisfies $RA \cup T \cup F$. (Recall that symmetry is already built into the notation.) We say that I is an *equality model* of N if it is an equality interpretation satisfying N. A set N is *equality satisfiable* if it has an equality model, and *equality unsatisfiable* otherwise. It can be shown that a set of clauses is equality satisfiable in our sense if and only if it is has a standard first-order model in which equality is interpreted as identity.

2.4 Associative-Commutative Rewriting

We have to reason about the satisfiability of clause sets $N \cup R \cup AC$, where $R \cup AC$ is a clausal specification of commutative rings. We describe Herbrand interpretations by (ground) rewrite systems; deal with interpretations indirectly, via rewriting; and design general inference rules that reflect these rewrite manipulations. The form of rewriting most appropriate for the class of problems we consider is associative-commutative rewriting.

If I is an equality interpretation then the set of all pairs (s,t) for which $s \approx t$ is true in I is a congruence relation on ground terms. Conversely, if $\sim$ is a congruence relation, then the set of all ground atoms $s \approx t$, for which $s \sim t$, is an equality interpretation. In short, equality interpretations can be described by congruence relations. Rewrite systems provide an effective tool for dealing with congruence relations.

A *rewrite system* is a binary relation on terms. The elements of a rewrite system are called (*rewrite*) *rules* and written $s \rightarrow t$. If R is a rewrite system, we denote by $\rightarrow_R$ the smallest rewrite relation containing R. The transitive-reflexive closure of $\rightarrow_R$ is denoted by $\rightarrow_R^*$; while $\leftrightarrow_R^*$ denotes the smallest congruence relation containing R. A rewrite system R is said to be *terminating* if the rewrite relation $\rightarrow_R$ is well-founded.

A function symbol f is said to be *associative* if it satisfies the axiom

$$f(x, f(y,z)) \approx f(f(x,y),z)$$

and *commutative* if it satisfies

$$f(x,y) \approx f(y,x).$$

Let AC be a set of such axioms. We write $f \in AC$, if AC contains the associativity and commutativity axioms for f, and also use AC to denote the set of rewrite rules $f(x, f(y,z)) \rightarrow f(f(x,y),z)$ and $f(x,y) \rightarrow f(y,x)$. We say that two terms u and v are *AC-equivalent* if $u \leftrightarrow_{AC}^* v$.

A reduction ordering $\succ$ is *AC-compatible* if $u' \leftrightarrow_{AC}^* u \succ v \leftrightarrow_{AC}^* v'$ implies $u' \succ v'$, for all terms u, u', v, and v'. If $\succ$ is AC-compatible, we write $u \succeq v$ to indicate that $u \succ v$ or $u \leftrightarrow_{AC}^* v$. We say that a rewrite system R is *AC-terminating* if it is contained in an AC-compatible reduction ordering.

Associativity and commutativity are built into rewriting via matching. If R is a rewrite system, we denote by $AC\backslash R$ the set of all rules $u' \rightarrow v\sigma$, such that $u' \leftrightarrow_{AC}^* u\sigma$ for some rule $u \rightarrow v$ in R and some substitution σ. The rewrite relation $\rightarrow_{AC\backslash R}$ corresponds to rewriting by R via AC-matching. We say that a term t can be *rewritten* (*modulo AC*), or is *AC-reducible*, if $t \rightarrow_{AC\backslash R} t'$. Terms that cannot be rewritten are said to be in *(AC-)normal form* or *(AC-)irreducible* (with respect to R). We write $u \downarrow_{AC\backslash R} v$ if u and v can be rewritten to AC-equivalent terms, i.e., if there exist terms u' and v' such that $u \rightarrow_{AC\backslash R}^* u' \leftrightarrow_{AC}^* v' \leftarrow_{AC\backslash R}^* v$. If R is AC-terminating and we have $u \downarrow_{AC\backslash R} v$, for all terms u and v with $u \leftrightarrow_{AC\cup R}^* v$, then R is called *AC-convergent*.

It is a standard result from the theory of term rewriting (see Dershowitz and Jouannaud 1990 for details and further references) that an AC-terminating rewrite system R is AC-convergent if (i) $u \downarrow_{AC\backslash R} v$ whenever $u \leftarrow_{AC\backslash R} t \leftrightarrow_{AC} v$ (a property called *local AC-coherence* of R) and (ii) $u \downarrow_{AC\backslash R} v$ whenever $u \leftarrow_{AC\backslash R} t \rightarrow_R v$ (a property called *local AC-confluence* of R).

Any rewrite system R can easily be extended to a locally AC-coherent system by a technique proposed by Peterson and Stickel (1981). An *extended rule* is a rewrite rule of the form $f(x,u) \to f(x,v)$, where $f \in AC$, u is a term $f(s,t)$, and x is a variable not occurring in u or v. We also say that $f(x,u) \to f(x,v)$ is an *extension* of $u \to v$. If R is a rewrite system, we denote by R^e the set R plus all extensions of rules in R. Any rewrite system R^e is locally AC-coherent: if $u \leftarrow_{AC\backslash R^e} t \leftrightarrow_{AC} v$, then $u \leftrightarrow^*_{AC} u' \leftarrow_{AC\backslash R^e} v$, for some term u'.

Checking for local AC-confluence is more difficult and usually involves the computation of so-called AC-critical pairs, which are obtained by the inference rule of AC-Superposition described next.

3 Associative-Commutative Superposition

3.1 Preliminaries

Two key aspects of the clause sets we have to deal with are the presence of equality and of associative-commutative function symbols. The standard inference system for dealing with equality in a clausal setting is paramodulation. The calculus we use as the deductive basis for our method is associative-commutative superposition (Bachmair and Ganzinger 1993). Superposition, as presented in (Bachmair and Ganzinger 1994c), is a refinement of paramodulation in which inferences are controlled by a selection function and a reduction ordering.

We call a literal L *maximal* in a clause $C \vee L$ if $L \not\prec L'$ for all literals L' in C. A *selection function* is a mapping that assigns to each clause a subset (possibly empty) of its negative literals. These negative literals are said to be *selected*. We assume that at least one literal is selected in each clause in which the maximal literal is negative. No literal needs to be selected in a clause whose maximal literal is positive. We say that a clause $C \vee s \approx t$ is *reductive* for $s \approx t$ (with respect to $\succ$) if there exists a ground instance $(C \vee s \approx t)\sigma$ such that $s\sigma \succ t\sigma$ and $(s \approx t)\sigma \succ C\sigma$ and no literal in C is selected. A clause C is called *universally reductive* if all ground instances of C are reductive and no literal in C is selected.

We say that $C \vee f(x,s) \approx f(x,t)$ is an *extension* of $C \vee s \approx t$ if $f \in AC$, s is a term $f(u,v)$, $C \vee s \approx t$ is reductive for $s \approx t$ and x is a variable not occurring in C, s, or t. In this case $C \vee f(x,s) \approx f(x,t)$ is called an *extended clause*. In an extended clause no literal may be selected.

Associativity and commutativity are built into the inference rules via AC-unification. Two terms u and v are *AC-unifiable* if $u\sigma \overset{*}{\leftrightarrow}_{AC} v\sigma$, for some substitution σ. If two terms u and v are AC-unifiable, then there exists a *complete set of AC-unifiers* $CSU_{AC}(u,v)$, such that for any substitution σ with $u\sigma \overset{*}{\leftrightarrow}_{AC} v\sigma$ there exist substitutions $\tau \in CSU_{AC}(u,v)$ and ρ, such that $x\sigma \overset{*}{\leftrightarrow}_{AC} (x\tau)\rho$, for all variables x in u and v. We assume that a function CSU_{AC} is given.

3.2 Inference Rules

The calculus $S^{\succ}_{AC}$ consists of the following inference rules. We assume that the premises of an inference share no common variables. If necessary the variables in one premise need to be renamed.

AC-Superposition

$$\frac{C \vee p \approx q \qquad D \vee u[p'] \approx r}{(C \vee D \vee u[q] \approx r)\sigma}$$

where (i) $\sigma \in CSU_{AC}(p, p')$, (ii) the clause $(C \vee p \approx q)\sigma$ is reductive for $(p \approx q)\sigma$, (iii) the clause $(D \vee u \approx r)\sigma$ is reductive for $(u \approx r)\sigma$, and (iv) p' is not a variable.

Negative AC-Superposition

$$\frac{C \vee p \approx q \qquad D \vee u[p'] \not\approx r}{(C \vee D \vee u[q] \not\approx r)\sigma}$$

where (i) $\sigma \in CSU_{AC}(p, p')$, (ii) the clause $(C \vee p \approx q)\sigma$ is reductive for $(p \approx q)\sigma$, (iii) $u[p'] \not\approx r$ is a selected literal in $D \vee u[p'] \not\approx r$, (iv) $u\sigma \not\preceq r\sigma$, and (v) p' is not a variable.

Reflective AC-Resolution

$$\frac{C \vee p \not\approx q}{C\sigma}$$

where (i) $\sigma \in CSU_{AC}(p, q)$, and (ii) $p \not\approx q$ is a selected literal in the premise.

AC-Factoring

$$\frac{C \vee p \approx q \vee p' \approx q'}{(C \vee q \not\approx q' \vee p' \approx q')\sigma}$$

where (i) $\sigma \in CSU_{AC}(p, p')$, (ii) $q\sigma \not\preceq q'\sigma$, (iii) the literal $(p \approx q)\sigma$ is maximal in $C\sigma$, and (iv) the premise contains no selected literals.

The calculus $S^{\succ}_{AC}$ is refutationally complete for clause sets $N \cup AC$. Other paramodulation-based calculi with built-in associativity and commutativity (Wertz 1992, Nieuwenhuis and Rubio 1994, Vigneron 1994) also embed relatively sophisticated control techniques in their inference rules. However, the efficiency of theorem provers usually depends not so much on the deductive inference rules that are employed than on the simplification mechanisms it implements. The concept of redundancy described next is sufficiently general and also flexible enough so that all necessary simplification techniques can be formulated conveniently.

3.3 Redundancy

Simplification techniques, such as tautology deletion, subsumption, demodulation, contextual rewriting, etc., represent an essential component of automated theorem provers. These techniques are based on a concept of redundancy (Bachmair and Ganzinger 1994c), which we have adapted to the AC-case in (Bachmair and Ganzinger 1993). The notion of redundancy will be of particular importance in the context of theorem proving for clause sets $N \cup R \cup AC$, as it will enable us to apply simplification techniques for ring theory in a meaningful way to the general clauses in N. In essence, we will extend techniques employed in constructing Gröbner bases for commutative rings to first-order clauses.

For any ground term p, let $T_{\preceq p}$ be the set of all ground instances $p_1 \not\approx p_2 \vee p_2 \not\approx p_3 \vee p_1 \approx p_3$ of the transitivity axiom for which $p \succeq p_i$ for $i \in 1 \ldots 3$; and $T_{\prec p}$ be the set of all ground instances for which $p \succ p_i$ for $i \in 1 \ldots 3$.

Let N be a set of clauses and C be a ground clause. Our intention is to specify when C is not needed for a potential refutation of $N \cup AC$. A ground clause C (which need not be an instance of N) is said to be *AC-redundant* with respect to N (and ordering $\succ$) if there exist ground instances $C_1, \ldots, C_k$ of N, such that $C \succ C_j$ for all $j \in 1 \ldots k$, and C is true in every model of $AC \cup RA \cup F \cup T_{\preceq p} \cup \{C_1, \ldots, C_k\}$, where p is the maximal term in C. A non-ground clause is called AC-redundant if all its ground instances are.

We emphasize that AC-redundancy is defined with respect to arbitrary interpretations, not just equality interpretations. In particular, there are restrictions on the use of the transitivity axiom. The restrictions are of more theoretical than practical significance, as all the simplification techniques that we will need can be formalized using AC-redundancy. In (Wertz 1992) and (Nieuwenhuis and Rubio 1994) a different notion of redundancy is used, where restrictions are imposed, not on transitivity, but instead on the use of the associativity and commutativity axioms. Our definition has the advantage that reduction modulo AC is a simplification, even in cases where the maximal term of a clause is reduced.

For example, consider the (unit) clauses $s[u'] \approx t$ and $u \approx v$, where $u' \leftrightarrow^*_{AC} u\sigma$, for some substitution σ. If $u\sigma \succ v\sigma$ and either $s \succ u\sigma$ or else $t \succ v\sigma$, then $s[u'] \approx t$ is AC-redundant with respect to any set N containing $u \approx v$ and $s[v\sigma] \approx t$. In practice, this allows one to replace $s[u'] \approx t$ by $s[v\sigma] \approx t$ in the presence of the equation $u \approx v$. In other words, the subterm u' can be rewritten modulo AC to a smaller term $v\sigma$. Simplification by rewriting modulo AC is admissible.

Let π be a ground inference with conclusion B and maximal premise C and let p be the maximal term in C. We say that π is *AC-redundant* with respect to N if there exist ground instances $C_1, \ldots, C_k$ of N, such that (a) B is true in every model of $AC \cup RA \cup F \cup T_{\prec p} \cup \{C_1, \ldots, C_k\}$, and either (b.i) both premises of π are ground instances of extended clauses and $\{\{\{p\}\}\} \succ C_j$,[7] for all j, or else (b.ii) $C \succ C_j$, for all j. A non-ground inference is called AC-redundant if all its ground instances are AC-redundant.

One way to render an inference in $\mathsf{S}^{\succ}_{AC}$ redundant is to add its conclusion to the set N. Thus, one may saturate any given set of clauses by systematically computing all possible inferences. (Since new clauses may enable new inferences, this process may continue indefinitely and result in an infinite saturated set.)

We say that a set of clauses N is *saturated up to AC-redundancy* if all inferences, the premises of which are non-redundant clauses in N or extensions of non-redundant clauses in N, are AC-redundant.

---

[7] Note that $\{\{\{p\}\}\} \succ C_j$ simply means that all terms in C_j are smaller than p.

Theorem 1 Bachmair and Ganzinger 1993. *Let N be a set of clauses that is saturated up to AC-redundancy with respect to the associative-commutative superposition calculus $\mathsf{S}^{\succ}_{AC}$. Then $N \cup AC$ is equality unsatisfiable if and only if it contains the empty clause.*

This theorem provides the basis for our refutational theorem proving method. It formally establishes the refutational completeness of the calculus $\mathsf{S}^{\succ}_{AC}$. To determine whether a given set of clauses is unsatisfiable, simply saturate it. If the set is indeed unsatisfiable, the empty clause (a contradiction) will eventually be generated.

It may seem strange that extended clauses are redundant, but inferences with them are not. But note that the above theorem requires extensions of *non-redundant* clauses only. Since extended clauses are redundant, extensions of extensions are consequently not needed. (It is important to avoid extensions of extensions, as the process may continue indefinitely and thus preclude the possibility of finitely saturating any non-trivial set of clauses.)

4 Commutative Rings

We assume that the first-order language under consideration contains function symbols 0, 1, $-$, $+$ and $\cdot$, which are intended to denote the operations of a commutative ring with unit, plus an additional constant -1 meant to denote $-(1)$. These are called *interpreted*, and all other function symbols are called *uninterpreted*. Also, terms with an interpreted or uninterpreted function symbol at the top will be called *interpreted* or *uninterpreted*, respectively. Moreover, we will also consider variables as uninterpreted terms.

The variety of commutative rings with a unit element can be specified by the set of equalities $R \cup AC$, where AC contains the associativity and commutativity axioms for addition and multiplication,

$$\begin{aligned} x + y &\approx y + x \\ x + (y + z) &\approx (x + y) + z \\ x \cdot y &\approx y \cdot x \\ x \cdot (y \cdot z) &\approx (x \cdot y) \cdot z \end{aligned}$$

and R is the set of equations

$$\begin{aligned} x + 0 &\approx x \\ -x + x &\approx 0 \\ x \cdot 1 &\approx x \\ x \cdot (y + z) &\approx (x \cdot y) + (x \cdot z) \end{aligned}$$

The defining equation for the constant -1 is

$$-(1) \approx -1.$$

Using standard techniques from associative-commutative rewriting, we obtain an AC-convergent rewrite system for the theory defined by the above equations. By $\mathcal{R}$ we denote the following set of rules:

$$x + 0 \rightarrow x \tag{1}$$
$$x \cdot 0 \rightarrow 0 \tag{2}$$
$$x \cdot 1 \rightarrow x \tag{3}$$
$$x \cdot (y + z) \rightarrow (x \cdot y) + (x \cdot z) \tag{4}$$
$$-x \rightarrow -1 \cdot x \tag{5}$$
$$1 + (-1) \rightarrow 0 \tag{6}$$
$$(-1) \cdot (-1) \rightarrow 1 \tag{7}$$
$$x + (-1 \cdot x) \rightarrow 0 \tag{8}$$

Lemma 2. *The rewrite system $\mathcal{R}^e$ is AC-convergent for the theory $R \cup AC$ over any language containing the function symbols from R plus any number of additional uninterpreted function symbols.*

The rewrite system $\mathcal{R}^e$ is similar to other convergent systems for commutative rings, except that we have extended the language by the constant -1 and rewrite $-x$ to a product, $-1 \cdot x$. From now on we may assume that terms and clauses do not contain the unary $-$ anymore.

Extensions are actually needed only for the rules (6)–(8), but not for (1)–(4). (The latter rules serve as their own extensions, so to say. For example, the extended rule $y + (x + 0) \rightarrow y + x$ is AC-equivalent to an instance, $(y + x) + 0 \rightarrow y + x$ of the original rule; for details see Bachmair 1991.)

From now on, we will denote arbitrary terms by p, q, r, u or v and uninterpreted terms by s or t. Terms of the form $t_1 \cdots t_m$ with all t_i different from -1 are called *products* and denoted by ϕ or ψ; terms of the form ϕ or $(-1) \cdot \phi$, *signed products* and denoted by μ or ν. In the notation for [signed] products we also admit $m = 0$, that is, a product denoted by ϕ may be 1, and a signed product μ may be 1 or -1. We often use juxtaposition to denote multiplication and simply write pq instead of $p \cdot q$. With this nomenclature, the normal forms defined by $\mathcal{R}^e$ are sums of signed products, $\mu_1 + \cdots + \mu_n$ where the uninterpreted terms in each signed product μ_i are in normal form. It should also be understood that we may have $n = 0$ in which case the sum is 0.

We will also use the following notation reminiscent of the algebraic notation for polynomials. If c is a positive integer and $t_1, \ldots, t_c$ are terms AC-equivalent to t, we write t^c to denote any product AC-equivalent to $t_1 \cdots t_c$ and ct to denote any sum AC-equivalent to $t_1 + \cdots + t_c$. Furthermore, we write dt, where d is the negative integer $-c$, to denote any sum AC-equivalent to $(-1)t_1 + \cdots + (-1)t_c$. Finally, if c is the number 0 and t is a product, then ct denotes 0 and $s + ct$ denotes s. For example, the term $((x \cdot f(x + y)) \cdot x) + ((x \cdot x) \cdot f(y + x))$ can be more concisely written as $2x^2 f(x + y)$.

If the given language contains no uninterpreted function symbols other than finitely many constants $X_1, \ldots, X_n$, then the *ground* expressions

$$c_1 X_1^{k_{11}} \cdots X_n^{k_{1n}} + \cdots + c_m X_1^{k_{m1}} \cdots X_n^{k_{mn}}$$

correspond to polynomials over indeterminates $X_1, \ldots, X_n$. We are specifically interested in adapting polynomial methods, such as Buchberger's algorithm for constructing Gröbner bases, to more general languages with function symbols and variables.

Termination

The AC-convergence of a rewrite system is established by three properties: local AC-coherence, local AC-confluence, and AC-termination. Extended rules ensure the first property. The second property requires checking of AC-critical pairs, which presents no difficulty in the case of $\mathcal{R}^e$; we refer the reader to the rewriting literature, e.g., (Dershowitz and Jouannaud 1990). For the third property we specify a suitable AC-compatible reduction ordering containing $\mathcal{R}$. This ordering will also play an important role in our deductive theorem proving method.

Theorem 3. *There exists an AC-compatible reduction ordering that is total up to AC on ground terms and contains all rewrite rules in $\mathcal{R}^e$.*

An ordering that fits the bill is any associative path ordering (APO, Bachmair and Plaisted 1985, Bachmair and Dershowitz 1986) based on a precedence on function symbols in which $f_1 \succ \cdots \succ f_n \succ - \succ -1 \succ 1 \succ 0 \succ \cdot \succ +$, where $f_1, \ldots, f_n$ are the given uninterpreted function symbols. Note that any such precedence is admissible for the associative path ordering, as there are no more than two AC-symbols and these are smaller than all other symbols. The uninterpreted function symbols may be listed in any order, but need to be assigned higher precedence than the interpreted symbols. Henceforth let $\succ$ be an APO based on such a precedence.

Convergent rewrite systems are also saturated:

Lemma 4. *$\mathcal{R}^e$ is saturated up to AC-redundancy with respect to $\mathsf{S}^{\succ}_{AC}$.*

In sum, the set $N \cup R \cup AC$ can be replaced by the equivalent set $N \cup \mathcal{R}^e \cup AC$. This provides us with at least two advantages. First, since $\mathcal{R}^e$ is already saturated, no further inferences need to be computed on it. (The replacement of R by $\mathcal{R}^e$ may also be thought of as a compilation process.) Secondly, the rewrite rules in $\mathcal{R}^e$ may be used to simplify clauses in N. The latter aspect will be discussed in the next section.

5 Specialized Simplification Techniques

So simplify the presentation for inferences, our meta-level notation will from now be modulo $AC1$ for $\cdot$ and $+$. That is, when we write $p = c\phi + p'$ then $c\phi$ denotes c products which are AC-equivalent to ϕ and which occur somewhere in the sum, not necessarily in front. Moreover, neither $c\phi$ nor p' need to be present. Thus p may also be of the form $c\phi$, p' or 0, depending on whether $p = 0$ and/or $c = 0$. Similarly, when we write $\phi = \phi_1\phi_2$ then ϕ_1 or ϕ_2 may be missing in which case $\phi_i = 1$.

This section lists the main simplifications such as cancellation that are afforded by the ring axioms. They are presented as rules of the

$$\frac{\{C\} \cup N}{\{D\} \cup N}.$$

Such a rule is called a *$\mathcal{R}$-simplification rule* whenever D is a logical consequence of $\{C\} \cup N \cup \mathcal{R}$ and C is AC-redundant in $\{D\} \cup N \cup \mathcal{R}$. A simplification rule, hence, denotes a legal move of the theorem prover during saturation by which C is replaced by D as the addition of D renders C redundant. Simplification rules may be applied eagerly in a don't care non-deterministic fashion without affecting refutational completeness.

In the simplification rules below, $\bowtie$ denotes either $\approx$ or $\not\approx$.

$\mathcal{R}$-Reduction $$\frac{\{u[l] \bowtie v \vee C\} \cup N}{\{u[r] \bowtie v \vee C\} \cup N}$$

if (i) $l \rightarrow_{AC\backslash\mathcal{R}^e} r$ and (ii) $u[l] \bowtie v \vee C \succ l \approx r$.

Cancellation $$\frac{\{c\phi + p \bowtie d\phi + q \vee C\} \cup N}{\{(c-d)\phi + p \bowtie q \vee C\} \cup N}$$

if (i) $|c| \geq |d| > 0$, and (ii) $\mathrm{sign}(c) = \mathrm{sign}(d)$.

Accumulation $$\frac{\{c\phi + p \bowtie -d\phi + q \vee C\} \cup N}{\{(c+d-1)\phi + p \bowtie (-1)\phi + q \vee C\} \cup N}$$

if $c \geq 1$ and $d \geq 2$.

Isolation $$\frac{\{c\phi + p \bowtie d\phi + q \vee C\} \cup N}{\{c\phi \bowtie d\phi + q + (-1)p \vee C\} \cup N}$$

if (i) $c > 0$ and $d = 0$ or $c = -1$ and $d \geq 0$, and (ii) $\phi \succ p$ and $\phi \succ q$.

Standardization $$\frac{\{(-1)\phi \approx q \vee C\} \cup N}{\{\phi \approx (-1)q \vee C\} \cup N}$$

if $\phi \approx (-1)q \vee C$ is universally reductive for $\phi \approx (-1)q$.

Lemma 5. *$\mathcal{R}$-Reduction, Cancellation, Accumulation, Isolation and Standardization are $\mathcal{R}$-simplification rules.*

Proof. This is easily verified. In the case of Standardization $\phi \approx (-1)q \vee C$ is used to reduce $(-1)\phi \approx q \vee C$. □

Note that for Accumulation $(c+1)\phi + p \bowtie q \vee C$ is in general *not* a simplification of $c\phi + p \bowtie (-1)\phi + q \vee C$. Although the former is smaller than the latter in the ordering on clauses, to prove $(c+1)\phi + p \bowtie q \vee C$ from $c\phi + p \bowtie -1\phi + q \vee C$ requires the instance $\phi + (-1)\phi \approx 0$ of $\mathcal{R}$, which is greater than $c\phi + p \bowtie -1\phi + q \vee C$.

6 Symmetrization

The *Symmetrization* of a ground clause C is the effect of partially saturating $\mathcal{R}^e \cup \{C\}$ until all inferences between the ring axioms and the original clause C, as well as the ones that have been derived from C as a result of the saturation process, become redundant. Symmetrization essentially consists of two phases. In the first phase, the clause is simplified until one of a few different so-called *sufficiently simplified* forms is reached. In the second phase, superposition inferences into $\mathcal{R}$ are taken care of by adding a suitable set of clauses.

6.1 Sufficiently Simplified Ground Clauses

In the previous section we have described a set of simplification rules which should be applied whenever possible. For a ground clause this will have the effect that, among others, the larger side of equations becomes irreducible by $\mathcal{R}^e$. Moreover, if $+$ occurs as the top symbol of the larger side, then the larger side is a sum of identical products, a monomial so to say. This syntactic form drastically restricts superposition inferences. Hence we would like to achieve this effect for all ground instances of any non-ground clause. It suffices to simplify those literals that may possibly engage in a superposition inference, and hence are either negative and selected, or else positive and contain the maximal product of their clause. To achieve our aim, certain instances of the above simplification rules will have to be lifted and restated as inferences that apply to general clauses. Before we actually define the lifted inferences, we shall first describe their ground instances. The additional ordering and selection restrictions avoid the computation of normal forms for literals that cannot engage in superposition.

Let p be a sum of signed products $c_1\phi_1 + \cdots + c_n\phi_n$ with coefficients c_i of the form 1 or -1. A signed product $c\psi$ is called *maximal in* p if $\psi \not\prec \phi_j$ for all j; and *strictly maximal in* p if $\psi \not\preceq \phi_j$ for all j. A signed product μ is called *maximal in a literal* $p \bowtie q$ if μ is maximal in p and q; and *maximal in a clause* C if μ is maximal in all literals of C. Note that on the ground level the ordering is total up to AC-equivalence. Thus the conditions for maximality or strict maximality translate to $\psi \succeq \phi_j$ or $\psi \succ \phi_j$, respectively.

Ground Product Reduction $$\frac{\mu[l] + p \bowtie q \vee C}{\mu[r] + p \bowtie q \vee C}$$

where (i) $l \rightarrow_{AC\backslash\mathcal{R}^e} r$, (ii) μ is maximal in p and q, and (iii) $\bowtie$ is $\not\approx$ and $\mu[l] + p \not\approx q$ is selected or else $\bowtie$ is $\approx$ and μ is maximal in C.

All the inferences are restricted so that only the selected literal or any positive literal that contains the maximal product of the premise needs to be considered. (iii), which formalizes this restriction, will apply, mutatis mutandis, to all the subsequent inferences and will, from now on, no longer be explicitly mentioned.

Ground Sum Contraction $$\frac{c\phi + (-d)\phi + p \bowtie q \vee C}{(c-d)\phi + p \bowtie q \vee C}$$

where (i) $c > 0$ and $d > 0$, (ii) ϕ is strictly maximal in p and maximal in q, and (iii) ϕ is irreducible with respect to $\mathcal{R}^e$.

Ground Cancellation $$\frac{c\phi + p \bowtie d\phi + q \vee C}{(c-d)\phi + p \bowtie q \vee C}$$

where (i) $|c| \geq |d| > 0$ and $\text{sign}(c) = \text{sign}(d)$, (ii) ϕ is strictly maximal in p and q, and (iii) ϕ is irreducible with respect to $\mathcal{R}^e$.

Ground Accumulation $$\frac{c\phi + p \bowtie -d\phi + q \vee C}{(c+d-1)\phi + p \bowtie (-1)\phi + q \vee C}$$

where (i) $c \geq 1$ and $d \geq 2$, (ii) ϕ is strictly maximal in p and q, and (iii) ϕ is irreducible with respect to $\mathcal{R}^e$.

Ground Isolation $$\frac{c\phi + p \bowtie d\phi + q \vee C}{c\phi \bowtie d\phi + q + (-1)p \vee C}$$

where (i) $c > 0$ and $d = 0$ or $c = -1$ and $d \geq 0$, (ii) ϕ is strictly maximal in p and q, and (iii) ϕ is irreducible with respect to $\mathcal{R}^e$.

Ground Standardization $$\frac{(-1)\phi \approx q \vee C}{\phi \approx (-1)q \vee C}$$

if (i) ϕ is irreducible with respect to $\mathcal{R}^e$, and (ii) $\phi \approx (-1)q \vee C$ is reductive for $\phi \approx (-1)q$.

With the exception of Ground Sum Reduction, the above inferences are special cases of the simplification rules in Section 5. Ground Sum Reduction can be obtained as a sequence of reductions with one of the inverse laws (6) or (8).

Applying these inferences exhaustively to a ground literal, we obtain an equivalent literal L in one of two possible so-called *sufficiently simplified forms* $L = c\phi \bowtie r$ or $L = (-1)\phi \bowtie (c-1)\phi + r$, with ϕ irreducible by $\mathcal{R}^e$, $\phi \succ r$, and $c > 0$. More generally, we call an arbitrary literal L *sufficiently simplified* if L is of the form $c\phi \bowtie r$ or $(-1)\phi \bowtie (c-1)\phi + r$, with ϕ irreducible by $\mathcal{R}^e$, ϕ strictly maximal in r, and $c > 0$. A (possibly non-ground) clause is called *sufficiently simplified* if it has a selected literal that is sufficiently simplified, or else if all positive literals that contain a maximal product are sufficiently simplified. The above inferences sufficiently simplify any given ground clause.

6.2 Superpositions into $\mathcal{R}$

We now analyze the critical pairs that are generated when $\{L\} \cup \mathcal{R}^e$ is saturated where L is a sufficiently simplified literal. $S(L)$, called the *symmetrization* of L, will denote the set of equations which we obtain, and is given below by a case analysis on the structure of L. Let L be of the form (i) $c\phi \approx r$ or else (ii) $(-1)\phi \approx (c-1)\phi + r'$, in which case we denote $(-1)r'$ by r. The definition of symmetrization will also apply to the non-ground case where we may have more than one strictly maximal product. Hence we only assume that ϕ is strictly maximal in L and irreducible by $\mathcal{R}^e$.

$$\mathcal{S}(L) = \{x \approx 0\} \qquad \text{if } c = 1 \text{ and } \phi = 1; \text{ or}$$

$$\mathcal{S}(L) = \{\phi \approx r\} \qquad \text{if } c = 1 \text{ and } \phi \neq 1; \text{ or}$$

$$\mathcal{S}(L) = \left\{ \begin{matrix} cx \approx 0 \\ (-1) \approx (c-1)1 \end{matrix} \right\} \qquad \text{if } c \geq 2 \text{ and } \phi = 1; \text{ or}$$

$$\mathcal{S}(L) = \left\{ \begin{matrix} c\phi \approx r \\ c(x \cdot \phi) \approx x \cdot r \\ (-1) \cdot \phi \approx (c-1)\phi + (-1)r \end{matrix} \right\} \text{ if } c \geq 2 \text{ and } \phi \neq 1.$$

If L is negative and of the above form there are no superpositions into positive literals. Since the maximal side $c\phi$ or $(-1)\phi$ of L is $\mathcal{R}^e$-reduced, there are also no superpositions into L by the rules in $\mathcal{R}^e$. Hence $\mathcal{S}(L)$ is simply defined as $\{L\}$.

Consider now a general clause C that is sufficiently simplified and of the form $C' \vee C''$ where either $C'' = L_1 = p \not\approx q$ and $p \not\approx q$ is selected in C; or else no literal is selected in C and $C'' = L_1 \vee \ldots \vee L_n$ contains all positive literals which contain the maximal product of C. As we have to symmetrize all the L_i, we define

$$\mathcal{S}(C) = \{\, C' \vee L_1^s \vee \ldots \vee L_n^s \mid L_i^s \in \mathcal{S}(L_i) \text{ for } i \in 1 \ldots n \,\}.$$

Symmetrization is defined only for clauses that are sufficiently simplified. A clause C is said to be *symmetrized* if it is in some $\mathcal{S}(D)$. Note that an AC-extension is needed for reductive clauses in $\mathcal{S}(C)$ where the maximal literal has a $+$ or $\cdot$ at the root of the left side. We shall also assume that if a literal is selected in C then the corresponding literal is selected in any of the symmetrizations of C.

Lemma 6. *If C is a ground clause then all superposition inferences in which one of the premises is in $\mathcal{S}(C)$ and the other is in $\mathcal{R}$ are redundant in $\mathcal{S}(C) \cup \mathcal{R}$.*

This lemma can be shown by a somewhat tedious but straightforward case analysis over all inferences.

6.3 Lifting Ground Simplification

In this section we are concerned with lifting ground simplification, which is the preparative step for symmetrization, to the non-ground level. The lifting becomes awkward in cases when a maximal product $xt_1 \ldots t_n$ in a sum contains a factor x that is just a variable. Such a variable may have to be instantiated with a sum of arbitrary length containing positive as well as negative terms. If $n \geq 1$ some of these instances will be computed by superposing with the distributivity rule, cf. Product Superposition below. For the remaining cases we will have to add an extra inference rule to achieve this effect. Clearly, application of these inferences, which are reminiscent of paramodulation with the functional-reflexive axioms for $+$ and $-$, needs to be controlled. It seems as if one could adopt a lazy strategy, by which these *unshielded occurrences* of a variable x are instantiated to a general sum just before they become instantiated by some other inference. For instance, cancelling ba on both sides of $xa \approx ba + c$ should produce $x'a \approx c$ rather than $0 \approx c$, representing the combined effect of instantiating x by $x' + x''$, unifying $x''a$ with ba and cancelling ba. Because of unshielded variables, cancellation and similar inferences have to proceed in a step-wise fashion.

Product Superposition $$\frac{\mu[l'] + p \bowtie q \vee C}{(\mu[r] + p \bowtie q \vee C)\sigma}$$

where (i) $l \to r$ is a rule in $\mathcal{R}^e$, (ii) $\sigma \in CSU_{AC}(l, l')$, (iii) l' is not a variable, (iv) $\mu\sigma$ is maximal in $p\sigma$ and $q\sigma$, and (v) $\bowtie$ is $\not\approx$ and $\mu[l'] + p \bowtie q$ is selected in $u[l'] + p \bowtie q \vee C$ or else $\bowtie$ is $\approx$ and $\mu\sigma$ is maximal in $C\sigma$.

Analogous to the ground case, the restriction (v), to the selected literal or to those positive literals that contain a maximal product, will, mutatis mutandis, apply to the subsequent inference rules. From now on, it will no longer be explicitly mentioned.

Sum Contraction 1 $$\frac{\mu + \phi + p \bowtie q \vee C}{(p \bowtie q \vee C)\sigma}$$

where (i) $\sigma \in CSU_{AC}(\mu, (-1)\phi)$, (ii) $\mu\sigma$ is maximal in $p\sigma$ and $q\sigma$, and (iii) $\mu\sigma$ is irreducible with respect to $\mathcal{R}^e$.

Sum Contraction 2 $$\frac{\mu_1 + \mu_2 + p \bowtie q \vee C}{(2\mu_1 + p \bowtie q \vee C)\sigma}$$

where (i) $\sigma \in CSU_{AC}(\mu_1, \mu_2)$, (ii) $\mu_1\sigma$ is maximal in $p\sigma$ and $q\sigma$, and (iii) $\mu_1\sigma$ is irreducible with respect to $\mathcal{R}^e$.

Cancellation $$\frac{\mu_1 + p \bowtie \mu_2 + q \vee C}{(p \bowtie q \vee C)\sigma}$$

where (i) $\sigma \in CSU_{AC}(\mu_1, \mu_2)$, (ii) $\mu_1\sigma$ is maximal in $p\sigma$ and $q\sigma$, and (iii) $\mu_1\sigma$ is irreducible with respect to $\mathcal{R}^e$.

Accumulation $$\frac{p \bowtie (-1)\phi_1 + (-1)\phi_2 + q \vee C}{(\phi_1 + p \bowtie (-1)\phi_1 + q \vee C)\sigma}$$

where (i) $\sigma \in CSU_{AC}(\phi_1, \phi_2)$, (ii) $\phi_1\sigma$ is maximal in $p\sigma$ and $q\sigma$, and (iii) $\phi_1\sigma$ is irreducible with respect to $\mathcal{R}^e$.

Isolation $$\frac{c\phi + p \bowtie d\phi + q \vee C}{c\phi \bowtie d\phi + q + (-1)p \vee C}$$

where (i) ϕ is strictly maximal in p and q, and (ii) ϕ is irreducible with respect to $\mathcal{R}^e$.

Standardization $$\frac{(-1)\phi \approx q \vee C}{\phi \approx (-1)q \vee C}$$

where (i) $\phi \approx (-1)q \vee C$ is reductive for $\phi \approx (-1)q$ and (ii) ϕ is irreducible with respect to $\mathcal{R}^e$.

Instantiation 1
$$\frac{x + p \approx q \vee C}{(x + p \approx q \vee C)\sigma}$$

where (i) σ sends x to $y + z$ with new variables y and z, and (ii) x is maximal in p and q.

Instantiation 2
$$\frac{\phi x + p \approx q \vee C}{(\phi x + p \approx q \vee C)\sigma}$$

where (i) σ sends x to $(-1)y$ with a new variable y, and (ii) ϕx is maximal in p and q.

The Instantiation and Sum Contraction 2 inferences are in addition problematic in that they are usually not *decreasing*. Hence the usual criterion of redundancy for inferences will never be satisfied, and saturation cannot be effectively achieved. These inferences have, therefore, to be equipped with a more restrictive notion of redundancy. They are called *AC-redundant* in a set of clauses N, if their respective conclusion is redundant in N, or else contained in N. Let us denote the inference system consisting of the inference rules Product Superposition, Sum Contraction 1 and 2, Cancellation, Accumulation, Isolation, Standardization, and Instantiation 1 and 2 by $\mathsf{Simp}^{\succ}_{\mathcal{R}}$. The following lemma expresses that the inference rules in $\mathsf{Simp}^{\succ}_{\mathcal{R}}$ allow to lift simplification in ring structures from the ground level to the first-order level.

Lemma 7. *Let N be a set of clauses which is saturated up to $\mathcal{R}$-redundancy with respect to $\mathsf{Simp}^{\succ}_{\mathcal{R}}$. Let C be a ground instance of a clause in N.*

1. *C is either redundant or else it is sufficiently simplified.*
2. *If C is non-redundant then C is an instance by σ of a clause $\hat{C}$ in N which is (i) sufficiently simplified, (ii) each maximal product ϕ in C is an instance $\hat{\phi}\sigma$ of a maximal product $\hat{\phi}$ in $\hat{C}$, and (iii) if ϕ and ψ are two maximal products in $\hat{C}$ which are different (modulo AC) then $\phi\sigma$ and $\psi\sigma$ are different products in C.*
3. *If N contains all symmetrizations of non-redundant and sufficiently simplified clauses in N then any $\mathsf{S}^{\succ}_{AC}$-inference between a clause in N and a rule in $\mathcal{R}^e$ is redundant.*

Proof. To show (1), suppose that C is not sufficiently simplified. Then C can be simplified to D by some ground simplification, which can be lifted to an inference in $\mathsf{Simp}^{\succ}_{\mathcal{R}}$. Since this inference is redundant, D is also a ground instance of N and C is redundant.

For (2), suppose that C is the ground instance $C'\sigma$ of a clause C' in N and that C' is not of the desired form. Then an inference with C' is possible, and since this inference is redundant but C itself is not redundant, N contains a clause $\hat{C}$ of the desired form.

(3) follows from Lemma 6. □

The significance of (2) lies in the fact that monomials on the ground level correspond to monomials on the level of general clauses. This is essential for being able to lift the inferences in the Gröbner base computation to equations with variables. To illustrate this, let us consider the example

$$ax + y + f(bz) + z \approx (-1)y + c \tag{9}$$

where $f \succ a \succ b \succ c$. This equation contains the unshielded variables x and y, and the shielded variable z. Maximal products are ax, y and $f(bz)$ and consequently many inferences are possible.

Product superpositions into the (signed) product ax in (9) are possible with the rules (2), (3) and (4) in $\mathcal{R}$, which yield

$$\begin{aligned} 0 + y + f(bz) + z &\approx (-1)y + c & (10)\\ a + y + f(bz) + z &\approx (-1)y + c \\ ax_1 + ax_2 + y + f(bz) + z &\approx (-1)y + c, & (11) \end{aligned}$$

where x is instantiated to 0, 1 or $x_1 + x_2$, respectively. Similar inferences are also possible for $(-1)y$ and below the uninterpreted function symbol f for bz. Also, the instantiation rules permit y to be instantiated to $y_1 + y_2$ or $(-1)y'$. To continue, we pick (11) and consider Sum Contraction inferences with that equation. Signed products obtained from ax_1, ax_2 and y are AC-unifiable in any combination, and we get

$$\begin{aligned} y + f(bz) + z &\approx (-1)y + c & (12)\\ ax_2 + f(bz) + z &\approx (-1)ax' + c \\ ax_1 + f(bz) + z &\approx (-1)ax' + c \\ 2ax_1 + y + f(bz) + z &\approx (-1)y + c \\ 2ax_1 + ax_2 + f(bz) + z &\approx (-1)y + c \\ ax_1 + 2ax_2 + f(bz) + z &\approx (-1)y + c. \end{aligned}$$

This time we pick (12)[8] and consider cancellation inferences. The only one is the one where z and $(-1)y$ are unified, which results in

$$y + f(bz) \approx c,$$

but we continue with (12). Accumulation is not applicable, since $(-1)y$ occurs only once on the right side. Isolation gives, with the choice of $(-1)y$ as the maximal product (and sides reversed),

$$(-1)y \approx y + f(bz) + z + (-1)c.$$

Standardization is not applicable here, since y occurs also on the right-hand side.

[8] We also obtain this clause more directly by choosing (10) in the previous step and simplification. This example shows that still a lot of redundant inferences are made. A careful analysis could exclude this case, but it would not be possible to represent the information about previous inferences in a standard first-order language. In a framework of superposition with constraints this superposition into the previously substituted part of a clause could be prevented by putting $x_1 \not\approx 0$ and $x_2 \not\approx 0$ into the constraint. With ordering constraints it would also be possible to enforce a consistent choice of the maximal product throughout a sequence of inferences.

7 Inferences on Sufficiently Simplified Clauses

At this point we have treated all AC-superposition inferences where at least one premise is from $\mathcal{R}^e$. It remains to consider the case where both premises are in N. We may assume that the original clauses have been replaced by the symmetrizations of their simplified forms, and now we have to analyse the overlaps between these. Notice that ground symmetrization produces up to 6 different versions of a literal. Many more versions of a clause are generated if more than one literal contains a maximal product. Simply computing all possible AC-superpositions between the various versions of a clause would give us a complete but not very efficient strategy. Indeed, it turns out that only a small fraction of all possible overlaps needs to be computed. This is described by the following inference rules:

Top Superposition $$\frac{c_1(y_1\phi) \approx y_1 p \vee C \qquad c_2(y_2\psi) \approx y_2 q \vee D}{((c_2 - c_1)(y_1\phi) + y_1 p \approx y_2 q \vee C \vee D)\sigma}$$

where (i) y_1 and y_2 are (different) variables which do not occur in ϕ, ψ, p, q, C or D, or denote 1[9] (ii) $\sigma \in CSU_{AC}(y_1\phi, y_2\psi)$ such that $y_1\sigma$ and $y_2\sigma$ share no common factor $\neq 1$, (iii) $(c_1(y_1\phi) \approx y_1 p \vee C)\sigma$ is symmetrized and reductive with respect to $(c_1(y_1\phi) \approx y_1 p)\sigma$, (iv) $(c_2(y_2\psi) \approx y_2 q \vee D)\sigma$ is symmetrized and reductive with respect to $(c_2(y_2\psi) \approx y_2 q)\sigma$, (v) no premise has a selected literal, and (vi) $c_2 \geq c_1$.

Deep Superposition $$\frac{p \approx q \vee C \qquad c\phi[p'] \approx r \vee D}{(c\phi[q] \approx r \vee C \vee D)\sigma}$$

where (i) $\sigma \in CSU_{AC}(p, p')$, (ii) $(p \approx q \vee C)\sigma$ is symmetrized and reductive with respect to $(p \approx q)\sigma$, (iii) $(c\phi[p'] \approx r \vee D)\sigma$ is symmetrized and reductive with respect to $(c\phi[p'] \approx r)\sigma$, (iv) the occurrence of p' in ϕ is not a variable and is is below an uninterpreted function symbol, and (v) no premise has a selected literal.

Negative Superposition $$\frac{p \approx q \vee C \qquad u[p'] \not\approx r \vee D}{(u[q] \not\approx r \vee C \vee D)\sigma}$$

where (i) $\sigma \in CSU_{AC}(p, p')$, (ii) $(p \approx q \vee C)\sigma$ is symmetrized and reductive with respect to $(p \approx q)\sigma$, and (iii) $u[p'] \approx r \vee D$ is symmetrized, (iv) $u[p'] \approx r$ is selected in $u[p'] \approx r \vee D$, (v) $u\sigma \not\preceq r\sigma$, and (vi) p' is not a variable.

Let $\mathsf{S}^{\succ}_{\mathcal{R}}$ consist of $\mathsf{Simp}^{\succ}_{\mathcal{R}}$ plus the inference rules Top Superposition, Deep Superposition, Negative Superposition, Reflective AC-Resolution and AC-Factoring. This inference system places strong restrictions on superposition at and above uninterpreted function symbols in the top region of terms. Superposition below uninterpreted function symbols and Negative Superposition is restricted only in that we require that the premises be symmetrized. In the present formulation of the inference system we have to consider all symmetrizations of the first premise, however. More work is needed to further strengthen the respective restrictions.

[9] We are saying that the meta-notation for the premises and the conclusion concerning the occurrences of variables y_1 and y_2 is modulo $AC1$.

Theorem 8. *Let $N \cup \mathcal{R}$ be a set of clauses that is saturated up to AC-redundancy with respect to $\mathsf{S}^{\succ}_{\mathcal{R}}$ and that contains all symmetrizations for any non-redundant and sufficiently simplified clause in N. Then $N \cup \mathcal{R}$ is saturated up to AC-redundancy with respect to $\mathsf{S}^{\succ}_{AC}$.*

Proof. We need to show that all AC-Superposition and all Negative AC-Superposition inferences from premises in $N^e \cup \mathcal{R}^e$ are AC-redundant.

If at least one premise is from $\mathcal{R}^e$ then such an inference is redundant by Lemma 7, since N is saturated with respect to $\mathsf{Simp}^{\succ}_{\mathcal{R}}$ and contains the symmetrizations of non-redundant, sufficiently simplified clauses.

It remains to consider the case where both premises are from N. If one of the premises is not symmetrized, it is redundant by Lemma 7 and the inference is redundant, too. Hence we need to consider only inferences between symmetrized clauses C_1 and C_2. Superposition inferences are restricted to the case where either L_2 is a selected literal in C_2 and C_1 is reductive for L_1, or where both C_1 and C_2 are reductive for L_1 and L_2, respectively.

A ground literal has, including extensions, up to six different forms after symmetrization. We consider the two most general cases where each L_i is of one of the two forms

$$x_i + c_i(y_i\phi_i) \bowtie x_i + y_i r_i \tag{13}$$

and

$$(-1)(y_i\phi_i) \bowtie (c_i - 1)(y_i\phi_i) + (-1)y_i r_i, \tag{14}$$

respectively, carrying extension variables x_i and y_i with respect to both $\cdot$ and $+$, respectively. Note that x_i and y_i do not occur inside ϕ_i, r_i or C_i'. Other forms may be seen as special cases, where extension variables are omitted, or where $c_i = 1$, or else where ϕ_i is missing. The analysis of these cases is essentially similar.

We distinguish three cases: (i) Two positive literals superpose, and the superposition is not below an uninterpreted function symbol, (ii) a positive literal superposes into another positive literal, but below an uninterpreted function symbol, and (iii) a positive literal superposes into a negative literal.

(i) Suppose L_1 and L_2 are positive literals.

(a) We start by considering the case where two ground clauses C_i of form (13) superpose.[10] Since AC-contexts can be moved into the substitution for the extension variables x_i and y_i, we need to consider only superpositions at the root in which the peak is an instance of both left-hand sides. The inference is symmetric, hence we may assume without loss of generality that $c_2 \geq c_1$.

If the sums $c_i y_i \phi_i$ did not overlap in some product, the superposition would be trivially redundant, as the substitution for the extension variables x_i would be reducible (Figure 1a). Since at least one product overlaps it follows that $(y_1\phi_1)\sigma =_{AC} (y_2\phi_2)\sigma$ (Figure 1b). By the same argument as before, the products ϕ_1 and ϕ_2 overlap in some term. We obtain the most general nontrivial

[10] This corresponds to the computation of S-polynomials in the Gröbner basis algorithm.

(a) A trivial overlap: $\begin{array}{l} abcy_1 + abcy_1 + \qquad\quad x_1 \\ \qquad x_2 \qquad + bcdy_2 + bcdy_2 + bcdy_2 \end{array}$

(b) A nontrivial overlap: $\begin{array}{l} abcy_1 + abcy_1 + \quad x_1 \\ \quad x_2 \;\; + bcdy_2 + bcdy_2 + bcdy_2 \end{array}$

(c) A maximal overlap: $\begin{array}{l} abcy_1 + abcy_1 + \; x_1 \\ bcdy_2 + bcdy_2 + bcdy_2 \end{array}$

Fig. 1. Overlaps of sums

overlap $(x_1 + c_1(y_1\phi_1))\sigma =_{AC} (x_2 + c_2(y_2\phi_2))\sigma$ where $x_i\sigma = (c - c_i)(y_i\sigma\phi_i)$ for some c. Consider the case where as many products as possible overlap, which implies $c = c_2$. Then $x_2\sigma = 0$ which corresponds to the use of the non-extended symmetrization $c_2(y_2\phi_2) \approx y_2r_2 \vee C_2'$ of C_2 (Figure 1c). Similarly, we require that ϕ_1 and ϕ_2 overlap as much as possible, i.e., $y_1\sigma$ and $y_2\sigma$ have no common factor. By making these restrictions we identify the smallest possible peak. The inference corresponding to this peak is the only one that actually needs to be computed, as it causes all other inferences to become redundant. This is exactly analogous to the situation in the Gröbner basis algorithm, where also only maximal overlaps are considered. In order to refer to this smallest peak in the following, let $\phi = y_1\sigma\phi_1$ and $\psi_i = y_i\sigma$ for $i \in 1, 2$ (Figure 2a). The superposition

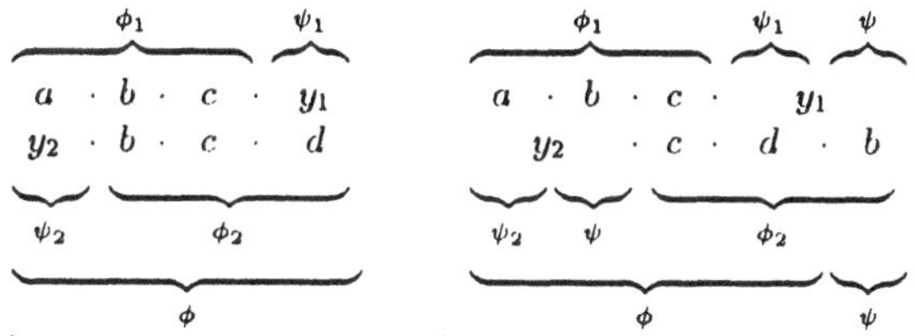

(a) A maximal overlap (b) A nonmaximal overlap

Fig. 2. Overlaps of products

inference in question is of the form

$$\frac{x_1 + c_1(y_1\phi_1) \approx x_1 + y_1r_1 \vee C_1' \qquad c_2(y_2\phi_2) \approx y_2r_2 \vee C_2'}{(c_2 - c_1)\phi + \psi_1r_1 \approx \psi_2r_2 \vee C_1' \vee C_2'} \tag{15}$$

Its conclusion can be obtained by top superposition with essentially the same premises, in particular the second, maximal premise is the same, and hence it is redundant.

We now show that other overlaps between clauses in the symmetrizations of the C_i are redundant, whenever inference (15) is redundant. Let us first consider other overlaps between the same two clauses.

(b) Assume that $y_1\sigma$ and $y_2\sigma$ share a common factor $\psi \neq 1$. Then $y_i\sigma = \psi\psi_i$ for $i = 1, 2$ (Figure 2b) and the inference is

$$\frac{x_1 + c_1(y_1\phi_1) \approx x_1 + y_1 r_1 \vee C_1' \qquad c_2(y_2\phi_2) \approx y_2 r_2 \vee C_2'}{(c_2 - c_1)\psi\phi + \psi\psi_1 r_1 \approx \psi\psi_2 r_2 \vee C_1' \vee C_2'} \tag{16}$$

The conclusion can be obtained from the conclusion of (15) by multiplying both sides with ψ, using the congruence law for multiplication, and using distributivity. The question is, whether this instance of distributivity is smaller than the maximal premise. The APO distributes $\cdot$ over $+$ and thus the left-hand side $\psi((c_2 - c_1)\phi + \psi_1 r_1)$ of the distributivity rule becomes $(c_2 - c_1)(\psi\phi) + \psi\psi_1 r_1$ which is smaller than $c_2(\psi\phi)$ in the maximal premise since there are $c_1 > 0$ occurrences less of the maximal power product in it. Since the bound on the redundancy proof for the inference (15) is lower than the bound here, we can reuse it. We conclude that the inference (16) is redundant.

(c) Assume that only $c_0 < c_1$ sum terms from C_1 overlap with C_2. We also allow that $y_1\sigma$ and $y_2\sigma$ share a common factor ψ as in (b). Then the inference is

$$\frac{x_1 + c_1(y_1\phi_1) \approx x_1 + y_1 r_1 \vee C_1' \qquad x_2 + c_2(y_2\phi_2) \approx x_2 + y_2 r_2 \vee C_2'}{(c_2 - c_0)\psi\phi + \psi\psi_1 r_1 \approx (c_1 - c_0)\psi\phi + \psi\psi_2 r_2 \vee C_1' \vee C_2'}$$

To show redundancy of this inference, we use the congruence law for $+$ to add $(c_1 - c_0)\psi\phi$ on each side of the conclusion of (16), for which we already have shown redundancy. The redundancy proof of (16) is with respect to a smaller maximal premise than here, so we are again allowed to reuse it.

(d) We now consider the overlap of a clause with a negative left-hand side into a clause which is extended with respect to multiplication. For the same reason as before, we need to consider only overlaps at the root of a product. Here we have $(-1)(y_1\phi_1) =_{AC} y_2\phi_2 =_{AC} (-1)\phi\psi$ and thus $y_1\sigma = \psi\psi_1$ and $y_2\sigma = (-1)\psi\psi_2$. We consider an arbitrary nontrivial but not necessarily maximal overlap and thus allow that $y_1\sigma$ and $y_2\sigma$ have a common factor ψ. We get the inference

$$\frac{(-1)(y_1\phi_1) \approx (c_1 - 1)(y_1\phi_1) + (-1)y_1 r_1 \vee C_1' \qquad c_2(y_2\phi_2) \approx y_2 r_2 \vee C_2'}{(c_1 - 1)\psi\phi + (-1)\psi\psi_1 r_1 + (c_2 - 1)(-1)\psi\phi \approx (-1)\psi\psi_2 r_2 \vee C_1' \vee C_2'}$$

Using the inverse law, the conclusion can be reduced to $(-1)\psi\psi_1 r_1 + (c_2 - c_1)(-1)\psi\phi \approx (-1)\psi\psi_2 r_2 \vee C_1' \vee C_2'$. We can multiply both sides of (16) by -1 and use distributivity to obtain the conclusion. Analogous to (b) the instance of distributivity used is again smaller than the maximal premise.

(e) If we overlap two symmetrizations with a negative left-hand side, that is, of the form $(-1)y_i\phi_i \approx y_i((c_i - 1)\phi_i + (-1)r_i) \vee C_i'$ for $i \in 1, 2$, then we obtain two more cases.

(e1) If the two occurrences of (-1) superpose then the overlapped term is $(-1)\phi\psi =_{AC} (-1)y_1\sigma\phi_1 =_{AC} (-1)y_2\sigma\phi_2$ and again we have $y_i\sigma = \psi\psi_i$ for $i = 1, 2$. This corresponds to the inference

$$\frac{(-1)y_1\phi_1 \approx y_1((c_1 - 1)\phi_1 + (-1)r_1) \vee C_1' \qquad (-1)y_2\phi_2 \approx y_2((c_2 - 1)\phi_2 + (-1)r_2) \vee C_2'}{\psi\psi_1((c_1 - 1)\phi_1 + (-1)r_1) \approx \psi\psi_2((c_2 - 1)\phi_2 + (-1)r_2) \vee C_1' \vee C_2'}$$

The conclusion can be rewritten to $(c_1 - 1)\phi\psi + \psi\psi_1(-1)r_1 \approx (c_2 - 1)\phi\psi + \psi\psi_2(-1)r_2 \vee C_1' \vee C_2'$ and, using the congruence law, simplified to $\psi\psi_1(-1)r_1 \approx (c_2 - c_1)\phi\psi + \psi\psi_2(-1)r_2$. Using instances of the inverse law (8) smaller than $\phi\psi$, we may move $\psi\psi_1(-1)r_1$ and $\psi\psi_2(-1)r_2$ to the other side of the equation. The result is $\mathcal{R}$-equivalent to the conclusion of (16) and thus redundant.

(e2) Otherwise, the peak becomes $(-1)(-1)\phi\psi$ which can be reduced by the smaller rule $(-1)(-1) \to 1$ in $\mathcal{R}$. Inferences in which the maximal term is reducible by a rule smaller than any of the premises are redundant.

(ii) Now suppose the superposition is below some uninterpreted function symbol. In this case it makes essentially no difference whether the premise is extended or not. For simplicity we carry out the proof for clauses which are not extended.

(a) Suppose the superposition is into a clause of the form (13), the inference is

$$\frac{l_1 \approx r_1 \vee C_1' \qquad c_2\phi_2[l_1\sigma] \approx r_2 \vee C_2'}{(c_2 - 1)\phi_2[l_1\sigma] + \phi_2[r_1\sigma] \approx r_2 \vee C_1' \vee C_2'}$$

where $l_1 \approx r_1 \vee C_1'$ may be any clause in the symmetrization and the occurrence of l_1 in ϕ_2 is below an uninterpreted function symbol. The substitution σ is needed to instantiate extension variables which may occur in l_1 and r_1 but not in C_1'. The other copies of $l_1\sigma$ in the conclusion $(c_2 - 1)\phi_2[l_1\sigma] + \phi_2[r_1\sigma] \approx r_2 \vee C_1' \vee C_2'$ can also be rewritten and we obtain $c_2\phi_2[r_1\sigma] \approx r_2 \vee C_1' \vee C_2'$. This is an instance of the conclusion of a Deep Superposition inference, which has the same premises and is redundant since N is saturated. Hence this inference is also redundant.

(b) If on the other hand the superposition is into a clause of the form (14), we get the inference

$$\frac{l_1 \approx r_1 \vee C_1' \qquad (-1)\phi_2[l_1\sigma] \approx (c_2 - 1)\phi_2[l_1\sigma] + (-1)r_2 \vee C_2'}{(-1)\phi_2[r_1\sigma] \approx (c_2 - 1)\phi_2[l_1\sigma] + (-1)r_2 \vee C_1' \vee C_2'} \tag{17}$$

where again the other copies of $l_1\sigma$ in the conclusion can be rewritten and we obtain $(-1)\phi_2[r_1\sigma] \approx (c_2 - 1)\phi_2[r_1\sigma] + (-1)r_2 \vee C_1' \vee C_2'$. Using the instance $\phi_2[r_1\sigma] + (-1)\phi_2[r_1\sigma] \approx 0$ of the inverse law, which is smaller than the maximal premise since the maximal product has been reduced, we obtain $0 \approx c_2\phi_2[r_1\sigma] + (-1)r_2 \vee C_1' \vee C_2'$. We may move $(-1)r_2$ to the other side and arrive at $c_2\phi_2[r_1\sigma] \approx r_2 \vee C_1' \vee C_2'$. This again is an instance of the conclusion of a Deep Superposition inference, which is redundant since N is saturated. Since its maximal premise $c_2\phi_2 \approx r_2 \vee C_2'$ is smaller than the maximal premise $(-1)\phi_2 \approx (c_2 - 1)\phi_2 + (-1)r_2 \vee C_2'$ of (17), this implies that (17) is redundant.

(iii) Let us now consider superpositions into a negative literal. In this case the symmetrization is obtained by simplification only, hence only one of the forms of a symmetrized clause needs to be present. All non-redundant inferences of this kind are lifted to Negative Superposition, which is Negative AC-Superposition restricted to symmetrized clauses. □

Corollary 9. *Let $N \cup \mathcal{R}$ be a set of clauses that is saturated up to AC-redundancy with respect to $\mathsf{S}^{\succ}_{\mathcal{R}}$ and that contains all symmetrizations for any* *non-redundant and sufficiently simplified clause in N. Then $N \cup \mathcal{R} \cup AC$ is equality unsatisfiable if and only if it contains the empty clause.*

8 A Simple Example

Let us conclude this section with an example. In boolean rings, each element is its own additive inverse. That is, if $xx \approx x$ for all x then $y + y \approx 0$ for all y. In clause form we get

$$xx \approx x \tag{18}$$

$$a + a \not\approx 0 \tag{19}$$

where a is a skolem constant. There are redundant ring theory superposition inferences of (18) with (2) yielding $0 \approx 0$, with (3) yielding $1 \approx 1$, with (4) yielding $((y+z)y) + ((y+z)z) \approx yy + yz + yz + zz$ and after reduction $yy + yz + yz + zz \approx yy + yz + yz + zz$, and a nonredundant one with (6) yielding

$$1 \approx -1. \tag{20}$$

Symmetrization produces

$$x + x \approx 0 \tag{21}$$

which can be used to derive the empty clause from (19).

9 Conclusion

We have proposed a specialized variant of the associative-commutative superposition calculus for commutative rings. We consider our investigation as a first step towards the integration of algebra and universal algebra in saturation-based theorem provers for first-order logic. We have shown that specialized simplification techniques eliminate the need for a large class of superposition inferences which involve the ring axioms. The number of inferences between other clauses is also considerably reduced by a process which we have called symmetrization, following (Le Chenadec 1984), and which represents a partial saturation of a clause with respect to the axioms of the theory. We have also shown that for top-level inferences between symmetrized clauses the effect of the many inferences between the possibly many symmetrizations of two clauses can be cast into on single, rather simple inference. The concept of saturation up to redundancy forms the main basis on which simplification and other optimization techniques may be justified.

This work is related to previous research in which the similarity between Buchberger's algorithm and Knuth-Bendix completion has been exploited. This similarity appears to have first been observed by (Loos 1981) and (Buchberger and Loos 1983). Since then a number of researchers have attempted to clarify, and formalize, the connection between the two methods; see (Buchberger 1987) for a discussion of the fundamental issues and further references. The free commutative ring over a set of free constants is isomorphic to a polynomial ring with coefficients in the integers. This in turn is a special case of a polynomial ring over an Euclidian coefficient ring which was investigated by (Kandri-Rody and Kapur 1988). The essential steps of one variant of their algorithm can be recovered from our calculus when we specialize it to unit equations over free constants. Our method is also an extension of work by (Marché 1994) who considers (possibly failing) Knuth-Bendix completion procedures for equations that contain a particular theory represented by a convergent rewrite system. In contrast, we deal with the non-failing case in the general setting of first-order clauses. Our own previous work on the relation between Gröbner basis methods and superposition (Bachmair and Ganzinger 1994a) has shown how to view the Gröbner basis computation for polynomials over a coefficient field B as a specialized strategy of $AC \cup B$-superposition. The concept of AC-superposition was extended so as to be able to model computation with coefficients as unification modulo the ground theory of B. We have also argued for a constraint-based approach in cases where the coefficient structure is merely a ring. The present paper considerably extends some of the ideas in the latter paper.

Future work will try to improve and extend the results of the present paper in various ways. For instance we would like to consider the case of fields for which one obtains a finite and saturated first-order presentation by simply adding the clause $x \approx 0 \vee x * x^{-1} \approx 1$ to the presentation of ring theory that we have been using here. The method of the present paper should easily extend to that case which can not be handled in a purely equational framework. We also hope to be able to combine our chaining methods for transitive (non-symmetric) relations with the method presented here. A problem of a similar nature has been solved in (Bachmair and Ganzinger 1994b) where we have shown, among other things, how to integrate the quantifier elimination procedure for dense total orderings without endpoints into chaining-based first-order theorem proving.

In this paper we have attempted to reuse previous results about the refutational completeness of our AC-superposition calculus. The completeness proof for the latter is based on a certain model construction technique which we did not want to repeat here. Now it seems to us as if we should rather have started from scratch and should have based the present investigation on a specific form of rewriting in rings. This would have induced an according modification of the model construction. On the other hand it might have saved us a lot of pain related to the concept of symmetrization. Symmetrized variants of clauses, like extensions in the AC-case, should better not be treated as first-class citizens. They should remain hidden. Moreover, replacing $(-1)\phi \approx (c-1)\phi+p$ by $c\phi \approx -p$ ought to be a simplification. This would be the case if all partial models in a modified model construction were rings so that redundancy proofs could apply ring axioms in an unrstricted manner. In such a setting Negative Superposition can be considerably restricted further. Finally, let us again mention the extremely prolific instantiation inferences for which one should try to find effective restrictions and control strategies. All in all we hope that it will be possible to arrive at a setting in which certain awkward technicalities of the present paper will disappear.

References

L. BACHMAIR AND N. DERSHOWITZ, 1986. Commutation, transformation, and termination. *Proc. 8th Conf. on Automated Deduction*, San Diego, CA, LNCS 230, pp. 5–20. Springer.

L. BACHMAIR AND H. GANZINGER, 1993. Associative-commutative superposition. Technical Report MPI-I-93-267, Max-Planck-Institut für Informatik, Saarbrücken. To appear in Proc. CTRS Workshop 1994.

L. BACHMAIR AND H. GANZINGER, 1994a. Buchberger's algorithm: A constraint-based completion procedure. *Proc. 1st Int. Conf. on Constraints in Computational Logics*, Munich, Germany, LNCS 845, pp. 285–301. Springer.

L. BACHMAIR AND H. GANZINGER, 1994b. Ordered chaining for total orderings. *Proc. 12th Int. Conf. on Automated Deduction*, Nancy, France, LNCS 814, pp. 435–450. Springer.

L. BACHMAIR AND H. GANZINGER, 1994c. Rewrite-based equational theorem proving with selection and simplification. *Journal of Logic and Computation* **4**(3): 217–247. Revised version of Technical Report MPI-I-93-250, Max-Planck-Institut für Informatik, Saarbrücken, 1993.

L. BACHMAIR AND D. PLAISTED, 1985. Termination orderings for associative-commutative rewriting systems. *Journal of Symbolic Computation* **1**: 329–349.

L. BACHMAIR, H. GANZINGER AND U. WALDMANN, 1994. Refutational theorem proving for hierarchic first-order theories. *Applicable Algebra in Engineering, Communication and Computing* **5**(3/4): 193–212. Earlier version: Theorem Proving for Hierarchic First-Order Theories. *Proc. 3rd Int. Conf. on Algebraic and Logic Programming*, Volterra, Italy, LNCS 632. Springer, 1992.

L. BACHMAIR, 1991. *Canonical Equational Proofs*. Birkhäuser, Boston.

R. S. BOYER AND J. S. MOORE, 1988. Integrating decision procedures into heuristic theorem provers: A case study of linear arithmetic. In J. E. Hayes, D. Michie and J. Richards (eds), *Machine Intelligence 11*, chapter 5, pp. 83–124. Clarendon Press, Oxford.

B. BUCHBERGER AND R. LOOS, 1983. Algebraic simplification. *Computer Algebra: Symbolic and Algebraic Computation*, 2nd edn, pp. 11–43. Springer.

B. BUCHBERGER, 1965. *An Algorithm for Finding a Basis for the Residue Class Ring of a Zero-Dimensional Ideal*, PhD thesis, University of Innsbruck, Austria. In german.

B. BUCHBERGER, 1985. Gröbner bases: An algorithmic method in polynomial ideal theory. In N. K. Bose (ed.), *Recent Trends in Multidimensional Systems Theory*, chapter 6, pp. 184–232. D. Reidel Publishing Company.

B. BUCHBERGER, 1987. History and basic features of the critical pair/completion procedure. *Journal of Symbolic Computation* **3**: 3–38.

H.-J. BÜRCKERT, 1990. A resolution principle for clauses with constraints. *Proc. 10th Int. Conf. on Automated Deduction*, Kaiserslautern, Germany, LNCS 449, pp. 178–192. Springer.

N. DERSHOWITZ AND J.-P. JOUANNAUD, 1990. Rewrite systems. In J. van Leeuwen (ed.), *Handbook of Theoretical Computer Science, Vol. B: Formal Models and Semantics*, chapter 6, pp. 243–320. Elsevier/MIT Press.

A. KANDRI-RODY AND D. KAPUR, 1988. Computing a Gröbner basis of a polynomial ideal over a euclidean domain. *Journal of Symbolic Computation* **6**: 19–36.

C. KIRCHNER, H. KIRCHNER AND M. RUSINOWITCH, 1990. Deduction with symbolic constraints. *Revue Française d'Intelligence Artificielle* **4**(3): 9–52. Special issue on automatic deduction.

P. LE CHENADEC, 1984. Canonical forms in finitely presented algebras. *Proc. 7th Int. Conf. on Automated Deduction*, Napa, CA, LNCS 170, pp. 142–165. Springer. Book version published by Pitman, London, 1986.

R. LOOS, 1981. Term reduction systems and algebraic algorithms. *Proc. 5th GI Workshop on Artificial Intelligence*, Bad Honnef, Informatik Fachberichte 47, pp. 214–234. Springer.

C. MARCHÉ, 1994. Normalised rewriting and normalised completion. *Proc. 9th Ann. IEEE Symp. on Logic in Computer Science*, Paris, pp. 394–403. IEEE Computer Society Press.

G. NELSON AND D. C. OPPEN, 1979. Simplification by cooperating decision procedures. *ACM Transactions on Programming Languages and Systems* **2**(2): 245–257.

R. NIEUWENHUIS AND A. RUBIO, 1994. AC-superposition with constraints: no AC-unifiers needed. *Proc. 12th Int. Conf. on Automated Deduction*, Nancy, France, LNCS 814, pp. 545–559. Springer.

S. OWRE, J. M. RUSHBY AND N. SHANKAR, 1992. PVS: A prototype verification system. *11th Int. Conf. on Automated Deduction*, Saratoga Springs, NY, LNCS 607, pp. 748–752. Springer.

G. E. PETERSON AND M. E. STICKEL, 1981. Complete sets of reductions for some equational theories. *Journal of the ACM* **28**(2): 233–264.

L. VIGNERON, 1994. Associative-commutative deduction with constraints. *Proc. 12th Int. Conf. on Automated Deduction*, Saratoga Springs, NY, LNCS 814, pp. 530–544. Springer.

U. WERTZ, 1992. First-order theorem proving modulo equations. Technical Report MPI-I-92-216, Max-Planck-Institut für Informatik, Saarbrücken.

Bulk Types and Query Language Design*

Catriel Beeri

Institute of Computer Science
The Hebrew University, Jerusalem, Israel

Abstract. Query languages have been a major research topic in the database area. Many results about the complexity and expressiveness of such languages have been obtained, both for the relational model and for various extensions. However, these results do not seem to provide sufficient guidelines for practical query language development. With the desirė to generalize from relational to general bulk types, the need for such design guidelines is felt. The paper surveys a recently proposed theory of query languages, based on basic notions from category theory, specifically on variants of monads, and argues that it provides a good framework for practical language design.

1 Introduction

Query languages have been, since the introduction of the relational model, an important area of study and development in the database field. A primary focus of attention for many years has been the study of the complexity and expressiveness of extensions of the relational calculus and algebra. However, as the interest in richer data models (so called *advanced models*) grew in the last decade, the issue of query language *design* has received increased attention. While expressiveness and complexity are important design criteria for such query languages as well, there are other important considerations, such as optimizability of queries, ease of use, ease of integration with the application development environment, and so on, and a need was felt for a re-examination of the basic ideas of query language design.

A query language is, by definition, a functional language, as it is used to define functions on databases (although SQL does also allow the specification of simple set-oriented updates). The simplicity of the relational model enabled essentially self-contained development and investigation of query languages, without any interesting connections to the theory of general or functional languages. But, one of the primary motivations for the generalization to advanced models was to bring the data model's type system closer to that of general programming languages, both to enhance its usability as a modeling tool, and to allow a seamless integration of the query and application development languages. With this direction of development, it is natural to expect deeper connections with the theory of programming languages. Such connections arise, for example, in the study of type systems (a relatively new subject for query languages), in transformational programming and its relationship to query optimization, and in the study of semantics.

* Work supported by a grant from GIF — The German Israeli Foundation for Scientific Research and Development.

This paper describes a recent approach to query language design for advanced models that is based on a rather simple idea from category theory — that of a *monad*. The approach provides a uniform foundation for the development of query constructs for a variety of data type constructors and includes, in particular, several languages, of low complexity, each of which can be used as a common query language for a model that allows some or all of these type constructors. The approach also promises to provide a good foundation for the study of query optimization, although this promise still waits to be substantiated.

As category theory has become a fundamental tool in the study of semantics of programming languages, it is only to be expected that it makes a debut in the database arena, where it has been long been shunned. For the benefit of those readers that have managed so far to avoid category theory, we emphasize that although category theory includes many abstract and sophisticated concepts and results, our interest here is only in some of the most basic notions of this theory. These are explained and motivated, so the paper is self-contained. To quote from [14], a category theorist would probably say about the results presented here: "well, yes, we knew that already;" and we would respond with: "as computing scientists, we have already declared our interest in the trivial." We hope our presentation convinces the reader that these notions are useful in the study of query languages and the modest effort needed to understand them pays off. The only non-trivial result is the translation of λ-calculi into algebraic languages. This technique seems to be closely related to query compilation, and is therefore worth understanding. In any case, this paper is a survey, emphasizing motivation and intuition; no proofs are presented.

The outline of the paper is the following. Section 2 presents the relational model and its query languages, and section 3 generalizes to complex values and bulk types. This sets the stage for the main body of the paper. Section 4 then presents monads and section 5 describes the query languages of monads, and presents some equivalence and normalization results. Section 6 summarizes the discussion of monads, and section 7 concludes.

2 The Relational Model and Query Languages

The relational model uses two type constructors, *tuple* and *set*. However, their use is severely restricted — only sets of tuples of atoms can be formed. Thus, 'type constructor' is not a common term in relational language theory. The basic theorem of this theory, that underlies much of the work on declarative query languages, and some of the work on query interpretation and compilation, is the equivalence of the relational calculus, denoted in this paper by rel–CALC, and the relational algebra, denoted rel–ALG. A related important result is that the complexity of this language is in logspace.

A detailed exposition of these and many related results can be found in [2]. In the rest of this section we expand on some of the details, with the goal of showing that despite the fact that this theory is well understood, it is somewhat problematic in that it does not provide a nice paradigm for practical query language design. This failure becomes more pronounced as we proceed in the sequel to consider advanced models.

2.1 Three Simple Languages

The most basic class of queries is CON, the class of *conjunctive* queries. These are the rel–CALC queries that can be expressed using only conjunction and existential quantification, and two kinds of atoms, namely relational atoms of the form $R(\bar{x})$, and equality/inequality atoms involving column names and constants. It is easy to see that each such query can be transformed to a normal form $\bar{x} \mid \exists \bar{y} \bigwedge_i atom_i(\bar{x}, \bar{y})$ (the list of free variables $\bar{x}$ is the *target list*).

There is also a simple sublanguage of rel–ALG, denoted by SPC or SPJ, namely the queries that can be expressed using only the operations *Select* (denoted σ), *Project* (denoted π), *Cross* (denoted $\times$), and *Join*,[2] where the selection condition is as described above. Here also there is a simple normal form: $\pi_{\ldots}(\sigma_{\ldots}(\times_i R_i))$. A third definition of a class of queries can be obtained from the commercial language SQL: Let (core–)SQL denote the queries that can be expressed using the block construction **select** *target-list* **from** *relation-list* **where** *condition*, in which *target-list* is a list of column names, and *condition* is a list of equalities and inequalities on column names and constants.

A fundamental theorem in the area of query languages is that these three languages are equivalent, they express the same class of queries:

$$\text{SQL} \equiv \text{CON} \equiv \text{SPJ} \ .$$

The proof is elegant and easy, especially when the normal forms above are used for the calculus and algebraic queries. In particular, when we consider the normal form for CON we observe that the existential quantifiers are redundant — as only existential quantifiers are used, a variable that does not appear in the target list is, by default, existentially quantified. The conjunction can be separated to a conjunction of relational atoms corresponding to the from-clause of SQL, and a conjunction of equalities/inequalities corresponding to the condition-clause. Thus, (core–)SQL can be viewed as a sublanguage of rel–CALC with some syntactic sugar. The translation from either CON or SQL to SPJ is also easy, and is close to translations performed in commercial systems.

2.2 Generalizations and Their Problems

We have identified a class of simple, common queries, expressible in at least three languages. But clearly, there is a need for more expressive power. For that, we first add disjunction: The *union* operator for the algebra, the disjunction for the calculus. Next, we add *set difference* to the algebra and negation to the calculus. It is tempting to state right away that the resulting languages are equivalent; but this is a bit premature, however. The two new constructs in the calculus enable us to write some queries that are generally considered *undesirable*. Two such queries are: $\{x, y, z \mid R(x, y) \vee S(y, z)\}$ and $\{x \mid \neg R(x)\}$. In the answer to the first query x and z can be assigned values that are not taken from or related to the database, and the same holds for x in the second query. In both cases the vagueness about the range of values for these variables makes us feel these queries are ill-defined.

[2] Only one of the last two is actually needed.

The problem is well known: rel–CALC queries need to be *domain independent*. That is, when we view a database as a logical structure, namely as a domain and some relations, then a query may return values from the domain that do not appear in the relations,[3] and these values in the result may change if we view the database as another structure with the same relations but a different domain. Even when the result values appear in the relations, the result may still be influenced by the choice of the domain. Queries that do not have this problematic behavior are called *domain independent*. Unfortunately, this property is undecidable. The solution is to impose syntactic restrictions on formulas that are a sufficient condition for domain independence. Several such conditions, of varying complexity, have been proposed in the literature, as early as in Codd's own pioneering papers [7]. They are generically known as *range restrictions*, as the main idea is to include in the formula restrictions on the ranges of variables.

Denoting the two notions by *di*, *rr* respectively, we can at last state the fundamental theorem:

$$\text{rel–CALC}_{di} \equiv \text{rel–CALC}_{rr} \equiv \text{rel–ALG} \ .$$

In summary, domain independence and range restrictions are esoteric, yet essential properties of the full relational calculus as a query language. Recalling that (core–)SQL can be viewed as a sublanguage of rel–CALC, how do these properties relate to extensions of SQL? Some of the main extensions of SQL are the addition of subqueries, and of various set-related operations such as *union*, $\in$ and $\subseteq$. These, however, are more algebraic than calculus-oriented. The notion of subquery brings to mind the concept of orthogonality, an important principle in programming language design, that does not seem to relate to the relational calculus. Other extensions of SQL include *aggregates* functions such as sum, maximum, average. These are ad-hoc extensions, not related to the main stream of query language theory as presented above. In short, it seems query language theory and practice have to some extent diverged.

3 Extending the Model and the Query Languages

The principle of orthogonality seems to (retroactively, to some extent) underlie many of the extensions to the relational model that were proposed during the eighties. The first modest step was done as early as 1977 [13], but the lead was seriously followed only in the early and mid-eighties. The *first normal form* property postulated by Codd states that entries in relations are atomic. This property simplifies the relational model, brings it theoretically very close to first-order predicate calculus, hence was (and still is) a key ingredient in its practical and theoretical success. Nevertheless, the new idea was to abandon this restriction, on the grounds that many applications require a richer data modeling facility, and that the application programming languages have a richer type system. Once this idea was abandoned, the way was opened to many new ideas concerning the data model. Some of these are reviewed here.

[3] When no function symbols are used in the query, such values are unrelated to the relations.

3.1 Complex Values

The first step was to allow relations as values in other relations. The next was to allow the use of the *tuple* and *set* type constructors in (almost) any order. Thus, a *complex value*[4] is obtained from atomic values by applying (possibly repeatedly) the two constructors, a relation is a set of such values, and a database is a vector of relations.

An extension of the model requires a corresponding extension of the query languages (or development of new ones). The calculus was extended firstly by making the variables typed, with the types ranging over the complex value types, and secondly by adding the predicate $\in$ — obviously needed for a model that has set values. Other additions, such as the predicate $\subseteq$ and set operations such as *union, intersection* were considered, but were shown to be expressible. This is essentially a ω-order predicate calculus. We denote it by co–CALC. ('co' stands for complex object, see footnote.)

The story of the algebra is more involved. A series of extensions were proposed. These included new operations, such as *nest* and *unnest*. The first allows to group values in a column of a relation based on common values in another column; it is very useful, for example, for depicting hierarchical relationships. The second is an inverse. While these two allow some creation and destruction of set values, they do not seem to satisfy all the needs of manipulating deeply nested set values. A facility to apply *project* to nested sets was proposed, then a facility for nested application of all rel–ALG operations. Quite surprisingly, it turned out that the algebras so obtained, even with rather modest extensions to rel–ALG are equivalent. However, while this observation lends some support to the claim that these algebras have the necessary expressive power, they do not seem to satisfy other requirements of language design, such as ease of use and orthogonality.

An approach that strives to take such considerations into account was proposed in [1]. The main idea is the replacement of the operation *project* by the higher-order function *map*.[5] This function is well-known in functional programming where it is used for lists, but it is equally useful for sets. Projections can be expressed by applying *map* to appropriate combinations of tuple selection and construction functions. The impact of this simple idea is far reaching, however; rather than using a set of fixed operations, each used for a single purpose, we now have the idea of a *programmable algebra*, as *map* can accept any (properly typed) function as argument. This generalization can be used in (at least) two ways. Firstly, it allows for an arbitrary algebra of basic types with operations and predicates to be given as the underlying universe of a database: Any of these 'built-in' functions can be used as an argument of *map*. Although built-in functions have been considered in the context of relational algebra and calculus, that was never a 'marriage based on love'. Secondly, a function constructed by applying *map* to a function can itself be an argument to *map*; thus, the problem of applying operations to deeply nested values is naturally solved. In short, the database algebra is finally recognized for what it is (or should be) — a special purpose functional language.

---

[4] These were called complex *objects* in [1], and this terminology is still widely used. However, they are just values, not objects as in 'object-oriented'.

[5] Similar ideas have been 'in the air', even published; see, for example, [15].

In addition to *map*, this algebra contains the usual rel–ALG operations. Additionally, it contains several constructors, selectors and and destructors for tuples and sets. We skip the detailed description — most of these operations are described in the sequel. Also included, for reasons to be discussed shortly, the operation $\mathcal{P}$, that constructs the powerset of a given set. We use co–ALG to denote the algebra without $\mathcal{P}$; it is equivalent in expressive power to the other proposals for a complex-value algebra above. We use co–ALG+$\mathcal{P}$ for the more powerful algebra.

Several questions come to mind as one views these developments: First, probably foremost, one would like to know whether the algebra can further be extended by adding other useful operations, and when can we be sure we have the right, the final algebra. Other, more technical questions, relate to the properties that have been considered for the relational case. Is the algebra (or some algebra) equivalent to the calculus? What is the expressiveness and complexity of these languages? Are there interesting sublanguages, similar to CON? Are there useful optimization strategies for these languages? We list here some of the known results about the first two questions. The third question is addressed by the approach and results described in the forthcoming sections. The last question is still a subject of research.

Regarding the relationship between the languages, we have the following results:

$$\text{co–ALG} + \mathcal{P} \equiv \text{co–CALC}_{di} \equiv \text{co–CALC}_{rr} \ .$$

As a matter of fact, the operation $\mathcal{P}$ was added to co–ALG specifically to achieve this result, as co–CALC, even with range restrictions, can express powerset. But, knowing that $\mathcal{P}$ has exponential cost, we can expect some bad news in terms of the expressive power of these languages. Indeed, in [1] it is shown that co–CALC can also express recursive queries, such as transitive closure, and is actually equivalent to complex-value stratified datalog with negation, quite a powerful language. In [9] it is shown that co–CALC can express all queries of elementary time[6] (or space) complexity. Obviously, the full co–CALC and the operation $\mathcal{P}$ are much more than we would like to have in a query language of reasonable complexity. Furthermore, although these languages are powerful and can express recursion, they do not seem to contain natural primitives for programming recursion.[7] The only piece of good news on the subject is that one can imose stronger range restrictions on the calculus, and then we have [8]

$$\text{co–ALG} \equiv \text{co–CALC}_{\textsf{strong}\ rr}$$

and further these restricted languages are in polynomial time.

In summary, the results so far indicate several problems. A naive extension of relational calculus has led to a calculus-based language that is prohibitively expressive, yet lacks appropriate programming primitives. Only by imposing strict (and presumably difficult to understand) constraints can one restrict the language to polynomial time. There does not seem to be any clear relationship between this language and the commercial language SQL, in particular, no generalization of CON was offered. The case with the algebra is somewhat better, but here also, by just considering the results mentioned above, it is not clear in what sense can we say this is **the** algebra for complex values.

---

[6] A function is in elementary time if it can be computed in time that is bounded by some tower of exponentials of fixed height.

[7] This fact has recently been formalized and proved in [19].

3.2 Bulk Types

Allowing relation entries to be complex values was just the first step. Once the barrier was broken, and it became clear that one could generalize the model and still support many of its positive properties, it was easy to conceive of other useful and interesting extensions. We mention here one direction, that will be the focus of attention for the sequel. Although one might naively believe that relational database systems use only sets (of tuples), in reality often *bag* semantics is used in query processing, both for ensuring correct results for aggregates and for avoiding the cost of duplicate elimination. The actual data storage is often serial, very close to lists. So why not deal with these data types in the open, at the conceptual level. Even more importantly, it is clear that if database technology is to be deployed and heavily used in areas outside its traditional business-oriented domain, such as engineering or scientific applications, it must support data types needed by these areas, which may include trees, ordered and unordered lists, arrays and so on.

These observations have recently led researchers to consider the general notion of *bulk type*. Intuitively, a data type is a bulk type if its instances are used to store elements of another type, and are unbounded in size. All the data types mentioned above fit this description. Some of the questions we would like to pose about bulk types are the following: What precisely is a bulk type? Do bulk types support declarative query languages? Can we find *one* language paradigm to fit all bulk types (probably with type-specific additions) or will we need different languages for different types? The latter option is clearly undesirable — we cannot expect users to learn a new language for each type. We would like bulk types to support some reasonable notion of uniform, polymorphic programming on instances of bulk types. We would like also to allow users to define bulk types specially tailored for their applications. Finally, we would like to understand more about the expressiveness and complexity of query language(s) for different types, and how query optimization may be performed.

At this point, we have completed the description of the background for the discussion of the main subject of this paper, which is a general framework recently proposed for bulk types and their associated query languages.

4 Monad-Based Data Types

A monad is a category with some additional structure. The proposal that monads can serve to describe properties of programming languages and constructs was made by Moggi [17], and further explored by Wadler [25]. Monads, and various variations, have been used to provide a definition for bulk types and a framework for the study of their query languages in many recent papers [5, 12, 11, 10, 18, 27, 20, 23, 21, 25, 26]; our discussion is based on these papers, mostly [5, 27, 20, 23, 21, 25].

4.1 Categories

A category consists of a set of *objects*, and a set of *arrows* between them, i.e., every arrow has a domain and co-domain. A very common case is that the arrows are functions, but they can also be relations, or other kinds of entities. A category is required to have an identity arrow for each object, and to have an associative composition operation on arrows (subject to the obvious domain/codomain compatibility restrictions).

Category theory has become a standard framework for theoretical studies of programming languages, especially of typed functional languages. A primary reason is that models for such languages are categories. Indeed, one can take the set of types of a language to be the set of objects of a category, and the set of functions of type $s \to t$ to be the set of arrows from s to t. As any reasonable functional language has an identity function for each type, and can express composition of functions, a semantic model of the language is a category. Although this observation, by itself, is rather uninspiring, experience has proved that the category-theoretic approach is useful in the study of programming languages and their semantics. Experience has also shown that the notion of a category, by itself, does not have enough structure to be very interesting. Useful properties of languages are modeled by additional structure of the category.

The observation above is valid in the context of database query languages. For example, for a relational framework, one can take (the types of) vectors of relations as the objects, and certain functions between them, such as the queries expressible in a given query language, as arrows. It is reasonable to assume that the query language can express the identity queries and composition of queries, hence this is indeed a category. As relations and their queries are simple and well-understood, one may feel that a category-based approach may not be beneficial. Furthermore, a category-based approach seems most useful when one wants to study a universes with a variety of structures and their relationships to each other. That does not seem to be the case with the relational model. However, the challenge we are facing, namely a characterization of the concept 'bulk type', with an emphasis on queries and query languages, calls for abstraction and generality. The use of 'category' abstracts away from the details of specific bulk types, and offers a convenient framework for studying the common features of a variety of bulk types.

Our task is, therefore, to find additional structure and properties of categories that reflect our understanding of bulk types, and that will enable us to understand and to reason uniformly about bulk types.

4.2 Monads, Ringads, ...

A *strong monad* is defined by the following three requirements:

Cat: It is a category, with *products*, and with *enough points* (that we denote below by **Cat**).

Products are used to create pairs and tuples. We might prefer to use labeled products, to construct records with attributes, but for the presentation of the ideas here simple products suffice. We assume that a type *unit* with a single element, denoted () is included. This type is the *empty product*. Having enough points is a technical condition. Its use is in that it enables one to prove that arrows in certain sets are distinct from each other.[8] It is not considered further in this paper

[8] It is somewhat problematic in that it rules out potentially interesting categories, so its precise role in the definition of (strong) monads merits further study.

Map: There exists an *endofunctor* M on the category.

A functor between categories is a category homomorphism. An endofunctor is a functor from a category to itself. Thus, M maps each object τ to another object: $\tau \mapsto M\tau$; and it maps every arrow between a pair of objects to an arrow between their images: $f : \tau \rightarrow \sigma \mapsto Mf : M\tau \rightarrow M\sigma$. Furthermore, M is a homomorphism, hence it preserves identity functions and composition of functions, see Fig. 4.2(a).[9]

For intuition, assume the objects are data types, and the arrows are functions (i.e., queries), as described above. Further, assume as a running example that we have a set type constructor. The existence of the constructor is modeled as a mapping from objects to objects: $M : \tau \mapsto set(\tau)$. However, the category-theoretic framework forces us to realize that a mapping on the types should be accompanied by a mapping on the functions. For the example, this is the higher-order function *map*, and indeed, if $f : \tau \rightarrow \sigma$ then $map(f) : set(\tau) \rightarrow set(\sigma)$.[10] Furthermore, *map* satisfies the equations of Fig. 4.2(a). It can be seen that *bag, list, tree* ... can replace *set*; a *map* function is naturally defined for each of our bulk type candidates. *Map* is an extension functional: it extends a function from a type to another to a function from the bulk type over the first type to the bulk type over the second. Another view is that *map* is an order-independent *iterator*. The existence of such an extension functional can be taken as one of the basic axioms of bulk types.

Natural: There exist three polymorphic operations, that are *natural transformations* between appropriate functors:
- $\eta_\sigma : \sigma \rightarrow M\sigma$.
- $\mu_\sigma : M^2\sigma \rightarrow M\sigma$.
- $\rho_{2\,\sigma} : \sigma \times M\sigma \rightarrow M\sigma$.

To see the need for additional operations, let us consider what is still missing in our characterization. We have given to M the intuition of a data type constructor, and a corresponding extension functional. But, such a constructor should be accompanied by data-level operations, specifically by constructors, selectors and destructors. For the *set* example, a function *single* that converts an element into a singleton set is a constructor; a function *set-collapse* that takes a set of sets into its union is a (partial) destructor. These are η, μ above, respectively. Of course, each is actually a family of functions, one for each type τ; in other words, each is a polymorphic function. Their properties, and in particular how they interact with the functor *map*, are stated in Fig. 4.2(b). As for ρ_2, it is an operation that relates M and the product. In the world of sets, we take $\rho_2(x, S) = \{(x, s) \mid s \in S\}$ — an unnesting operation.

Now we consider how these operations are natural transformations. A functor from a category to another can be viewed as embedding an image of the one in the other. Two functors create two images. A natural transformation between two functors expresses the intuition that the images are *uniformly* related. It is defined

[9] A full set of equations/diagrams for a strong monad can be found in [5]; we only give some of them in Fig. 4.2.

[10] Following category-theoretic notation we should have used *set* for both the mapping on the objects and the mapping on the functions. However, the notation we are using is common, actually standard, in the functional languages literature.

$$map(id_\tau) = id_{M\tau} \qquad\qquad map(f \circ g) = map(f) \circ map(g) \ .$$

(a)

$$\mu \circ \eta = id \qquad \mu \circ map(\eta) = id \qquad \mu \circ map(\mu) = \mu \circ \mu$$
$$(map(f)) \circ \eta = \eta \circ f \qquad (map(f)) \circ \mu = \mu \circ map(map(f)) \ .$$

(b)

Fig. 1 Equations for *map*, μ and η.

by a family of mappings, from the objects in the first image to those in the second image. Uniformity is expressed as follows: If P, Q, n are the two functors and the natural transformation, then for each $f : \tau \to \sigma$ in the source category, we have $Pf : P\tau \to P\sigma$, and $Qf : Q\tau \to Q\sigma$ in the target category. We further have two mappings $n_\tau : P\tau \to Q\tau$ and $n_\sigma : P\sigma \to Q\sigma$. Uniformity requires that the resulting diagram commutes.

Polymorphism is known to correspond closely to uniformity in this sense. In our case, we are dealing with endofunctors - functors from **Cat** to itself. If we denote by I the identity functor, the it can be seen that η_σ maps from $I\sigma$ to $M\sigma$, and is indeed a natural transformation. For example, consider the case when η is *single* and M corresponds to the *set* constructor. The functor I is the identity on types and functions; M maps the type τ to $set(\tau)$ and the function $f : \tau \to \sigma$ to $map(f) : set(\sigma) \to set(\tau)$. For an element $v : \tau$, we can either map it to $f(v) : \sigma$, then apply η_σ to obtain $\{f(v)\} : set(\sigma)$, or first apply η_τ to obtain $\{v\}$, then apply $map(f)$, to obtain the same value. This tells us that *map* treats its argument function as a black box, hence applying the function commutes with the application of the data type constructor.

Similarly, μ is a natural transformation from M^2 (the composition of M with itself) to M. For ρ_2, it is a natural transformation between the endofunctor on **Cat** that takes each object (τ, σ) (recall that **Cat** has products, so this is an object in the category) to $(I\tau, M\sigma)$ and the functor that takes each such object to $M(\tau, \sigma)$. The function ρ_2 has the polymorphic type $(\tau, M\sigma) \to M(\tau, \sigma)$, as required.

One may inquire why these operations and not others. The observant reader may also have noticed that η, μ are not really sufficient. For sets, we could add $\emptyset_{set(\tau)}$ as a constant, and $\cup_{set(\tau)}$ as a binary operation, for type τ. The triple *single*, $\emptyset$, $\cup$ is a *complete presentation* for sets: Given a domain τ, every set in $set(\tau)$ can be constructed from τ-elements by applying these operations. Furthermore, as noted below, $\emptyset$ and $\cup$ are independent from the monad operations (in a sense to be made more precise below). Thus, it makes sense to add them to the definition above. The interaction of these operations with M and with each other is expressed by additional equations, such as $map(f)(\emptyset) = \emptyset$ and $map(f)(S_1 \cup S_2) = map(f)(S_1) \cup map(f)(S_2)$, both re-emphasizing the treatment of f by *map* as a black box. A category with $M, \eta, \mu, \emptyset, \cup$ is called in [26] a *ringad*.

We defer a discussion of the choice of operations to follow the presentation of the languages in the next section. The results described in the sequel are not specific to monads, but apply to extensions thereof as well; to some extent they even hold for structures that are simpler than monads. For simplicity, in the sequel we use 'monad' as a generic name for these structures. Also, as our main interest is in queries, we use from now types and functions as synonyms to objects and arrows, respectively.

Given any collection of types with corresponding domains and functions (i.e. an algebra), one can construct a monad based on it by closing under M, and adding operations that are defined only for types of the form $M\tau$, such as $\emptyset, \cup$. From now we restrict attention to monads that are so constructed. The results described below hold for monads constructed over any such algebra of domains and functions. The underlying parameter algebra is described by a *parameter signature* Σ, containing *constants, base arrows (functions)*, possibly also equations describing their properties.

5 ...and Their Query Languages

Our interest in monads is motivated by the fact that they support several languages, that can be viewed as query languages. The languages are an algebra, a calculus, and a comprehensions language, denoted M–ALG, λ-M–CALC, M-COMP, respectively. We provide below a sketchy outline of the languages; full descriptions can be found in the references. For simplicity, we omit most type subscripts.

5.1 M–ALG

The algebraic language is *the language of the monad*. What that means is simply the following: Suppose that in considering a category we concentrate on the arrows; the collection of arrows is an algebra, with a collection of constants, namely the identity arrows, and one operation, namely composition. The language of the category consists of the constant names, and the composition operation. Terms in the language denote elements of the algebra, as usual. Obviously, the language as described so far, corresponding to a category with no additional structure, is extremely uninteresting. However, it becomes more interesting when the category has additional structure, that adds to the language additional constants and operations. This is precisely the case with monads.

Database folklore has it that relational algebra is called an 'algebra' since it is a small collection of operations on a collection of values, namely relations. We see here an additional, different, viewpoint: the language is an algebra because it is an *algebra of functions*, namely it has operations for creating new functions from given functions.

The first component is the constants and functions of the parameter Σ, the domain on which our database is constructed. All functions of Σ are constants in our algebra. As we want our language to be an algebra of functions, a domain constant c of type τ is represented as a *constant function*, of the form $Kc : unit \rightarrow \tau$. Next, we have the identity function *id* and the *composition* operation, denoted $\circ$. These give the part that corresponds to the fact that we have a category. As the category has products, we add *pair, 1st, 2nd*. However, while the projections remain ordinary functions, pairing is elevated to a functional; *pair*(f, g) is written in the outfix notation $< f, g >$. We next add the operations of the monad: *map*, μ, ρ_2, η, and also any additional monad -related operations such as $\emptyset$ and $\cup$ we want to have. Needless to say that the equational theory of the monad can be used to reason about expressions in the language. In particular, rewrite rules can be derived from the equations. This is relevant to query optimization.

Incidentally, note that we can now state formally what it means for operations not to be expressible by others. E.g. given only the operations listed above, without $\emptyset$ and $\cup$, are there expressions that correspond to these two operations? By 'correspond' we mean that the expression for $\emptyset$ has the same meaning on the *set* monad (and also on other monads such as *bag, list*). It turns out that these two cannot be expressed by the others. This can be proved for sets, hence is true generally. Note that μ can almost express $\cup$ — all that is required is, given expressions x, y that denote sets, to be able to create the set $\{x, y\}$; then an application of μ gives the desired expression. However, can we form such a 2-set?

For convenience in comparing to the other languages below, let us split the algebra into three groups: The first contains the constants and functions of Σ, *id*, $\circ$, *pair, 1st, 2nd, map* and ρ_2. This is the core of the language, representing a category with *map* and products, over Σ. The second group contains μ, and the third contains the rest of the operations, in our case $\eta, \emptyset, \cup$.

5.2 λ-M–CALC

The second language is a λ-calculus, enriched by some special operations on one hand, and restricted to have only first-order abstraction on the other hand. Its core, corresponding to the core of M–ALG above, contains the following: The constants and functions of Σ, *pair, 1st, 2nd, map*, first-order λ-abstraction, and application. By 'first-order' we mean that abstraction is allowed only on expressions that have a data type, but not on expressions that have a function type. A data type is either a base type (of Σ) or a type obtained from a data type by an application of M or product. (Thus, function type construction is excluded.) Note that ρ_2 is not included in the core — it can be expressed as $\lambda(x, S).map(\lambda s.(x, s))(S)$. The second and third groups are identical to those of the algebra.

In the literature, the calculus is often presented using an somewhat different operation set. It does not contain μ, and *map*; in their place it has an operation called *extend*, or *ext*, of type $(\tau \rightarrow M\sigma) \rightarrow M\tau \rightarrow M\sigma$. For example, for sets, if $f : \tau \rightarrow set(\sigma)$, then $ext(f)(S) = \bigcup\{f(s) \mid s \in S\}$. Thus, it extends a function in a manner very similar to *map*, except that it lifts only the domain type. The reason this operation is used rather than *map* is firstly, since it connects directly to one of the classical representations of monads, and secondly since it better connects to the third language we are about to introduce shortly. Both μ and *map* can be expressed in the *ext*-based representation: μ is expressed by $ext(\lambda x.x)$, where the identity function is of type $M\tau \rightarrow M\tau$, and $map(f) = ext(\lambda x.\eta(f(x)))$. On the other hand, $ext = \mu \circ map$. These interdependencies can be expressed in M–ALG as well. The results about inexpressibility of some operations by others are valid for this language as well.

The fundamental theorem about these languages is:

$$\text{M–ALG} \equiv \lambda - M - CALC \ .$$

The translations preserve the meanings of expressions, and also the equational theories. We do not present the proof here; see [5] for the details. We do make a few remarks, however. First, there is a well-known theorem of equivalence of typed λ-calculus with *cartesian-closed* categories (CCC's). Essentially it says that these categories are the models of the calculus, and it gives a translation of the calculus into the language of CCC's. The theorem above shows that this connection can be extended to a variety of calculi and categories. One might be tempted to say that the version of the theorem we have is a poor man's correspondence between λ-calculi and categories: The categories we consider do not have an exponentiation operation. On the other side, compensating for that lack, only first-order abstraction is allowed in the calculus. This implies a slightly different approach to proving that the algebra is functionally complete - the crux of the λ-M–CALC to M–ALG translation.

To what extent are these languages relevant to databases? Let us again consider the case of sets. It can be seen that M–ALG can express the well-known operations of *project, cross*. The first uses *map* and the pairing and projection functions. For example, to project a relation on the first and third columns, we take the projection function on the the two columns, pair them, and apply *map* to the resulting function. The second uses ρ_2 (wtice) to create a set of pairs of elements from a pair of sets. Assuming that Σ contains a type *bool* with its operations, it can also express *select*. For that, $\emptyset, \eta$ and the pair μ and *map*, or the equivalent *ext* are used: Given a predicate p, one defines a function whose value for an argument x is $\{x\}$ if $p(x)$ equals *true* and $\emptyset$ otherwise. The function is extended with *ext* to give the required selection. Some set operations are included: $\eta, \emptyset, \cup$. Assuming equality on base types is given, the language can express *membership, subset, intersection, difference, nest*. In short, we have all the operations of co–ALG. In fact, the paper [5] shows that suitable restrictions give precisely the power of rel–ALG or of co–ALG. The language not only has the same expressive power, it is actually very similar to the one of [1] (without $\mathcal{P}$). It is a polynomial-time language.

Let us denote the calculus with *map* and the additional set of operations above by λ-M–CALC($\mu, \emptyset, \eta, \cup, =_{base}$); a similar notation can be used for the algebra, with *map* and ρ_2 as built-in operations. Then, assuming Σ contains *bool*, we have the following basic result *for the set monad*:

$$\lambda - \text{M-CALC } (\mu, \emptyset, \eta, \cup, =_{base}) \equiv \text{M–ALG}(\mu, \emptyset, \eta, \cup, =_{base}) \equiv \text{co–ALG} \ .$$

5.3 M-COMP

But, even more interesting from the database point of view is the third language — M-COMP. Let us illustrate it first with a few examples:

$$R \times S \equiv \{(x, y) \mid x \leftarrow R, y \leftarrow S\} \ .$$

$$\sigma_{A=8} \equiv \{x \mid x \leftarrow R, x.A = 8\} \ .$$

These express relational queries. The next one expresses μ on a complex value database, in whic R is a set of sets:

$$\{y \mid x \leftarrow R, y \leftarrow x\} \ .$$

For the relational model, comprehensions have the same power as CON, the sublanguage of the relational calculus consisting of conjunctive queries. and can be seen as an intermediate form between CON and SQL. They share with SQL the property that no quantifiers are used, but avoid the use of key words. The full language is the same as λ-M–CALC, except that *ext* is not included; it is replaced by a new construct, the comprehension, of the form $\{e \mid x_1 \leftarrow e_1, \ldots, x_n \leftarrow e_n\}$. Its semantics is given by reducing it to *ext*, as follows:

$$\{e \mid x \leftarrow e_1\} \equiv ext(\lambda x.\{e\})(e_1) \quad (\equiv map(\lambda x.e)(e_1)) \ .$$

$$\{e \mid x_1 \leftarrow e_1, \ldots, x_n \leftarrow e_n\} \equiv \mu(\{\{e \mid x_2 \leftarrow e_2, \ldots, x_n \leftarrow e_n\} \mid x_1 \leftarrow e_1\})$$

$$\equiv ext(\lambda x_1.\{e \mid x_2 \leftarrow e_2, \ldots, x_n \leftarrow e_n\})(e_1) \ .$$

There is an obvious similarity here to the translation from SQL or CON to SPJ. Note that the minimum that is required in the calculus is to have *ext*, equivalently *map* and μ. As additional operations are added, they can be used in the e_i's.

The fundamental theorem is now extended to

$$\lambda - \text{M-CALC } (\mu, \emptyset, \eta, \cup, =_{base}) \equiv \text{M–ALG}(\mu, \emptyset, \eta, \cup, =_{base})$$

$$\equiv \quad \text{M-COMP}(\emptyset, \eta, \cup, =_{base}) \equiv \text{co–ALG} \ .$$

5.4 On Bags

While the languages above are general, the examples were all presented in terms of sets. We also presented one result that was specific to sets, namely the equivalence of $\lambda -$ M-CALC $(\mu, \eta, \cup, =_{base})$ with M–ALG$(\mu, \eta, \cup, =_{base})$, and the fact that these languages express all known 'reasonable' polynomial-time operations on sets. While the equivalence result is general, the second part of the claim is not, with bags as an example. There are many more polynomial-time operations on bags than on sets, since bags allow a form of counting. Libkin and Wong [12] present about ten or more such operations that cannot be expressed in the monad languages. They show that the two operations *unique* (i.e., *bag-to-set*) and *monus* (a form of bag difference) are independent, and with their addition the monad languages can express all other bag operations. Hence they propose that the monad languages extended with these two operations be taken as the standard polynomial bag query language.

5.5 Normalization

We mention briefly one more interesting property of the λ and comprehension based monad languages, which is also an extension of classical results about typed λ calculi. The result can be stated very simply: There is a set of rewrite rules, derived from the monad equations, such that the resulting system is strongly normalizing

[27]. Example rules are $1st(e_1, e_2) \leadsto e_1$, or $(\lambda x.e)e' \leadsto e[e'/x]$. Both are standard rules for λ-calculus with products. Other rules deal, for example, with *ext*, or with comprehensions, and allow unnesting of comprehension expressions. As we have two languages, and as some rules apply only to certain data types but not to others (e.g., $\cup$ over lists is *append*, which is not commutative, whereas the corresponding operations for sets and bags are), we actually have several strongly normalizing systems. The details and the proofs (which are of independent interest) can be found in [27]. We discuss here the meaning and significance of the result.

An important point to note is that, in contrast to the standard λ-calculus, the rewrite system here is not (a basis for) a computation system — the normal form is not the *result* of the computation. Rather, it is a simplification system, and the normal form is a simplified form of the query. Thus, the relationship is to query optimization more than to query evaluation. The reason is that the languages have built-in iterators (either *ext* or comprehensions), which are the main tool for accessing the data, and these are not evaluated or simplified.

Important consequences of the strong normalization property relate to the normal form. One important corollary that can be proved by analysis of the normal form is that the *set height* of intermediate data is bounded by the set height of the input (the database collections) and the output (the query result). Hence a query that contains subexpressions of 'large' set height can be simplified to a query without such subexpressions. This result contrasts sharply with the results of [9] that for co–CALC with relational (i.e., set height 1) input and output, increasing set height of intermediate types increases the expressive power. Another way of stating the result is that λ-M–CALC, hence also M–ALG, are conservative extensions of rel–ALG. In particular, for relational input and output, transitive closure and powerset cannot be expressed.

Another interesting corollary is that in comprehensions there is (almost) no need for λ-abstraction. It is essentially needed only for abstraction at the outermost level, on the database collections. This reinforces the claim that comprehensions is a good basis for developing user-level languages.

6 Discussion

We have seen enough results to try a summary of the overall picture. The general framework for bulk types and their query languages can be viewed as a tree. At the root of the tree we find a minimum set of operations and properties of bulk types, and we proceed from a node to a child by adding operations and/or properties. The general results about the tree nodes include the existence of equivalent algebraic and λ-calculus based languages, with a uniform translation between them that is preserved by the addition of operations to both languages, and preserves equational theories including those of the additional operations. Further, there is a node very close to the root such that for this node and its descendents we have a third language — comprehensions, with uniform translation to the other languages. The languages are all in polynomial time, that is, their expressions are efficiently evaluable.[11] Fi-

[11] This holds by construction; it is true for the root, and we add only polynomial time operations to descendents.

nally, we have for each language a collection of (node-specific) rewrite rules, and for two of them we have a strong normalization property, with a useful normal form.

Let us now consider the tree structure. The minimum basis for a bulk type is a category with products and enough points, a constructor M with the associated support of *map* and ρ_2, over a parameter signature that contains *bool* and has equality on its types. This can be taken as the root, and it supports minimal versions of M–ALG and λ-M–CALC, and the translation between them. These minimum languages can express cross products and projections. If μ is added, then we obtain the ability to express *ext* and comprehensions. Note that *sets, bags, lists, trees* and many other bulk types fit the root; however, while trees with data in the leaves support μ, it seems trees with data in internal nodes do not. The addition of $\emptyset, \eta$ allows us to construct expressions of M type, and in particular, combined with *bool* and *ext*, it allows us to express selection queries. For sets, since we have equality on base types, it also gives the ability to express membership, intersection and difference. These seem reasonable operations for any bulk type. So far, we have not seen much branching.

Now, to complete the collection of operations for sets, bags, lists, and many other types, we add a $\cup$ operation. Its interpretation depends, of course, on the type: *append* for lists, *merge* for ordered lists, and so on. Branching now occurs since for sets we seem to have reached a sufficiently powerful language, but for bags we need more operations. Furthermore, two-dimensional arrays can also be viewed as a bulk type, and for them it may be natural to consider two such operations — horizontal and vertical combination of arrays — another reason for branching. Another approach to arrays is to consider a two-dimensional array as a one-dimensional array of arrays. Despite being less symmetrical in the two dimensions, this approach seems to work fine [6]. Thus, from the node with $\emptyset, \eta$, we can expect type-specific branching. A catalogue of operations and their properties for specific types is still to be constructed.

7 Conclusions

The results described in this paper indicate recent developments in the database area, motivated by the need to generalize the relational model, that are pushing query languages closer to functional languages. The framework we described clearly benefits from bringing together ideas of the two domains. It also demonstrates that ideas from category theory can contribute to query language design, by providing a general framework, and abstraction. Another interesting point is that predicate calculus has been replaced in this framework by λ-calculus; declarative logic has been replaced by a computational logic. Issues like domain independence seem to become non-issue because of that.

It is interesting to note that our framework also includes results that are related to query optimization techniques. Monad equations can generate rewrite rules, resembling the algebraic rewrite rules of relational languages. The normalization algorithms resemble subquery elimination.

Among the many issues that still need to be addressed, we note the following:

- We have shown a general framework, but also that type-specific constructions are needed. A catalogue of such constructions, to serve as type-specific extensions of the general query languages needs to be developed.
- Although rewrite rules can potentially serve for query optimization, the use of monad rules for this purpose still need to be worked out. Additionally, query algebras generally use operations or clusters of operations for which several evaluation strategies are available. A case in point is product, which is often combined with selections and projections to be optimized together. The M–ALG operations seem to be of too fine a granularity. For example, it has no product, since that is expressed by using ρ_2. Finally, query systems use cost-based heuristics and intermediate data size estimates. it is not clear at all how to integrate these approaches into the monad-based framework.
- The framework needs to be extended to provide for recursion, as used in datalog and logic programming, and for aggregate functions, without allowing expensive operations like *powerset*. Some work in this direction has been reported in the literature, e.g., in [11, 18].

Note: The following references have not been mentioned in the paper: [3, 4, 16, 22, 24]

References

1. S. Abiteboul and C. Beeri. On the power of query languages for complex objects. *The VLDB Journal*, 1994. to appear.
2. S. Abiteboul, R. Hull, and V. Vianu. *Database Theory From A to F.* Addison-Wesley, 1994. to appear.
3. M. Atkinson, P. Richard, and P. Trinder. Bulk types for large scale programming. In *Proc. 1st Int'l East-West Database Workshop on Next Generation Information System Technology, Kiev, USSR, Oct. 9 -12, 1990*, volume 504 of *LNCS*, pages 229–250. Springer-Verlag, 1991.
4. V. Breazau-Tannen, P. Buneman, and S. Naqvi. Structural recursion as a query language. In P. Kanellakis and J. Schmidt, editors, *Proc. 3rd Int'l Workshop on Database Programming Languages, Nafplion, Greece, Aug. 27–30, 1991*, pages 9–19. Morgan Kaufmann Publishers, 1992.
5. V. Breazu-Tannen, P. Buneman, and L. Wong. Naturally embedded query languages. In *Proc. 4'th Int'l Conference on Database Theory, Berlin, Germany*, volume 646 of *LNCS*, pages 140–154. Springer-Verlag, Oct. 1992.
6. P. Buneman. The fast fourier transform as a database query. Unpublished, 1993.
7. E. F. Codd. Relational completeness of database sublanguages. In R. Rustin, editor, *Data Base Systems*, pages 65–98. Prentice-Hall, 1972.
8. S. Grumbach and V. Vianu. Tractable query languages for complex object databases. In *Proc. 10th ACM SIGACT-SIGMOD-SIGART Symposium on Principles of Database Systems (PODS), Denver, Colorado*, 1991.
9. R. Hull and J. Su. On the expressive power of database queries with intermediate types. *Journal of Computer and System Science*, 43:219–267, 1991.
10. L. Libkin and L. Wong. Semantic properties and query languages for or-sets. In *Proc. 12th ACM SIGACT-SIGMOD-SIGART Symposium on Principles of Database Systems (PODS), Washington, D.C.*, pages 37–48, May 1993.

11. L. Libkin and L. Wong. Aggregate functions, conservative extension, and linear orders. In *Proc. 4'th Int'l Workshop on Database Programming Languages, New York City*, pages 282–294. Springer-Verlag, 1994.
12. L. Libkin and L. Wong. Some properties of query languages for bags. In *Proc. 4'th Int'l Workshop on Database Programming Languages, New York City*, pages 97–114. Springer-Verlag, 1994.
13. A. Makinouchi. A consideration of normal form of not-necessarily-normalized relations in the relational data model. In *Proc. 3rd Int'l Conference on Very Large Databases, Tokyo, Japan*, pages 447–453, Oct. 1977.
14. G. Malcolm. Homomorphisms and promotability. In *Mathematics of Program Construction*, volume 375 of *LNCS*, pages 335–347. Springer-Verlag, 1989.
15. F. Manola and U. Dayal. PDM: An object-oriented data model. In *Int'l Workshop on Object-Oriented Database Systems*, pages 18–25. IEEE, 1986.
16. F. Matthes and J. Schmidt. Bulk types: Built-in or add-on? In *Proc. 3rd Int'l Workshop on Database Programming Languages, Nafplion, Greece, Aug. 27–30, 1991*, pages 33–54. Morgan Kaufmann Publishers, 1992.
17. E. Moggi. Notions of computation and monads. *Information and Computation*, 93:55–92, 1991.
18. D. Suciu. Bounded fixpoints for complex objects. In *Proc. 4'th Int'l Workshop on Database Programming Languages, New York City*, pages 263–281. Springer-Verlag, 1994.
19. D. Suciu and J. Paredaens. Any algorithm in the complex object algebra with powwerset needs exponential space to compute transitive closure. In *Proc. 13th ACM SIGACT-SIGMOD-SIGART Symposium on Principles of Database Systems (PODS), Minneapolis, MN*, pages 201–209, May 1994.
20. V. Tannen. Tutorial: Languages for collection types. In *Proc. 13th ACM SIGACT-SIGMOD-SIGART Symposium on Principles of Database Systems (PODS), Minneapolis, MN*, pages 150–154, May 1994.
21. P. Trinder. Comprehensions, a query notation for DBPLs. In P. Kanellakis and J. Schmidt, editors, *Proc. 3rd Int'l Workshop on Database Programming Languages, Nafplion, Greece, Aug. 27–30, 1991*, pages 55–68. Morgan Kaufmann Publishers, 1992.
22. P. Trinder and P. Wadler. List comprehensions and the relational calculus. In *Proc. 1988 Glasgow Workshop on Functional Programming, Rothesay, Scotland*, pages 115–123, Aug. 1988.
23. P. Trinder and P. Wadler. Improving list comprehension database queries. In *Proc. 4th IEEE Int'l Conference - Information Technologies for the 90's (TENCOM'89), Bombay, India*, pages 186–192, Nov. 1989.
24. P. Wadler. List comprehensions. In S. L. P. Jones, editor, *The Implementation of Functional Programming Languages (Chapt. 7)*, pages 127–138. Prentice Hall, 1987.
25. P. Wadler. Comprehending monads. *Mathematical Structures in Computer Science*, (2):461–493, 1992.
26. D. Watt and P. Trinder. Towards a theory of bulk types. Fide Technical Report 91/26, Department of Computing Science, University of Glasgow, July 1991.
27. L. Wong. Normal forms and conservative properties for query languages over collection types. In *Proc. 12th ACM SIGACT-SIGMOD-SIGART Symposium on Principles of Database Systems (PODS), Washington, D.C.*, pages 26–36, May 1993.

From Abstract Data Types to Logical Frameworks*

José Meseguer and Narciso Martí-Oliet

SRI International, Menlo Park, CA 94025, and
Center for the Study of Language and Information
Stanford University, Stanford, CA 94305

Abstract. This paper surveys ways in which the ideas and concepts developed in the research field of abstract data types have undergone a vigorous process of generalization that has led to the development of axiomatic notions of logic and of expressive multiparadigm logics.
On the one hand, the generalization from equational specifications to specifications in any logic requires general metalogical concepts making precise what logics are. Beginning with the notion of institution, several notions have been proposed to cover different needs arising in this task; we discuss these notions and summarize in particular the main ideas of the theory of general logics, which is a specific line of work in this area.
On the other hand, the extension of equational logic in several directions to make specifications and programs more expressive has given rise to powerful multiparadigm logics in which other specification and programming paradigms can be cleanly combined with the equational one; we discuss several of these extensions, including rewriting logic, which unifies equational, Horn, object-oriented, and concurrent specification and programming.
These two lines of research converge in the idea of a logical framework, that is, an expressive enough logic in which many other logics can be represented. We use notions from the theory of general logics to make precise the concept of a logical framework, and summarize our recent work on the use of rewriting logic as a logical framework as a promising particular approach.
Finally, we explain how these general concepts can help us achieve the practical goal of formal interoperability, that is, how they can provide a mathematical foundation to rigorously interoperate the different formalisms and tools that we need to use in order to formally specify and verify systems.

* Supported by Office of Naval Research Contracts N00014-90-C-0086 and N00014-92-C-0222, National Science Foundation Grant CCR-9224005, and by the Information Technology Promotion Agency, Japan, as a part of the Industrial Science and Technology Frontier Program "New Models for Software Architecture" sponsored by NEDO (New Energy and Industrial Technology Development Organization).

Table of Contents

1 Introduction

Since the emergence of the algebraic theory of abstract data types in the late 1970's, the field and its fundamental concepts have matured, and an impressive body of research has been developed thanks to the contributions of many people. The recent ADT Workshops bibliography compiled by Gogolla and Cerioli [49] as well as the survey and bibliography on algebraic specifications by Bidoit et al. [15] can give a feeling for some of the impressive research activity that has taken place.

In addition to the progress experienced within the specific area of abstract data types, some of the ideas and concepts developed for it have undergone a vigorous process of generalization that has greatly broadened their area of applicability far beyond data types. General theories of formal methods and specification languages, the notion of a logical framework, general notions of logic programming language, and unifications of programming and specification paradigms can be seen as emerging in some way from ideas originally developed in the theory of algebraic data types.

A good case in point is the generalization by Burstall and Goguen of the Clear equational specification language [19] to specification building operations in a general *institution* [54]. Many other contributions by other researchers have explored the general idea of making the logic of a specification language a parameter by developing adequate axiomatic notions of logic; several of these contributions are discussed in Section 2.1 below (see also [88]). In particular, it is possible to develop a theory of *general logics* in which the derivability relation, the proofs, and the models of a logic appear as different modular components of a logic in such a way that some lacking components can be added by adjoint constructions [96]. This has been exploited by Cerioli and Meseguer to obtain a general method of endowing a logic with additional structure by "borrowing" the missing structure from another logic [23, 24].

Another way in which ideas from algebraic data types have been generalized to attain wider applicability is by generalizing equational logic to more expressive logics that also have good properties such as the existence of initial and free models, but that support a wider range of applications. For example, many-sorted equational logic has been generalized to "sketchable" partial equational logic [118], and to order-sorted logic (see [60] and references there); and several higher-order extensions of equational logic that have initial models have been proposed. Similarly, order-sorted equational logic and Horn logic have been unified in order-sorted Horn logic with equality [59]. In this way, the equational and the Horn logic programming paradigms could be unified with an initial model semantics. These two paradigms and that of concurrent object-oriented programming have been recently unified by means of (order-sorted) rewriting logic [99, 100, 101], a logic of concurrent action in which equational and Horn logic are conservatively embedded, and which is very well suited for declarative specification and machine-independent programming of concurrent systems [83].

The two generalization efforts mentioned above, namely the search for a good theory of general logics and the progressive generalization of equational logic into increasingly more expressive extensions, can in fact be related in fruitful ways. Besides being able to use general logics as a metatheory supporting such multiparadigm generalization efforts [100], if an expressive enough logic $\mathcal{F}$ is found, it may be possible to use it as a *logical framework* in which many other logics can be represented by maps of logics. This is indeed the case for rewriting logic, as we have recently shown in [87, 88], where we show that rewriting logic can also be used as a general and expressive *semantic framework* in which a wide variety of systems and languages, including concurrent ones, can be naturally specified and prototyped.

What unique contributions to the broader area of software foundations and formal methods do these conceptual developments place us in a position to make? Probably many, but we believe that a particularly pressing problem that they could solve is the serious need for *formal interoperability* among different formal methods and specification formalisms, that is, the capacity to move in a mathematically rigorous way across the different formalizations of a system, and to use in a rigorously integrated way the different tools supporting such formalizations.

Indeed, it is a fact of life that different formal requirements of a software system such as functional correctness, real time behavior, concurrency, security, and fault tolerance are often expressed in *different* formal systems, and for very good reasons. There is no such thing as *the best* specification language for *all* purposes, only more or less adequate formalisms for some given purposes. Therefore, what we badly need in practice—and we do not have at present—is a way to rigorously interoperate the different formalisms and tools that we need to use in order to formally specify and verify systems. General axiomatic notions of logic and of map between logics, and logical frameworks allowing the representations of many logics can provide the necessary foundation upon which useful metatools providing automatic support for formal interoperability can be based.

As can be gathered from the table of contents, in Section 2 we discuss the generalization to general logics, in Section 3 we consider multiparadigm extensions of equational logic, in Section 4 we show how these two generalizations can be combined together in a logical framework, and in Section 5 we explain how these general concepts can help us achieve the goal of formal interoperability. We finish the paper with some concluding remarks.

Although this paper tries to give an overview of research developments in all the areas mentioned and we have tried to include references to the work of many authors, the bibliography is certainly not exhaustive. Besides, the paper includes sections written from a more personal perspective, in which we summarize our own specific proposals for solving particular problems.

2 From ADTs to General Logics

After a general discussion of institutions [54] and related notions, we give a brief summary of the theory of general logics [96], and of the process of borrowing logical structure along maps of logics [23].

2.1 Institutions and Generalizations

The Clear language [19] provided very useful mechanisms to structure algebraic specifications in a highly modular and parameterized way. A variety of other algebraic specification languages have since then further developed this approach. It was soon realized that the theory-combining operations underlying the semantics of Clear only depended on a few properties enjoyed by many other logics. This led to the theory of *institutions* [52, 54].

The relationship between institutions and abstract model theory is worth discussing. Barwise wrote a fundamental paper axiomatizing *abstract model theory* [9]. A key motivation was to make explicit what a wide variety of logics extending standard first order logic, such as second order logic, logics with generalized quantifiers, and infinitary logics, had in common, by developing an axiomatic framework in which all of them would fit. Barwise observed that certain properties of a logic were "soft" in the sense that they could be proved with very minimal assumptions in his general axiomatic setting, rather than depending on properties unique to a particular logic. Much research has been done in this area since the appearance of Barwise's axioms. An excellent overview of the field can be gained from the collection of papers in [10], which also contains a very complete bibliography.

In a certain sense, abstract model theory is not abstract enough. The key limiting assumption built into the framework is that models are typical set-theoretic structures as those used in first order logic, that is, a set, or a many-sorted collection of sets, together with functions and relations defined on such a set or sets. Although much useful work can be done under those assumptions, there are other logics whose models are of a different nature. Therefore, a fully general and abstract model theory should make very minimal assumptions about the models of a logic. Goguen and Burstall's notion of *institution* [52, 53, 54] provides precisely an axiomatization of abstract model theory in which the class of models associated to a given syntax only satisfies the minimal assumption of forming a category (which in particular could be just a set or a class if the category is discrete). Basically, an institution consists of a category **Sign** of signatures and a functor *sen* : **Sign** $\rightarrow$ **Set** associating to each signature a set of sentences, together with a functor **Mod** that associates to each signature Σ a category of *Σ-models*, and a binary relation $\models$ between models and sentences called *satisfaction* satisfying appropriate requirements. Goguen and Burstall have shown that institutions can be very useful in computer science in a variety of ways, including the definition of specification languages with powerful modularity and parameterization mechanisms (see also [123, 124] for examples of related work on applying institutions to software specification).

Subsequent work by a number of authors has shown that Barwise's observation about the possibility of "soft" proofs for properties of a logic remains true in the more general setting of institutions. For example, Tarlecki [131, 132, 133, 134] explores a number of such properties in an institutional framework, including the treatment of open formulae and universal quantification, free models, varieties and quasi-varieties, Craig's Interpolation Theorem, Robinson's Consistency Theorem, and Lindenbaum's Theorem. A careful study of Craig's Interpolation Theorem for institutions can be found in a more recent paper by Diaconescu, Goguen, and Stefaneas [31] (who also study modularity issues). Finally, an axiomatic study of the Löwenheim–Skolem Theorem has been presented by Salibra and Scollo [121, 122] in their somewhat more general preinstitution framework.

An important notion in the theory of institutions is that of *institution morphism* by which one institution can be related to another. Besides the original notion proposed by Goguen and Burstall, other related notions have been proposed, such as *preinstitution transformation* [122], *simulation* [5], *semi-institution morphism* [124], and *map of institutions* [96]. Cerioli's thesis [22] contains a good discussion of many of these notions and their relative advantages and disadvantages.

The notion of institution has been generalized in several ways. On the one hand, weaker notions such as those of *preinstitution* [122] relax the requirements that the satisfaction relation between models and sentences must meet, or do away with the satisfaction relation altogether, as in the case of *specification frames* [34]. On the other hand, the satisfaction relation can be enriched, so that instead of just assigning to a model and a sentence either *true* or *false*, a richer collection of truth values is used instead. Specifically, the poset formed by the two standard truth values can be replaced by a *category* of truth values. The first proposal for an enrichment of this kind was made by Mayoh with his notion of *gallery* [94]. This was later generalized by Goguen and Burstall [53] to the notion of *$\mathcal{V}$-institution*, where $\mathcal{V}$ is a category of values for the satisfaction relation. An even more ambitious generalization that uses indexed categories to take account of substitutions in formulas is provided by Poigné's notion of *foundation* [113].

The theory of institutions was primarily developed to axiomatize the model theory of logics in a general and flexible way. There are however other aspects of a logic quite different from its model theory, such as its entailment relation and its proof theory, that are also very important and are in addition very well suited for computational treatment. Although some aspects of deduction can be addressed using $\mathcal{V}$-institutions [53] and foundations [113], a promising alternative is to investigate such notions independently of the concept of institution, although in a similar spirit. In this way, a modular view of the different aspects of a logic such as its model theory, entailment relation, and proof theory can be developed, and appropriate notions of map preserving the logical structure of each aspect can be formulated. This is precisely the goal of the theory of general logics [96]; it tries to understand the different components of a logic (model theory, deducibility relation, proof theory) in a modular way, to allow focusing on those components relevant for each application. Section 2.2 below discusses in more detail the theory of general logics.

For the case of entailment systems, which focus on the entailment relation between a set of sentences and a consequence sentence, two other related notions that have been proposed in the literature are *π-institution* [40] (recently generalized in [39]) and *logical system* [67].

We can summarize our discussion of institutions and related notions by listing the following developments:

1. Weaker notions of institution and/or different notions of institution morphism:
   - simulations [5],
   - preinstitutions [121],
   - specification frames [34],
   - semi-institution morphisms [124],
   - map of institutions [96].
2. More general truth values:
   - galleries [94],
   - $\mathcal{V}$-institutions [53],
   - foundations [113].
3. Related notions for deducibility aspects of a logic:
   - π-institutions [40, 39],
   - logical systems [67, 68],
   - entailment systems [96],
   - proof calculi [96].

2.2 General Logics

A modular and general axiomatic theory of logics should adequately cover all the key ingredients of a logic. These include: a *syntax*, a notion of *entailment* of a sentence from a set of axioms, a notion of *model*, and a notion of *satisfaction* of a sentence by a model. The theory of *general logics* [96] provides axiomatic notions formalizing the different aspects of a logic and of their combinations into fuller notions of logic:

- An *entailment system* axiomatizes the consequence relation of a logic.
- The notion of *institution* [54] covers the model-theoretic aspects of a logic, focusing on the notion of satisfaction as discussed in Section 2.1.
- A *logic* is obtained by combining an entailment system and an institution.
- A *proof calculus* enriches an entailment system with an actual proof theory.
- A *logical system* is a logic with a choice of a proof calculus for it.

Here we give a brief review of the required notions; a detailed account with many examples can be found in [96] (see also [87, 88]).

Syntax can typically be given by a *signature* Σ providing a grammar on which to build *sentences*. We assume that for each logic there is a category **Sign** of possible signatures for it, and a functor *sen* assigning to each signature Σ the set $sen(\Sigma)$ of all its sentences. For a given signature Σ in **Sign**, *entailment* (also called *provability*) of a sentence $\varphi \in sen(\Sigma)$ from a set of axioms $\Gamma \subseteq sen(\Sigma)$ is a relation $\Gamma \vdash \varphi$ which holds if and only if we can prove φ from the axioms Γ using the rules of the logic. This relation must be reflexive, monotone, transitive, and must preserve translations between signatures. These components constitute an *entailment system*.

Combining an entailment system and an institution we obtain a *logic*, defined as a 5-tuple $\mathcal{L} = (\mathbf{Sign}, sen, \mathbf{Mod}, \vdash, \models)$ such that:

- $(\mathbf{Sign}, sen, \vdash)$ is an entailment system,
- $(\mathbf{Sign}, sen, \mathbf{Mod}, \models)$ is an institution,

and the following *soundness condition* is satisfied: for any $\Sigma \in |\mathbf{Sign}|$, $\Gamma \subseteq sen(\Sigma)$, and $\varphi \in sen(\Sigma)$,

$$\Gamma \vdash \varphi \implies \Gamma \models \varphi,$$

where, by definition, the relation $\Gamma \models \varphi$ holds if and only if $M \models \varphi$ holds for any model M that satisfies all the sentences in Γ.

The detailed treatment in [96] includes also a flexible axiomatic notion of a *proof calculus*—in which proofs of entailments, not just the entailments themselves, are first class citizens—and the notion of a *logical system* that consists of a logic together with a choice of a proof calculus for it.

One of the most interesting fruits of the theory of general logics is that it gives us a method for *relating* logics in a general and systematic way, and to exploit such relations in many applications. The key notion is that of a *mapping* translating one logic into another

$$\mathcal{L} \longrightarrow \mathcal{L}'$$

that preserves whatever logical properties are relevant, such as provability of formulas, or satisfaction of a formula by a model. Therefore, we have maps of entailment systems, institutions, logics, proof calculi, and logical systems. Such mappings allow us to relate in a rigorous way different logics, to combine different formalisms together, and to explore new logics for computational purposes. A detailed treatment of such maps is given in [96]; here we just give a brief sketch.

Basically, a map of entailment systems $(\Phi, \alpha) : \mathcal{E} \longrightarrow \mathcal{E}'$ maps the language of $\mathcal{E}$ to that of $\mathcal{E}'$ in a way that respects the entailment relation. This means that signatures of $\mathcal{E}$ are functorially mapped by Φ to signatures of $\mathcal{E}'$, and that sentences of $\mathcal{E}$ are mapped by α to sentences of $\mathcal{E}'$ in a way that is coherent with the mapping of their corresponding signatures. In addition, α must respect the entailment relations $\vdash$ of $\mathcal{E}$ and $\vdash'$ of $\mathcal{E}'$, i.e., we must have

$$\Gamma \vdash \varphi \Rightarrow \alpha(\Gamma) \vdash' \alpha(\varphi).$$

The map is *conservative* when this implication is an equivalence. For many interesting applications one needs to map signatures of $\mathcal{E}$ to *theories* of $\mathcal{E}'$, that is, Σ is mapped by Φ to (Σ', Γ'), with $\Gamma' \subseteq sen'(\Sigma')$. It is this more general notion of *map between entailment systems* that is axiomatized by the definition in [96].

A *map of institutions* $(\Phi, \alpha, \beta) : \mathcal{I} \longrightarrow \mathcal{I}'$ is similar in its syntax part to a map of entailment systems. In addition, for models we have a natural functor $\beta : \mathbf{Mod}'(\Phi(\Sigma)) \longrightarrow \mathbf{Mod}(\Sigma)$ "backwards" from the models in $\mathcal{I}'$ of a translated signature $\Phi(\Sigma)$ to the models in $\mathcal{I}$ of the original signature Σ, and such a mapping respects the satisfaction relations $\models$ of $\mathcal{I}$ and $\models'$ of $\mathcal{I}'$, in the sense that $M' \models' \alpha(\varphi) \iff \beta(M') \models \varphi$. Maps of institutions are different from the *institution morphisms* in [54].

A *map of logics* has now a very simple definition. It consists of a pair of maps: one for the underlying entailment systems, and another for the underlying institutions, such that both maps agree on how they translate signatures and sentences. There are also notions of *map of proof calculi* and *map of logical systems*, for which we refer the reader to [96].

In the theory of general logics, maps of entailment systems, institutions, logics, proof calculi, and logical systems are defined so that each of these notions gives rise to a category, and those categories are related by forgetful functors as shown in Figure 1.

The functors *inst*, *log*, *ent*, and (therefore also) *log;inst* have right adjoints, and *inst* has also a left adjoint [96].

The concepts of the theory of general logics have been applied to the axiomatization of a general notion of *logic programming language* in [96], and to the design of multiparadigm logic programming languages in [100]. They have also been applied by Bonacina and Hsiang [16] to the axiomatization of theorem-proving strategies, and by Darlington and Guo [28] to the semantics of constraint languages. Fiadeiro and Costa [38] use the notion of *categorical logic* in [96] to give an elegant account of the relation between temporal logic theories and concurrent processes.

The recent work of Gabbay [44, 43] on *labelled deductive systems* has some interesting parallels with work on general logics. Roughly speaking, a labelled deductive system consists of a language, a consequence relation, which need not

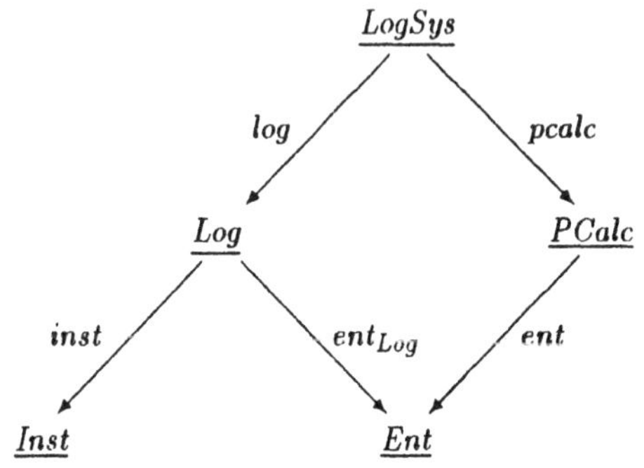

Fig. 1. Categories of logical structures and their relationships.

be monotonic, and an algebra of labels with deduction rules that show how labelled formulas can give rise to new labelled formulas. There is a parallel between Gabbay's consequence relation and the notion of entailment system, although to make the parallel closer entailment systems should be generalized so that monotonicity is not required. In a similar way, the labels on formulas and the rules to derive new labelled formulas from previous ones seem to provide the analogue of a proof calculus. It would be very worthwhile to explore further these, for the moment vague, analogies so as to obtain a precise understanding of the exact relationship between these two approaches.

2.3 Borrowing Logics

In practice, the theory of general logics can be used to relate in a correct way different formalisms, and to reuse the automated tools already existing for some of them in the context of other formalisms. The simplest instance of this idea is using a map at the appropriate level (entailment system, logic, proof calculus) to relate two logics and to reuse a tool—for example a theorem prover—belonging to the target logic in the context of the source logic. For things to work properly we want the map in question to be conservative.

We can generalize this situation to the case where the source logic in which we are interested has less logical structure than the target logic from which we wish to borrow both the extra structure and the tools already existing there. What can we do in this more general case?

The fact that the different components of a logical formalism (entailment system, proof calculus, logic) are modular in the precise sense of being, as it is the case for the functors *ent*, *inst*, *log*, and *log;inst* in Figure 1, related by adjoint functors allows adding the missing logical structure by means of universal constructions [96]. This gives us a hint for making the borrowing process universal in an appropriate sense. However, the desired enrichment of structure has to happen "along a map" and is therefore more general than that afforded by the above adjoint constructions.

Universal "borrowing" constructions in exactly this sense have been given by Cerioli and Meseguer [23, 24] for the cases involving *ent*, *inst*, *log*, and *log*;*inst*. The basic idea is that, under appropriate conditions satisfied in all those cases, the adjunctions can be generalized to more general adjunctions between appropriate comma categories [85] that make precise the notion of "borrowing along a map."

We focus below on a fibration property of the borrowing construction that affords a very simple explanation of the general process. We treat the case where our source formalism is an entailment system $\mathcal{E}$ and we wish to borrow a proof calculus structure from $\mathcal{P}$ along a map $\Phi : \mathcal{E} \longrightarrow ent(\mathcal{P})$; all the other cases are entirely similar [24].

As summarized in the following figure, we want to find a map $\hat{\Phi}$ in <u>*PCalc*</u> that "lifts" to the richer context of proof calculi our original map Φ in the precise sense that $ent(\hat{\Phi}) = \Phi$.

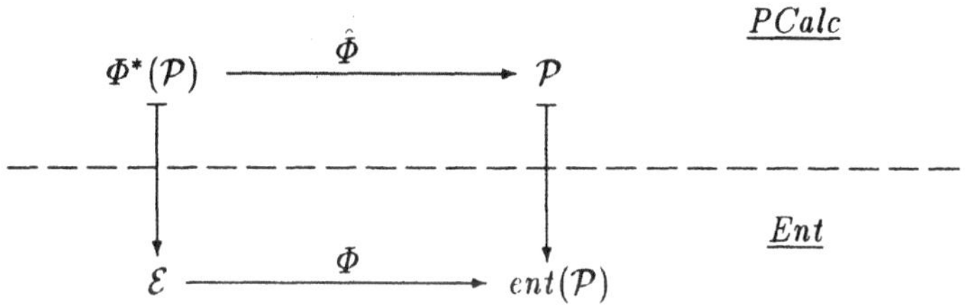

In fact we can find an optimal lifting of this kind that satisfies the universal "cartesian lifting" property described in the figure below, namely, that given a map of proof calculi $\chi : \mathcal{P}' \longrightarrow \mathcal{P}$ such that $ent(\chi) = \Psi;\Phi$ for some map of entailment systems $\Psi : ent(\mathcal{P}') \longrightarrow \mathcal{E}$, then there is a unique map of proof calculi $\tilde{\chi} : \mathcal{P}' \longrightarrow \Phi^*(\mathcal{P})$ such that $\chi = \tilde{\chi};\hat{\Phi}$ and $ent(\tilde{\chi}) = \Psi$.

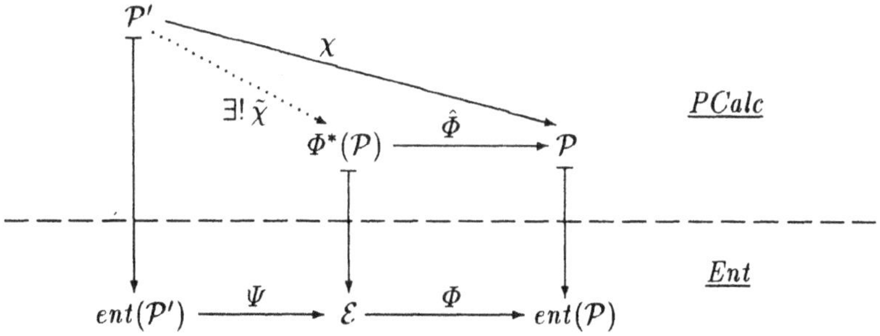

In the language of fibered categories [8, 70] all this can be summarized by saying that the functor ent : <u>*PCalc*</u> $\longrightarrow$ <u>*Ent*</u> is a *fibration*. Similarly, the functors *inst*, *log*, and *log*;*inst* are also fibrations [24].

3 From ADTs to Multiparadigm Logics

After discussing a variety of multiparadigm extensions of equational logic, we give a brief introduction to rewriting logic [99], a logic that unifies equational, Horn, object-oriented, and concurrent programming.

3.1 Multiparadigm Logics

In parallel with the search for axiomatic notions of logic, the need for more expressive logical formalisms to cover a wider range of applications in both specification and programming has led to investigating a variety of extensions of equational logic, including multiparadigm logics. Some of the extensions explored include the following, where we mention some references with no intention of being exhaustive.

1. Support of partiality and/or subtypes:
   - partial algebras [17, 3],
   - partial algebras with equationally defined domains [118, 115],
   - order-sorted algebras and related notions [50, 48, 60, 56, 72, 114, 128, 106].
2. Extensions to higher-order types (and subtypes):
   - higher-order types [112, 4, 95],
   - higher-order order-sorted types [116, 86].
3. Combinations of equational and Horn logics:
   - order-sorted Horn logic with equality [59, 127],
   - other extensions, including higher-order ones (see proceedings of recent logic programming conferences).
4. Unifications of equational and object-oriented programming:
   - hidden-sorted equational logic [55, 18],
   - rewriting logic (unifies also Horn logic and concurrent OOP) [99].

These extensions are not unrelated. Many of them can be systematically linked by *conservative* maps of logics. For example, the diagram of conservative maps in Figure 2 shows some of the logic extensions that have been developed, and, in boldface, some specification or logic programming languages that are based on such extensions.

In the diagram we can see the conservative extensions of untyped equational logic (*Eqtl*) into more expressive equational logic versions such as many-sorted (*MSEqtl*) [63], order-sorted (*OSEqtl*) [60], and equationally partial (*EqtlPart*, also called "essentially algebraic," or "sketchable") [118] equational logic; of course in all these logics one can have conditional equations, thus increasing the expressive power. All these extensions have equational specification and programming languages based on them. For example, the language of Hoffmann and O'Donnell [69, 100] and OBJ0 [51] are both untyped; Clear [19], OBJ1 [61], and Act One [35] are many-sorted; OBJ2-3 [41, 57, 64] are order-sorted, and Canons [118] is equationally partial.

The diagram also shows how the paradigms of equational and Horn logic programming can be unified by unifying their logics. Thus, unsorted equational logic and Horn logic (*Horn*) are unified in Horn logic with equality (*Horn*$^=$),

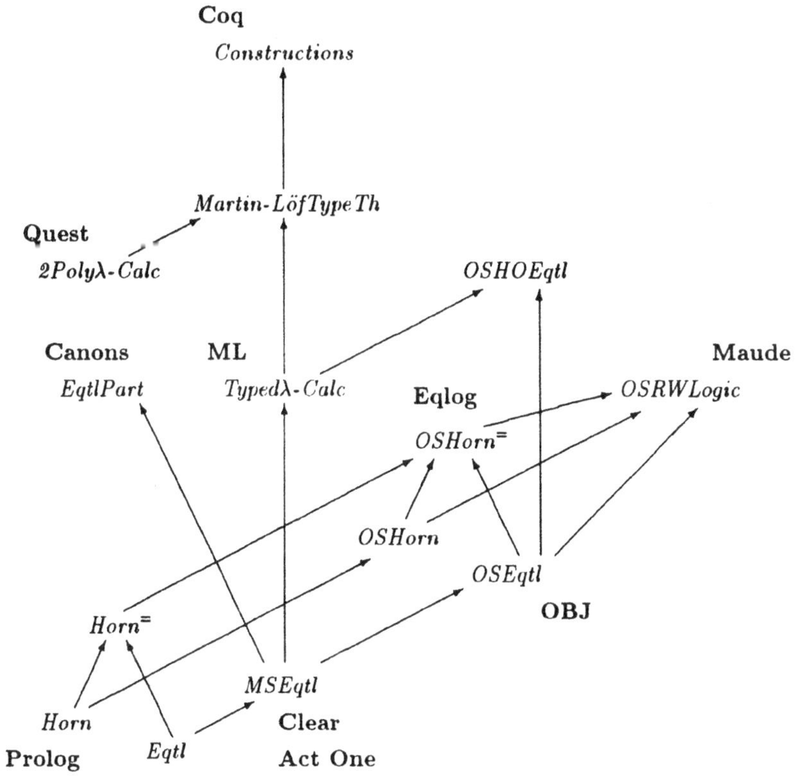

Fig. 2. A fragment of the space of logics and languages.

which it itself conservatively embedded in its many-sorted (not shown) and order-sorted ($OSHorn^=$) versions [59]. The area of integration of functional and Horn logic programming has been very active and many languages have been proposed; Eqlog [58] was the first such integration based on order-sorted Horn logic with equality.

Several extensions of the equational paradigm to higher order are also shown, including the simply typed lambda calculus (*Typedλ-Calc*), the Girard–Reynolds polymorphic lambda calculus (*2Polyλ-Calc*) [47, 120], Martin-Löf type theory (*Martin-LöfTypeTh*) [90, 92], the Coquand–Huet calculus of constructions (*Constructions*) [26], and order-sorted higher-order equational logic (*OSHOEqtl*) [86], which provides the semantic basis for a higher-order extension of OBJ3. Again, all the shown maps involving these logics are conservative; for example, the conservative map *2Polyλ-Calc* $\longrightarrow$ *Martin-LöfTypeTh* is defined and discussed in detail in [97], and the conservativity of the embedding of order-sorted equational logic into its higher-order version is proved in [86].

A number of systems for higher-order specification, verification, and programming have been proposed based on these higher-order logics. For example, the (pure) ML language [105] is closely related to the typed lambda calculus, but it is instead based on the *polymorphic* lambda calculus; expressions in general do not have one type, but a family of types that are the instances of a unique type expression involving type variables. The idea of programming with parametrically polymorphic types in the second-order lambda calculus goes back to Reynolds [120], and that of programming in Martin-Löf type theory to Martin-Löf himself [91]. Subsequent work, particularly in Scandinavia, has further explored the specification and programming uses of Martin-Löf type theory (see for example [108]); similarly, languages such as Quest [20] support programming in an extension of Girard's $F\omega$ with additional kind structure, subtypes, recursive types, and fixpoints. The Coq system [32] supports higher-order specification, verification, and programming in the calculus of (inductive) constructions.

Also present in the diagram is order-sorted rewriting logic (*OSRWLogic*) [99]. We can view it as a multiparadigm logic that unifies equational programming, Horn logic programming, and object-oriented programming, and that, in addition, is a logic of concurrent computation well suited for general parallel and distributed programming. The conservative embeddings of order-sorted equational logic and order-sorted Horn logic with equality into order-sorted rewriting logic are described in detail in [87]. The Maude language [101] supports executable specification of systems in rewriting logic, and its Simple Maude sublanguage can be used as a machine-independent parallel language on a wide variety of parallel machines [83, 84]. We further discuss rewriting logic in Section 3.2, and explain its capabilities as a logical framework in which many other logics can be represented in Section 4.3.

The above diagram illustrates an additional point, namely the use of maps of logics as a tool for defining new specification and programming languages with multiparadigm capabilities [100]. The search for such languages can be understood as the search for logics into which the logics of the paradigms that we want to unify can be embedded. Furthermore, all the logics in the diagram satisfy the requirements necessary for defining on each of them logic programming languages in the strong sense of [96, 100]. In particular, all of them have initial models. We can view the existence of initial models as a strong indication that these are particularly good extensions of standard equational logic.

We can understand the existence of initial models in all these logics in a compact and informative way by remarking that all of them are *categorical logics* in the sense of [96]. Indeed, for unsorted equational logic this goes back to Lawvere's thesis [78], for many-sorted equational logic to Bénabou's thesis [13], for equationally partial logic to Gabriel and Ulmer [45] (for a "sketchable" version see [7]), for Horn logic to Keane's work [71], and for the typed lambda calculus to work of Lambek [75]. Rewriting logic is presented as a categorical logic in Appendices A and B of [98]. A study of order-sorted and higher-order order-sorted equational logics as categorical logics can be found in [86]. The categorical logic character of Martin-Löf type theory has been studied by Cartmell [21] and by Seely [125], that of the second-order polymorphic lambda calculus by several authors [126, 97, 2], and that of the calculus of constructions by Ehrhard [33]. See also the excellent upcoming book by Jacobs [70] for a systematic categorical treatment of different type theories.

3.2 Rewriting Logic

A *signature* in (order-sorted) rewriting logic is an (order-sorted) equational theory (Σ, E), where Σ is an equational signature and E is a set of Σ-equations. Rewriting will operate on equivalence classes of terms modulo E. In this way, we free rewriting from the syntactic constraints of a term representation and gain a much greater flexibility in deciding what counts as a *data structure*; for example, string rewriting is obtained by imposing an associativity axiom, and multiset rewriting by imposing associativity and commutativity. Of course, standard term rewriting is obtained as the particular case in which the set of equations E is empty. Techniques for rewriting modulo equations have been studied extensively [30] and can be used to implement rewriting modulo many equational theories of interest.

Given a signature (Σ, E), *sentences* of rewriting logic are of the form

$$[t]_E \longrightarrow [t']_E,$$

where t and t' are Σ-terms possibly involving some variables, and $[t]_E$ denotes the equivalence class of the term t modulo the equations E. A *theory* in this logic, called a *rewrite theory*, is a slight generalization of the usual notion of theory in that, in addition, we allow the axioms $[t]_E \longrightarrow [t']_E$ (called *rewrite rules*) to be labelled, because this is very natural for many applications[2].

Given a rewrite theory $\mathcal{R}$, we say that $\mathcal{R}$ *entails* a sentence $[t] \longrightarrow [t']$, or that $[t] \longrightarrow [t']$ is a *(concurrent) $\mathcal{R}$-rewrite*, and write $\mathcal{R} \vdash [t] \longrightarrow [t']$ if and only if $[t] \longrightarrow [t']$ can be obtained by finite application of the following *rules of deduction* (where we assume that all the terms are well formed and $t(\overline{w}/\overline{x})$ denotes the simultaneous substitution of w_i for x_i in t):

1. **Reflexivity**. For each $[t] \in T_{\Sigma,E}(X)$, $\overline{[t] \longrightarrow [t]}$.
2. **Congruence**. For each $f \in \Sigma_n$, $n \in \mathbb{N}$,

$$\frac{[t_1] \longrightarrow [t'_1] \quad \ldots \quad [t_n] \longrightarrow [t'_n]}{[f(t_1, \ldots, t_n)] \longrightarrow [f(t'_1, \ldots, t'_n)]}.$$

[2] Moreover, the main results of rewriting logic have been extended to conditional rules in [99] with very general rules of the form

$$r : [t] \longrightarrow [t'] \ \textit{if} \ [u_1] \longrightarrow [v_1] \wedge \ldots \wedge [u_k] \longrightarrow [v_k].$$

This increases considerably the expressive power of rewrite theories.

3. **Replacement**. For each rule $r : [t(x_1, \ldots, x_n)] \longrightarrow [t'(x_1, \ldots, x_n)]$ in R,

$$\frac{[w_1] \longrightarrow [w'_1] \quad \ldots \quad [w_n] \longrightarrow [w'_n]}{[t(\overline{w}/\overline{x})] \longrightarrow [t'(\overline{w'}/\overline{x})]}.$$

4. **Transitivity**

$$\frac{[t_1] \longrightarrow [t_2] \quad [t_2] \longrightarrow [t_3]}{[t_1] \longrightarrow [t_3]}.$$

Rewriting logic is a logic for reasoning correctly about *concurrent systems* having *states*, and evolving by means of *transitions*. The signature of a rewrite theory describes a particular structure for the states of a system—e.g., multiset, binary tree, etc.—so that its states can be distributed according to such a structure. The rewrite rules in the theory describe which *elementary local transitions* are possible in the distributed state by concurrent local transformations. The rules of rewriting logic allow us to reason correctly about which *general* concurrent transitions are possible in a system satisfying such a description. Thus, computationally, each rewriting step is a parallel local transition in a concurrent system.

Alternatively, however, we can adopt a logical viewpoint instead, and regard the rules of rewriting logic as *metarules* for correct deduction in a *logical system*. Logically, each rewriting step is a logical *entailment* in a formal system. As we further discuss in Section 4.3 this second viewpoint is particularly fruitful when using rewriting logic as a logical framework [87, 88].

The computational and the logical viewpoints under which rewriting logic can be interpreted can be summarized in the following diagram of correspondences:

State	$\leftrightarrow$ *Term*	$\leftrightarrow$ *Proposition*
Transition	$\leftrightarrow$ *Rewriting*	$\leftrightarrow$ *Deduction*
Distributed Structure	$\leftrightarrow$ *Algebraic Structure*	$\leftrightarrow$ *Propositional Structure*

The last row of equivalences is actually quite important. Roughly speaking, it expresses the fact that a state can be transformed in a concurrent way only if it is nonatomic, that is, if it is *composed* out of smaller state components that can be changed independently. In rewriting logic this composition of a concurrent state is formalized by the *operations* of the signature Σ of the rewrite theory $\mathcal{R}$ that axiomatizes the system. From the logical point of view such operations can naturally be regarded as user-definable *propositional connectives* stating the particular structure that a given state has. See the papers [99, 89] for further discussion and examples illustrating the above correspondences between computational and logical concepts. Note that it follows from this discussion that rewriting logic is primarily a logic *of* change—in which the deduction directly corresponds to the change—as opposed to a logic to talk *about* change in a more indirect and global manner such as the different variants of modal and temporal logic. In our view these latter logics support a nonexecutable—as far as the system described is concerned—level of specification above that of rewriting logic. We are currently studying how these two levels can be best integrated within a unified wide-spectrum approach to the specification, prototyping, and declarative programming of concurrent systems.

Regarding the computational uses of rewriting logic, an obvious question to ask is how general and natural rewriting logic is as a *semantic framework* in which to express different languages and models of computation. Our experience in this regard is quite encouraging. In several papers [99, 101, 87] we have been able to show that a wide variety of models of computation, including concurrent ones, can be naturally and directly expressed as rewrite theories in rewriting logic without any encoding or artificiality. As a consequence, models hitherto quite distant from each other can be naturally unified and interrelated within a common framework. This is particularly useful in the field of concurrency, where alternative models proposed as "basic" by different authors differ greatly, and also in attempts at designing multiparadigm languages such as those combining functional and concurrent object-oriented programming.

In particular, we have shown that models and languages such as

- CCS [104],
- Petri nets [119],
- Actors [1],
- the UNITY language [25],
- the lambda calculus,
- equational languages, and
- concurrent object-oriented programming

can all be naturally expressed in rewriting logic. In addition, we have shown in [89] that rewriting logic has very good properties as a logic of change that avoids the *frame problem*, and that subsumes other logics previously proposed for this purpose.

The naturalness with which concurrent object-oriented programming can be expressed in rewriting logic and can be unified with equational programming is particularly encouraging, and has led to the design of the Maude specification language, its Simple Maude parallel sublanguage, and to the development of program transformation and compilation techniques that will allow efficient execution in a wide variety of parallel machines [101, 102, 83, 84]. In addition, rewriting logic and Maude have also been applied to the semantics of object-oriented databases [103].

Rewriting logic is being currently used by several researchers in a variety of ways. For example, C. Kirchner, H. Kirchner, and Vittek are using it as a foundation for their ELAN language and applying it to the specification of computational systems [73, 137, 74]; Futatsugi has adopted it as the semantic basis of his Cafe language [42]; Denker and Gogolla have used Maude to give semantics to the TROLL *light* object-oriented language [29]; Viry has developed useful program transformation techniques for rewrite theories using completion methods [136]; Laneve and Montanari have shown how the heavy notation of the residual calculus can be replaced by a simpler semantic account using rewriting logic [76, 77]; Corradini, Gadducci, and Montanari have studied its relationships with other categorical models and with event structures [27]; Levy and Agustí are applying it to their work on automated deduction [82, 80, 81]; Reichel has found it useful in his final coalgebra semantics for objects [117]; Lechner, Lengauer, and Wirsing have carried out an ambitious case study investigating the expressiveness of rewriting logic and Maude for object-oriented specification and have explored refinement concepts [79]; Talcott is using rewriting logic to give a concurrent semantics to actor systems [130]; and applications to Petri net algebraic specification have been developed by Battiston, Crespi, De Cindio, and Mauri [12], and by Bettaz and Maouche [14].

4 From ADTs to Logical Frameworks

After discussing work on logical frameworks and explaining how they can be conceptualized in the theory of general logics, we briefly summarize how rewriting logic can be used as a flexible and convenient logical framework.

4.1 Logical Frameworks

The two lines of research sketched in Sections 2 and 3, namely,

- the general axiomatization of logics, and
- the search for ever more expressive logics

come together in the notion of *logical framework*, that is, a "universal logic" $\mathcal{F}$ expressive and flexible enough so that a wide variety of other logics $\mathcal{L}$ can be faithfully represented in $\mathcal{F}$. The existence of frameworks of this kind does not imply that there is such a thing as a logic that is best in all aspects; although some logics may be well suited for representing many others, such logics do not directly support the more specialized reasoning for which the represented logics were explicitly designed, and usually cannot take advantage of the more efficient implementations that often can be developed because of special restrictions in a particular logic.

Much work has already been done in this area, including the Edinburgh logical framework LF [65, 6, 46]. The basic idea of the LF framework is to represent a logic as a signature in an appropriate higher-order type theory, in such a way that provability of a formula in the original logic can be reduced to provability of a type inhabitation assertion in the framework type theory. A categorical formalization of representations of logics in LF as appropriate conservative maps of "logical systems," which are similar to our conservative maps of entailment systems, has been given by Harper, Sannella, and Tarlecki in [67], and has been further extended to deal with open formulas and substitution in [66]. Other logical frameworks having some similarities with the LF framework include meta-theorem-provers such as Isabelle [110], λProlog [107, 37], and Elf [111], all of which adopt as framework logics different variants of higher-order logics or type theories. As further discussed in Section 4.3, rewriting logic can also be used as a logical framework [87, 88] enjoying good representational capabilities that in some respects compare favorably with higher-order logics.

There has also been important work on what Basin and Constable [11] call *metalogical* frameworks. These are frameworks supporting reasoning about the metalogical aspects of the logics being represented. Typically, this is accomplished by reifying as "data" the proof theory of the logic being represented in a process that is described in [11] as *externalizing* the logic in question. This is in contrast to the more *internalized* form in which logics are represented in LF and in meta-theorem-provers, so that deduction in the object logic is mirrored by deduction—for example, type inference—in the framework logic. Work on metalogical frameworks includes the already mentioned paper by Basin and Constable [11], who advocate constructive type theory as the framework logic, work of Matthews, Smaill, and Basin [93], who use Feferman's FS_0 [36], a logic designed with the explicit purpose of being a metalogical framework, earlier work by Smullyan [129], and work by Goguen, Stevens, Hobley, and Hilberdink [62] on the 2OBJ meta-theorem-prover, which uses order-sorted equational logic [60, 64].

4.2 The Idea of a Logical Framework

Viewed from the perspective of a general space of logics that can be related to each other by means of mappings, the quest for a logical framework, understood as a logic in which many other logics can be represented, can in principle—although perhaps not in all approaches—be understood as the search within such a space for a logic $\mathcal{F}$ (the *framework* logic) such that many other logics (the *object* logics) such as, say, $\mathcal{L}$ can be represented in $\mathcal{F}$ by means of mappings $\mathcal{L} \longrightarrow \mathcal{F}$ that have good enough properties.

The minimum requirement that seems reasonable to make on a representation map $\mathcal{L} \longrightarrow \mathcal{F}$ is that it should be a *conservative* map of entailment systems. Under such circumstances, we can reduce issues of provability in $\mathcal{L}$ to issues of provability in $\mathcal{F}$, by mapping the theories and sentences of $\mathcal{L}$ into $\mathcal{F}$ using the conservative representation map. Given a computer implementation of deduction in $\mathcal{F}$, we can use the conservative map to prove theorems in $\mathcal{L}$ by proving the corresponding translations in $\mathcal{F}$. In this way, the implementation for $\mathcal{F}$ can be used as a generic theorem-prover for many logics.

However, since maps between logics can, as we have seen, respect additional logical structure such as the model theory or the proofs, in some cases a representation map into a logical framework may be particularly informative because, in addition to being a conservative map of entailment systems, it is also a map of institutions, or a map of proof calculi. For example, when rewriting logic is chosen as a logical framework, appropriate representation maps for equational logic, Horn logic, and propositional linear logic can be shown to be maps of institutions also [87]. In general, however, since the model theories of different logics can be very different from each other, it is not reasonable to expect or require that the representation maps into a logical framework will always be maps of institutions.

The issue of whether, given an entailment system $\mathcal{E}$, a framework proof calculus $\mathcal{F}$, and a representation map $\Phi : \mathcal{E} \longrightarrow ent(\mathcal{F})$ that is a conservative map of entailment systems, proof calculi for $\mathcal{E}$ and $\mathcal{F}$ can be related in some way offers more hope. Using the Cerioli-Meseguer construction of Section 2.3 we can "borrow" the proof calculus of $\mathcal{F}$ in order to endow $\mathcal{E}$ with a proof calculus in such a way that the representation map then becomes a map $\hat{\Phi}$ of proof calculi.

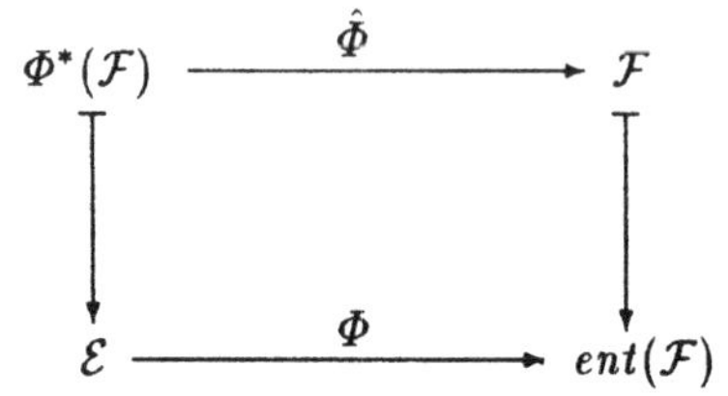

This method provides a very economic way of defining representations between logics, since only the entailment system part of the representation has to be specified. Furthermore, even when a representation already exists at the level of proof calculi the above construction remains useful and in a sense optimal. Suppose indeed that we are given a map of proof calculi $\Psi : \mathcal{P} \longrightarrow \mathcal{F}$ such that $ent(\Psi) = \Phi$. Then, by the cartesian lifting property of $\hat{\Phi}$ discussed in Section 2.3, there is a unique map of proof calculi $\tilde{\Psi} : \mathcal{P} \longrightarrow \Phi^*(\mathcal{F})$ such that $\Psi = \tilde{\Psi}; \hat{\Phi}$ and $ent(\tilde{\Psi}) = 1_{\mathcal{E}}$.

Having criteria for the adequacy of maps representing logics in a logical framework is not enough. An equally important issue is having criteria for the *generality* of a logical framework, so that it is in fact justified to call it by that name. That is, given a candidate logical framework $\mathcal{F}$, how many logics can be adequately represented in $\mathcal{F}$? We can make this question precise by defining the *scope* of a logical framework $\mathcal{F}$ as the class of entailment systems $\mathcal{E}$ having conservative maps of entailment systems $\mathcal{E} \longrightarrow ent(\mathcal{F})$. In this regard, the axioms of the theory of general logics that we have presented are probably too general; without adding further assumptions it is not reasonable to expect that we can find a logical framework $\mathcal{F}$ whose scope is the class of *all* entailment systems. A much more reasonable goal is finding an $\mathcal{F}$ whose scope includes all entailment systems of "practical interest," having finitary presentations of their syntax and their rules of deduction. Axiomatizing such finitely presentable entailment systems and proof calculi so as to capture—in the spirit of the more general axioms that we have presented, but with stronger requirements—all logics of "practical interest" (at least for computational purposes) is a very important research task.

Another important property that can help measuring the suitability of a logic $\mathcal{F}$ as a logical framework is its *representational adequacy*, understood as the naturalness and ease with which entailment systems can be represented, so that the representation $\mathcal{E} \longrightarrow ent(\mathcal{F})$ mirrors $\mathcal{E}$ as closely as possible. That is, a framework requiring very complicated encodings for many object logics of interest is less representationally adequate than one for which most logics can be represented in a straightforward way, so that there is in fact little or no "distance" between an object logic and its corresponding representation. Although at present we lack a precise definition of this property, it is quite easy to observe its absence in particular examples. We view representational adequacy as a very important practical criterion for judging the relative merits of different logical frameworks.

4.3 Rewriting Logic as a Logical Framework

A difficulty with systems based on higher-order type theory such as LF is that it may be quite awkward and of little practical use to represent logics whose structural properties differ considerably from those of the type theory. For example, linear and relevance logics do not have adequate representations in LF, in a precise technical sense of "adequate" [46, Corollary 5.1.8]. Since in metalogical frameworks a direct connection between deduction in the object and framework logics does not have to be maintained, they seem in principle much more flexible in their representational capabilities. However, this comes at a price, since the possibility of directly using an implementation of the framework logic to implement an object logic may be compromised.

In relation to this previous work, rewriting logic seems to have great flexibility to represent in a natural way many other logics, widely different in nature, including equational, Horn, and linear logics, and any sequent calculus presentation of a logic under extremely general assumptions about such a sequent presentation; moreover, quantifiers can also be treated without problems [87]. That is, rewriting logic seems to enjoy a good degree of representational adequacy as a logical framework. More experience in representing other logics is certainly needed, but we are encouraged by the naturalness and directness—often preserving the original syntax and rules—with which the logics that we have studied can be represented. This is due to the great simplicity and generality of rewriting logic, since in it all syntax and structural axioms are user-definable, so that the abstract syntax of an object logic can be represented as an algebraic data type. For example, a conjunction operator, or the set of formulas in a sequent, may be defined modulo structural axioms of associativity and commutativity; and the bookkeeping of substitutions and quantifiers can be encapsulated modulo appropriate equational axioms [87]. Then techniques for rewriting modulo structural axioms [30] can often be used to support an abstract view of formulas without having to descend into the details of equivalent representations. The simplicity of the representations is also due to the existence of only a few general "metarules" of deduction relative to the rewrite rules given by a specification, where such a specification can be used to describe with rewrite rules the rules of deduction of the object logic in question. There seems to be a certain tradeoff between the greater flexibility and representational generality of rewriting logic on the one hand, and the greater amount of built-in infrastructure and deductive power of the less flexible higher-order frameworks.

Given an implementation of rewriting logic, which can be accomplished using well-known rewrite rule implementation techniques, and given a conservative representation map from an object logic into rewriting logic, one can directly obtain a mechanized implementation of the object logic. Furthermore, given the directness with which logics can usually be represented, the task of proving conservativity is in many cases straightforward. Finally, externalization of logics using techniques such as reflection and induction on the externalized data (which relies on the existence of initial models) can be used to support metalogical reasoning in rewriting logic, in addition to the internalized logical representation of standard mappings. Some first steps in this direction, namely a representation of rewriting logic within itself, are taken in [88].

In summary, our experience with rewriting logic as a logical framework suggests that it has very good properties for this purpose in terms of:

- **Scope**. We actually conjecture that any finitely presented logic (for an adequate formal definition of "finitely presented logic" as a logic of practical interest) has a conservative representation in rewriting logic.
- **Representational adequacy**. The capacity for axiomatizing the syntactic constructs and structural properties of a logic as an order-sorted algebraic data type, and the rules of the logic as rewrite rules seems to make the "distance" between the logic and its representation negligible or non-existent in many cases.

Up to now, we have obtained [87, 88] representations by conservative maps of entailment systems—that in some cases are also maps of instiututions, and therefore maps of logics—for:

- equational logic,
- Horn logic with equality,
- linear logic,
- logics with quantifiers, such as first-order classical and linear logics,
- any logic describable with a sequent calculus, including first-order classical, modal, linear, and intuitionistic logics.

5 Formal Interoperability

At present, formal methods for software specification and verification are *monolithic*, in the sense that in each approach only one formal system or specification language is used to formalize the desired system properties. For this reason, although formal approaches are very useful at their appropriate level of abstraction, their formal systems, and the tools based on them, are as it were *autistic*, because they lack the theoretical basis for being related to other formalisms and to their supporting tools.

As a consequence, it is at present extremely difficult to integrate in a rigorous way different formal descriptions, and to reason across such descriptions. This situation is very unsatisfactory, and presents one of the biggest obstacles to the use of formal methods in software engineering because, given the complexity of large software systems, it is a fact of life that no single perspective, no single formalization or level of abstraction suffices to represent a system and reason about its behavior.

In practice we find ourselves in constant need of *moving back and forth* between different formalizations capturing different aspects of a system. For example, in a large software system we typically have very different requirements, such as functional correctness, proper real time behavior, concurrency, security, and fault-tolerance, which correspond to different views of the system and that are typically expressed in different formal systems. Often these requirements affect each other, but it can be extremely difficult to reason about their mutual interaction, and no tools exist to support such reasoning.

We need mathematical foundations, (meta)formal methods, and tools to achieve *formal interoperability*, that is, the capacity to move in a mathematically rigorous way across the different formalizations of a system, and to use in a rigorously integrated way the different tools supporting such formalizations. Axiomatic notions of logic, of mapping between logics, and of logical framework such as those discussed in this paper offer a good basis on which to build such foundations, and to develop very powerful and widely applicable *metatools* to support the formal interoperation of different formalisms and their associated tools. Metatools of this kind may include:

- **logical frameworks**, in which many different logics and specification languages can be defined, executed, and interoperated.
- **metalogical translators**, in which rigorous translations between any given pair of logical formalisms can be defined and automated. This can be extremely useful to vastly increase the applicability of tools, for example to use a theorem prover for one logic to prove theorems in a different logic.
- **metalogical module calculus tools**, which given specifications in an arbitrary logic, or in several logics, can support powerful parameterization and module composition operations to combine those specifications in a highly modular and reusable way.

The use of rewriting logic as a logical and semantic framework for applications such as those described above can be supported by tools such as a *rewriting logic interpreter*. In this way, we plan to combine different logics by combining their rewriting logic representations, and to executably interoperate such logics in combination. Similarly, we plan to combine and to interoperate executable specifications of different languages and systems. To accomplish these ambitious goals further research is needed, particularly in the areas discussed in Section 6.

The language design for such a rewriting logic interpreter, called Maude, is well advanced [101]. In addition, by using adequate program transformations [83] to move specifications into the Simple Maude sublanguage, it is possible to efficiently compile such a subset of rewriting logic on a wide variety of parallel architectures [84].

6 Concluding Remarks

This paper has tried to give an impressionistic view of several conceptual threads through which ideas that first emerged in the algebraic theory of data types have acquired a more general life of their own, and has suggested some ways in which these general ideas can be of great practical importance in software technology and in formal methods.

One such conceptual thread is the generalization from equational specifications to specifications in any logic, which requires metalogical concepts making precise what logics in general are. We have seen how, beginning with the notion of institution [52], a number of notions have been proposed in the literature to cover different needs arising in this task, and we have given an introduction to a particular line of work in this area that we and others have been developing, the theory of general logics [96].

Another thread is the extension of equational logic in several directions to make specifications and programs more expressive than it is possible when restricted to, say, many-sorted equational logic. In particular, we have considered *multiparadigm* extensions in which other specification and programming paradigms can be cleanly combined with the equational one. Two desirable properties of such extensions are their conservativity over equational logic and the existence of initial models in them, since their combination allows us to preserve as much as possible the good properties enjoyed by the equational paradigm. We have shown in concrete examples that it is indeed possible to achieve both conservativity and initiality in a wide range of such extensions, and that it is also possible to achieve powerful multiparadigm logics combining for example equational, Horn, object-oriented, and concurrent specification and programming, as it is the case in rewriting logic [99, 101, 100].

These two threads are tied together by the notion of a logical framework, in that, in the process of searching for more expressive logics, we can find a logic expressive enough to serve as a universal logic in which other logics can be represented. We have used notions from the theory of general logics to make precise the concept of a logical framework; and we have summarized our recent work on the use of rewriting logic as a logical framework [87, 88] as a particular promising approach.

We believe that these threads of conceptual development are not only beautiful and elegant, but that they are also eminently practical and that they hold much promise for solving important problems in software technology. One such problem, that we have described as the lack of *formal interoperability*, is the great difficulty at present for moving back and forth between different formalizations of a system and the lack of metatools supporting such reasoning across formalisms. Due to the inherent complexity of software systems, this problem is quite pressing because no logical formalism (specification language, prototyping language, etc.) will be best for all purposes. What exists is a *space* of possibilities (the universe of logics) in which careful choice of the formalisms that best suit some given purposes can be exercised. We have suggested that the ideas of general logics, maps of logics, and logical frameworks that we have discussed can play a crucial role as a theoretical foundation, and as the basis for the design of metatools, to achieve the goal of formal interoperability.

Of course, although we have dwelt to some extent in the past, our main concern is the future. Indeed, we believe that foundations should ***not*** be an academic exercise in describing past practice, some ***autopsy*** of the past. Their great *practical* importance is in *imagining the future*, in helping us find new, more powerful and general techniques and tools to specify, reason about, develop, evolve, and reuse software systems. Therefore, we hope that some of the ideas presented here will stimulate others as much as they stimulate us, because much work remains ahead of us to make a reality some of the promising possibilities that we have tried to suggest.

In particular, we can list, among others, the following technical problems that we think need to be solved in order to make further progress:

1. **Axiomatizing finitely presented logics**. The general logics axioms that we have presented are in a sense too general. The axiomatization in the same spirit, but with more specific requirements, of logics of "practical interest," having finitary presentations of their syntax and their rules of deduction and being in principle amenable to implementation on a computer, seems a very worthwhile research problem. Once an axiomatization of this kind is found and is justified as indeed capturing all logics of practical interest, we will have a good criterion for the generality of a logical framework, namely whether or not all such logics are within the scope of the framework, or what subclass of such logics is.
2. **Combining logics**. For example, a logic may be parameterized by another logic, or two logics may be combined together into a logic that extends both of them in a minimal way. Technically, these combinations are closely related to the existence of colimits, and in some cases limits, in the category of logics in question. Limits of institutions have been studied in [133, 135]; certain limits of logics and proof calculi are used in [23] to "borrow" logical structure missing in one logic from another logic. The problem, however, is that—due to the generality of the axioms used to formalize logics—in some cases the logics obtained through these categorical constructions are in a sense too poor. For example, logical connectives coming from two different logics may only exist in a disjoint and independent way in a combination defined this way, instead of interacting with each other as they should. Things are better when, as it has been done in LF [67, 68], a combination is performed not on the logics themselves, but on their representations inside a framework; but the constructions then dependent on the framework chosen. We conjecture that a satisfactory solution to the problem of combining logics will be found as a byproduct of the quest for appropriate axioms for logics of "practical use," because such a quest will lead to making explicit additional structure that is needed to define the right combination operations.
3. **Modular compositions**. Modularity and compositionality mechanisms for theories in a logic should be studied further. Indeed, this was one of the initial motivations for defining institutions, so that the theory-combining operations of the Clear language [19] would be independent of the logic, and much work has followed since the original Clear proposal (see for example the discussion and references in [54] and [31] for some recent ideas on modu-

larity issues). However, the search for more expressive specification and logic programming languages stimulates a corresponding search for a more powerful and expressive collection of theory-combining operations, which should of course remain independent of the logic as much as possible.

4. **Reflection.** This very important topic should be studied further. Reflection is indeed a very powerful technique both theoretically and for implementation purposes. It can in particular be extremely useful for treating metalogical aspects because it permits bringing down to the object level metalevel notions such as proof or theory. What seems to be needed is a more systematic study of reflection, perhaps in the axiomatic setting of general logics, to make explicit the essential characteristics of logical reflection in a logic-independent way.

Acknowledgements

Science is a collective enterprise and very much a dialogue. This becomes particularly evident when, as attempted to some extent here, some conceptual threads are followed for a sufficiently long period of time. We are therefore indebted to all those who have contributed and have helped sustain the scientific dialogue on these ideas; some of them have been mentioned in the references, but no attempt has been made to be exhaustive and all others are equally included. In addition, we wish to express our special gratitude to all our past and present collaborators, many of whom have also been cited in the references, since it is in joint work with them that many of our contributions to the dialogue have taken place. For example, joint work with Joseph Goguen on OBJ, Eqlog, and FOOPS stimulated us to pursue other multiparadigm extensions, and work with Maura Cerioli made possible the general borrowing technique summarized in Section 2.3. We are also very much indebted to Dr. Ralph Wachter for his continued encouragement and support of our work on the various directions discussed in this paper.

We also wish to express our thanks to the organizers and the participants of the tenth ADT meeting in Santa Margherita for giving us the chance of presenting these ideas there and for the many good comments and suggestions that we received during the workshop. In particular, we are grateful to Egidio Astesiano for gently encouraging us to produce a written version of the talk, and to José Fiadeiro for his technical suggestions to improve the exposition of the borrowing process. We thank also Manuel G. Clavel, Maura Cerioli, Hartmut Ehrig, and the referees for their very helpful comments and suggested improvements.

References

1. G. Agha. *Actors*. The MIT Press, 1986.
2. A. Asperti and S. Martini. Categorical models of polymorphism. *Information and Computation*, 99:1–79, 1992.
3. E. Astesiano and M. Cerioli. Free objects and equational deduction for partial conditional specifications. Technical Report 3, Dipartimento di Matematica, Università di Genova, 1990.

4. E. Astesiano and M. Cerioli. Partial higher-order specifications. *Fundamenta Informaticae*, 16(2):101–126, 1992.
5. E. Astesiano and M. Cerioli. Relationships between logical frameworks. In M. Bidoit and C. Choppy, editors, *Recent Trends in Data Type Specification*, volume 655 of *Lecture Notes in Computer Science*, pages 126–143. Springer-Verlag, 1993.
6. A. Avron, F. Honsell, I. A. Mason, and R. Pollack. Using typed lambda calculus to implement formal systems on a machine. *Journal of Automated Reasoning*, 9(3):309–354, December 1992.
7. M. Barr and C. Wells. *Toposes, Triples, and Theories*. Springer-Verlag, 1985.
8. M. Barr and C. Wells. *Category Theory for Computing Science*. Prentice-Hall, 1990.
9. J. Barwise. Axioms for abstract model theory. *Annals of Mathematical Logic*, 7:221–265, 1974.
10. J. Barwise and S. Feferman, editors. *Model-Theoretic Logics*. Springer-Verlag, 1985.
11. D. A. Basin and R. L. Constable. Metalogical frameworks. In G. Huet and G. Plotkin, editors, *Logical Environments*, pages 1–29. Cambridge University Press, 1993.
12. E. Battiston, V. Crespi, F. De Cindio, and G. Mauri. Semantic frameworks for a class of modular algebraic nets. In M. Nivat, C. Rattray, T. Russ, and G. Scollo, editors, *Proc. of the 3rd International AMAST Conference*, Workshops in Computing. Springer-Verlag, 1994.
13. J. Bénabou. Structures algébriques dans les catégories. *Cahiers de Topologie et Géometrie Différentielle*, 10:1–126, 1968.
14. M. Bettaz and M. Maouche. How to specify nondeterminism and true concurrency with algebraic term nets. In M. Bidoit and C. Choppy, editors, *Recent Trends in Data Type Specification*, volume 655 of *Lecture Notes in Computer Science*, pages 164–180. Springer-Verlag, 1993.
15. M. Bidoit, H.-J. Kreowski, P. Lescanne, F. Orejas, and D. Sannella, editors. *Algebraic System Specification and Development. A Survey and Annotated Bibliography*, volume 501 of *Lecture Notes in Computer Science*. Springer-Verlag, 1991.
16. M. P. Bonacina and J. Hsiang. A category theory approach to completion-based theorem proving strategies. Unpublished manuscript presented at *Category Theory 1991*, Mc Gill University, Montréal, Canada, 1991.
17. M. Broy and M. Wirsing. Partial abstract types. *Acta Informatica*, 18:47–64, 1982.
18. R. Burstall and R. Diaconescu. Hiding and behaviour: An institutional approach. Technical Report ECS-LFCS-92-253, Laboratory for Foundations of Computer Science, University of Edinburgh, December 1992.
19. R. Burstall and J. Goguen. The semantics of Clear, a specification language. In D. Bjørner, editor, *Proc. 1979 Copenhagen Winter School on Abstract Software Specification*, volume 86 of *Lecture Notes in Computer Science*, pages 292–332. Springer-Verlag, 1980.
20. L. Cardelli and G. Longo. A semantic basis for Quest. *Journal of Functional Programming*, 1(4):417–458, 1991.
21. J. Cartmell. Generalised algebraic theories and contextual categories. *Annals of Pure and Applied Logic*, 32:209–243, 1986.
22. M. Cerioli. *Relationships between Logical Formalisms*. PhD thesis, Technical Report TD-4/93, Dipartimento di Informatica, Università di Pisa, 1993.

23. M. Cerioli and J. Meseguer. May I borrow your logic? In A. M. Borzyszkowski and S. Sokołowski, editors, *Proc. 18th. Int. Symp. on Mathematical Foundations of Computer Science, Gdánsk, Poland, Aug/Sept 1993*, volume 711 of *Lecture Notes in Computer Science*, pages 342–351. Springer-Verlag, 1993.
24. M. Cerioli and J. Meseguer. May I borrow your logic? (Transporting logical structures along maps). Paper in preparation, 1995.
25. K. M. Chandy and J. Misra. *Parallel Program Design: A Foundation*. Addison-Wesley, 1988.
26. T. Coquand and G. Huet. The calculus of constructions. *Information and Computation*, 76(2/3):95–120, 1988.
27. A. Corradini, F. Gadducci, and U. Montanari. Relating two categorical models of term rewriting. To appear in *Proc. Rewriting Techniques and Applications, Kaiserslautern, April*, 1995.
28. J. Darlington and Y. Guo. Constrained equational deduction. In S. Kaplan and M. Okada, editors, *Proc. Second Int. Workshop on Conditional and Typed Rewriting Systems, Montreal, Canada, June 1990*, volume 516 of *Lecture Notes in Computer Science*, pages 424–435. Springer-Verlag, 1991.
29. G. Denker and M. Gogolla. Translating TROLL *light* concepts to Maude. In H. Ehrig and F. Orejas, editors, *Recent Trends in Data Type Specification*, volume 785 of *Lecture Notes in Computer Science*, pages 173–187. Springer-Verlag, 1994.
30. N. Dershowitz and J.-P. Jouannaud. Rewrite systems. In J. van Leeuwen, editor, *Handbook of Theoretical Computer Science, Vol. B*, pages 243–320. North-Holland, 1990.
31. R. Diaconescu, J. A. Goguen, and P. Stefaneas. Logical support for modularisation. In G. Huet and G. Plotkin, editors, *Logical Environments*, pages 83–130. Cambridge University Press, 1993.
32. G. Dowek, A. Felty, H. Herberlin, G. Huet, C. Paulin-Mohring, and B. Werner. The Coq proof assistant user's guide, version 5.6. Technical Report 134, INRIA-Rocquencourt, December 1991.
33. T. Ehrhard. A categorical semantics of constructions. In *Proc. Third Annual IEEE Symp. on Logic in Computer Science*, pages 264–273, Edinburgh, Scotland, July 1988.
34. H. Ehrig, M. Baldamus, and F. Orejas. New concepts of amalgamation and extension of a general theory of specifications. In M. Bidoit and C. Choppy, editors, *Recent Trends in Data Type Specification*, volume 655 of *Lecture Notes in Computer Science*, pages 199–221. Springer-Verlag, 1993.
35. H. Ehrig and B. Mahr. *Fundamentals of Algebraic Specification 1: Equations and Initial Semantics*. Springer-Verlag, 1985.
36. S. Feferman. Finitary inductively presented logics. In R. Ferro et al., editors, *Logic Colloquium'88*, pages 191–220. North-Holland, 1989.
37. A. Felty and D. Miller. Encoding a dependent-type λ-calculus in a logic programming language. In M. E. Stickel, editor, *Proc. 10th. Int. Conf. on Automated Deduction, Kaiserslautern, Germany, July 1990*, volume 449 of *Lecture Notes in Computer Science*, pages 221–235. Springer-Verlag, 1990.
38. J. Fiadeiro and J. Costa. Mirror, mirror in my hand: A duality between specifications and models of process behaviour. Research Report, DI-FCUL, Lisboa, Portugal, May 1994.
39. J. Fiadeiro and T. Maibaum. Generalising interpretations between theories in the context of (π-)institutions. In G. Burn, S. Gay, and M. Ryan, editors, *Theory and Formal Methods 93*, pages 126–147. Springer-Verlag, 1993.

40. J. Fiadeiro and A. Sernadas. Structuring theories on consequence. In D. Sannella and A. Tarlecki, editors, *Recent Trends in Data Type Specification*, volume 332 of *Lecture Notes in Computer Science*, pages 44–72. Springer-Verlag, 1988.
41. K. Futatsugi, J. Goguen, J.-P. Jouannaud, and J. Meseguer. Principles of OBJ2. In *Conf. Record 12th. Annual ACM Symp. on Principles of Programming Languages*, pages 52–66, New Orleans, Louisiana, January 1985.
42. K. Futatsugi and T. Sawada. Cafe as an extensible specification environment. To appear in *Proc. of the Kunming International CASE Symposium, Kunming, China, November*, 1994.
43. D. Gabbay. Fibred semantics and the weaving of logics 1. Unpublished manuscript, May 1993.
44. D. Gabbay. Labelled deductive systems. Volume 1: Foundations. Technical Report MPI-I-94-223, Max Planck Institut für Informatik, Saarbrücken, Germany, May 1994.
45. P. Gabriel and F. Ulmer. *Lokal Präsentierbare Kategorien*, volume 221 of *Lecture Notes in Mathematics*. Springer-Verlag, 1971.
46. P. Gardner. *Representing Logics in Type Theory*. PhD thesis, Technical Report CST-93-92, Department of Computer Science, University of Edinburgh, 1992.
47. J.-Y. Girard. *Interprétation Fonctionelle et Élimination des Coupures dans l'Arithmétique d'Ordre Supérieure*. PhD thesis, Université Paris VII, 1972.
48. M. Gogolla. Partially ordered sorts in algebraic specifications. In B. Courcelle, editor, *Proc. Ninth Colloquium on Trees in Algebra and Programming*, pages 139–153. Cambridge University Press, 1984.
49. M. Gogolla and M. Cerioli. What is an Abstract Data Type, after all? Manuscript, June 1994.
50. J. A. Goguen. Order sorted algebra. Technical Report 14, UCLA Computer Science Department, Semantics and Theory of Computation Series, 1978.
51. J. A. Goguen. Some design principles and theory for OBJ-0, a language for expressing and executing algebraic specifications of programs. In E. K. Blum, M. Paul, and S. Takasu, editors, *Proc. Mathematical Studies of Information Processing, Kyoto, Japan, August 1978*, volume 75 of *Lecture Notes in Computer Science*, pages 425–473. Springer-Verlag, 1979.
52. J. A. Goguen and R. M. Burstall. Introducing institutions. In E. Clarke and D. Kozen, editors, *Proc. Logics of Programming Workshop*, volume 164 of *Lecture Notes in Computer Science*, pages 221–256. Springer-Verlag, 1984.
53. J. A. Goguen and R. M. Burstall. A study in the foundations of programming methodology: Specifications, institutions, charters and parchments. In D. Pitt et al., editors, *Proc. Workshop on Category Theory and Computer Programming, Guildford, UK, September 1985*, volume 240 of *Lecture Notes in Computer Science*, pages 313–333. Springer-Verlag, 1986.
54. J. A. Goguen and R. M. Burstall. Institutions: Abstract model theory for specification and programming. *Journal of the Association for Computing Machinery*, 39(1):95–146, 1992.
55. J. A. Goguen and R. Diaconescu. Towards an algebraic semantics for the object paradigm. In H. Ehrig and F. Orejas, editors, *Recent Trends in Data Type Specification*, volume 785 of *Lecture Notes in Computer Science*, pages 1–29. Springer-Verlag, 1994.
56. J. A. Goguen, J.-P. Jouannaud, and J. Meseguer. Operational semantics of order-sorted algebra. In W. Brauer, editor, *Proc. ICALP'85*, volume 194 of *Lecture Notes in Computer Science*, pages 221–231. Springer-Verlag, 1985.

57. J. A. Goguen, C. Kirchner, H. Kirchner, A. Mégrelis, J. Meseguer, and T. Winkler. An introduction to OBJ3. In J.-P. Jouannaud and S. Kaplan, editors, *Proc. First Int. Workshop on Conditional Term Rewriting Systems, Orsay, France, July 1987*, volume 308 of *Lecture Notes in Computer Science*, pages 258–263. Springer-Verlag, 1988.
58. J. A. Goguen and J. Meseguer. Eqlog: Equality, types, and generic modules for logic programming. In D. DeGroot and G. Lindstrom, editors, *Logic Programming: Functions, Relations, and Equations*, pages 295–363. Prentice-Hall, 1986.
59. J. A. Goguen and J. Meseguer. Models and equality for logical programming. In H. Ehrig et al., editors, *Proc. Int. Joint Conf. on Theory and Practice of Software Development, Pisa, Italy, March 1987, Volume 2*, volume 250 of *Lecture Notes in Computer Science*, pages 1–22. Springer-Verlag, 1987.
60. J. A. Goguen and J. Meseguer. Order-sorted algebra I: Equational deduction for multiple inheritance, overloading, exceptions and partial operations. *Theoretical Computer Science*, 105:217–273, 1992.
61. J. A. Goguen, J. Meseguer, and D. Plaisted. Programming with parameterized abstract objects in OBJ. In D. Ferrari, M. Bolognani, and J. Goguen, editors, *Theory and Practice of Software Technology*, pages 163–193. North-Holland, 1983.
62. J. A. Goguen, A. Stevens, K. Hobley, and H. Hilberdink. 2OBJ: A meta-logical framework based on equational logic. *Philosophical Transactions of the Royal Society, Series A*, 339:69–86, 1992.
63. J. A. Goguen, J. Thatcher, and E. Wagner. An initial algebra approach to the specification, correctness and implementation of abstract data types. In R. Yeh, editor, *Current Trends in Programming Methodology IV*, pages 80–149. Prentice-Hall, 1978.
64. J. A. Goguen, T. Winkler, J. Meseguer, K. Futatsugi, and J.-P. Jouannaud. Introducing OBJ. Technical Report SRI-CSL-92-03, Computer Science Laboratory, SRI International, March 1992. To appear in J. A. Goguen, editor, *Applications of Algebraic Specification Using OBJ*. Cambridge University Press, 1995.
65. R. Harper, F. Honsell, and G. Plotkin. A framework for defining logics. *Journal of the Association for Computing Machinery*, 40(1):143–184, 1993.
66. R. Harper, D. Sannella, and A. Tarlecki. Logic representation in LF. In D. H. Pitt et al., editors, *Category Theory and Computer Science, Manchester, UK, September 1989*, volume 389 of *Lecture Notes in Computer Science*, pages 250–272. Springer-Verlag, 1989.
67. R. Harper, D. Sannella, and A. Tarlecki. Structure and representation in LF. In *Proc. Fourth Annual IEEE Symp. on Logic in Computer Science*, pages 226–237, Asilomar, California, June 1989.
68. R. Harper, D. Sannella, and A. Tarlecki. Structure theory presentations and logic representations. *Annals of Pure and Applied Logic*, 67:113–160, 1994.
69. C. M. Hoffmann and M. J. O'Donnell. Programming with equations. *ACM Transactions on Programming Languages and Systems*, 1(4):83–112, 1982.
70. B. Jacobs. *Categorical Logic and Type Theory*. North-Holland, 1995. To appear.
71. O. Keane. Abstract Horn theories. In F. W. Lawvere, C. Maurer, and G. C. Wraith, editors, *Model Theory and Topoi*, volume 445 of *Lecture Notes in Mathematics*, pages 15–50. Springer-Verlag, 1975.
72. C. Kirchner, H. Kirchner, and J. Meseguer. Operational semantics of OBJ-3. In T. Lepistö and A. Salomaa, editors, *Proc. ICALP'88*, volume 317 of *Lecture Notes in Computer Science*, pages 287–301. Springer-Verlag, 1988.

73. C. Kirchner, H. Kirchner, and M. Vittek. Designing constraint logic programming languages using computational systems. In F. Orejas, editor, *Proc. Second CCL Workshop, La Escala (Spain)*, September 1993.
74. H. Kirchner and P.-E. Moreau. Prototyping completion with constraints using computational systems. To appear in *Proc. Rewriting Techniques and Applications, Kaiserslautern, April*, 1995.
75. J. Lambek and P. J. Scott. *Introduction to Higher Order Categorical Logic*. Cambridge University Press, 1986.
76. C. Laneve and U. Montanari. Axiomatizing permutation equivalence in the λ-calculus. In H. Kirchner and G. Levi, editors, *Proc. Third Int. Conf. on Algebraic and Logic Programming, Volterra, Italy, September 1992*, volume 632 of *Lecture Notes in Computer Science*, pages 350–363. Springer-Verlag, 1992.
77. C. Laneve and U. Montanari. Axiomatizing permutation equivalence. *Mathematical Structures in Computer Science*, 1995. To appear.
78. F. W. Lawvere. Functorial semantics of algebraic theories. *Proceedings National Academy of Sciences*, 50:869–873, 1963.
79. U. Lechner, C. Lengauer, and M. Wirsing. An object-oriented airport. This volume.
80. J. Levy. A higher order unification algorithm for bi-rewriting systems. In J. Agustí and P. García, editors, *Segundo Congreso Programación Declarativa*, pages 291–305, Blanes, Spain, September 1993. CSIC.
81. J. Levy. *The calculus of refinements: a formal specification model based on inclusions*. PhD thesis, Universitat Politècnica de Catalunya, 1994.
82. J. Levy and J. Agustí. Bi-rewriting, a term rewriting technique for monotonic order relations. In C. Kirchner, editor, *Proc. Fifth Int. Conf. on Rewriting Techniques and Applications, Montreal, Canada, June 1993*, volume 690 of *Lecture Notes in Computer Science*, pages 17–31. Springer-Verlag, 1993.
83. P. Lincoln, N. Martí-Oliet, and J. Meseguer. Specification, transformation, and programming of concurrent systems in rewriting logic. In G. Blelloch, K. M. Chandy, and S. Jagannathan, editors, *Proc. DIMACS Workshop on Specification of Parallel Algorithms, Princeton, NJ, May 1994*, DIMACS Series in Discrete Mathematics and Theoretical Computer Science. American Mathematical Society, 1994.
84. P. Lincoln, N. Martí-Oliet, J. Meseguer, and L. Ricciulli. Compiling rewriting onto SIMD and MIMD/SIMD machines. In C. Halatsis et al., editors, *PARLE'94, Proc. Sixth Int. Conf. on Parallel Architectures and Languages Europe, Athens, Greece, July 1994*, volume 817 of *Lecture Notes in Computer Science*, pages 37–48. Springer-Verlag, 1994.
85. S. Mac Lane. *Categories for the Working Mathematician*. Springer-Verlag, 1971.
86. N. Martí-Oliet and J. Meseguer. Inclusions and subtypes. Technical Report SRI-CSL-90-16, Computer Science Laboratory, SRI International, December 1990. Revised May 1994.
87. N. Martí-Oliet and J. Meseguer. Rewriting logic as a logical and semantic framework. Technical Report SRI-CSL-93-05, Computer Science Laboratory, SRI International, August 1993.
88. N. Martí-Oliet and J. Meseguer. General logics and logical frameworks. In D. Gabbay, editor, *What Is a Logical System?*, pages 355–392. Oxford University Press, 1994.
89. N. Martí-Oliet and J. Meseguer. Action and change in rewriting logic. In R. Pareschi and B. Fronhoefer, editors, *Theoretical Approaches to Dynamic*

Worlds in Computer Science and Artificial Intelligence. Cambridge University Press, 1995. To appear.

90. P. Martin-Löf. An intuitionistic theory of types: Predicative part. In H. E. Rose and J. C. Shepherdson, editors, *Logic Colloquium'73*, pages 73–118. North-Holland, 1975.
91. P. Martin-Löf. Constructive mathematics and computer programming. In L. J. Cohen et al., editors, *Proc. 6th Int. Congress for Logic, Methodology, and Philosophy of Science, Hannover, 1979*, pages 153–175. North-Holland, 1982.
92. P. Martin-Löf. *Intuitionistic Type Theory*. Bibliopolis, 1984.
93. S. Matthews, A. Smaill, and D. Basin. Experience with FS_0 as a framework theory. In G. Huet and G. Plotkin, editors, *Logical Environments*, pages 61–82. Cambridge University Press, 1993.
94. B. Mayoh. Galleries and institutions. Technical Report DAIMI PB-191, Computer Science Department, Aarhus University, 1985.
95. K. Meinke. Universal algebra in higher types. *Theoretical Computer Science*, 100:385–417, 1992.
96. J. Meseguer. General logics. In H.-D. Ebbinghaus et al., editors, *Logic Colloquium'87*, pages 275–329. North-Holland, 1989.
97. J. Meseguer. Relating models of polymorphism. In *Proc. 16th. Annual ACM Symp. on Principles of Programming Languages*, pages 228–241, Austin, Texas, January 1989.
98. J. Meseguer. Rewriting as a unified model of concurrency. Technical Report SRI-CSL-90-02R, Computer Science Laboratory, SRI International, February 1990. Revised June 1990.
99. J. Meseguer. Conditional rewriting logic as a unified model of concurrency. *Theoretical Computer Science*, 96:73–155, 1992.
100. J. Meseguer. Multiparadigm logic programming. In H. Kirchner and G. Levi, editors, *Proc. Third Int. Conf. on Algebraic and Logic Programming, Volterra, Italy, September 1992*, volume 632 of *Lecture Notes in Computer Science*, pages 158–200. Springer-Verlag, 1992.
101. J. Meseguer. A logical theory of concurrent objects and its realization in the Maude language. In G. Agha, P. Wegner, and A. Yonezawa, editors, *Research Directions in Object-Based Concurrency*, pages 314–390. The MIT Press, 1993.
102. J. Meseguer. Solving the inheritance anomaly in concurrent object-oriented programming. In O. M. Nierstrasz, editor, *Proc. ECOOP'93, 7th European Conf., Kaiserslautern, Germany, July 1993*, volume 707 of *Lecture Notes in Computer Science*, pages 220–246. Springer-Verlag, 1993.
103. J. Meseguer and X. Qian. A logical semantics for object-oriented databases. In *Proc. Int. SIGMOD Conference on Management of Data*, pages 89–98. ACM, 1993.
104. R. Milner. *Communication and Concurrency*. Prentice Hall, 1989.
105. R. Milner, M. Tofte, and R. Harper. *The Definition of Standard ML*. The MIT Press, 1990.
106. P. Mosses. The use of sorts in algebraic specifications. In M. Bidoit and C. Choppy, editors, *Recent Trends in Data Type Specification*, volume 655 of *Lecture Notes in Computer Science*, pages 66–91. Springer-Verlag, 1993.
107. G. Nadathur and D. Miller. An overview of λProlog. In K. Bowen and R. Kowalski, editors, *Fifth Int. Joint Conf. and Symp. on Logic Programming*, pages 810–827. The MIT Press, 1988.

108. B. Nordström, K. Petersson, and J. Smith. *Programming in Martin-Löf's Type Theory: An Introduction.* Oxford University Press, 1990.
109. M. J. O'Donnell. *Equational Logic as a Programming Language.* The MIT Press, 1985.
110. L. Paulson. The foundation of a generic theorem prover. *Journal of Automated Reasoning*, 5:363–39, 1989.
111. F. Pfenning. Elf: A language for logic definition and verified metaprogramming. In *Proc. Fourth Annual IEEE Symp. on Logic in Computer Science*, pages 313–322, Asilomar, California, June 1989.
112. A. Poigné. On specifications, theories, and models with higher types. *Information and Control*, 68:1–46, 1986.
113. A. Poigné. Foundations are rich institutions, but institutions are poor foundations. In H. Ehrig et al., editors, *Categorical Methods in Computer Science with Aspects from Topology*, volume 393 of *Lecture Notes in Computer Science*, pages 82–101. Springer-Verlag, 1989.
114. A. Poigné. Parametrization for order-sorted algebraic specification. *Journal of Computer and System Sciences*, 40(2):229–268, 1990.
115. A. Poigné. Typed Horn logic. In B. Rovan, editor, *Proc. 15th. Int. Symp. on Mathematical Foundations of Computer Science, Banská Bystrica, Czechoslovaquia, August 1990*, volume 452 of *Lecture Notes in Computer Science*, pages 470–477. Springer-Verlag, 1990.
116. Z. Qian. Higher-order order-sorted algebras. In H. Kirchner and W. Wechler, editors, *Proc. Second Int. Conf. on Algebraic and Logic Programming, Nancy, France, October 1990*, volume 463 of *Lecture Notes in Computer Science*, pages 86–100. Springer-Verlag, 1990.
117. H. Reichel. An approach to object semantics based on terminal co-algebras. To appear in *Mathematical Structures in Computer Science*, 1995. Presented at *Dagstuhl Seminar on Specification and Semantics*, Schloss Dagstuhl, Germany, May 1993.
118. H. Reichel. *Initial Computability, Algebraic Specifications, and Partial Algebras.* Oxford University Press, 1987.
119. W. Reisig. *Petri Nets: An Introduction.* Springer-Verlag, 1985.
120. J. C. Reynolds. Towards a theory of type structure. In B. Robinet, editor, *Proc. Programming Symposium, Paris, April 1974*, volume 19 of *Lecture Notes in Computer Science*, pages 408–425. Springer-Verlag, 1974.
121. A. Salibra and G. Scollo. Compactness and Löwenheim-Skolem properties in pre-institution categories. Technical Report LIENS-92-10, Laboratoire d'Informatique de l'Ecole Normale Supérieure, Paris, March 1992.
122. A. Salibra and G. Scollo. A soft stairway to institutions. In M. Bidoit and C. Choppy, editors, *Recent Trends in Data Type Specification*, volume 655 of *Lecture Notes in Computer Science*, pages 310–329. Springer-Verlag, 1993.
123. D. Sannella and A. Tarlecki. Specifications in an arbitrary institution. *Information and Computation*, 76(2/3):165–210, 1988.
124. D. Sannella and A. Tarlecki. Toward formal development of programs from algebraic specifications: Implementations revisited. *Acta Informatica*, 25:233–281, 1988.
125. R. A. G. Seely. Locally cartesian closed categories and type theory. *Mathematical Proceedings of the Cambridge Philosophical Society*, 95:33–48, 1984.
126. R. A. G. Seely. Categorical semantics for higher order polymorphic lambda calculus. *Journal of Symbolic Logic*, 52(4):969–989, 1987.

127. G. Smolka. *Logic Programming Over Polymorphic Order-Sorted Types.* PhD thesis, Computer Science Department, University of Kaiserslautern, 1989.

128. G. Smolka, W. Nutt, J. A. Goguen, and J. Meseguer. Order-sorted equational computation. In H. Aït-Kaci and M. Nivat, editors, *Resolution of Equations in Algebraic Structures. Volume 2: Rewriting Techniques*, pages 297–367. Academic Press, 1989.

129. R. M. Smullyan. *Theory of Formal Systems*, volume 47 of *Annals of Mathematics Studies.* Princeton University Press, 1961.

130. C. Talcott. Heterogeneous component-based distributed computation. Paper in preparation, 1995.

131. A. Tarlecki. Free constructions in algebraic institutions. In M. P. Chytil and V. Koubek, editors, *Proc. Mathematical Foundations of Computer Science '84*, volume 176 of *Lecture Notes in Computer Science*, pages 526–534. Springer-Verlag, 1984.

132. A. Tarlecki. On the existence of free models in abstract algebraic institutions. *Theoretical Computer Science*, 37(3):269–304, 1985.

133. A. Tarlecki. Bits and pieces of the theory of institutions. In D. Pitt et al., editors, *Proc. Workshop on Category Theory and Computer Programming, Guildford, UK, September 1985*, volume 240 of *Lecture Notes in Computer Science*, pages 334–363. Springer-Verlag, 1986.

134. A. Tarlecki. Quasi-varieties in abstract algebraic institutions. *Journal of Computer and System Sciences*, 33(3):333–360, 1986.

135. A. Tarlecki, R. M. Burstall, and J. A. Goguen. Some fundamental algebraic tools for the semantics of computation. Part 3: Indexed categories. *Theoretical Computer Science*, 91:239–264, 1991.

136. P. Viry. Rewriting: An effective model of concurrency. In C. Halatsis et al., editors, *PARLE'94, Proc. Sixth Int. Conf. on Parallel Architectures and Languages Europe, Athens, Greece, July 1994*, volume 817 of *Lecture Notes in Computer Science*, pages 648–660. Springer-Verlag, 1994.

137. M. Vittek. *ELAN: Un cadre logique pour le prototypage de langages de programmation avec contraintes.* PhD thesis, Université Henry Poincaré — Nancy I, 1994.

Algebraic Specification Languages: An Overview

Martin Wirsing
Institut für Informatik
Ludwig-Maximilians-Universität München
Leopoldstr. 11 b, 80802 München, Germany
E-mail: wirsing@informatik.uni-muenchen.de

Abstract

Algebraic specification languages are characterised by their underlying logic, their constructs supporting a particular programming paradigm and their structuring mechanisms. In this paper a survey of algebraic specification languages is given together with hints to extensions towards imperative, object-oriented, concurrent, functional and logic programming. The main concepts for specification "in the small" and "in the large" are given and their representation in different specification languages is illustrated. A number of design decisions is listed which have to be considered for choosing a particular algebraic specification language. Finally, some trends and open questions concerning the development of algebraic specification languages are presented.

1. Introduction

Today requirements and design documents in software engineering are mostly informal, consisting of diagrams and natural language texts. However, it is recognized the functional properties of such requirements could, and should, be described by means of formal specifications in order to fix the meaning of the requirements exactly and to be able to analyse the specifications mathematically. Formal specifications are the only way to scientifically deal with rigorous proofs of properties and the correctness of software systems.

The size of the requirements and the design documents can be quite large; in the case of design it often comprises about the same number of pages as the final program. Classical mathematical notation has not enough structure for writing large specifications. So, already in the late seventies, the first specification languages emerged which provided appropriate means for writing and structuring specification documents formally. Since then, many specification languages have been designed. These can be classified into model-oriented, property-oriented and type-oriented ones. A model-oriented language such as VVSL [Mi 90] based on VDM [BJ 78], Z [Spi 89] or RAISE [HSP 93] is based on set theory: requirements are described by pre- and post-conditions or more generally by relations. Type-oriented languages such as ECC [Lu 90], DEVA [WSL 93] are based on type theory, i.e. a logic with a rich type structure. Here even formulas ("propositions") are considered as types.

The subject of this paper is property-oriented languages whose emphasis is on describing requirements and designs by axioms expressed in some logic, typically an extension of equational logic. In an *algebraic specification language* a software module is described by giving a signature consisting of sorts and operation symbols as a static interface. Equational axioms specify the required properties of the operations. Moreover, using structuring facilities specifications can be composed. The underlying logic allows one to prove properties of the specifications and hence gives the basis for validation and for the proof of correctness of refinements. Thus each algebraic specification language is characterized by its syntax, its semantics and its associated proof calculus. The differences between such languages originate from different factors such as their intended use in the software development process, the intended programming paradigm and the desired degree of tool support.

This paper presents a survey of the features of some of the most well-known algebraic specification languages with an emphasis on their underlying proof calculi. In particular, the following languages are considered: CLEAR, the Larch shared language LSL, OBJ, ASL, ACT, ASF, PLUSS, OBSCURE (for references see [W 90]), GSBL [CO 88], GLIDER [HL 94], SPECTRAL [KS 91] and SPECTRUM [Br et al. 93]. These languages are "pure" specification languages which are intended to support the style of "algebraic programming" as advocated e.g. in [GM 86] or [HG 89]; they are not oriented towards a "classical" programming style though their equational logic basis makes them very suitable for the development of functional programs. In order to support other programming paradigms, algebraic specification languages can be extended by specific notations and predefined specifications.

In Section 2, a survey of some well-known algebraic specification languages will be given together with an overview of extensions towards imperative, concurrent, object-oriented and functional programming. Sections 3 and 4 describe the concepts for specifying "in the small" data structures and algorithms and "in the large" systems of specifications. Thus Section 3 comprises equational logic, constraints, constructs for describing partial functions, infinite data, dynamic behaviour and features for relating and constructing sorts. Section 4 gives an overview of the use of specification-building operations and parameterisation,and shows how different levels of abstraction can be represented in some specification languages. In Section 5 an overview is given of design decisions which have to be considered in order to use or to develop a specification language. In particular, some design decisions concerning the use of specification languages in the software development process, design decisions with respect to syntax and semantics and design decisions for specification "in the small and "in the large" are mentioned. Finally, Section 6 presents some trends and open questions concerning the development of algebraic specification languages.

In particular in Sections 3 and 4 the reader is assumed to be familiar with the basic notions of universal algebra and logic such as signature Σ, Σ-algebra, the set $T(\Sigma,X)$ of Σ-terms with variables in X, Σ-formula, validity of a formula, model of a theory, free construction etc. For exact definitions see e.g. [EM 85], [W 90].

2. Survey of algebraic specification languages

The basic idea of algebraic specification is to specify an abstract data type by its signature and characteristic properties. Hence, the main concept of an algebraic specification language is the notion of axiomatic specification. The basic concepts of algebraic specification languages are outlined in Section 2.1. Section 2.2 gives an overview of current algebraic specification languages. In Section 2.3 some examples for specification languages supporting different programming styles are given.

2.1 Basic concepts

The basic syntactic form for specification "in the small" is given by a signature and a list of axioms. A signature consists of a list of declarations of sorts as names for carrier sets and of function symbols as names for operations. For each function symbol also the type or functionality is specified in the declaration. The axioms are correctly typed equational formulae. Moreover, many languages have a second kind of axioms, so-called constraints, which express properties of the carrier sets that can not be expressed in first-order logic. Two examples which have strongly influenced the design of specification languages are initial and generating constraints (for a third kind, so-called behavioural constraints, see Sections 3.2 and 4.1).

An initial constraint restricts a class of data structures to the (isomorphism class of) initial algebras characterised by "no junk" and "no confusion" (cf. [BG 80], [Sa 82]). "No confusion" means that the interpretation of two (ground) terms is the same only if this is provable from the axioms. "No junk" means that any element is denotable by a ground term. A generating constraint just requires the "no junk" property, leaving "no confusion" to be specified by "normal" axioms (for further details see Section 3).

The following example shows two specifications of the isomorphism class of natural numbers. The left one is an initial specification in CLEAR, the right one a loose specification in ASL. The keyword "**data**" indicates the initial constraint, "**reachable** ... **on** {Nat}" denotes the generating constraint.

```
const NAT =                          NATG = reachable
  theory                                    <( sort Nat,
    data                                       opns zero : →Nat
      sorts Nat                                     succ : Nat →Nat)
      opns  zero : →Nat                        axioms
            succ : Nat → Nat                   ¬ (zero = succ(x))
  endth                                        succ(x) = succ(y) ⇒x = y >
                                            on{Nat}
```

The semantic approach of an algebraic specification language is essentially determined by the kind of algebras chosen for interpreting the sorts and function symbols, the logic, and the semantics of a specification (see Section 3). For example one may choose between total, partial or order-sorted algebras. A specification expression may denote a class of algebras or a class of parameterised algebras; the class may consist of all algebras that satisfy the axioms (the so-called loose approach [Gu 75]) or be restricted to the isomorphism class of initial algebras (the so-called initial approach [GTWW 75]).

Each specification language has constructs for specification "in the large", i.e. for building specifications in a modular way. This includes constructs for extending a certain specification by new sorts, function symbols and axioms ("extension"), building a new specification by putting two specifications together ("sum"), renaming symbols of a specification ("rename"), restricting the signature of a specification by "exporting" a subsignature ("export") and abstracting from the required properties of a specification by considering its "observable" behaviour ("abstract"). The following example on the left written again in CLEAR describes an "extension" of the "sum" of NAT and a specification BOOL of truth values by a boolean function leq. The specification on the right, written in SPECTRUM, hides the function symbols zero and succ in the resulting specification. Only the sort Nat, the function symbol leq (and by default of SPECTRUM the sort and the function symbols of BOOL) are exported.

```
const NAT1 =
enrich NAT + BOOL by
      opns  leq :Nat, Nat → Bool
      eqns  leq (zero, n) = true
            leq (succ(n), zero) = false
            leq (succ(n), succ(m)) = leq (n, m)
   enden
```

```
NAT0 = export Nat, leq in NAT1
```

Semantically, all specification-building operations are derived from concepts of universal algebra and category theory in such a way that they are institution-independent. I.e. under mild assumptions on the underlying logic they can be defined independently of the logic.

Another important structuring concept is parameterisation. One distinguishes between implicit parameterisation where only an instantiation mechanism is given without any particular notation for abstraction and explicit parameterisation where syntactic constructs for procedural abstraction, and instantiation are given following either the "pushout" or the "λ-calculus approach". (For details see Section 4.) The example on the left shows a parameterised specification of lists over an arbitrary sort Elem in CLEAR. When LIST is supplied with an appropriate actual parameter specification, it gives the specification of lists over the sort which matches Elem in TRIV. The example on the right gives the specifications of lists over natural numbers and of lists over truth values.

```
proc LIST (X : TRIV) =
enrich X by    data
      sorts    List
      opns     nil: List
               cons: Elem, List → List
   enden
```

```
LIST_NAT    = LIST(NAT1[Elem is Nat])
LIST_BOOL   = LIST(NAT1[Elem is Bool])
```

where TRIV is the trivial specification declaring just the sort Elem:

```
meta TRIV = theory sort Elem endth
```

(The keyword "meta" indicates that TRIV describes a class of theories rather than a class of algebras.)

2.2 A genealogy of algebraic specification languages

In software development, design specifications and prototyping by executable specifications are supported by the initial approach; in the loose approach the aim is to cover the whole software development process including requirement specifications. As a consequence, algebraic specification languages can roughly be classified according to these two approaches, though most languages today include a loose part for specifying requirements and an executable sublanguage for prototyping.

Table 1 gives an overview of some well-known algebraic specification languages.

Historically speaking CLEAR [BG 77], developed by Burstall and Goguen, was the first language for constructing algebraic specifications in a modular way. CLEAR had considerable influence on the design of many other languages including OBJ and ASL. CLEAR has explicit parameterisation using the pushout approach and almost all structuring operators found in other specification languages are present in some form in CLEAR. It is also the first language which has been proved to be institution-independent. The concept of institution-independence was introduced by Burstall and Goguen in connection with the semantics of this language [BG 80].

Table 1: Algebraic specification languages

	Initial Algebra Approach			Loose Approach		
1977		CLEAR				
1978						
1979		OBJ0				
1980						
1981		OBJT				
1982	LOOK				ASL	
1983	ACT1			LSL	PLUSS	
1984						RAP
1985	OBSCURE	OBJ2	ASF	LSL/CLU		
1986					PLUSS(Meteor)	
1987						
1988	ACT1(rev.)/ACT2	OBJ3	GSBL			
1989					PLUSS(Bidoit)	
1990						GLIDER
1991				LSL/C		SPECTRAL
1992						
1993					SPECTRUM	

OBJ was originally designed by Goguen as an executable language for "error algebras": an attempt to handle errors and partial functions in a simple, uniform way by adding "error elements" to each sort. OBJ0 [Go 79] was based on unsorted equational logic, while OBJT designed by Tardo [T 81] used error algebras. OBJ2 [FGJM 85] was based on order-sorted algebras, rather than error algebras. The axioms are conditional equations. The structuring concepts include free, loose and protected (conservative) extension, sum, rename and pushout parameterisation. OBJ3 [GWMFJ 92] is very similar to OBJ2 but has a simpler implementation of order-sorted rewriting. OBJ2 and OBJ3 are executable and can both be seen as implementations of CLEAR for the case of order-sorted logic.

The language LOOK developed by Zilles, Lucas, Ehrig and Thatcher ([ZLT 82], [ETLZ 84]) was inspired by CLEAR but contains much simpler structuring operators consisting of free extension, renaming and sum. In particular, no "export" operation is available. The language ACT1 ([EFH 83], [EM 85]), developed by Ehrig, Fey and Hansen, takes parameterised specifications as the main syntactic construct; non-parameterised specifications are considered as a special case. ACT1 has structuring operations similar to LOOK. Its first version is based on pure initial algebra semantics where every specification denotes a free functor. The revised version also includes constraints [CEW 93]. Its successor, ACT2 ([Fe 88], [CEW 93]), extends it and provides constructs for writing modules and explicit parameterisation with an external ("export interface") and an internal description ("implementation specification") of a software system.

ASF [BHK 87, 89], developed by Bergstra, Heering and Klint, is based on a pure initial algebra approach and has structuring facilities similar to those of LOOK but with "export". It resolves overloading of names by the so-called "origin consistency". OBSCURE [LL 87] can be seen as an extension of ASF containing more powerful structuring mechanisms such as operators for constructing quotient algebras. As ASF it is executable. It has two semantics: an initial and a loose one.

GSBL [CO 88, 90] introduces a kind of inheritance as structuring facility based on the notion of subclass (cf. Section 4.1.4). Other constructs are loose and free extension, sum and renaming. Parameterisation is implicit.

ASL ([W 82], [SW 83]) was the first language with a "pure" loose semantics and first-order equational formulae as axioms. It is a kernel language with simple but powerful operations where every construct is considered as a specification-building operation. This includes the constructs for forming simple specifications from a signature and axioms, those for requiring constraints and the other structuring operators similar to those of CLEAR. In addition ASL offers behavioural abstraction. Parameterisation is based on the λ-calculus approach. ASL is institution-independent [ST 88] and has instantiations for total [SW 83] and partial algebras [W 86].

The goal of PLUSS ([Gau 84], [Bi 89]) is to support the specification development process in software engineering. Therefore it provides specific constructs called "draft" and "sketch" for specifications which are still under development. The other specification-building operations are derived from those of ASL. Parameterisation uses a refined form of the pushout approach.

RAP, developed by Broy's and the author's groups at the University of Passau [GeH 86], is probably the simplest language for which complex case studies have been written. It supports algebraic programming by hierarchical specifications with conditional equations and constructor constraints. The only structuring mechanism is enrichment (called "based on"). The corresponding RAP system implemented by Hußmann has been used for prototyping CIP-L and COLD specifications (for examples see [WB 89]).

Larch [GuH 86, 93] is a family of specification languages developed by Guttag, Horning and Wing which is based on Guttag's work on hierarchical data type specification. Each Larch specification has components written in two languages: one designed for a specific programming language, the so-called Larch interface language, and another common to all programming languages, the so-called Larch shared language LSL. Larch interface languages have been designed for CLU [GuH 86], C and Modula-3 [GuH 93]. Every interface language is an extension of a programming language with formal annotations instead of comments. LSL is a loose algebraic specification language with simple structuring operators (without "export" and without explicit parameterisation) but with a construct for observational abstraction called "partitioned by".

GLIDER ([DFSL 89], [HL 94]) is a language for requirement engineering based on loose semantics. It is a successor of GSBL, developed within the ESPRIT project ICARUS. The main difference to GSBL is the loose semantics and explicit parameterisation.

SPECTRAL [KS 91], developed by Krieg-Brückner and Sannella, is a powerful, compact specification language that includes partial higher-order functions, higher-order parameterisation by dependent types, subsorting and a form of inheritance. The design is based on Extended ML and PROSPECTRA (see Section 2.3), generalizing and extending both approaches.

SPECTRUM [Br et al. 93] is a language for developing executable specifications from requirement specifications. It contains explicit support for partial, continuous and higher-order functions, sort class polymorphism and infinite objects. Parameterisation is explicit. PLUSS and PA^{nn}DA-S [KH 93] can be seen as predecessors of SPECTRUM.

2.3 Support of programming paradigms

The languages mentioned above are all "pure" specification languages that support the algebraic programming style. Roughly, an *algebraic program* can be characterized as an executable specification which has first-order positive conditional equations as axioms. In this sense all languages which admit only such axioms (e.g. OBJ, RAP, OBSCURE, ACT, ASF and appropriate executable subsets of the other languages) can be considered as algebraic programming languages. In order to support also classical programming paradigms one has to extend a "pure" specification language with specific appropriate language constructs or to design a specification language that directly integrates the algebraic specification style with the programming concepts.

In the following table, we give some examples of specification languages that support imperative, object-oriented, concurrent, functional or logic programming.

Table 2: Support of Programming Styles

Imperative	Object-oriented	Concurrent	Functional	Logic
CIP-L	FOOPS	LOTOS	EML	SLog
Larch	OS	SMoLCS	SPECTRAL	LPG
COLD, RSL	TROLL	PSF, SCA	SPECTRUM	Eqlog
PA^{nn}DA	Maude	RSL		ALF
Z, VVSL		FOCUS		BABEL

Examples of specification languages supporting an *imperative programming style* are CIP-L [Ba et al. 81], COLD [J 89], Larch [GuH 86], VVSL [Mi 90] and Z [Spi 89]. The CIP-L language is a wide spectrum language which was designed within the project CIP aiming at the formal development of Algol-like programs from specifications by transformation. The RAP system was developed for prototyping hierarchical CIP-L specifications. PA^{nn}DA [KH 93], developed within the PROSPECTRA project, can be seen as the successor of CIP-L for the design of ADA programs. COLD is a design language developed in the framework of the ESPRIT project METEOR. Like CIP-L it supports loose algebraic specifications and imperative programs. The structuring constructs are derived from ASF. The underlying logic supports pre- and post-conditions and temporal operators based on infinitary predicate logic. In contrast to CIP-L and COLD (which integrate algebraic and imperative specifications) Larch separates them into two different languages (see above). RSL is the specification language of the RAISE method that is inspired by VDM; it is a wide spectrum language with facilities for structuring and concurrency; it offers constructs for loose abstract data type specification as well as for (recursive) type definitions and imperative specification. VVSL and Z are examples for model-based specification languages in which algebraic methods are used only for the formal semantics. VVSL is a formal specification language supporting VDM (cf. e.g. [BJ 78]). As for COLD its semantics is based on ASF and infinitary predicate logic. In Z the specification-building operators of CLEAR are used to give the semantics of the structuring constraints.

FOOPS [GM 87], OS [Bre 91], TROLL [EGS 93] and Maude [Me 95] are *object-oriented specification languages*. FOOPS and Maude are extensions of OBJ. Whereas FOOPS is just a notational extension to functional object-oriented programs, Maude introduces non-deterministic rewriting as a main feature. This also makes it suitable for concurrent programming. OS is an extension of ASL by operators for inheritance and clientship. TROLL uses the algebraic approach for the description of data structures and temporal logic for the behaviour of objects.

LOTOS, SMoLCS, PSF, FOCUS (for references see [AR 93]) and SCA [McT 93] provide examples of the support of *concurrent specifications*. LOTOS is an ISO-standard for the formal definition of protocols and services for computer networks. It uses ACT1 for the definition of data expressions and CCS for the description of concurrency. SMoLCS is a very powerful language which integrates labelled transition systems and algebraic specifications. It is based on partial higher-order algebras and uses ASL for structuring. PSF is a combination of ASF and ACP [BK 89]. Tucker uses initial algebraic specifications for describing synchronous concurrent automata (SCA). FOCUS is a methodology for specifying networks by properties of infinite streams of data. The underlying language is SPECTRUM.

Functional programming is the paradigm which corresponds most closely to algebraic specification. As algebraic programs functional programs consist of equations, but have a polymorphic type structure and higher-order functions. Examples for specification languages supporting functional programming are Extended ML, SPECTRUM, and SPECTRAL. Extended ML (short EML) designed by Sannella and Tarlecki enhances SML [Pau 91] by allowing axioms in SML-signatures and in SML-structures. The two other languages do not incorporate directly a functional language but they possess executable sublanguages which can be easily translated into a functional language.

For supporting *logic programming* one has to extend the notion of signature to contain function *and* predicate symbols. The languages SLog [Fr 85], EqLog [GM 86], LPG [BE 86], ALF [H 90] and BABEL [MR 92] follow this approach. All of them have conditional formulas in form of Horn clauses and conditional equations as axioms. They are based on initial semantics and possess execution mechanisms that combine term rewriting with resolution [H 94]. As a consequence these languages integrate the functional and the logic programming style and thus are called "functional-logic languages". SLog is similar to RAP but has predicates. LPG can be seen as an extension of both by explicit parameterisation. Eqlog is an extension of OBJ. ALF and BABEL support polymorphic higher-order functions.

3. Specification in the small

This Section gives a survey on the main concepts for algebraic specification "in the small". In Section 3.1 the different forms of equational axioms in algebraic specification languages are considered. Section 3.2 surveys the use of data constraints in specification languages.

Section 3.3 studies the treatment of partial functions and infinite data, Section 3.4 the representation of dynamic behaviour. Finally, in Section 3.5 different approaches for refining the sort structure are presented.

3.1 Equational Logic

Equational logic is the basis of the algebraic approach to specification. The seminal papers by Guttag [Gu 75] and the ADJ-group [GTWW 75] both introduced many-sorted equations for specifying the abstract properties of data structures axiomatically. This extension of untyped equational logic was the starting point of the abstract data type approach. Later, more complicated formulae have been used as axioms. A main characteristic is the treatment of the equality symbol as a predefined or universal symbol with fixed semantics. The following example describes a specification of pre-ordered sets in OBJ. Its models have a binary boolean infix operation "<=" that is reflexive and transitive. The keyword "th" indicates that PREORD denotes a first-order theory without any constraints. The models are all algebras of the appropriate signature that satisfy the axioms. The specification BOOL of truth values is a predefined specification.

```
th PREORD is
    sort Elem .
    op _<=_ : Elem Elem → Bool .
    vars E1 E2 E3 : Elem .
    eq E1 <= E1 = true .
    cq E1 <= E3 = true if E1 <= E2 and E2 <= E3 .
endth
```

3.1.1 Kinds of equational axioms

What kind of axioms one chooses depends on the intended use of specifications in the software development process. For writing executable design specifications, conditional equations have been chosen for two reasons: first, they are the most general form of equational axioms admitting initial algebras and, second, they are executable by conditional term rewriting and conditional narrowing strategies. For specifying requirements it soon became apparent that full first-order equational logic (with equality as only predicate symbol) was suitable [BDPW 79]. Generation constraints cannot be expressed in the first-order framework. Therefore, following the approach of Maibaum [MVS 85], infinitary equational logic [KR 89] has been used as a semantic basis for COLD and VVSL. Other extensions of first-order logic, such as dynamic and temporal logic and higher-order logic, are used for the support of particular programming paradigms. Table 3 gives an overview of the different kinds of axioms and their use in software development and specification languages (where only the most general class of formulae is mentioned).

Table 3: Kinds of axioms

Use	Kind of axiom	Syntax	Specification language
Universal algebra	One-sorted equations	$u = v$	
Abstract data types	Many-sorted equations	$u =_s v$	GSBL
Design specifications	Conditional equations	$\forall x_1{:}s_1,\ldots,x_m{:}s_m.$ $u_1=v_1 \wedge \ldots \wedge u_n=v_n \Rightarrow u =_s v$	OBJ, RAP,ASF LSL, ACT1 OBSCURE
Requirements	First-order equational logic	Formulae built from $=_s, \wedge, \neg, \forall$	CIP-L, ASL, ACT2, PLUSS, PA^{nn}DA, SPECTRAL, SPECTRUM
Requirements and constraints	Infinitary equational logic	First-order equ. logic + infinitary conjunctions $\bigwedge_{i \in N} \phi_i$	COLD, VVSL
Imperative, object-oriented or concurrency spec's	Dynamic and temporal logic	$[]\ \phi$, $<>\ \phi$, $[p]\ \phi$, $<p>\ \phi$,... where p is a program	Larch Interface languages, COLD, TROLL
Functional spec's	Higher-order logic	$\forall x{:}s \rightarrow s'$...	EML, SPECTRAL, SPECTRUM

3.1.2 Equational calculus

Birkhoff's classical calculus for one-sorted equations axiomatises the equality predicate as a reflexive, symmetric and transitive relation which is compatible with all function symbols and satisfies the substitution property. In order to extend this calculus to many-sorted equations one has to require compatibility for the function symbols of the appropriate signature. Unfortunately this extension is not consistent if one admits empty carriers set for the interpretation of sorts [HuO 80]. The solution is to record all variables used in the proof so far. In the following Birkhoff's axioms and rules for the one-sorted case are given (where x denotes a variable, $t,t',t'',t_1,u_1,...t_n,u_n$ denote terms, f an n-ary function symbol and $[x:=t]$ a substitution of x by t):

Reflexivity $\quad t=t$

Symmetry $\quad \dfrac{t=t'}{t'=t}$ $\qquad$ Transitivity $\quad \dfrac{t=t' \ , \ t'=t''}{t=t''}$

Compatibility $\quad \dfrac{t_1=u_1, \ldots, t_n=u_n}{f(t_1,\ldots,t_n)=f(u_1,\ldots,u_n)}$ $\qquad$ Substitution $\quad \dfrac{t=t'}{t[x:=t_1] = t'[x:=t_1]}$

The transitivity for the many-sorted case reads as follows (where s denotes a sort and X and Y are lists of sorted variables):

$$\frac{\forall X.\ t =_s t' \ , \ \forall Y.\ t' =_s t''}{\forall X \cup Y.\ t =_s t''}$$

A quantified variable can only be omitted if its sort is provably not empty. A sufficient condition is that there exists at least one ground term of this sort. In the following elimination rule $x_1,y_1,...x_n,y_n$ denote variables and $T(\Sigma)_{si}$ denotes the set of ground terms of sort s_i.

$$\frac{\forall x_1{:}s_1,\ldots,x_i{:}s_i,\ldots,x_n{:}s_n.\ t=t'}{\forall x_1{:}s_1,\ldots,x_{i-1}{:}s_{i-1},x_{i+1}{:}s_{i+1},\ldots,x_n{:}s_n.\ t=t'} \quad \text{if } T(\Sigma)_{si} \text{ is not empty}$$

In the presence of conditional axioms the following additional rule is sufficient for deriving (unconditional) equations (where X and Y are lists of sorted variables):

$$\frac{\forall X.\ u_1\sigma=v_1\sigma,\ldots,\ \forall X.\ u_n\sigma=v_n\sigma}{\forall X.\ u\sigma=v\sigma} \quad \begin{array}{l}\text{if } \sigma\text{: } X \to T(\Sigma,Y) \text{ is a substitution} \\ u_1=v_1 \wedge \ldots \wedge u_n=v_n \Rightarrow u=v \text{ an axion}\end{array}$$

If one admits only non-empty carrier sets then a calculus for many-sorted first-order equational logic can be obtained from any proof system for many-sorted first-order logic (see e.g. [Ba 77]). For specifying equality one does not take the Birkhoff rules directly, but one uses the corresponding axioms. To get a proof system in the general case one has to take care of the presence of empty carrier sets. One possibility is to use untyped first-order logic with a relativised quantification of the form $\forall x.\ x \in s \Rightarrow \phi$ for $\forall x{:}s.\ \phi$ [PaW 84].

Infinitary logic extends finitary first-order logic by infinitary conjunctions of the form $\bigwedge_{i \in N} \phi_i$ where all ϕ_i are themselves finitary or infinitary formulae. The proof rules are almost the same as for finitary first-order logic. The only difference is that in the rules for conjunction the index set I for conjunction is {1,2} in the finitary case and N in the infinitary case:

$\wedge$Introduction $\quad \dfrac{\phi_i \text{ for all } i \in I}{\bigwedge_{i \in I} \phi_i}$ $\qquad$ $\wedge$Elimination $\quad \dfrac{\bigwedge_{i \in I} \phi_i}{\phi_i}$ for all $i \in I$

All calculi mentioned above are complete (for equations and conditional equations see [Pa 88], for infinitary (partial) logic see [KR 89]). Finitary and infinitary first-order logic satisfy Craig's interpolation theorem [KR 89], which is important for proofs in structured specifications. This is true neither for many-sorted equations nor for many-sorted conditional equations [BHK 90]. (This may be one of the reasons for which languages such as ACT1 do not support the "export" operator.)

3.2 Constraints

Sort constraints are essential features of algebraic specifications for exact semantic modelling of the carrier sets of data structures. Except in ASL, where constraints are realised by specification-building operations, a constraint is considered as a special sentence or axiom which is determined by a list of function symbols and (generally implicitly) a sort or a list of sorts. Corresponding to the three main semantic approaches to abstract data types one can find three kinds of sort constraints: initial, generating and behavioural constraints. (For details see [EWT 83], [ST 87], [BHW 94].)

In Section 2.1 initial and generating constraints have been introduced for the case where all sorts satisfy such a constraint. More generally an *initial constraint* (as in the parameterised specification LIST where the sort Elem of TRIV is not constrained) denotes the free extension of the non-constrained sorts. In every model of LIST the carrier set interpreting List is the free extension of the carrier of Elem. In ACT1 one writes the initial constraint for lists with a sort List(Elem) as follows:

```
constructors
        nil : → List(Elem);
        cons : Elem, List(Elem) → List(Elem);
```

In general, function symbols such as "nil" and "cons" which generate the data elements of a sort are called "constructors". OBJ and ASF do not have a special notation for constructors. In OBJ the keyword "obj" indicates that all declared function symbols of the corresponding specification are constructors; in ASF all function symbols are constructors.

A *generating constraint* is weaker: it requires just a minimal extension ("no junk"). E.g. in the example of lists it requires that every element of the carrier of List(Elem) can be interpreted by a term t constructed from nil, cons and the elements of the carrier of Elem. In SPECTRUM (on the left) and in LSL (on the right) this is written as follows.

List **generated by** nil, cons;   List **generated by** [nil, cons]

LSL is the only language that supports *behavioural constraints* in form of assertions. In LSL, saying that a sort s is **partitioned by** a set of operations, Ops, asserts that if two terms of sort s are unequal, a difference can be observed using an operator in Ops. E.g.

```
NAT_EVEN : trait
   introduces
      zero : →Nat
      succ : Nat → Nat
      even : Nat → Bool
   asserts
      Nat partitioned by even
      ∀x : Nat
      even(zero) = true
      even(succ(zero)) = false
      even(succ(succ(x)))= even(x)
```

is a LSL specification that can be used to derive theorems such as

succ(succ(zero)) = zero.

In every model of NAT_EVEN two elements x, y are equal if they cannot be distinguished by even. In other words, for all x, y : Nat

$$x = y \Leftrightarrow \text{even}(x) = \text{even}(y).$$

Partitioned-by constraints can be axiomatised in first-order logic; generating constraints can be axiomatised in infinitary first-order logic [MVS 85], [KR 89]. Initial constraints are axiomatisable in (infinitary) first-order logic, if the induced congruence relation is definable in this logic.

Initial constraints are used in CLEAR, OBJ, ACT, ASF, GSBL and in a restricted form in SPECTRUM. Generating constraints are used in RAP, COLD, Larch, PLUSS, SPECTRAL, SPECTRUM, implicitly in CIP-L and as specification-building operations in ASL. Behavioural constraints occur in LSL and ASL and are used for the semantics of older versions of EML.

3.3 Partial functions and infinite data

In contrast to the theoretical approach to abstract data types which is based on total functions, the use of specifications in practical applications demands the ability to cope with partial functions. Therefore several languages including CIP-L, COLD, PA^{nn}DA, Z, VVSL, SPECTRAL, SPECTRUM introduce another universal predicate D, the so-called definedness predicate (written δ in SPECTRUM, "terminates" in EML and $\downarrow$ in COLD). OBJ uses subsorting to deal with partiality (cf. Section 3.5). For example, in SPECTRUM a partial predecessor function pred: Nat →Nat can be axiomatised as follows:

$\forall x : \text{Nat}$ **in** $(\delta\,(\text{pred}(x)) \Leftrightarrow \neg(x = \text{zero})) \wedge \text{pred}(\text{succ}(x)) = x;$

Partiality influences the interpretation of the equality symbol: in a two-valued interpretation one may choose between the *existential equality* [R 79] (where two terms are existentially equal if they are both defined and equal) and the *strong equality* [BW 82] (where two terms of the same sort are strongly equal if they are either both undefined, or both defined and equal).

Existential equality $=_e$ and strong equality $\cong$ satisfy the following properties (for all x,y:s):

$x =_e y \Rightarrow D(x) \wedge D(y);$

$x =_e x \Leftrightarrow D(x);$

$x \cong y \Leftrightarrow [(D(x) \vee D(y)) \Rightarrow x =_e y];$

The latter property shows that with the help of the definedness predicate D each equality relation can be expressed by the other.

Existential equality has the advantage of being semi-computable (in the initial model of a conditional equational specification) whereas strong equality may be non-computable. On the other hand strong equality represents the extensional equality between recursive functions and is therefore appropriate for use in program transformation. Existential equality is used e.g. in COLD and VVSL, strong equality in CIP-L, PA^{nn}DA, EML, SPECTRAL and SPECTRUM.

The main relation symbol in denotational semantics is not equality but a *complete partial order*. Hence for developing specifications of functional programs it is appropriate to choose the "less-defined" relation as an universal predicate symbol together with a constant $\bot$ denoting the least element of every sort. SPECTRUM and GLIDER are examples of specification languages based on this approach. As a consequence, non-strict functions such as "if.then.else" can be fully axiomatised in those languages. Also infinite data can be defined with the help of non-strict functions. For example, in SPECTRUM, if the sort Stream representing finite and infinite lists has the non-strict constructor function

$\&: \text{Nat} \times \text{Stream} \rightarrow \text{Stream}$,

then the equation

$a = \text{zero} \ \& \ a$

defines the infinite stream <zero,zero,...> consisting of infinitely many zero's.

3.4 Executable specifications and dynamic behaviour

For *executing algebraic specifications* automatically, Birkhoff-like calculi are not enough. Therefore prototyping systems use term rewriting and narrowing calculi where an equation t=t' is turned into an oriented equation of the form t⟶t'. Examples are the systems underlying RAP, PLUSS (the ASSPEGIQUE system) and ACT. The OBJ system and newer versions of the other systems use commutative and associative rewriting. Specifications written in these languages as well as in other languages based on the initial approach are executable: they can be interpreted via term rewriting and narrowing. Hence one can consider such a specification as a prototype of a system or even as program itself, a so-called "*algebraic program*" (cf. e.g. [GM 86], [HG 89]).

Implementation considerations often had strong influence on the design of programming languages. In the case of specification languages this has led to deep studies of rewriting. While confluent (and terminating) rewriting systems correspond exactly to equational axioms, non-confluent rewriting relations have a different semantics modelling the dynamic behaviour of non-deterministic rewriting. Among other reasons this has led to the introduction of a *second universal predicate symbol* into specification languages for describing *dynamic aspects of software systems*. We can distinguish three approaches:

- *labelled transition relations* of the form $t \text{-}^{a}\!\!\rightarrow t'$ are used for modelling dynamic behaviour of concurrent and object-oriented systems in SMoLCS [AGRZ 89];
- *non-deterministic rewriting* of the form t⟶t' is used in Maude for concurrent object-oriented specification, and more generally by Meseguer for modelling concurrency;
- *labelling* of the form $t \in l$ is used by Bernot/LeGall for modelling exceptions [BL 93].

For references and a comparison of the first two approaches see [AR 93]. In these approaches t, t' represent states and $t \text{-}^{a}\!\!\rightarrow t'$ (t⟶t', resp.) are used for modelling the transition from one state to the next. This leads to an operational description of the dynamic behaviour of a system which is based on an algebraic description of states and problem domain. Note the similarity to the "two-tiered" Larch approach. There, however, pre- and postconditions are used in interface languages for describing dynamic properties of a system. Other languages use dynamic and temporal logic (e.g. COLD) for this purpose. Only SPECTRUM remains entirely within the equational framework by the use of infinite streams.

3.5 Relating and constructing sorts

Simple, many-sorted signatures where sorts are (unstructured) names are used e.g. in CIP-L, RAP, ASF and COLD. Most other specification languages exploit refined sort disciplines. There are five approaches: subsorting, generic sorts, sort classes, dependent types and the semantic membership relation. (For a survey on subsorting and semantic membership see [Mo 93].)

For *subsorting* (OBJ, OS, GLIDER and Maude) a predicate symbol ≤ between sorts is introduced with the intended meaning that s≤s' holds if the carrier set interpreting s is a subset of the carrier of s'. The original reason for subsorting was to solve the problem of partial functions in the initial algebra approach: since any partial function, say f : s→s'', is total on its domain, dom(f), one can turn it into a total function by introducing a new subsort s_1 of s representing dom(f). For example in OBJ a specification of natural numbers with a predecessor function can be given by introducing a subsort Pnat for positive numbers:

```
obj NAT2 is sorts Nat Pnat .
    subsort Pnat < Nat .
    op zero : → Nat .
    op succ : Nat → Pnat .
    op pred : Pnat → Nat .
    var X : Nat .
    eq pred(succ(X)) = X .
endo
```

Other uses of subsorting are in refinement and for modelling class inheritance in object-oriented specification (e.g. in OS and Maude). A disadvantage is that static typechecking cannot be fully achieved.

The origin of *generic sorts* is parametric polymorphism. Sorts are not just constants: composed sort terms can be constructed with the help of predefined or user defined sort constructors, the generic sorts. The example below on the left shows a specification of loose polymorphic lists in SPECTRUM which declares a polymorphic sort List α. (The keywords **strict, total** indicate that cons is a strict and total function. For the semantics of the generating constraint see Section 3.2.) By instantiating the sort variable α in List α with List(Bool) one can construct the composed sort List(List (Bool)). Generic sorts are used implicitly in ACT1 (cf. the example with list constructors in 3.2) and GLIDER in connection with actualisation (for avoiding unnecessary renaming). *Parametric polymorphism* is used in EML and SPECTRUM. SPECTRUM employs also a more general form of parametric polymorphism: the notion of *sort class*. Here any sort s of a sort class C is equipped with function symbols and axioms defined in the declaration of C. For example the following SPECTRUM specification on the right defines a sort class PREO for sorts α which are pre-ordered:

```
POLY_LIST =
{   sort List α;
    nil : → List α;
    cons : α × List α → List α;
    cons strict total;
    List a generated by nil, cons;
}
```

```
PREORD = {
    class PREO;
    .<=.: α :: PREO ⇒ α × α → bool;
    axioms α :: PREO ⇒∀x,y,z:α in
    x <= x;
    x <= y ∧ y <= z ⇒ x <= z ;
    endaxioms; }
```

Dependent types admit more general sort constructors where the arguments can also be values, not only sorts. The classical example is an array sort of length n that can be expressed in SPECTRAL as follows

Array : (T : **type**) → (n : Nat)→ **type** = (v : List T || length v = n).

Dependent types are used in SPECTRAL for all kinds of objects, not only for sorts. Advantages of dependent types are that context conditions can be controlled on the level of signatures and more importantly that logic and structuring mechanisms are integrated into the same framework. A disadvantage is that all dependencies are made explicit leading to expressions with many parameters which may be difficult to read. Moreover, static type-checking cannot be achieved in the presence of subtypes defined by predicates.

In the *semantic membership* approach one considers membership t : s as an additional predicate symbol. There are several proposals for its axiomatisation including classified algebras, galactic algebras, equational type logic and unified algebras (for a survey see [Mo 93]). Mosses' language for action semantics is an example of the use of unified algebras. The advantage of these approaches lies in the fine-grain treatment of sorts: type declarations of functions are axioms in just the same way as equations. A problem is that the membership test is undecidable in general.

4. Specification "in the large"

Structuring is essential for being able to write, understand and analyse large specifications. Therefore all specification languages contain constructs for structuring specifications. In the following subsections the structuring concepts of specification languages are presented, classified into specification-building operators (Section 4.1), parameterisation (Section 4.2) and refinement (Section 4.3).

4.1 Specification-building operators

The abstract syntax for writing specifications in some specification languages can be seen as being given by a set of specification expressions which are generated by a set of specification-building operations. Any such operation allows one to construct a new specification from already existing specifications. Table 4 gives an overview of the different specification-building operators and lists some languages in which they occur.

For proving the validity of a formula in structured specifications two different techniques can be used: First one can reduce a structured specification to a non-structured normal form and prove the formula with the usual proof system of specification "in the small" (see [BHK 90] for ASF and [Bre 89] for ASL without behaviour). A drawback of this method is that it does not respect the modular structure of the specifications. Therefore by the second method, proofs are performed in accordance with the modular structure of the specification expressions (see [SB 82] for CLEAR, [ST 87] for behavioural abstraction, [Fa 92] for ASL, [HST 89], [W 93] and [Ce 94] for simplified versions of CLEAR and ASL). The idea in these proof systems is to

Table 4: Specification-building operations

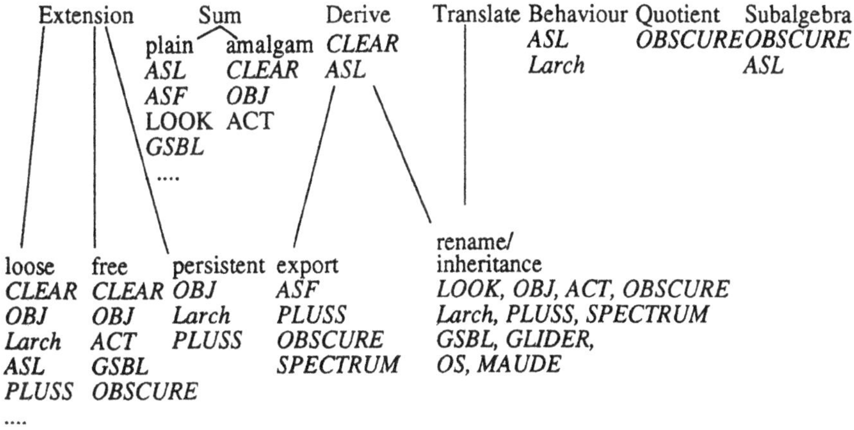

indicate by SP |– ϕ for any formula ϕ the specification expression SP in which ϕ is provable. Then for each specification-building operation γ the proof rules have the form

$$\frac{SP_1 \vdash \phi_1, \ldots, SP_n \vdash \phi_n}{\gamma(SP_1, \ldots, SP_n) \vdash \phi}$$

with the intended meaning: if $\phi_1, \ldots, \phi_n$ are valid in $SP_1, \ldots, SP_n$, then ϕ is valid in $\gamma(SP_1, \ldots, SP_n)$. A natural deduction calculus introducing proof terms for structured proofs is developed in [Pe 94].

4.1.1 Extension

All specification languages contain at least one form of extension. Semantically one has to be careful since an extension, say

SP1 = **extend** SP **by sorts** S **opns** F **axioms** E,

can have different meanings.

In the initial algebra approach it denotes the free construction (cf. e.g. [EM 85]) written "**enrich** SP **by data**..." in CLEAR, "extend SP by..." in ACT. The body of LIST (in 2.1) is an example of a free extension in CLEAR. In the loose approach, SP1 denotes an extension where every SP1-model restricted to the signature of SP is also a model of SP (written "**enrich** SP **by** ..." in CLEAR, "**includes** SP" in Larch, "**based on** SP" in CIP-L, "**enriches** SP" in PLUSS and SPECTRUM, "*WITH*" in GSBL).

Loose and free extension do not protect the original specification SP. The free construction may add new elements to the already declared sorts of SP. In the loose approach the interpretation of sorts and functions symbols of SP does not change; but because of the new axioms E, it may happen that not every model of SP can be extended to a model of SP1. To avoid such problems OBJ, Larch, PLUSS and EML introduce the concept of persistent extension (written "protecting" in OBJ, "**import**" in Larch, "**use**" in PLUSS). Such an extension protects all models of SP: each model of SP can be extended to a model of SP1 and each model of SP1 contains a model of SP as a reduct. In general, proving persistency is difficult and needs model-theoretic methods unless the axioms in E take the form of explicit definitions (i.e for each $f \in F$ the corresponding axiom has the form $f(x)=e$ or $f(x)=y \Leftrightarrow \phi$ where e and ϕ do not contain f).

The proof rule for loose and persistent extension is as follows:

$$\frac{SP \vdash \varphi}{\text{extend } SP \text{ by } \Delta \vdash \varphi}$$

The same rule holds for free extension if the formula φ is an equation.

4.1.2 Sum

The sum operator combines two specifications SP1 and SP2 to form a new specification written "SP1 + SP2" in CLEAR, OBJ and ASL, "union SP1 SP2 endunion" in ACT. Intuitively SP1 + SP2 denotes a specification whose signature is the union of the signatures of SP1 and SP2 and whose axioms are the union of the axioms of SP1 and SP2. This interpretation is correct for basic specifications consisting only of a signature and axioms. In the presence of subspecifications, however, there are different approaches to the treatment of shared subspecifications:

- *Disjoint union*: all symbols of SP1 are different from all symbols of SP2. This interpretation is not appropriate for shared subspecifications. For example if BOOL is a subspecification of SP1 and of SP2 then two copies of BOOL are created by SP1+SP2. Therefore none of the specification languages chooses disjoint union as semantics for the sum operator. But note that a dot notation as in SML [Pau 91] induces a disjoint union semantics for the sum. By the dot notation two copies SP1.BOOL.Bool and SP2.BOOL.Bool of the sort Bool of BOOL are created. In SML copying can be avoided by declaring a sharing constraint of the form SP1.BOOL.Bool = SP2.BOOL.Bool.
- *Set-theoretic union*: all shared symbols are identified. In this case only one copy of BOOL is created. However it may happen, that in SP1 and SP2 two different operations have been given the same name and therefore some unwanted identification may occur which, moreover, could create an inconsistency. Design languages such as COLD avoid the problem of unwanted identification by a so-called "origin consistency" which ensures that, in a composed specification, each applied function symbol refers to exactly one declaration. For requirements specification the origin consisteny is not adequate since one may want e.g. to compose a requirement for an equivalence relation from specifications of reflexivity, symmetry and transitivity so

that in all three subspecification declarations the same relation symbol occurs. Set-theoretic union is used in ASL, COLD, SPECTRUM and Larch.

- *Amalgamated sum*: given a (list of) shared subspecifications L, the amalgamated sum keeps just one copy of the symbols in L and builds the disjoint union of the symbols not occurring in L (for an exact definition see e.g. [EM 85]). This concept corresponds to the pushout approach and has a clean categorical foundation. A disadvantage is that name clashes are eliminated by automatically introducing new names without user interaction. The amalgamated sum concept is realised in CLEAR, OBJ and ACT and OBSCURE. The context conditions of OBSCURE ensure that no name clashes occur and therefore there is no difference to set-theoretic union.

The proof rules for set-theoretic union are as follows:

$$\frac{SP1 \vdash \phi}{SP1+SP2 \vdash \phi} \qquad \frac{SP2 \vdash \phi}{SP1+SP2 \vdash \phi}$$

The rules for disjoint union and amalgamated sum are similar but have to take the automatic renamings into account.

4.1.3 Derive and translate

The derive operation is used to forget some sorts or function symbols, possibly renaming those that remain. Mathematically it is defined as the reduct functor that is induced by a signature morphism $\sigma: \Sigma \rightarrow \Sigma'$. Given a specification SP' with signature Σ', the specification **derive** SP' **from** σ denotes the class of all Σ algebras that can be derived from models of SP' by interpreting a sort s as the interpretation of its image $\sigma(s)$ and a function symbol f by the interpretation of its image $\sigma(f)$. Only CLEAR and ASL use the derive operation directly. Other languages employ simpler variants of this operator: rename, export and forget can easily be expressed by derive using a bijective signature morphism or a canonical embedding. The rename operation has the obvious meaning, that is to rename sorts and function symbols in a consistent way; the export operation as well as the forget operation allow one to hide the non-exported symbols. An example for "export" is the specification NAT0 in Section 2.1.

The derive operator plays an important role for the notion of institution which makes specification languages independent from the underlying logic. The main consistency condition for an institution is the following property:

SP' $\vdash \sigma(\phi)$ if, and only, if **derive** SP' **from** $\sigma \vdash \phi$.

This condition leads to the proof rules for derive, export and rename:

$$\frac{SP' \vdash \sigma(\phi)}{\textbf{derive } SP' \textbf{ from } \sigma \vdash \phi} \qquad \frac{SP' \vdash \phi 0}{\textbf{export } \Sigma 0 \textbf{ from } SP' \vdash \phi 0} \qquad \frac{SP' \vdash \phi[a:= b]}{\textbf{rename } SP' \textbf{ by } [a : b] \vdash \phi}$$

where ϕ a Σ-formula, $\Sigma 0$ is a subsignature of the signature of SP', $\phi 0$ a $\Sigma 0$-formula and [a : b] denotes a signature morphism σ from Σ to Σ' with $\sigma(a) = b$ and $\sigma(x) = x$, otherwise.

From a logical point of view, the combination of export with sum is problematic. Semantically the following equation holds if Σ contains all shared symbols of SP1and SP2:

$$SP1|_\Sigma + SP2|_\Sigma = (SP1 + SP2)|_\Sigma$$

where $SP|_\Sigma$ stands for **export Σ from** SP and the equality asserts that the classes of models are the same. For proof systems the equivalence

$$SP1|_\Sigma + SP2|_\Sigma \models \phi \text{ if, and only, if } (SP1 + SP2)|_\Sigma \models \phi$$

holds only if the underlying logic satisfies Craig's interpolation theorem (for a detailed treatment see [BHK 90]).

The *translate operation* is similar to derive. It is a construction that is induced by a signature morphism. Given a specification SP and a signature morphism $\sigma: \Sigma \rightarrow \Sigma'$ the specification **translate** SP **by** σ denotes the class of all Σ'-algebras whose σ-reducts are models of SP. Translate can be used for defining renaming and for the notion of inheritance and subclassing e.g. in OS and GSBL. It is used as a basic semantic operation in LOOK and ACT1 but it does not appear directly in the syntax of these languages. The proof rule for translate is as follows:

$$\frac{SP \models \phi}{\textbf{translate}\ SP\ \textbf{with}\ \sigma \models \sigma(\phi)}$$

4.1.4 Renaming and inheritance

Although renaming can be derived from both "derive" and "translate", it is the central construct in algebraic specification for re-using pieces from other, previously existing specifications. It occurs in all specification languages listed in Section 2.2 (except CLEAR and ASL where it can be defined, cf. 4.1.3 and SPECTRAL where the higher-order constructs take care of renaming) with slightly different syntax: e.g. for constructing a new version of PREORD (cf. 3.1 and 3.5) with "<=" renamed to "eq" one writes

PREORD * (op _<=_ to eq)	in OBJ
PREORD (eq for <=)	in Larch
rename PREORD **by** [. <= . to eq]	in SPECTRUM

and similarly in the other languages. In the "object-oriented" languages OS and GSBL the name of a specification is also the name of the "sort of interest" of the specification. The example below to the left shows a class of pre-orders written in OS. OS introduces an inheritance mechanism where the sort of interest is automatically renamed. The example to the right defines a partial order relation as heir of Pre.

```
class spec Pre is
    opns .<=. : (Pre, Pre) → Bool
    axioms ∀x,y,z : Pre.
    ... as in PREORD ...
end class spec
```

```
class spec Po is
    inherits Pre
    axioms ∀x,y,z: Po.
    (x <= y) = true ∧ (y <= x) = true ⇒ x = y
end class spec
```

GSBL and Maude provide similar constructs. Maude also has constructs for redefining function symbols.

4.1.5 Other specification-building operators

There are three other specification-building operators: quotient, restrict and behaviour. Though these three operations are thoroughly studied in the literature they are practically not used in specification languages. Their importance originates from their use in semantics and refinements.

Quotient and *subalgebra operations* are needed in the most common notion for the change of data structures: the notion of implementation by "forget-restrict-identify" can be considered as a composition of export, subalgebra and quotient [SW 83]. Given a specification SP with signature Σ, subsignature Σ_0 and a set E of equations the specification **quotient** SP **by** E denotes the class of all algebras A/~ where A is a model of SP and ~ is the smallest congruence generated by E. In case ~ has an explicit definition of the form $x \sim y \Leftrightarrow \Psi[=]$ one can get a proof system of the quotient specification from this explicit definition and from the provable formulas of SP by renaming the equality relation "=" of SP into "$=_{SP}$".

$$\frac{\textbf{quotient}\ SP\ \textbf{by}\ E \vdash \forall x,y : s.\ x = y \Leftrightarrow \Psi[\text{“=”} := \text{“}=_{SP}\text{”}] \qquad SP \vdash \phi}{\textbf{quotient}\ SP\ \textbf{by}\ E \vdash \phi\,[\text{“=”} := \text{“}=_{SP}\text{”}]}$$

A quotient construction is offered in OBSCURE and can be derived in ASF, ACT and other languages as a special variant of free extension.

The specification **restrict** SP **to** Σ_0 denotes the class of all Σ_0-subalgebras of models of SP which are term generated by the operations of Σ_0. A subalgebra operation exists in OBSCURE and ASL. Universally quantified prenex formulas which are valid in SP remain valid in the restriction. No complete proof system for this operation is known to the author.

The *behaviour operation* is used to abstract from a class of models of a specification in order to get a wider class of models. The literature distinguishes two different approaches: In the so-called *abstractor semantics* one considers a notion of observational equivalence between *algebras*, in *behavioural semantics* one defines the semantics of a specification based on the notion of behavioural equivalence between *values*. (For details see [ONS 93].)

Abstractor semantics was chosen as operator in ASL [SW 83] and as semantic basis of EML [ST 85]. It includes the models of behavioural satisfaction. A drawback of abstractor semantics is that in general no convenient proof method is available (but see [ST 87]). Proof methods for behavioural satisfaction have been studied by Hennicker and Bidoit [BH 94]. Due to a new characterisation, these methods can be applied also to abstractor semantics [BHW 94]. Behavioural satisfaction is mainly used in connection with the notion of refinement. As far as the author knows, there is no specification language using this concept as a syntactic construct.

4.2 Parameterisation

In programming languages parameterisation means to abstract from particular input values of an algorithm by binding them in the parameter list of a procedure declaration. The corresponding basic syntactic constructs in imperative languages are procedure declaration and procedure call, in functional languages these are lambda-abstraction and function application.

The intention of parameterisation in a specification language is to abstract from a part of the specification in order to be able to instantiate it with different data types or specifications. This allows specifications to be defined in a generic fashion so that they may be applied in a variety of contexts which share some common characteristics. One distinguishes between explicit parameterisation where the parameter part is fixed by using a particular syntactic notation, and implicit parameterisation where only an instantiation mechanism is given without any particular notation for abstraction. The following table gives an overview of the parameterisation concepts in specification languages.

Table 5: Parameterisation concepts

Implicit parameterisation	Pushout approach	Lambda calculus approach
LOOK, Larch GSBL	CLEAR, OBJ, ACT, PLUSS	ASL, ASF, COLD SPECTRUM, SPECTRAL

4.2.1 Implicit parameterisation

Implicit parameterisation is used in languages for requirement specifications in order to re-use previously defined specifications. *Implicit parameterisation* can be seen as just another name for the renaming mechanism (cf. 4.1.4) in languages without explicit parameterisation such as LOOK, Larch and GSBL.

4.2.2 Explicit parameterisation

In *explicit parameterisation* there exists a syntactic construct for abstraction consisting of a formal parameter and a body. The formal parameter is usually given by a signature and a set of requirements. The syntax is similar in all specification languages. Compare the specification of parameterised lists in CLEAR with

LIST = **param** X = TRIV; **body** {enriches X; ... }	in SPECTRUM,
obj LIST [X :: TRIV] is sorts List ... endo	in OBJ,
type LIST [TRIV] is sorts List (Elem) ... endtype	in ACT,
LIST = λ X : TRIV. **enrich** X **by**	in ASL,
LIST : (X : TRIV) → **class** = **begin** ... **end**	in SPECTRAL.

However, the semantics is different. If parameter and body together are considered as a single specification one speaks of a *specification of parameterised objects* (e.g. parameterised algebras). If they are considered as a function from any kind of objects (e.g. algebras, specifications) to specifications one speaks of a *specification-valued function* (cf. [SST 92]). Moreover, one has to consider the way that actual parameters are instantiated. There are two different approaches: the pushout and the lambda calculus approach.

a) Pushout approach

In the pushout approach a *parameterised specification* PSP = (PAR, BODY) consists of a pair of specifications, where the body specification BODY is an extension of the formal parameter PAR. An example is the parameterised specification LIST in CLEAR (see Section 2.1) of the form (X : TRIV) B where B stands for "**enrich** X **by data** ...". PAR corresponds to TRIV and BODY to the expression B[X := TRIV] with TRIV substituted for X. In the model level semantics of ACT1, OBJ and PLUSS, the semantics of PSP is a functor F which defines for each model A of PAR a model F(A) of BODY. In the initial semantics, this functor is the free construction; in the loose semantics it is an arbitrary functor satisfying the axioms of BODY. In the example above A is an arbitrary set of data elements and the free construction F(A) is the set of all finite lists over A.

A parameterised specification PSP is instantiated by an actual parameter specification ARG with the help of a so-called "fitting morphism" h: PAR → ARG which defines the correspondence of the formal sorts and function symbols with those of the actual parameter. In order to obtain a correct instantiation ARG has to satisfy the requirements given by PAR. More formally this means that h is a *specification morphism*: all models of ARG are models of the translated formal parameter **translate** PAR **with** h. Then the result specification RES of the instantiation is defined as the pushout determined by the fitting morphism and the embedding morphism from PAR into BODY. The pushout is given by the following diagram:

$$\begin{array}{ccc} \mathrm{ARG} & \longrightarrow & \mathrm{RES} \\ h\uparrow & & \uparrow \\ \mathrm{PAR} & \longrightarrow & \mathrm{BODY} \end{array}$$

The category in which the pushout is formed depends on the semantics of the specification language. In CLEAR it is the category of theories as objects and specification morphisms as morphisms [Sa 82].

In ACT1 it is similar for the first level of semantics: instead of theories, specifications with conditional equational axioms are considered as objects. In this case the resulting specification (the pushout) can be constructed by textual substitution of PAR in BODY by ARG. In the model level semantics one constructs a lifting of the functor F to a functor F′ from the models of ARG to the models of RES; each model of RES can be interpreted as an amalgamated sum of corresponding models of BODY and ARG with a model of PAR as shared subpart.

In ACT1 PSP can be instantiated by a specification ARG or by another parameterised specification PSP1 = (PAR1, ARG). These actualisation mechanisms are called *standard* and *parameterised parameter* passing respectively.

An example for standard parameter passing is LIST_NAT (see Section 2.1). ARG corresponds to NAT1, the fitting morphism is given by the renaming [Elem to Nat]. An example for parameterised parameter passing in ACT1 would be the instantiation of PAR by parameterised sets leading to finite lists of sets over arbitrary data elements.

Main results for parameterisation with the pushout approach are existence and uniqueness (up to isomorphism) of free constructions, compositionality of parameter passing, associativity of parameterised parameter passing and several results concerning correctness with respect to suitable given model algebras [EM 85].

b) Lambda calculus approach

Parameterisation in the lambda calculus approach uses a *generalised form of lambda abstraction* written in COLD and ASL as

$$PSP = \lambda X : PAR.\ BODY(X)$$

where X is the name of the formal parameter, PAR is a specification expression, usually not containing free occurrences of X, and BODY(X) is a specification expression which may contain free occurrences of X.

Since BODY(X) is a specification, PSP is a specification-valued function, i.e. a function yielding a specification. In ASL, COLD and SPECTRUM the name X denotes a specification. The semantics of PSP is a function F that maps classes of algebras to classes of algebras such that for any specification ARG whose models are models of PAR, F(ARG) denotes the class of models of BODY[X := ARG].

Instantiation is made by partial β-reduction. If ARG satisfies the requirements of PAR (i.e. if the embedding of PAR into ARG is a specification morphism, written PAR ~~> ARG, see e.g. [SW83]) then the result of the instantiation PSP(ARG) is BODY[X := ARG]. The only difference to the classical lambda calculus is the parameter PAR restricting the admissible actual parameters which can be substituted for X [Fe 89]. As a consequence most features of the classical lambda calculus carry over to parameterised specifications; in particular, higher-order parameterisation (cf. [W 86], [SST 92], [Ce 94]) and (by using uncurrying) specifications with several parameters can be defined. SPECTRAL, EML and extensions of ASL [SST 92] use an even more refined type discipline based on dependent products.

A (relatively) complete proof calculus is given in [Ce 94]. It integrates a calculus for embeddings of the form PAR~~>ARG and uses contexts Γ of the form $X_1=N_1,\dots,X_n=N_n$ for assuming specification expressions as values for the free variables. The following (derived) rule can be used for proving the formula φ in the instantiation PSP(ARG).

$$\frac{\Gamma, X{=}ARG \mid\!> BODY \vdash \phi, \quad \Gamma \mid\!> PAR{\sim\sim>}ARG}{\Gamma \mid\!> (\lambda X : PAR.\ BODY)\ ARG \vdash \phi}$$

As in the pushout approach the signature of the actual parameter ARG may be different from the signature of PAR. Therefore the correspondence between both signatures has to be made explicit. In COLD this is done by renaming the lambda expression in a appropriate way before applying β-reduction. ASL, ASF and SPECTRUM use a fitting morphism. In contrast to the pushout approach name clashes between the symbols of ARG and the declared symbols of BODY have to be resolved explicitly by renaming BODY or ARG before performing the instantiation.

In the case where BODY[X := PAR] is an extension of PAR, this combination of renaming with β-reduction yields the same textual result as the pushout construction. But note that in general specification expressions may be more complicated than simple extension. In these cases the λ-calculus approach is more general than the pushout approach.

4.3 Relating different levels of abstraction

When constructing a software system it is not sufficient to construct just one specification but one has to develop different specifications ranging from abstract requirement specifications and design specifications to executable specifications or programs. In pure specification languages, such as ASL, CLEAR or ACT1, a specification is intended to describe only one level of abstraction of a software system at a time. Notions of refinement and implementation have been studied for these languages (see e.g. [SW 82], [SW 83], [Fa 92], [Ce 94]) but they are used on the meta-level in the specification development methodology. For example the development graph (see [PW 95]) of SPECTRUM relies on the notion of refinement as model class inclusion, where a specification SP1 is a refinement of a specification SP if any model of SP1 is also a model of SP.

However, some languages including COLD, ACT2, OBJ, EML, an extension of ASL [SST 92] and SPECTRAL offer features for representing two different levels of abstraction. COLD and ACT2 introduce notions of "component" (in COLD) and "module" (in ACT2) that relate internal and external descriptions of a software system. In COLD one writes

COMP x : K := L

for describing a so-called design component with name x, interface specification K and a specification L acting as implementation of K: the requirement is that L is a refinement of K.

In ACT2 a module consists of four parts:

MOD:

PAR	EXP
IMP	BOD

which are given by four algebraic specifications. The export EXP and the import IMP represent the interfaces of a module while the parameter PAR is a part common to both, import and export, and represents a part of the parameter of the whole system. The body BOD, which makes use of the resources provided by the import and offers the resources provided by the export, represents the implementation part of the module. As in COLD, the body is a refinement of the export part.

OBJ has the concept of "view" for defining fitting morphisms for parameter passing. It can also be used for representing a refinement between a OBJ-theory T and a OBJ-object O. A view denotes a specification morphism σ from T to O (cf. 4.2.2 a). The expression "view T as O via σ" is well defined if $\sigma : T \rightarrow O$ is a specification morphism from T to O.

An EML-signature corresponds to a specification. It extends the notion of SML-signature by axioms. An EML-structure denotes a class of algebras which satisfies an EML-signature if it is a subset of the model class of the signature. A functor in SML can be related with a specification of parameterised algebras in EML as follows. The EML-declaration

functor F(X : $<\Sigma, E>$) : RES = e

where $<\Sigma, E>$ denotes a SML-signature Σ with axioms E, RES an EML-signature and e an SML-structure expression, asserts that the SML-functor "functor F(X : Σ) = e" denotes a parameterised algebra such that for any model A of $<\Sigma,E>$ F(A) is a model of RES. Similarly in SPECTRAL one can declare a parameterised program of this specification as follows:

$$F: (X : <\Sigma, E>) \rightarrow RES\ X = e\ .$$

Note that the result specification RES X depends explicitly (unlike in EML) on the formal parameter X.

5. Design decisions

Algebraic specification languages are similar in many respects: all of them are typed languages, they are based on extensions of equational logic and have structuring facilities such as enrichment and sum. The differences between them originate from several factors such as their intended use in the software development process (Section 5.1), from design decisions with respect to syntax and semantics (Section 5.2) and from design decisions for specification "in the small" (Section 5.3) and "in the large" (Section 5.4).

5.1 Use of specification languages in the software development process

The use of a specification language for a particular software development depends on several properties of the language including

- the intended level of abstraction,
- the intended programming paradigm,
- the intended support of software engineering,
- the desired degree of tool support.

Depending on the *level of abstraction*, specification languages may aim at describing requirements, designs or programs. This influences the form of axioms and the kind of parameterisation. For requirement specifications general first-order axioms are employed (as e.g. in SPECTRUM) whereas for design specifications axioms may be restricted to conditional equations (as e.g. in OBJ) and for programs to a particular form of conditional equations (cf. e.g. [GHM 88]). Implicit parameterisation (as in Larch) seems to be appropriate for requirements specifications. More elaborate explicit parameterisation mechanisms are used for the design of components (such as for ACT2 and COLD); often it is influenced by the parameterisation concepts of the underlying programming language (as e.g. in EML).

As the examples in Section 2 show the *intended programming paradigm* such as imperative, functional, object-oriented or concurrent programming style may influence the whole specification language. For example in order to support functional programs higher-order function types are introduced in EML, SPECTRUM and SPECTRAL. Object-oriented specification languages like Maude and OS employ subsorting and structuring facilities for (class) inheritance. For writing pre- and post-conditions of imperative programs COLD introduces operators of dynamic logic whereas SMoLCS and Maude use labelled transition systems (SMoLCS) and term rewriting (Maude) for specifying sequential and concurrent state transitions. Moreover, languages which support imperative, object-oriented or concurrent programming include linguistic features for sequential or concurrent control flow.

The role of a *specification language in software engineering* depends on the particular development model.

In classical software process models such as the waterfall model or its refinements as well as in software developments methods based on structured analysis or object-orientation formal specification is not important today (cf. e.g. [So 92]); the situation could change, however, if formal methods can be integrated with pragmatic techniques and if practically usable tool support for formal specification will be available. Actually formal specifications are useful as a meta-tool for the formal foundation of pragmatic development models. E.g. In [Hu 94a,b] the pragmatic notations (including diagrams) of SSADM have been axiomatised in SPECTRUM which has led to several proposals for improvements of SSADM.

There are several software development methods based on formal approaches including the transformational approach of the CIP project, the B-method [Ab et al. 91], and the methods used in the projects RAISE, KORSO [PW 95], PROCOS [BLH 92]. One of the principal design decisions is whether there should be just one language supporting the whole software development process. In this case the language has to incorporate features for describing requirements, designs and programs. This leads to wide spectrum languages such as CIP-L, COLD, RSL, EML with complex semantics and proof rules. On the other hand if several languages and notations are used (as in the case of most pragmatic approaches) then one has to fix the semantic relationships between these notations, derive correctness criteria and to provide translations between the different languages. An important issue for the practical acceptance of formal techniques in the design and requirements phase is the graphical representation of formal descriptions (see e.g. [CEW 93]) and the integration of formal texts with usual semi-formal descriptions and diagrammatic notations (cf. [Wo 94]).

For the support of the development and the maintenance of specifications some languages include syntactic features for describing the evolution of a specification and the modification of existing specifications for new purposes. For example, PLUSS offers different syntactic constructs for denoting incomplete as well as complete specifications. Renaming, hiding and parameterisation provide means for controlled modification. Moreover some languages support refinement as an expressible relation between specifications (e.g. COLD) whereas others consider it as an external meta-relation (e.g. CLEAR, ASL).

Also the *desired tool support* such as executability of specifications, automatic or interactive proof, automatic type checking may influence the design of a specification languages. For example automatic type inference forbids the use of dependent types, executability is connected with the initial approach and requires specific forms of axioms and simple specification-building operations. Also one may hope for automatic proof only in the context of executable specifications.

There are other design decisions based on the *handling of the specification language*, e.g. whether one aims at easy readability, modifiability, writeability, verifiability. These choices often conflict: easy readability may require high-level, easy-to-use constructs, whereas easy verifiability demands a small language with few constructs. For example SPECTRUM and EML are languages with many high-level features making them suitable for use in practical applications but proving formulas is more difficult than e.g. in RAP.

5.2 Design decisions with respect to syntax and semantics

The design decisions concerning the *syntax* are similar to those in programming languages. Depending on the type system and the available parser, overloading, infix and mixfix notations can occur. The trade-off is between a simple syntax which is easy to parse but difficult to read and a complex syntax. The latter seems best since algebra is about terms and term manipulation and a flexible syntax is important for expressing terms readably.

A basic design decision is the *name structure* in large specifications. Most languages have a flat name structure (CLEAR, OBJ, SPECTRUM) whereas EML and SPECTRAL support the "do." notation. A flat name structure, in which every name is global, is not practical for large specifications. In order to avoid name clashes, a specifier has to know all occurring names. A possible solution is origin consistency as used in COLD, ASF and ACT. The same name can appear in different specifications as long as it is possible to compute uniquely its declaration (origin). Renaming is necessary only if this is impossible. In the dot notation every name, say n, is local to the specification, say SP, in which it is declared. To address it in another specification one has to call it by indicating it´s name together with the name of the specification where it is declared, in our example by SP.n. Renaming is not necessary..

In contrast to most programming languages the mentioned specification languages have a *formal semantics*. Several choices are possible: presentation semantics, model semantics, theory semantics and category-theoretic semantics.

- The *presentation semantics* defines a finite representation of a specification in terms of signatures and axioms. For presentation semantics it is necessary to "flatten" the specification expression of the language. This is possible only for languages with simple specification-building operations like ASF, ACT1 and LOOK.
- The *theory semantics* is similar but allows one to consider infinitely many axioms as needed for example for languages with more complex specification-building operations like e.g. CLEAR.
- In the *model semantics* a specification denotes a class of algebras (e.g. in ASL, SPECTRUM), a functor (e.g. OBJ and ACT1) or a class of functors (e.g. PLUSS).
- The *category theoretic semantics* is a form of semantics which is especially used if the language is *institution-independent*, that is if the language is independent of the particular logic. For example the specification-building operators of CLEAR, ASL are institution-independent [BG 80], [ST 88].

In general, the presentation semantics distinguishes more specifications than model semantics. Therefore ACT1 and several other languages have *two levels of semantics*: a presentation and a model semantics which have been proved to be consistent and complementary. Also other combinations are possible.

Executable specification languages, such as OBJ, have also an *operational semantics*. If the specification language is designed for a particular programming language the semantics of the programming language influences the semantics of the specification language. For example EML has a *"verification" semantics* in the style of the structural operational semantics of SML [KST 94].

Another important decision concerns the structure of the semantic description for (complex) specification languages. A convenient way is to define the semantics for a subset of the language, the so-called "kernel", and then to translate all syntactic constructs to this kernel (cf. the semantics of CIP-L, COLD and RSL). The problem is to choose the right size of the kernel: if it is too small the translation is too complex; if it is too large the semantics of the language becomes too complicated.

5.3 Design decisions for specification "in the small"

For specification "in the small" one has to decide about the kind of signature, the kind of logic and the semantic approach to simple specification.

Main decisions for signatures concern the *type structure*. Should signatures be one-sorted (i.e. untyped) or many-sorted (i.e. typed) and, if many-sorted, should there be simple sorts, polymorphism, subsorts, higher-order types or sort classes? The standard choice for specification languages is to have typed signatures. Defining types seems to be a natural part of writing specifications. The trade-off is between simplicity of typing and expressiveness of types. Simple type systems allow static type checking, automatic inference of types and automatic disambiguation of expressions. More complex type systems are more expressive but type checking is not static and turns out to be a form of theorem proving. Examples for that are the dependent types of SPECTRAL and the type system of action semantics, where types are particular values and the type of functions is given by a sentence.

Similarly for the *logic* there is a trade-off between a simple logic and a complex logic. A simple logic, such as equational logic with conditional equations as axioms, has a simple proof system that is complete but by which only simple properties can be expressed. Therefore additional structuring operators, such as hiding, and additional constraints are necessary for obtaining adequate axiomatisation of data structures. On the other hand a complex logic like higher-order logic requires powerful proof systems and is incomplete but term generating constraints can be expressed.

Particular design decisions concern the *treatment of partiality and equality*. Partial functions can be expressed either directly (see 3.3) or via subsorts (see 3.5). For the equality one has to distinguish the universal equality predicate and boolean functions for computing the equality between elements of particular datatypes. There is a subtle semantic difference (boolean functions are strict in contrast to the universal equality predicate) but this difference occurs only in connection with undefinedness and non-termination. Therefore e.g. SPECTRUM allows the overloading of both equalities.

The last item is the *semantic approach*. Should one choose loose or initial semantics? Requirements specification are naturally loose; programs are naturally initial; design specifications might be either loose if they describe only part of the structure of a program, or initial if they give a complete input/output definition.

5.4 Design decisions for specifications "in the large"

As described in Section 4 specification "in the large" concerns the structuring concepts of specification languages including specification-building operations, parameterisation and refinement.

The first question however is whether it is possible to express the structuring concepts by the underlying logic. In this case there would be no separation between specification "in the large" and "in the small" as in type-theory-based languages like DEVA [WSL 93]. In algebraic specification languages the distinction is always made.

All such languages contain at least *specification-building operations* for extension and sum.

Renaming is necessary for languages with simple logics but can be avoided in languages based on higher-order logic such as SPECTRAL. Export and hiding make proving more complicated (cf. 4.1.3). Therefore languages like Larch and ACT1 do not provide hiding whereas ACT2 realises hiding by attaching an interface to a specification (see 4.3). If one chooses even more powerful operations such as behavioural abstraction the structural concepts will be very expressive, but the proof systems become more complicated because the reduction of a specification to a flat normal form is impossible.

The different forms of parameterisation and refinements have been discussed in Section 4.2, and 4.3. But with respect to design decisions two further items should be considered. These are *polymorphism versus parameterisation* and *higher-order function versus parameterisation*. Polymorphism and even more sort classes model the concept of generic functions and generic sorts within specifications "in the small", whereas parameterised specifications model the same concept "in the large". A typical example are polymorphic lists. Consider the polymorphic specification POLY_LIST of Section 3.5 and the parameterised specification LIST of Section 2.1.

The main difference is in the way instantiations are made. In polymorphism several instantiations can be made within the same specification whereas the parameterised approach requires the construction of several actualisations of the parameterised specifications. Polymorphic languages like SPECTRUM or EML offer both concepts, where parameterisation is mainly included for interface descriptions of design specifications.

Also higher-order functions can be expressed by parameterisation. This is used in languages such as OBJ which rely on first-order logic. For example a higher-order function such as

$$\text{map} : (\alpha \to \beta) \to \text{List}\ \alpha \to \text{List}\ \beta;$$

can be expressed in OBJ as follows:

```
obj UNARY is
    sort Elem .
    op f : Elem →Elem .
endo
```

```
obj MAP [X :: UNARY] is
    protecting LIST[X] .
    op map: List →List .
    var Y : Elem . var L : List .
    eq map(nil) = nil .
    eq map(cons(Y, L)) = cons(f(Y), map(L)) .
endo
```

6. Trends

Specification languages which have been designed since 1990 such as SPECTRUM, SPECTRAL, GLIDER, ACT (revised version), Maude show a number of tendencies in the development of algebraic specification languages: all of them except Maude aim at covering the whole software development process starting from requirements up to executable specifications. They include constraints for the initial as well as for the loose approach and contain a well defined executable sublanguage. All of them support partial functions in some form and have simple specification-building operations. All of them contain concepts for explicit parameterisation and, with the exception of SPECTRUM, support specifications of parameterised programs. There is a trend to include features for particular programming styles, mainly for functional and object-oriented programming. The similarity between GLIDER, PLUSS and LPG has already been used to define an abstract common interchange format "FISC" which is used for communication between the development environments of these languages [Bi et al. 93].

An open question seems to be how to include descriptions of dynamic behaviour into specification languages. SPECTRUM and GLIDER favour infinite streams, COLD and the Larch interface languages use dynamic logic and pre- and post-conditions, whereas Maude and other concurrent specification languages choose non-deterministic rewriting or (labelled) transition systems.

Though currently studied in the literature [AC 93], [CM 93], [Hu 94a,b] the following aspects of programming are still not included in present algebraic specification languages: the integration of application dependent features such as description techniques for information systems or real time systems and the combination of different logics in a single specification language. The latter point seems especially important for the description of heterogeneous programming systems.

A major problem remains the acceptance of algebraic specification languages and techniques in software engineering. Today formal program development is practicable for middle size applications (cf. e.g. [GuM 94]) but it not suitable for writing e.g. a first sketch of the structure of a system nor for describing standardized architectures as used in large application systems. For the future it will be necessary to further improve the formal development methods with respect to practical applications and to enhance formal specification languages with graphical representations of static and dynamic views of the system under development.

Acknowledgements: This work has been partially sponsored by the ESPRIT working group COMPASS and the DFG project SPECTRUM.

Thanks to Michel Bidoit, Marie-Claude Gaudel, Jean-Marc Hufflen, Jeanine Souquieres, Don Sannella and all colleagues from the COMPASS-project for stimulating discussions and providing references. Special thanks to Egidio Astesiano for inviting me to write this paper, to Don Sannella for contributing many ideas to the section on design decisions and for careful reading a draft of this paper, to Maria-Victoria Cengarle, John Crossley and the anonymous referees for comments on a draft of this paper and last not least to my wife Sabine who helped me in preparing and typing this paper.

References

[Note: LNSC n = Springer Lecture Notes in Computer Science, Volume n]

[Ab et al. 91] J.-R. Abrial, M.K. Lee, D.S. Neilson, P.N. Scharbach, I.H. Sørensen:The B-method. In: S. Prehn, W.J. Toetenel (eds.): VDM '91 - Formal Software Development Methods, LNCS 552, 1991, 398-405.

[AC 93] E. Astesiano, M. Cerioli: Relationships between logical frameworks. In: [BC 93], 126-143.

[AGRZ 89] E. Astesiano, A. Giovini, G. Reggio, E. Zucca: An integrated algebraic approach to the specification of data types, objects and processes. In [WB 89], 1989, 91-116.

[AR 93] E. Astesiano, G. Reggio: Algebraic specification of concurrency. In: [BC 93], 1-39.

[Ba et al. 81] F. L. Bauer, M. Broy, W. Dosch, R. Gnatz, B. Krieg-Brückner, A. Laut, M. Luckmann, T. Matzner, B. Möller, H. Partsch, P. Pepper, K. Samelson, R. Steinbrüggen, M. Wirsing, H. Wössner: Programming in a wide spectrum language: A collection of example. In: Sci. Comput. Programming 1, 1981, 73-144.

[Ba 77] K. J. Barwise: Handbook of Mathematical Logic. Studies in Logic and the Foundations of Mathematics, Vol. 90, North-Holland, Amsterdam, 1977.

[BC 93] M. Bidoit, C. Choppy (eds): Recent Trends in Data Type Specification, LNCS 655, 1993.

[BDPW 79] M. Broy, W. Dosch, H. Partsch, P. Pepper, M. Wirsing: Existential quantifiers in abstract data types. In: H. A. Maurer (ed.): 6th ICALP. LNCS 71, 1979, 73-87.

[BE 86] D. Bert, R. Echahed: Design and implementation of a generic, logic and functional programming language. In: Proc. European Symposium on Programming, LNCS 213, 1986.

[BG 77] R. M. Burstall, J. A. Goguen: Putting theories together to make specifications. Proc. 5th Internat. Joint Conf. on Artificial Intelligence, Cambridge, MA, 1977, 1045-1058.

[BG 80] M. R. Burstall, J. A. Goguen: The semantics of CLEAR, a specification language. In: D. Björner (ed.): Proc. Advanced Course on Abstract Software Specifications. LNCS 86, 1980, 292-232.

[BHK 87] J.A. Bergstra, J. Heering, P. Klint: ASF - an algebraic specification formalism. CWI Amsterdam, Tech. Rep. CS-R8504, 1987.

[BHK 89] J.A. Bergstra, J. Heering, P. Klint: Algebraic Specification. New York, ACM Press, 1989.

[BHK 90] J.A. Bergstra, J. Heering, P. Klint: Module algebra. J. ACM 37, 1990, 335-372.

[BH 94] M. Bidoit, R. Hennicker: Proving behavioural theorems with standard first-order logic. In: G. Levi, M. Rodriguez-Artalejo(eds.): Algebraic and Logic Programming '94, LNCS 850, 1994, 41-58.

[BHW 94] M. Bidoit, R. Hennicker, M. Wirsing: Characterising behavioural semantics and abstractor semantics. In: ESOP 94, LNCS 788, 1994, 105-119.

[Bi 89] M. Bidoit: Pluss, un langage pour le developpement de specifications algebriques modulaires. These d'Etat, University Paris-Sud, 1989.

[Bi et al. 93] M. Bidoit, D. Bert, C. Choppy, R. Echahed, J.-M. Hufflen, J.-P. Jacquot, M. Lemoine, N. Lévy, J.-C. Reynaud, C. Roques, F. Voisin: Opération SALSA: Structure d'accueil pour spécification algébriques. Rapport final. In: Greco de Programmation, December 1993.

[BJ 78] D. Bjørner, C. B. Jones: The Vienna Development Method: the meta-language. LNCS 61, 1978.

[BK 89] J. Bergstra, J.W. Klop: ACP_t: A univ. axiom system for process specification. In [WB89], 447-465.

[BL 93] G. Bernot, P. Le Gall: Label algebras: a systematic use of terms. In: [BC 93], 144-163.

[BLH 92] D. Bjørner, H. Langmaack, C.A.R. Hoare: Provably Correct Systems. ProCoS I Final Delivery, 1992.

[Bre 89] R. Breu: A normal form for structured algeb. specifications. Univ. Passau, Tech. Rep. MIP-8917, 1989.

[Bre 91] R. Breu: Algebraic Specification Techniques in Object Oriented Programming Environments, LNCS 562, 1991.

[Br et al. 93] M. Broy, C. Facchi, R. Grosu, R. Hettler, H. Hußmann, D. Nazareth, F. Regensburger, O. Slotosch, K. Stølen: The Requirement and Design Specification Language SPECTRUM: An Informal Introduction, Version 1.0, Part I, TU München, Tech. Rep. TUM-I9311, 1993.

[BW 82] M. Broy, M. Wirsing: Partial abstract data types. In: Acta Inform. 18, 1982, 47-64.

[Ce 94] M.V. Cengarle: Formal specifications with higher-order parameterization. LMU München, Doktorarbeit, to appear.

[CEW 93] I. Claßen, H. Ehrig, D. Wolz: Algebraic Specification Techniques and Tools for Software Development. AMAST Series in Computing 1, Singapore, World Scientific, 1993.

[CM 93] M. Cerioli, J. Meseguer: May I borrow your logic? In: Proc. of MFCS 93, 18th International Symposium on Mathematical Foundations of Computer Science, LNCS 711, 1993, 342-351.

[CO 88] S. Clerici, F. Orejas: GSBL: an algebraic specification language based on inheritance. In: Proc. European Conf. on Object Oriented Programming, Oslo 88, LNCS 1988, 78-92.

[CO 90] S. Clerici, F. Orejas: The specification language GSBL. In: Recent Trends in Data Type Specification, 7th Workshop on Specification of Abstract Data Types, Wusterhausen, LNCS 534, 1990.

[DFSL 89] E. Dubois, J-P. Finance, J. Souquières, A. van Lamsweerde: First description of the ICARUS language kernel for the product level. ICARUS Preliminary Deliverable. SpecFun-005-R-June 1989.

[EFH 83] H. Ehrig, W. Fey, H. Hansen: ACT ONE: An algebraic specification language with two level of semantics. TU Berlin, FB 20, Tech. Rep. 80/03, 1983.

[EGS 93] H. Ehrig, M. Gogolla, A. Sernadas: Objects and their specification. In: [BC 93], 40-65.

[EM 85] H. Ehrig, B. Mahr: Fundamentals of Algebraic Specifications I, Equations and Initial Semantics. EATCS Monographs on Theoretical Computer Science 6, Springer, Berlin, 1985.

[EM 90] H. Ehrig, B. Mahr: Fundamentals of algebraic specification 2. In: EATCS Monographs of Theoretical Computer Science, vol. 21, Springer, Berlin 1990.

[ETLZ 84] H. Ehrig, J.W. Thatcher, P. Lucas, S.N. Zilles: Denotational and algebraic semantics of the algebraic specification language LOOK. TU Berlin, FB 20, Tech. Rep. 84/22, 1984.

[EWT 83] H. Ehrig, E. G. Wagner, J. W. Thatcher: Algebraic specifications with generating constraints. In: J. Diaz (ed.): 10th Internat. Coll. on Automata, Languages and Programming. Lecture Notes in Computer Science 154, Springer, Berlin, 1983, 188-202.

[Fa 92] J. Farres-Casals: Verification in ASL and related spec. languages. PhD thesis, Univ. of Edinburgh, 1992.

[Fe 88] W. Fey: Pragmatics, concepts, syntax, semantics, and correctness notions of ACT TWO: An algebraic module specification and interconnection language. TU Berlin, FB 20, Tech. Rep. 88/26, 1988.

[Fe 89] L. M. G. Feijs: The calculus λΠ. In [WB 89], 247-282.

[Fr 85] L. Fribourg: SLog: a logic programming language interpreter based on clausal superposition and rewriting. In: Proc. IEEE Internat. Symposium on Logic Programming, Boston, 1985, 172-184.

[FGJM 85] K. Futatsugi, J. Goguen, J.-P. Jouannaud, J. Meseguer: Principles of OBJ2. In: B. Reid (ed.): 12th ACM Symposium on Principles of Programming Languages, ACM, 1985, 52-66.

[Gau 84] M.-C. Gaudel: First introduction to Pluss, University of Paris Sud, Technical Report, L.R-I., 1984.

[GeH 86] A. Geser, H. Hußmann: Experiences with the RAP-system - a specification interpreter combining term rewriting and resolution. In: B. Robinet, R. Wilhelm (eds.): ESOP 86. LNCS 213, 1986, 339-350.

[GHM 88] A. Geser, H. Hußmann, A. Mück: A compiler for a class of conditional term rewriting systems. In: Conditional Term Rewriting Systems, LNCS 308, 1988, 84-90.

[GM 86] J. A. Goguen, J. Meseguer: Eqlog: equality, types, and generic modules for logic programming. In: D. Degroot, G. Lindstrom: Logic Programming, Functions, Relations, and Equations, Prentice Hall, N.J., 1986.

[GM 87] J. A. Goguen, J. Meseguer: Unifying functional, object-oriented and relational programming with logical semantics. In: B. Shriver, P. Wegner: Res. Dir. in Object-Oriented Programming, MIT Press 1987, 417-477.

[Go 79] J. Goguen: Some design principles and theory for OBJ-0, a language for expressing and executing algebraic specifications of programs. In: E. Blum, M. Paul, S. Takasu (eds.): Conference on Mathematical Studies of Information Processing, LNCS 75, 1979, 425-473.

[Gu 75] J. Guttag: The Specification and Application to Programming of Abstract Data Types. PhD Thesis, University of Toronto, Computer Science Dept. Report CSRG-59, 1975.

[GuH 86] J. Guttag, J. Horning: Report on the Larch shared language. Sci. Comp. Progr. 6,1986, 103-134.

[GuH 93] J. Guttag, J. Horning: Larch: Languages and Tools for Formal specification. Springer, 1993.

[GTWW 75] J. Goguen, J. Thatcher, E. Wagner, J. Wright: Abstract data types as initial algebras and the correctness of data representation. In A. Klinger (ed.): Computer Graphics, Pattern Recognition and Data Structures, IEEE, 1975, 89-93.

[GuM 94] G. Guiho, F. Meija: Operational safety critical software methods in railways. In: K. Duncan, K. Krueger: Information Processing '94, Vol. 3, North-Holland, 1994, 262-269.

[GW 88] J. A. Goguen, T. Winkler: Introducing OBJ3. SRI International, Tech. Rep. SRI-CSL-88-9, 1988.

[GWMFJ 92] J. Goguen, T. Winkler, J. Meseguer, K. Futatsugi, J.-P. Jouannaud: Introducing OBJ3. SRI International, Tech. Rep. SRI-CSL-92-03, 1992.

[H 90] M. Hanus: A functional and logic language with polymorphic types. In: Proc. Int. Symposium on Design and Implementation of Symbolic Computation Systems, LNCS 429, 1990, 215-224.

[H 94] M. Hanus: The integration of function into logic programming: a survey. To appear in: Journal of Logic Programming 1994.

[HG 89] H. Hußmann, A. Geser: The RAP system as a tool for testing COLD specifications. In [WB 89], 1989, 331-346.

[HL 94] J.-M. Hufflen, N. Lévy: The algebraic specification language GLIDER: a two-level language. Presented at the 10th ADT Workshop and 6th COMPASS Meeting, Santa Margherita Ligure, Draft version, 1994.

[HSP 93] A. Haxthausen, J. Pedersen, S. Prehn: RAISE: a product supporting industrial use of formal methods. TSI 12, 1993, 319-346.

[HST 89] R. Harper, D. Sannella, A. Tarlecki: Structure and representation in LF. In: Proc. 4th IEEE Symposium on Logics in Computer Science LICS 89, Asilomar, California, 1989, 226-237.

[Hu 94a] H. Hußmann: Formal foundations for SSADM. Habilitation thesis, TU München, 1994.

[Hu 94b] H. Hußmann: Formal foundations for pragmatic software engineering methods. In [Wo 94], 1994, 27-34.

[HuO 80] G. Huet, D. C. Oppen: Equations and rewrite rules: A survey. In: R. V. Book (ed.): Formal Language Theory: Perspectives and Open Problems. Academic Press, 1980.

[J 89] H.B.M. Jonkers: An introduction to COLD-K. In [WB 89], 139-206.

[KH] B. Krieg-Brückner, B. Hoffmann (eds.): PROgram development by SPECification and TRAnsformation, LNCS 680, 1993.

[KR 89] C.P.J. Koymans, G.R. Renardel de Lavalette: The logic MPL_w. In [WB 89], 247-282.

[KS 91] B. Krieg-Brückner, D. Sannella: Structuring specifications in-the-large and in-the-small: Higher-order functions, dependent types and inheritance in SPECTRAL. Proc. TAPSOFT 91, LNCS 1991.

[KST 94] S. Kahrs, D. Sannella, A. Tarlecki: The semantics of Extended ML: a gentle introduction. In: Int. Workshop on Specification Languages, Utrecht 1993, to appear.

[LL 87] T. Lehmann, J. Loeckx: The specification language OBSCURE. Universität des Saarlandes, Fakultät f. Informatik, Tech. Report A 87/07, 1987.

[Lu 90] Z. Luo: An extended calculus of constructions. PhD thesis, Univ. Edinburgh, 1990.

[McT 93] B. McConnell, J. V. Tucker: Infinite synchronous concurrent algorithms. In: F.L. Bauer, W. Brauer, H. Schwichtenberg (eds.): Logic and Algebra of Specification 1991, Springer, 1993, 321-376.

[Me 95] J. Meseguer: From abstract data types to logical frameworks. This volume.

[Mi 90] C.A. Middelburg: Syntax and Semantics of VVSL: A Language for structured VDM specifications. Doctoral Thesis, University of Amsterdam, 1990.

[Mo 93] P. D. Mosses: The use of sorts in algebraic specifications. In: [BC 93], 66-92.

[MVS 85] T.S. Maibaum, P. Veloso, M. Sadler: A theory of abstract data types for program development: bridging the gap? In: H. Ehrig, C. Floyd, M. Nivat, J.Thatcher: TAPSOFT '85, Vol.2. LNCS 186, 1985, 214-230.

[MR 92] J. J. Moreno-Navarro, M. Rodriguez-Artalejo: Logic programming with functions and predicates: the language BABEL. Journal of Logic Programming 12, 1992, 191-223.

[ONS 93] F. Orejas, M. Navarro, A. Sanchez: Implementation and beh. equivalence: a survey. In [BC93], 93-125

[PaW 84] P. Padawitz, M. Wirsing: Completeness of many-sorted equational logic revisited. Bull. EATCS 24, 1984, 88-94.

[Pa 88] P. Padawitz: Computing in Horn Clause Theories. EATCS Monographs 16, Springer, Berlin, 1988.

[Pau 91] L. Paulson: ML for the working programmer. Cambridge Univ. Press, 1991.

[Pe 94] H. Peterreins: A natural deduction calculus for structured specifications. Univ. München, Institut für Informatik, Tech. Report 9410, 1994.

[PW 95] P. Pepper, M. Wirsing et al.: KORSO: A methodology for the development of correct software. To appear in: M. Broy, S. Jähnichen(eds): KORSO: Correct Software by Formal Methods. 1995.

[R 79] H. Reichel: Theorie der Aequoide. Dissertation B. Humboldt-Universität Berlin, 1979.

[Sa 82] D. Sannella: Semantics, implementation and pragmatics of Clear, a program specification language. Ph.D. Thesis, Dept. of Computer Science, Univ. of Edinburgh, 1982.

[SB 83] D. Sannella, R. M. Burstall: Structured theories in LCF. In: G. Ausiello, M. Protasi (eds.): 8th CAAP, L'Aquila. LNCS 159, 1983, 377-391.

[So 92] I. Sommerville: Software Engineering, 4th edition, Wokingham: Addison Wesley, 1992.

[Spi 89] J. M. Spivey: The Z Notation - a reference manual. Prentice Hall 1989.

[SST 92] D. Sannella, S. Sokolowski, A. Tarlecki: Toward formal development of programs from algebraic specifications: parameterisation revisited. Acta Informatica 29, 1992, 689-736.

[ST 85] D. Sannella, A. Tarlecki: Program specification and development in Standard ML. Proc. 12th ACM Symp. on Principles of Programming Languages, New Orleans, 1985, 67-77.

[ST 87] D. Sannella, A. Tarlecki: On observational equivalence and algebraic specification. Journal of Computer and System Sciences, 34, 1987, 150-178.

[ST 88] D. Sannella, A. Tarlecki: Specifications in an arbitrary institution. Information and Computation 76, 1988, 165-210.

[SW 83] D. Sannella, M. Wirsing: A kernel language for algebraic specification and implementation. In: M. Karpinski (ed.): 11th Coll. on Foundations of Computation Theory. LNCS 158, 1983, 413-427.

[T 81] J. Tardo: The design, specification and implementation of OBJT: a language for writing and testing abstract algebraic program specifications. PhD Thesis, UCLA, Computer Science Department, 1981.

[W 82] M. Wirsing: Structured algebraic specifications. In: B. Robinet (ed.): AFCET Symposium for Mathematics in Computer Science, 1982, 93-108.

[W 86] M. Wirsing: Structured algebraic specifications: A kernel language. TCS 43, 1986, 123- 250.

[W 90] M. Wirsing: Algebraic specification. In: J. van Leeuwen (ed.): Handbook of Theoretical Computer Science, Amsterdam, North-Holland, 1990, 675-788.

[W 93] M. Wirsing: Structured specifications: syntax, semantics and proof calculus. In: F.L. Bauer, W. Brauer, H. Schwichtenberg (eds.): Logic and Algebra of Specification, Springer, 1993, 411-442.

[WB 89] M. Wirsing, J. Bergstra (eds.): Algebraic methods: theory, tools and applications. LNCS 394, 1989.

[WDCKWE 94] U. Wolter, K. Didrich, F. Cornelius, M. Klar, R. Wessäly, H. Ehrig: How to cope with the spectrum of SPECTRUM. TU Berlin, Tech. Rep. 94-22, 1994.

[Wo 94] B. Wolfinger (ed.): Innovationen bei Rechnern u. Kommunikationssystemen. Springer, 1994, 1-50.

[WSL 93] M. Weber, M. Simons, C. Lafontaine: The generic development language DEVA. LNCS 738, 1993.

[ZLT 82] S.N. Zilles, P. Lucas, J.W. Thatcher: A look at algebraic specifications. IBM Res. Rep. RJ 3568, 1982.

Types, Subtypes, and ASL+

David Aspinall

Department of Computer Science, University of Edinburgh, U.K.
e-mail: da@dcs.ed.ac.uk

Abstract. ASL+ is a formalism for specification and programming in-the-large, based on an arbitrary institution. It has rules for proving the satisfaction and refinement of specifications, which can be seen as a type theory with subtyping, including *contravariant refinement* for Π-abstracted specifications and a notion of *stratified equality* for higher-order objects. We describe the syntax of the language and a partial equivalence relation semantics. This style of semantics is familiar from subtyping calculi, but a novelty here is the use of a hierarchy of typed domains instead of a single untyped domain. We introduce the formal system for proving satisfaction and refinement and describe how it is linked to proof systems of the underlying programming and specification languages.

1 Introduction

There is a simple correspondence between the worlds of type theory and algebraic specification:

$$\begin{array}{ccc} \textit{elementhood},\ M : A & \Longleftrightarrow & \textit{satisfaction},\ M \in \textit{Mod}(A) \\ \textit{subtyping},\ A \leq A' & \Longleftrightarrow & \textit{refinement},\ A' \rightsquigarrow A \end{array}$$

The *elementhood* of a term M in a type A is like *satisfaction* of a specification A by a program M; to say that a type A is a *subtype* of another type A' is like saying that the specification A is a *refinement* of the specification A'. This connection holds because we take a model-theoretic approach to specification semantics: a specification amounts to the collection of models that are permissible implementations, and the refinement $A' \rightsquigarrow A$ just means that every model of A is also a model of A'. The difference is one of syntax and semantics: type theory is a game of symbol-pushing which often begins from syntactically defined relationships, whereas in our view of algebraic specification a model-theoretic semantics is paramount, and we search for *sound* proof-theoretic counterparts afterward.

An example of this is a formal system introduced by Sannella, Sokołowski, and Tarlecki [15] for proving satisfaction in ASL+, an extended version of the ASL specification language. The rules of their formal system are remarkably similar to those of a subtyping system with *power types*, designed by Cardelli as a programming language type-system [5]. Cardelli's system has terms of the form $\textit{Power}(A)$, which stands for the type of all subtypes of A. He uses the elementhood $A : \textit{Power}(A')$ to stand for the subtyping $A \leq A'$. In ASL+, there is a corresponding term written $\textit{Spec}(A)$, and $A : \textit{Spec}(A')$ is the syntactic counterpart of $A' \rightsquigarrow A$. Like Cardelli's system, ASL+ also has λ and Π-abstractions; we use them for expressing parameterised programs and specifications, and specifications of parameterised programs (an example follows below). The similarity between the systems of Cardelli and Sannella *et al.* is intriguing, because they were designed in isolation and from quite different motivations. It is explained, of course, by the correspondence above.

The work reported here is part of an attempt to consciously exploit this connection, by applying recent ideas from type theory to help understand and develop ASL+. The original treatment of the language and its formal systems was restricted in scope and depth. In particular, it turns out that the satisfaction system has a surprisingly complex meta-theory due to its combination of several concepts. The main focus of this paper, however, is on a new syntax and semantics for ASL+, which extend and improve the original treatment. The remainder of this section contains a brief overview of the framework; further explanation and motivations can be found in [15]. Section 2 describes the formal syntax of ASL+ and the kind-checking system used to define the semantics. In Section 3 we describe the semantics based on partial equivalence relations. Section 4 provides only an outline of the formal system for proving satisfaction; a fuller treatment will appear in [2]. Section 5 concludes.

1.1 Overview of the ASL+ framework

ASL+ is proposed as a kernel language for writing programs and specifications in-the-large; it extends the λ-calculus parameterisation mechanism of ASL. Suppose we wish to specify symbol tables for various kinds of lookup key: let KEY be a specification of a datatype of keys. A *parameterised specification* of symbol tables has the form:

$$SYMTAB =_{\text{def}} \lambda X \leq KEY \ . \ \ldots$$

Here the actual parameter that instantiates the variable X is required to be a specification that is a refinement of KEY. The body of the abstraction (indicated by dots) is a specification written using the parameter X. We can also write a *parameterised program* implementing symbol tables, parameterised on a program that implements the datatype KEY (this is like a *functor* in Standard ML):

$$SymTab =_{\text{def}} \lambda X : KEY \ . \ \ldots$$

But $SymTab$ isn't directly an implementation of $SYMTAB$ (even if it is correct); this is because $SYMTAB$ is a mapping from specifications to specifications, not a specification itself. To write a *specification of a parameterised program* (a *functor signature* in Extended ML), we use Π-abstraction:

$$SYMTAB^{\#} =_{\text{def}} \Pi X : KEY \ . \ \ldots$$

The denotation of $SYMTAB^{\#}$ is a collection of functions from algebras to algebras, which might include the function denoted by $SymTab$. Some parameterised specifications may be viewed as specifications of corresponding parameterised programs, but in general we need both; see [15] for further details, including an explanation of a meaning for '#' (which we use here simply as a part of the names for Π-abstractions).

ASL+ is a higher-order framework, so we may freely write higher-order specifications parameterised on $SYMTAB$, as well as specifications parameterised on KEY or $SYMTAB^{\#}$, and also higher-order parameterised programs. We now highlight some aspects connected with subtyping systems which will be important later.

Subsumption and Refinement. For reference sake, we recall the characteristic rule of subtyping systems, known as *subsumption*:

$$\frac{M : A \quad A \leq B}{M : B} \qquad (\text{SUB})$$

It expresses the idea that if A is a subtype of B, then every term of type A also has type B. In our setting, this rule is sound because of the definition of specification refinement.

Refinement of Π-specifications. There are two ways to refine specifications like $SYMTAB^{\#}$. First, we can make design decisions by imposing further constraints on the body. Alternatively, we can *remove* constraints from the argument specification KEY. Both result in a smaller class of models. A simple example is to imagine that KEY includes axioms that specify an ordering on keys. But we may wish to use an implementation *SymFinMap* of finite maps from some type ELT to symbols, which is surely good enough for the job, and satisfies a more general specification:

$$SYMFINMAP^{\#} =_{\text{def}} \Pi X : ELT \ldots.$$

If $KEY \leq ELT$, we have that $SYMFINMAP^{\#} \leq SYMTAB^{\#}$ and so via (SUB), $SymFinMap : SYMTAB^{\#}$ too (modulo some renaming, perhaps). The principle is captured by this rule (where Γ is a list of assumptions about variables):

$$\frac{\Gamma \vdash A' \leq A \quad \Gamma, X : A' \vdash B \leq B'}{\Gamma \vdash \Pi X{:}A.\, B \leq \Pi X{:}A'.\, B'} \qquad (\text{SUB-}\Pi)$$

This demonstrates the contravariance of the domain of function spaces. We might call this the rule of *contravariant refinement*, as its counterpart is known colloquially as the "contravariant rule" amongst subtyping enthusiasts.

Equality of models of Π-specifications. We would like to have a simple notion of equality on the terms of our calculus which entitles us to substitute like for like. Accepting (SUB-Π), we can go further than the usual β-conversion equalities. Suppose that we have two implementations *SymTab* and *SymFinMap*, and moreover, that these are equal as functions when restricted to the domain KEY. Then they are indistinguishable when used as implementations of $SYMTAB^{\#}$, and we write $SymTab = SymFinMap : SYMTAB^{\#}$ to mean that we may replace one for the other in any context which expects an implementation of $SYMTAB^{\#}$. The rule for equality of λ-terms is:

$$\frac{\Gamma \vdash A' \leq A \quad \Gamma, X : A' \vdash M = M' : B'}{\Gamma \vdash \lambda X{:}A.\, M = \lambda X{:}A'.\, M' \; : \Pi X{:}A'.\, B'} \qquad (\text{EQ-}\lambda)$$

When terms have several types, it is possible to have different equality relations at different types. The rule (EQ-λ) demonstrates that viewing terms in larger types can allow more terms to be considered equal; informally this is because there are fewer ways of distinguishing them. In general equalities become finer as the subtype hierarchy is descended. Conversely, moving from type to supertype equality is preserved; this monotonicity property that can be derived via (SUB) and the rules for β-conversion. These aspects of a *stratified equality* (stratified over a subtyping relation) are well known in subtyping type-systems.

2 The Formalism ASL+

ASL+ is based on an arbitrary institution [12], together with an associated programming language and specification language. This means we are given a collection of signatures $\Sigma \in$ **Sign**, and for each signature a collection of algebras $\mathbf{Alg}(\Sigma)$. The denotation of a program is an element of $\mathbf{Alg}(\Sigma)$ for some Σ, and the denotation of a specification is a collection of algebras, an element of $\mathbf{Spec}(\Sigma)$, writing $\mathbf{Spec}(\Sigma)$ as a shorthand for $Pow(\mathbf{Alg}(\Sigma))$. The underlying programming language is formalized as a collection of operations for putting together programs. An *arity* is an element of

$\mathbf{Sign}^* \times \mathbf{Sign}$. A *program building operator* (PBO) p with arity $(\Sigma_1 \cdots \Sigma_k, \Sigma)$ is a mapping $\mathbf{Alg}(\Sigma_1) \times \cdots \times \mathbf{Alg}(\Sigma_k) \to \mathbf{Alg}(\Sigma)$. Similarly, a *specification building operator* (SBO) s with the same arity is a mapping $\mathbf{Spec}(\Sigma_1) \times \cdots \times \mathbf{Spec}(\Sigma_k) \to \mathbf{Spec}(\Sigma)$.

The set $\mathcal{T}$ of *terms* of ASL+ is the least set such that:

1. $X \in \mathcal{T}$;
2. If $M_1 \in \mathcal{T} \ldots M_k \in \mathcal{T}$ then $p[M_1 \cdots M_k] \in \mathcal{T}$;
3. If $A_1 \in \mathcal{T} \ldots A_k \in \mathcal{T}$ then $s[A_1 \cdots A_k] \in \mathcal{T}$;
4. If $A \in \mathcal{T}$ and $M \in \mathcal{T}$ then $\lambda X{:}A.\, M \in \mathcal{T}$ and $\{M\}_A \in \mathcal{T}$;
5. If $M \in \mathcal{T}$ and $N \in \mathcal{T}$ then $MN \in \mathcal{T}$;
6. If $A \in \mathcal{T}$ and $B \in \mathcal{T}$ then $\Pi X{:}A.\, B \in \mathcal{T}$, $A \mathbin{\&} B \in \mathcal{T}$, and $Spec(A) \in \mathcal{T}$.

where X ranges over a fixed set of variables. The meta-variables A, B, M, N and variants range over $\mathcal{T}$; the intuition is that A and B stand for terms which are specifications (also called types because of the parallels drawn in Section 1). We write $\lambda X \le A.\, M$ as shorthand for $\lambda X{:}\,Spec(A).\, M$, and omit the empty bracket pairs from terms like $s[\,]$ and $p[\,]$.

A couple of term constructors were not mentioned in the previous section. $A \mathbin{\&} B$ is the *conjunction* of the specifications A and B: this can be thought of taking the union of the requirements of A with those of B, which corresponds to the intersection of model classes in the semantics; for this reason $A \mathbin{\&} B$ behaves as an *intersection type*. The *singleton type* $\{M\}_A$ provides a way of linking the levels of programs and specifications which is useful for writing Π-specifications. When $\{M\}_A \le B$ we know that M is an implementation of B. We treat the singleton type as the equivalence class of terms equal to M at the type A; the tag A is needed to keep track of which type we wish to think of M as inhabiting.

A *context* Γ is a list of declarations $X_1 : A_1, \ldots, X_n : A_n$ in which no variable X_i is declared more than once. We write $\langle\rangle$ for the empty context, $Dom(\Gamma)$ for the set $\{X_i \mid 1 \le i \le n\}$, and define the projection $\Gamma(X_i)$ to be A_i. A context Γ' *extends* another context Γ, written $\Gamma \subseteq \Gamma'$, if every declaration $X_i : A_i$ in Γ also appears in Γ'. The free and bound variables of a term are defined as expected. Syntactical identity is modulo alpha-convertibility, and $M[X := N]$ denotes the capture-avoiding substitution of the term N for the variable X inside the term M. Substitution extends to contexts pointwise on the A_i. There are three varieties of reduction on terms: β-reduction and η-reduction are as usual; additionally we use Γ-reduction, defined relative to a context Γ, as $\mathsf{C}[X] \longrightarrow_\Gamma \mathsf{C}[M]$ provided, for some M and A, $\Gamma(X) \equiv \{M\}_A$ ($\mathsf{C}[-]$ indicates a term with a hole in it). The idea behind Γ-reduction is that if we know a variable X inhabits a type $\{M\}_A$, then X must be equal to M.

Example 2.1 *ASL+ is intended to be instantiated with the institution independent SBOs of ASL described in [16]. These include families of operators such as the simple specification constructor $\langle\Sigma, \Phi\rangle$ which has arity (ϵ, Σ) where Φ is a set of Σ-sentences, and the hiding and renaming operator $D_\sigma \equiv$* **derive from** *–* **by** *σ which has arity (Σ', Σ) for each signature morphism $\sigma : \Sigma \to \Sigma'$. If we use the institution of equational logic $\mathcal{EQ}$, then signatures and algebras are the usual algebraic notions and sentences are equations; an orthogonal term rewriting system [9] is a suitable notion of program. PBOs might include $R_{\vec{\Phi}}$ with arity (ϵ, Σ) for a set of (oriented) Σ-equations $\vec{\Phi}$ that define an orthogonal term rewriting system, and $+_{\Sigma_1,\Sigma_2}$ with arity $(\Sigma_1\, \Sigma_2, \Sigma_1 \uplus \Sigma_2)$, for creating disjoint unions of rewrite systems.*

$$\frac{}{\langle\rangle\ \text{K-context}} \qquad (\text{K-EMPTY})$$

$$\frac{\Gamma \vdash A : \mathit{Spec}(K) \quad X \notin \mathit{Dom}(\Gamma)}{\Gamma, X : A\ \text{K-context}} \qquad (\text{K-EXTEND})$$

$$\frac{\Gamma\ \text{K-context} \quad \Gamma \equiv \Gamma_1, X : A, \Gamma_2 \quad \Gamma_1 \vdash A : \mathit{Spec}(K)}{\Gamma \vdash X : K} \qquad (\text{K-VAR})$$

$$\frac{\mathit{Arity}(p) = (\Sigma_1 \cdots \Sigma_k, \Sigma) \quad \text{for } 1 \le i \le k, \Gamma \vdash M_i : \Sigma_i \quad \Gamma\ \text{K-context}}{\Gamma \vdash p[M_1 \cdots M_k] : \Sigma} \qquad (\text{K-PBO})$$

$$\frac{\mathit{Arity}(s) = (\Sigma_1 \cdots \Sigma_k, \Sigma) \quad \text{for } 1 \le i \le k, \Gamma \vdash A_i : \mathit{Spec}(\Sigma_i) \quad \Gamma\ \text{K-context}}{\Gamma \vdash s[A_1 \cdots A_k] : \mathit{Spec}(\Sigma)} \qquad (\text{K-SBO})$$

$$\frac{\Gamma \vdash A : \mathit{Spec}(K) \quad \Gamma, X : A \vdash M : K'}{\Gamma \vdash \lambda X{:}A.\, M \ : K \to K'} \qquad (\text{K-}\lambda)$$

$$\frac{\Gamma \vdash M : K \to K' \quad \Gamma \vdash N : K}{\Gamma \vdash M\, N : K'} \qquad (\text{K-APP})$$

$$\frac{\Gamma \vdash M : K \quad \Gamma \vdash A : \mathit{Spec}(K)}{\Gamma \vdash \{M\}_A : \mathit{Spec}(K)} \qquad (\text{K-}\{\})$$

$$\frac{\Gamma \vdash A : \mathit{Spec}(K) \quad \Gamma \vdash B : \mathit{Spec}(K)}{\Gamma \vdash A \,\&\, B : \mathit{Spec}(K)} \qquad (\text{K-}\&)$$

$$\frac{\Gamma \vdash A : \mathit{Spec}(K) \quad \Gamma, X : A \vdash B : \mathit{Spec}(K')}{\Gamma \vdash \Pi X{:}A.\, B : \mathit{Spec}(K \to K')} \qquad (\text{K-}\Pi)$$

$$\frac{\Gamma \vdash A : \mathit{Spec}(K)}{\Gamma \vdash \mathit{Spec}(A) : \mathit{Spec}(\mathit{Spec}(K))} \qquad (\text{K-}\mathit{Spec})$$

Table 1: Kind checking in ASL+

2.1 Kind checking

The set $\mathcal{T}$ contains many nonsensical terms. Some of them are eliminated by *kind checking*, a syntax examination process that ensures structural well-formedness (*kindability*) of terms and contexts, by attaching a *kind* to each term according to the rules in Table 1. Kinds play a dual role, in fact; they are also used to define the semantic domains over which terms are interpreted. The kinds, ranged over by K, are formal expressions generated by the grammar:

$$K \ ::= \ \Sigma \ \mid \ K \to K \ \mid \ \mathit{Spec}(K)$$

where Σ ranges over **Sign**. Intuitively, a base kind Σ classifies terms that denote algebras with signature Σ; the arrow kind $K \to K'$ classifies mappings from terms with kind K to terms with kind K', and the specification kind $\mathit{Spec}(K)$ classifies collections of terms of kind K. Kind-checking involves two judgements:

Γ K-context	Γ is a kindable context.
$\Gamma \vdash M : K$	In context Γ, M has kind K.

In the case that the second judgement holds, we say that M is *kindable* in Γ.

We briefly describe the system. The rules (K-EMPTY) and (K-EXTEND) manage contexts. Each declaration in a context must have a *Spec*-kind, so $X : A$ means that

X has kind K when A has kind $Spec(K)$. The rule (K-VAR) derives this. The rules for PBOs (K-PBO) and SBOs (K-SBO) are similar: in each case, we must check that the operator is correctly instantiated and the final premise ensures that Γ is a kindable context in case $k = 0$. The rule (K-λ) gives an arrow kind to λ-abstractions; it should be compared with (K-Π) which shows that Π-abstractions stand for collections of mappings. The rule (K-APP) is the obvious rule for function application. A singleton term $\{M\}_A$ has kind $Spec(K)$ by (K-$\{\}$) when $M : K$ and $A : Spec(K)$, so A stands for a collection of terms with the same kind as M. By (K-&), we can only form conjunctions of specifications that have the same *Spec* kind. Finally, (K-*Spec*) characterises the *Spec* term constructor as forming collections of collections.

Example 2.2 *Suppose (for simplicity) that KEY is a nullary SBO s_k, with arity (ϵ, Σ_K). Let s_s be an SBO that builds symbol table specifications and p_s a PBO that builds symbol table implementations, with $Arity(s_s) = Arity(p_s) = (\Sigma_K, \Sigma_S)$. Now we have the following kindings:*

$() \vdash SYMTAB : Spec(\Sigma_K) \to Spec(\Sigma_S)$	$SYMTAB \equiv \lambda X \leq s_k.\, s_s[X]$
$() \vdash SymTab : \Sigma_K \to \Sigma_S$	$SymTab \equiv \lambda X{:}s_k.\, p_s[X]$
$() \vdash SYMTAB^\# : Spec(\Sigma_K \to \Sigma_S)$	$SYMTAB^\# \equiv \Pi X{:}s_k.\, s_s[\{X\}_{s_k}]$

Properties of kind-checking. The kind-checking system is well-behaved. The rules are *syntax-directed* by the term M and context Γ and so the kind of M is unique. The proposition below states desirable properties of the kind-checking system; the proofs are routine inductions on kinding derivations.

Proposition 2.3 (Kind-checking)

1. *Suppose Γ K-context, where $\Gamma \equiv X_1 : A_1, \ldots, X_n : A_n$. Then for all m such that $0 \leq m < n$, $X_1 : A_1, \ldots, X_m : A_m$ is also a kindable context and for some K_{m+1}, we have $X_1 : A_1, \ldots, X_m : A_m \vdash A_{m+1} : Spec(K_{m+1})$.*
2. *Suppose $\Gamma \vdash M : K$. Then (a) Γ K-context, and (b) $FV(M) \subseteq Dom(\Gamma)$.*
3. Weakening. *If $\Gamma \vdash M : K$, $\Gamma \subseteq \Gamma'$ and Γ' K-context, then $\Gamma' \vdash M : K$.*
4. Kind unicity. *If $\Gamma \vdash M : K$, then K is the unique such kind.*
5. Decidability. *It is decidable whether $\Gamma \vdash M : K$ for any given Γ, M, and K; furthermore, given just Γ and M, it is decidable whether there is such a K.*
6. Substitution. *If $\Gamma, X : A, \Gamma' \vdash M : K$, $\Gamma \vdash A : Spec(K')$ and $\Gamma \vdash N : K'$, then $\Gamma, \Gamma'[X := N] \vdash M[X := N] : K$.*
7. Single-step subject reduction. *Suppose $\Gamma \vdash M : K$. If any of $M \longrightarrow_\beta M'$, $M \longrightarrow_\eta M'$ or $M \longrightarrow_\Gamma M'$, then $\Gamma \vdash M' : K$ too.*

It is important to realise that kind checking is a necessary, but *not sufficient* condition to ensure that a term has a well-defined meaning. There are several ways that a kindable term may fail to have a denotation in the semantics given later:

- We can write λ-abstractions over specifications. In general, we have to check that a program satisfies a specification to see that an application of such a term is defined. For example, if s_0 is an inconsistent Σ-specification, and p denotes a Σ-algebra, so $Arity(s_0) = Arity(p) = \Sigma$, then $\vdash (\lambda X{:}s_0.\, X)\ p : \Sigma$ holds in the kind-checking system, but we choose to regard $(\lambda X{:}s_0.\, X)\ p$ as meaningless since p cannot satisfy s_0.

- A singleton specification $\{M\}_A$ denotes the collection of algebras equal to M which satisfy the specification A. Again, for this to be defined, we must check that M satisfies A, which is a stronger condition than the rule (K-{}) ensures.
- We allow for partiality of PBOs and SBOs so that some instantiations of an operator may fail to denote an algebra or collection of algebras. Whilst for specifications we might instead suppose that the operator returned the inconsistent specification, it is necessary for PBOs. For example, if we wished to allow a general union operation $\cup$ of term rewriting systems in $\mathcal{EQ}$, it may be that $P_1 \cup P_2$ is not confluent (hence not orthogonal); so $\cup$ is at best a partial operator.

3 Semantics of ASL+

The semantics presented here is an altered form of the set-theoretic semantics in [15]. Along lines suggested there, we use the institution to construct a hierarchy of set-like domains $\mathcal{D}_K$, indexed by kinds K. Programs built using PBOs have kind Σ for some specification Σ, and are interpreted as elements of $\mathcal{D}_K = \mathbf{Alg}(\Sigma)$. Rather than sets, specifications with kind $Spec(K)$ for some K are interpreted as partial equivalence relations (PERs) over $\mathcal{D}_K$ (for specifications built using SBOs, we have PERs over $\mathbf{Alg}(\Sigma)$ for some Σ). Parameterised terms with kind $K \rightarrow K'$ are interpreted as set-theoretic partial functions in $\mathcal{D}_K \rightharpoonup \mathcal{D}_{K'}$. We pause to explain these choices before presenting the definitions.

Partial equivalences. The use of partial equivalence relation models for interpreting subtyping and polymorphic type-systems is well-known (e.g., [6]). Recall that a *partial equivalence relation* R is a set $|R|$ (the carrier) together with a symmetric and transitive relation $-R- \subseteq |R| \times |R|$. The reason why we use PERs is that they model the typed equational theory of λ-calculi, and in a simple way that works well with subtyping. A type is interpreted as a PER over a set of values which are denotations of terms. Subtyping is just inclusion of PERs; if $A \leq B$ then for all a, b, $a\ [\![A]\!]\ b \Longrightarrow a\ [\![B]\!]\ b$ should hold. It follows that if two terms are equal at A, they are also equal at B. Typically, PER models follow an "untyped" approach, based on a global value space (e.g., the domain D of a model of the untyped λ-calculus) from which all types are carved out. Here we use the hierarchy $\mathcal{D}_K$, retaining a "typed" aspect; this is because algebras over different signatures live in different categories, so it seems natural to preserve the different value spaces in the semantics.

Partial functions. Partial functions are used because, as explained above, the true domain of a function with kind $K \rightarrow K'$ may be smaller than K. Their use also allows a neat way of capturing the rule (SUB-Π) shown in Section 1.1, via inclusion. If $\Pi X{:}A.\,B$ has kind $K \rightarrow K'$, then we let $[\![\Pi X{:}A.\,B]\!]$ stand for the collection of partial functions in $\mathcal{D}_{K \rightarrow K'}$ which are total *at least* on $[\![A]\!]$, and map elements $a \in [\![A]\!]$ to elements of $[\![B]\!]_{[X \rightarrow a]}$. So the inclusion $[\![\Pi X{:}A.\,B]\!] \subseteq [\![\Pi X{:}A'.\,B']\!]$ holds provided $[\![A']\!] \subseteq [\![A]\!]$ and $[\![B]\!]_{[X \rightarrow a]} \subseteq [\![B']\!]_{[X \rightarrow a]}$ for all $a \in [\![A']\!]$. Notice that this does not work if we define $[\![\Pi X{:}A.\,B]\!]$ as a set of total functions defined on exactly $[\![A]\!]$.

3.1 The semantic interpretation

We recall some nomenclature: the domain of a PER is $dom(R) = \{a \mid a\ R\ a\}$ and $a \in R$ abbreviates $a \in dom(R)$. If $a \in R$ then the equivalence class of a in R is $[a]_R = \{b \mid a\ R\ b\}$. Inclusion of PERs $R \subseteq R'$ is defined for PERs with the same carrier by $a\ R\ b \Longrightarrow a\ R'\ b$ for all a, b. PER$[A]$ stands for the set of all PERs with carrier A.

Domains for kinds and contexts. The semantic domain $\mathcal{D}_K$ associated to each kind K is a set defined by induction on the structure of K:

$$\begin{array}{lcl} \mathcal{D}_\Sigma & = & \mathbf{Alg}(\Sigma) \\ \mathcal{D}_{K \to K'} & = & \mathcal{D}_K \rightharpoonup \mathcal{D}_{K'} \\ \mathcal{D}_{Spec(K)} & = & \mathrm{PER}[\mathcal{D}_K] \end{array}$$

where $A \rightharpoonup B$ is the set of partial functions from A to B. We assume that for each $\Sigma \in \mathbf{Sign}$, the collection of algebras over Σ is built within some fixed universe, and so $\mathbf{Alg}(\Sigma)$ is a set; this provides a simplistic justification of the existence of the hierarchy $\mathcal{D}_K$.

Contexts are interpreted by PERs over products of sets: $A \times B$ is the set of all ordered pairs $\langle a, b \rangle$ with $a \in A, b \in B$ and π_1, π_2 are the projections. Let $1 =_{\mathrm{def}} \{*\}$ be a single point set. The domain $\mathcal{D}_\Gamma$ for a kindable context Γ is defined by induction on a kinding derivation:

$$\begin{array}{lcl} \mathcal{D}_{()} & = & 1 \\ \mathcal{D}_{\Gamma, X:A} & = & \mathcal{D}_\Gamma \times \mathcal{D}_K, \text{ where } \Gamma \vdash A : Spec(K) \end{array}$$

The free variables in a term will be interpreted by projection from an *environment*, which is a tuple g in the domain of some context. The projections along g corresponding to a context Γ are given by:

$$\begin{array}{lcl} g^{()}(Y) & & \text{undefined, for all } Y. \\ g^{\Gamma, X:A}(Y) & = & \begin{cases} \pi_2(g), & \text{if } Y \equiv X, \\ (\pi_1(g))^\Gamma(Y) & \text{if } Y \not\equiv X. \end{cases} \end{array}$$

We write $g_1{}^{\Gamma_1} \subseteq g_2{}^{\Gamma_2}$ if $g_1{}^{\Gamma_1}(X) = g_2{}^{\Gamma_2}(X)$ for all $X \in Dom(\Gamma_1)$.

Semantic constructions. Here are the semantic constructions used in the interpretation. The interpretation is partial (some terms fail to denote even if they are kindable, as we have explained), so we adopt the convention that the application of any of the constructions below to an undefined argument gives an undefined result.

Let A and B be sets; R, R' and R'' elements of PER$[A]$, $F \in dom(R) \rightharpoonup B$ and $G \in dom(R) \rightharpoonup \mathrm{PER}[B]$ such that $a\ R\ b$ implies $G(a) = G(b)$. Then:

- $Id(A, A') \in \mathrm{PER}[A]$ provided $A' \subseteq A$ and where:

$$a\ Id(A, A')\ a \qquad \text{for all } a \in A'$$

- $\{\}(R, a) \in \mathrm{PER}[A]$ provided $a \in A$, and where:

$$b\ \{\}(R, a)\ c \qquad \text{iff} \qquad b\ R\ c \text{ and } b\ R\ a$$

- $\lambda(R, F) \in A \rightharpoonup B$ is the partial function f defined by:

$$f(a) = \begin{cases} F(a) & \text{for all } a \in R \\ \text{undefined} & \text{otherwise.} \end{cases}$$

- $\Pi(R, G) \in \mathrm{PER}[A \rightharpoonup B]$ where:

$[\![\langle\rangle]\!]$	$=$	$Id(1,1)$
$[\![\Gamma, X : A]\!]$	$=$	$\Sigma([\![\Gamma]\!], [\![\Gamma \vdash A : Spec(K)]\!])$
$[\![\Gamma \vdash X : K]\!]_g$	$=$	$g^{\Gamma}(X)$
$[\![p[M_1 \cdots M_k] : \Sigma]\!]$	$=$	$[\![p]\!]([\![M_1 : \Sigma_1]\!], \ldots, [\![M_k : \Sigma_k]\!])$
$[\![s[A_1 \cdots A_k] : Spec(\Sigma)]\!]$	$=$	$Id(\mathcal{D}_\Sigma, [\![s]\!](dom([\![A_1 : Spec(\Sigma_1)]\!]), \ldots, dom([\![A_k : Spec(\Sigma_k)]\!])))$
$[\![\{M\}_A : Spec(K)]\!]$	$=$	$\{\}([\![A : Spec(K)]\!], [\![M : K]\!])$
$[\![A \mathbin{\&} B : Spec(K)]\!]$	$=$	$\cap([\![A : Spec(K)]\!], [\![B : Spec(K)]\!])$
$[\![Spec(A) : Spec(Spec(K))]\!]$	$=$	$\mathcal{P}([\![A : Spec(K)]\!])$
$[\![M\ N : K']\!]$	$=$	$[\![M : K \to K']\!]([\![N : K]\!])$
$[\![\Gamma \vdash \lambda X{:}A.M \ : K \to K']\!]_g$ $= \lambda([\![\Gamma \vdash A : Spec(K)]\!]_g, a \mapsto [\![\Gamma, X : A \vdash M : K']\!]_{\langle g, a\rangle})$		
$[\![\Gamma \vdash \Pi X{:}A.B \ : Spec(K \to K')]\!]_g$ $= \Pi([\![\Gamma \vdash A : Spec(K)]\!]_g, a \mapsto [\![\Gamma, X : A \vdash B : Spec(K')]\!]_{\langle g, a\rangle})$		

Table 2: Semantics of ASL+

$$f\ \Pi(R,G)\ g \quad \text{iff} \quad \forall a,b.a\ R\ b \Longrightarrow f(a)\ G(a)\ g(b)$$

- $\Sigma(R,G) \in \mathrm{PER}[A \times B]$ where:

$$c\ \Sigma(R,G)\ d \quad \text{iff} \quad \pi_1(c)\ R\ \pi_1(d) \quad \text{and} \quad \pi_2(c)\ G(\pi_1(c))\ \pi_2(d)$$

- $\cap(R,R') \in \mathrm{PER}[A]$ where:

$$a \cap(R,R')\ b \quad \text{iff} \quad a\ R\ b \quad \text{and} \quad a\ R'\ b$$

- $\mathcal{P}(R) \in \mathrm{PER}[\mathrm{PER}[A]]$ where:

$$R'\ \mathcal{P}(R)\ R'' \quad \text{iff} \quad R' = R'' \quad \text{and} \quad R' \subseteq R$$

Constructions such as λ, Π, Σ and $\cap$ are well-known. For example, $\Pi(R,G)$ is a PER in which two partial functions are related if they map related arguments to related results (and both must be defined on at least $dom(R)$). Less familiar ones include $Id(A,B)$, which is simply a PER over elements of A with domain B on which the equivalence relation is just identity; the PER $\{\}(R,a)$ which is the equivalence class of a in R, and $\mathcal{P}(R)$ in which two PERs are equivalent if they are equal as PERs and included in R. It is a simple matter to check that the constructions lead to values in the domains claimed, given defined arguments in the domains stated.

Definition of semantics. The interpretation of contexts and terms is defined in Table 2 by induction on kind-checking derivations. The interpretation of a context $[\![\Gamma]\!]$ is a PER over $\mathcal{D}_\Gamma$, and the interpretation of a term, $[\![\Gamma \vdash M : K]\!]$, is a map from $dom([\![\Gamma]\!])$ to $\mathcal{D}_K$. If $g \notin dom([\![\Gamma]\!])$, then $[\![\Gamma \vdash M : K]\!]_g$ is undefined by convention. There is an equation in the table for each kinding rule; for readability Γ and g are omitted when they don't play a part. We shall sometimes also omit K when it is clear from the context, writing just $[\![M]\!]$.

We rely upon an externally defined semantics for PBOs and SBOs: as mentioned before, $[\![p]\!]$ and $[\![s]\!]$ are partial maps between algebras or classes of algebras. SBOs ignore the equivalence relation on their arguments, and the instantiation of an SBO is interpreted as an identity PER. This means that two terms with kind Σ are equal just when they denote exactly the same algebra. (It would be interesting to extend this to allow coarser institution-dependent equalities, such as isomorphism, or even to allow $[\![s]\!]$ to be a PER constructor).

Example 3.1 *We calculate the meaning of the closed term $SYMTAB^{\#}$:*

$$\begin{array}{rcl} R =_{def} [\![s_k[\,]]\!] & = & Id(\mathcal{D}_{\Sigma_K}, [\![s_k]\!]) \\ [\![SYMTAB^{\#}]\!] & = & [\![\Pi X{:}s_k.\, s_s[\{X\}_{s_k}]]\!] \\ & = & \Pi(R,\, a \mapsto Id(\mathcal{D}_{\Sigma_S}, [\![s_s]\!](dom(\{\}(R, [\![X]\!]_{\langle\star,\, a\rangle}))))) \\ & = & \Pi(R,\, a \mapsto Id(\mathcal{D}_{\Sigma_S}, [\![s_s]\!](\{a\}))) \end{array}$$

By the definition of Π, $[\![SYMTAB^{\#}]\!]$ is interpreted as the set of partial functions f from $\mathbf{Alg}(\Sigma_K)$ to $\mathbf{Alg}(\Sigma_S)$ such that $\forall a \in [\![s_k]\!].\, f(a) \in [\![s_s]\!](\{a\})$. Two such functions f and f' are equivalent if they are equal as functions when restricted to $[\![s_k]\!]$.

Properties of the semantics. It would be nice to establish that the interpretation is well-defined in the sense that whenever $[\![M : K]\!]$ is defined, then $[\![M]\!] \in \mathcal{D}_K$. Unfortunately, this isn't true! The reason is that, because of the use of partial functions, a function application $f(a)$ in the semantics may be defined "by accident" without a being in the domain of the PER that f is assumed to inhabit. This isn't ensured by kind-checking or definedness of the interpretation function, but it is ensured by the stronger formal system of the next section. Some useful properties of the semantics can be established at this stage, nevertheless, under the assumption that everything we deal with is defined and in the domains required.

Lemma 3.2 (Semantic properties for well-defined interpretations)

1. Weakening. *Let Γ, Γ' be kindable contexts with $\Gamma \subseteq \Gamma'$. Let $g \in [\![\Gamma]\!]$ and $g' \in [\![\Gamma']\!]$ where $g^{\Gamma} \subseteq g'^{\Gamma'}$. Then $[\![\Gamma \vdash M : K]\!]_g = [\![\Gamma' \vdash M : K]\!]_{g'}$.*
2. Semantic contexts. *Let Γ be a kindable context and $\Gamma \vdash X : K$. Then: $\forall g_1, g_2.\, g_1 \; [\![\Gamma]\!] \; g_2 \Longrightarrow {g_1}^{\Gamma}(X) \; [\![\Gamma \vdash \Gamma(X) : Spec(K)]\!]_{g_1} \; {g_2}^{\Gamma}(X)$*
3. Semantic substitution. *Let $\Gamma, X : A, \Gamma' \vdash M : K'$, $\Gamma \vdash A : Spec(K)$, $g \in [\![\Gamma]\!]$, and let $n = [\![\Gamma \vdash N : K]\!]_g$. If $g_1 \in [\![\Gamma, \Gamma'[X := N]]\!]$, and $g_2 \in [\![\Gamma, X : A, \Gamma']\!]$, then:*
$$[\![\Gamma, \Gamma'[X := N] \vdash M[X := N] : K']\!]_{g_1} = [\![\Gamma, X : A, \Gamma' \vdash M : K']\!]_{g_2}$$
provided $g^{\Gamma} \subseteq {g_1}^{\Gamma,\Gamma'[X:=N]} \subseteq {g_2}^{\Gamma,X:SP,\Gamma'}$ and ${g_2}^{\Gamma,X:SP,\Gamma'}(X) = n$.
4. β and η-reduction. *Suppose $\Gamma \vdash M : K$ and $g \in [\![\Gamma]\!]$. If either $M \longrightarrow_{\beta} N$ or $M \longrightarrow_{\eta} N$, then $[\![M]\!]_g = [\![N]\!]_g$.*

4 Satisfaction in ASL+

So far we have a formal syntax of terms, and a semantics for the kindable terms. However, not all kindable terms have a denotation in the semantics, and we have no way of proving when a program satisfies a specification (elementhood in the semantics). We now introduce the system of rules[1] in Table 3 for proving satisfaction. Two judgements are defined:

[1]These are a re-design of those in [15], which had several omissions.

$$\begin{array}{ll} \Gamma \text{ Context} & \Gamma \text{ is a } \textit{denoting} \text{ context.} \\ \Gamma \vdash M : A & \text{In context } \Gamma,\ M \textit{ satisfies } A. \end{array}$$

and we use some derived judgements:

$$\begin{array}{lll} \Gamma \vdash A \leq B & =_{def} & \Gamma \vdash A : Spec(B) \\ \Gamma \vdash M = N : A & =_{def} & \Gamma \vdash M : \{N\}_A \\ \Gamma \vdash A & =_{def} & \Gamma \vdash A \leq B \text{ for some } B \end{array}$$

We have explained the "subtyping" abbreviation already. A relation of typed-equality $\Gamma \vdash M = N : A$ is included in the calculus via singleton types; this has been investigated elsewhere [1].

The judgement $\Gamma \vdash A$ asserts that A is a *denoting* type. More generally, a denoting term M is one for which there exists an A such that $\Gamma \vdash M : A$. Thus the rules in Table 3 can also be used to establish that a term has a denotation in the semantics. From the viewpoint of ASL+, a program term is meaningful just in case there is some specification that it satisfies, and similarly a specification is meaningful if there is another which it refines. This may seem like an odd way of determining which terms are well-formed, but typically the SBOs include operators for constructing trivial specifications, which for example may amount to some simple type-checking requirements. So if M is built from PBOs, it is natural to expect there to be some A built from SBOs such that $M : A$. Furthermore, we would expect $A \leq A$ if A is a well-formed specification. We examine this more closely next.

Basic programs and specifications. To do anything useful, we must first have some way to prove things about the underlying programming language and specification language. A *basic program* P is a term built using only PBOs and *basic program variables* from a **Sign**-sorted set V_{prog}; similarly a *basic specification* S (or T) is built using only SBOs and variables from a **Sign**-sorted set V_{spec}. We abstract away from the details of the underlying proof systems and assume that there are two *consequence relations* [3] which describe the properties of interest:

$$\begin{array}{ll} \Delta \models^{sat}_{V} P : S & \textit{basic satisfaction;} \\ \Delta \models^{ref}_{V} S \leq T & \textit{basic refinement.} \end{array}$$

In each case, V is the set of variables (from V_{prog} and V_{spec}) free in the program or specification terms and Γ is a finite set of statements with the same form as the right hand side. Variables are needed because it is essential to have *schematic* assertions that allow us to deal with SBOs and PBOs applied to ASL+ terms, and in particular, ASL+ variables. The rules (PBO) and (SBO) formalize this.[2] To apply one of these rules (backwards), one must find appropriate substitutions θ from variables in V to ASL+ terms which unify the right hand side of a sequent with the desired conclusion in ASL+. If the left hand side of the sequent Δ is non-empty, this leads to further statements to be proved in ASL+. (Of course, the substitutions θ must respect the sorts of the variables; we omit details here).

Example 4.1 *In $\mathcal{EQ}$, we would expect the consequence relations to include, for sets of sentences Φ_1, Φ_2 over signatures Σ_1, Σ_2: $\models^{sat}_{\{\}} R_{\vec{\Phi}_1} + R_{\vec{\Phi}_2} : \langle \Sigma_1 \uplus \Sigma_2, \Phi_1 \cup \Phi_2, \rangle$ (the union of two rewrite systems satisfies a specification consisting of a union of the equations), and $R_{\sigma(\vec{\Phi})} : S \models^{sat}_{\{S\}} R_{\vec{\Phi}} : D_\sigma(S)$ (which allows renaming), where*

[2] The vector notation $\bar{P}$, etc. abbreviates vectors of arguments to PBOs and SBOs. We have glossed over some details: there should be extra premises to ensure that the arguments are denotable: $\Gamma \vdash \bar{A}$ etc., and we should ensure that the arity of the operators is respected.

$$\frac{}{\langle\rangle \text{ Context}} \qquad (\text{EMPTY})$$

$$\frac{\Gamma \vdash A \quad X \notin Dom(\Gamma)}{\Gamma, X : A \text{ Context}} \qquad (\text{EXTEND})$$

$$\frac{\Gamma \text{ Context}}{\Gamma \vdash X : \Gamma(X)} \qquad (\text{VAR})$$

$$\frac{\Delta \models^{sat}_{V} p[\bar{P}] : s[\bar{S}] \quad \theta_p(\bar{P}) = \bar{M},\ \theta_s(\bar{S}) = \bar{A} \quad \Gamma \vdash \theta_p(\theta_s(\Delta)) \quad \Gamma \text{ Context}}{\Gamma \vdash p[\bar{M}] : s[\bar{A}]} \qquad (\text{PBO})$$

$$\frac{\Delta \models^{ref}_{V} s[\bar{S}] \leq t[\bar{T}] \quad \theta_s(\bar{S}) = \bar{A},\ \theta_s(\bar{T}) = \bar{B} \quad \Gamma \vdash \theta_s(\Delta) \quad \Gamma \text{ Context}}{\Gamma \vdash s[\bar{A}] : Spec(t[\bar{B}])} \qquad (\text{SBO})$$

$$\frac{\Gamma, X : A \vdash M : B}{\Gamma \vdash \lambda X{:}A.\, M : \Pi X{:}A.\, B} \qquad (\Pi\text{-I})$$

$$\frac{\Gamma \vdash M : \Pi X{:}A.\, B \quad \Gamma \vdash N : A}{\Gamma \vdash M\, N : B[X := N]} \qquad (\Pi\text{-E})$$

$$\frac{\Gamma \vdash M : A_1, A_2 \quad \Gamma \vdash A_1, A_2 : Spec(B)}{\Gamma \vdash M : A_1 \,\&\, A_2} \qquad (\&\text{-I})$$

$$\frac{\Gamma \vdash M : A_1 \,\&\, A_2 \quad j = 1, 2}{\Gamma \vdash M : A_i} \qquad (\&\text{-E})$$

$$\frac{\Gamma, X : A \vdash X : B \quad \Gamma \vdash B}{\Gamma \vdash A : Spec(B)} \qquad (Spec\text{-I})$$

$$\frac{\Gamma \vdash M : A \quad \Gamma \vdash A : Spec(B)}{\Gamma \vdash M : B} \qquad (Spec\text{-E})$$

$$\frac{\Gamma \vdash M : A \quad \Gamma \vdash N : A \quad M =_{\beta\eta\Gamma} N}{\Gamma \vdash M : \{N\}_A} \qquad (\{\}\text{-I})$$

$$\frac{\Gamma \vdash M : \{N\}_A}{\Gamma \vdash M : A} \qquad (\{\}\text{-E})$$

Table 3: Satisfaction Rules of ASL+

$\sigma : \Sigma \to \Sigma'$ is a signature morphism, Φ is a set of Σ-sentences and S stands for a basic Σ'-specification. Examples of proof rules which generate a consequence relation for $\models^{ref}$ on the institution independent operators of ASL can be found in [11].

Some assumptions must be made of $\models^{sat}$ and $\models^{ref}$, the most important of which is that they are sound with respect to the semantics of basic programs and specifications. For example, whenever $P_1 : S_1 \ldots P_n : S_n \models^{sat}_{V} P : S$ then

$$\forall \rho, \gamma.\, [\![P_1]\!]_\rho \in [\![S_1]\!]_\gamma \ \bigwedge \cdots \bigwedge\ [\![P_n]\!]_\rho \in [\![S_n]\!]_\gamma \Longrightarrow [\![P]\!]_\rho \in [\![S]\!]_\gamma$$

where ρ and γ are evaluations mapping Σ-variables from V_{prog} to Σ-algebras and Σ-variables from V_{spec} to sets of Σ-algebras. There are other requirements which reflect the ideas above: there should always be an S such that $\models^{sat}_{\{\}} P : S$ whenever P is a well-formed basic program with a denotation, and in this case we should have $\models^{ref}_{\{\}} S \leq S$ to indicate that S too is well-formed and has a denotation.

Higher-order constructors. In Table 3 there is a rule of *introduction* and a rule of *elimination* for each of the higher-order term constructors.

The rules for λ-introduction (Π-I) and elimination (Π-E) are usual in all type systems with dependent Π types. For conjunction the rules are also well-known, except that the introduction rule (&-I)[3] restricts intersections to being formed over types which have a common supertype. This reflects the semantics: we only form collections within the same value space.

The elimination rule (*Spec*-E) for the *Spec* operator is simply the subsumption rule in a different guise. The introduction rule (*Spec*-E) is rather unusual: it has a simple reading (if whenever X is assumed to inhabit A, it can be shown to also inhabit B, then deduce $A \leq B$), but its simplicity belies its power when combined with the other introduction and elimination rules. It is common in subtyping systems to axiomatise a separate subtyping relation with rules for each type constructor; this one rule captures the full relation. In particular, the (derived) relation $\leq$ is easily shown to be reflexive and transitive on denoting types, and familiar rules for subtyping intersection types follow. Also, the rule (SUB-Π) shown in Section 1.1 is admissible when we close the system under a rule of η-subject reduction.

The meaning of the singleton terms is captured by ($\{\}$-I). Whenever M is convertible to N via β,η or Γ reductions, and both satisfy S, we assert that M inhabits the singleton $\{N\}_S$: intuitively, M is in the equivalence class of terms equal to N when considered at S. The elimination rule is weaker, it just says that when $M : \{N\}_A$, then M must also satisfy A.

Example 4.2 *As a simple example, we can show that SymTab : SYMTAB*$^{\#}$*:*

$$\dfrac{\mathcal{P}:s_k,\mathcal{P}:\mathcal{S}\models^{sat}_{\{\mathcal{S},\mathcal{P}\}} p_s[\mathcal{P}]:s_s[\mathcal{S}] \quad \dfrac{\vdots}{X:s_k} \quad \dfrac{\vdots}{X:\{X\}_{s_k}} \quad \dfrac{\dfrac{\models^{ref}_{\{\}} s_k\leq s_k}{\vdash s_k \leq s_k}}{X:s_k}\ \text{Context}}{\dfrac{X:s_k \vdash p_s[X]:s_s[\{X\}_{s_k}]}{\langle\rangle \vdash \lambda X{:}s_k.\,p_s[X] : \Pi X{:}s_k.\,s_s[\{X\}_{s_k}]}}$$

(the dots are filled by repeating the few rules on the right, and using the rule ($\{\}$-I) *in the second case; we omitted the context* $X : s_k$ *in these branches too).*

This example serves to show how the proof theoretic side of the ASL+ framework is glued together, rather than illustrate the power of the language. We assumed that the main proof arises from a single sequent in $\models^{sat}$; in reality s_k and p_s would probably be composed of several SBOs and PBOs, and this proof could involve several invocations of the underlying proof systems.

Properties of satisfaction. Unlike the kind-checking system, it is not obvious how to apply the rules in the satisfaction system: for a given conclusion, several rules may be able to derive it. It would be interesting to examine ways of directing proof search in this system; this corresponds to looking for a type-checking algorithm for the related subtyping system. Of course, theorem proving is almost always needed at the level of basic programs and specifications anyway, so we can't hope for a complete algorithm.

[3]Notice that it has four premises, abbreviated in a hopefully obvious way.

Space precludes any treatment of the meta-theory of the rules here. We mention only the crucial aspect of the system mentioned at the outset: soundness with respect to the semantics defined in Section 3. This also establishes the well-definedness of the interpretation on denotable terms and contexts.

Proposition 4.3 (Soundness and Definedness properties)

1. Agreement with kind-checking.
   If Γ *Context, then* Γ *K-context.*
   If $\Gamma \vdash M : A$ *then for some (unique) kind* K, $\Gamma \vdash M : K$ *and* $\Gamma \vdash A : Spec(K)$.
2. Definedness.
   If Γ *Context, then* $[\![\Gamma]\!] \in \mathrm{PER}[\mathcal{D}_\Gamma]$.
   If $\Gamma \vdash M : A$ *and* $g \in [\![\Gamma]\!]$, *then* $[\![M : K]\!]_g \in \mathcal{D}_K$.
3. Γ-reduction.
   Suppose $\Gamma \vdash M : A$ *and* $g \in [\![\Gamma]\!]$. *Then* $M \longrightarrow_\Gamma N$ *implies* $[\![M]\!]_g\ [\![A]\!]_g\ [\![N]\!]_g$.
4. Soundness.
   If $\Gamma \vdash M : A$ *and* $g\ [\![\Gamma]\!]\ g'$, *then* $[\![M]\!]_g\ [\![A]\!]_g\ [\![M]\!]_{g'}$

The proofs proceed by induction on derivations in the satisfaction system. Part 1 uses Proposition 2.3; parts 2–4 are proved together, using Proposition 3.2. Now we have established:

Theorem 4.4 (Soundness of Satisfaction)

$\Gamma \vdash M : A$ *implies* $[\![\Gamma \vdash M : K]\!]_g \in [\![\Gamma \vdash A : Spec(K)]\!]_g$ *for all* $g \in [\![\Gamma]\!]$.

Proof. A corollary of the final part of Proposition 4.3, taking $g = g'$. □

5 Conclusions

ASL+ provides a unified framework for programming and specification in-the-large which seems powerful. Some larger and more detailed examples than those shown here have been studied in [17, 15, 2] but work is still needed to appreciate the practical merits of the different mechanisms of parameterisation. Real specification languages built on ASL+ might not use all of the parameterisation possibilities (Extended ML, for example, lacks parameterised specifications), but it makes sense to study a complete kernel formalism to see that the distinct mechanisms can be safely combined.

There are many avenues to be explored starting from the satisfaction system of Section 4. We would like to be able to characterise the relationship between the consequence relations for PBOs and SBOs and their corresponding fragments inside ASL+. The best case would be if the extension is conservative, and complete (i.e., a converse of Theorem 4.4 holds) when the underlying relations are complete. As mentioned, we should try to find ways of directing proof search in the system, so that showing satisfaction in ASL+ is reduced to showing underlying consequences in a canonical way. Unfortunately, similar things can be tricky to show for related subtyping systems [8, 14], and the added complication of dependent Π-types makes things harder still. Also, the concise presentation of the rules shown here is somewhat provisional; although it is nice to describe, it may prove more fruitful to study a longer equivalent version where more of the rules are spelled out.

Certain extensions of the satisfaction system would be interesting. One is to allow subtyping between signatures: whenever $\iota : \Sigma_1 \hookrightarrow \Sigma_2$ is an inclusion in a sub-category of signature inclusions, we can consider $\Sigma_2 \leq \Sigma_1$ by virtue of the reduct functor. This would allow many renamings to be avoided at the level of syntax; in the semantics, we would have to reconstruct them. The subtyping semantics in [4] uses a similar technique.

As well as subtyping parallels, there are some specification languages related to ASL+. Cengarle and Wirsing [7] describe a language with higher-order parameterisation, including parameterisation on signatures. Drossopoulou and Paterson [10] have explored similar type theory connections when designing a language for writing parameterised programs and their interfaces. SPECTRAL in [13] is a design for a rich language that combines an institution-level language that has subtyping, polymorphism and dependent types with a module-level language similarly endowed for specifications and programs.

Acknowledgements. I would like to sincerely thank Don Sannella, Benjamin Pierce and Andrzej Tarlecki for their coaching and encouragement during the course of this work. Thanks are also due to Claudio Russo and Martin Hofmann for discussions about ASL+, and to the anonymous referees of ADT'94 for suggestions to improve the presentation. I was supported by a UK EPSRC postgraduate studentship.

References

[1] David R. Aspinall. Subtyping with singleton types. Paper given at Computer Science Logic '94, Kazimierz, Poland, 1994.

[2] David R. Aspinall. Algebraic specification in a type-theoretic setting. Forthcoming PhD thesis, Department of Computer Science, University of Edinburgh, 1995.

[3] Arnon Avron. Simple consequence relations. *Information and Computation*, 92:105–139, 1991.

[4] Val Breazu-Tannen, Thierry Coquand, Carl A. Gunter, and Andre Scedrov. Inheritance as implicit coercion. *Information and Computation*, 93:172–221, 1991.

[5] Luca Cardelli. Structural subtyping and the notion of power type. In *Fifteenth Annual ACM Symposium on Principles of Programming Languages*, 1988.

[6] Luca Cardelli and Guiseppe Longo. A semantic basis for Quest. *Journal of Functional Programming*, 1(4):417–458, 1991.

[7] María Victoria Cengarle and Martin Wirsing. A calculus of parameterization for algebraic specifications. Technical Report 94/198, Department of Computer Science, Monsahs University, 1994.

[8] Pierre-Louis Curien and Giorgio Ghelli. Coherence of subsumption, minimum typing and type-checking in $F_{<}$. *Mathematical Structures in Computer Science*, 2:55–91, 1992. Also in Carl A. Gunter and John C. Mitchell, editors, *Theoretical Aspects of Object-Oriented Programming: Types, Semantics, and Language Design* (MIT Press, 1994).

[9] N. Dershowitz and J.-P. Jouannaud. Rewrite systems. In van Leeuwen et.al., editor, *Handbook of Theoretical Computer Science*, chapter 6. North-Holland, 1990.

[10] Sophia Drossopoulou and Ross Paterson. Higher order module parameterization. Technical report, Department of Computing, Imperial College, October 1993.

[11] Jorge Farrés-Cassals. *Verification in ASL and related Specification Languages.* PhD thesis, Edinburgh University, 1992.

[12] J. A. Goguen and R. M. Burstall. Institutions: abstract model theory for specification and programming. *Journal of the ACM*, 39:95–146, 1992.

[13] Bernd Krieg-Brückner and Donald Sannella. Structuring specifications in-the-large and in-the-small: Higher-order functions, dependent types and inheritance in SPECTRAL. In *TAPSOFT '91: Proc. Joint Conf. on Theory and Practice of Software Development*, Brighton, 1991.

[14] Benjamin C. Pierce. Bounded quantification is undecidable. *Information and Computation*, 112(1), July 1994.

[15] Donald T. Sannella, Stefan Sokołowski, and Andrzej Tarlecki. Toward formal development of programs from algebraic specifications: Parameterisation revisited. *Acta Informatica*, 29:689–736, 1992.

[16] Donald T. Sannella and Andrzej Tarlecki. Specifications in an arbitrary institution. *Information and Computation*, 76(2/3):165–210, 1988.

[17] Stefan Sokołowski. Parametricity in algebraic specifications: A case study. Technical report, Institute of Computer Science, Polish Academy of Sciences, Gdańsk, 1989.

On the Operational Semantics of the Algebraic and Logic Programming Language LPG

Didier Bert and Rachid Echahed

IMAG-LGI, CNRS, BP 53, 38041 Grenoble cedex 9, France
Email: {bert,echahed}@imag.fr

Abstract. This paper gives a brief description of the recent improvements of LPG, a programming language that integrates algebraic and logic programming paradigms. In this language, functions are defined by means of constructor-based conditional term rewriting systems and predicates are defined by means of Horn clauses where the bodies may contain classical literals as well as equations and negations of equations (disequations). The operational semantics of LPG is based on an extension of SLD–resolution which deals with equations and disequations by using a narrowing-based algorithm. We investigate such a narrowing-based algorithm for solving equations and disequations and give new sufficient conditions that ensure the completeness of narrowing strategies, in presence of *conditional* term rewrite systems. Similarities and differencies with other logic and functional languages are pointed out.

1 Introduction

After the proposal of the language LOGLISP by Robinson and Sibert [22], many languages have been proposed to combine functional and logic programming paradigms, see for instance [15] for a recent survey. We can mainly distinguish five classes of proposals : (1) languages that combine λ-calculus and Horn clause logic; (2) languages based on Horn clause logic with equality; (3) languages based on conditional logic; (4) constraint logic programming languages; (5) other languages that try to combine object-oriented, functional and logic paradigms. In this rough classification, LPG may be considered as an element of the second class, even if some features like the use of disequations are syntactically allowed.

LPG can be considered as an example of a language based on the notion of *strong logic programming* defined by Meseguer in [18]. In this framework a *program* P is a signature together with a finite set of sentences (axioms) in a logic $\mathcal{L}$. The *denotational semantics* of P is a model MS_P of P, which is standard in a well defined sense. For a program P, the user must be allowed to "test" or "evaluate" its program, i.e. to ask questions about the properties which hold in the model MS_P. If a *query* ϕ is provable in P by the entailment relation of the underlying logic $\mathcal{L}$, then it holds in the standard model by the soundness of $\mathcal{L}$, and the machine must be able to justify the truth of ϕ by giving a set of *answers*. So, the *operational semantics* of P is a proof algorithm based on the entailment relation that allows to prove queries and to give significant answers. Because of indeterminism of entailment relation, the implementation must find out strategies to achieve a relative efficiency in the proof, without loosing the "completeness" of the answers. This point is very important and difficult in practice. This is why, we focus on the rules and strategies used to answer queries in the system LPG. The main technical new result of this paper is an extension of "uniform" strategies which is proved to be complete for conditional term rewrite systems.

Informally, LPG (for *Langage de Programmation Générique*)[3, 5] is a generic, logic and functional programming language designed to experiment new concepts in the field of specification, prototyping and high-level programming languages. It is based on concepts of algebraic specifications, abstract data types and logic programming. Thus, with respect to functional languages, LPG offers the possibility to define predicates or relations. With respect to classical logic programming languages, LPG is generic, i.e. it offers the possibility to define predicates that can be parameterized by other predicates or functions. This feature allows to write "higher-order like" specifications such as the transitive closure of a relation given as parameter. It is strongly typed and admits user's definable types and functions. In LPG, functions are defined by conditional term rewrite systems and predicates are defined by Horn clauses whose bodies may include "classical" literals, equations or disequations (i.e. negations of equations). The operational semantics of LPG is intended to solve queries (usually called goals) i.e. conjunction of literals, equations or disequations including defined functions and logical variables. The proof theory for those general goals mixes the SLD-resolution principle with narrowing-based algorithms that are devoted to solve equations and disequations.

The paper is organized as follows : Section 2 briefly recalls some general background about algebraic specifications and rewrite systems. Section 3 gives a short presentation of the language. It outlines the denotational semantics of modules and particularly, of completely instantiated modules which are the "programs" for which the operational semantics is defined. Section 4 is devoted to the operational semantics of LPG. It presents the main rules of logical entailment that is to say the principle of resolution of literals augmented by an inference system for "solving" equations and disequations. This last system is based on *conditional* narrowing and uses narrowing-position selection strategies. The completeness of these strategies is investigated and sufficient conditions ensuring their completeness are given. At last, we conclude by a short comparison with other languages integrating functional and logic programming and give some insights into the possible future directions to improve the system.

2 Preliminaries

In this section, we recall some important notions and notations. See [6, 17] for the missing definitions about rewriting theory.

A many-sorted first order *signature* Σ is a tuple (S, Ω, Π) where S is a set of *sorts*, Ω is an S^*-indexed family of *operation* sets, and Π is an S^+-indexed family of *predicate* sets. For every sort $s \in S$, every set Π_{ss} includes the symbols of equality (==) and disequality (=/=). Let $\mathcal{X} = (\mathcal{X}_s | s \in S)$ be an S-sorted, countably infinite set of *variables*. We denote by $\mathcal{T}(\Sigma, \mathcal{X})_s$ the set of *terms* of sort s built from Σ and $\mathcal{X}$. $\mathcal{T}(\Sigma, \mathcal{X})$ denotes the set of all terms, i.e., the union $\cup_{s \in S} \mathcal{T}(\Sigma, \mathcal{X})_s$. By $\mathcal{V}ar(t)$ we denote the set of variables occurring in a term t. A term t is called *ground term* if $\mathcal{V}ar(t) = \emptyset$. A term is called *linear* if it does not contain multiple occurrences of one variable. An *equation* (resp. a *disequation*) is a pair denoted by t==t' (resp. t=/=t') where t and t' are terms. A specification is a tuple $SP = (\Sigma, E, Cl)$ where Σ is a first order signature, E is a set of conditional equations of the form l==r <== t_1==$t'_1, \ldots, t_n$==t'_n, and Cl is a set of Horn clauses of the form $P(t_1, \ldots, t_n)$ <== $A_1, \ldots, A_m$ where $P \in \Pi - \{==, =/=\}$ and each A_i may be an equation, a disequation or any other atom formed by predicates in Π.

Let SP be a specification. We denote by $\mathcal{S}ig(SP)$ the signature of SP and by $\mathcal{M}od(SP)$, the class of all models of SP. This class admits an initial model (up to isomorphism), also called *standard model* and noted SM_{SP}. Note that the existence of SM_{SP} is not guaranteed if we use disequations in the premises of conditional equations. Indeed, if we consider the conditional equation $f(x)$==2 <== $f(x)$=/=1, it is clear that there are models of this equation that are not comparable (by homomorphism). We denote by $=^i_E$ the inductive congruence generated by E over $\mathcal{T}(\Sigma, \mathcal{X})$ for any variable set $\mathcal{X}$. $\mathcal{T}(\Sigma)/E$ denotes the quotient term algebra. The relation $\neq^i_E$ is defined to be exactly the negation of $=^i_E$. In the standard model SM_{SP}, the predicates == and =/= are interpreted by the relations $=^i_E$ and $\neq^i_E$ respectively.

A signature $\Sigma = (S, \Omega, \Pi)$ is called *constructor-based* if the set of operations is split into two disjoint sets C and D. C is the set of constructors and D is the set of defined operations. A specifications SP is constructor-based if its signature is. A term t is called *innermost* if it is of the form $f(t_1, \ldots, t_n)$ such that $f \in D$ and every t_i does not contain any operation in D.

A *substitution* is a mapping $\sigma: \mathcal{X} \to \mathcal{T}(\Sigma, \mathcal{X})$ with $\sigma(x) \in \mathcal{T}(\Sigma, \mathcal{X})_s$ for all variables $x \in \mathcal{X}_s$ such that its *domain* $\mathcal{D}om(\sigma) = \{x \in \mathcal{X} \mid \sigma(x) \neq x\}$ is finite. Sometimes we will identify a substitution σ with the set $\{x \mapsto \sigma(x) \mid x \in \mathcal{D}om(\sigma)\}$. Substitutions are easily extended to endomorphisms over $\mathcal{T}(\Sigma, \mathcal{X})$. A substitution σ is called *ground substitution* if $\sigma(x)$ is a ground term for all $x \in \mathcal{D}om(\sigma)$. The *composition of two substitutions* σ and τ is defined by $(\sigma \circ \tau)(x) = \sigma(\tau(x))$ for all $x \in \mathcal{X}$. We also note the composition by $\sigma\tau$. We will note the identity substitution by id (for each x we have $id(x) = x$). The *restriction* $\sigma_{|V}$ of a substitution σ to a set V of variables is defined by $\sigma_{|V}(x) = \sigma(x)$ if $x \in V$ and $\sigma_{|V}(x) = x$ if $x \notin V$. If V is a set of variables, we write $\sigma = \sigma'[V]$ iff $\sigma_{|V} = \sigma'_{|V}$. $\leq$ denotes the usual preorder on substitutions: $\sigma \leq \sigma'[V]$ iff there exists β such that $\beta \circ \sigma = \sigma'[V]$. This preorder is extended to the equational theory $=^i_E$ as follows: $\sigma \leq^i_E \sigma'[V]$ iff $\exists \rho, \rho\sigma =^i_E \sigma'[V]$, where $\sigma =^i_E \sigma'[V]$ iff $\forall x \in V, \sigma(x) =^i_E \sigma'(x)$.

A *conditional rewrite rule* is a directed conditional equation of the form $l \to$

r <== t_1==$t'_1, \ldots, t_n$==t'_n such that l is not a variable, $\forall i \in \{1,..,n\}, \mathcal{V}ar(t_i$==$t'_i) \subseteq \mathcal{V}ar(l)$ and $\mathcal{V}ar(r) \subseteq \mathcal{V}ar(l)$. A *variant* of a rewrite rule r is obtained from r by a variable renaming. A conditional term rewrite system (CTRS for short) is a set of conditional rewrite rules. We denote by $Pos(t)$ the set of positions of subterms of t. $Pos^*(t)$ is a subset of $Pos(t)$ that includes the positions of non variable subterms of t. If $p \in Pos(t)$ then $t_{|p}$ is the subterm of t at position p and $t[s]_p$ is the term which is obtained by replacing the subterm at position p by the term s. The rewrite relation associated with a $CTRS$ R is obtained by interpreting the equality signs in the conditional part of a rewrite rule as joinability. That is to say, $t \rightarrow_R t'$ if there exists a position $p \in Pos^*(s)$, a variant $l \rightarrow r$ <== c of a rewrite rule in R and a substitution σ such that $t_{|p} = \sigma(l)$, $t' = t[\sigma(r)]_p$ and $\sigma(u) \downarrow_R \sigma(u')$ for every equation u==u' in c. The joinability of two terms t and t', denoted by $t \downarrow t'$, means that there exists a term u such that $t \rightarrow^*_R u$ and $t' \rightarrow^*_R u$ where $\rightarrow^*_R$ denotes the reflexive and transitive closure of $\rightarrow_R$. The relation $\rightarrow_R$ is terminating if there is no infinite derivation $t \rightarrow_R t_1 \rightarrow_R \ldots$. The relation $\rightarrow_R$ is confluent if $\forall t_1, t_2, t_3, t_1 \rightarrow^*_R t_2$ and $t_1 \rightarrow^*_R t_3 \Rightarrow \exists t_4 \mid t_2 \rightarrow^*_R t_4$ and $t_3 \rightarrow^*_R t_4$).

A *goal* is a conjunction of atoms $A_1, \ldots, A_m$, where A_i is either a literal (predicate symbol with arguments), an equation or a disequation, and where variables are existentially quantified. We say that a goal G (conditionally) narrows into a goal H if there exists an equation or disequation $e \in G$, a position $p \in Pos^*(e)$, a variant $l \rightarrow r$ <== c of a conditional rewrite rule in R and a substitution σ such that σ is the most general unifier of $e_{|p}$ and l, and $H = \sigma(G - \{e\} \cup \{e[r]_p\} \cup c)$. We write $G \rightsquigarrow_{[e,p,l \rightarrow r \text{ <== } c,\sigma]} H$ or $G \rightsquigarrow_\sigma H$. Let G be a goal, a substitution σ is a *solution* of G iff $\sigma(G)$ is valid in SM_{SP}. A set S of substitutions is called *complete set of solutions* of G iff every substitution σ in S is a solution of G (soundness) and for every ground solution of G, say θ, there exists a substitution β in S such that $\beta \leq^i_E \theta[\mathcal{V}ar(G)]$ (completeness).

3 The Language

The aim of this section is to give a flavour of the style of specification and programming in LPG through several examples. First of all, specifications are built up by composition of modules. There are three kinds of specification modules, namely *properties*, *types* and *enrichments*. All the modules are composed of a signature part and an axiomatization part. The signature part is a first-order signature. The axiomatization of operators is achieved by conditional equations whereas the predicates semantics is provided by Horn clauses, where the bodies of the clauses may include classical literals, equations (`t == t'`) and/or disequations (`t =/= t'`). The axiomatization is structured in two layers: the algebraic axiomatization of the operators, like in algebraic specification languages, without any reference to predicate symbols, and a second layer for the axiomatization of predicates which can mix all kinds of logical atoms.

Modules of "types" are designed to define abstract data types. In these modules, the list of operators is divided into *constructors* and *defined operators*. This

```
type Dot-Line
sorts
  dot, line
constructors
  c-dot: (nat,nat) → dot
  c-line : (dot,dot) → line
operators
  dist : (nat,nat) → nat
  sign : line → bool
  = : (dot,dot) → bool
predicates
  vertical, horizontal : line
  not-paral : (line,line)
variables
  i,j,k,l,m,n,o,p : nat
  a,b,c,d : dot
  q,r : line
equations
  1 : dist(i,j) ==> (i - j) + (j - i)
  2 : sign(c-line(c-dot(i,j),c-dot(k,l)))
              ==> (i <= k and j <= l) or (k <= i and l <= j)
  3 : c-dot(i,j) = c-dot(k,l) ==> i = k and j = l
clauses
  1: vertical(c-line(c-dot(i,j),c-dot(i,k))) <== k =/= j
  2: horizontal(c-line(c-dot(i,j),c-dot(k,j))) <== i =/= k
  3: not-paral(q,r) <== sign(q) =/= sign(r)
  4: not-paral(c-line(c-dot(i,j),c-dot(k,l)),c-line(c-dot(m,n),c-dot(o,p)))
              <== dist(i,k) * dist(m,o) =/= dist(j,l) * dist(n,p)
models
  Eq_dot: Equality[dot operators =]
end Dot-Line
```

Fig. 1. Data type of dots and lines.

means that the term algebra of the data type is generated by constructors only and that terms with other operators do have a meaning expressed solely with constructors. To weaken this constraint LPG allows to declare that some terms are "exception-terms" which have no standard meaning[1]. Modules of "enrichments" are used to declare only defined operators or predicates on types already declared. Consider the type module of Figure 1. It defines the sorts `dot` of dots with natural coordinates and `line` of straight lines. We assume that the data type of natural numbers with sort `nat` and usual operators on naturals as well as the data type of booleans with sort `bool` and boolean operators are already defined in the current context of modules. We also define a function `dist` that computes a "distance" between two naturals, the function `sign` that evaluates

[1] The preconditions and exceptions mechanism of LPG is not presented in this paper.

to **true** whenever the considered line has a positive slope, as well as the equality of two points (overloading is allowed for operators or predicates if they can be distinguished from sorts of the arguments). Then, several predicates on `line` are defined. In the equations of defined operators the equality symbol can be written as "==>" to mean that these axioms have to be used as rewrite rules from left to right. The left hand sides of such oriented rules must be innermost terms.

Modules of "properties" are designed to define first-order theories which characterize classes of types. For example, in Figure 2, we give two classical theories, namely `Equality` and `Total-Order`, that characterize respectively any set supplied with an equivalence relation[2] and any set supplied with an ordering.

Properties are used to specify generic parameters of generic types or enrichments. The generic parameters are introduced by the keyword "**requires**". Sorts, operators and predicates of the declaration `requires` are local declarations in the generic module and the axiomatization of the required property is inherited via the declared renaming. We show in figure 3 a generic module `Sorting` which requires a data type with total order to define the generic `sort` operator and the generic predicate `ordered` on sequences. This module uses the generic type of sequences which is available in the predefined library of LPG and values can be written as `[1,2,3]` instead of `cons(1,cons(2,cons(3,nil)))`. The notation `seq[elem]` stands for the sort of the sequences where the sort of elements is `elem`. In the module `Sorting`, the equation number 4 contains a conditional expression, like in functional languages. Such an equation is equivalent to the two following conditional rewrite rules :

```
add(x,cons(y,s)) → cons(x,cons(y,s)) <== x ≤ y == true
add(x,cons(y,s)) → cons(y,add(x,s))  <== x ≤ y == false
```

```
property Equality
sorts t
operators
   =: (t,t) → bool
variables
   x,y,z: t
equations
   1: x = x == true
   2: x = y == y = x
   3: (x = y and y = z)
          ⇒ (x = z) == true
end Equality
```

```
property Total-Order
sorts s
operators
   ≤,=: (s,s) → bool
variables
   x,y: s
equations
   1: x ≤ x == true
   2: x ≤ y and y ≤ x ⇒ x = y == true
   3: x ≤ y and y ≤ z ⇒ x ≤ z == true
   4: x ≤ y or y ≤ x == true
end Total-Order
```

Fig. 2. Definition of properties Equality and Total-Order

Other generic examples are presented in Figure 4. If a generic type/enrichment

[2] By convention in LPG, this property is used to define an operator which is supposed to give the observational equality on the elements of an abstract data type.

```
enrichment Sorting
requires Total-Order [elem operators ≤,eq]
operators
   sort: seq[elem] → [elem]
   add: (elem,seq[elem]) → seq[elem]
predicates
   ordered : seq[elem]
variables
   x,y: elem
   s: seq[elem]
equations
   1: sort(nil) ==> nil
   2: sort(cons(x,s)) ==> add(x,sort(s))
   3: add(x,nil) ==> [x]
   4: add(x,cons(y,s)) ==> if x≤y then cons(x,cons(y,s))
                              else cons(y,add(x,s)) endif
clauses
   1: ordered(s) <== sort(s) == s
end Sorting
```

Fig. 3. Definition of sorting of generic sequences

is parameterized by a property P, then it can be instantiated by any "model" of P. So, LPG allows to declare that data types and enrichments are models of properties. Actually, it is very useful to declare that a data type is a special case of a well known mathematical structure described by an LPG property, thus giving a better information on the type being specified. This is the idea of "views" in the OBJ language [12] and also in recent languages for computer algebra. A simple application of this method is to specify that some operators are commutative, or associative, or both, if they are models of the adequate property. Another example is the module `Dot-Line` (see Figure 1) which contains a model of the property `Equality` with the sort (or rather the elements of sort) `dot` and the operator `=` on dots. The syntactic form of model declarations in LPG looks like the generic parameters ones, after the keyword "**models**". Model declarations generate proof obligations. Such semantical verifications must be deferred to a prover not included in the current LPG system kernel.

A generic module can be instantiated by a model of its required property *by need*. The objects declared in the instantiated modules are available and can be used *directly* as non generic ones (for more information, see [5]). Several notations are available to denote such instantiated objects. Specially, a notation with explicit parameters is allowed; generic sorts are associated with sorts of the model, as in `seq[nat]` and operators or predicates are associated with effective operators and predicates of the parameter passing model, as in `sort[>=,=]([3,2,4])`, which is an occurrence of the operator declared in `Sorting` with the model of decreasing order on the natural numbers. In Figure 4, we present examples of definitions of generic predicates which can be used as "higher-order" predicates.

```
property Function
sorts t1,t2
operators
  f: t1 → t2
end Function
```

```
enrichment For-Graph
requires Function [t1,t2 operators f]
predicates              -- definition of
  graph: (t1,t2)        -- the graph of
variables               -- the function f.
  x : t1
clauses
  1: graph(x,f(x))
end For-Graph
```

```
property Bin-Relation
sorts t
predicates
  r: (t,t)
end Bin-Relation
```

```
enrichment Relation-Calculus1
requires Bin-Relation [t predicates r]
predicates
  reflex: (t,t)      -- reflex. closure of r.
  not-reflex: (t,t)  -- r without identity.
  inverse: (t,t)     -- inverse of r.
variables
  x,y : t
clauses
  1: reflex(x,x)
  2: reflex(x,y) <== r(x,y)
  3: not-reflex(x,y) <== r(x,y), x =/= y
  4: inverse(x,y) <== r(y,x)
end Relation-Calculus1
```

```
property Bin-Rel2
sorts t
predicates
  r1,r2: (t,t)
end Bin-Rel2
```

```
enrichment Relation-Calculus2
requires Bin-Rel2 [t predicates r1,r2]
predicates
  union: (t,t)       -- relation r1 or r2.
  inter: (t,t)       -- relation r1 and r2.
  compose: (t,t)     -- composition r1;r2.
variables
  x,y,z : t
clauses
  1: union(x,y) <== r1(x,y)
  2: union(x,y) <== r2(x,y)
  3: inter(x,y) <== r1(x,y), r2(x,y)
  4: compose(x,y) <== r1(x,z), r2(z,y)
end Relation-Calculus2
```

Fig. 4. Definition of "higher-order" predicates

Assume that the relation `id0` is simply the pair `{(0,0)}`, then the "predicate expression" `union[id0,inverse[graph[succ]]]` is the relation of the graph of the function `pred` on natural numbers (with `pred(0) == 0`). Another example of use of higher-order predicates, is the definition of family relationships. Given the following relationships on data type `person` :

```
husband: (person,person)
mother: (person,person)
```

where `husband(x,y)` (respectively `mother(x,y)`) means y is the husband (respectively, the mother) of x. Then the following other relationships can be defined as instances of generic predicates :

```
wife(x,y) <== inverse[husband](x,y)
spouse(x,y) <== union[husband,wife](x,y)
father(x,y) <== compose[mother,husband](x,y)
parents(x,y) <== union[father,mother](x,y)
grand-parents(x,y) <== compose[parents,parents](x,y)
children(x,y) <== inverse[parents](x,y)
brother-or-sister(x,y) <== not-reflex[compose[parents,children]](x,y)
```

A module SP is generally built over a set of submodules SP_j, which are instantiated and imported in it. The denotational semantics of a specification is a "modular semantics" in the sense that it is obtained by composition of the semantics of each individual module. The semantics of SP (noted $Sem(SP)$) depends on the semantics of the SP_j modules and on the constraints induced by parameterization and importations. Roughly, the denotational semantics of a property is the class of models of this property which respect (i.e. do not modify) the (semantics of) imported data types. The semantics of a generic data module is a strongly persistent free functor sending the class of models of the generic parameter to the class of models of the module [10]. But the operational semantics of the LPG language is defined for a single specification. So, for a modular specification SP, we need to compute a specification $\mathcal{F}lat(SP)$, which is the flattened specification associated to SP, when it exists. In LPG, for any completely instantiated module SP, the flattened specification $\mathcal{F}lat(SP)$ exists and $MS_{\mathcal{F}lat(SP)} \cong Sem(SP)$, i.e. the standard (initial) model of $\mathcal{F}lat(SP)$ is isomorphic to the modular semantics of SP. This is an expected result because of the semantics of generic modules. So, a completely instantiated modular specification is equivalent to a single flat specification obtained by gluing together basic specifications, enrichments and instantiated modules built by a translation via the parameter passing morphism (i.e. model), without duplication of the common submodules. Evaluations or resolutions are always performed in the *initial* model of the flattened specification. For instance, the resolution of the goal :

`union[id0,inverse[graph[succ]]](x,0) ?`

is equivalent to the resolution of : `union-i-igs(x,0) ?` in the context of declarations of Figure 5. This context contains the declarations of the module

Natural[3], the instance of **For-Graph** by the model **Function[nat,nat operators succ]**, the declarations of the module **Relation-Calculus1** instantiated by the model **Bin-Relation[nat predicates graph-succ]** and the declarations of the module **Relation-Calculus2** instantiated by the model **Bin-Rel2[nat predicates id0,inverse-gs]**. Names of predicate instances in the flattened specification are internal names. Correspondences are performed by the system between the "predicate expression" **graph[succ]** and the internal name **graph-succ** and so on, as indicated by comments in Figure 5.

```
type Evaluation_context
sorts nat
constructors
  0 : → nat
  succ : nat → nat
predicates
  id0 :             (nat,nat)    -- non generic predicate.
  graph-succ :      (nat,nat)    -- graph[succ].
  reflex-gs :       (nat,nat)    -- reflex[graph[succ]].
  not-reflex-gs :   (nat,nat)    -- not-reflex[graph[succ]].
  inverse-gs :      (nat,nat)    -- inverse[graph[succ]].
  union-i-igs :     (nat,nat)    -- union[id0,inverse[graph[succ]]].
  inter-i-igs :     (nat,nat)    -- inter[id0,inverse[graph[succ]]].
  compose-i-igs :   (nat,nat)    -- compose[id0,inverse[graph[succ]]].
variables
  x,y,z: nat
clauses
  1: id0(0,0)                                    -- def. id0.
  2: graph-succ(x,succ(x))                       -- def. graph[succ]
  3: reflex-gs(x,x)
  4: reflex-gs(x,y)       <== graph-succ(x,y)
  5: not-reflex-gs(x,y)   <== graph-succ(x,y), x =/= y
  6: inverse-gs(x,y)      <== graph-succ(y,x) -- def. inverse[graph[succ]].
  7: union-i-igs(x,y)     <== id0(x,y)        -- def. union[...,...].
  8: union-i-igs(x,y)     <== inverse-gs(x,y) -- def. union[...,...].
  9: inter-i-igs(x,y)     <== id0(x,y), inverse-gs(x,y)
  10: compose-i-igs(x,y) <== id0(x,z), inverse-gs(z,y)
end Evaluation_context
```

Fig. 5. Flattened context of evaluation of union[id0,inverse[graph[succ]]](x,0)

[3] Because the module is not given, it is restricted here to the constructors.

4 Operational Semantics of LPG

Let SP be a completely instantiated LPG specification, then there exists a basic specification $\mathcal{F}lat(SP)$ i.e. a collection of functions and predicates, which admits an initial (standard) model. Thus, queries can be "evaluated" in this standard model. Classical operational semantics of functional languages consists in a calculus that allows the "evaluation" (or normalization) of terms, whereas operational semantics of logic programming languages aims to solve goals. A functional logic programming language provides these two possibilities. In LPG, a goal is syntactically written as "$A_1, \ldots, A_m, \ldots, A_n$?" where every A_i is either an equation, a disequation or any other literal formed by predicates in SP. The LPG tool that solves goals is called *the solver* (see Figure 6 for a sample session). Note that the normalization of terms t is a particular case of solving a goal of the form "t==x?". In LPG system, when a term is ground, one may obtain its normal form by invoking a tool, called *the interpreter*, dedicated to such a task. This tool uses a compiled code of an abstract machine. By lack of place, the interpreter is not presented in this paper (see [3]).

```
{1} vertical (a) ?
for all k_1 : nat
for all j_1 : nat
for all i_1 : nat
a == c_line(c_dot(i_1,j_1),c_dot(i_1,k_1))
k_1 =/= j_1
more solutions? y
No more solutions.
```

```
{1} x + y == x * y ?
x == 0
y == 0
more solutions? y
x == 2
y == 2
more solutions? n
{1} cons(0, s) =/= [0] ?
s =/= nil
more solutions? y
No more solutions.
```

Fig. 6. Sample session of LPG solver.

The solver is based on one complete inference rule, an extension of the SLD-resolution, called SLDEI-resolution [8, 3]. This inference rule is parameterized by an algorithm solving equations and disequations in initial models and may be easily extended in order to cope with other new constraints. Results presented in this section are the following : proposition 4.2 states that SLDEI-resolution is sound and complete, then proposition 4.6 formulates that the entailment relation for solving equalities and disequalities is sound whereas proposition 4.7 states its completeness in presence of uniform strategies. New results are the presentation of a sound inference system for equalities and disequalities, the use of uniform strategies and the completeness of such strategies for conditional term rewriting systems. In the sequel we represent goals as multisets and denote them such as $\{A_1, \ldots, A_n\}$.

Definition 4.1 (*SLDEI*-**resolution**)
Let $SP = (\Sigma, E, Cl)$ be a constructor-based specification, G a goal and θ a substitution. The inference rules of SLDEI-resolution *are :*

- *Resolution:*

$$\frac{(G \cup \{P(t_1, \ldots, t_n)\}; \theta)}{(\sigma(G \cup \{D_1, \ldots, D_k\}); \sigma\theta)}$$

if $P \in \Pi$,
$P(v_1, \ldots, v_n)$<==$D_1, \ldots, D_k$ is a variant of a clause in Cl and σ belongs to a complete set of solutions of $\{v_1$==$t_1, \ldots, v_n$==$t_n\}$.

- *Unification:*

$$\frac{(G \cup \{t\texttt{==}t'\}; \theta)}{(\sigma(G); \sigma\theta)}$$

if σ belongs to a complete set of solutions of t==t'.

- *Disunification:*

$$\frac{(G \cup \{t\texttt{=/=}t'\}; \theta)}{(\sigma(G); \sigma\theta)}$$

if σ belongs to a complete set of solutions of t=/=t'.

We denote by $\longrightarrow_{SLDEI}$ the relation on goals and substitutions induced by the inference rules above. Then, we say that a substitution σ is *a solution computed by SLDEI-resolution* for a goal G if there exists a derivation

$$(G; id) \longrightarrow^{+}_{SLDEI} (\emptyset; \sigma)$$

Proposition 4.2 *Let $SP = (\Sigma, E, Cl)$ be a constructor-based specification and G a goal. The set of solutions computed by SLDEI-resolution for the goal G is a complete set of solutions of G.*

The proof of the completeness of SLDEI-resolution is quite similar to the one given in [8]. The consideration of disequations does not cause any substantial problem since the restriction of the use of disequations (Recall that disequations are not allowed in the bodies of conditional equations) ensures the existence of initial models. In other words, this syntactic condition on the use of disequations ensures in one hand the existence of one least congruence over terms, and on the other hand the continuity of a transformation on Herbrand E-models and then the existence of its least fixed point.

In order to define an effective operational semantics for our language, we need actual methods which compute complete sets of solutions of equations and disequations. In following, we present the inference rules that underlie such an algorithm which we have designed and implemented in LPG. This algorithm is based on narrowing [16]. It is well known that narrowing-based algorithms develop a very large search tree, computing very often redundant informations. Thus, many strategies of narrowing have been proposed. One of the most interesting improvement of narrowing-based algorithms consists in using the so called *narrowing position selection strategies* (or *narrowing strategies* for short) [21, 7].

The advantage of these strategies is undeniable. They can reduce drastically the narrowing search tree as they perform narrowing only at one chosen position. Formally, a narrowing strategy NS is a partial function from terms to positions (sequence of naturals). $NS : \mathcal{T}(\Sigma, \mathcal{X}) \to \mathcal{N}_{+}^{*}$. $NS(t)$ is defined to be a position p such that the term t is narrowable at position p. $NS(t)$ is defined if and only if such a position p exists. By abuse of notation, we extend the domain of strategies to atoms and goals as follows: We write $NS(t{==}t')$ resp. $NS(t{=/=}t')$ to denote a narrowing position either in t or in t' when it exists. For a goal G, we write $NS(G)$ to denote a narrowing position $NS(e)$ such that e is an equation or a disequation in G.

Unfortunately, the use of such strategies does not always preserve the completeness of narrowing algorithms (see [7] for a counterexample). So, sufficient conditions on specifications that ensure the completeness of such strategies (particularly the *outermost strategy*) have been proposed [7, 21, 9]. In this paper, we extend the conditions given in [9] to the case of CTRS's. In [9] we have proved that, in addition to termination and confluence of unconditional TRS's, a narrowing strategy is complete if it is uniform. A narrowing strategy NS is called ***uniform*** iff for any term $t \in \mathcal{T}(\Sigma, \mathcal{X})$, if $NS(t)$ is defined then for every ground normalized substitutions $\mu, \mu(t)$ is reducible at position $NS(t)$. When NS is uniform, a narrowing position such as $NS(t)$ is called ***uniform*** position.

The following example shows that these conditions do not ensure any more the completeness of narrowing strategies in the case of conditional TRS's.

Example 4.3 *Consider the following CTRS. It is borrowed from [19] and modified in order to satisfy the uniformity condition [9].*

$$\begin{array}{ll} f(d) & \to a <== d{==}b, d{==}c \\ f(c) & \to a \\ f(a) & \to c \\ d & \to b \\ d & \to c \\ b & \to c <== f(d){==}a \end{array}$$

This CTRS is confluent and terminating. Consider the goal $f(d){==}a$. The identity substitution is a solution for this goal. However, we can find some uniform narrowing strategy that leads to no solution. Indeed, consider the following derivation. At each step, we underline the equation we narrow.

$$\begin{array}{ll} \underline{f(d){==}a} & \leadsto a{==}a, \underline{d{==}b}, d{==}c \\ & \leadsto a{==}a, d{==}c, \underline{f(d){==}a}, d{==}c \\ & \leadsto \dots \end{array}$$

Hence we can manage to develop an infinite derivation that leads of course to no solution. However, at each step, the chosen position is uniform. To overcome this problem we need to reason upon a further rewrite relation [19] induced by CTRS's on goals. We note this relation $\mapsto$ which is defined by :

Definition 4.4 *Let R be a CTRS and S and T two goals. We write $S \mapsto_R T$ if there exists a goal e in S, a position $p \in Pos^*(e)$, a variant $l \rightarrow r$<==c of a rewrite rule in R and a substitution σ such that :*
1. $e_{|_p} = \sigma(l)$
2. $T = S - \{e\} \cup \{e[\sigma(r)]_p\} \cup \sigma(c)$
3. for every equation s==t *in* c, $\sigma(s) \downarrow_R \sigma(t)$

The advantage of this relation consists in having a simple correspondence between conditional narrowing and conditional rewriting [19] as it is the case for unconditional TRS's. Thus the completeness proof of conditional narrowing becomes quite similar to unconditional narrowing and the conditions for the completeness of narrowing strategies concern rather the relation $\mapsto_R$ than $\rightarrow_R$. Indeed, to ensure the completeness of a narrowing strategy NS, we require for $\mapsto_R$ to be confluent (which is implied by the confluence of $\rightarrow_R$) and terminating. Note that termination of $\rightarrow_R$ does not imply termination of $\mapsto_R$ (see the example above). From the narrowing strategy NS, we require uniformity between conditional narrowing and the relation $\mapsto_R$, i.e. if $NS(t)$ is defined, for every ground normalized substitution μ, $\mu(t)$ is reducible by $\mapsto_R$ at position $NS(t)$. For example, in the case of constructor-based CTRS when every defined function is total, innermost narrowing strategies are always uniform.

In the following definition we give the inference system $EQUALITY$ which consists of the main inference rules of the algorithm of solving equations and disequations we have implemented in LPG.

Definition 4.5 (Inference system $EQUALITY$)
Let $SP = (\Sigma, R, Cl)$ be a constructor-based specification such that $\mapsto_R$ is confluent and terminating, NS a uniform narrowing strategy, G a goal consisting of equations and disequations and θ a substitution. The inference rules of solving equations and disequations are :

– *Uniform Narrowing 1:*

$$\frac{(G \cup \{t\texttt{==}t'\}; \theta)}{(\sigma(G \cup \{(t\texttt{==}t')[r]_p\} \cup c); \sigma_{|V}\theta)}$$

$$\textit{if} \quad t\texttt{==}t' \leadsto_{[p, l \rightarrow r \texttt{<==} c, \sigma]} \sigma(\{t\texttt{==}t'[r]_p\} \cup c),\ p = NS(t\texttt{==}t') \ \textit{and}\ V = \mathcal{V}ar(t\texttt{==}t').$$

– *Uniform Narrowing 2:*

$$\frac{(G \cup \{t\texttt{=/=}t'\}; \theta)}{(\sigma(G \cup \{(t\texttt{=/=}t')[r]_p\} \cup c); \sigma_{|V}\theta)}$$

$$\textit{if} \quad t\texttt{=/=}t' \leadsto_{[p, l \rightarrow r \texttt{<==} c, \sigma]} \sigma(\{t\texttt{=/=}t'[r]_p\} \cup c),\ p = NS(t\texttt{=/=}t') \ \textit{and}\ V = \mathcal{V}ar(t\texttt{=/=}t').$$

– *Success 1:*

$$\frac{(G \cup \{t\texttt{==}t'\}; \theta)}{(G; \sigma\theta)}$$

if t and t' are not narrowable and σ = mgu(t, t')

- *Success 2:*

$$\frac{(G \cup \{k(t_1,\ldots,t_n)\text{=/=}k'(t'_1,\ldots t'_m)\};\theta)}{(G;\theta)}$$

if k and k' are two different constructors

- *Decomposition:*

$$\frac{(G \cup \{k(t_1,\ldots,t_n)\text{=/=}k(t'_1,\ldots t'_n)\};\theta)}{(G \cup \{t'_i\text{=/=}t'_i\};\theta)}$$

if k is a constructor and $1 \leq i \leq n$

- *Instantiation 1:*[4]

$$\frac{(G \cup \{x\text{=/=}k(t_1,\ldots,t_n)\};\theta)}{(\sigma(G) \cup \{k'(z_1,\ldots,z_m)\text{=/=}\sigma(k(t_1,\ldots,t_n))\};\sigma\theta)}$$

if x is a variable, k and k' are constructors, $z_1,\ldots,z_m$ are new variables and $\sigma = \{x \mapsto k'(z_1,\ldots,z_m)\}$

- *Instantiation 2:*

$$\frac{(G \cup \{x\text{=/=}y\};\theta)}{(\sigma(G) \cup \{k_1(x_1,\ldots,x_m)\text{=/=}k_2(y_1,\ldots,y_n)\};\sigma\theta)}$$

if x and y are different variables, k_1 and k_2 are constructors, $x_1,\ldots x_m, y_1,\ldots,y_n$ are new variables and $\sigma = \{x \mapsto k_1(x_1,\ldots,x_m), y \mapsto k_2(y_1,\ldots,y_n)\}$

We denote by $\longrightarrow_{EQU}$ the relation on goals and substitutions induced by the inference rules above. We denote by $\stackrel{i\text{-}f}{\longrightarrow}_{EQU}$ the instance-free subrelation of $\longrightarrow_{EQU}$. That is to say, $(G,\theta) \stackrel{i\text{-}f}{\longrightarrow}_{EQU} (G',\sigma)$ iff $(G;\theta) \longrightarrow_{EQU} (G';\sigma)$ and $\theta = \sigma$, in other words the derivation $\stackrel{i\text{-}f}{\longrightarrow}_{EQU}$ does not modify the substitution part of a pair $(G;\theta)$. Let G be a conjunction of equations and disequations. Then, we say that a substitution σ is *a solution computed by the system EQUALITY* for the goal G if there exists a derivation

$$(G;id) \longrightarrow^{+}_{EQU} (\emptyset;\sigma)$$

The soundness of the system *EQUALITY* is straightforward :

Proposition 4.6 *Let $SP = (\Sigma, R, Cl)$ be a constructor-based specification such that $\mapsto_R$ is confluent and terminating, G a goal consisting of equations and disequations. Then, every solution computed by the system EQUALITY for the goal G is a solution of G. Moreover, for any solution of G, say σ, we have the following derivation :*

$$(\sigma(G);id) \stackrel{i\text{-}f}{\longrightarrow}^{+}_{EQU} (\emptyset;id)$$

The completeness of the system *EQUALITY* is expressed by the following proposition. The proof is given in appendix (Section 6).

[4] Note that the corresponding rule in [11] is not sound.

Proposition 4.7 *Let $SP = (\Sigma, R, Cl)$ be a constructor-based specification such that $\mapsto_R$ is confluent and terminating, NS a uniform narrowing strategy, G a goal consisting of equations and disequations. Let σ be a ground solution of G. Then, there exists a substitution θ, computed by the inference system EQUALITY such that $\theta \leq^i_E \sigma[\mathcal{V}ar(G)]$.*

If we consider unconditional TRS's we can see that the system *EQUALITY* encompasses, on one hand the rules of solving equations using narrowing strategies [9] and on the other hand the rules of solving disequations given in [11] that we have corrected and improved by the use of narrowing strategies.

The LPG solver (see Figure 6 for a sample session) implements additional inference rules that improve the operational semantics. Actually, we rather use normal narrowing, i.e., after each narrowing step, the considered term is normalized. The use of inductive rules while normalization is also allowed. The soundness of the use of inductive rules is quite trivial since we transform a goal into another one which admits the same set of ground solutions. Other simplification rules are used such as :

- *Simplify 1:*
$$\frac{(G \cup \{t\texttt{==}t\}; \theta)}{(G; \theta)}$$

- *Simplify 2:*
$$\frac{(G \cup \{x\texttt{==}t)\}; \theta)}{(\sigma(G); \sigma\theta)}$$
if x is a variable such that $x \notin \mathcal{V}ar(t)$ and $\sigma = \{x \mapsto t\}$

- *Simplify 3:*
$$\frac{(G \cup \{x\texttt{=/=}t)\}; \theta)}{(G; \theta)}$$
if x is a variable such that $x \in \mathcal{V}ar(t)$ and t contains no defined operator (occur-check)

Other rules are used to detect failures such as :

- *Fail 1:*
$$\frac{(G \cup \{t\texttt{=/=}t\}; \theta)}{Failure}$$

- *Fail 2:*
$$\frac{(G \cup \{k_1(t_1, \ldots, t_n)\texttt{==}k_2(s_1, \ldots, s_m)\}; \theta)}{Failure}$$
if k_1 and k_2 are different constructors

A disequation of the form $x\texttt{=/=}t$ such that $x \notin \mathcal{V}ar(t)$ and t is a constructor term, i.e., t contains no defined operators, has an infinite set of solutions of the form $x\texttt{==}t'$ when x ranges over an infinite domain. To overcome this infinite computation, these kind of disequations are detected and presented as such in the solutions (see Figure 6).

5 Conclusion

In the paper, we have presented some aspects of the integration of algebraic and logic programming in a language supporting modular and generic specifications. In this language the semantics of completely instantiated specifications is isomorphic to the standard model of the flattened corresponding specification, thus giving a sound basis for the definition of the operational semantics. New results about the operational semantics are the presentation of a sound inference system for equalities and disequalities, the use of uniform strategies and the completeness of such strategies for conditional term rewriting systems.

Among the different proposals of functional logic programming languages, EQLOG [13] is by no means the closest to LPG. Both are based on Horn clause logic with equality and provide generic modules. However, EQLOG offers subsort facilities which lack in LPG whereas LPG allows the use of disequalities which is not possible in EQLOG. As far as we know, EQLOG has not been implemented and its operational semantics has been only sketched in [13] without any seek for optimization or so.

In LPG, predicates and functions are well distinguished. This fact allows the use of disequations within the bodies of Horn clauses without any problem. In other words, any completely instantiated LPG specification has an initial model. In languages based on conditional equational logic, the introduction of disequations in specifications is not so easy. In [2], an extension of BABEL [20] with disequations is sketched. Though traditional standard (initial) models do not always exist, the declarative semantics of BABEL ensures the existence of a kind of least model. In such a model some functions may be undefined (i.e., $f(x) = \perp$). The main drawback of this approach remains in the fact that the predicate =/= is not the negation of the predicate == as one may expect. This fact is not surprising. It is due to the interpretation of the predicate == in BABEL as what is called *strict equality*, which is not a congruence. Another difference between BABEL and LPG lies in the use of narrowing. BABEL uses lazy narrowing whereas LPG uses uniform narrowing strategies. This last point does not really matter, since one can easily augment BABEL environment with narrowing strategies and use them whenever the considered TRS is constructor-based. Another tentative to handle disequations is presented in [14]. This implementation, which follows [11], considers unconditional constructor-based TRS's and uses basic narrowing.

Finally, we review some possible improvements of the solving tool. The use of narrowing strategies allows to prune drastically the narrowing search tree. However, the condition of uniformity (totally defined functions over constructors) under which such strategies are applied may seem to be restrictive. Indeed, the existence of such strategies is ensured only when defined functions are total (not partial). When defined functions are partial, there are cases (goals) that cannot be solved completely by such strategies (see [9]). So, to consider a larger class of specifications where functions may be partial and TRS's are not even terminating, an extension of *needed narrowing* [1] to CTRS's will be a very good candidate. Another point is that narrowing strategies do not always avoid useless branches. Thus, other techniques can be used in order to detect wasted computations. In [4] we have started the investigation of a new method, based on abstract analysis techniques, which tries to avoid narrowing over some unsatisfiable equations or disequations. We plan to continue such investigations.

References

1. S. Antoy, R. Echahed, and M. Hanus. A needed narrowing strategy. In *Proc. of POPL'94*, pages 268–279, Portland, January 1994.
2. P. Arenas-Sanchez, A. Gil-Luezas, and J. Lopez-Fraguas. Combining Lazy narrowing with Disequality Constraints. In *Proc. of PLILP'94*, pages 385–399. LNCS 844, 1994.
3. D. Bert and R. Echahed. Design and implementation of a generic, logic and functional programming language. In *Proc. of ESOP'86*, pages 119–132. LNCS 213, 1986.
4. D. Bert, R. Echahed, and B. M. Østvold. Abstract rewriting. In *Proc. of WSA'93*, pages 178–192. LNCS 724, 1993.
5. D. Bert, R. Echahed, and J.-C. Reynaud. Reference manual of the LPG specification language and environment. Release with disequations. Technical report, IMAG, University of Grenoble, anonymous ftp distribution : at imag.fr,/pub/SCOP/LPG, 1994.
6. N. Dershowitz and J. Jouannaud. Rewrite systems. In J. van Leeuwen, editor, *Handbook of Theoretical Computer Science B: Formal Methods and Semantics*, chapter 6, pages 243–320. North Holland, Amsterdam, 1990.
7. R. Echahed. On completeness of narrowing strategies. In *Proc. CAAP'88*, pages 89–101. LNCS 299, 1988.
8. R. Echahed. Sur l'intégration des langages algébriques et logiques. Thèse de l'Institut National Polytechnique de Grenoble, 1990.
9. R. Echahed. Uniform narrowing strategies. In *Proc. of ALP'92*, pages 259–275. LNCS 632, 1992.
10. H. Ehrig and B. Mahr. *Fundamentals of Algebraic Specification 1: Equations and Initial Semantics*, volume 6 of *EATCS Monographs on Theoretical Computer Science*. Springer-Verlag, 1985.
11. M. Fernandez. Narrowing based procedures for equational disunification. Technical Report 764, LRI, University of Paris Sud, July 1992.
12. K. Futatsugi, J. A. Goguen, J.-P. Jouannaud, and J. Meseguer. Principles of OBJ2. In *Proc. of 12th ACM POPL*, pages 51-60. ACM, 1985.
13. J. A. Goguen and J. Meseguer. EQLOG: Equality, Types and Generic Modules for Logic Programming. In *Functional and Logic Programming, eds. DeGroot and Lindstrom*. Prentice-Hall, 1986.
14. M. Haberstrau. ECOLOG : an Environment for COnstraint LOGics. In *Proc. of CCL'94*, pages 237–252. Springer-Verlag, 1994.
15. M. Hanus. The integration of functions into logic programming: From theory to practice. *Journal of Logic Programming*, 19&20:583–628, 1994.
16. J.-M. Hullot. Canonical forms and unification. In *Proc. 5th Conference on Automated Deduction*, number 87, pages 318–334. LNCS 87, 1980.
17. J. W. Lloyd. *Foundations of Logic Programming*. Springer-Verlag, Berlin, 1984.
18. J. Meseguer. Multiparadigm logic programming. In *Proc. of ALP'92*, pages 158–200. LNCS 632, 1992.

19. A. Middeldorp and E. Hamoen. Counterexamples to completeness results for basic narrowing (extended abstract). In *Proc. of ALP'92*, pages 244–258. LNCS 632, 1992.
20. J. J. Moreno-Navarro and M. Rodríguez-Artalejo. Logic programming with functions and predicates: The language BABEL. *Journal of Logic Programming*, 12:191–223, 1992.
21. P. Padawitz. *Computing in Horn Clause Theories*, volume 16 of *EATCS Monographs on Theoretical Computer Science*. Springer-Verlag, 1988.
22. J.A. Robinson and E.E. Sibert. The LOGLISP user's manual. In *Report 12/81, Syracuse University, New York*, 1981.

6 Appendix

In this appendix we sketch the completeness proof of the system *EQUALITY* (proposition 4.7). For this aim, we establish first a correspondence between the relations $\longrightarrow_{EQU}$ and $\overset{i-f}{\rightarrow}_{EQU}$.

Lemma 1. *Let $SP = (\Sigma, R, Cl)$ be a constructor-based specification, NS a uniform narrowing strategy, G and T be goals consisting of equations and disequations, σ a normalized substitution and V a set of variables such that $\mathcal{V}ar(G) \cup \mathcal{D}om(\sigma) \subseteq V$ and $T = \sigma(G)$. If $(T; id) \overset{i-f}{\rightarrow}_{EQU} (T'; id)$ such that $NS(T) = NS(G)$ whenever T' is obtained from T by rewriting, then there exist a goal G' and substitutions σ' and θ such that :*
1. $(G; id) \longrightarrow^{+}_{EQU} (G'; \theta)$, *3. $\sigma'\theta = \sigma[V]$,*
2. $\sigma'(G') = T'$, *4. σ' is normalized*

Proof : We consider the case where the goal T is a single equation or disequation. The general case where T is a multiset of equations and disequations is then straightforward.

If T is an equation $T = t{==}t'$, then $(T'; id)$ can be deduced from $(T; id)$ by the relation $\overset{i-f}{\rightarrow}_{EQU}$ either by using the rule *Uniform Narrowing 1* or *Success 1*.

- Use of *Uniform Narrowing 1*. This case corresponds to rewriting T into T' using the relation $\mapsto_R$ (i.e., $T \mapsto_R T'$). This case has been proved in [19]. G' is deduced from G by the inference rule *Uniform Narrowing 1* using the same rewrite rule at the same position as in $T \overset{i-f}{\rightarrow}_{EQU} T'$. Notice that in the general case, the position p at which T may be reduced is not always uniform. That is why we required $NS(T) = NS(G)$. This assumption ensures the uniformity of the position p in G since the strategy NS is uniform, and then the validity of the inference rule *Uniform Narrowing 1*.
- Use of *Success 1*. In this case, the goal T' is empty and t and t' are syntactically equal. Since $\sigma(G) = T$, the goal G consists of an equation $g{==}g'$ and the terms g and g' are unifiable. Therefore we have $(G; id) \longrightarrow_{EQU} (\emptyset, \theta)$ using the rule *Success 1*, where $\theta = mgu(g, g')$. Since σ is also a unifier of g and g', we deduce the existence of a substitution σ' such that $\sigma'\theta = \sigma$. The normalization of σ' follows from that of σ.

If T is a disequation $T = t\texttt{=/=}t'$, then $(T';id)$ can be deduced from $(T;id)$ by the relation $\overset{i-f}{\rightarrow}_{EQU}$ either by using the rule *Uniform Narrowing 2*, *Success 2* or *Decomposition*.

- Use of *Uniform Narrowing 2*. This case corresponds to rewriting T into T' using the relation $\mapsto_R$. This case is similar to that of the rule *Uniform Narrowing 1* above.
- Use of *Success 2*. In this case $T = k(t_1,\dots,t_n)\texttt{=/=}k'(t'_1,\dots t'_m)$ where k and k' are constructors. and $T' = \emptyset$. There are three possibilities for G.
  1. $G = k(g_1,\dots,g_n)\texttt{=/=}k'(g'_1,\dots g'_m)$ where k and k' are constructors. In this case, θ is the identity and $\sigma' = \sigma$. We have $(G;id) \longrightarrow_{EQU} (\emptyset, id)$.
  2. $G = x\texttt{=/=}k'(g'_1,\dots,g'_m)$ where k' is a constructor. In this case, $\mathcal{D}om(\theta) = \{x\}$ and $\theta(x) = k(x_1,\dots,x_n)$ where the variables x_i are new. $\mathcal{D}om(\sigma') = \{x_1,\dots,x_n\}$ and $\sigma'(x_i) = g_i$. Thus $\sigma'\theta = \sigma[V]$. G' which is empty is deduced from G in two steps :
  $(G;id) \overset{i-f}{\rightarrow}_{EQU} (k(x_1,\dots,x_n)\texttt{=/=}k'(g'_1,\dots,g'_m);\theta) \overset{i-f}{\rightarrow}_{EQU} (\emptyset;\theta)$.
  The normalization of σ' follows from that of σ. Notice that the case $G = k(g_1,\dots,g_n)\texttt{=/=}x$ is the same as the current one.
  3. $G = x\texttt{=/=}y$. This case is quite similar to the previous one. So, $\mathcal{D}om(\theta) = \{x,y\}$ with $\theta(x) = k(x_1,\dots,x_n)$ and $\theta(y) = k(y_1,\dots,y_m)$ where the variables x_i and y_j are new. $\mathcal{D}om(\sigma') = \{x_1,\dots,x_n,y_1,\dots,y_m\}$ and $\sigma'(x_i) = g_i$ and $\sigma'(y_i) = g'_i$. Thus $\sigma'\theta = \sigma[V]$. G' which is empty is deduced from G in two steps :
  $(G;id) \overset{i-f}{\rightarrow}_{EQU} (k(x_1,\dots,x_n)\texttt{=/=}k'(g'_1,\dots,g'_m);\theta) \overset{i-f}{\rightarrow}_{EQU} (\emptyset;\theta)$.
  The normalization of σ' follows from that of σ.
- Use of *Decomposition*. In this case $T = k(t_1,\dots,t_n)\texttt{=/=}k(t'_1,\dots t'_n)$ where k is a constructor and $T' = t_i\texttt{=/=}t'_i$ for some i. There are three possibilities for G.
  1. $G = k(g_1,\dots,g_n)\texttt{=/=}k(g'_1,\dots g'_m)$ and $G' = g_i\texttt{=/=}g'_i$. In this case, θ is the identity and $\sigma' = \sigma$.
  2. $G = x\texttt{=/=}k'(g'_1,\dots,g'_m)$. In this case, $\theta(x) = k'(x_1,\dots,x_m)$ where the variables x_i are new and $\mathcal{D}om(\theta) = \{x\}$. $\mathcal{D}om(\sigma') = \{x_1,\dots,x_m\}$ and $\sigma'(x_i) = g_i$. Thus $\sigma'\theta = \sigma[V]$. G' is $x_i\texttt{=/=}g'_i$ and it is obtained from G in two steps :
  $(G;id) \overset{i-f}{\rightarrow}_{EQU} (k'(x_1,\dots,x_m)\texttt{=/=}k'(g'_1,\dots,g'_m);\theta) \overset{i-f}{\rightarrow}_{EQU} (x_i\texttt{=/=}g'_i;\theta)$.
  The normalization of σ' follows from that of σ.
  The case $G = k(g_1,\dots,g_n)\texttt{=/=}x$ is the same as the current one.
  3. $G = x\texttt{=/=}y$. In this case, $\mathcal{D}om(\theta) = \{x,y\}$ with $\theta(x) = k(x_1,\dots,x_n)$ and $\theta(y) = k(y_1,\dots,y_n)$ where the variables x_i and y_j are new. $\mathcal{D}om(\sigma') = \{x_1,\dots,x_n,y_1,\dots,y_n\}$ and $\sigma'(x_i) = g_i$ and $\sigma'(y_i) = g'_i$. Thus $\sigma'\theta = \sigma[V]$. G' is $x_i\texttt{=/=}y_i$ and it is obtained from G in two steps :
  $(G;id) \overset{i-f}{\rightarrow}_{EQU} (k(x_1,\dots,x_n)\texttt{=/=}k(y_1,\dots,y_n);\theta) \overset{i-f}{\rightarrow}_{EQU} (x_i\texttt{=/=}y_i;\theta)$.
  The normalization of σ' follows from that of σ. **End proof.**

Lemma 2. *Let $SP = (\Sigma, R, Cl)$ be a constructor-based specification, NS a uniform narrowing strategy, G_1 and T_1 be goals consisting of equations and disequations, σ_1 a normalized substitution and V a set of variables such that $\mathcal{V}ar(G_1) \cup \mathcal{D}om(\sigma_1) \subseteq V$ and $T_1 = \sigma_1(G_1)$. If $(T_1; id) \overset{i\text{-}f}{\twoheadrightarrow}_{EQU} (T_2; id) \overset{i\text{-}f}{\twoheadrightarrow}_{EQU} \ldots \overset{i\text{-}f}{\twoheadrightarrow}_{EQU} (T_n; id)$ then there exist a goal G_n and substitutions σ_n and θ_n such that : 1. $(G_1; id) \longrightarrow^*_{EQU} (G_2, \theta_2) \longrightarrow^*_{EQU} \cdots \longrightarrow^*_{EQU} (G_n, \theta_n)$,*
2. $\sigma_n(G_n) = T_n$,
3. $\sigma_n\theta_n = \sigma_1[V]$,
4. σ_n is normalized.

Provided that for each step $(T_i; id) \overset{i\text{-}f}{\twoheadrightarrow}_{EQU} (T_{i+1}; id)$ which corresponds to a rewriting step, $NS(T_i) = NS(G_i)$.

Proof : The proof is by induction on the length, l, of the derivation $(T_1; id) \overset{i\text{-}f^*}{\twoheadrightarrow}_{EQU} (T_n; id)$. The base case , $l = 0$, is trivial. For the induction step, let us assume $l = m + 1$. Then, there exists a goal T_1 such that $(T_1; id) \overset{i\text{-}f}{\twoheadrightarrow}_{EQU} (T_2; id) \overset{i\text{-}f^*}{\twoheadrightarrow}_{EQU} (T_n; id)$. From Lemma 1, there exist a goal G_2 and substitutions σ_2 and θ_2 such that :

- $(G_1; id) \longrightarrow^+_{EQU} (G_2; \theta_2)$,
- $\sigma_2\theta_2 = \sigma_1[V]$,
- $\sigma_2(G_2) = T_2$,
- σ_2 is normalized

On the other hand, by induction hypothesis we deduce the existence of a goal G_n and substitutions σ_n and β such that :

- $(G_2; id) \longrightarrow^*_{EQU} (G_n, \beta)$,
- $\sigma_n(G_n) = T_n$,
- $\sigma_n\beta = \sigma_2[V']$, where $V' = V - \mathcal{D}om(\theta_2) \cup \mathcal{I}m(\theta_2)$,
- σ_n is normalized

Now, let $\theta_n = \beta\theta_2$. By concatenating the two previous derivations $(G_1; id) \longrightarrow^+_{EQU} (G_2; \theta_2)$ and $(G_2; id) \longrightarrow^*_{EQU} (G_n, \beta)$ we obtain the demanded derivation $(G_1; id) \longrightarrow^*_{EQU} (G_2, \theta_n)$. It remains to show $\sigma_n\theta_n = \sigma_1[V]$. Since $V' = V - \mathcal{D}om(\theta_2) \cup \mathcal{I}m(\theta_2)$ we have $\sigma_n\beta\theta_2 = \sigma_2\theta_2[V]$. Thus $\sigma_n\theta_n = \sigma_2\theta_2 = \sigma_1[V]$. **End proof.**

Proof of Proposition 4.7 : Let σ' be the normalized form of σ. Since σ is a solution of G, so is σ' and then there exists a derivation : $(T_1; id) \overset{i\text{-}f^+}{\twoheadrightarrow}_{EQU} (\emptyset; id)$ (1), where $T_1 = \sigma'(G)$ such that the hypothesis of Lemma 2 concerning the positions given by the strategy NS are satisfied. Indeed, such a derivation always exists since the underlying CTRS is constructor-based which means that every non-constructor term contains at least one uniform narrowing position. So, from Lemma 2, derivation (1) may be constructed simultaneously with its corresponding derivation : $(G_1, id) \longrightarrow^!_{EQU} (\emptyset; \theta)$ (2), where $G_1 = C$, so that at each derivation step in (1) $(T_i; id) \overset{i\text{-}f}{\twoheadrightarrow}_{EQU} (T_{i+1}; id)$ which corresponds to a rewriting step, we have $NS(T_i) = NS(G_i)$. This is always possible because T_i is reducible at $NS(T_i)$ since NS is uniform. From Lemma 2, there exists a substitution σ'' such that $\sigma''\theta = \sigma'[\mathcal{V}ar(G)]$. Therefore, $\theta \leq \sigma'[\mathcal{V}ar(G)]$ and since σ' is the normal form of σ, we deduce $\theta \leq^i_E \sigma[\mathcal{V}ar(G)]$. **End proof.**

Behavioural Theories

Michel Bidoit[1] and Rolf Hennicker[2]

[1] LIENS, C.N.R.S. U.R.A. 1327 & Ecole Normale Supérieure
45, Rue d'Ulm, F-75230 Paris Cedex 05, France
[2] Institut für Informatik, Ludwig-Maximilians-Universität München
Leopoldstr. 11B, D-80802 München, Germany

Abstract. Behavioural theories are a generalization of standard theories where the equality predicate is interpreted by an arbitrary (possibly partial) congruence relation, called *behavioural equality*. In this paper we first show how to reduce the behavioural theory of any class C of Σ-algebras to (a subset of) the standard theory of some corresponding class of algebras. Then we consider infinitary axiomatizations of the behavioural equality and we define a general condition under which the infinitary axiomatization can be replaced by a finitary one. As a consequence, behavioural theorems over different kinds of specifications can be proved using standard proof techniques. All results are stated in an abstract way, i.e. independent of a particular behavioural equality. As an important example we can apply our results to observational theories where the behavioural equality is given by an observational equality between elements.

1 Introduction

Formal algebraic specifications provide an appropriate means for the development of correct software. Thereby an important role is played by correctness concepts which allow behavioural abstractions. The basic idea of these concepts is that a software product is regarded as a correct implementation of some given specification if it satisfies the intended behaviour independently of internal implementation details which may not satisfy all properties of the specification.

This idea has been formalized in several approaches in the literature (cf. e.g. [4, 9, 10, 8, 11]). For instance, in [10] a concrete specification SP' is called *abstractor implementation* of a given specification SP *via an abstractor* α (determined by an equivalence relation on the class of all Σ-algebras) if all models of SP' are models of the *abstractor specification* $\alpha(SP)$, i.e. are equivalent to a model of SP. A different approach, but guided by the same motivation, are *behavioural specifications*. Thereby the key idea is to relax the interpretation of the equality predicate $=$ and to use a *behavioural satisfaction relation* where the equality predicate is interpreted by a *behavioural equality* determined by an arbitrary (possibly partial) congruence relation on any Σ-algebra. (An important example are *observational equalities* which relate any two elements of an algebra which cannot be distinguished by observable computations, cf. e.g. [9, 1, 8].)

For performing correctness proofs in the case of behavioural specifications it is crucial to show that the axioms of a given specification are behaviourally satisfied by an implementation. In other words this means that the axioms of a given behavioural specification belong to the *behavioural theory* of the implementing specification where the behavioural theory of a class C of Σ-algebras is the set of all formulas that are behaviourally satisfied by all algebras of C. Since we know from a result in [2] that behavioural semantics is in many cases the same but (at most) more restrictive than abstractor semantics (for "factorizable" abstractors) this proof strategy is also correct for abstractor implementations.

Unfortunately it is usually difficult to prove that a formula ϕ belongs to the behavioural theory of a given class C of Σ-algebras. The behavioural satisfaction relation does not even fulfill the satisfaction condition of institutions. Therefore we are interested in finding "nice" characterizations of behavioural theories which allow us to prove behavioural theorems using standard proof techniques as implemented, for instance, in any available theorem prover for (standard) first-order logic. In [1] we have shown how this can be achieved in the particular case where C is the model class of a behavioural specification and where the behavioural equality is a total observational equality. It is the aim of this work to obtain a similar but more general result for arbitrary classes C of Σ-algebras (such that C can be instantiated by the model class of different kinds of specifications as e.g. standard specifications, abstractor specifications, behavioural specifications, "ASL-like" specifications) and for arbitrary (possibly partial) behavioural equalities (thus avoiding technicalities like "observable contexts" which appear in the observational framework).

For this purpose we proceed as follows:

In a first step (Section 4) we provide a general construction (the so-called "lift operator") which allows us to characterize the behavioural theory of a class C of Σ-algebras by (a subset of) the standard theory of a corresponding class $\mathcal{L}(C)$ of lifted algebras. More precisely, a formula ϕ is behaviourally valid in all algebras of C if and only if its lifted version $\mathcal{L}(\phi)$ is valid in the standard sense in all lifted algebras of $\mathcal{L}(C)$. The usefulness of this characterization of behavioural theories still depends on the possibility to prove standard theorems over $\mathcal{L}(C)$.

Therefore we introduce in a next step (Section 5) a general notion of (infinitary) axiomatization of behavioural equalities and we show that such an axiomatization is useful for characterizing the class $\mathcal{L}(C)$ of lifted algebras. In particular, we see that if C is axiomatizable (i.e. is the model class of a flat standard specification) and if an axiomatization of the behavioural equality is provided then $\mathcal{L}(C)$ is axiomatizable as well. However, we have still the problem that the axiomatization of the behavioural equality may be given by a set of *infinitary* formulas since in concrete examples (as in the case of observational equalities) only an infinitary axiomatization may be immediately deduced from the definition of the given behavioural equality.

Hence, in the last step (Section 6), it remains to get rid of such infinitary axiomatizations. For this purpose we consider conditional axiomatizations of the behavioural equality. The underlying idea is that if a class C of Σ-algebras satisfies a certain condition (represented by a set of finitary formulas) then the infinitary axiomatization of the behavioural equality can be replaced by a finitary one. Combined with the previous reduction of behavioural theories over C to standard theories over $\mathcal{L}(C)$ we can then prove behavioural theorems using standard proof techniques. As an example we consider in Section 7 the total observational equality and we show how one can reduce the observational theory of a multiset specification (which exports only a part of its operations) to a standard theory of another related specification.

2 Basic Notions

We assume that the reader is familiar with basic notions of algebraic specifications (cf. e.g. [3]) like the notions of (many sorted) *signature* $\Sigma = (S, F)$, *total Σ-algebra* $A = (\,(A_s)_{s\in S}, (f^A)_{f\in F}\,)$ where A_s are the carrier sets of A and f^A are the (total) operations, *Σ-term algebra* $T_\Sigma(X)$, *valuation* $\alpha : X \to A$ and *interpretation* $I_\alpha : T_\Sigma(X) \to A$. Throughout this paper we assume that the carrier sets A_s of a Σ-algebra A are not empty and $Alg(\Sigma)$ denotes the class of all such Σ-algebras. We assume also that $X = (X_s)_{s\in S}$ is a family of countably infinite sets X_s of variables of sort $s \in S$.

A *partial Σ-congruence* on a Σ-algebra A is a family $\approx_A = (\approx_{A,s})_{s\in S}$ of partial equivalence (i.e. symmetric and transitive) relations $\approx_{A,s}$ on A_s compatible with the signature Σ, i.e. for all $f \in F$ of arity $s_1 \dots s_n \to s$, for all $a_i, b_i \in A_{s_i}$, if $a_i \approx_{A,s_i} b_i$ then $f^A(a_1, \dots, a_n) \approx_{A,s} f^A(b_1, \dots, b_n)$.[3] A *$\Sigma$-congruence* $\approx_A$ is *total* if for all a in A, $a \approx_A a$. The "definition domain" of a partial congruence $\approx_A$, denoted by $\mathrm{Dom}(\approx_A)$, is defined by $\{a \in A \mid a \approx_A a\}$ and is a subalgebra of A (moreover $\approx_A$ is a total Σ-congruence on $\mathrm{Dom}(\approx_A)$). In the sequel $A/\!\approx_A$ denotes the quotient algebra of $\mathrm{Dom}(\approx_A)$ by $\approx_A$.

First-order Σ-formulas are defined as usual, from equations $l = r$, the logical connectives $\neg, \wedge, \vee, \dots$ and the quantifiers $\forall, \exists$. We will also use *infinitary Σ-formulas* of the form $\bigwedge_{i\in I} \phi_i$ and $\bigvee_{i\in I} \phi_i$, where $(\phi_i)_{i\in I}$ is a countable family of Σ-formulas. A *Σ-sentence* is a Σ-formula which contains no free variable. In the sequel $\mathrm{FreeVar}(\phi)$ denotes the set of the free variables of the formula ϕ and $\mathrm{Var}(t)$ denotes the variables of the term t.

The *(standard) satisfaction* of a Σ-formula ϕ (finitary or not) by a Σ-algebra A, denoted by $A \models \phi$, is defined as usual in the first-order predicate calculus where the predicate symbol $=$ is interpreted by the set-theoretic equality over the carrier sets of the algebra.

A *standard (algebraic) specification* SP is a tuple $\langle \Sigma, Ax \rangle$ where $\Sigma = (S, F)$ is a signature and Ax is a set of Σ-sentences, called *axioms* of SP. The *model class* of SP, denoted by $Mod(SP)$, is the class of all Σ-algebras which satisfy the axioms of SP, i.e. $Mod(SP) \stackrel{\text{def}}{=} \{A \in Alg(\Sigma) \mid A \models \phi \text{ for all } \phi \in Ax\}$.

A specification language is called *ASL-like* if to any specification SP is associated a signature, denoted by $Sig(SP)$, and a class of models, denoted by $Mod(SP)$, such that $Mod(SP) \subseteq Alg(Sig(SP))$, and if the language contains standard specifications and (at least) an operator $+$ for the combination

[3] In the sequel, for sake of clarity, we will often omit the subscript s and write $a \approx_A b$ instead of $a \approx_{A,s} b$.

of specifications SP and SP' such that $Sig(SP + SP') = Sig(SP) \cup Sig(SP')$ and $Mod(SP + SP') = \{A \in Alg(Sig(SP + SP')) \mid A|_{Sig(SP)} \in Mod(SP)$ and $A|_{Sig(SP')} \in Mod(SP')\}$.

The *(standard) theory* of a class $C \subseteq Alg(\Sigma)$ of Σ-algebras, denoted by $Th(C)$, is defined by $Th(C) \stackrel{\text{def}}{=} \{\Sigma\text{-formula } \phi \mid A \models \phi \text{ for all } A \in C\}$.
In the following $C \models \phi$ is an equivalent notation for $\phi \in Th(C)$ and similarly $SP \models \phi$ is an equivalent notation for $\phi \in Th(Mod(SP))$.

Note that we will always consider theories including infinitary Σ-formulas. However it is obvious that all our results remain valid if we restrict to first-order theories, i.e. theories consisting only of finitary (first-order) Σ-formulas.

3 Behavioural and Abstractor Specifications

In this section we summarize the basic definitions and results of [2] where the relationships between behavioural and abstractor specifications are studied.

Behavioural specifications are a generalization of standard specifications which allow to describe the behaviour of data structures and programs with respect to a given (partial) congruence relation. The essential difference to the standard case is that instead of the set-theoretic equality, the given congruence relation is used for the interpretation of the $=$ predicate symbol.

Another approach which also allows to relax the standard semantics of algebraic specifications are abstractor specifications (cf. [10]). In this case an equivalence relation between algebras is used for abstracting from the (standard) model class of a specification.

In the sequel of this paper we always assume given a family $\approx = (\approx_A)_{A \in Alg(\Sigma)}$ of (possibly partial) Σ-congruences on the algebras of $Alg(\Sigma)$ and an equivalence relation $\equiv$ on $Alg(\Sigma)$ such that $\equiv$ is *factorizable* by $\approx$, i.e.:
For all $A, B \in Alg(\Sigma)$, $A \equiv B$ if and only if $A/\approx_A$ and $B/\approx_B$ are isomorphic.

3.1 Behavioural and Abstractor Semantics

Definition 1 (Behavioural satisfaction relation). Let A be a Σ-algebra. Moreover, let $l, r \in T_\Sigma(X)_s$ be two terms of sort s, ϕ be an arbitrary Σ-formula, and $\alpha : X \to \mathrm{Dom}(\approx_A)$ be a valuation. The behavioural satisfaction relation w.r.t. $\approx$, denoted by $\models_\approx$, is defined as follows:

1. $A, \alpha \models_\approx l = r$ if and only if $I_\alpha(l) \approx_A I_\alpha(r)$.
2. $A, \alpha \models_\approx \phi$ is defined by induction on the structure of the formula ϕ.
3. $A \models_\approx \phi$ if and only if $A, \alpha \models_\approx \phi$, for all valuations $\alpha : X \to \mathrm{Dom}(\approx_A)$.

Hence Definition 1 is quite similar to the definition of the standard satisfaction relation, the only difference being for *(1)* where $I_\alpha(l) = I_\alpha(r)$ is replaced by $I_\alpha(l) \approx_A I_\alpha(r)$. Moreover, it is important to note that valuations have their range in $\mathrm{Dom}(\approx_A)$ and not in A, to take into account the partial nature of $\approx_A$.

Definition 2 (Behavioural specification). Let $SP = \langle \Sigma, Ax \rangle$ be a standard specification. Then:

1. The expression **behaviour** SP **w.r.t.** $\approx$ is a behavioural specification.
2. The model class of a behavioural specification is defined by
   $Mod(\textbf{behaviour } SP \textbf{ w.r.t. } \approx) \stackrel{\text{def}}{=} \{A \in Alg(\Sigma) \mid A \models_{\approx} \phi \text{ for all } \phi \in \mathcal{A}x\}$.

Definition 3 (Abstractor operator). For any class $C \subseteq Alg(\Sigma)$, $Abs_{\equiv}(C)$ denotes the closure of C under $\equiv$, i.e.:
$Abs_{\equiv}(C) \stackrel{\text{def}}{=} \{B \in Alg(\Sigma) \mid B \equiv A \text{ for some } A \in C\}$.

Definition 4 (Abstractor specification). Let $SP = \langle \Sigma, \mathcal{A}x \rangle$ be a standard specification. Then:

1. The expression **abstract** SP **w.r.t.** $\equiv$ is an abstractor specification.
2. The model class of an abstractor specification is defined by
   $Mod(\textbf{abstract } SP \textbf{ w.r.t. } \equiv) \stackrel{\text{def}}{=} Abs_{\equiv}(Mod(SP))$.

Fully abstract algebras play an important role for the characterization of behavioural semantics. Following Milner's notion (cf. [7]), we define full abstractness with respect to a given family $\approx$ of Σ-congruences as follows:

Definition 5 (Fully abstract algebra).

1. A Σ-algebra A is called fully abstract with respect to $\approx$ (or briefly fully abstract) if $\approx_A$ coincides with the set-theoretic equality over the carrier sets of A. (In particular $\approx_A$ is total.)
2. For any class $C \subseteq Alg(\Sigma)$ of Σ-algebras, $FA_{\approx}(C)$ denotes the subclass of the fully abstract algebras of C, i.e. $FA_{\approx}(C) \stackrel{\text{def}}{=} \{A \in C \mid A \text{ is fully abstract}\}$.

Definition 6 (Regularity). A family $\approx = (\approx_A)_{A \in Alg(\Sigma)}$ of Σ-congruences is called regular if, for any Σ-algebra A, the quotient algebra $A/\approx_A$ is fully abstract.

Definition 7 (Behavioural quotient operator). For any class $C \subseteq Alg(\Sigma)$, $C/\approx$ denotes the behavioural quotient of C, i.e.: $C/\approx \stackrel{\text{def}}{=} \{A/\approx_A \mid A \in C\}$.

Definition 8 (Behaviour operator). For any class $C \subseteq Alg(\Sigma)$,
$Beh_{\approx}(C) \stackrel{\text{def}}{=} Abs_{\equiv}(FA_{\approx}(C))$.

A central result of [2] is the following characterization of behavioural semantics:

Theorem 9. *If the family* $\approx$ *is regular, then*
$Mod(\textbf{behaviour } SP \textbf{ w.r.t. } \approx) = Beh_{\approx}(Mod(SP))$.

Example 1. An important example in which all our results apply is the *partial observational equality* of elements as defined e.g. in [8].

Formally, let $\Sigma = (S, F)$ be a signature, $Obs \subseteq S$ be a set of observable sorts, and $In \subseteq S$ be a set of input sorts. Let X_{In} be the S-sorted family of variables defined by $(X_{In})_s = \emptyset$ if $s \notin In$ and $(X_{In})_s = X_s$ if $s \in In$ (where $X = (X_s)_{s \in S}$ is the generally assumed family of countably infinite sets of variables of sort s), and let $Z = (\{z_s\})_{s \in S}$ be a disjoint S-sorted family of singleton sets. Then:

1. An *observable Σ-context* is a Σ-term $C \in T_\Sigma(X_{In} \cup Z)$ of observable sort which contains besides input variables in X_{In} exactly one distinguished variable z_s (called *context variable*) of some sort $s \in S$.[4] The application of a context C with context variable z_s to a term t of sort s is denoted by $C[t]$. The set of observable contexts with context variable of sort s and input variables in In is denoted by $\mathcal{C}_s^{Obs,In}$.
2. If A is a Σ-algebra then two elements $a, b \in A_s$ are observationally equal, denoted by $a \approx_{Obs,In,A} b$, if:
   (a) There exists a term $t \in T_\Sigma(X_{In})_s$ and a valuation $\alpha : X_{In} \to A$ such that $I_\alpha(t) = a$, and similarly for b.
   (b) For all contexts $C \in \mathcal{C}_s^{Obs,In}$ with context variable z_s, for all valuations $\alpha : X_{In} \to A$, we have $I_{\alpha_1}(C) = I_{\alpha_2}(C)$, where $\alpha_1, \alpha_2 : X_{In} \cup \{z_s\} \to A$ are the unique extensions of α defined by $\alpha_1(z_s) = a$ and $\alpha_2(z_s) = b$.
3. The family $(\approx_{Obs,In,A})_{A \in Alg(\Sigma)}$ of partial observational equalities (which in particular are partial Σ-congruences) is denoted by $\approx_{Obs,In}$. Dom$(\approx_{Obs,In,A})$ is the smallest subalgebra of A which is generated by the values of input sorts.
4. A special important case is obtained by chosing $In = S$. In that case the associated observational equality is a total Σ-congruence and correspond to the (total) observational equality of elements as defined in e.g. [9, 1].

3.2 Behavioural Theories

According to the generalization of the standard satisfaction relation to the satisfaction relation with respect to a family $\approx$ of Σ-congruences we consider the theory with respect to $\approx$ of a given class C of Σ-algebras.

Definition 10 (Behavioural theory). Let $C \subseteq Alg(\Sigma)$ be a class of Σ-algebras. The behavioural theory of C, denoted by $Th_\approx(C)$, is defined by:
$Th_\approx(C) \stackrel{\text{def}}{=} \{\Sigma\text{-formula } \phi \mid A \models_\approx \phi \text{ for all } A \in C\}$.
In the following $C \models_\approx \phi$ is an equivalent notation for $\phi \in Th_\approx(C)$.

Another central result of [2] is the following theorem which leads to a characterization of behavioural theories:

Theorem 11. *For all Σ-algebras A, B and Σ-formulas ϕ the following holds:*
1. *$A \models_\approx \phi$ if and only if $A/\approx_A \models \phi$.*
2. *If $A \equiv B$ then $A \models_\approx \phi$ if and only if $B \models_\approx \phi$.*
3. *If A is fully abstract then $A \models_\approx \phi$ if and only if $A \models \phi$.*

Corollary 12. *For any class C of Σ-algebras, we have:*
1. $Th_\approx(C) = Th(C/\approx)$.
2. $Th_\approx(Abs_\equiv(C)) = Th_\approx(C)$.
3. $Th_\approx(FA_\approx(C)) = Th(FA_\approx(C))$.
4. $Th_\approx(Beh_\approx(C)) = Th_\approx(Abs_\equiv(FA_\approx(C))) = Th(FA_\approx(C))$.

[4] By exception, in the sequel Var(C) will denote the set of variables occurring in C *but* the context variable of C.

In practice it is usually difficult to prove behavioural theorems due to the generalized satisfaction relation. Although Corollary 12(1) shows that in principle behavioural theories can be reduced to standard theories this result is of little practical interest because even if the class C is axiomatizable we have (in general) no straightforward proof system for the standard theory of the class $C/\approx$ (since the formation of quotients does not preserve the validity of arbitrary Σ-formulas). Therefore we are interested in finding other characterizations of behavioural theories which allow us to prove behavioural theorems using standard proof techniques. For this purpose our general strategy is first to reduce the behavioural theory $Th_{\approx}(C)$ of some class C of Σ-algebras to (a subset of) the standard theory $Th(D)$ of some other class D of algebras and then to look for an appropriate axiomatization (or a proof system) for D (provided that an axiomatization or a proof system for C is given). According to the previous results we know that this strategy works well in the following case: If C is a class of **fully abstract** algebras then we know by Corollary 12(3) that $Th_{\approx}(C) = Th(C)$ i.e. in this case the behavioural theory of C can be reduced to the standard theory of C. Moreover we have shown in [1] that if $C = FA_{\approx_{Obs,S}}(Mod(SP))$ is the class of the fully abstract models of a standard specification SP where $\approx_{Obs,S}$ is a total observational equality defined by a set Obs of observable sorts (cf. Example 1) then C can be axiomatized by a set of infinitary Σ-formulas which under some condition (the so-called *observability kernel* assumption) can be replaced by a finitary axiomatization.

It is the aim of this work to obtain a similar result for arbitrary classes C of Σ-algebras and arbitrary families $\approx$ of partial Σ-congruences.

4 The Lift Operator

In a first step we introduce a "lift" operator which provides an explicit denotation for the given family $\approx \; = (\approx_A)_{A \in Alg(\Sigma)}$ of partial Σ-congruences. For this purpose we use predicate symbols to denote the equivalence relations and their domains.[5]

Definition 13 (Lift operator). Given a signature Σ, a Σ-algebra A, a class C of Σ-algebras and a Σ-formula ϕ we define their lifted versions as follows:

1. $\mathcal{L}(\Sigma) \stackrel{\text{def}}{=} \Sigma \cup \{\sim_s : s\ s\}_{s \in S} \cup \{D_s : s\}_{s \in S}$, i.e. $\mathcal{L}(\Sigma)$ is the signature Σ enriched by, for each sort s in S, a binary predicate $\sim_s : s\ s$ (to denote the behavioural equality) and a unary predicate D_s (to denote the definedness of $\sim_s$). We will adopt an infix notation for the binary predicates $\sim_s$, i.e. we write $l \sim_s r$ instead of $\sim_s (l, r)$.
2. $\mathcal{L}(A)$ is the unique $\mathcal{L}(\Sigma)$-algebra extension of A defined by:
   (a) $\mathcal{L}(A)|_{\Sigma} \stackrel{\text{def}}{=} A$

[5] We assume the reader to be familiar with the usual notions of predicates and their interpretations.

(b) For any s in S, $\sim_s^{\mathcal{L}(A)} \stackrel{\text{def}}{=} \approx_{A,s}$,
i.e. for any a, b in $\mathcal{L}(A)_s$ $(= A_s)$, $a \sim_s^{\mathcal{L}(A)} b$ if and only if $a \approx_{A,s} b$.

(c) For any s in S, for any a in $\mathcal{L}(A)_s$ $(= A_s)$, $D_s^{\mathcal{L}(A)}(a)$ if and only if $a \approx_{A,s} a$ (hence if and only if $a \sim_s^{\mathcal{L}(A)} a$).

3. $\mathcal{L}(C) \stackrel{\text{def}}{=} \{\mathcal{L}(A) \mid A \in C\}$.
4. $\mathcal{L}(\phi) \stackrel{\text{def}}{=} \left[\left(\bigwedge_{y:s \in \mathrm{FreeVar}(\phi)} D_s(y)\right) \Rightarrow \phi^*\right]$, where ϕ^* is defined by induction on the structure of ϕ as follows:[6]
   (a) If ϕ is an equation $l = r$ between two terms of sort s, then ϕ^* is $l \sim_s r$,
   (b) $(\neg\phi)^* = \neg(\phi^*)$, $(\phi_1 \wedge \phi_2)^* = (\phi_1^*) \wedge (\phi_2^*)$, $(\phi_1 \vee \phi_2)^* = (\phi_1^*) \vee (\phi_2^*)$, and similarly for infinite conjunctions and disjunctions,
   (c) $(\forall x{:}s.\phi)^* = \forall x{:}s.[D_s(x) \Rightarrow \phi^*]$.
   Note that if ϕ is a closed Σ-formula then $\mathcal{L}(\phi)$ coincides with ϕ^*.

Definition 14. Given a class D of $\mathcal{L}(\Sigma)$-algebras, we define:
$Th^{\mathcal{L}}(D) \stackrel{\text{def}}{=} \{\Sigma\text{-formula } \phi \mid \mathcal{L}(\phi) \in Th(D)\}$.

The following theorem shows that for any class C of Σ-algebras the behavioural theory of C consists of all Σ-formulas ϕ whose lifted version $\mathcal{L}(\phi)$ belongs to the standard theory of $\mathcal{L}(C)$.

Theorem 15. *For any Σ-algebra A and Σ-formula ϕ,*
$A \models_{\approx} \phi$ if and only if $\mathcal{L}(A) \models \mathcal{L}(\phi)$.
Hence, for any class C of Σ-algebras,
$C \models_{\approx} \phi$ if and only if $\mathcal{L}(C) \models \mathcal{L}(\phi)$, i.e. $Th_{\approx}(C) = Th^{\mathcal{L}}(\mathcal{L}(C))$.

Proof. Relies on the following lemmas:

Lemma 16. *Let A be a Σ-algebra and ϕ be a Σ-formula. For all valuations $\alpha : X \to \mathrm{Dom}(\approx_A)$, the following conditions are equivalent:*

1. $A, \alpha \models_{\approx} \phi$
2. $\mathcal{L}(A), \alpha \models \phi^*$
3. $\mathcal{L}(A), \alpha \models \mathcal{L}(\phi)$

Lemma 17. *Let A be a Σ-algebra and ϕ be a Σ-formula. The following conditions are equivalent:*

1. *For all valuations $\alpha : X \to \mathrm{Dom}(\approx_A)$: $\mathcal{L}(A), \alpha \models \mathcal{L}(\phi)$*
2. *For all valuations $\beta : X \to \mathcal{L}(A)$: $\mathcal{L}(A), \beta \models \mathcal{L}(\phi)$* □

Remark. Let C be a class of fully abstract Σ-algebras. By Theorem 15 we have $Th_{\approx}(C) = Th^{\mathcal{L}}(\mathcal{L}(C))$. Moreover, $Th^{\mathcal{L}}(\mathcal{L}(C)) = Th(C)$ because for any fully abstract algebra A, $A \models \phi$ if and only if $\mathcal{L}(A) \models \mathcal{L}(\phi)$. Hence we obtain in this particular case again our previous result $Th_{\approx}(C) = Th(C)$.

[6] Similar constructions, called relativizations, were used in [12] and recently in [6].

Theorem 15 provides a means for reducing the set of behavioural theorems over an arbitrary class C of Σ-algebras to a set of standard theorems over a corresponding class $\mathcal{L}(C)$ of $\mathcal{L}(\Sigma)$-algebras.[7] However, the usefulness of this reduction still depends on the possibility to perform proofs of standard theorems over $\mathcal{L}(C)$. Since $\mathcal{L}(C)$ is constructed on top of C by introducing a denotation for the behavioural equality we claim that for proving standard theorems over $\mathcal{L}(C)$ we need, on one hand, a proof system for proving standard theorems over C (in the best case C is axiomatizable) and, on the other hand, we need an axiomatization of the behavioural equality which will be considered in the next section.

Example 2.

1. Let $C = Mod(SP)$ be the model class of a standard specification $SP = \langle \Sigma, \mathcal{A}x \rangle$. Then, by Theorem 15, $Th_{\approx}(Mod(SP)) = Th^{\mathcal{L}}(\mathcal{L}(Mod(SP)))$ and we will see in the next section that $\mathcal{L}(Mod(SP))$ can be axiomatized with the help of an axiomatization of the behavioural equality.
   More generally, if SP is a structured ASL-like specification (cf. Section 2) we will see that $\mathcal{L}(Mod(SP))$ can be expressed by a specification of the ASL-like language as soon as an axiomatization of the behavioural equality is provided (cf. Example 7).
2. Let $C = Abs_{\equiv}(C')$ for some class C' of Σ-algebras. Then an immediate application of Theorem 15 would lead to $Th_{\approx}(Abs_{\equiv}(C')) = Th^{\mathcal{L}}(\mathcal{L}(Abs_{\equiv}(C')))$. But even if C' is axiomatizable there is no simple proof system for $Abs_{\equiv}(C')$ and hence also not for $\mathcal{L}(Abs_{\equiv}(C'))$. However, in this case we know, by Corollary 12(2), that $Th_{\approx}(Abs_{\equiv}(C')) = Th_{\approx}(C')$ and hence we can apply Theorem 15 to C' instead of $Abs_{\equiv}(C')$. Thus we obtain $Th_{\approx}(Abs_{\equiv}(C')) = Th_{\approx}(C') = Th^{\mathcal{L}}(\mathcal{L}(C'))$. Hence for abstractor specifications we have:
   $Th_{\approx}(Mod(\textbf{abstract } SP \textbf{ w.r.t. } \equiv)) = Th_{\approx}(Mod(SP)) = Th^{\mathcal{L}}(\mathcal{L}(Mod(SP)))$, i.e. this case can be reduced to the case considered in Part 1 of the example.
3. Let $C = Beh_{\approx}(C')$ for some class C' of Σ-algebras. Then an application of Theorem 15 would lead to $Th_{\approx}(Beh_{\approx}(C')) = Th^{\mathcal{L}}(\mathcal{L}(Beh_{\approx}(C')))$ which again is not a useful reduction. However, in this case we know, by Corollary 12(4), that $Th_{\approx}(Beh_{\approx}(C')) = Th(FA_{\approx}(C'))$. In this case we are interested in an axiomatization of full abstractness. In particular, **if the family $\approx$ is regular** then $Th_{\approx}(Mod(\textbf{behaviour } SP \textbf{ w.r.t. } \approx)) = Th(FA_{\approx}(Mod(SP)))$. (Note that in this case we do not actually use Theorem 15 but rather the more specific Theorem 9 together with Corollary 12(4).)
4. Let C be a class of Σ-algebras such that $Abs_{\equiv}(C) = Beh_{\approx}(C)$ (see [2] for simple necessary and sufficient conditions). Then we have:
   $Th_{\approx}(C) = Th_{\approx}(Abs_{\equiv}(C)) = Th_{\approx}(Beh_{\approx}(C)) = Th(FA_{\approx}(C))$.

5 Axiomatization of the Behavioural Equality

In the previous section we have shown how to replace the behavioural theory of some given class C of Σ-algebras by (a subset of) the standard theory of another

[7] In [6] it is shown how a similar result for "expressible" behavioural equalities can be obtained in the framework of higher-order logic.

related class of algebras. The next step is to provide a characterization of this class of algebras in terms of an axiomatization of the behavioural equality.

Definition 18 (Axiomatization of the behavioural equality). An axiomatization of the behavioural equality $\approx$ is a family of (possibly infinitary) Σ-formulas $(Beh_s^\infty(x_s, y_s))_{s\in S}$ (where x_s and y_s are the only free variables, of sort s, of $Beh_s^\infty(x_s, y_s)$) such that, for any Σ-algebra A, any sort s in S and any valuation $\alpha : X \to A$, $A, \alpha \models Beh_s^\infty(x_s, y_s)$ if and only if $\alpha(x_s) \approx_A \alpha(y_s)$. Whenever such an axiomatization exists, we say that the behavioural equality $\approx$ is axiomatizable.

In the following, we assume given an axiomatization $(Beh_s^\infty(x_s, y_s))_{s\in S}$ of the behavioural equality $\approx$.

Example 3 (Observational equality).

- The (total) observational equality $\approx_{Obs,S}$ induced by a set Obs of observable sorts (cf. Example 1) is axiomatized by the following infinitary formulas: $Beh_s^\infty(x_s, y_s) \stackrel{\text{def}}{=} \bigwedge_{C\in\mathcal{C}_s^{Obs,S}} \forall \mathrm{Var}(C) \,.\, C[x_s] = C[y_s]$. Note that if s is an observable sort then $Beh_s^\infty(x_s, y_s)$ is equivalent to $x_s = y_s$, i.e. for observable elements the observational equality coincides with the set-theoretic equality.
- The (partial) observational equality $\approx_{Obs,In}$ induced by a set Obs of observable sorts and a set In of input sorts (cf. Example 1) is axiomatized by the following infinitary formulas:
  $Beh_s^\infty(x_s, y_s) \stackrel{\text{def}}{=} Def_s(x_s) \wedge Def_s(y_s) \wedge \bigwedge_{C\in\mathcal{C}_s^{Obs,In}} \forall \mathrm{Var}(C) \,.\, C[x_s] = C[y_s]$,
  where $Def_s(x_s)$ is an abbreviation for $\bigvee_{t\in T_\Sigma(X_{In})_s} \exists \mathrm{Var}(t) \,.\, x_s = t$.
  Note that if s is an input sort, then $Beh_s^\infty(x_s, y_s)$ is equivalent to $\bigwedge_{C\in\mathcal{C}_s^{Obs,In}} \forall \mathrm{Var}(C) \,.\, C[x_s] = C[y_s]$; if s is an observable sort then $Beh_s^\infty(x_s, y_s)$ is equivalent to $Def_s(x_s) \wedge Def_s(y_s) \wedge x_s = y_s$. Moreover, $Beh_s^\infty(x_s, x_s)$ is always equivalent to $Def_s(x_s)$.

Before we come back to the general case of lifted algebras in Section 5.3 we will consider the usefulness of an axiomatization of the behavioural equality in the case of fully abstract algebras.

5.1 Case of Fully Abstract Algebras

The following proposition provides an obvious characterization of full abstractness in terms of an axiomatization of the behavioural equality.

Proposition 19 (Characterization of fully abstract algebras).
A Σ-algebra A is fully abstract if and only if, for all s in S,
$A \models \forall x_s, y_s{:}s.\, [Beh_s^\infty(x_s, y_s) \Leftrightarrow x_s = y_s]$. □

From Proposition 19 we directly deduce the following result which says that for any class C of Σ-algebras the subclass of the fully abstract algebras of C can be characterized using an axiomatization of the behavioural equality. This fact will be used when considering the particular case of behavioural theories of behavioural specifications (cf. Example 4(3)).

Theorem 20. *Let FA^{∞} be the following formula:*
$\bigwedge_{s \in S} \forall x_s, y_s{:}s. [Beh_s^{\infty}(x_s, y_s) \Leftrightarrow x_s = y_s]$.
Then for any class C of Σ-algebras, $FA_{\approx}(C) = C \cap Mod(\langle \Sigma, FA^{\infty} \rangle)$.
In particular, if $C = Mod(\langle \Sigma, Ax \rangle)$ then $FA_{\approx}(C) = Mod(\langle \Sigma, Ax \cup FA^{\infty} \rangle)$. □

5.2 Invariance and Regularity

The results for fully abstract algebras are the basis for the characterization of behavioural theories of behavioural specifications since in this case we have $Th_{\approx}(Mod($**behaviour** SP **w.r.t.** $\approx)) = Th(FA_{\approx}(Mod(SP)))$ whereby it is crucial that the given family $\approx$ is regular (cf. Example 2(3)). The aim of this section is to point out that whenever an axiomatization of the behavioural equality is provided one can characterize the regularity of $\approx$ by a certain property (called invariance) of this axiomatization.

Definition 21 (Invariant formula). A formula ϕ is called invariant w.r.t. $\approx$ if, for any Σ-algebra A and valuation $\alpha : X \to \text{Dom}(\approx_A)$, $A, \alpha \models_{\approx} \phi$ if and only if $A, \alpha \models \phi$.

The following lemmas will be used for proving the characterization of regularity given in Proposition 24.

Lemma 22. *The axiomatization of the behavioural equality $\approx$ is invariant if and only if, for any Σ-algebra A and any sort s in S:*
$A \models_{\approx} \forall x_s, y_s{:}s. [Beh_s^{\infty}(x_s, y_s) \Leftrightarrow x_s = y_s]$.

Proof. Let A be a Σ-algebra and $\alpha : X \to \text{Dom}(\approx_A)$ be an arbitrary valuation.
$\Longrightarrow$: $A, \alpha \models_{\approx} Beh_s^{\infty}(x_s, y_s)$ iff (by invariance) $A, \alpha \models Beh_s^{\infty}(x_s, y_s)$ iff $\alpha(x_s) \approx_A \alpha(y_s)$ iff $A, \alpha \models_{\approx} x_s = y_s$.
$\Longleftarrow$: $A, \alpha \models_{\approx} Beh_s^{\infty}(x_s, y_s)$ iff (by assumption) $A, \alpha \models_{\approx} x_s = y_s$ iff $A, \alpha \models Beh_s^{\infty}(x_s, y_s)$. Hence the axiomatization is invariant. □

Lemma 23. *The axiomatization of the behavioural equality $\approx$ is invariant if and only if, for any Σ-algebra A and any sort s in S:*
$A/{\approx_A} \models \forall x_s, y_s{:}s. [Beh_s^{\infty}(x_s, y_s) \Leftrightarrow x_s = y_s]$.

Proof. Follows from Theorem 11.1 and Lemma 22. □

Proposition 24. *The behavioural equality $\approx$ is regular if and only if its axiomatization is invariant.*

Proof. The behavioural equality $\approx$ is regular if and only if, for any Σ-algebra A, $A/{\approx_A}$ is fully abstract. According to Proposition 19 and Lemma 23, this is equivalent to the invariance of the axiomatization. □

It is therefore easy to show that the observational equality $\approx_{Obs,In}$ is always regular (cf. Example 3). In the following we always assume that the family $\approx$ is regular or equivalently that the axiomatization of the behavioural equality is invariant.

5.3 General Case

We will now generalize the results obtained for fully abstract algebras to the lifting operator. In a first step we obtain an appropriate characterization of lifted algebras.

Proposition 25 (Characterization of lifted algebras). *Let B be an arbitrary $\mathcal{L}(\Sigma)$-algebra. Then $B \in \mathcal{L}(Alg(\Sigma))$ (i.e. B is a lifted algebra) if and only if, for all $s \in S$:*
$B \models \forall x_s, y_s{:}s.[Beh_s^\infty(x_s, y_s) \Leftrightarrow x_s \sim_s y_s]$ *and* $B \models \forall x_s{:}s.[x_s \sim_s x_s \Leftrightarrow D_s(x)]$.

Proof. Let A be a Σ-algebra. Since A and $\mathcal{L}(A)$ have the same carrier sets, it is not necessary to distinguish between valuations from X to A and valuations from X to $\mathcal{L}(A)$. In the following we will denote such valuations by $\alpha : X \longrightarrow A, \mathcal{L}(A)$.

$\Longrightarrow$: Assume $B \in \mathcal{L}(Alg(\Sigma))$ and let $A \in Alg(\Sigma)$ such that $B = \mathcal{L}(A)$. Let $\alpha : X \longrightarrow A, \mathcal{L}(A)$ be an arbitrary valuation. $\mathcal{L}(A), \alpha \models Beh_s^\infty(x_s, y_s)$ iff (since $Beh_s^\infty(x_s, y_s)$ is a Σ-formula) $A, \alpha \models Beh_s^\infty(x_s, y_s)$ iff (by Definition 18) $\alpha(x_s) \approx_A \alpha(y_s)$ iff (by Definition 13) $\alpha(x_s) \sim_s^{\mathcal{L}(A)} \alpha(y_s)$ iff $\mathcal{L}(A), \alpha \models x_s \sim_s y_s$. Hence $B \models \forall x_s, y_s{:}s.[Beh_s^\infty(x_s, y_s) \Leftrightarrow x_s \sim_s y_s]$. The fact that $B \models \forall x_s{:}s.[x_s \sim_s x_s \Leftrightarrow D_s(x)]$ follows directly from Definition 13(2.c).

$\Longleftarrow$: Assume $B \models \forall x_s, y_s{:}s.[Beh_s^\infty(x_s, y_s) \Leftrightarrow x_s \sim_s y_s]$ and $B \models \forall x_s{:}s.[x_s \sim_s x_s \Leftrightarrow D_s(x)]$. Let $A = B|_\Sigma$. We prove that $B = \mathcal{L}(A)$. For this it is enough to show that for all $s \in S$ and for all $a, b \in B_s$ $(= A_s = \mathcal{L}(A)_s)$ $a \sim_s^B b$ iff $a \sim_s^{\mathcal{L}(A)} b$ and $D_s^B(a)$ iff $D_s^{\mathcal{L}(A)}(a)$.
Let $\alpha : X \to B, A, \mathcal{L}(A)$ be a valuation such that $\alpha(x_s) = a$ and $\alpha(y_s) = b$. Then $a \sim_s^B b$ iff $B, \alpha \models x_s \sim_s y_s$ iff $B, \alpha \models Beh_s^\infty(x_s, y_s)$ iff $A, \alpha \models Beh_s^\infty(x_s, y_s)$ iff $a \approx_A b$ iff $a \sim_s^{\mathcal{L}(A)} b$. Moreover, $D_s^B(a)$ iff $B, \alpha \models D_s(x)$ iff $B, \alpha \models x_s \sim_s x_s$ iff $a \sim_s^B a$ iff $a \sim_s^{\mathcal{L}(A)} a$ iff $D_s^{\mathcal{L}(A)}(a)$. Hence $B = \mathcal{L}(A)$. □

From Proposition 25 we directly obtain that for any class C of Σ-algebras the class $\mathcal{L}(C)$ of lifted algebras can be characterized using an axiomatization of the behavioural equality.

Theorem 26. *Let BEH^∞ be the following formula:*
$\bigwedge_{s \in S} \forall x_s, y_s{:}s.[Beh_s^\infty(x_s, y_s) \Leftrightarrow x_s \sim_s y_s] \wedge \bigwedge_{s \in S} \forall x_s{:}s.[x_s \sim_s x_s \Leftrightarrow D_s(x_s)]$.
For any class C of Σ-algebras, let $Ext(C) \stackrel{\text{def}}{=} \{B \in Alg(\mathcal{L}(\Sigma)) \mid B|_\Sigma \in C\}$. Then $\mathcal{L}(C) = Ext(C) \cap Mod(\langle \mathcal{L}(\Sigma), BEH^\infty \rangle)$.
In particular, if $C = Mod(\langle \Sigma, Ax \rangle)$ then $Ext(C) = Mod(\langle \mathcal{L}(\Sigma), Ax \rangle)$, hence $\mathcal{L}(C) = Mod(\langle \mathcal{L}(\Sigma), Ax \cup BEH^\infty \rangle)$. □

5.4 Application to Various Classes of Algebras

We can apply the previous theorems to various classes of algebras of special interest.

Example 4. Let $SP = \langle \Sigma, Ax \rangle$ be a standard specification.

1. If $C = Mod(SP)$ then, by Theorem 26,
$\mathcal{L}(Mod(SP)) = Mod(\langle \mathcal{L}(\Sigma), Ax \cup BEH^{\infty} \rangle)$ and hence, by Theorem 15,
$Th_{\approx}(Mod(SP)) = Th^{\mathcal{L}}(Mod(\langle \mathcal{L}(\Sigma), Ax \cup BEH^{\infty} \rangle))$.
2. If $C = Mod($**abstract** SP **w.r.t.** $\equiv)$ then
$Th_{\approx}(Mod($**abstract** SP **w.r.t.** $\equiv)) =$ (cf. Example 2(2)) $Th_{\approx}(Mod(SP)) =$ (cf. Case 1) $Th^{\mathcal{L}}(Mod(\langle \mathcal{L}(\Sigma), Ax \cup BEH^{\infty} \rangle))$.
3. If $C = Mod($**behaviour** SP **w.r.t.** $\approx)$ then
$Th_{\approx}(Mod($**behaviour** SP **w.r.t.** $\approx)) =$ (cf. Example 2(3))
$Th(FA_{\approx}(Mod(SP))) =$ (cf. Theorem 20) $Th(Mod(\langle \Sigma, Ax \cup FA^{\infty} \rangle))$.
4. Assume that $Mod($**abstract** SP **w.r.t.** $\equiv) = Mod($**behaviour** SP **w.r.t.** $\approx)$ (see [2] for simple necessary and sufficient conditions). Then
$Th_{\approx}(Mod(SP)) = Th(Mod(\langle \Sigma, Ax \cup FA^{\infty} \rangle))$ (cf. Example 2(4) and Case 3).

6 The Behavioural Kernel

As we have seen in Example 4, the combination of the results in Section 4 and Section 5 allows us to characterize behavioural theories in terms of standard theories using an axiomatization of the behavioural equality. In particular, we have seen how we can axiomatize fully abstract algebras (through FA^{∞}) and lifted algebras (through BEH^{∞}). However, in general these axiomatizations are infinitary ones. To perform proofs is therefore still difficult. One possibility is to replace these infinitary formulas by infinitary proof rules (such as *context induction*) and to show that the resulting proof system is sound and complete (cf. [5]). Another possibility, studied in this section, is to find special (but general enough) cases where the infinitary axiomatization can be replaced by a finitary one.

In practice it may be simple to find an infinitary axiomatization of the behavioural equality (indeed in the observational framework this axiomatization is directly deduced from the definition of the observational equality). Unfortunately it is usually impossible to find a finitary axiomatization of $\approx$ which for any Σ-algebra A is equivalent to the infinitary one. But since we are always interested in the behavioural theory of some given class C of Σ-algebras we do not really need a finite axiomatization of the behavioural equality for any arbitrary Σ-algebra but rather for the algebras in the class C we are interested in. In several examples it turns out that if the class C satisfies some simple properties, then we can find a finitary axiomatization of the behavioural equality for the algebras belonging to C. This is formalized as follows:

Definition 27 (Conditional axiomatization of the behavioural equality). A conditional axiomatization of the behavioural equality $\approx$ is a pair $(BK, (Beh_s^F(x_s, y_s))_{s \in S})$, where BK is a finitary first-order Σ-formula and $(Beh_s^F(x_s, y_s))_{s \in S}$ is a family of finitary first-order Σ-formulas (where x_s and y_s are the only free variables, of sort s, of $Beh_s^F(x_s, y_s))$ such that:
For any Σ-algebra A, **if** $A \models BK$ **then** for any s in S and valuation $\alpha : X \to A$, $A, \alpha \models Beh_s^F(x_s, y_s)$ if and only if $\alpha(x_s) \approx_A \alpha(y_s)$.
BK is called the behavioural kernel of the conditional axiomatization.

From the definition above one may think that, given a class C of algebras, one has to look for an adequate conditional axiomatization $(BK, (Beh_s^F(x_s, y_s))_{s\in S})$ such that each A in C satisfies BK. In practice we work the other way round, i.e. we start from a given infinitary axiomatization $(Beh_s^\infty(x_s, y_s))_{s\in S}$ and then we will look for some syntactical transformations leading to a (finitary) conditional axiomatization $(BK, (Beh_s^F(x_s, y_s))_{s\in S})$ such that whenever a Σ-algebra A satisfies the condition BK the finitary axiomatization is equivalent to the infinitary one. More precisely:

Lemma 28. *$(BK, (Beh_s^F(x_s, y_s))_{s\in S})$ is a conditional axiomatization of the behavioural equality if and only if, for any Σ-algebra A:*
If $A \models BK$ **then** *for any s in S and valuation $\alpha : X \to A$,*
$A, \alpha \models Beh_s^F(x_s, y_s)$ *if and only if* $A, \alpha \models Beh_s^\infty(x_s, y_s)$. □

Example 5. In the case of the total observational equality $\approx_{Obs,S}$ a conditional axiomatization is given in [1] using as a condition the so-called *observability kernel*. For a concrete instantiation of this axiomatization see Section 7. To provide a conditional axiomatization for a partial observational equality $\approx_{Obs,In}$ is still a matter of further research.

It is obvious that all results obtained in the previous section carry over to conditional axiomatizations.

Theorem 29. *Let $(BK, (Beh_s^F(x_s, y_s))_{s\in S})$ be a conditional axiomatization of the behavioural equality. Let A be a Σ-algebra, B be a $\mathcal{L}(\Sigma)$-algebra and C be a class of Σ-algebras such that $A \models BK$, $B \models BK$ and $C \models BK$.*

1. *A is fully abstract if and only if, for all s in S,*
   $A \models \forall x_s, y_s{:}s.\, [Beh_s^F(x_s, y_s) \Leftrightarrow x_s = y_s]$.
2. *Let FA be the following formula:*
   $\bigwedge_{s\in S} \forall x_s, y_s{:}s.\, [Beh_s^F(x_s, y_s) \Leftrightarrow x_s = y_s]$.
   Then $FA_{\approx}(C) = C \cap Mod(\langle\Sigma, FA\rangle)$.
3. *In particular, if* $C = Mod(\langle\Sigma, Ax\rangle)$ *then* $FA_{\approx}(C) = Mod(\langle\Sigma, Ax \cup FA\rangle)$.
4. $B \in \mathcal{L}(Alg(\Sigma))$ *(i.e. B is a lifted algebra) if and only if, for all $s \in S$,*
   $B \models \forall x_s, y_s{:}s.\, [Beh_s^F(x_s, y_s) \Leftrightarrow x_s \sim_s y_s]$ *and*
   $B \models \forall x_s{:}s.\, [x_s \sim_s x_s \Leftrightarrow D_s(x)]$.
5. *Let BEH be the following formula:*
   $\bigwedge_{s\in S} \forall x_s, y_s{:}s.\, [Beh_s^F(x_s, y_s) \Leftrightarrow x_s \sim_s y_s] \wedge \bigwedge_{s\in S} \forall x_s{:}s.\, [x_s \sim_s x_s \Leftrightarrow D_s(x_s)]$.
   Then $\mathcal{L}(C) - Ext(C) \cap Mod(\langle\mathcal{L}(\Sigma), BEH\rangle)$
6. *In particular, if* $C = Mod(\langle\Sigma, Ax\rangle)$ *then* $\mathcal{L}(C) = Mod(\langle\mathcal{L}(\Sigma), Ax \cup BEH\rangle)$.

In the following examples we assume given a conditional axiomatization of the behavioural equality with behavioural kernel BK.

Example 6. Let $SP = \langle\Sigma, Ax\rangle$ be a standard specification such that $SP \models BK$. Then we obtain the same results as in Example 4 but with BEH (FA resp.) instead of BEH^∞ (FA^∞ resp.).

Example 7. Let SP be an ASL-like specification such that $SP \models BK$. It is easy to show that $Ext(Mod(SP)) \cap Mod(\langle \mathcal{L}(\Sigma), BEH \rangle) = Mod(SP + \langle \mathcal{L}(\Sigma), BEH \rangle)$. Then Theorem 29(5) shows that $\mathcal{L}(Mod(SP)) = Mod(SP + \langle \mathcal{L}(\Sigma), BEH \rangle)$ and hence, by Theorem 15, $Th_{\approx}(Mod(SP)) = Th^{\mathcal{L}}(Mod(SP + \langle \mathcal{L}(\Sigma), BEH \rangle))$. Hence $SP \models_{\approx} \phi$ if and only if $(SP + \langle \mathcal{L}(\Sigma), BEH \rangle) \models \mathcal{L}(\phi)$, where BEH is a first-order formula. As an important consequence of this result we obtain that whenever $SP \models BK$ we can use any proof system for ASL-like specifications (cf. e.g. [12]) for proving behavioural theorems over SP.

7 Example: A Behavioural Theory of Multisets

Let us consider the following specification of multisets:

```
spec : MULTISET
 use : ELEM, NAT, BOOL
 sort : Multiset
 operations :
  ∅ : → Multiset
  insert : Elem Multiset → Multiset
  _∈_ : Elem Multiset → Bool
  occurs : Elem Multiset → Nat
 axioms :
    ∀ M : Multiset, e,e' : Elem .
  e ∈ ∅ = false
  e ∈ insert(e,M) = true
  e ≠ e' ⇒ e ∈ insert(e',M) = e ∈ M
  occurs(e,∅) = 0
  occurs(e,insert(e,M)) = occurs(e,M) + 1
  e ≠ e' ⇒ occurs(e,insert(e',M)) = occurs(e,M)
  insert(e,insert(e',M)) = insert(e',insert(e,M))
end MULTISET.
```

The last axiom says that the order of inserting elements into a multiset is irrelevant. However, note that two multisets can be distinguished by the number of occurrences of elements. Hence MULTISET $\not\models$ insert(e,insert(e,M)) = insert(e,M). In fact adding this equation to the MULTISET specification would lead to an inconsistency (because, e.g., occurs(e,insert(e,insert(e,∅))) = 2 while occurs(e,insert(e,∅)) = 1).

We are now interested to study the behaviour of multisets if we forget the operation occurs. For instance, if one would like to use multisets for an implementation of sets then no occurs operation would be required. Formally, we consider the signature Σ-Set which consists of all sorts and operations of the MULTISET signature but the function symbol occurs and we consider the specification MULTISET$|_{\Sigma\text{-Set}}$ which is the restriction of MULTISET to the signature

Σ-`Set` and whose model class is defined (as usual) by:
$Mod(\texttt{MULTISET}|_{\Sigma\text{-Set}}) \stackrel{\text{def}}{=} \{A|_{\Sigma\text{-Set}} \mid A \in Mod(\texttt{MULTISET})\}$.

The behavioural theory of $\texttt{MULTISET}|_{\Sigma\text{-Set}}$ will now be studied w.r.t. the total observational equality $\approx_{Obs,S}$ induced on Σ-`Set`-algebras by $Obs = \{$ `Elem, Nat, Bool`$\}$ and $S = Obs \cup \{$`Multiset`$\}$. This observational equality is a family of total Σ-`Set`-congruences (cf. Example 1).

To apply Theorem 29, we must provide a conditional axiomatization of the observational equality. But before we note that we can apply some obvious simplifications. First, the observational equality we consider is a total one, hence the predicates D_s are not necessary. Moreover, on observable sorts the observational equality coincides with the set-theoretic equality, hence the predicates $\sim_s$ are not necessary either when s is an observable sort. This means that we can considerably simplify the lifting operator (for algebras and formulas), the axiomatization of the observational equality and the induced formula *BEH* by using just one predicate $\sim_{\texttt{Ms}}$ (for sake of clarity we abbreviate the sort `Multiset` by `Ms`). In the following we will use this simplification without further notice.

Now, to find a conditional axiomatization we apply a result of [1] which leads to:

- The behavioural kernel (called here observability kernel) is the following formula BK:
  $\forall$ `M,M':Ms`. [($\forall$ `e:Elem`. `e` $\in$ `M` $=$ `e` $\in$ `M'`) $\Rightarrow$
  ($\forall$ `e,e':Elem`. `e` $\in$ `insert(e',M)` $=$ `e` $\in$ `insert(e',M')`)].
- $Beh^{F}_{\texttt{Ms}}(\texttt{M},\texttt{M'}) \stackrel{\text{def}}{=}$ ($\forall$ `e:Elem`. `e` $\in$ `M` $=$ `e` $\in$ `M'`).

It is not difficult to prove that $\texttt{MULTISET}|_{\Sigma\text{-Set}} \models BK$. Therefore, following Example 7, we can conclude that, for any Σ-`Set` formula ϕ:
$\texttt{MULTISET}|_{\Sigma\text{-Set}} \models_{\approx_{Obs,S}} \phi$ iff
$(\texttt{MULTISET}|_{\Sigma\text{-Set}} + \langle \mathcal{L}(\Sigma\text{-}\texttt{Set}), BEH\text{-}\texttt{Set}\rangle) \models \mathcal{L}(\phi)$ iff
$\texttt{MULTISET}^* \models \mathcal{L}(\phi)$, where:

- *BEH*-`Set` $\stackrel{\text{def}}{=}$ $\forall$ `M,M':Ms`. [($\forall$ `e:Elem`. `e` $\in$ `M` $=$ `e` $\in$ `M'`) $\Leftrightarrow$ `M` $\sim_{\texttt{Ms}}$ `M'`].
- `MULTISET`* is the enrichment of the `MULTISET` specification by the predicate $\sim_{\texttt{Ms}}$ and the axiom *BEH*-`Set`.

For instance, we can prove that
$\texttt{MULTISET}|_{\Sigma\text{-Set}} \models_{\approx_{Obs,S}}$ `insert(e,insert(e,M)) = insert(e,M)`
by proving `MULTISET`* $\models$ `insert(e,insert(e,M))` $\sim_{\texttt{Ms}}$ `insert(e,M)`
which is not difficult to show according to the axioms of `MULTISET`*.

8 Conclusion

In this paper we have studied how to prove behavioural theorems over different kinds of specifications using standard proof techniques. Our approach is abstract because we have considered behavioural equalities which are determined by arbitrary partial congruence relations. Thus our results can be instantiated by different kinds of behavioural equalities.

Important examples are the total observational congruence considered e.g. in [9] and the partial observational congruences of e.g. [8, 2]. In [1] we have shown how to build a conditional axiomatization for total observational congruences. How to construct a conditional axiomatization for partial observational congruences has still to be investigated.

Acknowledgements: This work is partially supported by the French-German cooperation programme PROCOPE and by the ESPRIT Working Group COMPASS II.

References

1. M. Bidoit and R. Hennicker. Proving behavioural theorems with standard first-order logic. In *Proc. of ALP'94*, pages 41–58. Springer-Verlag L.N.C.S. 850, 1994.
2. M. Bidoit, R. Hennicker, and M. Wirsing. Behavioural and abstractor specifications. Technical Report LIENS–94–10, 1994. A short version appeared as: Characterizing behavioural semantics and abstractor semantics, in *Proc. of ESOP'94*, Springer-Verlag L.N.C.S. 788, pages 105–119, 1994.
3. H. Ehrig and B. Mahr. *Fundamentals of algebraic specification 1. Equations and initial semantics*, volume 6 of *EATCS Monographs on Theoretical Computer Science*. Springer-Verlag, 1985.
4. J. Goguen and J. Meseguer. Universal realization, persistent interconnection and implementation of abstract modules. In *Proc. of 9th ICALP*, pages 265–281. Springer-Verlag L.N.C.S. 140, 1982.
5. R. Hennicker and M. Wirsing. *Behavioural specifications*. Proof and Computation, International Summer School Marktoberdorf 1993. Springer-Verlag, 1995.
6. M. Hofmann and D. Sannella. On behavioural abstraction and behavioural satisfaction in higher-order logic. In *Proc. of TAPSOFT'95*. Springer-Verlag L.N.C.S., 1995. To appear.
7. R. Milner. Fully abstract models of typed λ-calculi. *Theoretical Computer Science*, 4:1–22, 1977.
8. P. Nivela and F. Orejas. Initial behaviour semantics for algebraic specification. In *Recent Trends in Data Type Specification*, pages 184–207. Springer-Verlag L.N.C.S. 332, 1988.
9. H. Reichel. Initial restrictions of behaviour. In *Proc. of IFIP Working Conference, The Role of Abstract Models in Information Processing*, 1985.
10. D. Sannella and A. Tarlecki. Toward formal development of programs from algebraic specification: implementation revisited. *Acta Informatica*, 25:233–281, 1988.
11. O. Schoett. Behavioural correctness of data representation. *Science of Computer Programming*, 14:43–57, 1990.
12. M. Wirsing. *Structured specifications: syntax, semantics and proof calculus*. Logic and Algebra of Specification, International Summer School Marktoberdorf 1991. Springer-Verlag, 1993.

Equations for Describing Dynamic Nets of Communicating Systems[1)]

Manfred Broy

Institut für Informatik, Technische Universität München
80290 München, Germany

Abstract. We give a notation and a logical calculus for the description and deductive manipulation of dynamic networks of communicating components. We represent such nets by hierarchical systems of recursive equations for streams. We give logical rules that describe the communication within a net and the dynamic creation of components, channels and rearrangement of the net structure. Such net transformations are based on a calculus of declarations of identifiers for data elements and especially for streams and equational logic. We demonstrate the modelling of interactive systems that correspond to dynamically changing net structures as obtained in systems with dynamic process creation (such as in object oriented approaches) within a framework of classical equational logic.

1. Introduction

It is one of the central issues of computing science to model distributed interactive information processing systems in terms of their static and dynamic properties. The description of systems by formal texts or graphics is static in nature, of course. The dynamic aspects of a system are also called its behaviour. For its description we need special techniques that allow to capture dynamic properties by static description techniques.

There are two options for describing the behaviour of networks of communicating agents:

- mathematical structures ("data structures") for the representation of the behaviour of systems (such as streams, traces, event structures, computation sequences) in terms of their histories,
- rules that reflect the changes (the computation steps) in a system (such as state machines, transition systems, operational semantics).

---

1) This work was partially sponsored by the Sonderforschungsbereich 342 "Werkzeuge und Methoden für die Nutzung paralleler Rechnerarchitekturen" and by the EC BRA Working Group COMPASS.

Typically some aspects of a system are of static nature (do not change over the life time of the system) while others are of dynamic nature.

So far we used the terms static and dynamic in a rather informal way. A formalization of these notions is hardly possible without choosing a formal model or a formal description technique for systems. But even then a characterisation of the notion of dynamic and static aspects is not obvious. Is a system invariant that asserts that the reachable system states always show a specific property considered as a static or a dynamic property?

Nevertheless, in spite of our difficulties to formally define the notions static and dynamic it is considered an important characteristic of a system which of its properties are of a static and which of a dynamic nature. Therefore it might be helpful to classify some basic system concepts. We may distinguish between external and internal properties of a system. External properties of a system are:

- the syntactic interface given by its communication channels to the outside world with their sorts.

Internal properties of a distributed interactive system are among others:

- the number of its subcomponents,
- the connections of its subcomponents (channels),
- the state shape (attributes and sorts).

In the following we give an approach based on logic for the description of interacting distributed systems of communicating components. We describe such systems by nets. We describe nets by hierarchical sets of equations which are logical formulas of a specific syntactic form.

The paper is structured as follows. In section 2 we introduce a very simple notation for data flow nets. Using this notation we describe nets by defining equations for streams. More precisely, we use a notation that allows to write hierarchical systems of equations for streams. With each such system of equations we associate a data flow graph that visualises the components and the communication structure of the described system model. This is worked out in section 3. In section 4 we give logical inference rules for the hierarchical systems of equations. These rules allow us to transform the syntactic structure of the equations without changing their logical meaning. The rules allow us in particular to change the structure of the network associated with the formulas. This allows to model the dynamic creation and deletion of channels and components. In section 5 we show how the rules can be generalised for changing also the syntactic interface of components to model the dynamic change of interfaces.

We treat mobile communication as a more elaborate example in section 6. In section 7 we show how to extend the approach to nondeterministic systems. In an appendix the most important notions for streams are given.

2. Representation of Nets

In this section we introduce a logical notation that allows us to describe data flow nets. We use specific logical formulas for the description of nets. A net description is given by a set of declarations. Declarations are equations for data elements, in our case equations for streams in a specific syntactic form. The equations contain free identifiers. The structure of the equations allows us to isolate a subset of these identifiers which we call *declared* or *output channels* while we call the others *input channels*.

The declarations on one hand define semantically a family of streams (one for each output channel) for any given assignment of streams to its input channels. The streams associated with the output channels denote the output histories of the described system.

The syntactic structure of the set of equations determines a data flow net which represents a communication structure of a system in terms of its components and communication channels.

2.1 Nets as Sets of Equations

We study equations formed by identifiers and terms built by the function symbols of a given signature Σ. A signature $\Sigma = (S, F)$ consists of a set S of sorts (including the specific sort Stream) and a set F of function symbols for which functionalities are specified.

Given a signature $\Sigma = (S, F)$ and a set X of S-sorted identifiers we can form terms over the function symbols in Σ and the identifiers in X. Every term has an individual sort.

Given terms t_1 and t_2 of the same sort we can form equations $t_1 = t_2$. An equation $x = t$ where x is an identifier and t is a term is called *explicit*.

Let $Z \subseteq X$ be a set of identifiers. For every identifier $z \in Z$ let t_z be a term of the same sort as z. Let

$$E = \{z = t_z : z \in Z\}$$

denote a set of explicit equations. The set E contains exactly one equation for every identifier in the set Z. Let the set

$$\text{Free}(E)$$

denote the set of identifiers obtained by the union of set Z and the set of free variables in the terms t_z. The set Z denotes the set of identifiers declared in E. Formally, we define this set of declared identifiers of the set of explicit equations E as follows:

$$\text{Dec}(E) = Z.$$

A set of explicit equations E where its set of declared identifiers Z are of sort Stream can be understood as the description of an interactive system. Each identifier $z \in Z$ stands for a communication channel, each equation stands for a computation node in the network. Every channel has exactly one source which is the equation in which it occurs on the left hand side and it has all nodes as targets which are the equations in which it occurs on the right hand side. This way a set of explicit equations can be understood as a network. Such a network can be represented more explicitly by a directed graph. The net can be understood as an interactive system that produces the streams assigned as the values of the declared identifiers as output. We formally associate a net to sets of equations in section 3.

However, often not all values of declared identifiers of a set of equations should be exported as output. Let $O \subseteq \text{Dec}(E)$ be the set of identifiers that we want to export as output. We denote a component with the channels in the set O of exported identifiers by the following expression:

O: E

O is called the set of *output channels* of the component O: E (where E is a set of explicit equations). The channels in the set

Dec(E)\O

are called *hidden*. The identifiers in the set Dec(E)\O are also called the *internal channels* of the net represented by E.

The set In(O: E) of *input channels* of the component described by O: E is defined by the following equations:

In(O: E) = Free(E) \ Dec(E)

Logically the effect of hiding channels can be expressed by existential quantification over the identifiers that are to be hidden. Let $\{x_1, ..., x_n\}$ be the set of hidden identifiers in the net O: E. Logically the term O: E is syntactic sugar. It represents the formula:

$$\exists\, x_1, ..., x_n: E$$

We define the set of externally visible declared identifiers for the term O: E as follows:

Dec(O: E) = O

If the set O, that is used to hide channels, is omitted, then this is equivalent to a component denotation where O = Dec(E).

2.2 Composition of Nets

We are not only interested in data flow nets with a flat communication structure as induced by the sets of explicit equations, but also in hierarchical nets that consist of components that again consist of networks of interacting components. Such *hierarchical nets* are obtained by putting nets together by parallel composition.

Let N_1 and N_2 be formulas denoting nets with disjoint sets of output identifiers for N_1 and N_2, in mathematical terms $Dec(N_1) \cap Dec(N_2) = \emptyset$. We write

$$N_1 \parallel N_2$$

for the parallel composition of the nets N_1 and N_2.

The parallel composition operator leads to a simple formal notation for describing systems by hierarchical nets. With the possibilities to denote nets by sets of equations as introduced so far we obtain the following syntax for expressions denoting nets:

‹Net expression› ::=	‹ID-Set›: ‹Net expression› |
	‹EQ-Set› |
	‹Net expression› || ‹Net expression›

‹EQ-Set› ::= { ‹explicit equation› [, ‹explicit equation›]* }

‹ID-Set› :: = { ‹id› [, ‹id›]* }

‹explicit equation› ::= ‹id› = ‹term›

We even allow the recursive declaration of such nets. For this purpose, we introduce identifiers for nets and write explicit (recursive) equations for nets. Given a net identifier f and a net expression N we write the equation

$$f = N_0$$

to associate a recursively declared net to the net identifier f. We, in addition, allow parameters in such equations for nets. For recursive nets we obtain the following syntax:

‹Net expression› ::= ‹ID-Set›: ‹Net expression› |

‹EQ-Set› |

‹Net expression› || ‹Net expression› |

‹Net-ID› {(‹term› {, ‹term› }*)}

where the nets associated to net identifiers are defined by net equations:

‹Net equation› ::= ‹Net-ID› { (‹id› {, ‹id› }*) } = ‹Net expression›

For a recursively defined net described by the net equation

$$f = N$$

we define the set of declared identifiers (along the lines of least fixpoint concepts) by the inclusion least set D for which the following formula holds:

$$\mathrm{Dec}(f) = D \Rightarrow D = \mathrm{Dec}(N)$$

The generalisation of this definition to parameterized net declarations is straightforward. Our notation for nets uses nothing than equational logic plus some syntactic sugar for hiding channels which logically can be replaced by existential quantification.

3. Nets as Hierarchical Data Flow Graphs

A net has a topological structure that can be represented by a directed graph where each arc has one component as its source and a set of components as its targets (a stream can be shared and consumed by several components). A special source of an arc (then we speak of an *input arc*) and a special target of an arc (then we speak of an *output arc*) is the environment of the net. Arcs are also called channels and logical represented by identifiers for data elements and in particular for streams.

With every net expression we associate a hierarchical data flow graph. This graph is defined as follows.

(1) With the net expression O: E formed of a set of equations E with output channels O we associate a node with the set O as output arcs and the set (O ∪ Free(E))\Dec(E) as input arcs.

(2) With every expression O: (C_1 ‖ ... ‖ C_n) we associate a node with a data flow graph that has n nodes and the set

$$\cup (\{Dec(C_i): 1 \leq i \leq n\} \cup \{In(C_i): 1 \leq i \leq n\})$$

as its arcs (its channels).

By this definition we associate a hierarchical data flow graph with every net expression. However, a net expression can not only be seen as a net but also be understood as a logical formula. Every logical inference rule that is applied to transform the formula leads to a new formula and this way also to a new data flow net. To explain how nets are associated with systems of explicit equations we consider a simple example.

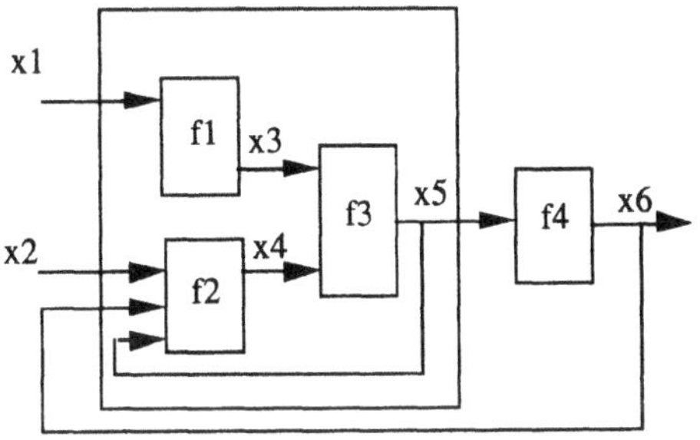

Fig. 1 A hierarchical data flow net

The hierarchical data flow net given in Fig. 1 corresponds to the following net expression:

$$\{x6\}: ((\{x5\}: \{x3 = f1(x1), x4 = f2(x2, x6, x5), x5 = f3(x3, x4)\}) \parallel \{x6 = f4(x5)\})$$

This example demonstrates how systems of explicit equations can be understood as a representation of a hierarchical data flow nets of interactive components.

4. A Calculus for Dynamic Nets

A set of explicit equations can be understood logically as a formula consisting the equations composed by logical conjunction. The notation

$$O: \{x_1 = t_1, ..., x_n = t_n\}$$

is understood as syntactic sugar for the logical formula

$$\exists z_1, ..., z_k: x_1 = t_1 \wedge ... \wedge x_n = t_n$$

where the set $\{z_1, ..., z_k\} = \{x_1, ..., x_n\} \setminus O$ denotes the set of internal channels.

Parallel composition of two networks corresponds to logical composition by logical conjunction of the respective equations.

Since our notation for nets can be understood as formulas in equational logic, we can use the calculus of equational logic to manipulate net expressions. We are in particular interested in logical inference rules that correspond to well-known transformations modelling the dynamic behaviour of communicating systems.

Given a net in terms of hierarchical sets of equations we apply substitutions to manipulate these equations. These substitutions can be used to mimic communication as well as the transformation of the net structure.

(1) *Rule of renaming of internal channels* (logical principle: α-renaming, renaming of bound identifiers): The following rule allows to rename an internal channel z to the identifier x provided x is a fresh identifier.

$$\frac{z \in \mathrm{Dec}(E)\backslash O \qquad\qquad x \notin O \cup \mathrm{free}(E)}{O\!: E = O\!: E[x/z]}$$

(2) *Rule of internal communication* (logical principle: redefining the stream x declared by the equation x = a & R to x = R and replacing simultaneously all occurrences of the identifier x on the right hand side of equations by the term a & x): The following rule allows to communicate the first message in a stream to all consumers of that stream.

$$\frac{(x = a \,\&\, R) \in E \qquad\qquad x \notin O \qquad\qquad x \notin \mathrm{Free}(a)}{O\!: E = O\!: (E\backslash\{x = a \,\&\, R\})[(a \,\&\, x)/x] \cup \{x = R[(a \,\&\, x)/x]\}}$$

Note that a may be an arbitrary expression as long as the identifier x does not occur free in a.

(3) *Scope sharing* (logical principle: fusion of existential quantifiers): The following rule allows to share two disjoint scopes. By this rule a hierarchical data flow graph can be turned into a flat one.

$$\frac{(O_1 \cup \mathrm{Dec}(E_1)) \cap (O_2 \cup \mathrm{Dec}(E_2)) = \varnothing}{(O_1\!: E_1) \parallel (O_2\!: E_2) = (O_1 \cup O_2)\!:\ (E_1 \cup E_2)}$$

(4) *Nesting scopes* (logical principle: elimination of existentially quantified variables that do not occur free): This is a very simple rule that allows to simplify nested hiding.

$$O_1\!: O_2\!: E = O_1 \cap O_2\!: E$$

(5) *Local channel elimination/introduction* (logical principle: fold/unfold, replacing equal by equal): The following rule allows to introduce a channel or to eliminate a channel by introducing/eliminating a declaration.

$$\frac{(z = t) \in E \qquad\qquad z \notin O \cup \mathrm{Free}(t)}{O\!: E = O\!: (E\backslash\{z = t\})\, [t/z]}$$

This rule can be applied to declarations for arbitrary elements including streams.

(6) *Recursion* (logical principle: unfold rule): Recursively defined networks can be unfolded according to the following rule.

$$\frac{f(x) = N}{O\!: (E \parallel f(t)) \;= O\!: (E \parallel N[t/x])}$$

These rules induce an equivalence relation on nets. These rules can be used to change the data flow graphs associated with a net.

(7) *Elimination of unused channels* (logical principle: elimination of conjunctions of existential quantified formulas that evaluate to true): The following rule allows to eliminate parts of a net (this may change the input alphabet).

$$\frac{\mathrm{Dec}(E_2) \cap (O \cup \mathrm{Free}(E_1)) = \varnothing}{O{:}\ E_1 \cup E_2 = O{:}\ E_1}$$

This rule allows in particular to eliminate net fragments that do not contribute to the output channels.

Our set of rules can be extended by rules that state least fixpoint principles for explicit equations (that can be viewed as declarations) and recursive equations for nets. We do not present such an extension here, since for our goals the simple set of rules given above is sufficient.

Especially interesting are the rules of communication and the rule of internal channel elimination and introduction. The rule of communication is demonstrated by the following simple example.

Example: Demonstration of the rule of communication. Let the function

succ*: Stream Nat → Stream Nat

be specified by the axiom;

succ*(n & s) = (n+1) & succ*(s)

The net expression

{y}: { x = 1 & succ*(x)} || { y = succ*(ft(x) & y) }

can be transformed by the rule of internal communication to the following logically equivalent expression:

{y}: { x = succ*(1 & x) } || { y = succ*(ft(1 & x) & y) }

which can be reduced by the axioms given for the function succ* and the function ft (see appendix) to the expression

{y}: { x = 2 & succ*(x) } || { y = 2 & succ*(y) } □

Let E1, E2 and E3 be sets of explicit equations. The application of the rule of internal channel elimination and introduction is illustrated by Fig. 2.

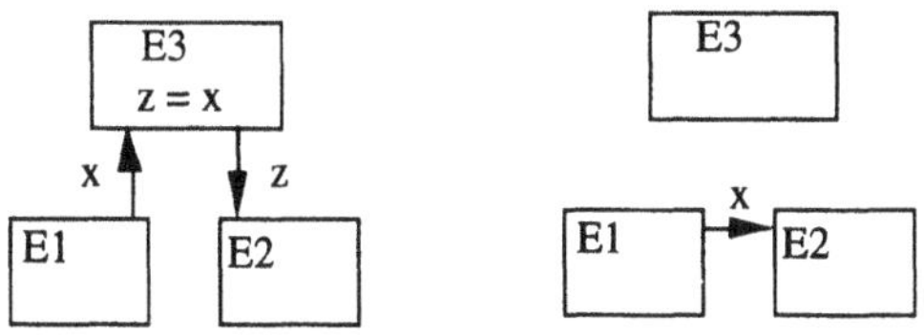

Fig. 2 Application of the rule of local channel elimination; we assume that z and x do not occur in E3

To illustrate our approach we use as a simple and well known example the sieve of Erathostenes.

Example: Sieve of Eratosthenes. Let the following function

$$\text{filter: Nat} \rightarrow (\text{Stream Nat} \rightarrow \text{Stream Nat})$$

be given. We specify it by the following axioms:

$$m \textbf{ mod } n = 0 \Rightarrow \text{filter}(n).(m \,\&\, s) = \text{filter}(n).s$$

$$m \textbf{ mod } n > 0 \Rightarrow \text{filter}(n).(m \,\&\, s) = m \,\&\, \text{filter}(n).s$$

We can use the function sieve to define a recursive net:

$$\text{sieve}(x, y) \equiv \{y\}\text{: } \{y = \text{ft}.x \,\&\, r,\ z = \text{filter}(\text{ft}.x).x\} \parallel \text{sieve}(z, r)$$

We obtain the sieve of Eratosthenes by the following net expression:

$$\{p\}\text{: } x = 2 \,\&\, \text{succ}^*(x)\} \parallel \text{sieve}(x, p)\,.$$

This net generates as output on its output channel p the stream of prime numbers in ascending order. This is not difficult to prove.

We demonstrate how we mimic the execution of the concurrent program associated with the net by our logical inference rules. We introduce an auxiliary identifier y for p such that p can accumulate the result stream:

$\{p\}$: $\{p = y, x = 2 \,\&\, \text{succ}^*(x)\} \parallel \text{sieve}(x, y)$

$\equiv$ {*unfolding sieve*}

$\{p\}$: $\{p = y, x = 2 \,\&\, \text{succ}^*(x)\} \parallel \{y\}$:$\{y = \text{ft}.x \,\&\, r, z = \text{filter}(\text{ft}.x).x\} \parallel \text{sieve}(z, r)$

$\equiv$ {*simplifying the result*}

$\{p\}$: $\{p = y, x = 2 \,\&\, \text{succ}^*(x), y = \text{ft}.x \,\&\, r, z = \text{filter}(\text{ft}.x).x\} \parallel \text{sieve}(z, r)$

$\equiv$ {*communication over x and simplifying the result*}

$\{p\}$: $\{p = y, x = \text{succ}^*(2 \,\&\, x), y = 2 \,\&\, r\ , z = \text{filter}(2).x\} \parallel \text{sieve}(z, r)$

$\equiv$ {*communication over y and simplifying the result*}

$\{p\}$: $\{p = 2 \,\&\, y, x = \text{succ}^*(2 \,\&\, x), y = r, z = \text{filter}(2).x\} \parallel \text{sieve}(z, r)$

$\equiv$ {*renaming r to y, eliminating z, unfolding succ**}

$\{p\}$: $\{p = 2 \,\&\, y, x = 3 \,\&\, \text{succ}^*(x)\} \parallel \text{sieve}(\text{filter}(2).x, y)$

$\equiv$ {*communication over x, unfolding filter, simplifying the result*}

$\{p\}$: $\{p = 2 \,\&\, y, x = \text{succ}^*(3 \,\&\, x)\} \parallel \text{sieve}(3 \,\&\, \text{filter}(2).x, y)$

$\equiv$ {*simplifying the result, unfolding sieve*}

$\{p\}$: $\{p = 2\&y, x = \text{succ}^*(3\&x), y = 3\&r, z = \text{filter}(3).(3\&\text{filter}(2).x)\} \parallel \text{sieve}(z, r)$

$\equiv$ {*unfolding filter, communication over y, eliminating r*}

$\{p\}$: $\{p = 2 \,\&\, 3 \,\&\, y, x = \text{succ}^*(3 \,\&\, x), z = \text{filter}(3).\text{filter}(2).x\} \parallel \text{sieve}(z, y)$

$\equiv$ ...

These rewriting technique can easily be used as the basis for an inductive proof that shows that the output stream p is the stream of all prime numbers. □

The example demonstrates that an appropriate application of the logical inference rules allows to mimic the computation of the net.

5. Components with Dynamic Interfaces

So far we have given logical inference rules that correspond to equivalence transformations of hierarchical systems of equations that change the internal structure of the net associated with the formula but do not change its syntactic interface. In this section we show how to deal with dynamic interfaces in our setting.

The syntactic interface of a component represented by a set of equations is determined by its set of free identifiers, their sorts, and the information whether an identifier represents an output channel (is declared) or an input channel (is free, but not declared). As well understood in logic, we cannot replace a logical formula by a logically equivalent one which has a different set of free identifiers[1]. Therefore we cannot change the syntactic interface of nets by logical rules. However, if we have additional logical propositions we can change a formula. Consider the formula

(*) $x = a + b$

If we know in addition to (*) that

(**) $y = x - b + c$

holds, then under this assumption the formula (*) is equivalent to the formula

$$x = a + b \wedge y = a + c$$

This formula contains the free identifiers y and c not contained in (*). We can obviously replace a formula by a logical equivalent one, containing a different set of free identifiers if we have additional propositions as assumptions. This idea will be used in the following to manipulate components with dynamic changing interfaces in given contexts.

5.1 Streams of Streams

The access interface of a system is determined by its set of input and output channels. For describing systems that are dynamically changing their access interface, we have to be able to change these sets in communication steps.

To increase the number of input channels of a component is not a problem, if we allow to transmit input channels (represented by identifiers) as values. Assume x has the sort Stream Stream M and y has the sort Stream M. Then we may allow defining equations for the stream ft.x of the form

---

[1] We may at most eliminate or introduce identifiers for which the formula does not contain any specific logical proposition. For instance, we can always add or eliminate tautologies such as $x = x$ as long as we assume that all domains are nonempty.

ft.x = ...

When allowing these equations we can no longer guarantee the consistency of the logical formulas with such simple syntactic means as used so far. We may, however, use more sophisticated syntactical conditions to ensure consistency. We do not go into the discussion of such conditions, but rather give rules for dealing with systems of equation in the context of equations.

(1) *Rule of input channel renaming* (logical principle: equal for equal): If y is an input channel and from the context it is known that y = x holds then we can use x instead of y wherever we want.

$$\frac{y = x \qquad y \notin O \qquad x \notin \text{Free}(E)}{O\!: E = O\!: E[x/y]}$$

(2) *Rule of output channel renaming* (logical principle: equal for equal): An output channel y can be replaced by the channel x if x = y is ensured in the context.

$$\frac{x = y \qquad y \in O \qquad x \notin \text{Free}(E)}{O\!: E = (O\backslash\{y\}) \cup \{x\}\!: E[x/y]}$$

(3) *Rule of input channel introduction by communication* (logical principle: equal for equal): If x is a stream of streams and y is its first element then we can replace y by ft.x, if y is not an output channel.

$$\frac{x = y \,\&\, R \qquad y \notin O \qquad x \notin \text{Free}(E)}{O\!: E[\text{ft}.x/y] = O\!: E}$$

(4) *Rule of output channel introduction by communication* (logical principle: equal for equal): If y is the first element of stream x which is a stream of streams and x is an output channel then y can be added to the output channels.

$$\frac{y = \text{ft}.x \qquad x \in O \qquad y \notin \text{Dec}(E)\backslash O}{O\!: E \cup \{\text{ft}.x = R'\} = O \cup \{y\}\!: E \cup \{y = R'\}}$$

These rules allow to change the syntactic interface of components under certain context constraints that are again expressed by logical conditions.

5.2 Channels as Data Elements

In a more radical approach to systems with the behaviour of dynamic networks we may introduce a specific sort of channel names. Then channel names are data elements like other data, too. This has the disadvantage, however, that all the rules from equational logic, that are immediately available in the case of equational presentations of systems, now have to be redefined.

Similar to the π-calculus of Robin Milner (see [Milner et al. 92]) we now consider channels no longer as identifiers in logic but as elements of a set of channel names that can be both used as values and as identifiers. These elements then can be in particular communicated like values. For instance we write

$$\exists\, x\!: \{x = c \,\&\, D,\ \text{ft}.x = D'\}$$

The rule of communication allows us to change this formula to

$$\exists\, x: \{x = D[c \,\&\, x / x],\ c = D'[c \,\&\, x / x]\}$$

We may even recursively introduce an unbounded number of channels

$$\exists\, x: \{x = c \,\&\, D\} \parallel X \qquad \textbf{where} \qquad X = \{ft.x = D',\ X[rt.x/x]\}$$

A further possibility to model changing syntactic interfaces is to allow equations (nets) be transferred as messages. We may write then

$$\exists\, x: \{x = \{y = D'\} \,\&\, D,\ ft.x\}$$

and obtain by the rule of communication

$$\exists\, x: \{x = D,\ y = D'\}$$

However, we pay a high prize by introducing an explicit sort of channel names, since now all the logical rules of channels which above are introduced just as special cases of inference rules of equational logic have to be stated axiomatically. This would lead to a calculus with some similarity to π–calculus.

6. Example: Mobile Communication

In this section we give an extended example. We treat a system that consists of a number of mobile communication units (mcu), a number of transmission stations (ts), and of a transmission centre (tc). The system can be described by the net expression

$$tc \parallel ts_1 \parallel \ldots \parallel ts_n \parallel mcu_1 \parallel \ldots \parallel mcu_m$$

We describe a mobile communication unit by the function car:

$$car(x, y) = \{y\}: y = f^*(x)$$

where the function f* mimics the response of cars to input. For simplicity let us assume the following equation for f* (let f be some given function):

$$f^*(d \,\&\, x) = f(d) \,\&\, f^*(x)$$

Fig. 3 shows the structure of our network for mobile communication.

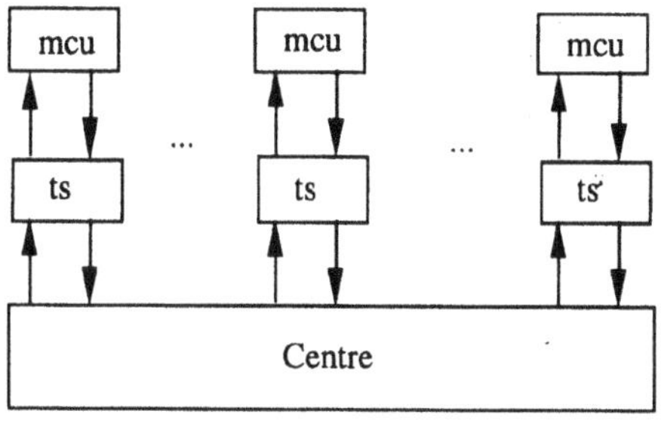

Fig. 3 Mobile Communication

We describe the transmission stations with the help of the function station. In the net expression

$$\text{station}(r, x, y, z)$$

the channels r and x serve as input channels and y and z serve as output channels. The channel r is supposed to carry the input from the transmission centre.

The input channel r of a station can carry messages of the following forms

connect(x, y)

disconnect

message(d)

The message connect(x, y) advises the station to work from now on with a car with input stream y and output stream x. In other words y is declared by the station and x is used. The message disconnect advises the station to drop its current connection and to send its current connection channels back to the centre via channel z using the message connect(x, y). The data message (d) is transmitted to the car it is connected to.

The defining equations for the stations are given in the following:

Establish car connection:

$$\text{station}(\text{connect}(x, y) \,\&\, r, x', y', z) \equiv \text{station}(r, x, y, z)$$

Disconnect car connection (x' and y' are internal channels):

$$\text{station}(\text{disconnect} \,\&\, r, x, y, z) \equiv$$

$$\{y, z\}\text{: } \{z = \text{connect}(x, y) \,\&\, z'\} \parallel \text{station}(r, x', y', z)$$

Transmit message to car and from car

$$\text{station}(\text{message}(d) \,\&\, r, x, y, z) \equiv$$

$$\{y, z\}\text{: } \{y = d \,\&\, y', z = \text{ft}.x \,\&\, z'\} \parallel \text{station}(r, \text{rt}.x, y', z')$$

We define

$$\text{mcu}_i = \text{car}(x_i, y_i)$$

$$\text{ts}_i = \text{station}(x_i, z_i, r_i, y_i)$$

Now the structure of the network can be changed individually according the messages send by the centre. We just show the interaction of the station with a mobile communication unit with the help of the following subsystem:

$$\{\text{out}\}\text{: } \{ r = \text{connect}(x, y) \,\&\, \text{message}(d) \,\&\, \text{disconnect} \,\&\, r, \text{out} = z\} \parallel \text{station}(r, x', y', z) \parallel \text{car}(y, x)$$

$\equiv$ *{communication on r}*

$$\{\text{out}\}\text{: } \{ r = \text{message}(d) \,\&\, \text{disconnect} \,\&\, r', \text{out} = z\} \parallel \text{station}(\text{connect}(x, y) \,\&\, r, x', y', z) \parallel \text{car}(y, x)$$

$\equiv$ *{unfold station}*

$$\{\text{out}\}\text{: } \{ r = \text{message}(d) \,\&\, \text{disconnect} \,\&\, r', \text{out} = z\} \parallel \text{station}(r, x, y, z) \parallel \text{car}(y, x)$$

≡ {communication on r}

{out}: { r = disconnect & r', out = z} || station(message(d) & r, x, y, z) || car(y, x)

≡ {unfold station}

{out}: { r = disconnect & r', out = z} ||
{y, z}: {y = d & y', z = ft.x & z'} || station(r, rt.x, y', z') || car(y, x)

≡ {simplification, communication on y, elimination of x'}

{out}: { r = disconnect & r', out = z, z = ft.x & z'} ||
station(r, rt.x, y, z) || car(d & y, x)

≡ {unfold car, simplification}

{out}: { r = disconnect & r', out = z, z = ft.x & z', x = f*(d & y)} ||
station(r, rt.x, y, z)

≡ {unfold f*, communication over x, simplification}

{out}: { r = disconnect & r', out = z, z = f(d) & z', x = f*(y)} || station(r, x, y, z)

≡ {communication over z, elimination of z', simplification}

{out}: { r = disconnect & r', out = f(d) & z, y = f*(x)} || station(r, x, y, z)

≡ {communication over r}

{out}: { r = r', out = f(d) & z, y = f*(x)} || station(disconnect & r, x, y, z)

≡ {unfold station}

{out}: { r = r', out = f(d) & z, y = f*(x)} ||
{y, z}: {z = connect(x, y) & z'} || station(x, z', r, y')

≡ {communication over z, simplification}

{out}: { r = r', out = f(d) & connect(x, y) & z', y = f*(x)} || station(x, z', r, y')

≡ ...

This example shows how the creation of new channels is treated in our calculus of declarations. All we have used here are rules of equational logic.

7. Extension to Nondeterministic Systems

Following [Broy 87a] we understand and specify nondeterministic components by sets of deterministic components. A deterministic component is represented by an equation

$$x = f(x_1, ..., x_n)$$

A nondeterministic component is represented by the following logical formula

$$\exists f: x = f(x_1, ..., x_n) \wedge Q.f$$

along the lines of [Broy 87a] where the predicate Q specifies a set of functions. The calculus introduced so far carries over to nondeterministic components in a straightforward way since logically all the rules for manipulating equations can also be applied if the respective equation is inside of existentially quantified formulas of the form given above.

Logically a nondeterministic component does not uniquely define its output streams. Therefore some of the steps of inference are not equivalence transformations but implication steps. Given a "nondeterministic system" represented by

$$x = E_1 \vee x = E_2$$

in a decision step we may replace it by

$$x = E_1$$

or by

$$x = E_2$$

as well. This shows that also from an operational point of view nondeterminism is adequately modelled that way.

8. Conclusion

It is interesting to observe that the logical notions of scope and equations can be made the basis for the dynamics of communicating systems. This is not surprising, since scoping and name spaces are essential for mobile communication and also an integral part of predicate logic.

Logic is very flexible. If the equation

$$x = t$$

holds in a particular scope, we can use x instead of t and vice versa everywhere in this scope without changing the meaning of the terms. This holds of course also, when the term t contains free identifiers as long as there are no scope conflicts.

Of course using logical rules in a flexible way does not lead to an operational semantics. Only if we add a strategy that expresses which rule is to be used in which situation a concrete operational semantics is obtained. A concrete operational semantics is given by the concurrent constraint logic approaches (cf. [Saraswat 89] and [Smolka 94]).

The relationship between logical inference rules and execution steps for interactive systems as well as the relation between logical expressions and networks gives an interesting way to model dynamic networks of communicating systems.

Software engineers have a very specific intuitive understanding of the dynamic behaviour of interactive systems when they talk about the creation and deletion of components. Obviously, they think about dynamically changing networks and with respect to components with dynamic changing interfaces. They like to think about situations, where suddenly there is a new channel created that they can use to communicate and also that a channel is deleted. This fits very well with the operational understanding of systems, where the system changes step by step its state. And the state is determined by the network of currently active and existing components.

It is quite clear that there are many ways to model such systems mathematically. For instance, such systems can of course be simply modelled by state machines where there is one state component which denotes the set of existing components.

What is the best way to represent the behaviour of dynamically changing systems is an open question. It is completely unclear whether it is better to find just very straightforward mathematical representations in terms of well-known structures where the dynamic behaviour is represented quite implicitly or if it is much better to have special calculi like Milner's π–calculus to represent the behaviour of such systems.

Acknowledgement

I thank Radu Grosu, Ketil Stølen, Klaus Dendorfer and Cliff Jones for stimulating discussions.

Appendix: Streams

Streams are used to denote histories of communications on channels. Given a set M of messages a stream over M is a finite or infinite sequence of elements from M. Let

$$(M \cup \{\perp\}, \sqsubseteq)$$

be a partially ordered set with least element $\perp$ which is complete (every directed set has a least upper bound).

By M^* we denote the finite sequences over M. M^* includes the empty sequence which is denoted by $\langle\rangle$.

By M^∞ we denote the infinite sequences over the set M. M^∞ can be understood to be represented by the total mappings from the natural numbers $\mathbb{N}$ into M. We denote the set of streams over the set M by M^ω. Formally we have

$$M^\omega =_{def} M^* \cup M^\infty.$$

We introduce a number of functions on streams that are useful in system descriptions.

A classical operation on streams is the *concatenation* of two streams which we denote by ˆ. The concatenation is a function that takes two streams (say s and t) and produces a stream as result starting with s and continuing with t. Formally the concatenation has the following functionality:

$$.\hat{}.: M^\omega \times M^\omega \to M^\omega$$

If s is infinite, then concatenating s with t yields s again:

$$s \in M^\infty \Rightarrow s\hat{}t = s$$

Concatenation is associative and has the empty stream $\langle\rangle$ as its neutral element:

$$r\hat{}(s\hat{}t) = (r\hat{}s)\hat{}t, \qquad \langle\rangle\hat{}s = s = s\hat{}\langle\rangle,$$

For $m \in M$ we denote by $\langle m\rangle$ the one element stream. We write m & s for $\langle m\rangle\hat{}s$.

On the set M^ω of streams we define a *prefix ordering* $\sqsubseteq$. We write $s \sqsubseteq t$ for streams s and t to express that s is a *prefix* of t. Formally we have for streams s and t:

$$s \sqsubseteq t \text{ iff } \exists\, r, s' \in M^\omega: s'\hat{}r = t \land \forall\, i \in \{1,..., \#s\}: s.i \sqsubseteq s'.i.$$

The prefix ordering defines a partial ordering on the set M^ω of streams. If $s \sqsubseteq t$, then we also say that s is an *approximation* of t. The set of streams ordered by $\sqsubseteq$ is complete in the sense that every directed set $S \subseteq M^\omega$ of streams has a *least upper bound* denoted by lub S. A nonempty subset S of a partially ordered set is called *directed*, if

$$\forall x, y \in S: \exists z \in S: x \sqsubseteq z \wedge y \sqsubseteq z .$$

By least upper bounds of directed sets of finite streams we may describe infinite streams. Infinite streams are also of interest as (and can also be described by) fixpoints of prefix monotonic functions. The streams associated with feedback loops in interactive systems correspond to such fixpoints.

A *stream processing function* is a function

$$f: M^\omega \to M^\omega$$

that is *prefix monotonic* and *continuous*. The function f is called prefix *monotonic*, if for all streams s and t we have

$$s \sqsubseteq t \Rightarrow f.s \sqsubseteq f.t .$$

For better readability we often write for the function application f.x instead of f(x). The function f is called *continuous*, if for all directed sets $S \subseteq M^\omega$ of streams we have

$$\text{lub } \{f.s: s \in S\} = f.\text{lub } S .$$

If a function is continuous, then its results for infinite input can be already predicted from its results on all finite approximations of the input.

By $\perp$ we denote the pseudo element which represents the result of diverging computations. We write $M^\perp$ for $M \cup \{\perp\}$. Here we assume that $\perp$ is not an element of M. On $M^\perp$ we define also a simple partial ordering by:

$$x \sqsubseteq y \quad \text{iff } x = y \vee x = \perp$$

We use the following functions on streams

$$\text{ft}: M^\omega \to M^\perp,$$

$$\text{rt}: M^\omega \to M^\omega.$$

They are defined as follows: the function ft selects the first element of a stream, if the stream is not empty. The function rt deletes the first element of a stream, if the stream is not empty. The properties of the functions can be expressed by the following equations that can also be used as defining axioms for them (let $m \in M$, $s \in M^\omega$):

$$\text{ft}.\langle\rangle = \perp, \qquad \text{rt}.\langle\rangle = \langle\rangle, \qquad \text{ft}(m\hat{\ }s) = m, \qquad \text{rt}(m\hat{\ }s) = s.$$

The concept of sequences is essential for modelling the stepwise proceeding of computations. When modelling a system component by a state machine or a transition system we obtain finite or infinite computations in the form of sequences of states.

References

[Broy 85]
M. Broy: Specification and top down design of distributed systems. In: H. Ehrig et al. (eds.): Formal Methods and Software Development. Lecture Notes in Computer Science 186, Springer 1985, 4-28, Revised version in JCSS 34:2/3, 1987, 236-264

[Broy 86]
M. Broy: A theory for nondeterminism, parallelism, communication and concurrency. Habilitation, Fakultät für Mathematik und Informatik der Technischen Universität München, 1982, Revised version in: Theoretical Computer Science 45 (1986) 1-61

[Broy 87a]
M. Broy: Semantics of finite or infinite networks of communicating agents. Distributed Computing 2 (1987), 13-31

[Broy 87b]
M. Broy: Predicative specification for functional programs describing communicating networks. Information Processing Letters 25 (1987) 93-101

[Dybier, Sander 88]
P. Dybier, H. Sander: A functional programming approach to the specification and verification of concurrent systems. Chalmers University of Technology and University of Göteborg, Department of Computer Sciences 1988

[Grosu 94]
R. Grosu: A formal foundation for concurrent object oriented programming. Ph. D. Thesis, Technische Universität München, Fakultät für Informatik, submitted 1994

[Kahn, MacQueen 77]
G. Kahn, D. MacQueen: Coroutines and networks of processes, Proc. IFIP World Congress 1977, 993-998

[Milner et al. 92]
R. Milner, J. Parrow, D. Walker: A calculus of mobile processes. Part i + ii, Information and Computation, 100:1 (1992) 1-40, 41-77

[Saraswat 89]
V.A. Saraswat: Concurrent constraint programming languages. Ph. D. Thesis, School of Computer Science, Carnegie Mellon University, Pittsburgh, CA, 1989

[Smolka 94]
G. Smolka: A calculus for higher order concurrent constraint programming with deep guards. DFKI Research Report RR-94-03

A Lazy Approach to Partial Algebras *

M. Cerioli

DISI–Dipartimento di Informatica e Scienze dell'Informazione, Università di Genova
Viale Benedetto XV, 3 - 16132 Genova - Italy
e-mail: cerioli@disi.unige.it

Abstract. Starting from the analysis of which features are required by an algebraic formalism to describe at least the more common data types used in imperative and functional programming, a framework is proposed, collecting many techniques and ideas from the algebraic community, with the capability for an immediate representation of partiality and error-recovery. This formalism, of so called lazy algebras, inherits mainly from two parents: partial and label algebras; from the former especially on a technical side and from the later from a philosophical point of view. But, as all children, it has its own individuality and in particular an original mechanism to represent lazy evaluation in an algebraic framework has been introduced.

Introduction

This paper aims at the definition of an algebraic formalism providing tools for the immediate representation of the most common data types used in imperative and functional programming. In order to decide which features are needed by such an algebraic framework, the starting point is the analysis of the steps a user of a specification language goes through, toward the formal description of the required data type. First of all names for the types and operations are decided; moreover for every operation the number (and usually the type) of the arguments are fixed. Then among the strings on that alphabet a subset is chosen, of the "well-formed" terms, that are usually (a subset of) the many-sorted terms on those functions; this corresponds to the static check and should get rid of the real junk, i.e. of all those sequences of symbols that are meaningless and whose nonsense can be decided. Notice that if the data type under construction has only total functions, then static check suffices to eliminate all meaningless terms. Otherwise among the well-formed terms there are still strings that are not intended to represent correct values, but that could be needed as error messages or in order to apply some kind of error-recovery strategy. Thus the following design step is the division of well-formed terms into "ok" and "possibly errors" and then equivalences onto the two classes are defined to describe the semantics. Therefore a "user-friendly" formalism should provide tools to concisely describe well-formed terms, i.e. some kind of signature, to partition terms into "ok" and errors, to give semantics to the "ok" ones and to deal with errors in a twofold way: on one side error terms should disappear, in the sense that they have

* This work has been partially supported by ESPRIT BRA WG n. 6112 COMPASS, HCM-Medicis and MURST 40% Modelli della computazione e dei linguaggi di programmazione

no place in the carriers of the models, but on the other side they are needed for error-recovery.

Trying to collect bits of known formalisms to build a powerful framework, it is easy to find tools for the syntactical analysis; indeed it is immediate to check that standard many-sorted features are easy to use and allow to eliminate most of the junk. It is worth noting that pure order-sorted approaches are, from this point of view too restrictive, as the "errors" are (or should be in principle) avoided, narrowing the domain of "partial" functions, and hence errors are prevented at a syntactical level. On the other side using one-sorted formalisms is too weak, as even trivially uncorrect strings are considered correct terms and must be taken in account; for example search space for inference systems dramatically increases.

Using partiality it is also easy to manage error terms that do not appear in the carriers, but this seems contradictory w.r.t. error recovery; indeed if an error does not exist how can it be recovered? The innovative idea of the framework proposed here is exactly a way to conciliate the partiality of function interpretation in the models with an error-recovery purely syntactic, with the flavor of lazy valuation.

The main results of the paper, besides the introduction of the *lazy partial algebra* framework (Section 1), are the existence of initial and free objects (Section 2) and an alternative characterizations of such objects through a sound and complete inference system (Section 4). In Section 3 a few examples, showing the great usage facility of the proposed formalisms, are given. Proofs are omitted, but a large use of lemmas should suggest the structure of the more relevant theorems.

1 The Lazy framework

1.1 Motivations

Analyzing the most common data types present in computer science, (at least) three features appear to be mandatory for a specification language and hence for an algebraic formalism designed to give semantics to the language.

Typing. After a long time of many-sorted frameworks, recently homogeneous approaches have been presented (see e.g. [13, 11, 12]), where the freedom given by the lack of typing is used to enlarge the expressive power of the language. In most of these approaches sorts and elements float together in the carrier of any model, so that, for example, functions apply to sorts too and hence dependent types are available and operations between sorts, like intersection or sum, can be defined; moreover an operation on elements can result in a sort, or better a subsort, so that non-determinism and (if the sort is empty) non-termination are immediately at hand. But this power has a price: first of all static check, i.e. well formedness of terms, is limited to the number of arguments and this means a smaller help for the language users in "debugging" their specifications; moreover the carrier of any model has to be very large. This can be thought irrelevant, as most users could be interested only on the logical side, especially if a tool for prototyping would be available; but the proliferation of elements, all denoted by terms, makes the search space unmanageable and hence prevents a concrete use of such tools. Therefore we prefer to have a typing system, forfeiting the extra-power.

On the other side a too strict typing mechanism can be as dangerous as its absence. Indeed think for example of a pure order sorted approach to the specification of natural numbers with a predecessor operation; as the predecessor of 0 is undefined, a subsort of non-zero natural numbers is introduced, built by the successor applied to any natural argument. Then terms with two predecessors in a row are not well-formed, as the result of a predecessor is a (possibly zero) natural number and hence has not the correct type for another predecessor to be applied. Moreover if possibly incorrect terms are prevented, then error-recovery is impossible, as there is nothing to be recovered. Note that, using the retract mechanism (see [10]), an implicit and unavoidable error-recovery strategy is imposed and the only improvement w.r.t. standard many-sorted approaches is the uniformity of the error-detection, as a term represent an error iff it cannot be reduced to a form without retracts.

On the base of this analysis (for a longer and deeper discussion on the use of sorts to classify elements and restrain errors see [14]), in the sequel a standard many-sorted typing is adopted.

Partiality. As the data types used in programming languages are inherently partial, partiality must be taken in account. Note that the partiality introduced to allow a top-down development, where reasonably many details are not decided at the top level, but left free for the designer of lower modules to fix, is a feature of the language that does not need, in principle, to have a corresponding feature at the semantic level; indeed it is a tool for helping the design of the project, whose use disappears at the last stage, where the system is built bottom-up and every detail has been fixed. But the partiality due to the need for representing a semicomputable (and non computable) function persists to the last moment and cannot be eliminated, although in many cases (but not in all interesting ones) can be dealt with in an indirect way. As the theory of partial algebras is nowadays well established ([16, 7, 19]), using an indirect representation of partiality seems unreasonable.

Although, having partial functions, semidecidable boolean relations can be easily simulated (at least if their falsity is never tested), by representing every relation as a "boolean" function, with a special boolean sort, (see [8] and [9] for a similar approach in a total framework), predicates have been considered necessary, because of their recently increasing use in specifications, for example to represent transitions in concurrency, or the typing relation. In particular the use of predicates allows specifications of many simple data types, where boolean functions are the unique partial functions, whose truth can be decided, while the falsity cannot, to be described as total specification, avoiding the proliferation of errors.

Non strictness. Roughly speaking there are two kinds of non-strict functions widely used in programming languages: the "don't care", like the famous **if then else** or boolean **and**, or with lazy valuation, and the "error handling". "Don't care" is characterized by resulting in the same value whatever it is substituted for the missing value, while "error handling" corresponds to recover a value, after an erroneous computation, mainly by means of projections, as for example by instantiating the equations $x * 0 = 0$ or $pop(push(x, s)) = s$ for "erroneous" values of x.

Analyzing the examples of both kind of non-strictness it is easy to note that a non-strict function is needed only to represent some kind of *lazy valuation* (call by need, call by name ...) or simplification and hence its standard representation using totality plus a labeling of values to describe that some states (or computations or values) are erroneous is unsatisfactory, because it makes the models full of junk and does not meet the intuition. If just the "don't care" kind of non-strictness is needed, then there are approaches that avoid to introduce values to represent the missing arguments of the non-strict function (see e.g. [1]), although the implicit monotonicity condition raises some troubles. But if "error recovery" is needed, then apparently there is no way to avoid the "erroneous" values; indeed, for example, if positive integers are considered, then to have that the evaluation of $t = pred(zero) * zero$ is 0, the evaluation of $pred(zero)$ should be a value a such that the interpretation of the $*$ operation on a and 0 yields 0, as the interpretation in a model A of t is $pred^A(zero^A) *^A zero^A$, by compositionality.

But this approach does not meet the intuition that a simplification of t to $zero$, by the rule $x * zero = zero$, as been performed *on terms*, so that the evaluation of t reduces to the evaluation of $zero$. To stay close to this notion, algebras are endowed with a congruence on terms, representing the preprocessing (or compilation, or simplification) that transforms a term into a simpler one, so that the evaluation of a term becomes the easier evaluation of its simplification.

1.2 Lazy Signatures and Structures

Lazy signatures are usual many sorted signatures with predicates.

Definition 1. A *signature* Σ consists of a set S of *sorts*, an $S^* \times S$-indexed family F of *operation symbols* and an S^+-indexed family P of *predicate symbols*. If $f \in F_{(s_1 \ldots s_n, s)}$, then we write $f: s_1 \times \ldots \times s_n \to s$ and say that $s_1 \times \ldots \times s_n$ is the *arity* of f and s is the *type* of f; analogously if $p \in P_{s_1 \ldots s_n}$, then we write $p: s_1 \times \ldots \times s_n$ and say that $s_1 \times \ldots \times s_n$ is the *arity* of p.

Given a signature $\Sigma = (S, F, P)$, a family X of variables for Σ in an S-sorted family of disjoint sets X_s of new symbols, i.e. s.t. $X_s \cap (\cup_{w \in S^*, s' \in S} F_{w,s'} \cup \cup_{w \in S^+} P_w) = \emptyset$ for all $s \in S$. □

As in the sequel we will use the definition of congruence both in the total and in the partial frameworks, let us recall these notions in order to fix the notation.

Definition 2. Given a signature $\Sigma = (S, F, P)$ and a total algebra A over (S, F), a *partial congruence* $\equiv^A$ on A is an S-indexed family of symmetric and transitive relations $\{\equiv^A_s \subseteq s^A \times s^A\}_{s \in S}$ s.t. if $f \in F_{(s_1 \ldots s_n, s)}$ and $t_i \equiv^A_{s_i} u_i$ for $i = 1, \ldots, n$, then either $f(t_1, \ldots, t_n) \equiv^A_s f(u_1, \ldots, u_n)$ or both $f(t_1, \ldots, t_n)$ and $f(u_1, \ldots, u_n)$ do not belong to the *domain* of $\equiv^A$, where, given a partial congruence $\equiv^A$, its *domain*, denoted by $Dom(\equiv^A)$, consists of all elements τ s.t. $\tau \equiv^A \tau$.

Moreover a partial congruence $\equiv^A$ on A is called a *total congruence* iff its domain is A, i.e. if every $\equiv^A_s$ is reflexive. □

Let us introduce the model theoretic ingredients of the lazy framework.

Definition 3. Given a signature $\Sigma = (S, F, P)$, a *lazy algebra* $\mathcal{A}$ on Σ consists of:

- a partial algebra A on the signature Σ, i.e. $A = (\{s^A\}_{s\in S}, \{f^A\}_{f\in F})$, where s^A is a set for every $s \in S$, said the *carrier of sort* s in A and $f^A: {s_1}^A \times \ldots \times {s_n}^A \to s^A$ is a partial function for every $f \in F_{(s_1\ldots s_n,s)}$; in particular if $n = 0$, i.e. if $f \in F_{(\Lambda,s)}$, then f^A is either undefined or an element of s^A.
- a total congruence $\equiv^A$ on $T_\Sigma(A)$, the algebra ofII terms built on the variable family $\{s^A\}_{s\in S}$, *compatible* with the interpretation of function symbols in A, i.e. s.t. if $t^A, u^A \in s^A$, then $t\equiv^A u$ iff $t^A = u^A$, where for a term $\tau \in T_\Sigma(A)$ we denote by τ^A the standard evaluation of the term τ in the partial algebra A w.r.t. the identity evaluation of variables in A.
- an interpretation $\mathcal{P}^A$, associating every predicate symbol $p \in P_{s_1\ldots s_n}$ with its *truth-set* $\mathcal{P}^A(p) \subseteq {s_1}^{T_\Sigma(A)} \times \ldots \times {s_n}^{T_\Sigma(A)}$; moreover the interpretation $\mathcal{P}^A$ is required to be *sound* w.r.t. $\equiv^A$, i.e. if $t_i \equiv^A_{s_i} u_i$ for $i = 1 \ldots n$ then $(t_1, \ldots, t_n) \in \mathcal{P}^A(p)$ iff $(u_1, \ldots, u_n) \in \mathcal{P}^A(p)$, for every $p \in P_{s_1\ldots s_n}$.

Given lazy algebras $\mathcal{A} = (A, \equiv^A, \mathcal{P}^A)$ and $\mathcal{B} = (B, \equiv^B, \mathcal{P}^B)$ on Σ, a *lazy homomorphism* $h: \mathcal{A} \to \mathcal{B}$ is a homomorphism $h: A \to B$ between partial algebras, i.e. an S-indexed family of total functions $h_s: s^A \to s^B$ s.t. if $f^A(a_1, \ldots, a_n) = a \in s^A$, then $f^B(h_{s_1}(a_1), \ldots, h_{s_n}(a_n)) = h_s(a)$, preserving simplification and predicates, i.e. s.t. $t\equiv^A u$ implies $h(t)\equiv^B h(u)$ and $(t_1, \ldots, t_n) \in \mathcal{P}^A(p)$ implies $(h_{s_1}(t_1), \ldots, h_{s_n}(t_n)) \in \mathcal{P}^B(p)$, where h is extended by freeness on terms in $T_\Sigma(A)$. □

Note that predicates are interpreted as their truth-set, but apply to *terms* instead of values; this is a slight generalization of the ideas behind label algebras (see e.g. [6]), where only unary predicates, called label indeed, where allowed. A relevant difference w.r.t. label algebra approach is that term evaluating to the same value are indistinguishable by predicates, while labeling disregards the equalities between terms. Thus predicates here are a bit more general than in standard approaches, because properties of undefined terms can be stated too, but less flexible than labeling; this restriction has been introduced in order to avoid (pathological) examples as the following.

Example 1. Let us consider the following label specification, with just one label b.

spec Sp =
  sorts s, s'
  opns $a: \to s$
    $f: s \times s \times s \to s'$
  axioms $x = a$
    $f(x, x, y) : b$
    $f(x, y, x) : b$
    $f(y, x, x) : b$

Although labeling disregards equalities between values, and hence should in some sense be unaffected by the requirement $x = a$, in all models $f(x, y, z) : b$ holds for lack of values to instantiate x, y and z. Indeed, because of the first axiom, all models have a one-point carrier of sort s, so, recalling that evaluations are made on terms built from the elements of the algebra as variables, there are two elements to evaluate x, y and z on, that are the element of the carrier (seen as a variable) and the constant a; hence for every valuation for x, y and z (at least) one among the last three axioms applies so that $f(x, y, z) : b$ holds. But note that if another constant of sort s is introduced, whose interpretation must be the same value as that of a by the first axiom, then three terms of sort s exist and hence none of the axioms applies, so that $f(x, y, z) : b$ does not hold anymore, even if the models have the same carriers and function interpretation as before. In other words adding syntax, even if in every model such new terms reduce to values already denoted by old terms, can change the validity of labeling. □

Since the definition of lazy homomorphism is obviously satisfied by the identity and by the composition of lazy homomorphisms, we can define the category of lazy algebras and inherit the notion of initial (free) object in a class.

Definition 4. Given a signature Σ, the category $\mathbf{CAlg}(\Sigma)$ has lazy algebras as objects and lazy homomorphisms as arrows; identities are the families of identity maps $\{I_s \mid s \in S\}$ and composition is defined componentwise.

Let C be a subclass of $\mathbf{CAlg}(\Sigma)$ objects and X be an S-sorted family of variables; then a pair $(\mathcal{F}, E)$ is *free* for X in C iff $\mathcal{F} = (F, \equiv^F, \mathcal{P}^F) \in$ C, with $E: X \to F$, and for every $\mathcal{A} = (A, \equiv^A, \mathcal{P}^A)$ in C and every $V: X \to A$ there exists a unique homomorphism $h_V: \mathcal{F} \to \mathcal{A}$ s.t. $h_V \cdot E = V$.

If X is empty (i.e. $X_s = \emptyset$ for every $s \in S$), then a free pair is called *initial*. □

Note that, since the definition of free (initial) coincides with the standard one in category theory, the properties of free (initial) objects applies to our framework too; in particular any two free (initial) objects are isomorphic.

Notation. In the sequel for every lazy algebra $\mathcal{A} = (A, \equiv^A, \mathcal{P}^A)$ and every $\tau \in T_\Sigma(A)$ the evaluation τ^A is inductively defined by $a^A = a$ for all $a \in A$ and $f(t_1, \ldots, t_n)^A = f^A(t_1^A, \ldots, t_n^A)$, i.e. is the standard evaluation for the identical valuation of variables in A as elements of A.

Moreover if $(\sigma: X \to T_\Sigma(Y))$ $\sigma: T_\Sigma(X) \to T_\Sigma(Y)$ and t is a term on X, then $\sigma(t)$ denotes the image of t along (the free extension of) σ.

Finally for every valuation $V: X \to T_\Sigma(A)$ and every term $t \in T_\Sigma(X)$, we will denote by $t^{A,V}$ the evaluation $V(t)^A$, that is the standard evaluation for the valuation $id_A \cdot V$. □

Note that $t^{A,V}$ is a value (or is undefined), while $V(t)$ is a term (and it is always defined).

As in more standard algebraic frameworks, an initial (free) object in a class, if any, is minimally defined and satisfies as few identities between defined terms as possible; moreover the interpretation of predicates and the simplification relation (i.e. the error-recovery) are minimal too.

Theorem 5. *Given a signature Σ, a subclass of* $\mathbf{CAlg}(\Sigma)$ *objects* C *and an S-sorted family of variables X, if $(\mathcal{F}, E)$ is free for X in* C, *then for every $\mathcal{A} = (A, \equiv^A, \mathcal{P}^A) \in$* C, *every valuation $V: X \to T_\Sigma(A)$ and every $t, t', t_1, \ldots, t_n \in T_\Sigma(X)$ the following conditions hold:*

minimal definedness *if $t^{F,E}$ is defined, then $t^{A,V}$ is defined too;*
no-confusion *if $t^{F,E} = t'^{F,E} = a \in F$, then $t^{A,V} = t'^{A,V}$;*
minimal simplification *if $E(t) \equiv^F E(t')$, then $V(t) \equiv^A V(t')$;*
minimal truth *if $(E(t_1), \ldots, E(t_n)) \in \mathcal{P}^F(p)$, then $(V(t_1), \ldots, V(t_n)) \in \mathcal{P}^A(p)$.* □

2 A logic of simplifications

The main interest is on the definition of basic specifications taking advantage of the tools introduced so far. As usual in algebraic specification, we consider Horn-Clauses, built starting from three different kinds of atoms: (existential) equality between values, equivalence between terms and predicate application. As in our framework the result of an operation depends not only on the values of its arguments, but also on the history of such values, the valuations for variables have to be made not in the carriers of the models, but on *terms*; in other words we substitute computations, instead of values, for variables.

2.1 Formulas and Specifications

Definition 6. Let $\Sigma = (S, F, P)$ be a signature and X be a family of variables for Σ. Then the set $Atoms(\Sigma, X)$ of *atoms* over Σ and X consists of

Existential equalities: $t =_e t'$, where t, t' are terms on X of the same sort;
Simplifications: $t \equiv t'$, where t, t' are terms on X of the same sort;
Predicates: $p(t_1, \ldots, t_n)$, where t_i are terms of sort s_i on X and $p \in P_{s_1 \ldots s_n}$.

Moreover the set $HC(\Sigma, X)$ of *positive conditional formulas* over Σ and X consists of all formulas of the form $\Delta \supset \epsilon$, where $\Delta \subseteq Atoms(\Sigma, X)$ and $\epsilon \in Atoms(\Sigma, X)$, too. If $\Delta = \emptyset$, then $\Delta \supset \epsilon$ is simply written as ϵ, so that $Atoms(\Sigma, X) \subseteq HC(\Sigma, X)$.

In the sequel for every formula $\phi = \Delta \supset \epsilon$ we will denote by $Var(\phi)$ the set of variables that appear in ϕ, by $Prem(\phi)$ the set Δ of the *premises* of ϕ and by $Cons(\phi)$ the atom ϵ, called the *consequence* of ϕ. Moreover the existential equalities of the form $t =_e t$, where both sides are the same term, are denoted by $D(t)$.

Let $\mathcal{A} = (A, \equiv^A, \mathcal{P}^A)$ be a lazy algebra, ϕ be a positive conditional formula over Σ and X and $V: Y \to T_\Sigma(A)$ be a valuation, with $Var(\phi) \subseteq Y$; then $\mathcal{A}$ *satisfies* ϕ w.r.t. V, denoted by $\mathcal{A} \models_V \phi$, according with the following conditions:

- $\mathcal{A} \models_V t =_e t'$ iff $t^{A,V}$ and $t'^{A,V}$ are the same value in A;
- $\mathcal{A} \models_V t \equiv t'$ iff $V(t) \equiv^A V(t')$;
- $\mathcal{A} \models_V p(t_1, \ldots, t_n)$ iff $(V(t_1), \ldots, V(t_n)) \in \mathcal{P}^A(p)$;
- $\mathcal{A} \models_V \Delta \supset \epsilon$ iff $\mathcal{A} \models_V \epsilon$ or $\mathcal{A} \not\models_V \delta$ for some $\delta \in \Delta$.

Then $\mathcal{A}$ *satisfies* ϕ, denoted by $\mathcal{A} \models \phi$, iff $\mathcal{A} \models_V \phi$ for all V: $Var(\phi) \to T_\Sigma(A)$. □

Remark. Lazy signature, algebras and formulas do not form an institution. Indeed, since variable valuations range on terms and not on values, the satisfaction condition does not hold, not even for signature inclusions, as the forgotten syntax can increase the number of possible instantiations; the problems are the same as for label algebras. However the lazy framework forms an rps preinstitution (see e.g. [17]) and this property suffices to guarantee that the models of a larger specification, hierarchically built on a smaller one, can be restricted to models of the smaller, so that modular constructions are meaningful. Thus, although the theory of institution independent specification languages ([18, 3, 4]) does not apply directly to the lazy framework, the most relevant part of such theory can be rephrased for rps preinstitutions and hence, in particular, for the lazy formalism. □

Lemma 7. *Let $\Sigma = (S, F, P)$ be a signature and X be a family of variables for Σ; for every lazy algebra $\mathcal{A} = (A, \equiv^A, \mathcal{P}^A)$ on Σ, every positive conditional formula ϕ over Σ and X and all valuations $V: X \to T_\Sigma(A)$, $\sigma: Y \to T_\Sigma(X)$ we have that $\mathcal{A} \models_{V \cdot \sigma} \phi$ iff $\mathcal{A} \models_V \sigma(\phi)$.* □

Definition 8. A *specification* Sp consists of a signature Σ and a set of positive conditional formulas over Σ and any family X of variables, called the *axioms* of Sp.

Given a specification $Sp = (\Sigma, Ax)$, the *model class* of Sp, denoted by $\mathbf{Mod}(Sp)$, consists of all lazy algebras over Σ satisfying all formulas in Ax. □

2.2 Initial and free models

As more standard frameworks, lazy specifications admit initial and free models, characterized by properties like "no-junk" and "no-confusion" (see e.g. Theorem 5). Moreover the proof follows a classical pattern: the quotient of the term algebra w.r.t. the *minimal congruence* is shown to be free.

Definition 9. Let $\Sigma = (S, F, P)$ be a signature and X be a family of variables for Σ; then a *lazy congruence* over $T_\Sigma(X)$ consists of

- a *partial* congruence $\approx$ on $T_\Sigma(X)$ containing $X \times X$.
- a *total* congruence $\cong$ on $T_\Sigma(X)$ s.t. $\approx \subseteq \cong$ and if $t \cong u$ with t and u belonging to the domain of $\approx$, then $t \approx u$.
- for every $p \in P_{s_1 \ldots s_n}$ a set $\bar{p} \subseteq T_\Sigma(X)_{s_1} \times \ldots \times T_\Sigma(X)_{s_n}$ s.t. if $t_i \cong_{s_i} u_i$ for $i = 1 \ldots n$ and $(t_1, \ldots, t_n) \in \bar{p}$, then $(u_1, \ldots, u_n) \in \bar{p}$.

Given a lazy congruence $\Re = (\approx, \cong, \{\bar{p}\})$ over $T_\Sigma(X)$, the *quotient lazy algebra* $\mathcal{A} = T_\Sigma(X)/\Re$ consists of:

- for every $s \in S$, denoting by $[t]$ the equivalence class of t in $\approx$, $s^A = \{[t] \mid t \in Dom(\approx)\}$;
- for every $f \in F_{s_1 \ldots s_n, s}$, and every t_i in the domain of $\approx$, $f^A([t_1], \ldots, [t_n])$ is $[f(t_1, \ldots, t_n)]$, if $f(t_1, \ldots, t_n)$ belongs to the domain of $\approx$, is undefined otherwise.
- $t \equiv^A t'$ iff $\tau \in \rho(t)$ and $\tau' \in \rho(t')$ exist s.t. $\tau \cong \tau'$, where ρ is defined below.
- for every $p \in P_{s_1 \ldots s_n}$, $(t_1, \ldots, t_n) \in \mathcal{P}^A(p)$ iff $\tau_i \in \rho(t_i)$, for $i = 1 \ldots n$, exist s.t. $(\tau_1, \ldots, \tau_n) \in \bar{p}$, where ρ is defined below.

For every term $t \in T_\Sigma(A)$ let $\rho(t)$ denote the set of terms on $T_\Sigma(X)$ obtained by removing brackets in t, i.e. $\rho(t)$ is inductively defined by $\rho([t]) = \{t' \mid t' \in [t]\}$ if $t \in A$ and $\rho(f(t_1, \ldots t_n)) = \{f(t'_1, \ldots t'_n) \mid t'_1 \in \rho(t_1) \ldots t'_n \in \rho(t_n)\}$;

Moreover in the sequel $\overline{V}: X \to T_\Sigma(A)$ will denote the evaluation defined by $\overline{V}(x) = [x]$ for all $x \in X$. □

The evaluation of terms in a quotient is strongly related to the evaluation within the term algebra.

Lemma 10. *Let $\Re = (\approx, \cong, \{\bar{p}\})$ be a lazy congruence over $T_\Sigma(X)$, $\mathcal{A}$ be the lazy algebra $T_\Sigma(X)/\Re$ and $V: Var(\phi) \to T_\Sigma(A)$ be a valuation. Then for every valuation $U: Var(\phi) \to T_\Sigma(X)$ s.t. $U(x) \in \rho(V(x))$ for all $x \in X$ we have:*

- $t^{A,V} = U(t)^{A,\overline{V}}$ *for every* $t \in T_\Sigma(Var(\phi))$;
- $\overline{V} \cdot U(t) \equiv^A V(t)$ *for every* $t \in T_\Sigma(Var(\phi))$. □

Definition 11. Let $\Sigma = (S, F, P)$ be a signature, X be a family of variables for Σ, $\mathcal{A} = (A, \equiv^A, \mathcal{P}^A)$ be a lazy algebra and $V: X \to A$ be a valuation. Then the ***kernel*** $k(\mathcal{A}, V)$ of the evaluation w.r.t. $\mathcal{A}$ and V is the congruence $(\approx, \cong, \{\bar{p}\})$ over $T_\Sigma(X)$ defined by:

- $t \approx_s u$ iff $t^{A,V} = u^{A,V} \in s^A$.
- $t \cong_s u$ iff $V(t) \equiv^A V(u)$.
- for every $p \in P_{s_1 \ldots s_n}$, $(t_1, \ldots, t_n) \in \bar{p}$ iff $(V(t_1), \ldots, V(t_n)) \in \mathcal{P}^A(p)$.

Let Sp be a specification over Σ and X be a family of variables for Σ; then the lazy congruence $K(Sp, X)$ is the (componentwise) intersection of $k(\mathcal{A}, V)$ for all $\mathcal{A} \in \text{Mod}(Sp)$ and all valuations $V: X \to A$. □

It is immediate to check that the kernels are congruences and that the intersection of congruences is a congruence too.

As quite common in algebraic frameworks, the free object is the quotient of the corresponding term algebra w.r.t. the "minimal" kernel.

Theorem 12. *Let* Sp *be a specification over* $\Sigma = (S, F, P)$ *and* X *be a family of variables for* Σ. *Then* $(T_\Sigma(X)/K(Sp, X), \overline{V})$ *is free for* X *in* $\text{Mod}(Sp)$. □

3 Using Lazy Specifications

Let us first of all note that every total and partial specification can be immediately and automatically translated[2] into a lazy specification, by adding the definedness of variables in the premises, to make their instantiation range on values, and axioms of the form $p(x_1, \ldots, x_n) \supset D(x_i)$ to restrict predicates to work on values; moreover, for total specifications, axioms of the form $D(x_1) \wedge \ldots \wedge D(x_n) \supset D(f(x_1, \ldots, x_n))$ have to be added, too, to have that the interpretation of function symbols are total functions in all models. As most specifications are total or partial, a specification language based on the lazy framework should provide facilities to concisely describe those requirements. It is interesting to note that, from a practical point of view, stating the definedness of variables in the premises does not increase the number of checks; indeed the typing verification needed in any framework is here replaced by the definedness check.

But lazy specifications also allow the definition of evaluation strategies. For instance, let us assume given a specification Sp_B for the boolean expressions of a programming language, including the constants **true** and **false**, but possibly with other (partial) operations, and enrich it by an **and** construct. Then many different evaluation strategies can be defined. Each of the following groups of axioms presents one of the more usual strategies, assuming that all defined terms reduces either to

[2] This indeed is a particular case of logical simulation (see e.g. [8]) and its existence not only guarantees that the lazy framework is at least as expressive as the total and partial ones, but also allows the use of multiparadigm specification languages (see e.g. [4])

true or to **false**; but it is easy to see that others (e.g. "right to left") could be axiomatized as well.

$$\left.\begin{array}{l} D(x) \wedge y = \mathbf{true} \supset x \text{ and } y = x \\ D(x) \wedge y = \mathbf{false} \supset x \text{ and } y = \mathbf{false} \end{array}\right\} \text{strict evaluation}$$

$$\left.\begin{array}{l} x = \mathbf{true} \supset x \text{ and } y \equiv y \\ x = \mathbf{false} \supset x \text{ and } y \equiv \mathbf{false} \end{array}\right\} \text{left to right evaluation, strict on the first argument}$$

$$\left.\begin{array}{l} \mathbf{true\ and}\ x \equiv x \\ \mathbf{false\ and}\ x \equiv \mathbf{false} \end{array}\right\} \text{non-strict left to right evaluation}$$

$$\left.\begin{array}{l} \mathbf{true\ and}\ x \equiv x \\ \mathbf{false\ and}\ x \equiv \mathbf{false} \\ x\ \mathbf{and\ true} \equiv x \\ x\ \mathbf{and\ false} \equiv \mathbf{false} \end{array}\right\} \text{parallel non-strict evaluation}$$

Notice the difference between $x = \mathbf{true} \supset x$ **and** $y \equiv y$ and **true and** $y \equiv y$; indeed in the first case x is required to be defined, while the later allows the simplification of x **and** y to y even if x is undefined, provided that x simplifies to **true** (as from $x \equiv$ **true**, also x **and** $y \equiv$ **true and** y follows, by congruence, and hence x **and** $y \equiv y$ is required by transitivity).

Another interesting point is the interaction between error-recovery and modularity (see [15]). A classical example of this problem is the definition of the stacks (see [5] for a full discussion on the possible specifications of stacks). Indeed the stack data type is parametric w.r.t. the specification of its elements; thus *a priori* there is no way to define the value of the top of the empty stack without destroying the sufficient completeness property; indeed it should be a new error of the primitive type of elements. In many total approaches the solution is to reduce it to any previously existing error value, but there are no guarantees that such value exists. Using partial specifications, it is easy to have that top and pop are defined only on non-empty stacks, saving the sufficient completeness; consider indeed the following standard partial specification, parametric on the specification of the elements, that is supposed to have a principal sort, `elem`.

```
spec Sp1 =  enrich Elem by
    sorts   stack
    opns    empty: → stack
            push: elem × stack → stack
            top: stack → elem
            pop: stack → stack
    axioms  D(empty)
            D(x) ∧ D(s) ⊃ D(push(x, s))
            D(x) ∧ D(s) ⊃ top(push(x, s)) = x
            D(x) ∧ D(s) ⊃ pop(push(x, s)) = s
```

If error recovery is required, then the only way to deal with it in partial (as well as in order-sorted) frameworks is to add the definedness (well-formedness) of "errors", destroying the sufficient completeness, together with recovery axioms, so that the framework is in no way different w.r.t. the standard many-sorted approach. Using lazy algebras, instead, it is possible to introduce simplification on terms.

```
spec Sp2 =  enrich Sp1 by
    axioms  top(push(x, s)) ≡ x
            pop(push(x, s)) ≡ s
```

Notice that in Sp_2 for example the term τ = **top(push**(t, **pop(empty)))** simplifies, in all models, to t, but, even if t is defined, τ is undefined; indeed τ represents a "recovered" computation. The strictness of functions prevents τ to be defined, unless **pop(empty)** is defined too. In other words the initial model of Sp_2 consists of the same partial algebra as the initial model of Sp_1, but the simplification relation has been enlarged to recover some errors.

Note that finer error-recovery strategies can be defined as well; for example the following specification corresponds to the recovery of just one level of error due to **pop** and **top**.

$$
\begin{array}{lll}
\text{spec } Sp_3 = & \text{enrich } Sp_1 \text{ by} \\
\quad\text{axioms} & D(s) \wedge D(x) \supset \mathbf{top}(\mathbf{push}(x, \mathbf{pop}(s))) \equiv x \\
 & D(s_1) \wedge D(s_2) \supset \mathbf{pop}(\mathbf{push}(\mathbf{top}(s_1), s_2)) \equiv s_2
\end{array}
$$

A third kind of problem comes from the definition of *limited* data types, for example limited stacks. The intuition is that after a phase of top-down design, during which the stacks were regarded as their "ideal" model, in the bottom-up development stacks should be replaced by a more "real" and limited model. But in all algebraic approaches this step cannot be done painlessly. Indeed terms that were seen as perfectly correct (i.e., depending on the framework, as defined, well-formed, labeled by "ok" and so on) should be moved in the "incorrect" part of the type, loosing so, in some sense, a property, while all frameworks are incremental and only allow to increase the properties of any term. This reflects in the need for a heavy modification of the original specification (e.g. by decorating the axioms in order to apply them only to those arguments that do not raise an overflow), against any notion of modularity.

Analyzing this phenomenon, it is easy to see that the original specification is overdefined; indeed if the knowledge about which terms represent values and which errors is reached only at the last stage of design, then it is incorrect, and indeed it is a source of troubles, to define **push** as a total function, because it is not total in limited models. But the standard approaches require the terms to be defined (well formed/labeled with "ok"...) in order to apply simplifying axioms to them, so that the contradiction between the need for delaying the decision about definedness and the capability to state equalities among terms is inescapable. Using lazy specification, instead, the specification Sp_1 can be rephrased with equality replaced by the simplification relation, capturing in this way the intuition that the axioms state an equivalence on computation and that the definedness is only added at the last possible moment.

$$
\begin{array}{ll}
\text{spec } Sp_1' = & \text{enrich } \mathtt{Elem} \text{ by} \\
\quad\text{sorts} & \mathtt{stack} \\
\quad\text{opns} & \mathtt{empty}\colon \to \mathtt{stack} \\
 & \mathtt{push}\colon \mathtt{elem} \times \mathtt{stack} \to \mathtt{stack} \\
 & \mathtt{top}\colon \mathtt{stack} \to \mathtt{elem} \\
 & \mathtt{pop}\colon \mathtt{stack} \to \mathtt{stack} \\
\quad\text{axioms} & \mathbf{top}(\mathbf{push}(x, s)) \equiv x \\
 & \mathbf{pop}(\mathbf{push}(x, s)) \equiv s
\end{array}
$$

Now the definition of the stacks large at the most **max** elements, with the convention that $\mathbf{push}^n(x_1, \ldots, x_n, s)$ is the term inductively defined by $\mathbf{push}^0(\lambda, s) = s$ and $\mathbf{push}^{n+1}(x_1, \ldots, x_{n+1}, s) = \mathbf{push}^n(x_1, \ldots, x_n, \mathbf{push}(x_{n+1}, s))$ for every term s of sort stack, is the following enrichment:

spec $Sp_2' =$ enrich Sp_1' by
axioms $D(x_1) \wedge \ldots \wedge D(x_{\mathbf{max}}) \supset D(\mathbf{push}^n(x_1, \ldots, x_{\mathbf{max}}, \lambda))$

By strictness the definition of all the subterms is given. Notice that the axioms of Sp_1' define a strong error-recovery strategy as the definedness of variables is not required in the premises; adding such premises, the error-recovery can be weakened, and even, adding the definedness of all subterms instead of variables, completely banished.

4 A Sound and Complete Calculus

It is implicit in the nature of algebraic specifications, seen as tools for reasoning on programs, the need for a calculus to help the understanding of the specification basic properties, possibly with the related definition of a tool. A calculus is doubly needed in this framework, that is based on the concept of simplification.

We are mainly interested in formulas where most variables can only range on *defined* elements, represented in the form $\{D(x_1), \ldots, D(x_n)\} \supset \epsilon$, or on subsets described by predicates. Thus, although atomic deduction would suffice for the definition of the initial object, the calculus presented here is strictly conditional. This, moreover, enables a concise description of variables used in deduction already utilized for the partial approach (see e.g. [2]), in order to avoid well known problems related to empty-carriers.

Definition 13. Let $\Sigma = (S, F, P)$ be a signature, X an S-sorted family of denumerable variable sets and Ax a set of positive conditional formulas over Σ and X.

Then the inference system $CL(Sp)$, where $Sp = (\Sigma, Ax)$ consists of Ax and of the following rules, where $t, t', t'', t_1, \ldots, t_n, t_i'$ are terms on Σ and X:

Existential equality rules

$$\overline{t =_e t' \supset t' =_e t} \qquad \overline{t =_e t' \wedge t' =_e t'' \supset t =_e t''} \qquad \overline{D(f(t_1, \ldots, t_n)) \supset D(t_i)}$$

$$\overline{t_i =_e t_i' \wedge D(f(t_1, \ldots, t_n)) \supset f(t_1, \ldots, t_n) =_e f(t_1, \ldots, t_{i-1}, t_i', t_{i+1} \ldots, t_n)}$$

Simplification rules

$$\overline{t \equiv t} \qquad \overline{t \equiv t' \supset t' \equiv t} \qquad \overline{t \equiv t' \wedge t' \equiv t'' \supset t \equiv t''}$$

$$\overline{t_1 \equiv t_1' \wedge \ldots \wedge t_n \equiv t_n' \supset f(t_1, \ldots, t_n) \equiv f(t_1', \ldots, t_n')}$$

$$\overline{t \equiv t' \wedge D(t) \wedge D(t') \supset t =_e t'} \qquad \overline{t =_e t' \supset t \equiv t'}$$

Predicate rule

$$\overline{t_1 \equiv t_1' \wedge \ldots \wedge t_n \equiv t_n' \wedge p(t_1, \ldots, t_n) \supset p(t_1', \ldots, t_n')}$$

Substitution rule

$$\frac{\phi}{\sigma(\phi)} \quad \sigma \text{ term substitution}$$

Modus Ponens

$$\frac{\Delta \supset \epsilon, \Gamma \supset \delta}{\Delta - \{\delta\} \cup \Gamma \cup \Theta \supset \epsilon} \quad \Theta = \{x \equiv x \mid x \in Var(\delta) - (Var(\Delta - \{\delta\} \cup \Gamma \supset \epsilon))\}$$

If ϕ is inferred by $CL(Sp)$, then we write $CL(Sp) \vdash \phi$. □

It is worth noting that the side condition of the Modus Ponens rule guarantees that variables can be eliminated, during a deduction, only if a substitution takes place. This suffices for inconsistent deductions to be avoided even in the case of empty carriers and non-sensible signatures.

The above calculus is sound, as the following proposition will show.

Proposition 14. *Let $Sp = (\Sigma, Ax)$ be a specification; then $CL(Sp) \vdash \phi$ implies that $\mathcal{A} \models_V \phi$ for all $\mathcal{A} \in$ **Mod**(Sp) and all $V: Var(\phi) \to T_\Sigma(A)$.* □

We are mainly interested in atomic completeness, as an atomically-complete calculus gives the free (initial) model, that satisfies as few atoms as possible, but, since in our framework the variables used in the deduction that cannot be eliminated (as values for their instantiation are missing) are kept track of by atoms of the form $x \equiv x$ (if the variable can be instantiated on every term) or $x =_e x$ (if the variable can be instantiated only on defined term) in the premises, we should regard

$$x_1 \equiv x_1 \wedge \ldots \wedge x_n \equiv x_n \wedge y_1 =_e y_1 \wedge \ldots \wedge y_m =_e y_m \supset \epsilon$$

as an *atom* in the notation $\forall x_1 \ldots x_n : T_\Sigma(A); \forall y_1 \ldots y_m : A.\epsilon$. But if the x have to be instantiated on terms built from the values of A (and hence from the y), their presence in the premises does not increase the number of elements needed in the carriers in order to make the deduction possible. Hence we are interested in an easier form of formulas, those that in the premises have only definedness assertions.

Notation. Every ϕ of the form $x_1 =_e x_1 \wedge \ldots \wedge x_n =_e x_n \supset \epsilon$ is called *basically atomic* and if $CL(Sp) \vdash \phi$, then we say that $CL(Sp) \vdash_X \epsilon$ holds for each $X \supseteq \{x_1 \ldots x_n\}$. □

The above calculus is complete w.r.t. basically atomic sentences; the proof is done by constructing a model satisfying only the deduced atoms.

Definition 15. Let $Sp = (\Sigma, Ax)$ be a specification and X be a family of variables; then $K(CL(Sp), X)$ is the lazy congruence $(\approx, \cong, \{\bar{p}\})$ defined by:

- $t \approx t'$ iff $CL(Sp) \vdash_X t =_e t'$ for all $t, t' \in T_\Sigma(X)$;
- $t \cong t'$ iff $CL(Sp) \vdash_X t \equiv t'$ for all $t, t' \in T_\Sigma(X)$;
- $(t_1, \ldots, t_n) \in \bar{p}$ iff $CL(Sp) \vdash_X p(t_1, \ldots, t_n)$ for all $t_i \in T_\Sigma(X)$ and $p \in P$;

Moreover let $\mathcal{G}(Sp, X)$ be the quotient lazy algebra $T_\Sigma(X)/K(CL(Sp), X)$ and let $E: X \to G(Sp, X)$ be the evaluation defined by $E(x) = [x]$ for all $x \in X$. □

Let us remark that $K(CL(Sp),X)$ is a lazy congruence. Indeed, because of modus ponens and of the rules for existential equality, $\approx$ is a partial congruence, whose domain includes X; moreover, because of modus ponens and of the rules for simplification, $\cong$ is a total congruence, $\approx \subseteq \cong$ and if $t \cong t'$, with $t \approx t$ and $t' \approx t'$, then $t \approx t'$. Finally, the predicate interpretation is well defined w.r.t. simplification, because of the rules for predicate and modus ponens.

Proposition 16. *Let $Sp = (\Sigma, Ax)$ be a specification, X be a family of variables and $V\colon Var(\phi) \to T_\Sigma(G(Sp,X))$ be a valuation. Then $\mathcal{G}(Sp,X) \models_E \epsilon$ iff $CL(Sp) \vdash_X \epsilon$, for every atom ϵ over X.* □

Note that, in particular, $\mathcal{G}(Sp,X) \models_E x =_e x$ for all $x \in X$, because of the symmetry rule for existential equality.

Proposition 17. *Let $Sp = (\Sigma, Ax)$ be a specification and X be a family of variables. Then $\mathcal{G}(Sp,X)$ is a model of Sp.* □

We are finally able to show the completeness of the calculus w.r.t. basically atomic formulas.

Theorem 18. *Let $Sp = (\Sigma, Ax)$ be a specification and ϕ be $\Delta \supset \epsilon$, where $\Delta = \{D(x_1), \ldots, D(x_m)\}$; if $\mathcal{A} \models_V \phi$ for all $\mathcal{A} \in \mathrm{Mod}(Sp)$ and all $V\colon X \to T_\Sigma(A)$, then $CL(Sp) \vdash_X \epsilon$, where $X = Var(\phi)$.* □

The calculus gives the free models.

Theorem 19. *Let Sp be a specification over $\Sigma = (S, F, P)$ and X be a family of variables for Σ. Then $(\mathcal{G}(Sp,X), E)$ is free for X in $\mathrm{Mod}(Sp)$.* □

Conclusions and Further Developments

Having proposed an algebraic framework to easily deal with the features of an imperative or functional programming language, the next step should be the definition of a user-friendly specification language, whose semantics will be defined in terms of lazy specifications. This will lead to investigate about rewriting techniques for the lazy framework and, possibly, to an implementation. To this aim it could be useful to modify the simplification relation, dropping the requirement that it is a congruence, and making it a "rewrite" relation.

Acknowledgments. I would like to thank my office-mate, Elena Zucca, for patiently debating with me the original, vague and confused intuitions that brought to the definition of the lazy frame. Moreover I'm indebted to Gianna Reggio for carefully reading a draft of this paper and to Egidio Astesiano for a continuous stimulus to research.

References

1. E. Astesiano and M. Cerioli. Non-strict don't care algebras and specifications. In S. Abramsky and T.S.E. Maibaum, editors, *Proceedings of TAPSOFT'91*, number 493 in Lecture Notes in Computer Science, pages 121–142, Berlin, 1992. Springer Verlag.

2. E. Astesiano and M. Cerioli. Free objects and equational deduction for partial conditional specifications. *Theoretical Computer Science*, 1995. To appear.
3. E. Astesiano and M. Cerioli. Relationships between logical frames. In *Recent Trends in Data Type Specification*, number 655 in Lecture Notes in Computer Science, pages 126–143, Berlin, 1993. Springer Verlag.
4. E. Astesiano and M. Cerioli. Multiparadigm specification languages: a first attempt at foundations. In D.J. Andrews, J.F. Groote, and C.A. Middelburg, editors, *Semantics of Specification Languages (SoSL'93)*, Workshops in Computing, pages 168–185. Springer Verlag, 1994.
5. J.A. Bergstra and J.V. Tucker. The inescapable stack: an exercize in algebraic specification with total functions. Technical Report P8804, University of Amsterdam; Programming Research Group, 1988.
6. G. Bernot and P. Le Gall. Label algebras: a systematic use of terms. In *Recent Trends in Data Type Specification*, number 655 in Lecture Notes in Computer Science, pages 144–163, Berlin, 1993. Springer Verlag.
7. P. Burmeister. *A Model Theoretic Oriented Approach to Partial Algebras*. Akademie Verlag, Berlin, 1986.
8. M. Cerioli. *Relationships between Logical Formalisms*. PhD thesis, Universities of Genova, Pisa and Udine, 1993. Available as internal report of Pisa University, TD-4/93.
9. R. Diaconescu. The logic of Horn clauses is equational. Submitted for publication, 1992.
10. J.A. Goguen and R. Diaconescu. A survey of order sorted algebra. Draft, 1992.
11. V. Manca, A. Salibra, and G. Scollo. Equational type logic. *Theoretical Computer Science*, 77:131–159, 1990. Special Issue dedicated to AMAST'89.
12. A. Mégrelis. *Algèbre galactique - Un procédé de calcul formel, relatif aux semi-functions, à l'inclusion et à légalité*. PhD thesis, University of Nancy I, 1990.
13. P. Mosses. Unified algebras and institutions. In *Proceedings of 4th Annual IEEE Symposium on Logic in Computer Science*, pages 304–312, 1989.
14. P. Mosses. The use of sorts in algebraic specifications. In *Recent Trends in Data Type Specification*, number 655 in Lecture Notes in Computer Science, pages 66–92, Berlin, 1993. Springer Verlag.
15. A. Poigné. Partial algebras, subsorting, and dependent types: Prerequisites of error handling in algebraic specifications. In *Recent Trends in Data Type Specification*, number 332 in Lecture Notes in Computer Science, pages 208–234, Berlin, 1987. Springer Verlag.
16. H. Reichel. *Initial Computability, Algebraic Specifications, and Partial Algebras*. Akademie Verlag, 1986.
17. A. Salibra and G. Scollo. A soft stairway to institutions. In *Recent Trends in Data Type Specification*, number 655 in Lecture Notes in Computer Science, pages 310–329, Berlin, 1992. Springer Verlag.
18. D. Sannella and A. Tarlecki. Specifications in an arbitrary institution. *Information and Computation*, 76:165–210, 1988.
19. M. Wirsing. Algebraic specification. In *Handbook of Theoretical Computer Science* North Holland, 1990.

Transactions in Object-Oriented Specifications

G. Denker *

Technische Universität Braunschweig, Informatik, Abt. Datenbanken
Postfach 3329, D–38023 Braunschweig, Germany
e–mail: denker@idb.cs.tu-bs.de

Abstract. The formal step by step development of implementations from specifications is necessary to allow the incremental description of large software systems and hence split the software development process in manageable portions. Due to the complex notion of objects as units of structure and behavior, the refinement process has to be reconsidered in the object-oriented framework. Apart from refining structure the behavioral part gives rise to refine actions by transactions. Referring to information systems as application domain, concurrency control aspects come into play because of shared resources. We present an approach to incorporate transactions into object-oriented specification and illustrate the main problems of synchronizing them on commonly used resources. The aim is that independent actions of different transactions, i.e., actions which are not accessing the same sources, may be arbitrarily interleaved. We envisage a denotational semantics based on event structures in which the sequential composition of transactions can be appropriately liberalized and outline the ideas by giving some examples.

1 Introduction

Traditionally, the software development process runs through several phases, starting with a first informal requirement analysis, passing conceptual modeling stages, and ending up with an implementation of the system. During these steps a variety of documents is produced which are related in different ways. Some of them are more detailed description, some are extension or revised versions of other ones. For large applications, like safety critical or data-intensive high integrity systems, this process can become confusing and hardly manageable. Therefore, the demand for formal specification techniques ensuring the correctness of each step is indispensable and will have a long term impact on software development methods.

We are interested in designing information systems, i.e., reactive systems with an underlying database and application programs. Conventionally, data and operations are designed independently and under different paradigms such that the resulting database system and applications programs do not fit. The object-oriented paradigm promises to solve this problem by encapsulating data

* Work reported here was partially supported by CEC under ESPRIT-II Basic Research Working Group No. 6112 COMPASS and by CEC under ESPRIT BRA WG 6071 IS-CORE

and operations in the notion of an object and regarding a system as a community of interacting objects. By means of this it represents a combination of ideas from different fields, such as programming languages, theory of abstract data types and database systems.

Given this situation the notion of refinement has to be reconsidered. Due to the more complex notion of an object data and operations can be refined concurrently. Moreover, the refinement step possibly comprises a change of granularity in the design process. We will focus on the latter and refer to this in the following as reification. This paper proposes an approach to formalize the notion of reification in object-oriented specifications.

Since objects are understood as processes endowed with data, refinement results from process theory as well as from theory of abstract data types could be helpful. Refinement of abstract data types has been already investigated in 1972 by Hoare [Hoa72] and, moreover, in [Nip86, ST88, EGL89, EM90] and others. There has also been done a lot of work on refinement in process theory. For example, based on the semantic background of labelled transition system Aceto and Hennessy [AH93] introduced a refinement equivalence to support the refinement of an action by a process and Jifeng [Jif89] proposed a concept of simulation and proved it to be sound for correctness of implementation. Moreover, causality based models have been studied with respect to refinement (e.g., [vGG90, Vog90]). Although several work has been done on refinement issues in the theory of abstract data types and in process theory an adequate semantic framework encapsulating aspects of both applicable to objects is lacking.

Additionally, the aimed application domain of information system design gives rise to look at the development of refinement in database theory. For example Schewe, Schmidt and Wetzel [SSW91] outline a set of standard refinement rules to support the steps from conceptual database design to efficient extended relational implementations. Object-oriented investigations have also been made, e.g., [SGG+91, SGS92, ES90] give semantic foundations of reification of (abstract) objects over (a community of base) objects. The work in [FM90, FSMS92] also deals with implementing objects. In [FM94] actions are considered as objects and by means of this the refinement of atomic actions by continuing transactions is investigated. But the mentioned approaches abstract from synchronization problems which arise when several transactions concurrently access shared data in information systems. That is why reifying actions by transactions forces to take care of concurrency control issues.

Since our main concern is object-oriented specification of information systems, in this paper we will deal with the following problems:

Firstly, we aim at introducing transactions into object-oriented specifications. We will give an idea how the reification step from actions to transactions can be expressed in object-oriented specifications like TROLL [HSJ+94] which is the language we use for illustration purposes. We present specifications of an abstract object and base objects and explain how the latter can serve for implementing the behavior of the former. For that reason we specify another object, the reification of the abstract object, which is a composition of base objects with some further conditions.

Secondly, by example we will explain the main problems of synchronizing transactions emerged from reifying abstract actions to transactions composed of base actions. Moreover, correct interleavings of transactions are discussed. For a given sequence of transactions all independent actions, i.e., actions which are not accessing the same resources, may be arbitrarily interleaved without changing the overall effect. We intend to reflect this in the models of the reified object.

Thirdly, we will envisage a semantic domain for object-oriented specifications based on event structures. Because of the three-layered reification approach, i.e., abstract, base, and reified objects, we will relate this model to these three kinds of objects. The aim is that the mentioned interleaving possibilities of transactions should be expressed in the model of the reified object.

Finally, we will give a general condition for a correct reification relation between abstract, base, and reified models.

The remainder of the paper is organized as follows. In Sect. 2 the main problems of reification combined with synchronization aspects are motivated by an illustrating example. The object-oriented specification language TROLL is mentioned in passing. Furthermore, the basic idea of causally (in)dependent actions is described, which enables us to distinguish between valid and wrong interleavings of transactions. We will show how transactions can be introduced syntactically in TROLL. In Sect. 3 we shortly outline the underlying framework of event structures and apply it to the running example to show how an object can be explained semantically. In the rest of the paper we will concentrate on reification issues. Sect. 4 points out which effects transaction specifications as a means of action reification have on the corresponding models. The model of the reified object is illustrated by example. More generally, we will give a semantic reification condition relating abstract, base, and reified models in Sect. 5. Describing open problems and future work in Sect. 6 closes the paper.

2 Action Reification and Concurrency Control

We will give an example using a TROLL [HSJ+94] similar language to motivate the ideas of action reification in object-oriented specifications. Because of space restrictions some language specific details are missing and some ad hoc notations are introduced in order to focus on the illustration of the examples.

The first example specifies `Step` objects, which are able to change their attribute `quantity` by performing increasing (`inc`) or decreasing (`dec`) actions. The specified axioms (***enabled, changing***) establish the intended behavior of these actions, i.e., `inc` events increase `quantity` by one and `dec` events, which are only enabled if the `quantity` attribute is greater than zero, decrease it by one. Moreover, two actions are specified for creating and destroying `Step` objects.

```
template Step
  attributes quantity:nat initialized 0 .
  actions
    create birth .
    inc
      changing quantity:=succ(quantity) .
    dec
      enabled quantity>0
      changing quantity:=pred(quantity) .
    reset
      changing quantity:=0 .
    destroy death .
end template Step
```

The next example describes `Counter` objects which memorize natural numbers. We will exploit this later on to count how often a specific action has been executed. The `remainder` attribute can be initialized with a natural number and each execution of a `tic` action decreases it until it equals zero. The axiom expresses that as long as `remainder>0` a `tic` action will occur sometimes in the future.

```
template Counter
  attributes remainder:nat initialized 0 .
  actions
    create birth .
    init(n:nat)
      changing remainder:=n .
    tic
      enabled remainder>0
      changing remainder:=pred(remainder) .
    destroy death .
  axioms
    {remainder>0} F tic .
end template Counter
```

Let be $T1, T2, T3, T4$ four transactions composed of `Step` and `Counter` actions. We will use them to illustrate the idea of transactions and possible interleavings of independent actions of transactions. `St,Ct1,Ct2` are objects of type `Step` and `Counter`, respectively (; is sequential compositions and || denotes parallelism):

$T1$ = `St.create`
$T2$ = `Ct1.create;Ct1.init(2);Ct1.tic||St.inc;Ct1.tic||St.inc`
$T3$ = `Ct2.create;Ct2.init(1);Ct2.tic||St.dec`
$T4$ = `St.reset`

Executing these transactions in sequence cause the following observations qi of the attribute quantity after each Ti $(i = 1, \ldots, 4)$:

$$q1 = 0; q2 = 2; q3 = 1; q4 = 0$$

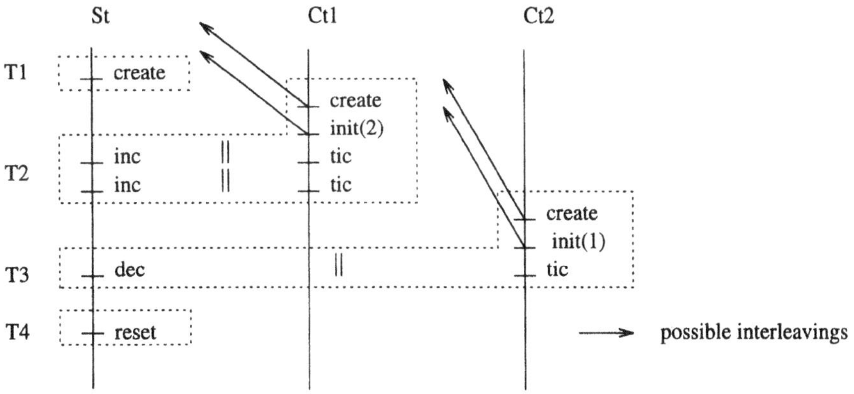

Fig. 1. Interleaving of independent actions

Thus, after initializing the quantity with zero in $T1$, two is added to it by $T2$, afterwards $T3$ subtract one, and finally quantity is reset to zero by $T4$. The sequence `create;add(2);sub(1);reset` will assist as our running example later on. We will built out of `Step` and `Counter` a new object where transactions as $T1, \ldots, T4$ become reifications of abstract actions. Assuming that such an object with definitions $T1, T2, T3, T4$ is given. Executing the sequence $T1; T2; T3; T4$ in this object would yield the same overall effect as if priority would be given to some actions through interleaving as depicted in Fig. 1. For instance, one of the possible correct interleavings of $T1; \ldots; T4$ is

```
Ct1.create;Ct2.create;Ct2.init(1);Ct1.init(2);St.create;
    St.inc||Ct1.tic;St.inc||Ct1.tic;St.dec||Ct2.tic;St.reset.    (1)
```

This is known as correct interleaving of sequential composed transactions in concurrency theory (cf for instance [LMWF94, Elm92]). It is based on the fact that actions which do not access the same resources may change the execution order without changing the overall visible effect. In this sense they are independent. For instance, actions operating on different objects are independent. Furthermore, actions operating on different attributes of one objects are also independent. The latter case is not reflected in Fig. 1. Thus, synchronization problems arise when different transactions access shared data. This is the fact for the transactions $T1, \ldots, T4$ which are all changing the quantity attribute in St. The idea of introducing a dependency relation on actions to weaken serial composition has been investigated already in different contexts, as for example in process algebra [RW94] or in database theory [Kat94].

Let us now come to the reification of actions by transactions. As mentioned before, the specified transactions $T1, \ldots, T4$ simulate initialization ($T1$), addition of two ($T2$), subtraction of one ($T3$), and reset ($T4$). This way, we implemented a specific behavior of an Adder presupposing the following specification:

```
template Adder
  attributes quantity:nat initialized 0 .
  actions
    create birth .
    add(n:nat)
      changing quantity:=quantity+n .
    sub(n:nat)
      enabled quantity-n>=0
      changing quantity:=quantity-n .
    reset
      changing quantity:=0 .
    destroy death .
end template Adder
```

The idea is to exploit services of Step and Counter to implement Adder. In order to achieve this we have to express abstract actions (e.g., add, sub) through transactions combined of Step and Counter actions. We have already touched on this in the definitions of $T1, \ldots, T4$. More generally, it could be done as follows (Adder-R stands for reified Adder):

```
template Adder-R
  components St: Step
             Ct: Counter set
  attributes quantity:nat derived St.quantity.
  actions
    create TRAC CREATE .
    add(n:nat) TRAC ADD(n:nat) .
    sub(n:nat) TRAC SUB(n:nat)
      enabled quantity-n>=0.
    ...
  process declaration
    CREATE = St.create .
    ADD(n:nat) = Cti.create -> Cti.init(n) -> INCSEQ .
    INCSEQ = {Cti.remainder>0} Cti.tic || St.inc -> INCSEQ .
    ...
end template Adder-R
```

Intuitively, the specified Adder-R object has the same observable behavior as Adder. Whenever an abstract action like add(n), sub(n) or reset is performed in `Adder` and `Adder-R` objects, respectively, the possible observations of `quantity` will be the same. `Adder-R` represents a reification of `Adder` on the basis of `Step` and `Counter` because it preserves the visible effect of abstract actions.

Before we roughly present the chosen semantic domain of event structures in the next section we shortly outline our aims. The `Adder` object is a fully sequential object which will be reflected by the models presented in the following section. This means that `Adder` is described as a set of possible life cycles, i.e., sequences of actions. `Adder-R` composed of `Step` and `Counter`, each also sequential objects, should implement the behavior of `Adder`. Substituting in all `Adder` life cycles for every abstract `Adder` action the appropriate transaction of `Step` and `Counter` actions would also result in a fully sequential behavior for `Adder-R`. Instead we would like to take the ideas of concurrency control into account expressing that some actions in `Adder-R` are independent and may be executed in arbitrary order. Thus, the models of `Adder-R` should take into consideration that the execution order of some actions is free. So, the models should reflect all possible correct interleavings of transactions. Consequently, the model class of `Adder-R` will contain not only life cycles received from abstract life cycles through substitution of abstract actions by concrete transactions, but also life cycles which represent correct interleavings. For instance, the life cycle in (1) should be in the model class of `Adder-R`.

In the next section the main ideas of the semantic model are presented and they are applied to single objects, as `Adder`, `Step`, and `Counter`. The model of the reified object `Adder-R` is presented in Sect. 4. The relations between the models of abstract, base and reified objects is outlined in Sect. 5.

3 Object Specification – An Event Based Model

For specifying local properties of objects we use linear temporal logic. Appropriate interpretation structures for this kind of logic are life cycles, i.e., linear traces of events. Therefore, single objects are assumed to be sequential. Concurrency comes into play by composing objects to systems. The points of communication are specified through calling mechanism stating which events should happen synchronously. Correspondingly, semantics is given to systems of objects by global webs which are composed of the local life cycles glued together at shared communication events. This semantic approach fits into the more general framework of locally sequential event structures.

In [ES95] one can find the detailed definitions of the chosen model of locally sequential event structures and the distributed temporal logic (DTL) going with this model. Moreover, some general results about the mathematics of this semantic framework are presented in [ES95]. DTL is a modification of the temporal logic for describing agents defined in [Thi94]. For providing semantics to object-oriented specifications a first approach towards translating specifications written in a TROLL-like toy language to formal DTL specifications is given in [ESSS94]. This work is still in progress. Because of space limitations we will only present parts of the semantic framework which are used in the following paper to formalize the reification condition. Since we focus on reification issues we will illustrate the intended models by example. The details about the construction of the models are given in [ES95] where the reader can also find the following definitions.

The semantic description starts with the notion of a so called instance signature. An instance signature is a pair (Id, Ac), where Id is a set of identities and $Ac = \{Ac_i\}_{i \in Id}$ is an Id-indexed family of action alphabets. Communication is set up by actions shared among several objects. The set of possible identities can be derived from the users specification. In our example we only have one instance of type **Adder**, so that we skipped the details about possible identities in the specification. The action alphabet for objects of one template is derived from the specified action symbols, where each of those action symbols gives rise to a set of actions; e.g., **add(n:nat)** induces actions **add(1)**, **add(2)**, ...

For a given instance signature $\Sigma_I = (Id, Ac)$ we construct a Σ_I-event structure $E = \bigcup_{i \in Id}(Ev_i, \rightarrow_i)$ where each $(Ev_i, \rightarrow_i)$ is a sequential event structure (for construction details see [ES95]).

A sequential event structure E is a pair $(Ev, \rightarrow)$ where Ev is the set of events and $\rightarrow$: $Ev \times Ev$ is the "step" causality relation. Thus, causality $\rightarrow^*$ is the transitive, reflexive closure of $\rightarrow$. Sequential event structures are the models of single objects. Since we assume no intra-object concurrency conflict is a derived concept, i.e., $e \# f$ iff $\neg(e \rightarrow^* f \vee f \rightarrow^* e)$. Moreover, sequential event structures fulfill the following two conditions: (1) there exists a unique minimal element $\epsilon \in Ev$ and (2) every local configuration $\downarrow e = \{e' \mid e' \rightarrow^* e\}$ of an event e is totally ordered.

In a Σ_I-event structure two events e, f are globally in conflict $(e \# f)$ iff $\exists i \in Id, \exists e', f' \in Ev_i: e' \# f' \wedge e' \rightarrow^* e \wedge f' \rightarrow^* f$. Two events e, e' are concurrent $(e \ co \ e')$ iff $\neg(e \rightarrow^* e' \vee e' \rightarrow^* e \vee e \# e')$.

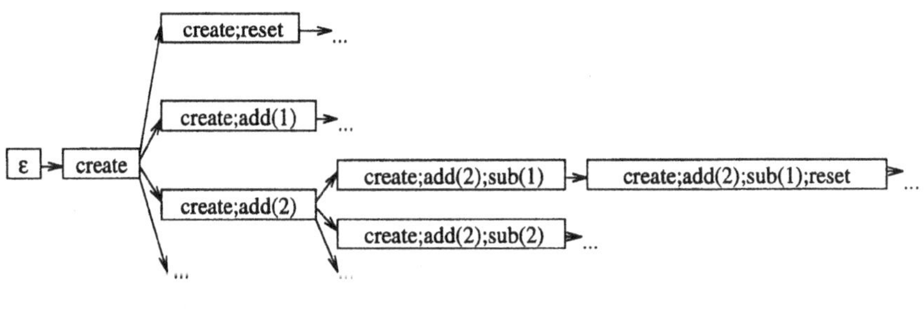

Fig. 2. Event structure of Adder objects

We show the sequential event structure associated with **Adder** objects. In Fig. 2 events are framed and arrows denote causality. The sequential event structure reflects the idea that **Adder** objects may perform **add** and **reset** actions at any point in time, whereas **sub** actions may only be performed when enough

add actions have already been occurred (since then the **quantity** attribute is greater than zero). Therefore, it is not possible to have an event **create;sub(1)** in Fig. 2 which is causally dependent from the event **create**. Thus, **Adder** is semantically described by a locally sequential event structure that takes all specified axioms (e.g., *enabled, changing*) into considerations. The two conditions for locally sequential event structures are fulfilled in the **Adder** event structure: (1) the minimal element is ϵ and (2) there are no concurrent events since all local configurations are totally ordered. For instance, the local configuration $\downarrow$ **create;add(2);sub(1)** = {**create;add(2);sub(1), create;add(2), create**} is totally ordered.

With these preliminaries we will now investigate the specified **Adder-R** template and the semantics of objects of this type. This way, we will show how locally sequential event structures are glued together at some points to build a global event structure where concurrency arises. Moreover, we will point out the role of process declarations as a means of action reification and work towards the formalization of the relationship between the models of abstract, concrete, and base objects.

4 Semantics of Transaction Specifications

As already mentioned, composed objects are semantically described as a concurrent combination of the corresponding locally sequential event structures satisfying the specified axioms. More precisely, webs are built out of local life cycles of the involved objects. Some of the events are shared by different objects by means of overlapping life cycles.

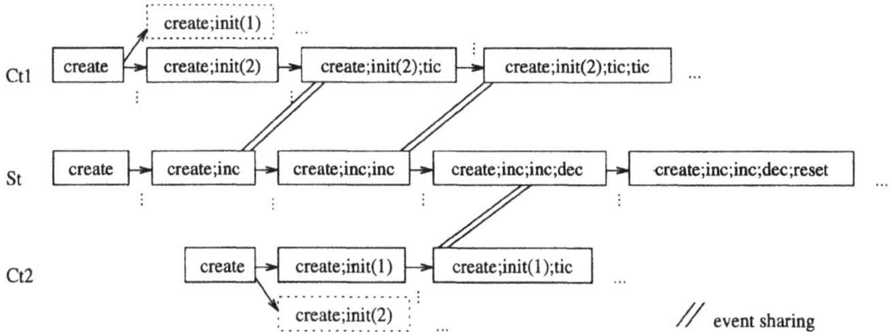

Fig. 3. Event structure of Adder-R objects

Adder-R is a composition of **Step** and **Counter**. **Step** and **Counter** are each interpreted through locally sequential event structures analogously to **Adder**. The locally sequential event structures are concurrently combined to a (global) event structure by composing them to **Adder-R**. The locally sequential event.

They are identified at shared events. The knotting points are specified in the process declaration part of `Adder-R` via parallelism (||).

The specification of processes to restrict the intended behavior is motivated by convenience. It is just more natural to specify certain patterns instead of many temporal axioms. Though it is equivalently expressible with temporal logic formulae that an object has a very determined behavior. Therefore, the process declaration in `Adder-R` on the one hand restricts the possible behavior to sequences of `Step` and `Counter` actions which represent `add`, `sub`, ... actions and on the other hand ties the event structures together at shared events. E.g., the statement `St.inc`||`Cti.tic`) in the process declaration of `Adder-R` says that those events where the `St.inc`-action in the `Step` event structure and the `Cti.tic`-action in the `Counteri` event structure occurs, respectively, should happen synchronously. Thus, the event structures are identified at those points.

Let us take the transaction sequence `CREATE;ADD(2);SUB(1);RESET` already mentioned in Sect. 2. Executing this sequence in `Adder-R` would imply the execution of several `Step` and `Counter` actions. To give a fully detailed account it is

```
St.create;Ct1.create;Ct1.init(2);St.inc||Ct1.tic;St.inc||Ct1.tic;
        Ct2.create;Ct2.init(1);St.dec||Ct2.tic;St.reset.
```

Projecting this sequence to events of the involved objects `St,Ct1,Ct2` gives exactly the web of three life cycles in Fig. 3. The information about event sharing in different locally sequential event structures is pictured by double bars between these events. `St.inc`||`Ct1.tic` and `St.dec`||`Ct2.tic` occur simultaneously. We only depicted parts of the incorporated locally sequential event structures by focussing on the specific transaction sequence. The whole global event structure of `Adder-R` consists of a combination of locally sequential event structures for `Step` and `Counter` interconnected at some events. The dotted-framed events indicate that the locally sequential event structures of the involved objects are themselves complex structures.

One can see that knotting together the locally sequential event structures like this keeps the relation between events as flexible as possible. That means that events are only ordered or identified via sharing if necessary. All other events are concurrent. The independence of actions of different objects is preserved as far as possible by composing the local event structures in a concurrent manner. Only necessary causalities are propagated through event sharing. E.g., in Fig. 3 the `create;init(2)` event of `Ct1`, the `create` event of `St`, and the `create;init(1)` event of `Ct2` are concurrent.

Up to now we constructed from locally sequential event structures a concurrent global event structure for `Adder-R`. Let us come back to the idea that independent actions of different transactions may be executed in any order. The possible interleavings of transactions can be obtained by flattening the global concurrent event structure to a sequential one. On this intention we substitute every global (concurrent) life cycle of the global (concurrent) event structure by a set of totally ordered life cycles in the following way: concurrency of two events in a global life cycle gives rise to two new life cycles where theses events appear in any order.

Given an event structure $E = (Ev, \rightarrow)$, a locally sequential event structure $E_{seq} = (Ev_{seq}, \rightarrow_{seq})$ is called a sequentialization of E iff (1) $Ev = Ev_{seq}$ and (2) $\forall e, f \in Ev : e \rightarrow^* f \Rightarrow e \rightarrow^*_{seq} f$.

With respect to the example in Fig. 3 the sequentialization of this event structure would contain as an interleaving sequence also the one intuitively wanted (cf Fig 1 and equation (1) in Sect. 2). Therefore, `Adder-R` is semantically described on the one hand as a concurrent composition of sequential objects, but on the other hand one can also look at it as a sequential object, i.e., as the set of all interleaving sequences derived by flattening from the possible distributed life cycles of its event structure. This means that the reified object `Adder-R` allows for more liberal sequences than those resulting from substituting the refinement transactions in the sequential life cycles of the abstract object.

We have only shown by example that our proposal of taking transaction specifications as a reason to identify events in the corresponding event structures is successful with respect to liberalizing sequential composition. Subsequently, we will investigate more generally the relation between the different models of abstract, base and reified objects and formulate a condition, when reification is semantically correct.

5 Semantic Reification Condition

Our approach to reification is 3-layered. We specify an abstract object (`Adder`) and try to use base objects (`Step` and `Counter`) to implement the abstract behavior by importing them in a reified object as components (`Adder-R`). Further restrictions on the behavior of the components (e.g., process declarations) might be specified in the reified object. We gave an exemplary outline of the semantics of the reified object in the last section. Now we will investigate the general relationship between the models of abstract, base, and reified objects and establish a reification condition between them.

In Sect. 3 we already mentioned that the specification of the abstract object type (e.g., template `Adder`) determines an instance signature $\Sigma_{Abs} = (Id_{Abs}, Act_{Abs})$ plus a set of axioms ϕ_{Abs}. For the running example it turns out that $\Sigma_{Adder} = (Id_{Adder}, Act_{Adder})$ where Id_{Adder}={`Ad`}, Act_{Adder} ={`create`,`add(1)`,`add(2)`,..., `sub(1)`,..., `reset`} and ϕ_{Adder} = {∀ `n:nat (Y(quantity=v)` ∧ `add(n))`⇒ `quantity=v+n`,...} (*changing* axiom of `Adder`, `Y` temporal previous operator).

The semantics of an abstract object is a locally sequential event structure $E_{Abs} = (Ev_{Abs}, \rightarrow_{Abs})$ where events are occurrences of Act_{Abs}-actions. The event structure reflects the specified axioms, i.e., all possible life cycles fulfill the axioms (cf Fig. 2). Analogously, each base object type Bas_i, $i = 1, \ldots, n$ (e.g., `Step` and `Counter`) is syntactically fixed through a signature $\Sigma_{Bas_i} = (Id_{Bas_i}, Act_{Bas_i})$

and a set of axioms ϕ_{Bas_i}. Correspondingly to the abstract objects, semantics is given by locally sequential event structures $E_{Bas_i} = (Ev_{Bas_i}, \rightarrow_{Bas_i})$, $i = 1, \ldots, n$.

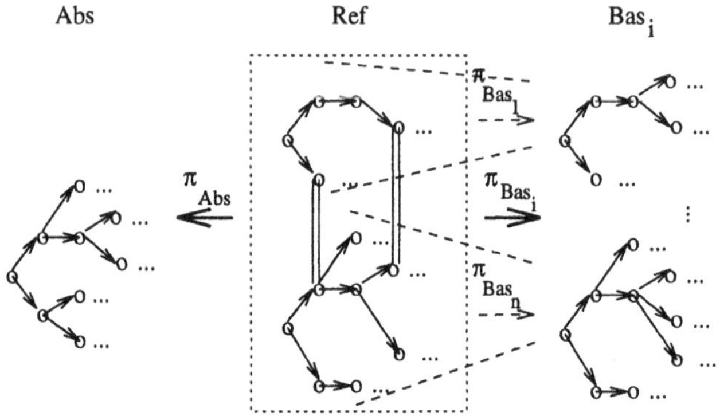

Fig. 4. Relationship between abstract, base and reified models

The reified object is defined as a combination of base objects plus possibly additionally specified attributes, actions, and axioms. Accordingly, the signature of the reified object partly ensues from the signatures of the base objects: $\Sigma_{Ref} = (Id_{Ref}, Act_{Ref}) = (Id_{Ref}, \bigcup_i Act_{Bas_i} \cup Act_{Ref'})$ and $\phi_{Ref} = \bigcup_i \phi_{Bas_i} \cup \phi_{Ref'}$.

The corresponding event structure $E_{Ref} = (Ev_{Ref}, \rightarrow_{Ref})$ has to fulfill the following conditions to be a reification of the abstract object on top of the base objects (see Fig. 4): (1) Given a (distributed) life cycle in E_{Ref}, the projections to Bas_i events ($i = 1, \ldots, n$) must result in valid life cycles of the corresponding E_{Bas_i} event structures, but not all life cycles of E_{Bas_i} must show up in E_{Ref}. This means, that the reified object may only further restrict the behavior of base objects, but may not change the behavior of the involved base objects. The semantics of base objects can only be limited, but cannot be changed completely. As such the behavior of the base objects is inherited to the reified object; (2) the mapping of events to the corresponding abstract event must fit into the abstract behavior, i.e., the reified behavior simulates the abstract behavior. This is a highly non-injective map since several events in the reified event structure belong to one transaction and therefore, they are mapped to the same abstract event. Moreover, abstracting the reified behavior to abstract behavior must be surjective. This is due to the fact that we do not cope with nondeterminism in our models, so that the reification can not choose between some non-deterministic abstract behavior. All abstract life cycles represent behavior which has to be implemented.

Formalizing these points results in the following reification condition:

Definition 1 *Given event structures* $E_{Abs}, \bigcup_i E_{Bas_i} (i = 1, \ldots, n)$, *and* E_{Ref}.

The corresponding set of life cycles are denoted as $\Lambda_{Abs}, \Lambda_{Bas_i}$, *and* Λ_{Ref}, *respectively.*

E_{Ref} *is a reification of* E_{Abs} *on top of* $\bigcup_i E_{Bas_i}$ *iff there exist order-preserving (partial) maps* $\pi_{Abs} : Ev_{Ref} \rightarrow Ev_{Abs}$ *and* $\pi_{Bas_i} : Ev_{Ref} \rightarrow Ev_{Bas_i}$ $(i = 1, \ldots, n)$ *s.t. for all (distributed) life cycle* $\lambda_{Ref} \in \Lambda_{Ref}$ *the following two conditions hold:*

$$\pi^*_{Bas_i}(\lambda_{Ref}) \in \Lambda_{Bas_i}$$
$$\pi^*_{Abs}(\Lambda_{Ref}) = \Lambda_{Abs}$$

where $\pi^*_{Abs}, \pi^*_{Bas_i}$ *are extensions of* π_{Abs}, π_{Bas_i}, *respectively, to (sets of) life cycles.*

The first condition states that the semantics of the components of the reified object are not altered. Thus, the behavior of a *Ref* object is composed out of behavior of Bas_i objects. At the most the Bas_i behavior is restricted. New events may occur because of executing additionally specified actions. The second condition reflects the surjectivity condition described above. The mapping of the behavior of the reified object to abstract behavior reaches all life cycles of the abstract object.

6 Concluding Remarks and Future Work

In this paper we presented an approach for integrating transactions into the object-oriented specification language TROLL and applied these notations to express action reification. The accompanying problems of concurrency control were illustrated by example and the intended aim of liberalizing sequential composition of transactions was explained. After we have presented a sketch of the underlying semantic framework of event structures applicable to TROLL specifications, we pointed out how the raised problems can be solved. Our proposal for the treatment of transaction specifications as a means of action reification constitutes a possibility to reach the wanted weak serial composition. We illustrated the intended models for transaction declarations and how they realize the liberal sequential composition. Furthermore, we generally described the correct relation between the models of objects participating in a reification process.

Still a lot of work remains to be done. We only considered the semantic aspect of reification up to now. On the syntactical side we intend to work on the nature of reification functions. We will establish a language for describing (systems of) objects in which reification is declared. We are interested in the kind of formulas for which validity remains after application of reification, i.e., proofs of formulas commute with applications of reification functions. We would like to adopt process languages like CSP [Hoa78] or CCS [Mil80] to built a general structure for expressing action reification syntactically. Thus, we will be able to describe more formally how actions are reified by process descriptions than shown in the TROLL specifications. On this basis we will investigate when action reification works out, i.e.,

$$S \models \varphi$$
$$\Updownarrow$$
$$Ref(S) \models Ref(\varphi)$$

where S is a process algebraic term, $Ref(S)$ is the corresponding reified term, φ a formula, and $Ref(\varphi)$ the refined formula. Work in this direction has been done by [RW94, Weh93] which we would like to take as a starting point. Using the semantic framework of event structures they provide results on the refinement of formulas formulated in a variant of the trace based extension of PTL [Thi94].

Acknowledgements

Special thanks are due to Hans-Dieter Ehrich whose work on DTL was the starting point for the presented investigations. Several fruitful and encouraging discussions on semantics and logics helped a lot to clarify the understanding of the general framework. [ES95] was the basis for investigations concerning reification in object-oriented specifications. Thanks to our Braunschweig colleagues who helped a lot to improve this paper by critical and constructive remarks. Furthermore, our partners from the IS-CORE and COMPASS projects contributed to this work with fruitful discussions on semantics and reification topics. Especially J. Fiadeiro, U. Goltz, M. Huhn, P. Niebert, and H. Wehrheim gave valuable support with their comments and questions concerning reification issues.

References

[AH93] L. Aceto and M. Hennessy. Towards Action-Refinement in Process Algebras. *Information and Computation*, 103:204–269, 1993.

[EGL89] H.-D. Ehrich, M. Gogolla, and U.W. Lipeck. *Algebraische Spezifikation abstrakter Datentypen – Eine Einführung in die Theorie.* Teubner, Stuttgart, 1989.

[Elm92] A.K. Elmagarmid, editor. *Database Transaction Models for Advanced Applications.* Data Management Systems. Morgan Kaufmann, San Mateo, California, 1992.

[EM90] H. Ehrig and B. Mahr. *Fundamentals of Algebraic Specification 2: Modules and Constraints.* Springer, Berlin, 1990.

[ES90] H.-D. Ehrich and A. Sernadas. Algebraic Implementation of Objects over Objects. In J. W. deBakker, W.-P. deRoever, and G. Rozenberg, editors, *Proc. REX Workshop "Stepwise Refinement of Distributed Systems: Models, Formalisms, Correctness"*, pages 239–266. LNCS 430, Springer, Berlin, 1990.

[ES95] H.-D. Ehrich and A. Sernadas. Local Specification of Distributed Families of Sequential Objects. This volume.

[ESSS94] H.-D. Ehrich, A. Sernadas, G. Saake, and C. Sernadas. Distributed Temporal Logic for Concurrent Object Families. In R. Wieringa and R. Feenstra, editors, *Working papers of the International Workshop on Information Systems - Correctness and Reusability*, pages 22–30. Vrije Universiteit Amsterdam, RapportNr. IR-357, 1994.

[FM90] J. Fiadeiro and T. Maibaum. Describing, Structuring and Implementing Objects. In J.W. de Bakker, W.P. de Roever, and G. Rozenberg, editors, *Foundations of Object-Oriented Languages (Proc. REX/FOOL Workshop, Noordwijkerhood (NL))*, pages 274–310. Springer, Berlin, LNCS 489, 1990.

[FM94] J.L. Fiadeiro and T. Maibaum. Sometimes "Tommorrow" is "Sometime" – Action Refinement in a Temporal Logic of Objects. In D. M. Gabbay and H. J. Ohlbach, editors, *Proc. First Int. Conf. on Temporal Logic, ICTL, Bonn, Germany, July 1994*, pages 48–66. Springer, 1994. LNAI 827.

[FSMS92] J. Fiadeiro, C. Sernadas, T. Maibaum, and A. Sernadas. Describing and Structuring Objects for Conceptual Schema Development. In P. Loucopoulos and R. Zicari, editors, *Concepual Modeling, Databases, and CASE: An Integrated View of Information Systems Development*, pages 117–138. John Wiley & Sons, Inc., 1992.

[Hoa72] C.A.R. Hoare. Proof of Correctness of Data Representations. *Acta Informatica*, 1:271–281, 1972.

[Hoa78] C.A.R. Hoare. Communicating Sequential Processes. *Communications of the ACM*, 21(8):666–677, 1978.

[HSJ+94] T. Hartmann, G. Saake, R. Jungclaus, P. Hartel, and J. Kusch. Revised Version of the Modelling Language TROLL (Version 2.0). Informatik-Bericht 94–03, Technische Universität Braunschweig, 1994.

[Jif89] H. Jifeng. Various Simulations and Refinements. In J.W. de Bakker, W.-P. de Roever, and G. Rozenberg, editors, *Stepwise Refinement of Distributed Systems: Models, Formalism, Correctness, Proc. REX Workshop, Mook, The Netherlands, May/June 1989*, pages 340–360. Springer, 1989. LNCS 430.

[Kat94] S. Katz. Global Equivalence Proof for ISTL. In D. M. Gabbay and H. J. Ohlbach, editors, *Proc. First Int. Conf. on Temporal Logic, ICTL, Bonn, Germany, July 1994*, pages 17–29. Springer, 1994. LNAI 827.

[LMWF94] N. Lynch, M. Merritt, W. Weihl, and A. Fekete. *Atomic Transactions.* Data Management Systems. Morgan Kaufmann, San Mateo, California, 1994.

[Mil80] R. Milner. *A Calculus of Communicating Systems.* Springer, Berlin, 1980.

[Nip86] T. Nipkow. Nondeterministic data types: models and implementations. *Acta Informatica*, 22:629–661, 1986.

[RW94] A. Rensink and H. Wehrheim. Weak Sequential Composition in Process Algebras. In B. Jonsson and J. Parrow, editors, *Proc. Fifth Int. Conf. on Concurrency Theory, Concur'94, Uppsala, Sweden*, pages 226–241. Springer, August 1994. LNCS 836.

[SGG$^+$91] C. Sernadas, P. Gouveia, J. Gouveia, A. Sernadas, and P. Resende. The Reification Dimension in Object-oriented Data Base Design. In D.J. Harper and M.C. Norrie, editors, *Specifications of Database Systems, Glasgow*, pages 275–298. Springer, 1991. Workshop in Computing.

[SGS92] C. Sernadas, P. Gouveia, and A. Sernadas. Refinement: Layered Definition of Conceptual Schemata. In E.D. Falkenberg, C. Rolland, and E.N. El-Sayed, editors, *Information System Concepts: Improving the Understanding*, pages 19–51. North-Holland, 1992. IFIP Transactions.

[SSW91] K.-D. Schewe, J.W. Schmidt, and I. Wetzel. Specification and Refinement in an Integrated Database Application Environment. In S. Prehn and W.J. Toetenel, editors, *Proc. VDM'91, Formal Software Development Methods*. Springer, 1991. LNCS 551/552.

[ST88] D. Sannella and A. Tarlecki. Towards formal development of programs from algebraic specifications: implementations revisited. *Acta Informatica*, 25:233–281, 1988.

[Thi94] P.S. Thiagarajan. A Trace Based Extension of Linear Time Temporal Logic. In *Proc. 9th annual IEEE Symposium on Logic in Computer Science, CNAM, Paris, France*, pages 438–447. IEEE Computer Society Press, July 4-7 1994.

[vGG90] R. van Glabbeck and U. Goltz. Equivalences and Refinement. In I. Guessarian, editor, *Semantics of Systems of Concurrent Processes*, pages 309–333. Springer, April 1990. LNCS 469.

[Vog90] W. Vogler. Bisimulation and Action Refinement. Technical Report SFB 342/10/90 A, Technische Universität München, Mai 1990.

[Weh93] H. Wehrheim. Parametric Action Refinement. Technical Report 18, Universität Hildesheim, Institut für Informatik, Postfach 101363, 31113 Hildesheim, November 1993. Hildesheimer Informatik Berichte.

Local Specification of Distributed Families of Sequential Objects*

Hans-Dieter Ehrich[1] and Amílcar Sernadas[2]

[1] Abteilung Datenbanken, Technische Universität
Postfach 3329, D-38023 Braunschweig, Germany
[2] Departamento de Matemática, Instituto Superior Técnico
Av. Rovisco Pais, P-1096 Lisboa Codex, Portugal

Abstract. Fully concurrent models of distributed object systems are specified using linear temporal logic that does not per se cope with concurrency. This is achieved by employing the principle of local sequentiality: we specify from local viewpoints assuming that there is no intra-object concurrency but full inter-object concurrency. Local formulae are labelled by identity terms. For interaction, objects may refer to actions of other objects, e.g., calling them to happen synchronously. A locality predicate allows for making local statements about other objects. The interpretation structures are global webs of local life cycles, glued together at shared communication events. These interpretation structures are embedded in an interpretation frame that is a labelled locally sequential event structure. Two initiality results are presented: the category of labelled locally sequential event structures has initial elements, and so has the full subcategory of those satisfying given temporal axioms. As in abstract data type theory, these initial elements are obvious candidates for assigning standard semantics to signatures and specifications.

1 Introduction

In abstract data type theory, higher-order model classes like isomorphism classes of many-sorted algebras are specified with (conditional) equational logic that does not per se allow for specifying such classes. The trick is to employ some general higher-order principle to specifiable classes. A popular principle of this kind is initiality, i.e., restriction to initial models.

This paper suggests an analogous trick for distributed systems specification. The higher-order principle is *local sequentiality*. Employing local sequentiality, we can specify fully concurrent models of distributed computation using a logic that does not per se cope with concurrency.

Local sequentiality means that we distinguish between local objects and global families of objects, making the general assumption that there is no intra-object concurrency but full inter-object concurrency.

* This work was partly supported by the EU under ESPRIT-III BRA WG 6071 IS-CORE (Information Systems - COrrectness and REusability) and BRA WG 6112 COMPASS (COMPrehensive Algebraic approach to System Specification and development) and by ESDI under research contract OBLOG (OBject LOGic).

Objects are locally specified in a sequential process logic, linear temporal logic in our case. Local formulae are labelled by identity terms. Interaction is specified by locally referring to actions of other objects, e.g., calling them to happen synchronously. For making statements about other objects, a locality predicate is introduced.

The interpretation structures for linear temporal logic are life cycles, i.e., linear causality chains of events. Accordingly, our interpretation structures for local specification are global webs of local life cycles, glued together at shared communication events. These interpretation structures are embedded in an interpretation frame that is a labelled locally sequential event structure. Interpretation frames are models of processes.

This extends the simple models we used in our previous work where interpretations were (sets of) life cycles [SEC90, EGS91] or menues [ES91]. The life cycle model has been used as a semantic basis for object specification languages OBLOG [SSE87, SSG+91], TROLL [JSHS91, SJE92, Ju93, HSJHK94], TROLL *light* [CGH92, GCH93], and GNOME [SR94].

Our work has been greatly influenced by related work on specification languages and theoretical foundations. In a sense, we integrate work on algebraic specification of data types [EGL89, EM85, EM90] and databases [Eh86, EDG88], process specification [Ho85, Mi89], the specification of reactive systems [Se80, MP89, Sa91a], conceptual modeling [Ch76, Bo85, EGH+92, SF91, SJH93] and knowledge representation [ST89, MB89].

Approaches to logic and algebraic foundations of object-orientation and concurrency have given essential input to the work reported here. The results in [FSMS91, FM91, FM92, SSC92] have been influential. FOOPS [GM87, GW90] has provided insights in the algebraic nature of objects. Algebraic approaches to concurrency are given in [AR92, MM93, Br93].

The local specification logic and interpretation structures put forward in this paper are influenced by the n-agent logic in [LMRT91], but we deviate from that logic in essential respects: we have more elementary temporal operators, and our interpretations are quite different.

In a companion paper [ESSS95], the foundations outlined here are applied to the semantic description of an abstract object specification language.

2 Object signatures and interpretations

2.1 Data signatures

We assume that the reader is familiar with data signatures and their algebraic interpretations, but we briefly introduce our notation and terminology.

A *data signature* is a pair $\Sigma_D = (S_D, \boldsymbol{\Omega}_D)$ where S_D is a set of *data sorts*, and $\boldsymbol{\Omega}_D = \{\Omega_{x,s}\}_{x \in S_D^*, s \in S_D}$ is an $S_D^* \times S_D$-indexed family of sets of *data operation symbols*. Given an S_D-indexed set $\boldsymbol{X} = \{X_s\}_{s \in S_D}$ of variable symbols, the Σ_D-*terms over* $\boldsymbol{X}$ are denoted by $\boldsymbol{T}_{\Sigma_D}(\boldsymbol{X})$.

If $x = s_1 \ldots s_n$, we write $\omega : s_1 \times \ldots \times s_n \to s$ or $\omega : x \to s \, [\in \Omega]$ for $\omega \in \Omega_{s_1 \ldots s_n, s}$.

An *interpretation* of Σ_D is a Σ_D-algebra $\boldsymbol{U}$ with carrier sets s_U for each $s \in S_D$, and operations $\omega_U : x_U \to s_U$ for each operator $\omega : x \to s \in \boldsymbol{\Omega}$. If $x = s_1 \ldots s_n \in S_D^*$, then $x_U = s_{1U} \times \ldots \times s_{nU}$ is the cartesian product. The interpretation of a term $t \in \boldsymbol{T}_{\Sigma_D}(\boldsymbol{X})$ in $\boldsymbol{U}$ with a given variable assignment θ is denoted by t_U^θ.

The class of all Σ_D-algebras is structured by Σ_D*-algebra morphisms*. A Σ_D-algebra morphism $\boldsymbol{h} : \boldsymbol{U} \to \boldsymbol{V}$ is a family of maps $\boldsymbol{h} = \{h_s : s_U \to s_V\}_{s \in S_D}$ such that, for each operator $\omega : x \to s \in \boldsymbol{\Omega}$ and each element $\boldsymbol{a} \in x_U$, we have $h_s(\omega_U(\boldsymbol{a})) = \omega_V(\boldsymbol{h}_x(\boldsymbol{a}))$.

The nice properties of the category Σ_D-**alg** of Σ_D-algebras and Σ_D-algebra morphisms are well known and have been utilized for elegant semantic constructions for abstract data type specifications [EGL89, EM85, EM90].

2.2 Class and instance signatures

Classes in the sense of what follows are *object* classes, not classes in the sense of set theory.

Definition 1. Let Σ_D be a data signature. A *class signature over* Σ_D is a triple $\Sigma_C = (S_O, I, A)$ where S_O is a set of *object sorts*, $I = \{I_{x,b}\}_{x \in S_{DO}^*, b \in S_O}$ is an $S_{DO}^* \times S_O$-indexed set family of *instance operators*, and $A = \{A_{x,b}\}_{x \in S_{DO}^*, b \in S_O}$ is an $S_{DO}^* \times S_O$-indexed set family of *action operators*. Here, $S_{DO} = S_D \cup S_O$.

Like for data operators, we use the notation $i : x \to b$ for $i \in I_{x,b}$ and $a : x \to b$ for $a \in A_{x,b}$.

Example 1. We give a signature for a class of flip-flops using an intuitive ad-hoc notation that easily translates to our formalism. The specification says that flip-flops can be created, set, reset and destroyed. Moreover, we have an infinite set of flip-flop identities: F1, F2, R(n) for all natural numbers n, and a "next" flip-flop N(f) for every flip-flop f. Each flip-flop identity is associated with a flip-flop instance. This does not necessarily mean that the system has infinitely many flip-flops, an instance may have several "alias" names. This aspect is not persued in the present paper.

```
class flip-flop;
   object sort FF;
   data sort nat;
   actions create, set, reset, destroy;
   instances F1, F2, R : nat, N : FF;
end flip-flop.
```

The notation is intended to mean the following class signature. The underlying data signature is assumed to contain the sort nat of natural numbers.

$S_O = \{\mathtt{FF}\}$

$I = \{\mathtt{F1} : \to \mathtt{FF},\ \mathtt{F2} : \to \mathtt{FF},\ \mathtt{R} : \mathtt{nat} \to \mathtt{FF},\ \mathtt{N} : \mathtt{FF} \to \mathtt{FF}\}$

$A = \{\mathtt{create} : \to \mathtt{FF},\ \mathtt{destroy} : \to \mathtt{FF},\ \mathtt{set} : \to \mathtt{FF},\ \mathtt{reset} : \to \mathtt{FF}\}$

There are infinitely many flip-flop identities, e.g., `F1`, `F2`, `R(0)`, `R(1)`, ... , `N(F1)`, `N(F2)`, `N(R(0))`, `N(N(R(0)))`, etc.

flip-flops can be created, set, reset, and destroyed. The "value" of a flip-flop is represented by the fact that `set` or `reset`, respectively, is *enabled* (cf. section 3). □

The interpretation of a class signature Σ_C is indirectly given by (1) extending the underlying data signature Σ_D to cover the identities and actions specified in the class signature, and (2) deriving an instance signature Σ_I for the identities and individual action alphabets of all object instances.

The data signature extension is defined as follows. Each object sort b goes with the two data sorts of object identities b^i and object actions b^a, respectively. Thus, the object sorts S_O give rise to two sets of data sorts called S_O^i and S_O^a. Let $S^i = S_D \cup S_O^i$ and $S^a = S_D \cup S_O^a$. For $x = s_1 \ldots s_n \in S_{DO}^*$, we define $x^i = s_1^i \ldots s_n^i \in S^{i*}$ where, for $j \in \{1, \ldots, n\}$, $s_j^i = s_j$ if $s_j \in S_D$. The notation x^a is defined correspondingly.

Definition 2. Given a data signature $\Sigma_D = (S_D, \boldsymbol{\Omega}_D)$ and a class signature $\Sigma_C = (S_O, I, A)$ over Σ_D, the *extended data signature* $\Sigma = (S, \boldsymbol{\Omega})$ is given by

$$S = S_D \cup S_O^a \cup S_O^i$$

where $S_O^a = \{b^a \mid b \in S_O\} \cup \{ac\}$ and $S_O^i = \{b^i \mid b \in S_O\} \cup \{id\}$, and

$$\boldsymbol{\Omega} = \boldsymbol{\Omega}_D \cup \boldsymbol{\Omega}_O^a \cup \boldsymbol{\Omega}_O^i \cup \boldsymbol{\Omega}_O^{ai}$$

where, for every object sort $b \in S_O$ and every $x \in S_{DO}^*$, we have $\Omega^a_{O;b^i x^a, b^a} = A_{x,b}$, $\Omega^i_{O;x^i,b^i} = I_{x,b}$; $\Omega^{ai}_{O;b^a p^i, bool} = \{ai_{bp}\}$. The other sets in the families are empty. Moreover, for every object sort $b \in S_O$, we assume $b^i \leq id$ and $b^a \leq ac$.

Before we explain the transformation, we illustrate it by the `flip-flop` example.

Example 2. The `flip-flop` class signature in example 1 transforms to the following data signature extension.

sorts $\mathtt{FF}^i \leq \mathtt{id}$, $\mathtt{FF}^a \leq \mathtt{ac}$
ops `F1, F2 :` $\rightarrow \mathtt{FF}^i$
`R : nat` $\rightarrow \mathtt{FF}^i$
`N :` $\mathtt{FF}^i \rightarrow \mathtt{FF}^i$
`create, set, reset, destroy :` $\mathtt{FF}^i \rightarrow \mathtt{FF}^a$
$\mathtt{ai}_{\mathtt{FF},\mathtt{FF}}$ `:` $\mathtt{FF}^a \times \mathtt{FF}^i \rightarrow \mathtt{bool}$ □

The sort *id* is to be interpreted by all identities in the system. Because of the standard unique naming assumption in object-oriented systems, this should be the disjoint union of the interpretations of the sorts b^i for $b \in S_O$. Using order sorting, we have $b^i \leq id$ for every object sort $b \in S_O$.

The sort ac is to be interpreted by all actions in the system, i.e., by the union of the interpretations of the sorts b^a for $b \in S_O$. We do not require disjointness here, we will allow for overlap expressing that actions are shared among objects. But still, using order sorting, we have $b^a \leq id$ for every object sort $b \in S_O$.

The data identity operators $i : x^i \to b^i \in \Omega_O^i$ are derived from the object identity operators $i : x \to b \in I$. They may be parameterized over data, including identities but not actions. So we can cope with objects identified by other objects.

The data action operators $a : b^i \times x^a \to b^a \in \Omega_O^a$ are derived from the object action operators $a : x \to b \in A$. They may have actions ("methods") as parameters. Implicitly, this allows for identity parameters as well since each action carries the identity of its object with it. Data action operators are associated with object instances, so we have identities of sort b as additional parameter. If $a(i, t_1, \ldots, t_n) \in T_\Sigma(\boldsymbol{X})_{b^a}$, we call i the *identity of action* $a(i, t_1, \ldots, t_n)$.

For any object sorts $b, p \in S_O$, the id-of-action operators $ai_{bp} : b^a \times p^i \to bool$ are to be interpreted by relations associating with each individual action the identities of its objects. Of course, the equation $ai_{bb}(a(u, y), u) = true$ should hold for every $a : b^i \times x^a \to b^a \in \Omega_O^a$. Moreover, if the occurrence of action a' of sort $i' : b'$ implies the occurrence of action a'' of sort $i'' : b''$ (e.g., via synchronous action calling), then a' should also belong to the actions of i'', i.e., $ai_{b'b''}(a', i'') = true$. The idea is that $ai_{bp}(a, i) = true$ should hold whenever action a affects object i.

Definition 3. An *instance signature* is a pair $\Sigma_I = (Id, \boldsymbol{Ac})$ where Id is a set of *identities*, and $\boldsymbol{Ac} = \{Ac_i\}_{i \in Id}$ is an Id-indexed family of *action alphabets*.

An instance signature is a distributed action alphabet, providing a local action alphabet for each object. Communication is established by actions shared among two or more objects.

Definition 4. The *partners* of an action α are $P(\alpha) = \{i \in Id \mid \alpha \in Ac_i\}$.

Let $\Sigma_C = (S_O, I, A)$ be a class signature over the data signature $\Sigma_D = (S_D, \boldsymbol{\Omega}_D)$. Let $\boldsymbol{U}$ be an interpretation of the extended data signature Σ.

Definition 5. The *instance signature* determined by Σ and $\boldsymbol{U}$ is $\Sigma_I = (Id, \boldsymbol{Ac})$ where $Id = id_U$ is the global set of identities, and $\boldsymbol{Ac} = \{Ac_i\}_{i \in Id}$ is the Id-indexed family of action alphabets $Ac_i = \{\alpha \in ac_U \mid ai_{qb}(\alpha, i) = true$ for some sort $q \in S_O$ and the sort b of $i\}$.

2.3 An event-based interpretation of instance signatures

The interpretations of instance signatures are concurrent processes synchronized via shared events, i.e., action occurrences.

Suitable interpretation structures can be based on any distributed process model, for instance Petri nets or distributed transition systems. But the interpretation structures should fit to the specification logic. Choosing the latter suggests the appropriate process model.

As an example, for simplicity, and because of its proven practicality [MP89, Se80, Sa91a, Sa91b], we use linear temporal logic for specifying the local properties of individual objects. The suitable interpretation structures for linear temporal logic are linear traces of events, also called life cycles [SEC90, EGS91].

There is an obvious distributed model based on individual life cycles and event sharing, namely global webs of life cycles glued together at shared communication events. This is the model we adopt here. A frame for this model is an event structure that is locally sequential.

Event structures were introduced by Winskel [Wi80]. A recent survey of models for concurrency including event structures is [WN93]. We briefly give the definition and introduce our notation. Our main deviation from standard notation is that we use $\rightarrow^*$ for causality instead of the usual $\leq$ because we use the latter for order sorting, and we want to use event structures where causality is the reflexive and transitive closure of a base relation $\rightarrow$ of "step" causality. The following definition is taken from [WN93].

Definition 6. A (discrete prime) *event structure* is a triple $E = (Ev, \rightarrow^*, \#)$ where Ev is a set of events and $\rightarrow^*, \# \subseteq Ev \times Ev$ are binary relations called *causality* and *conflict*, respectively. Causality $\rightarrow^*$ is a partial ordering, and conflict $\#$ is symmetric and irreflexive. For each event $e \in E$, its *local configuration* $\downarrow e = \{e' \mid e' \rightarrow^* e\}$ is finite. Conflict propagates over causality, i.e., $e \# e' \rightarrow^* e'' \Rightarrow e \# e''$ for all $e, e', e'' \in Ev$. Two events $e, e' \in Ev$ are *concurrent*, $e\, co\, e'$ iff $\neg(e \rightarrow^* e' \vee e' \rightarrow^* e \vee e \# e')$.

In the sequel, the order-theoretic notions refer to causality.

Definition 7. Let E be an event structure. A *life cycle* in E is a maximal totally ordered sub-event structure of E.

Definition 8. A *sequential* event structure E is an event structure in which (1) there is a unique minimal element $\varepsilon \in Ev$, (2) every local configuration $\downarrow e$ is totally ordered, and (3) causally independent events are always in conflict, i.e., for all events $e, f \in Ev$, we have $e \# f$ iff neither $e \rightarrow^* f$ nor $f \rightarrow^* e$ holds. The events $Ev_+ = Ev - \{\varepsilon\}$ are called the *proper* events.

Intuitively, the causally minimal event represents an imaginary "initial event" where no action occurred so far. This represents the "pre-natal" state of an object where nothing happened yet (not even a "birth" action).

With respect to causality, a sequential event structure E is a rooted tree. It represents a set of life cycles grouped together by equal prefixes. A single life cycle is also a sequential event structure.

Sequential event structures are our model of objects. There is no intra-object concurrency. Thus, conflict is a derived concept. We omit it from notation. Assuming that causality $\rightarrow^*$ is the reflexive and transitive closure of a base relation $\rightarrow$ of "step" causality, we arrive at the notation

$$E = (Ev, \rightarrow)$$

for sequential event structures. We will extend this notation to any event structure where conflict is determined from causality by a general assumption. Actually, this holds for all event structures we consider here.

The interpretation structures we envisage for a given instance signature Σ_I are labelled locally sequential Σ_I-event structures. This is our model for fully concurrent families of sequential objects. For modelling communication, the local event sets Ev_i may overlap: an event $e \in Ev_i \cap Ev_j \cap \dots$ is shared by objects $i, j, \dots \in Id$.

We make these notions precise, but first we need some notation. Given a set I and an I-indexed family $\boldsymbol{M} = \{M_i\}_{i \in I}$ of sets, we denote their union by $\bigcup \boldsymbol{M} = \bigcup_{i \in I} M_i$. If $\boldsymbol{E} = \{E_i\}_{i \in I}$ is a family of event structures, we denote their union by $\bigcup \boldsymbol{E} = (\bigcup_{i \in I} Ev_i, \bigcup_{i \in I} \rightarrow_i)$.

The notation is justified by the assumption that global conflicts are only those inherited by local conflicts: for all events $e, f \in E$, we have $e \# f$ iff, for some object i and some events $e', f' \in Ev_i$, we have a local conflict $e' \#_i f'$ while $e' \rightarrow^* e$ and $f' \rightarrow^* f$. That is, we globally assume $e\, co\, f$ as a default.

Definition 9. Let $\Sigma_I = (Id, \boldsymbol{Ac})$ be an instance signature. A *Σ_I-event structure* E is the union $\bigcup \boldsymbol{E}$ of an Id-indexed family $\boldsymbol{E} = \{E_i\}_{i \in I}$ of sequential event structures where $E_i = (Ev_i, \rightarrow_i)$. The set family of proper events is denoted by $\boldsymbol{Ev}_+ = \{Ev_{i+}\}_{i \in Id}$, and $Ev_+ = \bigcup \boldsymbol{Ev}_+$.

That is, Σ_I-event structures are *locally sequential*. This model is similar to the n-agent model described in [LMRT91].

Definition 10. Given a Σ_I-event structure E, a *distributed life cycle* $L = (Lc, \rightarrow)$ *in* E is an event structure $L \subseteq E$ that is the union of a family $\boldsymbol{L} = \{L_i\}_{i \in Id} \subseteq \boldsymbol{E}$ of life cycles in E, i.e., $L_i \subseteq E_i$ for every $i \in Id$.

A distributed life cycle is a system of life cycles for the individual objects, glued together at shared "communication" events.

Our interpretation structures are *labelled* distributed life cycles within labelled Σ_I-event structures, so we have to introduce labelling.

Definition 11. Let $E = (Ev, \rightarrow)$ be a Σ_I-event structure. A *labelling for* E is a map $\bar{\alpha} : Ev_+ \rightarrow \bigcup \boldsymbol{Ac}$ that is the union $\bar{\alpha} = \bigcup \boldsymbol{\alpha}$ of a family of maps $\boldsymbol{\alpha} = \{\alpha_i : Ev_{i+} \rightarrow Ac_i\}_{i \in Id}$ satisfying the following condition: for all events $e', e'' \in Ev$, we have $\bar{\alpha}(e') \neq \bar{\alpha}(e'')$ whenever there is an event $e \in Ev$ such that $e \rightarrow e'$ and $e \rightarrow e''$.

Intuitively, each proper event is the occurrence of an action, and the label is supposed to be this action. The imaginary start events ε_i do not have labels. The labels of the immediate successors of an event e are the actions *enabled* at e (cf. definition 21). These must be distinct for different successor events.

Definition 12. An *interpretation frame* for a given instance signature Σ_I is a labelled Σ_I-event structure $\bar{E} = (E, \bar{\alpha})$. An *interpretation structure* within $\bar{E}$ is a labelled distributed life cycle $\bar{L} = (L, \bar{\alpha}\,|_L)$ where $L \subseteq E$.

Now we define one particular interpretation frame determined by a given instance signature Σ_I. The idea is obvious: the events are defined to be all possible occurrences of actions.

However, not every combination of local configurations is a meaningful context for an action to occur. For instance, if I invite you to meet, then both of us must "remember" that invitation, otherwise the meeting cannot take place. More precisely, when we meet, the two of us must not be in local configurations where you are sure I invited you, and I am sure I never did.

The relevant concept is that of a consistent configuration for an action in which it can possibly occur. In such a configuration, any two objects must agree on their past communication. Generalizing the notation for local configurations $\downarrow e$ to sets, we define $\downarrow C = \{e' \mid \exists e \in C : e' \rightarrow^* e\}$ for any subset $C \subseteq Ev$ of events.

Definition 13. Given a Σ_I-event structure $E = (Ev, \rightarrow)$, a *configuration in* E is a set of events $Cf \subseteq Ev$ with the properties (1) $Cf = \downarrow Cf$ and (2) Cf is conflict-free, i.e., $(Cf \times Cf) \cap \# = \emptyset$. If $I \subseteq Id$ is a set of object identities, then a *configuration for* I in E is a configuration that is the range $\gamma(I)$ of a map $\gamma : I \rightarrow Ev$ such that $\gamma(i) \in Ev_i$ for every $i \in I$.

A configuration Cf for I in E contains one event $e_i = \gamma(i) \in Ev_i$ for every $i \in I$. These events e_i need not be distinct. Two different objects $i, j \in I$ may share an event in Cf, i.e., we may have $e_i \in Ev_j$ as well. In this case, e_i and e_j must be causally related because otherwise they would be in conflict.

Definition 14. Given an instance signature $\Sigma_I = (Id, \boldsymbol{Ac})$, the *interpretation frame* $\bar{E}(\Sigma_I) = (E(\Sigma_I), \bar{\alpha})$ is inductively defined as follows. $E(\Sigma_I) = \bigcup \boldsymbol{E}(\Sigma_I)$ where $\boldsymbol{E}(\Sigma_I) = \{E_i\}_{i \in Id}$ where $E_i = (Ev_i, \rightarrow_i)$, for each object $i \in Id$.

(1) $\varepsilon_i \in Ev_i$ for every object $i \in Id$.
(2) if α is an action and Cf is a configuration for α's partners $P(\alpha)$, then $Cf\,\alpha \in Ev_i$ for every partner $i \in P(\alpha)$; as for labelling and causality: we have $\bar{\alpha}(Cf\,\alpha) = \alpha$, and $e \rightarrow_i Cf\,\alpha$ for every $e \in Cf \cap Ev_i$ and every $i \in P(\alpha)$.

The basis of this inductive definition is given by birth events that happen in configurations consisting of one or more "initial events" ε_i. The event $Cf\,\alpha$ represents α occurring in the configuration Cf. This event is shared by the partners of α.

We prove that the construction is sound.

Theorem 15. *For each instance signature Σ_I, $\bar{E}(\Sigma_I)$ is an interpretation frame for Σ_I.*

Proof: We have to show that every local event structure $E_i = (Ev_i, \rightarrow_i)$, $i \in Id$, is sequential, and that the labels are ok, i.e., immediate successors have different labels.

We prove the first by induction over the structure of $\bar{E}(\Sigma_I)$.

Let $i \in Id$ be an identity, and let $e \in E_i$. If $e = \varepsilon_i$, then $\downarrow_i e = \{\varepsilon_i\}$ is trivially totally ordered, where $\downarrow_i e = \downarrow e \cap E_i$. Otherwise, we have $e \in Cf\,\alpha$ for some action $\alpha \in Ac_i$ and some configuration Cf for $P(\alpha)$. Assume that every life cycle prefix so far, i.e., every local configuration $\downarrow_j f$ for $f \in Cf$ and $j \in P(\alpha)$, is totally ordered. Then we have to show that $\downarrow_j Cf\,\alpha$ is totally ordered as well for every $j \in P(\alpha)$.

Assume that, for some partner $j \in P(\alpha)$, $g, g' \in \downarrow_j Cf$. Since $\downarrow_j Cf$ is a linear trace, g and g' are causally related in E_j, say $g \rightarrow_j^* g'$. Since both are causal for $Cf\,\alpha$, $\downarrow_j Cf\,\alpha$ is totally ordered as well.

As for labelling, we have to show that labels of events with a common immediate predecessor are different. But this is obvious from construction since the events are *defined* by the actions applied to the configurations representing the current states of the action's partners. □

Labelled Σ_I-event structures are related by *morphisms*. Adapting general event structure morphisms from [WN93] to our structures, we arrive at the following definition. Let $\Sigma_I = (Id, \boldsymbol{Ac})$ be an instance signature.

Definition 16. Let $E_1 = (Ev_1, \rightarrow_1)$ and $E_2 = (Ev_2, \rightarrow_2)$ be two Σ_I-event structures. A *Σ_I-event structure morphism* $h : E_1 \rightarrow E_2$ is the union $\bigcup \boldsymbol{h}$ of an Id-indexed family of partial surjective maps $\boldsymbol{h} = \{h_i : Ev_{1i} \cdots\twoheadrightarrow Ev_{2i}\}_{i \in Id}$ such that $h : Ev_1 \cdots\twoheadrightarrow Ev_2$ is a partial surjective map, and for all $e_1, e_2 \in Ev_1$, if $h(e_1)$ and $h(e_2)$ are both defined, then $h(e_1) \rightarrow_2 h(e_2)$ iff $e_1 \rightarrow_1 e_2$.

These morphisms are easily extended to *labelled* Σ_I-event structures: if $h(e)$ is defined, then $\bar{\alpha}_2(h(e)) = \bar{\alpha}_1(e)$.

Labelled Σ_I-event structures and their morphisms form a category Σ_I-**evt**. We cannot go into a detailed analysis of this category, we just mention that it has initial elements[3]. In fact, we can prove that the labelled Σ_I-event structure constructed in definition 14 is an initial element.

Theorem 17. *$\bar{E}(\Sigma_I)$ is initial in Σ_I-**evt**.*

Proof: The initial morphism $h : \bar{E}(\Sigma_I) \rightarrow \bar{F}$ to some labelled Σ_I-event structure $\bar{F}$ is defined by sending the minimal element ε_i to the corresponding minimal element in F_i, for every $i \in Id$. The other events are mapped as follows. If $h(Cf)$ is defined for (every event in) a configuration Cf, then we define, for every action α, $h(Cf\,\alpha) = h(Cf)\alpha$ if the latter exists, otherwise $h(Cf\,\alpha)$ is undefined. By $h(Cf)\alpha$ we mean the immediate successor of all events in $h(Cf)$ labelled α. It is not hard to see that this defines a morphism and that it is unique. □

3 Object specification

Our logic for object class specification is a linear temporal logic with locality. We illustrate the idea by means of the `flip-flop` example.

[3] For obvious reasons, we avoid the usual term "object" for an element of a category.

It is beyond the scope of this paper to develop an abstract specification language for class signatures like the one in the `flip-flop` example 1 (cf. [ESSS95]). We give the "target" logic directly into which such a language is to be translated.

That is, we give a specification logic for the extended data signature $\Sigma = (S, \boldsymbol{\Omega})$.

The S-indexed family $\boldsymbol{T}_\Sigma(\boldsymbol{X})$ of sets of *terms* is defined as usual, employing an S-indexed family $\boldsymbol{X}$ of sets of *variables*.

Definition 18. The set $L_\Sigma(\boldsymbol{X})$ of *formulae* is inductively defined as follows:

- $(t_1 =_{ss} t_2) \in L_\Sigma(\boldsymbol{X})$ provided that $t_1, t_2 \in T_\Sigma(\boldsymbol{X})_s$;
- $\tau(i) \in L_\Sigma(\boldsymbol{X})$ provided that $i \in T_\Sigma(\boldsymbol{X})_{id}$;
- $\alpha(i)$, $\triangleright\alpha(i) \in L_\Sigma(\boldsymbol{X})$ provided that $\alpha(i) \in T_\Sigma(\boldsymbol{X})_{ac}$ where $i \in T_\Sigma(\boldsymbol{X})_{id}$ is the identity of α;
- $(\neg\varphi) \in L_\Sigma(\boldsymbol{X})$ provided that $\varphi \in L_\Sigma(\boldsymbol{X})$;
- $(\varphi \Rightarrow \varphi') \in L_\Sigma(\boldsymbol{X})$ provided that $\varphi, \varphi' \in L_\Sigma(\boldsymbol{X})$;
- $(\exists x\ \varphi) \in L_\Sigma(\boldsymbol{X})$ provided that $x \in X_s$ for some $s \in S$ and $\varphi \in L_\Sigma(\boldsymbol{X})$;
- $(\mathsf{X}_i\,\varphi), (\mathsf{F}_i\,\varphi), (\mathsf{Y}_i\,\varphi), (\mathsf{P}_i\,\varphi) \in L_\Sigma(\boldsymbol{X})$ provided that $i \in T_\Sigma(\boldsymbol{X})_{id}$ and $\varphi \in L_\Sigma(\boldsymbol{X})$.

Definition 19. The set $L_\Sigma^\tau(\boldsymbol{X})$ of *local formulae* is the set $\{i : \varphi \mid i \in T_\Sigma(\boldsymbol{X})_{id}, \varphi \in L_\Sigma(\boldsymbol{X})\}$.

The locality predicate $\tau(i)$ says that the formula is local to i, i.e., the "owner" of the local formula is communicating with i. The predicate $\alpha(i)$ means that action α has just occurred in object i. The predicate $\triangleright\alpha(i)$ means that action α is enabled in object i, i.e., it may happen next. Of course, actions must be enabled when they occur (i.e., just before they have just occurred). The symbols for the local temporal operators have the following meaning: X_i means next in i, F_i means sometime in the future of i, P_i means sometime in the past of i, and Y_i means previous (*yesterday*) in i. X_i and Y_i are meant to be the strong versions, i.e., the next and previous states, respectively, have to exist.

We apply the usual rules for omitting brackets, and we introduce further connectives through abbreviations, e.g., $(\varphi \vee \varphi')$ for $((\neg\varphi) \Rightarrow \varphi')$. The same applies to temporal operators, e.g., $(\mathsf{X}_i^?\,\varphi)$ for $(\neg(\mathsf{X}_i(\neg\varphi)))$, $(\mathsf{G}_i\,\varphi)$ for $(\neg(\mathsf{F}_i(\neg\varphi)))$, $(\mathsf{Y}_i^?\,\varphi)$ for $(\neg(\mathsf{Y}_i(\neg\varphi)))$, and $(\mathsf{H}_i\,\varphi)$ for $(\neg(\mathsf{P}_i(\neg\varphi)))$.

Definition 20. An *object specification* is a pair $Ospec = (\Sigma, \Phi)$ where Σ is an extended data signature, and $\Phi \subseteq L_\Sigma^\tau(\boldsymbol{X})$ is a set of local formulae as axioms.

Example 3. We specify a class of flip-flops, based on the signature given in example 2.

sorts nat, $\mathrm{FF}^i \le$id, $\mathrm{FF}^a \le$ac

ops F1, F2 : $\to \mathrm{FF}^i$
R : nat $\to \mathrm{FF}^i$
N : $\mathrm{FF}^i \to \mathrm{FF}^i$

$$\texttt{create, set, reset, destroy} : \texttt{FF}^i \rightarrow \texttt{FF}^a$$
$$\texttt{ai}_{\texttt{FF},\texttt{FF}} : \texttt{FF}^a \times \texttt{FF}^i \rightarrow \texttt{bool}$$

axioms $\forall f, g$:FF, n:nat

f: $\texttt{create}(g) \Rightarrow \tau(g)$
f: $\texttt{set}(g) \Rightarrow \tau(g)$
f: $\texttt{reset}(g) \Rightarrow \tau(g)$
f: $\texttt{destroy}(g) \Rightarrow \tau(g)$

f: $\triangleright\texttt{create}(f) \Leftrightarrow \neg\triangleright\texttt{set}(f) \wedge \neg\triangleright\texttt{reset}(f)$
f: $\texttt{create}(f) \Rightarrow \mathsf{Y}_f \triangleright\texttt{create}(f)$
f: $\texttt{create}(f) \Rightarrow \triangleright\texttt{set}(f)$
f: $\texttt{create}(f) \Rightarrow \mathsf{G}_f(\neg\mathsf{P}_f\,\texttt{destroy}(f) \Rightarrow \neg(\triangleright\texttt{set}(f) \Leftrightarrow \triangleright\texttt{reset}(f)))$
f: $\texttt{set}(f) \Rightarrow \mathsf{Y}_f \triangleright\texttt{set}(f)$
f: $\texttt{set}(f) \Rightarrow \triangleright\texttt{reset}(f)$
f: $\texttt{reset}(f) \Rightarrow \mathsf{Y}_f \triangleright\texttt{reset}(f)$
f: $\texttt{reset}(f) \Rightarrow \triangleright\texttt{set}(f)$
f: $\texttt{destroy}(f) \Rightarrow \mathsf{Y}_f \triangleright\texttt{destroy}(f)$
f: $\texttt{destroy}(f) \Rightarrow \neg\triangleright\texttt{set}(f) \wedge \neg\triangleright\texttt{reset}(f)$

f: $\texttt{set}(f) \Rightarrow \mathsf{X}_f\,\texttt{set}(\texttt{N}(f))$

F1: $\texttt{set}(\texttt{F1}) \Rightarrow \texttt{set}(\texttt{F2})$
F2: $\texttt{destroy}(\texttt{F2}) \Rightarrow \mathsf{P}_{\texttt{F1}}\,\texttt{set}(\texttt{F1})$

R(n): $\texttt{set}(\texttt{R}(n)) \Rightarrow \mathsf{F}_{\texttt{R}(n)}\,\texttt{set}(\texttt{R}(n+1))$

The first four axioms say that only shared actions may occur locally. Actually, these axioms need not be given explicitly because they are satisfied anyway in every interpretation (cf. definition 21 below).

Axiom five gives a necessary and sufficient condition for a flip-flop's creation to be enabled: it must neither be in a set nor in a reset state. Axiom six is the instance of a general rule: no action occurs unless it is enabled. Axioms seven and eight describe the state after creation: the flip-flop is set, and from now on it is always either set or reset as long as it is not destroyed. Axioms nine to twelve give the obvious preconditions and effects of set and reset. Axiom thirteen is another instance of the general rule mentioned. The fourteenth axiom puts a flip-flop after destruction in the same state as before creation: resurrection is possible!

The fifteenth axiom puts a clockwork of flip-flops into operation: flip-flops in the chain N are set step by step, one after the other, once an initial one is set.

The sixteenth axiom talks about two particular flip-flops, it says that whenever F1 has been set, then F2 has been set at the same time. This is an instance of synchronous *action calling*. As a consequence, we have $\texttt{set}(\texttt{F1}) \Rightarrow \tau(\texttt{F2})$ and thus $ai_{\texttt{FF},\texttt{FF}}(\texttt{set}(\texttt{F1}),\texttt{F2}) = \textbf{true}$, i.e., set(F1) is also an action of F2. The seventeenth axiom says that F2 can only be destroyed if it has at least once been set by F1 via action calling.

The eighteenth and last axiom says that whenever R(n) has been set, then

R$(n+1)$ will eventually be set. R is a "lazy" version of clockwork N. Consider the following alternative:

$$\mathtt{R}(n) : \mathtt{set}(\mathtt{R}(n)) \Rightarrow \mathsf{F}_{\mathtt{R}(n+1)}\, \mathtt{set}(\mathtt{R}(n+1))$$

This does not say the same: in the former case, a communication between R(n) and R$(n+1)$ is required at the moment when R$(n+1)$ is set. In the latter case, the communication must take place *right now* and reassure R(n) that its successor R$(n+1)$ will eventually be set.

Here is a simple fact that is entailed by the axioms:

$$\mathtt{F1} : \mathtt{set}(\mathtt{F1}) \Rightarrow \tau(\mathtt{F2}) \wedge \mathsf{P}_{\mathtt{F2}}\, \mathtt{create}(\mathtt{F2}).$$

□

The logic $L_\Sigma(\boldsymbol{X})$ over an extended data signature is interpreted over an instance signature $\Sigma_I = (Id, \boldsymbol{Ac})$ based on a data signature Σ_D and a data universe $\boldsymbol{U}$, and an interpretation structure $\bar{L} = (L, \bar{\alpha}\mid_L)$ within an interpretation frame $\bar{E} = (E, \bar{\alpha})$, as described in section 2. Please remember that $L = \bigcup\{L_i\}_{i\in Id}$ where $L_i = (Lc_i, \rightarrow_i)$, and $E = \bigcup\{E_i\}_{i\in Id}$ where $E_i = (Ev_i, \rightarrow_i)$.

In particular, the local formulas are interpreted in a local configuration $\downarrow e$ of L and a variable assignment θ. Of course, data terms are to be interpreted globally in $\boldsymbol{U}$.

Definition 21. The *satisfaction* relation $\models$ is inductively defined by the following rules:

- $\bar{L}, \downarrow e, \theta \models i : (t_1 =_{ss} t_2)$ iff ${t_1}^{\theta}_{U} = {t_2}^{\theta}_{U}$;
- $\bar{L}, \downarrow e, \theta \models i : \tau(j)$ iff $e \in Lc_{i^\theta_U} \cap Lc_{j^\theta_U}$;
- $\bar{L}, \downarrow e, \theta \models i : \alpha(j)$ iff $e \in Lc_{i^\theta_U}$ and $\bar{\alpha}(e) = \alpha(j)$;
- $\bar{L}, \downarrow e, \theta \models i : \rhd\alpha(j)$ iff $e \in Lc_{i^\theta_U}$ and, for some $e' \in Ev_{i^\theta_U}$, $e \rightarrow_{i^\theta_U} e'$ and $\bar{\alpha}(e') = \alpha(j)$;
- $\bar{L}, \downarrow e, \theta \models i : (\neg\varphi)$ iff $e \in Lc_{i^\theta_U}$ and not $\bar{L}, \downarrow e, \theta \models i : \varphi$;
- $\bar{L}, \downarrow e, \theta \models i : (\varphi \Rightarrow \varphi')$ iff $e \in Lc_{i^\theta_U}$ and $\bar{L}, \downarrow e, \theta \models i : \varphi'$ or not $\bar{L}, \downarrow e, \theta \models i : \varphi$;
- $\bar{L}, \downarrow e, \theta \models i : (\exists x\ \varphi)$ iff $e \in Lc_{i^\theta_U}$ and $\bar{L}, \downarrow e, \theta' \models i : \varphi$ for some x-equivalent assignment θ';
- $\bar{L}, \downarrow e, \theta \models i : (\mathsf{X}_j\, \varphi)$ iff $e \in Lc_{i^\theta_U}$ and $\bar{L}, \downarrow e', \theta \models j : \varphi$ for some event $e' \in Lc_{j^\theta_U}$ such that $e \rightarrow_{i^\theta_U} e'$ or $e \rightarrow_{j^\theta_U} e'$;
- $\bar{L}, \downarrow e, \theta \models i : (\mathsf{F}_j\, \varphi)$ iff $e \in Lc_{i^\theta_U}$ and $\bar{L}, \downarrow e', \theta \models j : \varphi$ for some event $e' \in Lc_{j^\theta_U}$ such that $e \rightarrow^* e'$;
- $\bar{L}, \downarrow e, \theta \models i : (\mathsf{Y}_j\, \varphi)$ iff $e \in Lc_{i^\theta_U}$ and $\bar{L}, \downarrow e', \theta \models j : \varphi$ for some event $e' \in Lc_{j^\theta_U}$ such that $e' \rightarrow_{i^\theta_U} e$ or $e' \rightarrow_{j^\theta_U} e$;
- $\bar{L}, \downarrow e, \theta \models i : (\mathsf{P}_j\, \varphi)$ iff $e \in Lc_{i^\theta_U}$ and $\bar{L}, \downarrow e', \theta \models j : \varphi$ for some event $e' \in Lc_{j^\theta_U}$ such that $e' \rightarrow^* e$.

This requires some explanation.

The first rule is straightforward, equations between data terms are interpreted globally. The second rule says that j is local in i iff i's current event is shared by j. The third rule says that, in any local configuration of a proper event, there is precisely one action that just occurred (possibly shared with some other object j), given by the label.

The forth rule is a little unusual in that it is not interpreted in an isolated life cycle but in a life cycle *in context.* Intuitively, $\alpha(j)$ is enabled if it may happen in some next step in the *frame*, not necessarily in the life cycle. A more classic way to capture this would use life cycles with one-step look-ahead ("barbed wires") as interpretation structures.

Rules five to seven are adapted from predicate calculus.

The eighth rule requires some thought: the events e and e' may belong to different life cycles! For i to know that φ holds for j tomorrow, i and j may communicate either today or tomorrow.

Also in the nineth rule, e and e' may belong to different objects. $i : \mathsf{F}_j\, \varphi$ holds in a local configuration $\downarrow\!e$ for i iff $j : \varphi$ holds in some future configuration $\downarrow\!e'$ for j where e' causally depends on e. This causal dependency may involve a chain of objects $i = i_1, \ldots, i_n = j$ where successive objects communicate via some shared event.

The last two rules are the past-directed analoga of future-directed rules eight and nine.

Definition 22. A labelled distributed life cycle $\bar{L}$ *satisfies* a local formula $i : \varphi$, written $\bar{L} \models i : \varphi$, iff $\bar{L}, \downarrow\!e, \theta \models i : \varphi$ for every local configuration $\downarrow\!e$ and every variable assignment θ. A local formula $i : \varphi$ is *valid* in the interpretation frame $\bar{E}$, written $\bar{E} \models i : \varphi$, iff $\bar{L} \models i : \varphi$ for every distributed life cycle $\bar{L}$ in $\bar{E}$.

Interpretation structures represent single runs of processes. Since we are interested in entire processes, we may ask which interpretation frames represent specified processes, i.e., have the property that all axioms are valid. In particular, it is interesting to look at these interpretation frames within the category Σ_I**-evt** of all interpretation frames, with morphisms as defined in definition 16. Since there is an initial element in Σ_I**-evt** (theorem 17), the obvious question to ask is whether the same holds for the subcategory of interpretation frames satisfying given axioms Φ. The answer is positive.

Let $Ospec = (\Sigma, \Phi)$ be an object specification (cf. definition 20), and let Σ_I be the instance signature determined by Σ and a given data universe $\boldsymbol{U}$ (cf. definition 5). Let ***Ospec*-evt** be the full subcategory of all elements in Σ_I**-evt** satisfying Φ.

Theorem 23. ***Ospec-evt*** *has initial elements.*

Proof idea: an initial element is given by the largest labelled sub-event structure of $\bar{E}(\Sigma_I)$, the initial element of Σ_I**-evt** (cf. theorem 17), containing all distributed life cycles satisfying all axioms in Φ. □

As in abstract data type theory, the initial elements of Σ_I-**evt** and ***Ospec*-evt** are obvious candidates for assigning standard semantics to signatures and specifications, respectively.

4 Concluding Remarks

The local specification logic and distributed semantics presented in this paper deserve further study. An obvious next step is to provide a proof system. [LMRT91] give a sound and complete proof system for their propositional n-agent logic, but that does not carry over to our case. It is not clear whether a complete proof system for our logic exists. But still, there are software tools for analysing and animating temporal logic specifications [Sa91b] that can be adapted to our approach.

Our theory will be extended towards *structured* specifications. That means that we have to introduce and study appropriate signature and specification morphisms and corresponding forgetful functors on interpretation frames and structures. This would provide the basis for studying composition as well as parameterization. For composition, there are two aspects: composing sequential objects from components [ESSS95], and composing concurrent families from subfamilies.

There is work in progress to incorporate reification issues in our framework [De94, De95]. It is well known that the temporal operators of our logic are not suitable for action refinement, the logic in [CE94] (which is similar to Hennessy-Milner logic [HM85]) may be better suited. This is an indication that we should work in a family of related logics, as put forward in [MM94].

While reification requires a more "operational" logic, specification expressiveness and comfort suggest to move in the opposite direction. An obvious extension of our logic is to introduce branching-time operators. Branching-time formulae cannot be interpreted in single life cycles. That means that our interpretation frames will play the role of interpretation structures.

Acknowledgments

The authors are grateful to their colleagues in the IS-CORE and COMPASS projects for inspiration about the nature of objects and how to reason about them. Special thanks are due to Cristina Sernadas and Gunter Saake for attention, hints, suggestions, objections, and understanding. The work of José Fiadeiro and Tom Maibaum has been influential. Also many thanks to Grit Denker, and to the Hildesheim process logic group of Ulla Goltz for surprising insights in the nature of process logics, concurrency, and locality. Finally, we are grateful to the anonymous referees for friendly comments and constructive criticism.

References

[AR92] E. Astesiano and G. Reggio. Algebraic Specification of Concurrency. Recent Trends in Data Type Specification, LNCS 655, Springer-Verlag, Berlin 1992

[Bo85] A. Borgida. Features of Languages for the Development of Information Systems at the Conceptual Level. *IEEE Software* 2 (1985), 63-73

[Br93] M. Broy. Functional Specification of Time-Sensitive Communicating Systems. *ACM Transactions on Software Engineering and Methodology* 2 (1993), 1-46

[CE94] S. Conrad and H.-D. Ehrich. An Elementary Logic for Object Specification and Verification. In U. Lipeck and G. Vossen, editors, *Workshop Formale Grundlagen für den Entwurf von Informationssystemen, Tutzing*, pages 197–206. Technical Report Univ. Hannover, No. 03/94, 1994

[CGH92] S. Conrad, M. Gogolla, and R. Herzig. TROLL *light*: A Core Language for Specifying Objects. Informatik-Bericht 92–02, TU Braunschweig, 1992

[Ch76] P. P Chen. The Entity-Relationship Model—Toward a Unified View of Data. *ACM Transactions on Database Systems*, Vol. 1, No. 1, 1976, 9–36

[De94] G. Denker. Object Reification (Extended Abstract). Working Papers of the International Workshop on Information Systems - Correctness and Reusability, IS-CORE'94. R. Wieringa and R. Feenstra, eds. Technical Report IR-357, VU Amsterdam 1994

[De95] G. Denker. Transactions in Object-Oriented Specifications. This volume

[EDG88] H.-D. Ehrich, K. Drosten, and M. Gogolla. Towards an Algebraic Semantics for Database Specification. In: R. Meersmann and A. Sernadas (eds.). *Proc. 2nd IFIP WG 2.6 Working Conf. on Database Semantics "Data and Knowledge" (DS-2)*, Albufeira (Portugal), 1988. North-Holland, Amsterdam, 119-135

[EGH+92] G. Engels, M. Gogolla, U. Hohenstein, K. Hülsmann, P. Löhr-Richter, G. Saake, and H.-D. Ehrich. Conceptual modelling of database applications using an extended ER model. *Data & Knowledge Engineering, North-Holland*, Vol. 9, No. 2, 1992, 157-204

[EGL89] H.-D. Ehrich, M. Gogolla, and U. Lipeck. Algebraische Spezifikation Abstrakter Datentypen. Teubner–Verlag, Stuttgart 1989

[EGS91] H.-D. Ehrich,J. Goguen, and A. Sernadas. A Categorial Theory of Objects as Observed Processes. Proc. REX/FOOL School/Workshop, J. W. deBakker et. al. (eds.), LNCS 489, Springer-Verlag, Berlin 1991, 203-228

[Eh86] H.-D. Ehrich. Key Extensions of Abstract Data Types, Final Algebras, and Database Semantics. In: D. Pitt et al. (eds.): *Proc. Workshop on Category Theory and Computer Programming*. Springer, Berlin, LNCS series, 1986, 412-433

[EM85] H. Ehrig and B. Mahr. Fundamentals of Algebraic Specification 1. Springer-Verlag, Berlin 1985

[EM90] H. Ehrig and B. Mahr. Fundamentals of Algebraic Specification 2. Springer-Verlag, Berlin 1985

[ES91] H.-D. Ehrich and A. Sernadas. Fundamental Object Concepts and Constructions. Information Systems - Correctness and Reusability, Proc. ISCORE Workshop'91 (G. Saake and A. Sernadas, eds.), Informatik-Berichte 91-03, Techn. Univ. Braunschweig 1991, 1-24

[ESSS95] H.-D. Ehrich, G. Saake, A. Sernadas, and C. Sernadas. Distributed Temporal Logic for Concurrent Object Families (Extended Abstract). Proc. ISCORE Workshop '94, R. Wieringa, ed. World Scientific Publishers. To appear 1995

[FM91] J. Fiadeiro and T. Maibaum. Towards Object Calculi. Information Systems – Correctness and Reusability, Proc. ISCORE Workshop'91 (G. Saake and A. Sernadas, eds.), Informatik-Berichte 91-03, Techn. Univ. Braunschweig 1991, 129-178

[FM92] J. Fiadeiro and T. Maibaum. Temporal Theories as Modularisation Units for Concurrent System Specification. *Formal Aspects of Computing* 4 (1992), 239-272

[FSMS91] J. Fiadeiro, C. Sernadas, T. Maibaum, and G. Saake. Proof-Theoretic Semantics of Object-Oriented Specification Constructs. In: R. Meersman, W. Kent, and S. Khosla (eds.). *Object-Oriented Databases: Analysis, Design and Construction (Proc. 4th IFIP WG 2.6 Working Conference DS-4, Windermere (UK))*, Amsterdam, 1991. North-Holland, 243-284

[GCH93] M. Gogolla, S. Conrad, and R. Herzig. Sketching Concepts and Computational Model of TROLL *light*. In A. Miola, editor, *Proc. 3rd Int. Conf. Design and Implementation of Symbolic Computation Systems (DISCO'93)*, pages 17-32. Springer, LNCS 722, 1993

[GM87] J. A. Goguen and J. Meseguer. Unifying functional, object-oriented and relational programming with logical semantics. *Research Direction in Object-Oriented Programming*, B.Shriver,P.Wegner (eds.), MIT Press 1987, 417-477

[GW90] J. A. Goguen and D. Wolfram. On Types and FOOPS. In: R. Meersman, W. Kent, and S. Khosla (eds.). *Object-Oriented Databases: Analysis, Design and Construction (Proc. 4th IFIP WG 2.6 Working Conference DS-4, Windermere (UK))*, Amsterdam, 1991. North-Holland

[HM85] M. Hennessy and R. Milner. Algebraic Laws for Nondeterminism and Concurrency. Journal of the ACM 32 (1985), 137-161

[Ho85] C. A. R. Hoare. Communicating Sequential Processes. Prentice-Hall, Englewood Cliffs, NJ, 1985

[HSJHK94] T. Hartmann, G. Saake, R. Jungclaus, P. Hartel, and J. Kusch. Revised Version of the Modeling Language TROLL. Informatik-Bericht 94-03, TU Braunschweig 1994

[JSHS91] R. Jungclaus, G. Saake, T. Hartmann, and C. Sernadas. Object-Oriented Specification of Information Systems: The TROLL Language. Informatik-Bericht 91-04, TU Braunschweig, 1991

[Ju93] R. Jungclaus. Modeling of Dynamic Object Systems, a Logic-based Approach. Advanced Studies in Computer Science. Vieweg Verlag, Braunschweig/Wiesbaden, 1993

[LMRT91] K. Lodaya, M. Mukund, R. Ramanujam, and P.S. Thiagarajan. Models and Logics for True Concurrency. in P.S. Thiagarajan (ed.): Some Models and Logics for Concurrency. Advanced School on the Algebraic, Logical and Categorical Foundations of Concurrency. Gargnano del Garda, 1991

[MB89] J. Mylopoulos and M. Brodie, (eds.). Readings in Artificial Intelligence & Databases. Morgan Kaufmann Publ. San Mateo, 1989

[Mi89] R. Milner. Communication and Concurrency. Prentice-Hall, Englewood Cliffs, 1989

[MM93] N. Martí-Oliet and J. Meseguer. Rewriting Logic as a Logical and Semantic Framework. Report SRI-CSL-93-05, SRI International, Menlo Park 1993

[MM94] N. Martí-Oliet and J. Meseguer. General Logics and Logical Frameworks. In: D. M. Gabbay (ed.). *What is a Logical System?*. Oxford University Press 1994. To appear

[MP89] Z. Manna and A. Pnueli. The Anchored Version of the Temporal Framework. In: J. deBakker, W. deRoever, and G. Rozenberg (eds.). *Linear Time, Branching Time and Partial Order in Logics and Models for Concurrency.* LNCS 354, Springer-Verlag, Berlin, 1989, 201-284

[Sa91a] G. Saake. Conceptual Modeling of Database Applications. In: Karagiannis, D. (ed.): *Proc. 1st IS/KI Workshop, Ulm (Germany), 1990.* Springer, Berlin, LNCS 474, 1991, 213-232

[Sa91b] G. Saake. Descriptive Specification of Database Object Behaviour. *Data & Knowledge Engineering* 6 (1991), 47-74

[Se80] A. Sernadas. Temporal Aspects of Logical Procedure Definition. *Information Systems*, Vol. 5, 1980, 167–187

[SEC90] A. Sernadas, H.-D. Ehrich, and J.-F. Costa. From processes to objects. *The INESC Journal of Research and Development 1:1*, pages 7-27, 1990

[SF91] C. Sernadas and J. Fiadeiro. Towards Object-Oriented Conceptual Modelling. *Data & Knowledge Engineering* 6 (1991), 479-508

[SJE92] G. Saake, R. Jungclaus, and H.-D. Ehrich. Object-Oriented Specification and Stepwise Refinement. In J. de Meer, V. Heymer, and R. Roth, editors, *Proc. Open Distributed Processing, Berlin (D), 8.-11. Okt. 1991 (IFIP Transactions C: Communication Systems, Vol. 1)*, pages 99-121. North-Holland, 1992

[SJH93] G. Saake, R. Jungclaus, and T. Hartmann. Application Modelling in Heterogenous Environments Using an Object Specification Language. *International Journal of Intelligent and Cooperative Information Systems* 2 (1993), 425-449

[SR94] A. Sernadas and J. Ramos. The GNOME Language: Syntax, Semantics and Calculus. Tech. Report, Instituto Superior Técnico, Lisboa 1994

[SSC92] A. Sernadas, C. Sernadas, and J.F. Costa. Object Specification Logic. Internal report, INESC, University of Lisbon, 1992. (to appear in Journal of Logic and Computation)

[SSE87] A. Sernadas, C. Sernadas, and H.-D. Ehrich. Object-Oriented Specification of Databases: An Algebraic Approach. In P.M. Stoecker and W. Kent, editors, *Proc. 13th Int. Conf. on Very Large Databases VLDB'87*, pages 107-116. VLDB Endowment Press, Saratoga (CA), 1987

[SSG+91] A. Sernadas, C. Sernadas, P. Gouveia, P. Resende, and J. Gouveia. OBLOG – Object-Oriented Logic: An Informal Introduction. Technical report, INESC, Lisbon, 1991

[ST89] J. W. Schmidt and C. Thanos (eds.). Foundations of Knowledge Base Management. Springer-Verlag, Berlin, 1989

[Wi80] G. Winskel: Events in Computation. PhD thesis, University of Edinburgh

[WN93] G. Winskel and M. Nielsen. Models for Concurrency. Report DAIMI PB – 463, Computer Science Department, Aarhus University 1993

Dynamic Abstract Data Types Based on Algebraic Graph Transformations

Hartmut Ehrig
TU Berlin

Michael Löwe
ISST Berlin

Fernando Orejas
Univ. of Catalunya

ABSTRACT: The concept of dynamic abstract data types was recently proposed by two of the authors as a dynamic extension of the well-known concept of abstract data types, motivated by several recent approaches in the areas of algebraic specifications, object-orientation, evolving algebras and graph transformations. The basic idea of dynamic abstract data types is to extend abstract data types by dynamic operations which are transformations between abstract data types. In this paper we consider a specific kind of dynamic abstract data types where the transformations are defined by rules in the sense of algebraic graph transformations. The concept of attributed graph transformations is used to define this new version of dynamic abstract data types and to show some important properties of the corresponding transition category. The constructions are illustrated by a small example from the area of data bases.

1. Introduction

The concept of abstract data types as developed in the 70'ies is today well-known and accepted in the computer science community. In addition to several other specification techniques the theory of algebraic specifications has become an essential part of the theory of abstract data types. In contrast to other specification techniques like VDM or Z, which are based implicitly or explicitly on states, algebraic specifications of abstract data types can be given in an axiomatic style avoiding the notion of a state. For the specification of systems with dynamic behaviour, however, it seems to be necessary to have a notion of state and some kind of dynamic operations which are able to change the state. Although states can be modelled explicitly by suitable state sorts within standard algebraic specifications it has turned out that for systems with dynamic behaviour such specifications with explicit state sorts and corresponding read and update operations become rather long and tedious (see [DG 94]). This means that algebraic specifications and abstract data types in the classical sense are in principle able to model systems with dynamic behaviour but in general not necessarily convenient for this purpose. Meanwhile there are several proposals in the literature to overcome this difficulty, which have motivated us to propose a dynamic extension of abstract data types, called dynamic abstract data types [EO 94].

Our proposal is mainly motivated by the concept of algebraic specifications with implicit state in the sense of Dauchy and Gaudel [DG 94] and that of D-oids given by Astesiano and Zucca in [AZ 92, 94]. In both cases states of systems are represented by algebras and dynamic operations of the system by transformations between algebras. In [DG 94] the emphasis is more on the syntactical level extending algebraic specifications by access functions and modifiers with specific semantical interpretation, while the D-oids in [AZ 94] provide a very general semantical model for dynamic data types without syntactical level. The idea of formalizing states as algebras and operations as transformations between algebras has been used already in the area of programming language semantics:

On one hand the treatment of declarations in imperative programming languages by Wagner [Wag 89], on the other hand the notion of "evolving algebras" in the sense of Gurevitch [Gur 91, 94] which have been applied successfully to different languages, like PROLOG, OCCAM and others and object-oriented data models [GKS 92].

Another main motivation for our concept of dynamic abstract data types is the idea to provide abstract data types with distinguished instances of types, sometimes called objects, and to allow concurrent access to operations. In the framework of algebraic module specifications this idea is the basic concept of "concurrently executable modules" proposed by Weber and Ehrig in [WE 88]. A first approach to formalize these ideas is given by Große-Rhode in [GR 90] using a combination of algebraic specifications and projection specifications. Another extension of algebraic module specifications towards object based specifications is given by Parisi-Presicce and Pierantonio in [PPP 91/94] where the approach in [PPP 94] is closely related to D-oids in [AZ 94]. The specification of parallel state dependent systems by Große-Rhode in [GR 94] is influenced by [GR 90], [DG 94] and [AZ 92, 94].

Last but not least our concept of dynamic abstract data types is motivated by the algebraic theory of graph transformations [Ehr 79] and especially attributed graph transformations [LKW 93] which are studied in the COMPUGRAPH working group [EL 93]. Graph transformations are used to model the operational semantics of object-based systems in the sense of ACTOR-systems, [Kor 94] and TROLL-light [WG 94]. Attributed graphs are specific algebras with graphical components allowing to model objects in the graphical and values in the data part. Dynamic operations can be modelled by rules in attributed graph transformation systems such that the application of dynamic operations leads to a transformation between attributed graphs. Since attributed graphs are algebras modelling the state of a system, attributed graph transformations might be used to model transformations of states in dynamic abstract data types. In fact, the theory of algebraic graph transformations seems to be very useful to analyse properties concerning independence, parallelism and concurrency of dynamic operations in dynamic abstract data types.
In this paper we want to show how dynamic abstract data types can be defined using attributed graph transformations and how the theory of algebraic graph transformations can be applied to show several important properties.
The main aspects of this paper are the following:

1. We want to review the new concept of dynamic abstract data types, which supports the idea of state-as-algebra and dynamic operation as transformation between algebras.
2. In the theory of graph transformations the idea a is state-as-graphs approach where dynamic changes are modelled by application of graph rewriting rules.
3. The main aim of this paper is to show that the graph transformation approach can be presented within the state-as-algebra approach and hence within the framework of dynamic abstract data types.
   This main idea is supported on one hand by the fact that the algebraic theory of graph transformations is not only applicable to classical graphs, but also to attributed graphs, a suitable integration of graphs and algebras. On the other hand there is a well-developed theory of graph transformations concerning independence, parallelism and concurrency of transformations which can be applied to transformations of dynamic abstract data types.
   Hence the concept of dynamic abstract data types based on algebraic graph transformations is a fruitful integration of the field "algebraic specification of abstract data types" with that of "algebraic graph transformation".

In section 2 and 3 we review the concepts of dynamic abstract data types, algebraic, and attributed graph transformations in the sense of [EO 94] and [LE 91, LKW 93] respectively. In section 4 we define our new concept of dynamic abstract data types (DADT) based on attributed graph transformations (AGT). We study independence of dynamic operations and discuss several interesting examples. In section 5 we construct and show some important properties of transition categories, the semantics of DADT's. Finally we summarize in the conclusion the benefits of combining algebraic graph transformations with dynamic abstract data types and discuss several extensions of our version of DADT's introduced in section 4 in view of more complex practical examples as studied in [BE 94].

ACKNOWLEDGEMENTS

This paper was partially supported by ESPRIT Basic Research WG's COMPASS and COMPUGRAPH. We are grateful to several members of these WG's and the IFIP WG's 2.1, 2.2, 2.3, 14.3 for fruitful discussions in Santa Margharita Ligure and San Miniato and to the referees for useful comments. Special thanks to Ms. H. Barnewitz for excellent typing and figure drawing.

2. Dynamic Abstract Data Types

In this section we review the 4-level proposal in [EO 94] for dynamic abstract data types, short DADT's, in a slightly revised version and discuss briefly some approaches in the literature which -at least to some extend- can be considered as different versions of DADT's.
The main intention of DADT's is to provide a framework for specification and semantics of systems with static data values and dynamic behaviour, i.e. with distinguished static and dynamic parts. In the 4-level proposal for DADT's in [EO 94] the first two levels correspond to classical algebraic specifications with fixed resp. loose semantics and the last two levels are specifying dynamic operations on different levels.
The specification DYNSPEC of a DADT D consists of three parts DYNSPEC = (VSPEC, ISPEC, DSPEC) given in levels 1 - 3 for DADT's below. Moreover, level 4 of DADT's is a higher level specification HSPEC for a family of DADT's.

2.1 Level 1 of DADT's: Value Type Specification VSPEC

The value type specification VSPEC of the DADT D is an algebraic specification with fixed semantics, i.e. the semantics of VSPEC is a classical abstract data type defined (up to isomorphism) by a given VSPEC-algebra A, e.g. the quotient term algebra T_{VSPEC} defining the initial semantics of VSPEC or any other fixed VSPEC-algebra A. Sorts and operations in VSPEC are called value sorts and value operations respectively.

2.2 Level 2 of DADT's: Instant Structure Specification ISPEC

The instant structure specification ISPEC of the DADT D is an algebraic specification with constraints in the sense of [EM 90] which is an extension of the value type specification VSPEC. The additional sorts and operations in VSPEC are called class sorts and access or attributed functions. The semantics SEM(ISPEC) of ISPEC is loose, i.e. it consists of all ISPEC-algebras IA, called instant structures.
Instant structures are intended to model the states of the system given by the DADT D. For consistent states we require especially that the value type algebra A is protected, i.e. IA restricted to VSPEC is isomorphic to A. Inconsistent states are ISPEC-algebras violating some of the constraints of ISPEC.

2.3 Level 3 of DADT's: Dynamic Operations Specification DSPEC

Dynamic operations of the DADT D are intended to define transformations between instant structures IA of D, i.e. state transformations. The dynamic operation specification DSPEC is not restricted to be an algebraic specification, but may be a suitable extension of algebraic specifications or an integration with other specification techniques. DSPEC includes dynamic generators g_{op}:w and dynamic operations d_{op}:w, where w = s1...sn is a string of value or class sorts.
For each (syntactic) dynamic operation d_{op}:w in DSPEC we have a (semantic) dynamic operation dop_D in the DADT D, which is partially defined on instant structures IA and arguments $ai \in IA_{si}$(i = 1,...,n). If dop_D is defined for IA at (a1,...,an) we obtain a new instant structure IB and a transformation t:IA $\rightarrow$ IB, i.e. dop_D(IA, a1,...,an) = (IB, t). In this case the transformation t is denoted for short by

$$dop_D(a1,\ldots,an):IA \rightarrow IB$$

A transformation t:IA $\rightarrow$ IB between instant structures IA and IB is a morphism in a suitable category, but not necessarily an instant structure homomorphism from IA to IB.
The basis of the semantics of DSPEC is an instant structure transition system, where the states are instant structure and the transitions are transformations defined by dynamic operations (see figure 1). In general the semantics of DSPEC is a transition category where the objects are instant structures or suitable equivalence classes of them and the morphisms are composite transformations generated by dynamic operations. We also consider variants of DADT's where dynamic operations are allowed to be nondeterministic, i.e. (IB, t) is not uniquely defined by (IA, a1,...,an), or to compute also values, i.e. dop_D(IA, a1,...,an) = (IB, t, b) for some value b in IB.

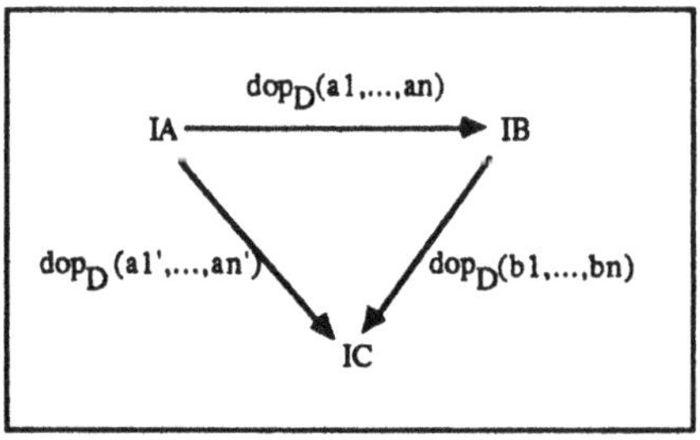

Figure 1: Instant Structure Transition System of D

2.4 Level 4 of DADT's: Higher Level Dynamic Specification HSPEC

The higher level dynamic specification HSPEC defines a family $(Di)_{i \in I}$ of DADT's. It includes higher level dynamic generators for the creation of Di-objects and higher level dynamic operations for update, composition and communication of different Di-objects. Instances and hence Di-objects may be either elements of a new class sort di for Di or copies of Di($i \in I$). It might be possible that HSPEC for level 4 can be expressed using the specification techniques for levels 1-3 on a higher level.

2.5 Different Versions of DADT's

In the following we give a short overview how far different approaches in the literature - most of them mentioned already in the introduction - can be considered as different versions of DADT's in the sense of 2.1 - 2.4 above.

1. Algebraic specifications with implicit state in the sense of Dauchy and Gaudel [DG 94] fit nicely into levels 1-3 of DADT's, where "access functions" and "modifiers" are in level 2 and 3 respectively. Note, that in [DG 94] no new sorts in level 2 are introduced, but only operations. Transformations on level 3 are given by "modifiers" which are sequential compositions of "elementary modifiers" corresponding to "elementary access functions" on level 2.
2. D-oids in the sense of Astesiano and Zucca [AZ 92, 94] are a perfect semantical model of levels 1-3 of DADT's, where a separation of levels 1 and 2 in [AZ 94] is optional. The second level is given by a suitable institution with explicit sorts, so that all kinds of specification techniques in the sense of institutions can be used. The dynamic operations of [AZ 94] in the third level are allowed to define not only new algebras as states but also new data as values. The transformations are given by tracking maps, which are partial functions between the carriers of the algebras.
3. The approaches of Große-Rhode [GR 94], Parisi-Presicce and Pierantonio [PPP 94, Pie 94], and Gogolla [Gog 94] can also be considered as algebraic techniques for the specification of DADT's, where transformations in the third level are defined by method expressions, quasi-homomorphisms and algebras respectively. Note, that [GR 94] provides a sound and complete calculus for transformations, in [Pie 94] the specification of dynamic operations is induced by that of operations on level 2, and in [Gog 94] also level 4 of DADT's is considered. An early example to model states as algebras and state changes as transformations in a pure algebraic framework is given already by Wagner in [Wag 89] where transformations are "generalized homomorphisms", a combination of specification morphisms and homomorphisms.
4. The concept of "evolving algebras" [Gur 91, 94] is based on concrete algebras and transition rules defining transformations between algebras by pointwise updates of operations and extensions of domains. Combining evolving algebras with algebraic notions of abstraction should lead to very promising variants of DADT's. In [Gur 94] it is pointed out that concepts of concurrency and distribution within evolving algebras are important extensions which are presently discussed but not yet formalized.
5. In the area of algebraic graph transformation concepts of independence, parallelism, concurrency and distribution of states and transformations have been studied already [Ehr 79, LE 91, EL 93]. In the subsequent sections of this paper we introduce a new interesting variant of DADT's based on attributed graph transformations in the sense of [LKW 93] where these concepts have not been studied up to now.

3. Algebraic Graph Transformations

In this section we introduce the basic notions, constructions and results in the theory of algebraic graph transformations as far as they are needed in the following sections. For a general overview of theory and applications of graph transformations in general and the algebraic approach in particular we refer to our survey [EL 93]. In particular we concentrate on transformations of attributed graphs [LKW 93], a combination of graphical and algebraic structures, and transformations via pushouts based on partial homomorphisms, called single-pushout approach [Löw 90, LE 91].

In the following we consider signatures SIG and SIG-algebras in the sense of total algebras [EM 85], but partial homomorphisms $f{:}A \to B$ between SIG-algebras A and B. This means that we

have a total homomorphism $f!:A(f) \to B$, where $A(f)$ is a subalgebra of A, called domain of f in A, with inclusion $A(f) \to A$.
Note that the notation $A(f)$ for the domain is dual to $f(A)$ for the range of f. Instead of "homomorphisms" we sometimes speak of "morphisms" only. The category of all SIG-algebras and all partial homomorphisms between them is denoted by $\mathbf{SIG^P}$. **SIG** denotes the subcategory of $\mathbf{SIG^P}$ with the same class of objects and all total homomorphisms. It is well-known that directed graphs can be seen as algebras with respect to the following signature

GRAPH = Sorts: V, E

Opns: s, t: $E \to V$

If we replace the set E of edges by a family $(E_{n,m})_{n,m \in \mathbb{N}}$ of hyperedges with n source and m target vertices we obtain the following signature for hypergraphs

HYPERGRAPH = Sorts: V, $(E_{n,m})_{n,m \in \mathbb{N}}$

Opns: $(s1,\ldots,sn, t1,\ldots,tm: E_{n,m} \to V)_{n,m \in \mathbb{N}}$

The signatures of graphs and hypergraphs are important special cases of graph structure signatures defined by the property that they contain unary operation symbols only.

3.1 Definition (Graph Structure Signature and Graph Structures)

A graph structure signature GS is a signature which contains unary operation symbols only, i.e. no constants and no n-ary operation symbols with $n \geq 2$. GS-algebras are called graph structures. The category of graph structures with partial homomorphisms is denoted $\mathbf{GS^P}$.

The general idea of algebraic graph transformations is to define transformations via pushouts. The algebraic approach, introduced in [Ehr 79], uses total morphisms and two pushouts, now called double pushout approach. The single pushout approach in [LE 91] on the other hand is defined for each transformation by a single pushout based on partial homomorphisms. The following fundamental result for the single pushout approach proven in [Löw 90] shows that graph structures with partial homomorphisms are the adequate framework for this approach.

3.2 Theorem (Co-completeness of $\mathbf{SIG^P}$)

The category $\mathbf{SIG^P}$ of SIG-algebras and partial homomorphisms is finitely cocomplete if and only if SIG is a graph structure GS.

The explicit construction of pushouts in $\mathbf{GS^P}$ is essentially more complex than that in the total case.

3.3 Construction (Pushouts in Graph Structures)

Let GS be a graph structure signature and $f:A \to B$, $g:A \to C \in \mathbf{GS^P}$. The pushout of f and g in $\mathbf{GS^P}$, i.e. $(D, f^*:C \to D, g^*:B \to D)$, can be constructed in four steps:

a. Construction of the gluing object: Let $\underline{A}$ be the greatest subalgebra of A satisfying (i) $\underline{A} \subseteq A(f) \cap A(g)$ and (ii) $x \in \underline{A}$, $y \in A$ with $f(x) = f(y)$ or $g(x) = g(y)$ implies $y \in \underline{A}$.
b. Construction of the definedness area of f^* and g^*: Let $B(g^*)$ be the greatest subalgebra of B whose carriers are contained in $B - f(A - \underline{A})$. Symmetrically, $C(f^*)$ is the greatest subalgebra in $C - g(A - \underline{A})$.
c. Gluing: Let $D = (B(g^*) \uplus C(f^*))/_{\equiv}$, where $\equiv$ is the least equivalence relation containing $\sim$, where $x \sim y$ if there is $z \in \underline{A}$ with $f(z) = x$ and $g(z) = y$.
d. Pushout morphisms: f^* is defined for all $x \in C(f^*)$ by $f^*(x) = [x]_{\equiv}$. The morphism g^* is defined symmetrically.

If the definedness areas of partial homomorphisms are explicitly represented by inclusion morphisms, the whole situation in construction 3.3 can be visualized in **GS** as it is done in figure 2. Note that the squares (1), (2), and (3) commute and (4) is a pushout in **GS** due to 3.3 (c + d).

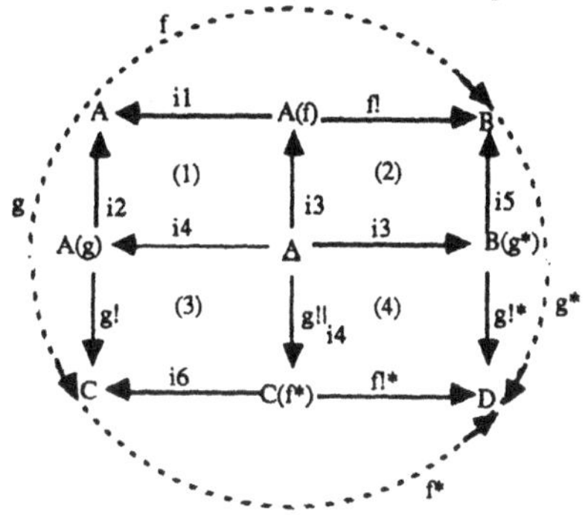

Figure 2: Pushout construction in $\mathbf{GS^P}$

These complex types of pushout construction perform deletion, gluing, and addition of graphical elements within a single colimit construction. Hence they can be used to mathematically define the operational behavior of graph rewriting and transformations of dynamic operations in a precise way.

3.4 Definition (Rule, Occurrence, Derivation of Graph Structures)

Let GS be a graph structure signature. A rewriting rule $r:L \rightarrow R$ is a partial morphism in $\mathbf{GS^P}$. An occurrence for r in an object $G \in \mathbf{GS^P}$ is a total morphism $m:L \rightarrow G$. The direct derivation of G with the rule r at an occurrence m is the pushout of m and r in $\mathbf{GS^P}$ written $G \Rightarrow H$ via (r, m). The corresponding pushout object H in figure 3 is called derived graph.

The intuition of a rule $r:L \rightarrow R$ is that all objects in L - L(r) shall be deleted, all objects in R - r(L) shall be added and L(r) resp. r(L) provides the gluing context. Note that the derivation with r deletes destructively due to construction 3.3 (b), in the sense that all objects in G pointing (for example by source or target mappings) to deleted objects are deleted themselves; if two objects $x \in L - L(r)$ and $y \in L(r)$ in a rule's left hand side are identified by an occurrence, the effect of deletion is dominant.

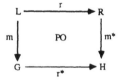

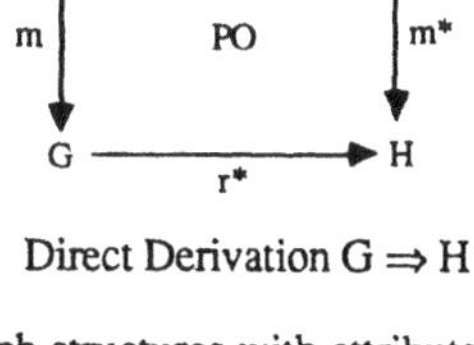

Figure 3: Direct Derivation $G \Rightarrow H$ via (r,m)

Now we are going to combine graph structures with attributed algebras leading to the notion of attributed graphs as introduced in [LKW 93].

3.5 Definition (Attributed Graph Specifications and Attributed Graphs and Morphisms)

1. An attributed graph specification

   ATTR = (GS, SPEC, ATTROP)

   consists of a graph structure signature GS = (S1, OP1) an algebraic specification SPEC = (S2, OP2, E2), and a family of attribute assignment functions

   $$\text{ATTROP} = (attr_s{:}s \rightarrow s2_s)_{s \in S} \text{ with } S \subseteq S1 \text{ and } s2_s \in S2$$

2. An attributed graph is an ATTR-algebra A.
3. An attributed graph morphism $f{:}A \rightarrow B$ (short ATTR-morphism) is a partial morphism

whose SPEC-part is total, i.e. a pair f = (f1, f2) of a partial morphism $f1:A_{GS} \rightarrow B_{GS}$ between the GS-parts of A and B, and a total morphism $f2:A_{SPEC} \rightarrow B_{SPEC}$ between the SPEC-parts which are compatible with ATTROP:

4. The category **ATTR** of attributed graphs consists of objects and morphisms as defined in 2 and 3 above.

The main result needed for the theory of attributed graph transformations is the following existence and construction of pushouts in **ATTR**.

3.6 Theorem (Pushouts of Attributed Graphs)

Let ATTR = (GS, SPEC, ATTROP) be an attributed graph specification. Pushouts in the category **ATTR** exists and they can be constructed componentwise in the category $\mathbf{GS^P}$ of graphical structures with partial morphisms, and in the category **SPEC** of SPEC-algebras with total morphisms. □

Proof: *Note that ATTR cannot be defined as a comma category in an obvious way, because of specific choices of partial and total morphisms in* ***ATTR****. But an explicit proof using the existence in each component and the construction in 3.3 for the GS-part leads to the desired result. This is shown for ATTR = (GS, SIG, ATTROP) with a signature SIG in the algebraic part in [LKW 93] but can be extended to our case with SPEC instead if SIG.*

In the following version of attributed graph transformations we do not use the full generality of theorem 3.6 for conceptual reasons. In fact, we restrict the rules $r:L \rightarrow R$ to have as SPEC-part the quotient term algebra $T_{SPEC}(X)$ over some variables X and the occurrence morphisms $m:L \rightarrow G$ as total morphisms in ***ATTR****, i.e. also total in the GS-part (see 3.4). This implies that the derived attributed graph H can be chosen to have the same SPEC-part A as G, i.e. $A = G_{SPEC} = H_{SPEC}$ can be considered as a fixed attribute algebra for all attributed graphs in one derivation sequence. This reflects the intuitive idea that only the graphical part and the attribute functions should be changed within a derivation sequence. The following definition for attributed graphs is an extension of the corresponding definitions in 3.4 for graph structures.*

3.7 Definition (Rule, Occurrence, Derivation of Attributed Graphs)

Let ATTR = (GS, SPEC, ATTROP) be an attributed graph specification. A rewriting rule $r:L \rightarrow R$ is an **ATTR**-morphism where the SPEC-component r_{SPEC} is the identity of the quotient term algebra $T_{SPEC}(X)$ over some finite set of variables X. An occurrence $m:L \rightarrow G$ of r in an attributed graph G is an **ATTR**-morphism whose GS-component m_{GS} is total, s.t. both components m_{GS} and m_{SPEC} of m are total. The direct derivation of G with the rule r at an occurrence m is the pushout of m and r in ATTR (see figure 3), written $G \Rightarrow H$ via (r, m), where w.l.o.g. we have $r^*_{SPEC} = id$ on G_{SPEC}.

3.8 Example (Attributed Graphs and Transformations Based on ER-Schemes)

In [CLWW 94] the static and dynamic semantics of entity-relationship models is defined using attributed graphs and transformations. In this paper we will show how this can be represented by dynamic abstract data types based on attributed graph transformations. For reasons of simplicity we discuss all constructions using an instructive example.

In a first step we present an attributed graph specification ATTR which is derived from an entity-relationship schema for persons living in a city given in figure 4.

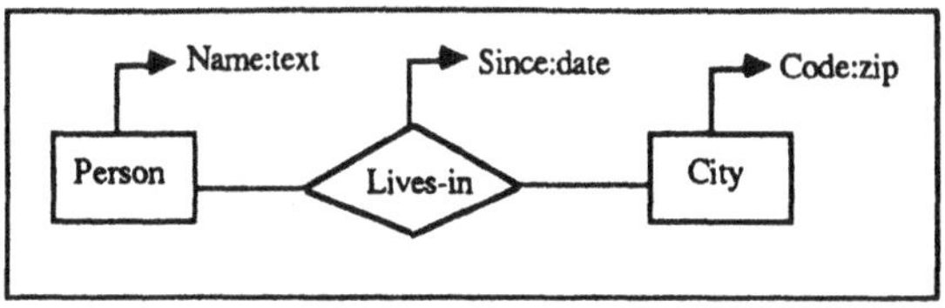

Figure 4: ER-Schema

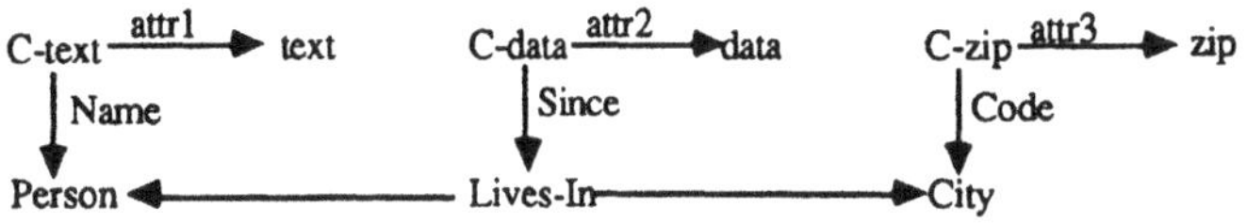

Figure 5: Attribute Graph Specification ATTR

The attributed graph specification ATTR = (GS, SPEC, ATTROP) is shown in figure 5 where SPEC consists of the sorts text, data, zip (and suitable data type operations and equations which are not shown), ATTROP consists of attribute functions attr1, attr2, attr3. All the remaining sorts and operation symbols belong to the graphical part GS. Especially we have attribute carrier sorts C-text, C-data, C-zip. Intuitively elements of attribute carrier domains can be regarded as objects holding an attribute value which may change in time.

Let us assume to have persons Harry and Sally living since 1/1/85 and 8/2/86 in a city with zip-code 10629. This can be represented by the ATTR-algebra G and deletion of Sally leads to the ATTR-algebra H in figure 6.
The representation of G and H in figure 6 is similar to the notation of ATTR in figure 5. Moreover, we show an ATTR-morphism $r^*:G \rightarrow H$ with domain $G(r^*) = H$ in figure 6. The ATTR-algebras G and H share the same SPEC-part A the initial SPEC-algebra T_{SPEC}. For simplicity we only show those elements of the SPEC-algebra A explicitly which are in the image of the attribute functions.

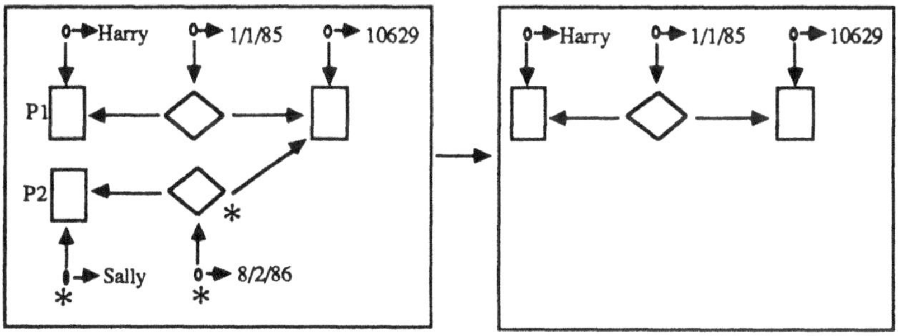

Figure 6: ATTR-morphism $r^*:G \rightarrow H$

The rewriting rule $r:L \rightarrow R$ for the deletion of a person is given in figure 7, where except of $p \in L_{Person}$ all domains of graphical sorts in L and R are empty. The SPEC-parts of L and R is the initial SPEC-algebra T_{SPEC}, i.e. $X = \emptyset$. The morphism r = (r1, r2) is undefined on the GS-part r1 and identical on SPEC-part r2.

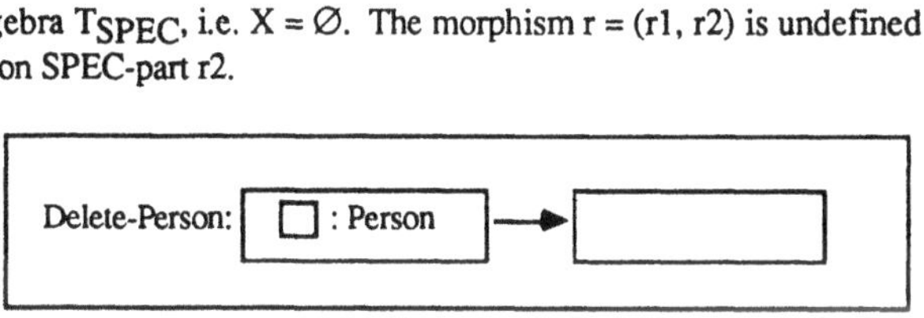

Figure 7: Rule $r:L \rightarrow R$ for Deletion of Persons

The delete-person rule $r:L \to R$ can be applied with occurrence $m = (m1, m2)\ L \to G$, defined by $m1(\square) = p2$ and $m2:T_{SPEC} \to A$ the initial homomorphism, to the attributed graph G in figure 6 leading to H and the ATTR-morphism r^* in figure 6. As a side effect to the deletion of p2 also the three items marked by * in G are deleted (see remark following definition 3.4).

4. Concept of Dynamic Abstract Data Types Based on Attributed Graph Transformations

In this section we combine the concept of attributed graph transformations, short AGT's, presented in the previous section with that of dynamic abstract data types, short DADT's, in section 2 to define an interesting new version of DADT's based on AGT's. The main idea is to use rewriting rules for AGT's as specification for dynamic operations in level 3 and construction mechanisms for AGT's in level 4. Especially we are able to study independence of dynamic operations using techniques from the theory of algebraic graph transformations. This is an important new aspect for DADT's, going beyond classical ADT's, which can be studied in our version of DADT's. Other important aspects will be discussed as extensions of our concept in the conclusion.

We start with the notion of an attributed graph transformation system which is based on the concepts introduced in section 3.

4.1 Definition (Attributed Graph Transformation System)

An attributed graph transformation system, short AGT-system,

$$AGT = (ATTR, START, RULES)$$

consists of an attributed graph specification ATTR = (GS, SPEC, ATTROP), a set START of attributed graphs G which are ATTR-algebras sharing the same attribute algebra A as SPEC-part, i.e. $G_{SPEC} = A$, and a set RULES of rewriting rules $r:L \to R$ with finite graphical parts.

Remark: *For conceptual reasons we assume that the graphical parts L_{GS} and R_{GS} of L and R are finite because this reflects the idea of local applicability and local change.*

4.2 Example (AGT-System Based on ER-Schemas)

Using the notation introduced in example 3.8 we define the following AGT-system AGT = (ATTR, START, RULES): ATTR is the attributed graph specification in figure 5 based on the ER-schema in figure 4. START consists of the start graph G0 with algebraic part $G0_{SPEC} = A = T_{SPEC}$ and empty graphical part, i.e. $G0_{GS} = \emptyset$. The set RULES, partly shown in figures 7 and 8 consists of 9 rules, which are the insert rules (Insert-Person, Insert-City, Insert-Lives-In) for the insertion of persons, cities and lives-in-relationships, the delete rules (Delete-Person, Delete-City, Delete-Lives-In) for the deletion of items and the update rules (Update-Name, Update-Since, Update-Code) for the update of the corresponding data attributes.

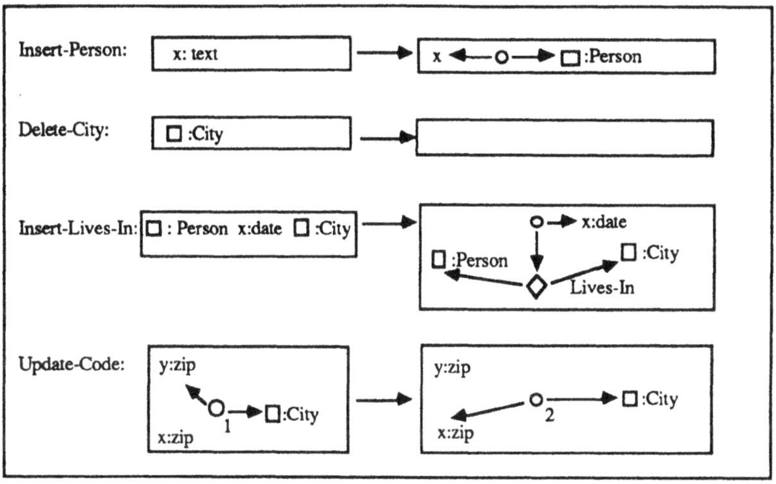

Figure 8: AGT-Rules

Each of the insert and update rules has one variable x:data of the corresponding data sort while the delete rules have no data variables. The morphisms $r:L \to R$ for the insert rules are total inclusions, for the delete rules partial inclusions undefined on the GS-part, and for the update rules the attribute object 1 on the left hand side is deleted and a new attribute object 2 on the right hand side is created. This allows to model the update of attributes as partial homomorphisms. In fact the application of the update-code rule to the graph G in figure 6 with occurrence morphism $m:L \to G$ and $m(x) = 10630$ leads to a new graph H' and a partial homomorphism $r':G \to H'$. This partial homomorphism r' is undefined on the attribute object 1 with $attr3_G(1) = 10629$ and creates a new attribute object 2 in H' with $attr3_{H'}(2) = 10630$.

4.3 Construction (Dynamic Operations Associated to Rules)

Given a rule $r:L \to R$ in an AGT-system AGT we want to construct a dynamic operation $d_{op}:s1...sn$ in the sense of DADT's such that each application of the rule r to an attributed graph G with result H leads to a transformation $d_{op}^*(a1,...,an):G \Rightarrow H$ between attributed graphs as instant structures in the sense of DADT's.

For each rule $r:L \to R$ we have a finite set X of variables, s.t. the SPEC-component of L and R is equal to the quotient term algebra $T_{SPEC}(X)$. This means that for each occurrence $m:L \to G$ the SPEC-component $m2 = m_{SPEC}:L_{SPEC} \to G_{SPEC}$ is uniquely determined by an assignment $asg:X \to A$ with $A = G_{SPEC}$.

In order to fix also the GS-component $m1 = m_{GS}$ of an occurrence morphism $m:L \to G$ we select $m \geq 0$ redex elements x1,...,xm in L of graphical sorts s1,...,sm in GS, i.e. $xi \in L_{si}$ ($i = 1,...,m$), in the following way: For each attributed graph G and each choice of graphical values ai $\in G_{si}$ ($i = 1,...,m$) there is at most one GS-morphism $m_{GS}:L_{GS} \to G_{GS}$ with $m_{GS}(xi) = ai$ ($i = 1,...,m$).

According to this choice the associated dynamic operation d_{op} of the rule $r:L \to R$ has the signature

$$d_{op}:s1...sn \ (n \geq 0)$$

where s1,...,sm ($m \geq 0$) are the graphical sorts and s(m+1)...sn ($m \leq n$) are the data sorts of the data variables in X. For notational reasons we have now $X = \{x(m+1),...,xn\}$ while x1,..,xm are elements in L_{GS} which do not belong to the data variables X.

Given an attributed graph G and elements $ai \in G_{si}$ (i = 1,...,n) the dynamic operation d_{op}:s1...sn of rule r:L → R is applicable to G with arguments a1,...,an if there is an occurrence morphism m:L → G with m(xi) = ai (i = 1,...,n). In this case we have a transformation

$$d_{op}^*(a1,...,an):G \Rightarrow H$$

which is defined by the pushout of figure 9 in the category **ATTR** using the notation of remark 5 below.

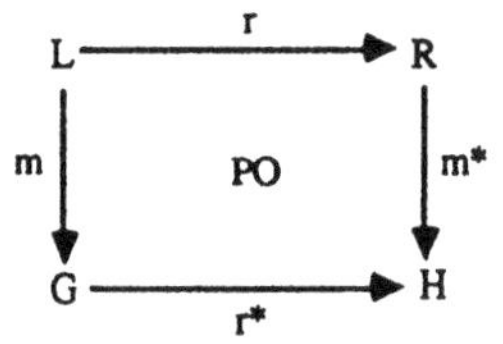

Figure 9: Transformation $d_{op}^*(\underline{a}):G \Rightarrow H$ with Dynamic Operation d_{op}:w of Rule r:L → R and Occurrence m:L → R defined by $m(\underline{x}) = \underline{a}$

Remarks:

1. *There is always a possible choice of $m \geq 0$ redex elements x1,...,xm in L with the desired property. Of course the idea is to take a minimal number m of redex elements, e.g. m = 0 if possible. In the worst case m is equal to the number of all elements in the domains of L_{GS}, which are finite by assumption (see remark of 4.1).*
2. *If the dynamic operation d_{op}:s1...sn is applicable to G with arguments a1,...,an the transformation d_{op}^*(a1,...,an) is uniquely determined (up to isomorphism) because the occurrence morphism m is determined by a1,...,an and pushouts are unique (up to isomorphism).*
3. *The transformation $d_{op}^*(a1,...,an):G \Rightarrow H$ has an underlying partial homomorphism r^*:G → H with $r^*_{SPEC} = id_A$ for its SPEC-part which is determined by the pushout in figures 3 and 9.*
4. *If we do not fix graphical sorts we obtain in general a nondeterministic transformation defined by a nondeterministic choice of m:L → G with $m(\underline{x}) = \underline{a}$.*
5. *For notational convenience we abbreviate n-tuples (x1,...,xn) by $\underline{x}$, (a1,...,an) by $\underline{a}$, s1,...,sn by w and write $m(\underline{x}) = \underline{a}$ instead of m(xi) = ai for (i = 1,...,n).*

4.4 Fact (Dynamic Operations Associated to Rules)

For each rule r:L → R of an AGT-system there is a dynamic operation d_{op} of rule r with signature

$$d_{op}:w \quad w = s1...sn \ (n \geq 0)$$

s.t. for each application of r to an attributed graph G with occurrence morphism m:L → G and direct derivation G ⇒ H via (r, m) there are elements $ai \in G_{si}$ (i = 1,...,n) defining $\underline{a}$ = (a1,...,an) and a transformation

$$d_{op}^*(\underline{a}):G \rightarrow H$$

given by the pushout in figure 9. Vice versa given G and $ai \in G_{si}$(i = 1,...,n) there is at most one occurrence morphism m:L → G with $m(\underline{x}) = \underline{a}$. In this case $d_{op}*(\underline{a})$ is defined as above.

Proof

See construction 4.3. □

4.5 Example (Dynamic Operations for ER-Schema)

The dynamic operations for the rules of the AGT-system in example 4.2 are given in figure 10 according to construction 4.3.

Name	:	Signature
Insert-Person	:	text
Insert-City	:	zip
Insert-Lives-In	:	Person City date
Delete-Person	:	Person
Delete-City	:	City
Delete-Lives-In	:	Lives-In
Update-Name	:	C-text text
Update-Since	:	C-date date
Update-Code	:	C-zip zip

Figure 10: Dynamic Operations d_{op}:w for ER-Schema

4.6 Definition (Independence of Transformations)

Let d_{op}:w and d_{op}':w' be the dynamic operations of rules p:L → R and q:M → S. Two transformations $d_{op}*(\underline{a})$:G ⇒ H and $d_{op}'*(\underline{a}')$:G ⇒ H' given by pushouts (1) and (2) respectively in figure 11 are called parallel independent if the composite partial homomorphisms $q^* \circ m$ and $p^* \circ n$ are total.

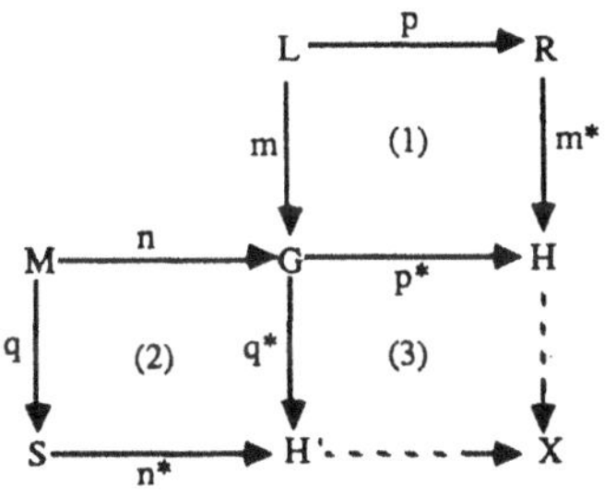

Figure 11: Parallel Independence of Transformations

Remarks:

1. *The parallel independence of two transformations requires that both occurrences are preserved by the other transformation such that we obtain inherited occurrences, which are called residuals. In fact, this must only be checked for the graphical parts of the morphisms, since the algebraic parts are total in any case. Intuitively this means that the intersection of the occurrences m(L) and n(M) in G is included in the intersection m($\underline{L}$) and n($\underline{M}$) of the translated gluing points $\underline{L}$ of p and $\underline{M}$ of q, where the gluing points are defined as $\underline{A}$ in 3.3.*
2. *Given transformations $d_{op}*(\underline{a})$:G ⇒ H and $d_{op}'*(\underline{a}')$:H ⇒ X we are able to define sequential independence as in [Löw 90] and to show that sequential independent transformations can also be applied in opposite order leading to the same result.*

4.7 Theorem (Local Church-Rosser Property)

For two parallel independent transformations $d_{op}*(\underline{a})$:G ⇒ H and $d_{op}'*(\underline{a}')$:G ⇒ H' as given in figure 11 there is an attributed graph X and transformations $d_{op}*(q^*(\underline{a}))$:H' ⇒ X and $d_{op}'*(p^*(\underline{a}'))$:H ⇒ X as shown in figure 12

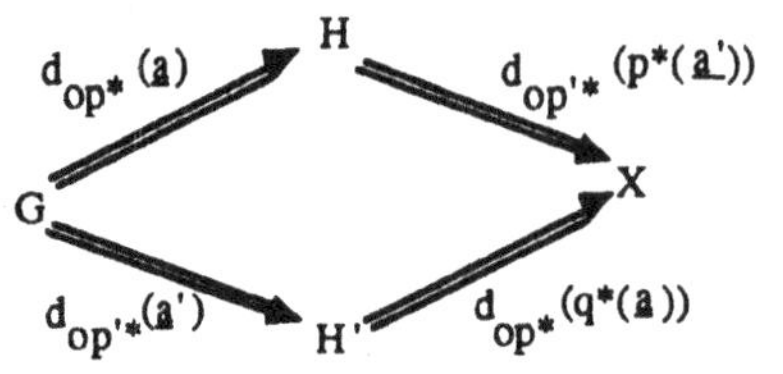

Figure 12: Independent Transformations

Proof: *Due to parallel independence the morphisms $q^* \bullet m$ and $p^* \bullet n$ in figure 11 are total and by definition of transformations (see figure 9) we have $m(\underline{x}) = \underline{a}$ and $n(\underline{x}') = \underline{a}'$. This implies that $p^*(\underline{a}') = p^* \bullet n(\underline{x}')$ and $q^*(\underline{a}) = q^* \bullet m(\underline{a})$ are well-defined. Now we construct the attributed graph X as pushout of q^* and p^* in (3) of figure 11. The composite pushouts of (1) and (3) resp. (2) and (3) are defining the transformations $d_{op}*(q^*(\underline{a})):H' \Rightarrow X$ and $d_{op}{}'*(p^*(\underline{a}')):H \Rightarrow X$ shown in figure 12.* □

4.8 Construction (Dynamic Abstract Data Type Based on an Attributed Graph Transformation System)

Given an attributed graph transformation system AGT = (ATTR, START, RULES) as in 4.1 we give a specification DYNSPEC = (VSPEC, ISPEC, DSPEC) for a dynamic abstract data type D = D(AGT) and HSPEC for corresponding families of DADT's in the sense of section 2.

Level 1 of D(AGT): Value Type Specification VSPEC

The value type specification VSPEC is the specification SPEC of the attributed graph specification ATTR = (GS, SPEC, ATTROP). The semantics of VSPEC = SPEC is fixed to be the attributed algebra A which is shared by all the attributed graphs G in START. If START is empty we choose the initial SPEC-algebra A = T_{SPEC}.

Level 2 of D(AGT): Instant Structure Specification ISPEC

The instant structure specification ISPEC is the attributed graph specification ATTR, i.e. ISPEC = ATTR. This means that ISPEC-algebras (instant structures) are attributed graphs G. The only constraint we require at this moment for attributed graphs G is the fact that they protect the attributed algebra A, i.e. G_{SPEC} = A. Additional constraints, especially for the graphical part G_{GS}, will be discussed in the conclusion.

Level 3 of D(AGT): Dynamic Operations Specification DSPEC

The specification DSPEC consists of all dynamic generators and dynamic operations defined as follows:

For each attributed graph G in START we define a dynamic generator g_{op}:λ with semantics gop_D = G. For each rule r:L → R in RULES we take the dynamic operation d_{op}:w of rule r as defined in 4.3. Given an attributed graph G and arguments $\underline{a}$ = (a1,...,an) in G of sorts w = s1...sn the dynamic operation d_{op}:w can be applied to G if the rule r is applicable to G with an occurrence morphism m:L → G determined by $\underline{a}$. In this case the transformation $dop_D(\underline{a}) = d_{op}*(\underline{a}):G \Rightarrow H$ is defined by the pushout of figure 9 in the category **ATTR**. Parallel independence of transformations as defined as in 4.6 allows to apply both transformations in arbitrary order due to the local Church-Rosser Property shown in figure 12 of theorem 4.7. In fact both transformation sequences in figure 12 are sequential independent (see remark 2 of 4.6) which means that they can be commuted.

The semantics of DSPEC is the instant structure transition category to be defined in section 5 which roughly corresponds to the derivation category in the sense of graph grammars which has been studied up to now only in the double-pushout approach of graph grammar [CELMR 94].

Level 4 of D(AGT): Higher Level Dynamic Specification HSPEC

Concerning level 4 of dynamic abstract data types based on AGT's we only give some basic ideas which may be a starting point for mechanisms to create, combine and transform AGT's and the corresponding DADT's:

A higher level dynamic specification HSPEC for AGT's consists of higher level dynamic generators, creating a family $(AGTi)_{i \in I}$ of AGT-systems with dynamic abstract data types D(AGTi) ($i \in I$) in the sense of level 1-3, and higher level dynamic operators which are operators on AGT's and the corresponding DADT's in the following sense where extension can be considered as a special case of union:

1. Extension of AGT's by adding new start graphs and rules.
2. Union of AGT's (with the same attributed graph specification ATTR and attribute algebra A) defined by union of start graphs and rules.
3. Transformation of AGT's by change of attribute algebras (see section 5).
4. Transformation of AGT's by morphisms of AGT's (see section 6).

4.9 Example (Dynamic Abstract Data Types Based on AGT-System for ER-Schemas)

The AGT-system AGT in example 4.2 defines a dynamic abstract data type D(AGT) with a dynamic generator generating the start graph G0 and dynamic operations as given in example 4.5.

5. Transition Category of Dynamic Abstract Data Types Based on Attributed Graph Transformations

In this section we define the transition system and the transition category of a dynamic abstract data type D(AGT) based on an attributed graph transformation system AGT. The transition category TRANSCAT(AGT) is the semantics of D(AGT) in the sense of dynamic abstract data types. Since each AGT-system is based on a specific attribute algebra A, written AGT(A), we will study the relationship between the transition categories induced by a change of attribute algebras given by a SPEC-homomorphism $f:A \rightarrow B$. In fact, we obtain an induced functor F_f between the transition categories TRANSCAT(AGT(A)) and TRANSCAT(AGT(B)). This relationship leads to a category TRANSCATCAT(AGT) of transition categories and to a functor TRANSCAT from the category SPEC of SPEC-algebras to TRANSCATCAT(AGT) which - under certain conditions - becomes an isomorphism of categories. This seems to be significant for DADT's in general because a similar isomorphism for a different version of DADT's is shown in [GR 94].

5.1 Definition (Transition System and Transition Category)

1. Given an AGT-system AGT = (ATTR, START, RULES) the transition system TRANS(AGT) of AGT is a (meta-)graph, where the nodes are attributed graphs, i.e. ATTR-algebras and the edges are all transformations $d_{op}{}^*(\underline{a}):G \Rightarrow H$ with dynamic operations $d_{op}:w$ of the rules $r \in$ RULES in the sense of 4.3 and 4.4. More precisely the nodes of TRANS(AGT) are all the attributed graphs G in START and all other attributed graphs H reachable by finite sequences of transformations.
2. The transition category TRANSCAT(AGT) of AGT is the category freely generated by the transition system TRANS(AGT) according to the well-known free construction between graphs and categories.

Remarks:

1. *In section 4 we have discussed parallel and sequential independence of transformations. Figure 12 shows that independent transformation sequences can be commuted, taking into account adaption of the arguments* $\underline{a}$ *and* $\underline{a}'$ *by* $q^*(\underline{a})$ *and* $p^*(\underline{a}')$ *respectively. In other words both sequences are shift equivalent w.r.t. shift of independent transformations. This shift equivalence can be extended to become a congruence of morphisms in TRANSCAT(AGT) leading to a quotient category CTRANSCAT(AGT) of concurrent transformation sequences in the spirit of interleaving semantics.*
2. *These constructions are similar to those of derivation categories and derivation categories modulo shift in the double-pushout approach [CELMR 94]. The construction of corresponding abstract derivation categories needs special care concerning the notion of equivalence of derivations w.r.t. isomorphisms.*

5.2 Remark and Definition (Change of Attribute Algebras)

Note that all attributed graphs in the set START of an AGT-system share a common attribute algebra A and the attribute algebra is preserved under all transformations (see 3.7). This implies that all attributed graphs in the transition system TRANS(AGT) and the transition category TRANSCAT(AGT) share the same attribute algebra A. To express this fact we will now write AGT(A) and START(A) instead of AGT and START and study the effect of changing the attribute algebra by a SPEC-homomorphism $f:A \to B$. Let **ATTR(A)** be the subcategory of **ATTR** (see 3.5) consisting of all objects and morphisms with SPEC-part equal to A resp. id_A.

5.3 Fact (Change of Attribute Algebras for AGT-Systems)

Given an AGT-system AGT(A) = (ATTR, START(A), RULES) and a SPEC-homomorphism $f:A \to B$ then there is an induced functor E_f:**ATTR(A)** $\to$ **ATTR(B)**, called extension of attribute algebras by f, and an induced AGT-system AGT(B) = (ATTR, START(B), RULES) with

$$START(B) = \{E_f(G) / G \in START(A)\}$$

Proof: *The attributed graph specification ATTR is given by ATTR = (GS, SPEC, ATTROP) (see 4.1). For each object G in* ***ATTR(A)*** *we define* $E_f(G) = G'$ *in* ***ATTR(B)*** *by* $G'_{GS} = G_{GS}$, $G'_{SPEC} = B$ *and for all* $attr{:}s \to s'$ *in ATTROP, with sorts s and s' in GS and SPEC respectively, let* $attr_{G'}{:}G'_s \to G'_{s'}$ *be defined by* $attr_{G'} = f_{s'} \circ attr_G$. *This is well-defined because of* $G'_s = G_s$ *according to the fact that sort s is in GS. Moreover we have a total* ***ATTR****-morphism* $f(G){:}G \to G'$ *defined by* $f(G)_{GS} = id$ *and* $f(G)_{SPEC} = f$ *which is compatible with ATTROP by definition of* $attr_{G'}$. *For each morphism* $h{:}G \to H$ *in* ***ATTR(A)*** *we define* $E_f(h) = h'{:}G' \to H'$ *by* $h'_{GS} = h_{GS}$ *and* $h'_{SPEC} = id_B$ *which can be shown to be compatible with ATTROP and leads to a commutative diagram in figure 13.*

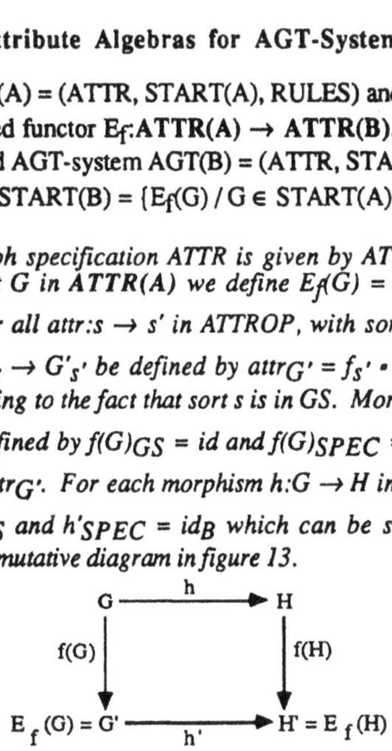

Figure 13: Change of Attribute Algebras by $f:A \to B$

5.4 Theorem (Change of Attribute Algebras for Transition Categories)

Given an AGT-system AGT(A) and a SPEC-homomorphism $f:A \to B$ then there is an induced functor

$$F_f{:}TRANSCAT(AGT(A)) \to TRANSCAT(AGT(B))$$

where AGT(B) is the induced AGT-system (see 5.3).

Proof: *We show that the induced functor* F_f*:****ATTR(A)*** $\to$ ***ATTR(B)*** *leads to a graph morphism between the transition system TRANS(AGT(A)) and TRANS(AGT(B)) which can be freely extended to the functor* F_f *between the transition categories. On objects G in TRANSCAT(AGT(A)), which are equal to the nodes in TRANS(AGT(A)), we define* $F_f(G) = E_f(G)$. *It remains to show that for each transformation* $d_{op}{}^*(\underline{a}){:}G \Rightarrow H$ *in TRANSCAT(AGT(A)) with dynamic operation* $d_{op}{:}w$ *of a rule* $r{:}L \to R$ *in AGT(A) as shown in figure 9 we obtain a transformation* $d_{op}{}^*(f(G)\,(\underline{a})){:}G' \Rightarrow H'$ *in TRANSCAT(AGT(B)) where* $F_f(G) = E_f(G) = G'$ *and* $F_f(H) = E_f(H) = H'$ *and* $f(G){:}G \to G'$ *is the total* ***ATTR****-morphism defined in the proof of 5.3. In fact, it suffices to show that the diagram in figure 13 is a pushout in* ***ATTR****, because the composition of this pushout with that in figure 9 leads to the pushout in* *figure 14 defining the transformation* $d_{op}{}^*(f(G)\,(\underline{a})): G' \Rightarrow H'$. *But the diagram in figure 13 is a pushout in **ATTR** by theorem 3.6 because it is a pushout in the GS-component* ($f(G)_{GS} = id$, $f(H)_{GS} = id$, $h_{GS} = h'_{GS}$) *and in the SPEC-component* ($h_{SPEC} = id$, $h'_{SPEC} = id$, $f(G)_{SPEC} = f = f(H)_{SPEC}$). □

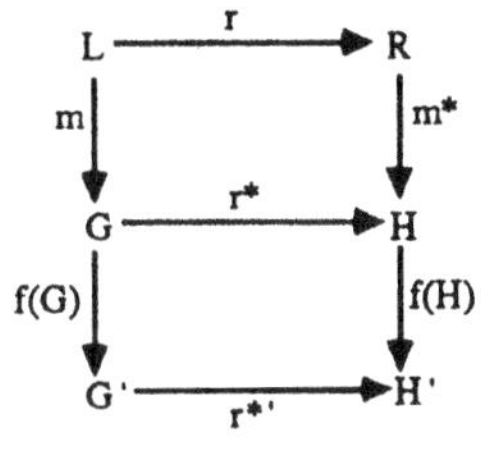

Figure 14: Induced Transformation $d_{op}{}^*(f(G)(\underline{a})):G' \Rightarrow H'$

5.5 Definition (Category of Transition Categories and Transition Category Functor)

Given an AGT-system AGT with attribute algebra $I = T_{SPEC}$, the initial SPEC-algebra. For each SPEC-algebra A there is a unique SPEC-homomorphism $h:I \to A$ leading to an induced AGT-system AGT(A) (see 5.3). The category TRANSCATCAT(AGT) of transition categories of AGT has as objects all transition categories TRANSCAT(AGT(A)) and as morphisms all functors F_f:TRANSCAT(AGT(A)) → TRANSCAT(AGT(B)) induced by SPEC-homomorphisms $f:A \to B$ in **SPEC**. Defining TRANSCAT(A) = TRANSCAT(AGT(A)) and TRANSCAT(f) = F_f we obtain a functor

TRANSCAT:**SPEC** → TRANSCATCAT(AGT)

called <u>transition category functor of AGT</u>.

5.6 Theorem (Transition Category Functor)

The transition category functor TRANSCAT of an AGT-system AGT = (ATTR, START, RULES) is a well-defined functor and we have the following properties if START is nonempty:

1. TRANSCAT is bijective on objects and surjective on morphisms, but in general not bijective.
2. TRANSCAT is an isomorphism of categories if the following attribute condition is satisfied for ATTR = (GS, SPEC, ATTROP):

For each data type sort s' in SPEC and each SPEC-algebra A the family of attribute functions

$$[attr_G:G_s \to G_{s'}]_{G \in \mathbf{ATTR(A)}}$$

is surjective, i.e. for each $a \in A_{s'} = G_{s'}$ there is a **ATTR(A)**-algebra G and $b \in G_s$ for some graphical sort s s.t. $attr_G(b) = a$.

Remark: *If START is empty then TRANSCAT(AGT(A)) is empty for each SPEC-algebra A.*

Proof:

1. *TRANSCAT is a well-defined functor because it preserves identities and composition of SPEC-morphisms by construction of* E_f *and* F_f *in 5.3 and 5.4. Moreover, TRANSCAT is surjective on objects and morphisms by construction. TRANSCAT is injective on objects because TRANSCAT(A) = TRANSCAT(B) implies by nonemptiness of START the existence of* $G \in START(A)$ *which is an object of TRANSCAT(A) and hence also of TRANSCAT(B). Hence we have for the SPEC-part of G* $G_{SPEC} = A$ *and also* $G_{SPEC} = B$ *which implies A = B.*
But in general TRANSCAT is not injective on morphisms due to the following counterexample. Take ATTROP = ∅ and X = ∅ for all rules. Then we have for all

SPEC-homomorphisms f, g:A → B equality of the functors F_f, F_g, i.e. $F_f = F_g$. On objects G we have $F_f(G) = F_g(G)$ because the construction of $F_f(G) = E_f(G)$ does not depend on f due to ATTROP = ∅. For morphisms $d_{op}*(a):G \Rightarrow H$ in TRANSCAT(AGT(A)) given by the upper pushout in figure 14 the composite pushouts for f and g are equal because $f(G)_{GS} = id = g(G)_{GS}$ and the SPEC-parts of f(G) • m and g(G) • m are equal due to initiality of $L_{SPEC} = T_{SPEC}(X) = T_{SPEC}$ for X = ∅.

2. *It remains to show that the attribute condition implies that TRANSCAT is injective on morphisms. Given f, g:A → B with $F_f = F_g$ we have to show f = g. For each data type sort s' in SPEC and each $a \in A_{s'}$ the attribute condition implies that we have an ATTR(A)-algebra G, an attribute function $attr_G:G_s \to G_{s'}$ and some $G \in G_s$ s.t. $attr_G(b) = a$. Now $F_f(G) = F_g(G)$ implies $attr_{G'} = attr_{G''}$ for $F_f(G) = G'$ and $F_g(G) = G''$. By construction in 5.3 we have $attr_{G'} = f_{s'} \bullet attr_G$ and $attr_{G''} = g_{s'} \bullet attr_G$. But this implies $f_{s'}(a) = g_{s'}(a)$ and hence f = g.* □

6. Conclusion

In this paper we have reviewed the concept of dynamic abstract data types (DADT's) and introduced a new variant of DADT's based on attributed graph transformations (AGT's), which are a combination of algebraic specifications and algebraic graph transformations.
Although the concept of DADT's has been proposed in [EO 94] as a common frame for several recent approaches in the area of algebraic specifications, object-orientation, evolving algebras and graph transformations, discussed in sections 1 and 2, we are convinced that it is too early to come up with a formal definition and a general theory of DADT's.
Presently it seems to be much more important to relate existing approaches to the concept of DADT's (announced by H. Reichel [Rei 94], H.D. Ehrich [Ehr 94], and J. Padberg [Pad 94] and to study specific versions of DADT's in more detail. In fact most of the approaches - although very promising - still have to be extended to study independence of dynamic operations leading to suitable notions of parallelism, concurrency and distribution for DADT's. These notions, on the other hand, have been studied in the theory of algebraic graph transformations already. In this paper we have reviewed some basic concepts of algebraic and attributed graph transformations in section 3 and have started to extend the notions concerning independence, parallelism and concurrency to attributed graph transformations as well as dynamic operations and transformations of the corresponding DADT's in section 4.
The main contribution of this paper is the presentation of a dynamic abstract data type D(AGT) based on a general AGT-system AGT, illustrated by a specific AGT-system from the area of data bases. Moreover, we have introduced the transition category of the dynamic abstract data type D(AGT) and studied its properties concerning the change of attribute algebras of the given AGT-system.
In view of the specification of DADT's for more complex practical examples, like the shipping software in [BE 94], it seems to be important to extend DADT's based on AGT-systems by the following concepts:

1. Constraints for attributed graph specifications as defined in [EM 90] for general algebraic specifications in order to express integrity constraints for the attributed graphs modelling the instant structures of the system.
2. Application conditions for dynamic operations expressible on a graphical or a logic/algebraic level.
3. Parallelism and synchronization of dynamic operations and transformations corresponding to parallel and amalgamated rules and derivations in the sense of algebraic graph transformations.
4. Dynamic operations defined by programmed graph transformation rules which allow to model not only basic transformations (actions) corresponding to one rule, but also complex transformations (transactions) defined by a sequence of rules.
5. Morphisms of DADT's, based on morphisms of AGT-systems, which are able to express extensions of DADT's by additional dynamic operations in order to support stepwise development and refinement.

In fact, most of these concepts have been studied in theory of algebraic graph transformations to some extend already. Most recently concepts 2 to 4 have been extended to attributed graph transformations in [HMTN 94] including some basic first results which seem to be very useful for our framework of DADT's. Moreover, we have already more specific ideas and preliminary results concerning concepts 1 and 5. A more detailed presentation of these topics, however, goes beyond the scope of this paper.

7. References

[AZ 92] Astesiano, E., Zucca, E.: *A Semantic Model for Dynamic Systems.* Springer Workshops in Computing, 1992/93, pp. 63-80

[AZ 94] Astesiano, E., Zucca, E.: *D-oids: A Model for Dynamic Data Types.* Special Issue of MSCS, accepted for publication 1994

[BE 94] Bardohl, R., Ehrig, H.: *Specification of Shipping Software Using Dynamic Abstract Data Types.* In preparation (1994)

[CELMR 94] Corradini, A., Ehrig, H., Löwe, M., Montanari, U., Rossi, F.: *Abstract Graph Derivations in the Double-Pushout Approach.* Proc. Graph Grammar Workshop Dagstuhl 1993, Springer LNCS 776 (1994), pp. 86-103

[CLWW 94] Claßen, I., Löwe, M., Waßerroth, S., Wortmann, J.: *Static and Dynamic Semantics of Entity-Relationship Models Bassed on Algebraic Methods,* Proc. IFIP-Congress and GI-Fachgespräche, Hamburg 1994, to appear

[DG 94] Dauchy, P., Gaudel, M.G.: *Algebraic Specifications with Implicit State.* Techn. Report, Univ. Paris-Sud, 1994

[Ehr 79] Ehrig, H.: *Introduction to the algebraic theory of graph grammars (A Survey)* in: Graph Grammars and Their Application to Computer Science and Biology, Springer LNCS 73, (1979), 1-69

[Ehrich 94] Ehrich, H.D.: *Modular Semantics for Concurrent Families of Sequential Objects,* Lecture at ADT-COMPASS Workshop, Santa Margharita Ligure, 1994

[EL 93] Ehrig, H., Löwe, M.: *The ESPRIT BRWG COMPUGRAPH "Computing by Graph Transformations": A Survey.* TCS 109 (1993), pp. 3-6

[EM 85] Ehrig, H., Mahr, B.: *Fundamentals of Algebraic Specification 1. Equations and Initial Semantics.* EATCS Monographs on Theoretical Computer Science, Vol. 6, Springer (1985)

[EM 90] Ehrig, H.; Mahr, B.: *Fundamentals of Algebraic Specification 2. Module Specifications and Constraints.* EATCS Monographs on Theoretical Computer Science, Vol. 21, Springer-Verlag (1990)

[EO 94] Ehrig, H., Orejas, F.: *Dynamic Abstract Data Types: An Informal Proposal,* Bull. EATCS 53 (1994), pp. 162-169

[GKS 92] Gottlieb, G., Kappel, G., Scheff, M.: *Semantics of Object Oriented Data Models - The Evolving Algebra Approach.* Springer LNCS 504 (1992), pp. 144-160

[Gog 94] Gogolla, M.: *An Algebraic Semantics for the Object Specification Language TROLL-light,* Lecture at ADT-COMPASS Workshop, Santa Margharita Ligure, 1994

[GR 90] Große-Rhode, M.: *Towards Object-Oriented Algebraic Specifications.* Recent Trends in Data Type Specifications, Springer LNCS 534, 1990, pp. 98-116

[GR 94] Große-Rhode, M.: *Specification of Parallel State Dependent Systems.* TU Berlin, 1994, in preparation

[Gur 91] Gurevitch, Y.: *Evolving Algebras, A Tutorial Introduction.* Bull. EATCS 43 (1991), pp. 264-284

[Gur 94] Gurevitch, Y.: *Evolving Algebra 1993.* In Boerger (ed.): Specification and Validation Methods, Oxford University Press, to appear 1994

[HMTW 94] Heckel, R., Müller, J., Taentzer, G., Wagner A.: *Attributed Graph Transformations with Controlled Application of Rules,* Proc. Graph Grammar Workshop, Mallorca 1994, to appear

[Kor 94] Korff, M.: *Single Pushout Transformations of Equationally Defined Graph Structures with Applications to Actor Systems.* Proc. Graph Grammar Workshop Dagstuhl 1993, Springer LNCS 776, 1994, pp. 234-247

[LE 91] M. Löwe, H. Ehrig: *Algebraic Approach to Graph Transformation Based on Single Pushout Derivations,* in: 16th Int. Workshop on Graph-Theoretic Concepts in Comp. Sci., Springer LNCS 484,pp. 338-353, 1991.

[LKW 93] Löwe, M., Korff, M., Wagner, A.: *An Algebraic Framework for the Transformation of Attributed Graphs.* In M.R. Sleep et.al. (eds.) Term Graph Rewriting: Theory and Practice, Wiley, London (1993), pp. 185-199

[Löw 90] Löwe, M.: *Extended Algebraic Graph Transformations*, PhD thesis, TU Berlin 1990, short version in TCS 109, pp. 181-224

[Pad 94] Padberg, J.: *Abstract Data Type Semantics for Algebraic High-Level Nets Using Dynamic Abstract Data Types*, Proc. Int. Workshop on Quality of Communication Based Systems, Berlin 1994, to appear

[Pie 94] Pierantonio, A.: *Making Static Dynamic: Towards an Axiomatization for Dynamic ADT's*. Proc. Int. Workshop on Quality of Communication Based Systems, Berlin 1994, to appear

[PPP 91] Parisi-Presicce, F., Pierantonio, A.: *An Algebraic Approach to Inheritance and Subtyping*. Proc. ESEC 1991, Springer LNCS 550, 1991, pp. 364-379

[PPP 94] Pierantonio, A., Parisi-Presicce, F.: *On the Algebraic Specification of Object Dynamics in Object-Oriented Systems*. Lecture at joint COMPASS-ISCORE workshop, Lisbon 1994, paper in preparation 1994

[Rei 94] Reichel, H.: *An Approach to Object Semantics Based on Terminal Co-Algebras*. Special Issue of MSCS, to appear 1994

[Wag 89] Wagner, E.: *On Declarations*; Springer LNCS 393, 1989, pp. 261-277

[WE 88] Weber, H., Ehrig, H.: *Specification of Concurrently Executable Modules and Distributed Modular Systems*. Proc. Workshop Future Trends of Distr. Comp. Systems in the 1990's, HongKong, 1988, pp. 202-215

[WG 94] Wagner, A., Gogolla, M.: *Defining Operational Behaviour of Object Specifications by Attributed Graph Transformations*. Internal Report, 1994

Modular Termination of Term Rewriting Systems Revisited *

Maribel Fernández and Jean-Pierre Jouannaud[1]

Laboratoire de Recherche en Informatique, Bât. 490
CNRS et Université de Paris Sud, 91405 Orsay, France
email: {maribel,jouannau}@lri.fr

1 Introduction

Confluent and terminating term rewriting systems are a major tool for prototyping algebraic specifications. This paper is concerned with the impact of stepwise development methodologies on prototyping.

Assume given two modules, each one specifying a set $\mathcal{D}_i$ $(i = 0, 1)$ of *defined functions* with respect to a given set $\mathcal{C}_i$ of *constructors* by means of a set R_i of rewrite rules. By definition, $\mathcal{D}_i$ is the set of symbols heading the left-hand sides of rules, the other symbols being in $\mathcal{C}_i$. The set $\mathcal{F}_i = \mathcal{C}_i \cup \mathcal{D}_i$ is called the *signature* of the module. Putting these two modules together results in the union of the two rewriting systems R_0 and R_1, written $R_0 \cup R_1$. In the unions we consider, $\mathcal{D}_0 \cap \mathcal{D}_1 = \emptyset$. We distinguish three kinds of unions of increasing generality:

Disjoint union, denoted by $R_0 \oplus R_1$, if $\mathcal{F}_0 \cap \mathcal{F}_1 = \emptyset$.

Combined union, denoted by $R_0 \uplus R_1$, if $\mathcal{F}_0 \cap \mathcal{F}_1 = \mathcal{C}_0 \cap \mathcal{C}_1$, i.e. in this class of unions only constructors may be shared.

Hierarchical union, denoted by $R_0 + R_1$, if $\mathcal{F}_0 \cap \mathcal{D}_1 = \emptyset$, but $\mathcal{F}_1 \cap \mathcal{D}_0 \neq \emptyset$, that is, the systems may share constructors, and moreover the defined symbols of R_0 may be constructors of R_1. In $R_0 + R_1$, R_0 is the *base*, and R_1 the *enrichment*. There may be several successive enrichments in a hierarchical union.

Since obtaining a confluent and terminating rewriting system from a set of equations may be a hard task, it is desirable that both properties are closed under these unions. A property of term rewriting systems is *modular* if it is closed under union. Neither termination nor confluence is closed under arbitrary union. However, it is well known that confluence is a modular property of disjoint unions, a celebrated result of Toyama [25]. This is not true of combined union, as pointed out by Kurihara and Ohuchi [13]. In contrast, termination is not a modular property, even of disjoint unions [24]:

$$R_0 = \{f(0, 1, x) \to f(x, x, x)\}, \quad R_1 = \{g(x, y) \to x, \ g(x, y) \to y\}$$

Indeed, there is the following infinite reduction sequence:

$$f(g(0,1), g(0,1), g(0,1)) \to f(0, g(0,1), g(0,1)) \to f(0, 1, g(0,1)) \to f(g(0,1), g(0,1), g(0,1)) \ldots$$

* This work was partly supported by the "Greco de programmation du CNRS", and the ESPRIT Basic Research Action COMPASS.

Contradicting hopes, the above example can be refined so as to have confluent definitions for both rewrite systems [4]:

$$R_0 = \{f(0,1,x) \rightarrow f(x,x,x),\ f(x,y,z) \rightarrow 2,\ 0 \rightarrow 2,\ 1 \rightarrow 2\}$$

$$R_1 = \{g(x,y,y) \rightarrow x,\ g(y,y,x) \rightarrow x\}$$

for which there is again an infinite reduction sequence originating from $f(g(0,2,1), g(0,2,1), g(0,2,1))$.

It however turns out that the *existence* of normal forms for all terms is a modular property of disjoint unions [17]. So, if two rewrite systems are both confluent and terminating, their disjoint union enjoys unique normal forms even when there are infinite reduction sequences. For example, reducing all subterms of $f(g(0,2,1), g(0,2,1), g(0,2,1))$ in the above sequence to 2 yields the normal form 2. Using implicitely a result of Rusinowitch [23] for *non-duplicating* disjoint unions, Kurihara and Ohuchi pointed out that a very simple strategy allows to compute this normal form: *shared rewriting* in which different occurrences of a same variable in a right-hand side of rule are shared. This strategy is indeed implemented in any rewriting software for efficiency reasons. So, prototyping disjoint unions operates safely. This is also true of combined unions [13], and can be generalized to even more complex situations [17].

Our goal is to work out a comprehensible theory of modularity of termination, by presenting all these results in a coherent framework[2]. Let us call *homogeneous* in a union $R_0 \cup R_1$ a term which uses function symbols of one signature only, and does not use defined symbols that belong also to the other signature. Non-homogeneous terms can be split into a maximal homogeneous top part called *cap* and a multiset of pending subterms called *aliens*. Roughly speaking, a rewrite relation on terms is *alien-decreasing* if rewriting inside the cap of a term does not increase the multiset of aliens with respect to the subterm relation. This abstract property of rewrite relations is the key to modularity of disjoint and combined unions, and also plays a role for the modularity of hierarchical unions.

A key contribution of this paper is a simple proof of modularity of termination of unions of alien-decreasing rewrite relations, see section 4. This result subsumes previous results applying to disjoints unions [23], combined unions [13] and *crosswise disjoint unions* [19], since shared rewrite systems, non-duplicating rewrite systems and crosswise disjoint systems are alien-decreasing, as shown in section 3. It also may apply to hierarchical or even more general unions.

For hierarchical unions, we present a second modularity result that applies when the base is alien-decreasing and enrichments obey a generalised primitive-recursive schema, see section 6. This yields new modularity results, related to the recent results of Krishna Rao [20, 21], Gramlich [7] and Dershowitz [2].

The above results generalize to reductive conditional rewrite systems [10], and to rewriting modulo equations whose congruence classes are finite.

---

[2] There are other results in this area, which do not relate directly to ours, however, and are not discussed here for lack of space.

2 Preliminaries

We assume the reader familiar with the basic concepts and notations of term rewriting systems. We refer to [3] for missing definitions and notations.

A *signature* $\mathcal{F}$ is a finite set of *function symbols* together with their (fixed) arity. $\mathcal{X}$ denotes a denumerable set of *variables*, $T(\mathcal{F})$ denotes the set of *ground terms* over $\mathcal{F}$ and $T(\mathcal{F},\mathcal{X})$ denotes the set of *terms* built up from $\mathcal{F}$ and $\mathcal{X}$.

Terms are identified with finite labelled trees as usual. *Positions* are strings of positive integers. Λ denotes the empty string (root position) and "." denotes string concatenation. We use $\mathcal{P}os(t)$ for the set of positions in t, and $\mathcal{FP}os(t)$ for its set of non-variable positions. The prefix ordering (resp. lexicographic ordering) on positions is denoted by $>$ (resp. $>^{N}_{lex}$) and the strict subterm relationship by $\lhd$. The encompassment ordering, denoted by $\blacktriangleleft$, is the strict part of the quasi-ordering: $u \trianglelefteq v$ if $v|_p = u\sigma$ for some position p and substitution σ and its equivalence corresponds to variable renaming. Subsumption is a special case of encompassment (in which u is an instance of v). We use $root(t)$ for the variable or function symbol at the root of t. The *subterm* of t at position p is denoted by $t|_p$ and the result of replacing $t|_p$ with u at position p in t is denoted by $t[u]_p$. This notation is also used to indicate that u is a subterm of t. $\mathcal{V}ar(t)$ denotes the set of variables appearing in t. A term is linear if variables in $\mathcal{V}ar(t)$ occur at most once in t. If t is non-linear, it can be linearized resulting in a linear term t' such that $t = t'\xi$, where ξ is a substitution from $\mathcal{V}ar(t')$ to $\mathcal{V}ar(t)$.

Substitutions are written as in $\{x_1 \mapsto t_1, \ldots, x_n \mapsto t_n\}$ where t_i is assumed different from x_i. We use greek letters for substitutions and postfix notation for their application.

A *term rewriting system* is a set of rewrite rules $R = \{l_i \to r_i\}_i$, where $l_i \notin \mathcal{X}$ and $\mathcal{V}ar(r_i) \subseteq \mathcal{V}ar(l_i)$. A term t rewrites to a term u at position p with the rule $l \to r$ and the substitution σ, written $t \xrightarrow[l\to r]{p} u$, or simply $t \to_R u$, if $t|_p = l\sigma$ and $u = t[r\sigma]_p$. Such a term t is called *reducible*. Irreducible terms are said in *normal form*. A term t is *strongly normalizable* if every reduction sequence out of t is finite, hence ends in a normal form of t. A substitution γ is strongly normalizable if $x\gamma$ is strongly normalizable for all x. We denote by $\to^{+}_{R}$ (resp. $\to^{*}_{R}$) the transitive (resp. transitive and reflexive) closure of the rewrite relation $\to_R$. The subindex R will be omitted when it is clear from the context.

A term rewriting system R is

- *confluent* if $t \to^* u$ and $t \to^* v$ implies $u \to^* s$ and $v \to^* s$ for some s,
- *terminating* (or *strongly normalizing*) if all reduction sequences are finite,
- *convergent* if it is confluent and terminating,
- *collapsing* if it contains a rule whose right-hand side is a variable,
- *conservative* (also called *non-duplicating*) if for all $l \to r \in R$ and for all $x \in \mathcal{V}ar(l)$, the number of occurrences of x in r is less than or equal to the number of occurrences of x in l.

3 Alien-decreasing unions

We first need some vocabulary. Given a term rewriting system R, recall that its signature $\mathcal{F}$ is partitioned into a set $\mathcal{D} = \{f \in \mathcal{F} \mid f = root(l), l \to r \in R\}$ of *defined symbols* and a set $\mathcal{C} = \mathcal{F} - \mathcal{D}$ of *constructors*. We may write $\mathcal{D} \cup \mathcal{C}$ for $\mathcal{F}$.

Definition 1. Let R_0 and R_1 be two rewrite systems over the respective signatures $\mathcal{F}_0 = \mathcal{C}_0 \cup \mathcal{D}_0$ and $\mathcal{F}_1 = \mathcal{C}_1 \cup \mathcal{D}_1$ such that $\mathcal{D}_0 \cap \mathcal{D}_1 = \emptyset$. Let $R = R_0 \cup R_1$ be the union of the two rewrite systems, $\mathcal{F} = \mathcal{F}_0 \cup \mathcal{F}_1$ be the union of the two signatures, and $\mathcal{S} = \mathcal{C}_0 \cap \mathcal{C}_1$ the set of shared constructors. A term in $\mathcal{T}(\mathcal{F}, \mathcal{X})$ is *homogeneous* if it uses function symbols of $\mathcal{F}_0 - \mathcal{D}_1$ or $\mathcal{F}_1 - \mathcal{D}_0$ exclusively (it is homogeneous with respect to the signature $\mathcal{F}_0$ in the first case, and with respect to $\mathcal{F}_1$ in the latter). A term in $\mathcal{T}(\mathcal{F}, \mathcal{X})$ is *quasi-homogeneous* if it has the form $s[t_1, \ldots, t_n]_{p_1, \ldots, p_n}$, where $s[x_1, \ldots, x_n]_{p_1, \ldots, p_n} \in \mathcal{T}(\mathcal{S}, \mathcal{X})$, and $\{t_i : i \in [1..n]\}$ is a multiset of homogeneous terms. Derivations using rules in R are *homogeneous* if all terms in the sequence are homogeneous with respect to the same signature.

For combined unions, our definition of homogeneous terms corresponds to the usual definition (i.e. a term $t \in \mathcal{T}(\mathcal{F}, \mathcal{X})$ is homogeneous in a combined union if $t \in \mathcal{T}(\mathcal{F}_0, \mathcal{X}) \cup \mathcal{T}(\mathcal{F}_1, \mathcal{X})$). For more general unions, note that a term built up with symbols from $\mathcal{F}_0$ (resp. $\mathcal{F}_1$) may be non-homogeneous.

Non-homogeneous derivations may be homogenized by computing *caps* and *aliens*. The cap of a term is its maximal (with respect to subsumption) topmost quasi-homogeneous part, the subterms pending from the cap being called aliens.

Definition 2. Let ξ be a one to one correspondence between the set of terms $\mathcal{T}(\mathcal{F}, \mathcal{X})$ and a denumerable set $\mathcal{Y} \supseteq \mathcal{X}$, such that $\xi(x) = x$ for all $x \in \mathcal{X}$.
If t is quasi-homogeneous, then $cap(t) = t$ and $aliens(t) = \emptyset$.
Otherwise, $t = s\sigma$, where $s \in \mathcal{T}(\mathcal{F}, \mathcal{Y})$ is quasi-homogeneous and maximal with respect to subsumption, and $\forall y \in \mathcal{V}ar(s), y\sigma = \xi(y)$.
We define $cap(t)$ to be the term s and $aliens(t)$ to be the multiset of terms $\{y\sigma \mid y \in (\mathcal{Y} - \mathcal{X}) \cap \mathcal{V}ar(s)\}$ where each term $y\sigma$ appears as many times as the number of occurrences of y in s.
Let c_i a new constructor symbol added to F_i, and $c_i(s)$ the cap of the term $c_i(t)$. We define $cap(t, i)$, the cap of t w.r.t. R_i (resp. $aliens(t, i)$, the multiset of aliens of t w.r.t. R_i), to be the term s (resp. the multiset of terms $aliens(t)$).

Example 1. Let $\mathcal{F}_0 = \{f, c\}, \mathcal{F}_1 = \{g, c\}, \mathcal{X} = \{x\}, \mathcal{Y} \supset \{x, y\}$. Then $cap(c(f(g(x)), g(x))) = c(f(y), g(x))$, and $cap(c(f(g(x)), g(x)), 0) = c(f(y), y)$. Assume now we have the rule $f(f(x)) \to c(f(x), x)$. Then, $f(f(g(x)))$, whose cap is homogeneous, rewrites to $c(f(g(x)), g(x))$, whose cap is quasi-homogeneous, but not homogeneous.

Note that the cap of a term is defined up to renaming of variables in $\mathcal{Y} - \mathcal{X}$, since the one to one correspondance ξ is arbitrary on $\mathcal{Y} - \mathcal{X}$.

Definition 3. A relation $\to$ on terms in the union is *alien-decreasing* if $s \to t$ in a cap position of s with a rule of R_i implies $aliens(s, i) \rhd_{mul} aliens(t, i)$, or $aliens(s, i) =_{mul} aliens(t, i)$ and $cap(s, i) \to^{+} \cup \trianglerighteq cap(t, i)$.

Note that instead of the ordering $\rightarrow^+ \cup \triangleright$, we could use any well-founded extension of $\rightarrow^+$ provided it is compatible with $\triangleright$. The above is the only one known, but recent results of Rubio may change this situation [22].

Quasi-homogeneous terms may have symbols from both $\mathcal{D}_0$ and $\mathcal{D}_1$ provided their root is a shared constructor. Rewriting a quasi-homogeneous term amounts to rewrite one of its homogeneous subterms and results in a quasi-homogeneous term if the rules are alien-decreasing. In this sense, quasi-homogeneous terms behave like homogeneous ones for alien-decreasing rules, therefore:

Property 4. *If R_0, R_1 are terminating and alien-decreasing, then $R_0 \cup R_1$ is terminating on quasi-homogeneous terms.*

We now start investigating particular cases of alien-decreasing unions.

3.1 Conservative combined unions

It is rather straightforward to see that a combined union is alien-decreasing iff it is conservative. Of particular interest is the case of shared rewriting, that is, rewriting on directed acyclic graphs (dags) representing terms (see [13, 5] for details). In this way, multiple occurrences of a subterm may be simultaneously reduced to a common term. In a shared-reduction step, subterms that are covered by the same variable in the left-hand side of the rule are not copied but shared in the resulting dag, even if the right-hand side of the rule has multiple occurrences of this variable. Hence, shared-rewriting is alien-decreasing for combined unions, or more generally, when the right-hand sides of the rules are homogeneous terms. So, all results applying to conservative combined unions apply as well to combined unions with shared rewriting.

3.2 Conservative stratified unions

We can relax the hypothesis that we have a combined union, by assuming that the right-hand sides of rules are homogeneous, and that the left-hand sides may not be, yielding a *stratified union*. Still, we need the conservativity condition (or sharing) for those variables whose all occurrences appear immediately below the cap of the left hand side. Again, such rules are alien-decreasing.

The *crosswise disjoint unions* defined by D. Plump [18, 19] as unions $R_0 \cup R_1$ such that the right-hand sides of R_i have no common function symbol with the left-hand side of R_{1-i}, are particular cases of conservative stratified unions, in which shared constructors cannot appear in right-hand sides.

Example 2. Let $\{R_1 = f(h(x), c(c(x))) \rightarrow f(x, c(x))\}$. The right-hand side $f(x, c(x))$ is homogeneous in a union $R_0 \cup R_1$ for any rewrite system R_0 which does not have f and c as defined symbols. E.g. if we take $\{R_0 = h(c(x)) \rightarrow x\}$ then we obtain a conservative stratified union, which is neither a combined union nor a crosswise disjoint union.
Starting from the term $f(h(h(x)), c(c(h(x))))$ whose cap is $f(y, c(c(z)))$ and multiset of aliens is $\{h(h(x)), h(x)\}$, we obtain by R_1 $f(h(x), c(h(x)))$ whose cap is $f(z, c(z))$ and multiset of aliens is $\{h(x), h(x)\}$.

3.3 Alien-decreasing hierarchical unions

In a hierarchical union $R_0 + R_1$ the rules in R_0 are homogeneous, but the rules in R_1 may not be (of course, not all hierarchical unions are alien-decreasing).

Since in the previous example R_0 is homogeneous, $R_0 + R_1$ is an alien-decreasing hierarchical union, as well as a conservative stratified union. But there are hierarchical unions that are not stratified and vice-versa.

Example 3. Take $\{R_1 = f(c(x), h(h(x))) \rightarrow f(x, h(x))\}$. R_1 is alien decreasing for any rewrite system that has h or c as defined symbol, because alien subterms decrease strictly in the subterm relationship. E.g., if $\{R_0 = h(c(x)) \rightarrow x\}$, $R_0 + R_1$ is an alien-decreasing hierarchical union which is neither a combined union nor a stratified union.
Starting from the term $f(c(c(x)), h(h(c(x))))$ whose cap is $f(c(c(x)), y)$ and multiset of aliens is $\{h(h(c(x)))\}$, we obtain by R_1 $f(c(x), h(c(x)))$ whose cap is $f(c(x), y')$ and multiset of aliens is $\{h(c(x))\}$.
Keeping the same set R_0, the example $\{R_1 = f(c(x), h(x)) \rightarrow f(x, h(x))\}$ is also alien-decreasing under the same hypothesis, because aliens are equal and the cap decreases strictly in the encompassment ordering.

3.4 General alien-decreasing unions

Alien-decreasing unions need not be hierarchical or stratified:

Example 4. As before, we take $\{R_1 = f(c(x), h(h(x))) \rightarrow f(x, h(x))\}$. Since R_1 is alien decreasing for any rewrite system that has h or c as defined symbol, the union $R_0 \cup R_1$ where $\{R_0 = h(f(c(x), c(x))) \rightarrow x\}$ is an alien-decreasing union which is neither combined nor stratified nor hierarchical.

We can indeed characterize the alien-decreasing property on the rules themselves. First of all, since the rule $l \rightarrow r \in R_0$ is itself a particular rewrite, it must satisfy the alien-decreasing condition. Now, since we need stability of the condition under instanciation, we must add to the multiset of aliens, the multiset of variables of l which are not in $alien(l)$. Let $M(t)$ be the multiset $alien(t) \cup (cap(t) \cap \mathcal{X})$. Then R_0 is alien-decreasing iff for every rule $l \rightarrow r \in R_0$, $M(l) \rhd_{mul} M(r)$ or $M(l) =_{mul} M(r)$ and $cap(l)(\rightarrow^{+}_{R_0 \cup R_1} \cup \rhd)cap(r)$.

4 Termination of alien-decreasing unions

Termination is not a modular property even in the case of disjoint unions. However, it becomes modular under various hypotheses. The first result was obtained by Rusinowitch: termination is a modular property of non-duplicating disjoint unions [23]. Kurihara and Ohuchi then showed that termination of shared-rewriting is a modular property of combined unions [13], and Plump gave a proof of the modularity of termination of shared rewriting for crosswise disjoint unions [18, 19].

We give here an abstract version of these properties: termination is modular for *alien-decreasing general unions*. Note that systems in such unions may share constructors as well as defined operators. We derive all previous modularity results as restricted cases. Besides, our proof abstracts from useless details in [13, 19, 23] by being based on a stronger induction argument traditional in proof theory (see, e.g. [6]).

Theorem 5. *Let R_0, R_1 be terminating term rewriting systems over $T(\mathcal{D}_0 \cup \mathcal{C}_0, \mathcal{X})$ and $T(\mathcal{D}_1 \cup \mathcal{C}_1, \mathcal{X})$ respectively, where $\mathcal{D}_0 \cap \mathcal{D}_1 = \emptyset$. If $\rightarrow_{R_0}$, $\rightarrow_{R_1}$ are alien-decreasing then $\rightarrow_{R_0 \cup R_1}$ is terminating.*

Proof. In order to show that any term is strongly normalizable in $R_0 \cup R_1$, we shall prove a stronger property: *For any term t and strongly normalizable substitution γ, $t\gamma$ is strongly normalizable.* The theorem follows directly, by taking the identity substitution for γ.

We proceed now by noetherian induction. We interpret a term $t\gamma$ by the pair $\mathcal{I}(t\gamma) = \langle t, \{\gamma\}\rangle$, where $\{\gamma\}$ denotes the multiset $\{x\gamma \mid x \in Var(t)\}$. These pairs are compared in the ordering $(\trianglerighteq, (\rightarrow_{R_0 \cup R_1})_{mul})_{lex}$, denoted $\gg$ in the following. Recall that $\trianglerighteq$ stands for the encompassment ordering. Besides, since $\rightarrow_{R_0 \cup R_1}$ is well-founded on γ by assumption, $\gg$ is well-founded.

We distinguish three cases in the proof, depending on the properties of $t\gamma$.

1. $t\gamma$ reduces at a position p inside γ. There are two cases:
   If t is not linear, let t' be a linearized version of t, and γ' be such that $t\gamma = t'\gamma'$. Clearly, γ' is strongly normalizable since γ is, and $t \trianglerighteq t'$. Hence $\langle t, \{\gamma\}\rangle \gg \langle t', \{\gamma'\}\rangle$, and $t\gamma = t'\gamma'$ is strongly normalizable by the induction hypothesis. Note how we used here the fact that the same term may be decomposed in several ways, hence have several interpretations.
   If t is linear, then $t\gamma$ reduces to $t\gamma'$. Then $\langle t, \{\gamma\}\rangle \gg \langle t, \{\gamma'\}\rangle$, hence $t\gamma'$ is strongly normalizable by the induction hypothesis.
2. $t\gamma$ reduces to t' at a position $p \neq \Lambda$ of t. Then $t \trianglerighteq t|_p$, hence $\langle t, \{\gamma\}\rangle \gg \langle t|_p, \{\gamma\}\rangle$, hence $t|_p\gamma = (t\gamma)|_p$ is strongly normalizable. Let z be a new variable and $u = t[z]_p$. Let $\gamma' = \gamma \cup \{z \mapsto (t\gamma)|_p\}$. γ' is strongly normalizable, and $t \trianglerighteq u$, hence $\langle t, \{\gamma\}\rangle \gg \langle u, \{\gamma'\}\rangle$, hence $u\gamma' = t\gamma$ is strongly normalizable.
3. $t\gamma$ reduces to t' at $p = \Lambda$. There are two subcases:
   (a) $t = f(t_1, \ldots, t_n)$ and t is not a variable renaming of $u = f(x_1, \ldots, x_n)$. Since $\langle t, \{\gamma\}\rangle \gg \langle t_i, \{\gamma\}\rangle$ for $1 \leq i \leq n$, $\gamma' = \{x_1 \mapsto t_1\gamma, \ldots, x_n \mapsto t_n\gamma\}$ is strongly normalizable. Since $t \trianglerighteq u$, $\langle t, \{\gamma\}\rangle \gg \langle u, \{\gamma'\}\rangle$, hence $u\gamma' = t\gamma$ is strongly normalizable.
   (b) $t = f(x_1, \ldots, x_n)$. Since γ is strongly normalizable by assumption, the subterms of the terms $x_i\gamma$ are strongly normalizable as well. Then $t\gamma$ is strongly normalizable by Lemma 6 below.

In all cases $t\gamma$ is strongly normalizable or reduces to strongly normalizable terms. Hence $t\gamma$ is strongly normalizable.

Lemma 6. *Let R_0, R_1 be terminating term rewriting systems over $T(\mathcal{D}_0 \cup \mathcal{C}_0, \mathcal{X})$ and $T(\mathcal{D}_1 \cup \mathcal{C}_1, \mathcal{X})$ respectively, where $\mathcal{D}_0 \cap \mathcal{D}_1 = \emptyset$. If $\rightarrow_{R_0}$, $\rightarrow_{R_1}$ are alien-decreasing then any term whose alien subterms are strongly normalizable with respect to $\rightarrow_{R_0 \cup R_1}$ is strongly normalizable with respect to $\rightarrow_{R_0 \cup R_1}$.*

Proof. We interpret a term t by the pair $\mathcal{I}(t) = \langle aliens(t), cap(t) \rangle$ of the multiset of its alien subterms and its cap. Multisets of alien subterms are compared in the multiset extension of $\rightarrow_{R_0 \cup R_1} \cup \rhd$, where $\lhd$ denotes the strict subterm relation, and caps are compared in the reduction ordering $\rightarrow_{R_0 \cup R_1} \cup \blacktriangleright$, i.e. we use $((\rightarrow_{R_0 \cup R_1} \cup \rhd)_{mul}, \rightarrow_{R_0 \cup R_1} \cup \blacktriangleright)_{lex}$ for the ordering on interpretations. This is a well-founded ordering because $\rightarrow_{R_0 \cup R_1}$ is terminating on alien subterms by assumption, $cap(t)$ is a quasi-homogeneous term and R_0, R_1 are terminating, and the union of the encompassment relation (which includes $\rhd$) with a terminating rewrite relation is well-founded [3].

Now, if $t \rightarrow_{R_i} t'$ $(i \in \{0, 1\})$ there are two possibilities:

1. It is a reduction in the cap, then there are two subcases. If $aliens(t) \rhd_{mul} aliens(t')$, then $\mathcal{I}(t) > \mathcal{I}(t')$. This is in particular the case if the cap shrinkes. Otherwise, $aliens(t) =_{mul} aliens(t')$ since R_0 and R_1 are alien-decreasing. We must therefore compare the caps. By assumption, $cap(t) \rightarrow_{R_i} cap(t')$ or $cap(t) \blacktriangleright cap(t')$. In both cases, the cap has decreased in our ordering, hence $\mathcal{I}(t) > \mathcal{I}(t')$.
2. It is a reduction inside an alien of t, then $aliens(t)(\rightarrow_{R_0 \cup R_1} \cup \rhd)_{mul} aliens(t')$. Then $\mathcal{I}(t) > \mathcal{I}(t')$. Note that we need to consider $\rhd$ since the result of reducing an alien subterm of t can be a term whose root belongs to the same signature as $cap(t)$ (in particular, could be a constructor), and so only its strict subterms are alien subterms of t' in this case.

In both cases the interpretation is strictly decreasing, which proves the claim.

Compare this proof structure with [23], [13] and [18], and note that lemma 6 is an interesting tool on its own: we do not use the notion of "rank" for the induction argument, which makes our proof much less technical.

Assume now that both rewrite systems $\mathcal{R}_0$ and $\mathcal{R}_1$ are *simply terminating*, that is, can be shown terminating by use of a simplification ordering. Let P_f be the rewrite system made of the projection rules $f(x_1, \ldots, x_n) \rightarrow x_i$ for all $1 \leq i \leq n$. Since a set R of rules is simply terminating iff $R \cup \bigcup_{f \in \mathcal{F}} P_f$ is terminating, it suffices to note that the obtained set of rules is alien-decreasing when the starting set R is, in order to prove that simple termination is a modular property of alien-decreasing unions.

In the case of combined unions, Kurihara and Ohuchi proved that simple termination is modular [14], without assuming the alien-decreasing property. On the other hand, rewriting becomes compatible with embedding for simply terminating systems, hence we can use embedding in our induction ordering instead of subterm or encompassement. As a consequence, we can relax the alien-decreasing assumption, but cannot get rid of it.

5 Cap-decreasing unions

Rusinowitch [23] also showed that termination of disjoint unions is modular for non-collapsing rewrite rules, and conjectured that modularity is true when one system is non-duplicating and non-collapsing, which was later proved by Middeldorp [16]. Rusinowitch second result can be proved by changing the interpretation in the proof of lemma 6, by putting the cap first, and the multiset of aliens second.

In fact, disjoint unions of non-collapsing systems are a particular case of *cap-decreasing* general unions: a reduction in a term in the union either decreases the cap or does not change the cap but decreases the aliens. Formally:

Definition 7. A relation $\rightarrow$ on terms in a union $R_0 \cup R_1$ where $\mathcal{D}_0 \cap \mathcal{D}_1 = \emptyset$ is *cap-decreasing* if $s \rightarrow_p t$ implies that $cap(s)$ and $cap(t)$ are terms in the same signature, and if $p \in \mathcal{FP}os(cap(s))$ then $cap(s) \rightarrow \cup \trianglerighteq cap(t)$, otherwise $cap(s) = cap(t)$.

Besides the class of non-collapsing disjoint unions, the class of non-collapsing combined unions is cap-decreasing when there are no constructor-lifting rules (i.e. when no right-hand side is rooted by a shared constructor). There are more general cap-decreasing unions: if R_0, R_1 are neither collapsing nor constructor-lifting and their left-hand sides are homogeneous, then $R_0 \cup R_1$ is cap-decreasing even if defined symbols of one system are used as constructors in the other.

Theorem 8. *Let R_0, R_1 be terminating term rewriting systems over $T(\mathcal{D}_0 \cup \mathcal{C}_0, \mathcal{X})$ and $T(\mathcal{D}_1 \cup \mathcal{C}_1, \mathcal{X})$ respectively, where $\mathcal{D}_0 \cap \mathcal{D}_1 = \emptyset$. If $\rightarrow_{R_0}$, $\rightarrow_{R_1}$ are cap-decreasing then $\rightarrow_{R_0 \cup R_1}$ is terminating.*

Proof. The same as Theorem 5 but using Lemma 9 below instead of Lemma 6 at the end of the proof.

Lemma 9. *Let R_0, R_1 be terminating term rewriting systems over $T(\mathcal{D}_0 \cup \mathcal{C}_0, \mathcal{X})$ and $T(\mathcal{D}_1 \cup \mathcal{C}_1, \mathcal{X})$ respectively, where $\mathcal{D}_0 \cap \mathcal{D}_1 = \emptyset$. If $\rightarrow_{R_0}$, $\rightarrow_{R_1}$ are cap-decreasing then any term whose alien subterms are strongly normalizable with respect to $\rightarrow_{R_0 \cup R_1}$ is strongly normalizable with respect to $\rightarrow_{R_0 \cup R_1}$.*

Proof. By noetherian induction, interpreting a term t by the pair $\mathcal{I}(t) = \langle cap(t), aliens(t) \rangle$, and using the ordering $(\rightarrow_{R_0 \cup R_1} \cup \trianglerighteq, (\rightarrow_{R_0 \cup R_1})_{mul})_{lex}$, which is well founded since R_0 and R_1 are terminating and caps are quasi-homogeneous, and $\rightarrow_{R_0 \cup R_1}$ is terminating on alien subterms by assumption.

As already mentioned, non-collapsing disjoint unions are cap-decreasing:

Corollary 10. *[23] Termination is a modular property of non-collapsing disjoint unions.*

The technique used in the proofs of the last theorems can be easily adapted to the case of combined unions where one system is both alien-decreasing and cap-decreasing:

Theorem 11. *Let R_0, R_1 be terminating term rewriting systems over $\mathcal{T}(\mathcal{D}_0 \cup \mathcal{C}_0, \mathcal{X})$ and $\mathcal{T}(\mathcal{D}_1 \cup \mathcal{C}_1, \mathcal{X})$ respectively, where $\mathcal{D}_0 \cap \mathcal{D}_1 = \emptyset$. If either $\rightarrow_{R_0}$ or $\rightarrow_{R_1}$ is both cap-decreasing and alien-decreasing, then $\rightarrow_{R_0 \cup R_1}$ is terminating.*

Proof. W.l.g. we are going to assume that $\rightarrow_{R_0}$ is cap-decreasing and alien-decreasing. To prove termination of $R_0 \uplus R_1$ we use a sort of combined interpretation which will choose the appropriate order between cap and aliens:

$$\mathcal{I}(t) = \langle rank(t), aliens_0(t), cap(t), aliens(t) \rangle$$

where $rank(t) = 1$ if t is homogeneous and $rank(t) = 1 + max_{s \in aliens(t)}(rank(s))$ otherwise, and $aliens_0(t)$ is the multiset of aliens of t if $cap(t) \in \mathcal{T}(\mathcal{F}_0, \mathcal{X})$ and the empty multiset otherwise. The proof of the lemma is done by noetherian induction on the well-founded ordering

$$(>_N, (\rightarrow_{R_0 \cup R_1} \cup \rhd)_{mul}, \rightarrow_{R_0 \cup R_1} \cup \blacktriangleright, (\rightarrow_{R_0 \cup R_1})_{mul})_{lex}.$$

We get Middeldorp's result for disjoint unions [16] as a corollary.

6 Hierarchical unions

The alien-decreasing property is not a real restriction in the case of combined unions since shared rewriting is alien-decreasing. In contrast, it is a severe restriction in the case of hierarchical unions since it applies to all systems in the hierarchy. Indeed, there are very few hierarchical systems which are alien-decreasing. For example, the system below, defining addition and multiplication is not. In this section we will prove a modularity result for a sequence of rewrite systems the base of which is alien-decreasing. Practice favours this kind of hierarchical combination, since it corresponds to the so-called incremental development methodology of algebraic specifications.

Let $R_0, R_1, \ldots, R_n$ be term rewriting systems over $\mathcal{T}(\mathcal{D}_0 \cup \mathcal{C}, \mathcal{X})$, $\mathcal{T}(\mathcal{D}_1 \cup (\mathcal{D}_0 \cup \mathcal{C}), \mathcal{X})$, ..., $\mathcal{T}(\mathcal{D}_n \cup (\mathcal{D}_{n-1} \cup \ldots \cup \mathcal{D}_0 \cup \mathcal{C}), \mathcal{X})$ respectively. The corresponding *hierarchical union* $R_0 + \ldots + R_n$ has R_0 for *basis*, and $R_1, \ldots, R_n$ for *incremental developments*.

Example 5. A very simple (and well-known) hierarchical system is the following, where the basis defines the addition of natural numbers, and in the second level the product of natural numbers is defined using the addition.

$$\mathcal{C} = \{S, 0\},\ \mathcal{D}_0 = \{+\},\ \mathcal{D}_1 = \{\times\},\ \mathcal{D}_2 = \{!\}.$$

$$R_0 = \begin{cases} 0 + x \rightarrow x \\ S(x) + y \rightarrow S(x + y) \end{cases} \qquad R_1 = \begin{cases} 0 \times x \rightarrow 0 \\ S(x) \times y \rightarrow x \times y + y \end{cases}$$

$$R_2 = \begin{cases} 0! \rightarrow 1 \\ S(x)! \rightarrow S(x) \times x! \end{cases}$$

The termination of $R_0 + R_1 + R_2$ is modular as a consequence of theorem 14 below, since it is an example of the *multiset schema* defined next.

6.1 Statuses and orderings

Function symbols in an incremental development will be assigned a status, that will be used to build up an ordering. We allow for a complex notion of status (e.g. the usual multiset status, or the left-to-right lexicographic status, or a term like $lex(x_2, x_4, mul(x_3, x_1)))$, allowing us to tune up the comparison of lists according to practical needs. For example, comparing the lists of terms l_1, l_2, l_3, l_4 and r_1, r_2, r_3, r_4 according to the above status and the ordering $\rhd$ generates the comparison of l_2 and r_2 first, then of l_4 and r_4 if l_2 and r_2 are equivalent under variable renaming, and if this is also true of l_4 and r_4, then the two multisets $\{l_3, l_1\}$ and $\{r_3, r_1\}$ are compared.

Definition 12. Let *mul* and *lex* be varyadic symbols. A *status* of arity n is a term $stat \in \mathcal{T}(\{mul, lex\}, \mathcal{X})$ such that $\mathcal{V}ar(stat) = \{x_1, \ldots, x_n\}$ and in normal form with respect to the rewrite system R_{stat}:

$$\begin{array}{rcl}
lex(x_1, \ldots, x_m, lex(y_1, \ldots, y_n), z_1, \ldots, z_p) & \to & lex(x_1, \ldots, x_m, y_1, \ldots, y_n, z_1, \ldots, z_p) \\
mul(x_1, \ldots, x_m, mul(y_1, \ldots, y_n), z_1, \ldots, z_p) & \to & mul(x_1, \ldots, x_m, y_1, \ldots, y_n, z_1, \ldots, z_p) \\
lex(x_1, \ldots, x_m, mul, z_1, \ldots, z_p) & \to & lex(x_1, \ldots, x_m, z_1, \ldots, z_p) \\
mul(x_1, \ldots, x_m, lex, z_1, \ldots, z_p) & \to & mul(x_1, \ldots, x_m, z_1, \ldots, z_p) \\
lex(x) \to x & & mul(x) \to x
\end{array}$$

To each function symbol f of arity n, we associate a status (i.e. a tree) $stat_f$ of the same arity. The status is called *multiset* (respectively *lexicographic*) if equal to $mul(x_1, \ldots, x_n)$ (respectively $lex(x_{\xi(1)}, \ldots, x_{\xi(n)})$, where ξ is a permutation of $[1..n]$). The status of a constant symbol is therefore equal to *lex* or *mul*, while the status of a unary symbol is the variable x_1.
Given a term t whose variables occur at positions $p_1, \ldots, p_m$ such that $p_i <^N_{lex} p_{i+1}$, its status $stat_t$ is the normal form according to R_{stat}, of $stat(t, \Lambda, \{p_1, \ldots, p_m\})$, where *stat* is defined by:

$$stat(f(t_1, \ldots, t_n), p, l) = stat_f\{x_1 \mapsto stat(t_1, p.1, l), \ldots, x_n \mapsto stat(t_n, p.n, l)\}$$
$$stat(x, p, l) = x_i \text{ if } p = p_i \in l$$

Example 6. Let f, g and a have the respective statuses $lex(x_1, x_2, x_3)$, $mul(x_1, x_2)$ and *lex*. Then, $f(x, y, g(x, y))$ has the status $lex(x_1, x_2, mul(x_3, x_4))$, while $f(x, g(a, y), g(a, a))$ has the status $lex(x_1, x_2)$.

Statuses allow us to extend well-founded orderings on sets to well-founded orderings on sequences. Given a set S equipped with a well-founded ordering $>$, a status *stat* depending on n variables $x_1, \ldots, x_n$ and two lists of elements of S of length n, we define the ordering $>_{stat}$ as follows:

$$\{l_1, \ldots, l_n\} >_{stat} \{r_1, \ldots, r_n\} \quad \text{iff}$$

$$stat\{x_1 \mapsto l_1, \ldots, x_n \mapsto l_n\} >_{rpo} stat\{x_1 \mapsto r_1, \ldots, x_n \mapsto r_n\}$$

As a particular case of recursive path ordering, this ordering on sequences is of course well-founded if the starting ordering on S is, and is closed under instantiation [1]. Note that this ordering boils down to the usual lexicographic or multiset ordering in case the status is a term of height one.

6.2 General Recursive Schema

In this section we consider *hierarchical unions* in which

- R_0 is terminating, and alien-decreasing or cap-decreasing, and
- each incremental development satisfies the *general recursive schema* defined below:

Definition 13. Let R be a rewrite system on $T(\mathcal{F}, \mathcal{X})$, and assume that f is a new function symbol, i.e. $f \notin \mathcal{F}$, equipped with a status $stat_f$. Then we can define f with a finite set of rewrite rules satisfying the following *General (recursive) Schema*:

$$f(l_1, \ldots, l_n) \to v$$

where $l_1, \ldots, l_n \in T(\mathcal{F}, \mathcal{X})$, $v \in T(\mathcal{F} \cup \{f\}, \mathcal{X})$, and for all subterms of the form $f(r_1, \ldots, r_n)$ in v, $\{l_1, \ldots, l_n\} \rhd_{stat_f} \{r_1, \ldots, r_n\}$.

We will term the general schema the *multiset schema* (resp. *lexicographic schema*) when all statuses are multiset (resp. lexicographic). The multiset schema was first presented in [9] under the name of *general schema*. Note that the multiset schema is primitive recursive because terms in $\vec{l}$ may not contain any f by definition, hence the same is true of terms in $\vec{r}$ due to the multiset comparison. This is no more true in case of a lexicographic comparaison, hence embedded recursive calls become possible with the lexicographic schema, henceforth for the general schema. One could think that the hypothesis $f(l_1, \ldots, l_n) \to r_i$ which is necessary for the definition of the recursive path ordering [11] is also necessary here. But this is not the case, since we require that $\{l_1, \ldots, l_n\} \rhd_{stat_f} \{r_1, \ldots, r_n\}$ for all subterms of the form $f(r_1, \ldots, r_n)$ in v. So, if a term v_i is not reached in the comparison, either it has no subterm headed by f, or it has some which will be compared.

There are only two restrictions in the general schema: mutually recursive definitions are forbidden, since we define a new function f each time; terms in $\vec{r_i}$ must be smaller in a precise sense (using the subterm relationship) than terms in $\vec{l}$. The first restriction can be removed by packing mutually recursive definitions in a same tuple of definitions satisfying the general schema. The second appears to be essential to our proof, although we believe it can be relaxed.

Example 7. The following is a rewrite program to sort a list of natural numbers by inserting elements one by one into position. *cons* and *nil* are the list constructors, and s and 0 are the constructors for natural numbers. We use x and y for arbitrary natural numbers, and l for an arbitrary list of natural numbers.

$$\begin{aligned} max(0, x) &\to x & min(0, x) &\to 0 \\ max(x, 0) &\to x & min(x, 0) &\to 0 \\ max(s(x), s(y)) &\to s(max(x, y)) & min(s(x), s(y)) &\to s(min(x, y)) \end{aligned}$$

$$\begin{array}{rcl} insert(x, nil) & \rightarrow & cons(x, nil) \\ insert(x, cons(y, l)) & \rightarrow & cons(max(x, y), insert(min(x, y), l)) \\ sort(nil) & \rightarrow & nil \\ sort(cons(x, l)) & \rightarrow & insert(x, sort(l)) \end{array}$$

Here, *insert* must have a lexicographic status, from right to left, while *min*, *max* and *sort* may have a multiset status (or a lexicographic one).

Note that most examples of hierarchical systems found in the literature (e.g. [15]), and the above one, are indeed constructor systems, but our result does not require this restriction. We now turn to the main result of this section:

Theorem 14. *Let $R = R_0 + R_1 + \ldots + R_m$ be a hierarchical union such that R_0 is terminating and alien-decreasing (resp. cap decreasing), and $R_1, \ldots, R_m$ are incremental developments satisfying the general recursive scheme. Then $\rightarrow_R$ is terminating.*

Proof. We have to prove that for all t in the union, t is strongly normalizable with respect to R. As previously, we shall prove the stronger property: *For all strongly normalizable substitution γ, $t\gamma$ is strongly normalizable.*

The proof is by noetherian induction. We interpret the term $t\gamma$ by the triple $< i, t, \{\gamma\} >$, where i is the maximal index of the function symbols belonging to t and $\{\gamma\}$ is the list of terms obtained from $t\gamma$ by searching t depth first: $\{t\gamma|_{p_1}, \ldots, t\gamma|_{p_n} : t|_p \in \mathcal{X} \text{ iff } \exists i \in [1..n] p = p_i \text{ and } p_1 <^N_{lex} \cdots <^N_{lex} p_n\}$

Note that a term may have several interpretations, depending on how it is viewed as an instance of some term t by a strongly normalizable substitution γ. This pecularity will be heavily used in the proof.

The triples are compared in the ordering $(>_N, \trianglerighteq, (\rightarrow_R \cup \triangleright)_{stat})_{lex}$, denoted by $\gg$ in the following and by $\gg_n$ when we want to indicate that the nth element of the triple has decreased but not the $(n-1)$ first ones. Here, *stat* stands for the status $stat_t$ of the second element t in the triple $< i, t, \{\gamma\} >$. Note that since triples are compared lexicographically, this status is the same in both triples when the comparison reaches $\{\gamma\}$ (as in case (3.c) below), since both second elements of the triples must then be equal modulo variable renaming. Besides, since γ is strongly normalizable by assumption, and because the union of the strict subterm relationship with a rewrite relation is well-founded [3], the relation $(\rightarrow_R \cup \triangleright)_{stat}$ is well-founded on γ. Hence, $\gg$ is a well-founded ordering on the triples.

For simplicity, we will abuse the notations by comparing terms, instead of their interpretations.

There are three cases in the proof, depending on the properties of $w = t\gamma$.

1. $t\gamma$ reduces at a position p inside γ. There are two cases:
   If t is not linear, let t' be a linearized version of t and γ' be such that $t\gamma = t'\gamma'$. Clearly γ' is strongly normalizing since γ is, and $t \trianglerighteq t'$. Hence $t\gamma \gg_2 t'\gamma'$, and $t\gamma = t'\gamma'$ is strongly normalizable by the induction hypothesis.
   If t is linear, then $t\gamma$ reduces to $t\gamma'$. Then $t\gamma \gg_3 t\gamma'$, hence $t\gamma'$ is strongly normalizable by the induction hypothesis.

2. $t\gamma$ reduces to t' at a position p of t with $p \neq \Lambda$.
   Then $t \rhd t|_p$, hence $t\gamma \gg t|_p\gamma = (t\gamma)|_p$, and $(t\gamma)|_p$ is strongly normalizable. Let z be a new variable and $u = t[z]_p$. Let $\gamma' = \gamma \cup \{z \mapsto (t\gamma)|_p\}$. γ' is strongly normalizable, and $t \rhd u$, then $t\gamma \gg u\gamma' = w$, hence w is strongly normalizable.
3. $t\gamma$ reduces to t' at $p = \Lambda$. Now, there are three subcases:
   (a) $t = f(t_1, \ldots, t_n)$ and t is not a variable renaming of $u = f(x_1, \ldots, x_n)$. Then $t\gamma \gg t_i\gamma$ for $1 \leq i \leq n$, hence $\gamma' = \{x_1 \mapsto t_1\gamma, \ldots, x_n \mapsto t_n\gamma\}$ is strongly normalizable. Since $t \rhd u$, $u\gamma'$ is strongly normalizable, and $u\gamma' = t\gamma$.
   (b) $t = f(x_1, \ldots, x_n)$ and $f \in \mathcal{F}_0$. Since γ is strongly normalizable by assumption, the subterms of the terms $x_i\gamma$ are strongly normalizable as well. Then $t\gamma$ is strongly normalizable by Lemma 15 below.
   (c) $t = f(x_1, \ldots, x_n)$ and $f \notin \mathcal{F}_0$. Then $f(x_1, \ldots, x_n)\gamma = f(l_1, \ldots, l_n)\gamma' \rightarrow v\gamma'$ where $f(l_1, \ldots, l_n) \rightarrow v$ is a rule defining f. As subterms of $\{\gamma\}, l_1\gamma', \ldots, l_n\gamma'$ as well as terms in $\{\gamma'\}$ are strongly normalizable by assumption. We now prove the following property (P):
   for any term w and substitution θ satisfying:
   (i) θ is strongly normalizable, and
   (ii)$\{l_1\gamma', \ldots, l_n\gamma'\} \rhd_{stat_f} \{u_1\theta, \ldots, u_n\theta\}$, for all subterms $f(u_1, \ldots, u_n)$ of w,
   $w\theta$ is strongly normalizable.
   The proof is by induction on the number of recursive calls to f in w.

   - Assume that f has no occurrence in w. Then the interpretation of $w\theta$ is strictly smaller than the interpretation of $f(x_1, \ldots, x_n)\gamma$, and since θ is strongly normalizable, we can conclude by the outer induction hypothesis.
   - Otherwise, we eliminate an innermost recursive call by moving its instance by θ to the substitution part. Let $f(u_1, \ldots, u_n)$ be a recursive call at position p in w such that f does not occur in any u_i. Hence $f(x_1, \ldots, x_n)\gamma \gg_1 u_i\theta$, and $u_i\theta$ is strongly normalizable by the outer induction hypothesis. Hence, the substitution $\theta' = \{x_1 \mapsto u_1\theta, \ldots, x_n \mapsto u_n\theta\}$ is strongly normalizable. Now, $\{x_1\gamma, \ldots, x_n\gamma\} = \{l_1\gamma', \ldots, l_n\gamma'\} \rhd_{stat_f} \{u_1\theta, \ldots, u_n\theta\} = \{x_1\theta', \ldots, x_n\theta'\}$ by assumption on w. Therefore $f(x_1, \ldots, x_n)\gamma \gg_3 f(x_1, \ldots, x_n)\theta'$, hence $f(x_1, \ldots, x_n)\theta' = f(u_1\theta, \ldots, u_n\theta)$ is strongly normalizable by the outer induction hypothesis.
     We can now move the instantiated recursive call $f(u_1\theta, \ldots, u_n\theta)$ to θ (abusing names) by adding a new variable z to its domain and letting $z\theta = (w|_p)\theta = f(u_1, \ldots, u_n)\theta$, yielding a strongly normalizable substitution θ such that $w\theta = w[z]_p\theta$. We now prove property (ii) for $w[z]_p$. But this follows from the fact that any recursive call to f at position q in $w[z]_p$ is a recursive call to f at position q in w, hence their instances by θ are identical terms. Since the recursive call in w satisfies (ii), so does the recursive call in $w[z]_p$.

Since $w[z]_p$ has one recursive call to f less than w, we can apply the inner induction hypothesis and conclude that $w[z]_p\theta = w\theta$ is strongly normalizable, and we are done with the proof of (P).

Note now that the pair (v, γ') satisfies (i) as already noticed and (ii) by definition of the general schema, and because $\triangleright_{stat_f}$ is closed under instantiation. Taking v for w and γ' for θ finishes the proof of this case.

In each case $t\gamma$ is strongly normalizable or reduces to strongly normalizable terms. Then $t\gamma$ is strongly normalizable.

This proof is indeed a specialization of [9] to the case of first-order rules, but allows for a more sophisticated notion of status to the price of some complications in case 3c of the proof. But these complications arise as soon as we allow for a lexicographic status, which is crucial for practical needs.

Lemma 15. *Let $R = R_0 + R_1 + \ldots + R_n$ be a hierarchical system such that R_0 is terminating and alien-decreasing (resp. cap-decreasing). If $f \in \mathcal{F}_0$ then any instance of $f(x_1, \ldots, x_n)$ is strongly normalizable (with respect to R) whenever its alien subterms are strongly normalizable (with respect to R).*

Proof. Straightforward adaptation of the proof of lemma 6.

7 Extensions

Our results generalize easily to other forms of rewriting: conditional rewrite systems that are *reductive*, and rewriting modulo a set of *regular* equations. Reductive rewrite systems [10] generalize the notion of simplifying rewrite systems of Kaplan [12].

7.1 Conditional rewriting

Definition 16. A *conditional rewrite system* R is a set $\{\rho_i\}_i$ of conditional rules of the form:

$$\rho = l \to r \text{ if } u_1 \downarrow v_1 \wedge \ldots \wedge u_n \downarrow v_n$$

where $\downarrow$ is interpreted as joinability with respect to R.

To the rule ρ, we associate the term rewriting system $\hat{\rho} = \{l \to r, l \to u_1, l \to v_1, \ldots, l \to u_n, l \to v_n\}$, and to the set $R = \{\rho_i\}_i$ of rules we associate the set $\hat{R} = \bigcup_i \hat{\rho}_i$ of rules.

We say that R is *reductive* (resp. *alien-decreasing, cap-decreasing*) if $\hat{R}$ is terminating (resp. alien-decreasing, cap-decreasing). Reductive systems are of course terminating [10].

We say that R satisfies the general schema iff the associated rewrite system $\hat{R}$ satisfies the schema.

Theorem 17. *Termination is a modular property of alien-decreasing (resp. cap decreasing) unions of reductive rewrite systems.*
Termination is a modular property of hierarchical reductive systems having an alien-decreasing (resp. cap-decreasing) base.

Proof. We simply apply theorems 5 (resp. 8), or 14, to $\hat{R}$ which shows that R is reductive.

Hierarchical unions of conditional rewrite systems have also been investigated by Middeldorp and Gramlich, with a different notion of reductive conditionnal rewriting system for which modularity results are problematic.

7.2 Rewriting modulo

Associative-commutative rewriting is very important in practice. We can also generalize easily our results for this case, actually for rewriting modulo a congruence whose equivalence classes are finite. This implies in particular that this congruence is generated by *regular* equations, that is equations $l = r$ such that $\mathcal{V}ar(l) = \mathcal{V}ar(r)$.

It is important here that the subterm and encompassment orderings are still compatible (with respect to well-foundedness) with the rewriting relation on congruence classes of terms, which in turns requires that the congruence classes are finite [8]. It is also important that equivalent terms are built up from the same set of function symbols in order for our interpretation to be compatible with the congruence, which follows from the regularity condition. The finiteness condition on congruence classes is therefore all we need.

Theorem 18. *Termination is a modular property of alien-decreasing (resp. cap decreasing) unions of reductive rewrite systems modulo a congruence whose equivalence classes are finite.*
Termination is a modular property of hierarchical reductive systems modulo a congruence whose equivalence classes are finite, provided the base is alien-decreasing (resp. cap-decreasing).

8 Conclusion

We have identified a property of rewrite relations, the alien-decreasing property, that turns out to be a key for the modularity of termination of disjoint, combined and even hierarchical unions. We have shown a simple proof of the modularity of termination of general unions $R_1 \cup R_2$ ($\mathcal{D}_1 \cap \mathcal{D}_2 = \emptyset$) of alien-decreasing systems, and we also showed that many known sufficient conditions for the modularity of termination [23, 13, 18, 19] are in fact consequences of this result.

The modularity result of [23] for disjoint unions without collapsing rules is instead obtained as a consequence of another general result: modularity of general unions of cap-decreasing systems.

The proof technique applied to obtain the modularity of systems satisfying the abstract property of cap-decreasingness or alien-decreasigness is interesting on its own, and it yields simple proofs of other modularity results, such as [16].

For hierarchical systems with an alien-decreasing base, we have given sufficient conditions for the modularity of termination related with the form of the recursive rules in the enrichments: when these rules satisfy the general recursive scheme then the whole system terminates. Although hierarchical systems arise naturally in practice, for instance in the development of functional programs or algebraic specifications, modular aspects of hierarchical systems have deserved little attention until now. Previous results on modularity of hierarchical systems were given by Krishna Rao in [20], where sufficient conditions for modularity of convergence of a restricted class of hierchical systems are shown, and in [21], where he characterizes a class of hierarchical systems for which syntactical sufficient conditions for modularity of simple termination can be given. Another class of hierarchical systems for which termination is modular is described in [2]. The results presented in [20, 21, 2] and here are not easily comparable because there are systems whose termination can be established by one result and not by the others. In particular, we accomodate mutually recursive definitions easily, which causes difficulties to finding simplification orderings, as in [21]. We can also generalize our results to the case of conditional rewriting modulo a congruence whose equivalence classes are finite. This was done without effort, thanks to our powerful proof technique.

Acknowledgments: To Bernhard Gramlich and Ralph Matthes for their careful reading.

References

1. Nachum Dershowitz. Orderings for term rewriting systems. *Theoretical Computer Science*, 17(3):279–301, March 1982.
2. Nachum Dershowitz. Hierarchical termination. Draft, 1994.
3. Nachum Dershowitz and Jean-Pierre Jouannaud. Rewrite systems. In J. van Leeuwen, editor, *Handbook of Theoretical Computer Science*, volume B, pages 243–309. North-Holland, 1990.
4. K. Drosten. *Termerssetzungssysteme*. PhD thesis, University of Passau, Germany, 1989. In german.
5. M. Fernandez and J.-P. Jouannaud. Modularity properties of term rewriting systems revisited. Technical Report 875, Laboratoire de Recherche en Informatique, November 1993.
6. J.-Y. Girard, Y. Lafont, and P. Taylor. *Proofs and Types*. Cambridge Tracts in Theoretical Computer Science. Cambridge University Press, 1989.
7. B. Gramlich. A structural analysis of modular termination of term rewriting systems. Research Report SR-91-15, University Kaiserslautern, 1991.
8. Jean-Pierre Jouannaud and Hélène Kirchner. Completion of a set of rules modulo a set of equations. *SIAM Journal on Computing*, 15(4), November 1986.

9. Jean-Pierre Jouannaud and Mitsuhiro Okada. Executable higher-order algebraic specification languages. In *Proc. 6th IEEE Symp. Logic in Computer Science, Amsterdam*, pages 350–361, 1991.
10. Jean-Pierre Jouannaud and B. Waldmann. Reductive conditional term rewriting systems. In *Proc. Third IFIP Working Conference on Formal Description of Programming Concepts*, Ebberup, Denmark, 1986.
11. S. Kamin and Jean-Jacques Lévy. Two generalizations of the recursive path ordering. Available as a report of the department of computer science, University of Illinois at Urbana-Champaign, 1980.
12. Stephane Kaplan. Conditional rewrite rules. *Theoretical Computer Science*, 33:175–193, March 1984.
13. Mahahito Kurihara and Azuma Ohuchi. Non-copying term rewriting and modularity of termination. Hokkaido University.
14. Mahahito Kurihara and Azuma Ohuchi. Modularity of simple termination of term rewriting systems with shared constructors. *Theoretical Computer Science*, 103:273–282, 1992.
15. A. Middeldorp and Y. Toyama. Completeness of combinations of constructor systems. In *Proc. 4th Rewriting Techniques and Applications, LNCS 488*, Como, Italy, 1991.
16. Aart Middeldorp. A sufficient condition for the termination of the direct sum of term rewriting systems. In *Proc. of the 4th IEEE Symposium on Logic in Computer Science, Pacific Grove*, pages 396–401, 1989.
17. Aart Middeldorp. *Modular Properties of Term Rewriting Systems*. PhD thesis, Free University of Amsterdam, Netherland, 1990.
18. Detlef Plump. Implementing term rewriting by graph reduction: Termination of combined systems. In *Proc. Conditional and Typed Rewriting Systems, LNCS 516*, 1991.
19. Detlef Plump. Collapsed tree rewriting: Completeness, confluence and modularity. In *Proc. Conditional Term Rewriting Systems, LNCS 656*, 1993.
20. M.R.K. Krishna Rao. Modular proofs for completeness of hierarchical systems. to appear, 1993.
21. M.R.K. Krishna Rao. Modular proofs for simple termination of hierarchical systems. to appear, 1993.
22. Albert Rubio. Automated deduction with constrained clauses. PhD Thesis, Univ. de Catalunya, 1994.
23. Michaël Rusinowitch. On termination of the direct sum of term rewriting systems. *Information Processing Letters*, 26:65–70, 1987.
24. Y. Toyama. Counterexamples to termination for the direct sum of term rewriting systems. *Information Processing Letters*, 25:141–143, April 1987.
25. Y. Toyama. On the Church-Rosser property for the direct sum of term rewriting systems. *Journal of the ACM*, 34(1):128–143, April 1987.

Institutions for Behaviour Specification(*)

J.L.Fiadeiro and **J.F.Costa**

ILTEC & Dept. Informatics
Faculty of Sciences, University of Lisbon,
Campo Grande, 1700 Lisboa, PORTUGAL
{llf,fgc}@di.fc.ul.pt

Abstract. Capitalising on the profusion of modal logics that have been proposed for reactive system specification since [Pnueli 77], on current work that explores categorical formalisations of models of concurrency such as [Sassone et al 93], and on our own past work relating specification logics and such process models [Fiadeiro and Costa 93, Fiadeiro et al 93, Sernadas et al 94], we develop a notion of institution of behaviour in which structural properties of logics and models that are relevant for specifying system behaviour can be formalised and discussed. In this framework, we characterise and relate the existence of adjoint situations between theories and models with the existence of terminal models and the difference between underspecification and nondeterminism.

1 Introduction

This paper is a preliminary account of a systematic study of the relationships between models of reactive system behaviour and their specifications taken as theories in a given logic. The overall aim of this work is to provide, for reactive system development, the same kind of formal support as has been provided for relational systems through the various algebraic techniques that have been proposed for Abstract Data Type (ADT) specification, namely in what concerns structure and modularity.

The work on ADT specification led to the proposal of institutions [Goguen and Burstall 92] as a means of defining specification concepts and techniques independently of the underlying logic. Our specific purpose in this paper is to put forward a specialisation of the notion of institution as a means of capturing the kind of structural properties that arise in modelling systems that are reactive. The motivation for this specialisation has its origins in three different sources.

Firstly, there is a large body of work on reactive system specification, be it *behaviour oriented*, i.e. based on a process language and mathematical models like transition systems,

(*) This work was partially supported by the Esprit BRAs 6071 (ISCORE) and 8035 (MODELAGE), the HCM Scientific Network MEDICIS, and JNICT under contract PBIC/C/TIT/1227/92.

or *logic oriented*, i.e. based on the use of formulas of some logic to specify properties of systems. The use of modal logics, namely temporal logics, has been proposed for this purpose since Pnueli's seminal paper [Pnueli 77]. The relationship between behaviours and formulas of the logic can be established by a *satisfaction relation*. This relation can be defined directly over the syntax of a process language (e.g. [Barringer et al 85] for CSP) or via a correspondence between the process algebra and the semantic structures of the logic (e.g. [Hennessy and Milner 85]).

Secondly, recent work on the behaviour side of concurrency [Sassone et al 93] has shown that category theory can be used to provide an abstract characterisation of typical constructions in process models (e.g. limits in suitable categories characterise parallel composition of processes) and a way of relating different models of concurrency (through adjunctions). Such categorial characterisations bring the field much closer to Goguen's categorial approach to General Systems Theory [Goguen and Ginali 78], and make the semantic domains much easier to "institutionalise".

Thirdly, the work developed in the IS-CORE project (BRA 3023/6071) has investigated categorial techniques on both sides of the satisfaction relation, having built several institutions for object specification based on modal logics [e.g. Fiadeiro and Maibaum 91, 92, Sernadas et al 94] and proposed several categorial models of process and object behaviour [e.g. Ehrich et al 91, Costa et al 92]. In particular, we have recently concerned ourselves with the relationship between the two sides [Fiadeiro et al 93], and have established an adjunction between the theories of a linear temporal logic and a trace-based model of behaviour [Fiadeiro and Costa 93] suggesting that the categorial approach provides a very expressive framework for relating behaviour models and logics.

Questions which arise immediately are "what can be generalised (and how) to other logics and behaviour models?" and "how does the categorial approach compare with the more classical approaches?". Our purpose in this paper is to investigate how the institutional framework can be used to start answering these questions by clarifying what the notion of "categorial approach to behaviour specification" might be.

More precisely, we put forward a notion of institution of behaviour (β-institution) that characterises a subclass of institutions that have the structural properties that we have found useful for modelling behaviour and which are related to well known properties of Kripke semantics of modal logics. We then begin exploring the structural properties of β-institutions, discussing in particular the relationship between "programs/systems" and "specifications", and characterising and relating adjoint situations between theories and models with underspecification and nondeterminism. In the concluding remarks, we discuss some of the future lines of research that we intend to undertake.

2 Institutions of behaviour

We have already mentioned that, following the work of Pnueli and others, we take modal logics as a starting point for the definition of β-institutions. The idea, however, is not to specialise the grammar and model functors of institutions in order to encode Kripke structures and their corresponding modal operators, but to capture the structural properties of Kripke semantics that we have found important for modelling behaviour.

We shall, therefore, dedicate very little attention to the syntactic aspects and adopt, as for institutions, a category SIGN of signatures and a grammar functor Sen: SIGN→SET for the syntactic structures of a β-institution. As an example, we may take any propositional modal logic: SIGN consists of SET (every signature consists of the set of atomic formulae of the logic) and Sen provides, for every choice of atomic formulae, the set of formulae that they generate using a fixed collection of logical connectives.

Let us then concentrate on the model theory of β-institutions. Let us recall some definitions from Kripke semantics of modal logics taken from [Goldblatt 87]:

Definition 2.1: A *frame* is a pair <S,R> where S is a set and R a binary relation on S ($R \subseteq S \times S$). ∎

The set S is the set of possible worlds (or points, or states) and R is the accessibility relation between worlds.

For instance, frames for linear temporal logic can be defined as follows [Wolper 89]:

Definition 2.2: A frame for linear temporal logic is a pair <S,R> such that R is a total function. ∎

We have already stated that we are interested in the structural property of frames and, hence, on the mappings between frames that preserve such structures. In the mathematical logic literature, frames come equipped with a notion of morphism known as *p-morphism* [Goldblatt 87] or *zigzag morphism* [van Benthem 84]:

Definition 2.3: Let $<S_1,R_1>$ and $<S_2,R_2>$ be frames. A *p-morphism* $f:<S_1,R_1>\rightarrow<S_2,R_2>$ is a function $f:S_1\rightarrow S_2$ satisfying:

- sR_1t implies $f(s)R_2f(t)$;
- $f(s)R_2u$ implies the existence of t such that sR_1t and $f(t)=u$. ∎

The second condition is a kind of "conservativeness" requirement on the translation between possible worlds. It says that no new alternative worlds are provided in $<S_2,R_2>$ for the worlds which come from S_1. In terms of system behaviour, this means that nondeterminism cannot be increased. We shall see later on why this condition is important and what its impact is on the relationship between specifications and behaviours.

Categorially speaking, we have the following characterisation:

Proposition 2.3: Frames and p-morphisms constitute a category KRI. This category is concrete over SET. ∎

The frames which typically arise in models of system behaviour usually have a different presentation. For instance, consider the model of process behaviour that we adopted in [Fiadeiro and Costa 93]:

Definition 2.4: A process behaviour (or process, for short) is a pair <E,Λ> where E is a pointed set (i.e. a set with a distinguished element $\bot_E$) and Λ is a subset Λ of E^ω (i.e., each $\lambda \in \Lambda$ is a function $\lambda:\omega\rightarrow E$, an infinite sequence of elements of E). ∎

Given a process $P=<E,\Lambda>$ we refer to E as P_α — the *alphabet* of P — and we refer to Λ as P_Λ — the *language* of P. The elements of E are called *events*. The designated event $\perp_E$ corresponds to idle steps of the process (steps that are performed by the environment).

Such process models usually induce frames. For instance, there is a canonical way of generating from a process a frame for linear temporal logic:

Definition/Proposition 2.5: Given a process $P=<E,\Lambda>$, the corresponding frame is $Kri(P)=<S_P,R_P>$ defined as follows:

- $S_P=\{<\lambda,i> \mid \lambda\in\Lambda, i\in\omega\}$
- $<\lambda,i>R_P<\mu,j>$ iff $\lambda=\mu$ and $j=i+1$

The relation R_P thus defined is a total function and, hence, we obtain a frame for linear temporal logic as defined in 2.2. ∎

Models of process behaviour also come equipped with morphisms (see [Sassone et al 93] for a classification of several such categories corresponding to different models). Morphisms for the trace-based model defined in 2.4 are defined as follows [Fiadeiro and Costa 93] (also explored in [Dionísio 91]):

Definition 2.6: Let h be a morphism from a pointed set A to a pointed set B (i.e. h is a total function $A\rightarrow B$ such that $f(\perp_A)=\perp_B$). The *extension* of h to A^ω is the function $h^\omega:A^\omega\rightarrow B^\omega$ defined by $h^\omega(\lambda)=\lambda;h$. A *process morphism* $h:<P_\alpha,P_\Lambda>\rightarrow<Q_\alpha,Q_\Lambda>$ is a morphism $h:P_\alpha\rightarrow Q_\alpha$ of pointed sets such that $h^\omega(P_\Lambda)\subseteq Q_\Lambda$. ∎

A morphism $h:<P_\alpha,P_\Lambda>\rightarrow<Q_\alpha,Q_\Lambda>$ can be seen as a way of making Q a *component-of* P, or a way in which P can *simulate* Q.

Proposition 2.7: Processes and process morphisms constitute a category PROC. There is a forgetful functor $U_\perp$:PROC$\rightarrow$SET$_\perp$ that sends each process P to its alphabet P_α (where SET$_\perp$ is the category of pointed sets). This functor is faithful, making PROC concrete over SET$_\perp$. ∎

The fact that processes behave as frames for linear temporal logic corresponds to the following result:

Proposition 2.8: Let $h:<P_\alpha,P_\Lambda>\rightarrow<Q_\alpha,Q_\Lambda>$ be a process morphism. Let Kri(h) be the mapping $S_P\rightarrow S_Q$ defined by $Kri(h)(\lambda,i)=(h^\omega(\lambda),i)$. The mapping Kri that acts on processes as defined in 2.4. and on morphisms as above is a functor PROC$\rightarrow$KRI.
proof: We have to check that every mapping Kri(h) satisfies the conditions for a p-morphism. The first condition is trivially verified. In order to check conservativeness, let $(h^\omega(\lambda),i)R_Q(\mu,j)$. By definition of R_Q, $\mu=h^\omega(\lambda)$ and $j=i+1$, i.e. $(\mu,j)=Kri(h)(\lambda,i+1)$. But $(\lambda,i)R_P(\lambda,i+1)$ by definition. ∎

Following the motivation given in the introduction and at the beginning of the section, our idea is to adopt for the "semantic" component of β-institutions categories BEHA of process behaviour such as PROC. If, indeed, the logical language is a modal one, then it should be possible to establish a functor BEHA$\rightarrow$KRI such as for PROC above in order to provide the semantic structures that are necessary to interpret the language. We shall, however, abstain from making commitments on the existence and the nature of any relationship between BEHA and KRI. The reasons for doing so are twofold. On the one hand, many logics work with more than one accessibility relation, requiring more than one functor mapping BEHA to KRI to exist. On the other hand, we would not like to rule out non-modal formalisms if they satisfy the structural properties that we are going to lay down for β-institutions. However, in the definition of these structural properties, we shall draw on the characteristics of modal logics.

Consider now the relationship between syntax and semantics. In modal logics, language is interpreted over a *model* for the atomic formulae [Goldblatt 87]:

Definition 2.9: Given a signature (set of atomic formulae) Σ, a *Σ-model* is a triple $<S,R,V>$ where $<S,R>$ is a frame and $V: \Sigma \rightarrow 2^S$ is a (total) function. ∎

Hence V is a function assigning to every atomic formula $p \in \Sigma$ a subset V(p) of S that stands for the worlds in which p is true (in the case of linear temporal logic interpreted over PROC, propositions correspond to actions so that V(p) returns the events during which action p occurs).

The way V extends to formulae is logic-dependent. It gives rise to a S-indexed family of truth relations $\models_s$ between models and formulae. This relation gives rise to another truth relation $\models$ between models and formulae defined by $M \models A$ iff $M \models_s A$ for every $s \in S$. It is the "truth in a model" relation that we adopt for β-institutions in order to abstract from the choice of the space of possible worlds. This relation will henceforth be called "satisfaction relation" to keep faithful to the traditional terminology of institutions.

It still remains to abstract the notion of model, namely the function V, from standard Kripke semantics to β-institutions. In order to give further motivation of the solution that we adopted, consider the extension of the notion of p-morphism to models [Goldblatt 87]:

Definition 2.10: Let $<S_1,R_1,V_1>$ and $<S_2,R_2,V_2>$ be Σ-models. A p-morphism $f:<S_1,R_1,V_1> \rightarrow <S_2,R_2,V_2>$ is a frame p-morphism $f:<S_1,R_1> \rightarrow <S_2,R_2>$ such that $s \in V_1(p)$ iff $f(s) \in V_2(p)$ for every $p \in \Sigma$. ∎

If we write the condition in the following equivalent way:

$$V_1 = V_2;f^{-1}$$

we see that the contravariant power-set functor is being applied to functions between possible worlds as a means of connecting the domains of the two valuation functions. The same functor appears in the definition of valuation functions (2.9) operating on possible worlds. This suggests that the relationship between syntax and semantics in a β-institution be based on a functor Sign: BEHA $\rightarrow$ SIGN^{op}.

Models over a signature Σ can now be defined as in 2.9: a Σ-model is a pair $<\sigma,B>$ where B is a behaviour and $\sigma:\Sigma \rightarrow Sign(B)$. According to 2.10, a morphism $f: <\sigma_1,B_1> \rightarrow <\sigma_2,B_2>$ is now a morphism $f:B_1 \rightarrow B_2$ such that $\sigma_1=\sigma_2;Sign(f)$. That is, the category Mod(Σ) of models for a signature Σ is the comma category $(Sign \downarrow \Sigma)$.

Given a signature morphism $\sigma:\Sigma \rightarrow \Sigma'$, we can easily defined the associated reduct functor as mapping every Σ'-model $<\sigma,B>$ to the Σ-model $<\mu;\sigma,B>$. That is, we define

Mod:SIGN→CAT^{op} to be the functor (Sign↓_).

Given these definitions, the satisfaction condition of institutions translates to:

for every $\sigma:\Sigma\rightarrow\Sigma'$, $\mu:\Sigma'\rightarrow Sign(B)$ and $A\in Sen(\Sigma)$, $<\mu,B>\models_{\Sigma'}\sigma(A)$ iff $<\sigma;\mu,B>\models_{\Sigma}A$

We can now make precise the definition that we have been progressively building:

Definition 2.11: An institution of behaviour (β-institution) consists of:

syntax:

- a category SIGN (of signatures)
- a functor Sen: SIGN → SET (grammar)

semantics:

- a category BEHA (of behaviours)
- a functor Sign: BEHA→$SIGN^{op}$

model-theory:

- a |SIGN|-indexed family of satisfaction relations $<\sigma,B>\models_{\Sigma}A$ where $A\in Sen(\Sigma)$ and $\sigma:\Sigma\rightarrow Sign(B)$, satisfying the following property: for every $\sigma:\Sigma\rightarrow\Sigma'$, $\mu:\Sigma'\rightarrow Sign(B)$ and $A\in Sen(\Sigma)$, $<\mu,B>\models_{\Sigma'}\sigma(A)$ iff $<\sigma;\mu,B>\models_{\Sigma}A$ ∎

As examples of β-institutions we have, as expected, modal logics for which BEHA is a subcategory of KRI whose objects are the frames which satisfy the intended requirements on the accessibility relation (e.g. linearity as in 2.2). In the case of propositional logics, SIGN is SET and Sign is the power-set functor applied to the forgetful functor that projects frames into their underlying sets of possible worlds as discussed above.

As an example of a β-institution built over a process model, we have linear temporal logic over PROC as defined in [Fiadeiro and Costa 93]. Another example is given in [Sernadas et al 94] for a category of labelled transition systems. There are other obvious associations of logics with some of the process models defined in [Sassone et al 93] to form β-institutions, e.g. branching time logic for synchronisation trees, but no systematic assignment as been attempted yet.

As intended, β-institutions are a specialisation of the notion of institution:

Definition and Proposition 2.12: Every β-institution defines a corresponding institution as follows:

- its category of signatures is SIGN as for the β-institution;
- its grammar functor is Sen as for the β-institution;
- its model functor is (Sign↓_): SIGN→CAT^{op};
- its family of satisfaction relations is ⊨ as for the β-institution ∎

3 Specifications and the p-property

All the components of β-institutions were motivated with standard notions of the model theory of modal logics except for the satisfaction condition. This property has no counterpart in modal logics because changes of language, as captured by signature morphisms, are not usually studied in mathematical and philosophical logic.

There is, however, an important structural property satisfied by Kripke structures and which is not captured in definition 2.11:

Proposition 3.1: Let $f:<S_1,R_1,V_1>\rightarrow<S_2,R_2,V_2>$ be a morphism of Σ-models and A a formula over Σ. For any $s\in S_1$, $<S_1,R_1,V_1> \models_s A$ iff $<S_2,R_2,V_2> \models_{f(s)} A$. ∎

This property, taken from [Goldblatt 87], cannot be directly formulated for β-institutions. It admits, however, the following corollary (which in [van Benthem 84] is attributed to Segerberg):

Corollary 3.2: Let $f:<S_1,R_1,V_1>\rightarrow<S_2,R_2,V_2>$ be a morphism of Σ-models. For any formula A over Σ, $<S_1,R_1,V_1> \models A$ if $<S_2,R_2,V_2> \models A$. ∎

This property is now generalisable to β-institutions:

Definition 3.3: We say that a β-institution has the *p-property* iff it satisfies the following condition: for every signature Σ, Σ-models $<\sigma_1,B_1>$ and $<\sigma_2,B_2>$, and morphism f: $<\sigma_1,B_1> \rightarrow <\sigma_2,B_2>$, if $<\sigma_2,B_2>\models A$ then $<\sigma_1,B_1>\models A$ for every $A\in Sen(\Sigma)$. ∎

It is this property that requires conservativeness with respect to nondeterminism of p-morphisms as defined in 2.3. This is intuitive if we think in terms of process behaviour and, using the terminology put forward in [Kuiper 89], distinguish between *required* nondeterminism and *allowed* nondeterminism. Required nondeterminism is nondeterminism which any implementation must possess because the specification requires so. It translates into branching of the accessibility relation. Allowed nondeterminism is the freedom that is left to the implementor due to the vagueness of the specification, which results in the existence of more than one model to the specification.

The p-property implies that if a process P_1 simulates a process P_2, then any property satisfied by P_2 is also satisfied by P_1. Hence, because required nondeterminism is a property, it cannot decrease from P_2 to P_1: if behaviour morphisms allowed for further branching in P_2, then P_2 would show more properties (the existence of more alternative behaviours) than P_1.

This means that if we are working over a process model BEHA which is rich enough to model required nondeterminism (e.g. labelled transition systems as defined in [Sassone et al 93]) and we want to define a β-institution over that process model in such a way that it has the p-property (we shall see that there are good reasons for doing so), then we have to select a subcategory of BEHA with the same objects but only those morphisms that do not allow for nondeterminism to be increased.

If, however, the logical language is not rich enough for requiring nondeterminism (as, for instance, in [Sernadas et al 94] where linear temporal logic is interpreted over labelled transition systems), then there is no need for moving to a subcategory. (The linear tense operators are not interpreted directly over a transition system but over the sets of runs generated from that transition system.) The p-property is, indeed, a relationship between syntax and semantics, not a property of models alone.

The interest of the p-property lies in the acquired structural properties of the category of theories (specifications) of the β-institution. We discuss now some of these properties.

Definition 3.4: The category THEO of the theories of a β-institution is defined as for its corresponding institution. The objects of THEO are pairs $<\Sigma,\Gamma>$ where $\Gamma \subseteq Sen(\Sigma)$ is closed under consequence, i.e. $A \in \Gamma$ whenever, for every $M \in Mod(\Sigma)$, $M \models_\Sigma \Gamma$ implies $M \models_\Sigma A$. A theory morphism $\sigma:<\Sigma_1,\Gamma_1> \rightarrow <\Sigma_2,\Gamma_2>$ is a signature morphism $\sigma:\Sigma_1 \rightarrow \Sigma_2$ such that $Sen(\sigma)(\Gamma_1) \subseteq Sen(\sigma)(\Gamma_2)$. ∎

A particularly interesting class of β-institutions consists of those for which the functor $Sign:BEHA \rightarrow SIGN^{op}$ can be lifted to a functor $Spec:BEHA \rightarrow THEO^{op}$ such that Mod itself can be lifted to THEO as $Mod(T)=(Spec \downarrow T)$. The intuition for this interest is that we should be able to associate with every behaviour B a canonical specification Spec(B) so that every morphism $T \rightarrow Spec(B)$ identifies T as a specification of B and, dually, B as a realisation of T. In this case, the models of T correspond to all possible refinements of T into programs. Identifying BEHA with (the behaviours of) programs (or processes), this corresponds to the idea that programs can themselves be regarded as specifications, and that the models of a specification can be identified with the programs which, in some sense, "complete" the specification.

Notice that the relationships between processes and specifications which can be found in the literature (e.g. [Hennessy and Milner 85, Pnueli 85, Graf and Sifakis 89]) are also based on the existence of a way of associating a set of formulas Spec(B) with every behaviour B. Although, in these approaches, the main interest is in discussing the relationship between the equivalence relation induced by Spec and the one inherent from BEHA, Pnueli already suggests in [Pnueli 85] that the induced orderings be compared as well. The functoriality of Spec is a kind of correctness requirement on these orderings, namely that if B_1 simulates B_2 then $Spec(B_2)$ "implies" $Spec(B_1)$. We shall further discuss other requirements on Spec below.

Although it is always possible to define a mapping that associates a theory Spec(B) with every behaviour B – the obvious candidate assigns to Spec(B) the signature Sign(B) and theorems $\{A \in Sen(Sign(B)): <id,B> \models A\}$ – it is not always possible to extend it to a functor that lifts Sign, i.e. such that $Spec(h:B \rightarrow B')=Sign(h)$. In order to motivate why this is so, assume that we have a functor $Spec:BEHA \rightarrow THEO^{op}$ and consider a morphism $h:B' \rightarrow B$. Because Spec is a functor, we have $Spec(h):Spec(B) \rightarrow Spec(B')$. Hence, if B is a model of a specification T, i.e. if we have a morphism $\sigma:T \rightarrow Spec(B)$, then B' is also a model of T through the morphism $\sigma;Spec(h)$. In particular this implies that, for every signature Σ and $A \in Sen(\Sigma)$, if $<\sigma,B> \models_\Sigma A$ then $<\sigma;Sign(h),B'> \models_\Sigma A$. That is, the β-institution is required to have the p-property.

Proposition 3.5: If the satisfaction relation has the p-property, then the mapping Spec defined by

- for every B:BEHA, $Spec(B)=<Sign(B),\{A \in Sen(Sign(B)): <id,B> \models A\}>$
- for every $h:B \rightarrow B'$, $Spec(h:B \rightarrow B')=Sign(h)$

is a functor $BEHA \rightarrow THEO^{op}$.

proof: it is sufficient to prove that $Spec(h:B \rightarrow B')$ is, indeed, a theory morphism $Spec(B') \rightarrow Spec(B)$. Let $A' \in Spec(B')$. Then, $<id,B'> \models A'$. The p-property implies that $<Sign(h),B> \models A'$. The satisfaction condition then implies $<id,B> \models Sen(Sign(h))(A')$. ∎

Definition 3.6: Given a theory $T=<\Sigma,\Gamma>$, Mod(T) is defined as for the corresponding institution, i.e. as the full subcategory of Mod(Σ) which consists of the Σ-models which satisfy T. ∎

Proposition 3.7: If the satisfaction relation has the p-property, then Mod(T)=(Spec↓T).

proof:

1. Let $<\sigma,B>\in$ Mod(T), i.e. $<\sigma,B>\models A$ for every $A\in T$. Then, by the satisfaction condition, $<id,B>\models\sigma(A)$ for every $A\in T$, i.e. $\sigma(T)\in$ Spec(B), which means that σ is a theory morphism $T\rightarrow$Spec(B).
2. Let $T\rightarrow$Spec(B) and $A\in T$. Then, because σ is a theory morphism, $\sigma(A)\in$ Spec(B), i.e. $<id,B>\models\sigma(A)$. The satisfaction condition then implies that $<\sigma,B>\models A$. Hence, $<\sigma,B>\in$ Mod(T). ∎

Corollary 3.8: If the satisfaction relation has the p-property, Mod=(Spec↓_) ∎

It is well known that (Spec↓_) is a pullback-preserving functor and, hence, the p-property leads to an exact institution [Meseguer 89]. This is a particularly important property on the modularity allowed by the formalism because it tells us that the models of a composite specification (taken as a colimit) are all the possible compositions (taken as limits) of the models of the components. That is, in order to develop a system that satisfies a composite specification, we may put together any models of the component specifications.

Corollary 3.9: If a β-institution has the p-property then it is exact. ∎

As already mentioned, the p-property has an interesting interpretation from the point of view of behaviour specification. Intuitively, this property corresponds to an "open semantics" of behaviour: any behaviour that simulates a model is itself a model; or: if a component of a system is a model of a specification, then the system itself is a model for that specification. We say that this corresponds to an open semantics of behaviour because it implies that if one is satisfied with a process (because it meets a certain specification), then one must be satisfied with any other process which simulates it; it is not possible to specify a process in isolation.

By the way it is defined, Spec satisfies one of the compatibility requirements for *expressivity* of the logic for the domain BEHA as defined by Pnueli [Pnueli 85]. Adapting to our context, namely to the use of theories instead of formulae as the target of Spec, this is the property

$<\sigma,B>\models A$ iff $\sigma(A)\in$ Spec(B)

The other requirement, that B_1 and B_2 be "equivalent" (isomorphic) whenever B_1 is a model of Spec(B_2) is, however, a little awkward in our setting because morphisms provide a much finer spectrum of relationships between behaviours. A formulation which we think is in the spirit of Pnueli's requirement is:

if $<\sigma$:Sign(B_2)$\rightarrow$Sign(B_1),$B_1>\in$ Mod(Spec(B_2))
then there is $h:B_1\rightarrow B_2$ such that Sign(h)=σ.

This says that B_1 is related to B_2 whenever B_1 is a model of Spec(B_2). Because $<\sigma$:Sign(B_2)$\rightarrow$Sign(B_1),$B_1>\in$ Mod(Spec(B_2)) iff σ:Spec(B_2)$\rightarrow$Spec(B_1), this requirement corresponds to fullness of Spec. It is also in the spirit of the notion of expressiveness proposed by Pnueli that Spec be faithful, as it corresponds to saying that distinctions between behaviours are not ignored by their specifications.

Definition 3.10: A β-institution is said to be *expressive* iff it has the p-property and Spec is full and faithful. ∎

The classification on the relationship between the logic and the process models put forward in [Hennessy and Milner 85] concerns just the equivalence relations of the process model and the one induced on them by the logic:

Definition 3.11: A β-institution is said to be *adequate* iff it has the p-property and Spec reflects isomorphisms, i.e. if whenever h is a behaviour morphism such that Spec(h) is a theory isomorphism, then h is itself an isomorphism. ∎

Notice that functors always preserve isomorphisms. Hence, adequacy means that two behaviours are isomorphic iff their specifications are isomorphic.

Because faithful and full functors reflect isomorphisms, the relationship between expressiveness and adequacy is as in [Pnueli 85]:

Proposition 3.12: Every expressive β-institution is adequate. ∎

The problems of characterising the equivalences imposed on models by temporal logics and of developing logics which are expressive for given process models are well documented in the literature (e.g. [Goltz et al 92], [Graf and Sifakis 89]).

4 Programs, adjointness and fibrations

We have seen that, under the p-property, the models of a specification T can be associated with all the possible refinements of T into specifications which correspond to "programs". Intuitively, a specification T should correspond to a program when it has a "canonical" model. Because models of a specification are closed under morphisms (simulation) this corresponds to the existence of a behaviour [T] such that every other model is a simulation of [T]. In categorial terms:

Definition 4.1: We say that a specification T is a program iff Mod(T) has a terminal object (which we denote by [T]). ∎

A typical β-institution, i.e. a typical formalism for behaviour specification, will be such that not every specification is a program. Indeed, the idea of working with specifications is to be able to start from "loose" requirements which do not identify a single program, and refine them, by adding detail, until a "program" is obtained, i.e. a specification to which a program can be assigned.

A β-institution which corresponds to a formalism for "programming", i.e. such that every specification has a canonical realisation as a program, is then an institution with a terminal semantics:

Definition 4.2: A β-institution is said to have a terminal semantics iff, for every T:THEO, Mód(T) has a terminal object. ▮

If a β-institution has a terminal semantics, then a functor Beha: THEO→$BEHA^{op}$ can be defined which returns the behaviour that corresponds to every program (theory):

Proposition 4.3: Consider a β-institution with terminal semantics. The mapping Beha defined by

- for every P:THEO, Beha(P) is the behaviour of "the" terminal object of Mod(P);
- for every $\sigma:P_1 \to P_2$, Beha(σ) is the unique morphism $Beha(P_2) \to Beha(P_1)$ that results from $Beha(P_1)$ being terminal in $Mod(P_1)$ and $Beha(P_2)$, through the reduct functor associated with σ, being a model of P_1;

is a functor THEO→$PROG^{op}$.

proof: We shall just detail the construction of Beha(σ). Let $<\mu_i, Beha(P_i)>$ be terminal in $Mod(P_i)$. By the reduct functor associated with σ, $<\sigma;\mu_2, Beha(P_2)>$ is a model of P_1. Hence, because $<\mu_1, Beha(P_1)>$ is terminal in $Mod(P_1)$, there is a unique $h:Beha(P_2) \to Beha(P_1)$ such that $\sigma;\mu_2;Sign(h)=\sigma;\mu_1$. We take Beha(σ) to be h. ▮

Thanks to the p-property, β-institutions with terminal semantics have very strong structural properties:

Proposition 4.4: A β-institution with the p-property has a terminal semantics iff the functor Spec: BEHA→$THEO^{op}$ has a right adjoint.

proof: This is a consequence of a general result of category theory – a functor F:C→D has a right adjoint iff for every object B of D there is a terminal object in the category (F↓B). See [Crole 93] for a proof. ▮

Corollary 4.5: A β-institution with the p-property has a terminal semantics iff Beha is a right adjoint of Spec. ▮

These results on adjointness and exactness (3.9), which generalise [Fiadeiro and Costa 93], are one of the motivating forces behind the construction of β-institutions, as they have always been perceived as important structural properties for behaviour specification. Notice that this adjoint situation does not follow from the usual Galois correspondence of logics because we are dealing with models and not sets of models.

The existence of this adjointness implies that the model functor Mod: $THEO^{op}$→CAT can be factorised as Beha;(BEHA↓_) which characterises the β-institution as follows:

Corollary 4.6: A β-institution with the p-property has a terminal semantics iff it is categorical, in the sense of [Meseguer 89], on BEHA. ▮

That is, categoricity characterises "programmability".

As an example of a β-institution which has terminal semantics we have linear temporal logic with trace-based semantics as defined in [Fiadeiro and Costa 93]. The construction and proof of the existence of the adjunction can also be found in that paper. The intuitive interpretation of this result is the well known fact that linear temporal logic does not distinguish between underspecification and nondeterminism! That is, the existence of several models of a linear temporal theory can always be attributed to nondeterminism. We shall return to this distinction later on.

Expressive β-institutions, as defined in 3.10, satisfy a stronger property:

Proposition 4.7: If an expressive β-institution has a terminal semantics, every behaviour B is isomorphic to Beha(Spec(B)), i.e. Spec(B) is a program whose behaviour is B.
proof: This is a consequence of the fact that, in an adjunction, the left adjoint is faithful and full iff the unit is a natural isomorphism. ∎

The proof shows that the converse is also true: if a β-institution with the p-property has a terminal semantics, then it is expressive if $B \approx Beha(Spec(B))$ for every B:BEHA.

Proposition 4.7 is somewhat surprising as it might be expected that the specification of a behaviour be a program! It is certainly true that B is a model of Spec(B), but it may not be the maximal one if the logic and the process model are not fully compatible. For instance, the process model may assign more structure to behaviours than what is needed for interpreting the logic (e.g. transition systems interpreting linear temporal logic as in [Sernadas et al 94]). In this case, a subcategory of BEHA would be needed where, by removing some of the morphisms, the notion of equivalence is coarser.

We shall now attempt at further characterising the specifications (theories) that are programs, i.e. that have terminal models. We are going to provide that characterisation in the context of additional structural properties of the β-institution. These structural properties are of two kinds.

First we are going to assume that the functor Sign: $BEHA \rightarrow SIGN^{op}$ can be factorised as $BEHA \xrightarrow{Alph} ALPH \xrightarrow{F} SIGN^{op}$. The category ALPH captures the notion of alphabet. We shall further require that Alph be faithful, making BEHA concrete over ALPH. All models presented in [Sassone et al 93] are indeed concrete categories. In the case of the trace-based model that we defined in 2.4 and 2.6, alphabets are pointed sets (of events).

Definition 4.8: We say that a β-institution is factorised over a category ALPH iff the functor Sign: $BEHA \rightarrow SIGN^{op}$ can be factorised as $BEHA \xrightarrow{Alph} ALPH \xrightarrow{F} SIGN^{op}$ where Alph is faithful. ∎

We did not define β-institutions using this factorisation from the beginning because results so far did not depend on it. Factorised β-institutions also have the advantage of exhibiting a pleasing symmetry between syntax and semantics, both being given through faithful functors (concrete categories) $THEO \rightarrow SIGN$ and $BEHA \rightarrow ALPH$. The relationship between syntax and semantics is then left to the functor $F: ALPH \rightarrow SIGN^{op}$.

The first structural property that we shall require is that $F: ALPH \rightarrow SIGN^{op}$ admits a right adjoint. The motivation for this condition is that the "distance" between specifications and models should lie in the axioms of the specification and the behaviours of the model, not in signatures and alphabets. Hence, the difference between programs and specifications should not be reflected in the signatures but in the axiomatisations: a specification is refined into a program essentially by addition of detail (axioms). (The fact that we work with an adjunction and not an equivalence means that there is still some transformation to be performed on the signatures but that this tranformation is well determined.) In the case of linear temporal logic over trace-based models of behaviour as defined in [Fiadeiro and

Costa 93], the adjunction between $SET_\perp$ and SET^{op} is established through the contravariant power-set functor. That is, events are taken as sets of action propositions.

The right adjoint to the functor F, which we shall denote by G, fixes the alphabet of the terminal model of a specification T, if it exists. The second structural property will allow us to determine the behaviour of the terminal model among the behaviours over the chosen alphabet. That is, it will allow us to choose the terminal behaviour over the subcategory of models whose alphabet is the one determined by the functor G.

Definition 4.9: For every theory T, we define $Mod^*(T)$ to be the (full) subcategory of Mod(T) whose objects are of the form $<\varepsilon_\Sigma:\Sigma\rightarrow Sign(B), B>$ where Σ is the signature of T, $\varepsilon_\Sigma:\Sigma\rightarrow F(G(\Sigma))$ is the co-unit of the adjunction, and $G(\Sigma)$ is the alphabet of B. ∎

The category $Mod^*(T)$ is, therefore, defined over the fibre $Alph^{-1}(G(\Sigma))$, i.e. over the behaviours whose alphabet is $G(\Sigma)$. Because the refinement morphism is now fixed to ε_Σ, we have the following characterisation for $Mod^*(T)$:

Proposition 4.10: $Mod^*(T)$ is isomorphic to a subcategory of $Alph^{-1}(G(\Sigma))$: the full subcategory whose objects are the $G(\Sigma)$-behaviours B such that $<\varepsilon_\Sigma,B>\models A$ for every $A\in T$. ∎

Because the typical behaviour categories with which we deal are fibre-small, we may assume that $Mod^*(T)$ is itself small. Moreover, because fibres are partial orders, $Mod^*(T)$ is also a partial order.

The second structural property requires Alph:BEHA→ALPH to be a split cofibration [Barr and Wells 90]. Intuitively, this property implies that, given an alphabet morphism $h:\alpha\rightarrow\alpha'$, and a behaviour B such that $Alph(B)=\alpha$, we can find its "image" h(B), i.e. a behaviour whose alphabet is α' and is "closest" to B. In this case, closest means that: (1) h is itself a morphism between B and h(B); (2) for every other behaviour B' over α' for which h is a morphism from B to B', there is a unique morphism $h(B)\rightarrow B'$ which is projected to $id_{\alpha'}$.

Proposition 4.11: A functor $\_^\bullet$: $Mod(\Sigma)\rightarrow Mod^*(\Sigma)$ is defined as follows:

- $<\sigma:\Sigma\rightarrow Sign(B),B>^\bullet$ is $<\varepsilon_\Sigma:\Sigma\rightarrow F(G(\Sigma)), \sigma^+(B)>$ where ε_Σ is the co-unit of the adjunction and σ^+ is the unique morphism $Alph(B)\rightarrow G(\Sigma)$ such that $(\varepsilon_\Sigma;F(\sigma^+)=\sigma)$;
- given models $<\sigma,B>$ and $<\sigma',B'>$ and $h:B\rightarrow B'$ such that $\sigma=\sigma';F(h)$, $h^\bullet$ is the unique morphism $\sigma^+(B)\rightarrow\sigma'^+(B')$ such that $(h;\sigma'^+)=\sigma^+;h^\bullet$.

This functor is a left-adjoint of the inclusion functor of $Mod^*(\Sigma)$ into $Mod(\Sigma)$. ∎

This functor translates every model to another model over the canonical alphabet $G(\Sigma)$.

Corollary 4.12: $Mod^*(\Sigma)$ is a reflective sub-category of $Mod(\Sigma)$. ∎

In order to lift the functor $(\_^\bullet)$ from signatures to theories, i.e. to obtain, for every theory T, $Mod^*(T)$ as a (full) reflective subcategory of Mod(T), we have to require that the satisfaction relation be compatible with the cofibration:

Definition 4.13: A factorised β-institution is said to be fibred iff

- Alph:BEHA→ALPH is a split cofibration;

- for every signature Σ, $A \in Sen(\Sigma)$, $\sigma:\Sigma \to F(\alpha)$ and morphism $h:Alph(B) \to \alpha$, $<\sigma;F(h),B> \models A$ implies $<\sigma,h(B)> \models A$. ∎

Notice that the satisfaction condition implies that we have an equivalence.

As an example of a fibred β-institution we have linear temporal logic over PROC as defined in [Fiadeiro and Costa 93]. In this case, Alph is even topological. Another example is given in [Sernadas et al 94] for labelled transition systems.

Proposition 4.14: In a fibred factorised β-institution, if $<\sigma:\Sigma \to Sign(B),B>$ is a model of $T=<\Sigma,\Gamma>$, then $<\sigma:\Sigma \to Sign(B),B>^{\bullet}$ is also a model of T.
proof: Let $A \in \Gamma$. We want to prove that $<\varepsilon_\Sigma,\sigma^+(B)> \models A$. Because the satisfaction relation is compatible with the cofibration, it is sufficient to prove that $<\varepsilon_\Sigma;F(\sigma^+),B> \models A$. But, by definition, $\varepsilon_\Sigma;F(\sigma^+)=\sigma$, and $<\sigma,B> \models A$ because $<\sigma:\Sigma \to Sign(B),B>$ is a model of T. ∎

Corollary 4.15: In a fibred factorised β-institution, $Mod^*(T)$ can be characterised as a (full) reflective subcategory of Mod(T). ∎

Suppose now that $Mod^*(T)$ has a terminal object T^*. Let $<\sigma,B>$ be a model of T (which implies that $<\varepsilon_\Sigma,\sigma^+(B)>$ is also a model of T). Because T^* is terminal in $Mod^*(T)$ there is a unique morphism $h:\sigma^+(B) \to T^*$ such that $F(h)=id_\Sigma$ where Σ is the signature of T. The composition $\sigma^+;h$ gives us a morphism $B \to T^*$. Moreover, $\varepsilon_\Sigma;F(\sigma^+;h)= \varepsilon_\Sigma;(F(\sigma^+);F(h))=\varepsilon_\Sigma;F(\sigma^+)=\sigma$. On the other hand, suppose we have another morphism $g:B \to T^*$ such that $\varepsilon_\Sigma;F(g)=\sigma$. Then, necessarily, g=h because of the adjunction. Hence, $<\varepsilon_\Sigma,T^*>$ is a terminal object of Mod(T).

Proposition 4.16: In a fibred factorised β-institution, if $Mod^*(T)$ has a terminal object than so does Mod(T) and they coincide. ∎

We have thus reduced the problem of finding a terminal object for Mod(T) to determining a terminal object for $Mod^*(T)$.

Being small and a partial order, a sufficient condition for $Mod^*(T)$ to admit a terminal model is that $Mod^*(T)$ admits (small) colimits. In fact, this is equivalent to admitting small coproducts. Indeed, because $Mod^*(T)$ is a partial order, the uniqueness condition for the morphisms into the colimit of the whole category is automatically satisfied and, hence, its colimit is a terminal object.

Proposition 4.17: In a fibred factorised β-institution, a theory T has a terminal model if $Mod^*(T)$ is closed under small coproducts. ∎

This condition, i.e. that $Mod^*(T)$ admits arbitrary (but small) coproducts, has an intuitive interpretation. Indeed, like products correspond to parallel composition, coproducts correspond, in most process models, to *nondeterministic choice*. Hence, the condition requires that $Mod^*(T)$ be closed under choice, i.e. that any arbitrary choice between models of T be still a model of T. Intuitively, this means that we obtain a program when we have eliminated all the underspecification, the remaining models being able to be reduced to one via a choice operator. It is important to notice that this choice operator is internalising part of what we called *allowed nondeterminism* in section 3, i.e. that nondeterminism which, as opposed to *required nondeterminism*, originates in the vagueness of the specification and not in specific requirements of the specification for nondeterministic behaviour.

It is interesting to note that, for linear temporal logic, programs coincide with theories because the logic does not distinguish between nondeterminism and underspecification. The same, however, is not true, for instance, for branching time logic or the μ-calculus, which allow for required nondeterminism but, depending on how their model theory is defined, may or may not internalise allowed nondeterminism. We are currently working on the categorial characterisations of the two kinds of nondeterminism and their relationships with theories.

5 Concluding remarks

In this paper, we showed how an abstract and general account of the relationships between process models and logics for the specification of reactive system behaviour can be given in the context of a specialisation of the notion of institution. The notion of β-institution was proposed taking into account the structural properties of traditional Kripke semantics of modal logics, the recent work on categorial models of concurrency [Sassone et al 93], and our own past work on the modularisation of temporal specifications [Fiadeiro and Maibaum 92] and on relating logics and models of reactive behaviour [Fiadeiro et al 93, Fiadeiro and Costa 93]. We were thus able to establish abstract characterisation of some of the concepts and techniques that have been proposed for reactive system development, and lay the foundations for future work.

As an example of the expressive power of this framework, we showed how concepts that have been put forward for relating behavioural and logical approaches based on notions of observational equivalence [Hennessy and Milner 85, Pnueli 85, Graf and Sifakis 87] can be formalised and refined in the context of β-institutions. As part of future research, we intend to explore this new added expressive power in the generalisation of these studies, namely in a classification of logics of concurrency in the spirit of [Goltz et al 92].

As another application, we explored the structural properties of the category of theories of β-institutions to characterise exactness and the existence of adjoint situations between theories and models (not sets of models as in the standard Galois correspondence). Exactness is a property of β-institutions that satisfy an important structural property (the p-property of Kripke structures). The existence of such adjoint situations was shown to be equivalent to the availability of terminal models for specifications (meaning that every specification denotes a canonical program). We also showed how the existence of terminal models of specifications is related to the elimination of underspecification in favour of nondeterminism. Further work is necessary in order to characterise the difference between required and allowed nondeterminism (as in [Kuiper 89]) in the context of the adopted categorial approach. We also intend to explore other aspects of β-institutions, namely mappings between β-institutions as a means of establishing a proof-theoretic counterpart to the classification mechanisms developed in [Sassone et al 93] for concurrency models.

It is only fair to say that other applications of algebraic techniques to concurrency do exist, notably the work developed in Genova [e.g. Reggio 91] around entity institutions. The application of the institutional framework that these authors have developed is different from ours in that their starting point is an algebraic specification of the Kripke structures of the logic, thus developing an ontology (dynamic entities) which in our approach is missing: whereas in entity institutions "processes" are denoted by terms, in β-institutions they are denoted by theories. This is also the difference between exogeneous and endogeneous applications of logic to system modelling. It seems worth developing a more formal relationship between the two approaches, as they seem to complement each other, entity institutions providing a way of dealing explicitly with the external structure (configuration) of complex systems, and β-institutions providing a more abstract framework in which to discuss the structural properties of specifications and their underlying formalisms.

Acknowledgements

We are grateful to Tom Maibaum for many fruitful discussions.

References

[Barr and Wells 90]
M.Barr and C.Well, *Category Theory for Computing Science*, Prentice-Hall 1990

[Barringer et al 85]
H.Barringer, R.Kuiper and A.Pnueli, "A Compositional Temporal Approach to a CSP-like Language", in E.Neuhold and G.Chroust (eds) *Formal Models in Programming*, North-Holland 1985, 207-227

[Costa *et al* 92]
J.F.Costa, A.Sernadas, C.Sernadas and H.-D.Ehrich, "Object Interaction", in *Proc. MFCS'92*, LNCS 629, Springer-Verlag 1992, 200-208.

[Crole 93]
R.Crole, *Categories for Types*, Cambridge University Press 1993

[Dionísio 91]
F.M.Dionísio, *Um Modelo e Submodelos Categoriais de Processos Concorrentes*, MSc. Thesis, Dept.Mathematics, Fac.Engineering, Technical University of Lisbon, 1991.

[Ehrich et al 91]
H.-D.Ehrich, J.Goguen and A.Sernadas, "A Categorial Theory of Objects as Observed Processes", in J.deBakker, W.deRoever and G.Rozenberg (eds) *Foundations of Object-Oriented Languages*, LNCS 489, Springer Verlag 1991, 203-228.

[Fiadeiro and Costa 93]
J.Fiadeiro and J.F.Costa, *Mirror, mirror in my hand: a topological adjunction between temporal theories and processes*, Research Report, DI-FCUL, March 1993.

[Fiadeiro and Maibaum 91]
J.Fiadeiro and T.Maibaum, "Describing, Structuring, and Implementing Objects", in J.deBakker, W.deRoever and G.Rozenberg (eds) *Foundations of Object-Oriented Languages*, LNCS 489, Springer-Verlag 1991, 274-310.

[Fiadeiro and Maibaum 92]
J.Fiadeiro and T.Maibaum, "Temporal Theories as Modularisation Units for Concurrent System Specification", *Formal Aspects of Computing* 4(3), 1992, 239-272.

[Fiadeiro et al 93]
J.Fiadeiro, J.F.Costa, A.Sernadas and T.Maibaum, "Process Semantics of Temporal Logic Specification", in M.Bidoit and C.Choppy (eds) *Recent Trends in Data Type Specification*, LNCS 655, Springer-Verlag 1993, 236-253.

[Goguen and Burstall 92]
J.Goguen and R.Burstall, "Institutions: Abstract Model Theory for Specification and Programming", *Journal of the ACM* 39(1), 1992, 95-146

[Goguen and Ginali 78]
J.Goguen and S.Ginali, "A Categorical Approach to General Systems Theory", in G.Klir (ed) *Applied General Systems Research*, Plenum 1978, 257-270.

[Goldblatt 87]
R.Goldblatt, *Logics of Time and Computation*, CSLI 1987.

[Goltz et al 92]
U.Goltz, R.Kuiper, W.Penczek, "Propositional Temporal Logics and Equivalences", in W.Cleaveland (ed) *CONCUR'92*, LNCS 630, Springer-Verlag 1992, 222-236.

[Graf and Sifakis 89]
S.Graf and J.Sifakis, "An Expressive Logic for a process Algebra with Silent Actions", in B.Banieqbal, H.Barringer and A.Pnueli (eds) *Temporal Logic in Specification*, LNCS 398, Springer-Verlag 1989, 44-61.

[Hennessy and Milner 85]
M.Hennessy and R.Milner, "Algebraic Laws for Nondeterminism and Concurrency", *Journal of the ACM* 32(1), 1985, 137-161

[Kuiper 89]
R.Kuiper, "Enforcing Nondeterminism via Linear Temporal Logic Specifications using Hiding", in B.Banieqbal, H.Barringer and A.Pnueli (eds) *Temporal Logic in Specification*, LNCS 398, Springer-Verlag 1989, 295-303.

[Meseguer 89]
J.Meseguer, "General Logics", in H.-D.Ebbinghaus et al (eds) *Logic Colloquium 87*, North-Holland 1989.

[Pnueli 77]
A.Pnueli, "The Temporal Logic of Programs", in *Proc 18th Annual Symposium on Foundations of Computer Science*, IEEE 1977, 45-57.

[Pnueli 85]
A.Pnueli, "Linear and Branching Structures in the Semantics and Logics of Reactive Systems", in *ICALP'85*, LNCS 194, Springer-Verlag 1985, 15-32.

[Reggio 91]
G.Reggio, "Entities: an Institution for Dynamic Systems", in H.Ehrig, K.Jankte, F.Orejas and H.Reichel (eds) *Recent Trends in Data Type Specification*, LNCS 534, Springer-Verlag 1991, 244-265

[Sassone et al 93]
V.Sassone, M.Nielsen and G.Winskel , "A Classification of Models for Concurrency", in E.Best (ed) *CONCUR'93*, LNCS 715, Springer-Verlag 1993, 82-96.

[Sernadas et al 94]
A.Sernadas, J.F.Costa and C.Sernadas, "An Institution of Object Behaviour", in H.Ehrig and F.Orejas (eds) *Recent Trends in Data Type Specification*, LNCS 785, Springer-Verlag 1994.

[van Benthem 84]
J.van Benthem, "Correspondence Theory", in D.Gabbay and F.Guenthner (eds) *Handbook of Philosphical Logic* vol II, Reidel 1984, 167-247.

[Wolper 89]
P.Wolper, "On the Relation of Programs and Computations to Models of Temporal Logic", in B.Banieqbal, H.Barringer and A.Pnueli (eds) *Temporal Logic in Specification*, LNCS 398, Springer-Verlag 1989, 75-123.

An Algebraic Semantics for the Object Specification Language TROLL *light**

Martin Gogolla & Rudolf Herzig

Universität Bremen, FB Mathematik und Informatik
AG Datenbanksysteme, Postfach 330440, D-28334 Bremen, Germany
e-mail: gogolla@informatik.uni-bremen.de

Abstract. Within the KORSO project we have developed the object specification language TROLL *light* which allows to describe the part of the world to be modeled as a community of concurrently existing and communicating objects. Recently, we have worked out the basic notions of a pure algebraic semantics for our language. The main underlying idea is to present a transition system where the states represent the states of the specified information system, and state transitions are caused by the occurrence of finite sets of events. This semantics is formulated by representing states and state transitions as algebras. The various constructs of TROLL *light* are unified to general axioms restricting the possible interpretations for TROLL *light* object descriptions.

1 Introduction

The information system development process can be divided into two phases: The requirements and the design engineering phase. At the end of the requirements engineering phase, a first formal description of the system to be developed should be the "contract" for further development. Therefore, the task of delivering this first formal specification is of central concern.

One language designed for this task is the object description language TROLL *light* [CGH92, GCH93, HCG94], a dialect of OBLOG [SSE87] and TROLL [JSHS91]. Other recent object specification languages are ABEL [DO91], CMSL [Wie91], GLIDER [CJO94], MONDEL [BBE+90], OCS [AAR94], OS [Bre91], and Π [Gab93]. Our language TROLL *light* incorporates ideas from algebraic specification [EM85, EM90, Wir90], semantic data models [HK87, PM88], and process theory [Hoa85, Hen88, Mil89]. It is a language for describing static and dynamic properties of objects. This is achieved by offering language features to specify object structure as well as object behavior. The main advantage of following the object paradigm is the fact that all relevant information concerning one object can be found within one single unit and is not distributed over a variety of locations.

* Work reported here has been partially supported by the CEC under Grant No. 6112 (COMPASS).

We explain the essential characteristics of TROLL *light* by means of an example. This small example will be used throughout in order to explain all details of our approach. In Fig. 1 binary trees, where the nodes carry boolean information, are

```
TEMPLATE Node
  DATA TYPES   Bool;
  ATTRIBUTES   Content:bool;
  SUBOBJECTS   Left, Right:node;
  EVENTS       BIRTH create;
                     createLeft;
                     createRight;
                     update(Content:bool);
               DEATH destroy;
  VALUATION    [ create ] Content=true;
               [ update(B) ] Content=B;
  INTERACTION createLeft >> Left.create;
               createRight >> Right.create;
  BEHAVIOR     PROCESS Node =
                 ( create -> NodeLife );
               PROCESS NodeLife =
                 ( createLeft, createRight, update -> NodeLife |
                   { UNDEF(Left) AND UNDEF(Right) }
                     destroy -> Node );
END TEMPLATE
```

Fig. 1. TROLL *light* example template

specified as object types (or templates as object types are called in TROLL and TROLL *light*).

DATA TYPES: In TROLL *light* data types are employed for various purposes. Data types are assumed to be specified with a data type specification language. Their signature is made known in a template with the DATA TYPES section.

ATTRIBUTES: The Node template uses the data type Bool in order to define one attribute Content of data sort bool.

SUBOBJECTS: For templates (or object types) we employ the same naming convention as for data types. Template names are written capitalized, and each template (Node) induces a corresponding object sort written exactly as the template but with a starting lower case letter (node). A Node object is allowed to have two local subobjects, namely Left and Right, of sort node.

EVENTS: The things which can happen to Node objects are called events. Node objects can be created, their left and right subnodes can be created, they can be updated, and they can be destroyed.

VALUATION: Valuation rules serve to define the effect of events on attributes. They specify the value an attribute has after the occurrence of an event.

INTERACTION: Interaction rules are used to describe the synchronization of events. For instance, whenever the **createLeft** event occurs in the parent object, the **create** event must occur for the left subobject. New objects can only be created as subobjects of existing objects by this mechanism which is called birth event calling.

BEHAVIOR: Possible life cycles, i.e., sequences of allowed events, are specified in the behavior part. For a given template there is always a process with the same name which is the initial process for objects belonging to the template. An objects' life starts with a BIRTH event and possibly ends with a DEATH event, which in this case is only allowed to occur when there are no subobjects. In between, the events **createLeft**, **createRight**, and **update** can occur, but due to the interaction rule, for instance, **createLeft** can only occur if the called event **create** fits into the subobjects' life cycle.

Above, we have shown a simple example of a TROLL *light* template for introductory purposes. For more sophisticated applications, we have to refer to [CGH92, GCH93, HCG94, GHC+94]. There, you find for instance parameterized attributes and subobject symbols, complex attributes, and non-trivial event synchronization.

An attractive specification language on its own is not enough. It must be completed by specification tools. Therefore TROLL *light* comes along with a development environment offering special tools for verification and validation purposes. In order to support verification, the TROLL *light proof support system* solves verification tasks given by the user. It checks whether the desired properties are fulfilled by the specified TROLL *light* object descriptions. The TROLL *light animator* is designed to simulate the behavior of a specified object community. By this, the informal view of the real-world fragment to be modeled is validated against the current specification. Details of the development environment can be found in [GVH+94].

The remainder of this paper is organized as follows. In Sect. 2 we explain the basic ingredients of our approach to object specification, namely object signatures and models for such signatures. Section 3 introduces axioms in order to restrict the class of models for object signatures and explains how a standard model for TROLL *light* specifications is obtained. In Sect. 4 we shortly compare our approach with other proposals which appeared in recent literature. Section 5 closes the paper with some concluding remarks and mentions future work to be done.

2 Signatures and Models

Here, we introduce the main components of our approach. First, we introduce data signatures and data algebras. Second, signatures for object communities including attributes and events are proposed. These object signatures are reduced to conventional algebraic signatures. Doing this, we can afterwards define models, namely object communities, as special algebraic transition systems.

Definition 1. A **data signature** $D\Sigma = (DS, \Omega)$ consists of a set of data sorts DS and a family of sets of operation symbols $\Omega = \langle \Omega_{w,ds} \rangle_{w \in DS^*, ds \in DS}$. A **$D\Sigma$-model** $M_{D\Sigma}$, i.e., an algebra, is given by a family of sets $\langle M_{ds} \rangle_{ds \in DS}$ and a family of functions $\langle F_{w,ds} \rangle_{w \in DS^*, ds \in DS}$ such that for $\omega : ds_1 \times ... \times ds_n \rightarrow ds \in \Omega$ domain and range of ω_M are determined by $\omega_M : M_{ds_1} \times ... \times M_{ds_n} \rightarrow M_{ds}$. The category of all $D\Sigma$-models is denoted by $ALG_{D\Sigma}$. We assume one data signature $D\Sigma$ and one data algebra DA to be fixed.

Example 2 (Data signature and data algebra). The above TROLL *light* template uses the data type *Bool* with the following data signature.

data sorts bool
operations $false, true, bottom :\rightarrow bool$

The data algebra for this signature is the term algebra $T_{D\Sigma}$. As an alternative to completing signatures and algebras with bottom elements, we could use partial algebras. However, we want to be as close as possible to our implementation [HG94b] which allows bottom expressions, for instance, as user input representing information that is unknown.

Definition 3. Let a data signature $D\Sigma$ be given. An **object signature** $O\Sigma = (OS, A, E)$ over the data signature $D\Sigma$ consists of a set of object sorts OS, a family of sets of attribute symbols $A = \langle A_{os,w,s} \rangle_{os \in OS, w \in S^*, s \in S}$, and a family of sets of event symbols $E = \langle E_{os,w} \rangle_{os \in OS, w \in S^*}$, where S refers to the union of DS and OS, i.e., $S := DS \cup OS$.

Example 4 (Object signature). The above template did not mention the object sort for which the attributes and events of the template are defined. This is now done explicitly in the corresponding object signature. For the time being, we treat TROLL *light* subobject symbols like attribute symbols. The distinction between both will become clear later in Requirement 25 concerning the interpretation of subobject symbols.

object sorts	*node*
attributes	$left, right : node \rightarrow node$
	$content : node \rightarrow bool$
events	$create : node$
	$createLeft, createRight : node$
	$update : node \times bool$
	$destroy : node$

Definition 5. Let an object signature $O\Sigma$ be given. The **attribute signature** $A\Sigma$ induced by $O\Sigma$ consists of S, i.e., the union of data and object sorts, and the union of operation and attribute symbols, i.e., $A\Sigma = (DS \cup OS, \Omega \cup A)$.

As already proposed in [Gog89], attribute algebras belonging to attribute signatures are used to describe the states of a system. Thus a single algebra represents the system state in one instant of time.

Example 6 (Attribute signature and attribute algebra). The attribute signature for our running example has the following shape.

sorts *bool*, *node*
operations $false, true, bottom :\to bool$
$left, right : node \to node$
$content : node \to bool$

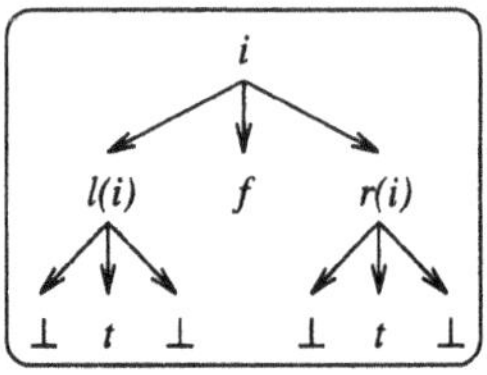

Fig. 2. Example of an attribute algebra $M_{A\Sigma}$

In Fig. 2 we graphically show one attribute algebra $M_{A\Sigma}$ whose data part is required to be isomorphic to the term algebra of the data signature, i.e., $U_{A\Sigma \to D\Sigma}(M_{A\Sigma}) = T_{D\Sigma}$[2]. The algebra $M_{A\Sigma}$ has three "proper" node objects $(i, l(i), r(i))$ and one special object representing undefined $(\bot)$. The functions in $M_{A\Sigma}$ are understood to be defined as described in the table in Fig. 3. In the graphical representation, left arrows represent the function $left_{M_{A\Sigma}}$, middle arrows the function $content_{M_{A\Sigma}}$, right arrows the function $right_{M_{A\Sigma}}$, and the undefined object $\bot$ is duplicated as it is needed.

$n \in M_{A\Sigma,node}$	$left_{M_{A\Sigma}}(n)$	$right_{M_{A\Sigma}}(n)$	$content_{M_{A\Sigma}}(n)$
i	$l(i)$	$r(i)$	$false$
$l(i)$	$\bot$	$\bot$	$true$
$r(i)$	$\bot$	$\bot$	$true$
$\bot$	$\bot$	$\bot$	$bottom$

Fig. 3. Definition of functions in $M_{A\Sigma}$

Definition 7. Let an object signature $O\Sigma$ be given. The **event signature** $E\Sigma$ induced by $O\Sigma$ consists of the attribute signature extended by one special sort symbol $\hat{e}$ for events and an appropriate family of event symbols $\hat{E}$, i.e., $E\Sigma = (DS \cup OS \cup \{\hat{e}\}, \Omega \cup A \cup \hat{E})$ with $\hat{E} = \langle \hat{E}_{os,w,\hat{e}} \rangle_{os \in OS, w \in S^*}$ and $\hat{E}_{os,w,\hat{e}} := E_{os,w}$.

Algebras of event signatures describe possible transitions caused by the set of events in the interpretation of sort $\hat{e}$.

Example 8 (Event signature and event algebra). For the running example the event signature given in Fig. 4 shows up.

[2] $U_{A\Sigma \to D\Sigma}$ denotes the forgetful functor from $A\Sigma$-algebras to $D\Sigma$-algebras.

sorts	*bool, node, ê*	
operations	*false, true, bottom* :→ *bool*	$(f, t, \bot)$
	left, right : *node* → *node*	(l, r)
	content : *node* → *bool*	(ct)
	create : *node* → *ê*	(c)
	createLeft, createRight : *node* → *ê*	(cL, cR)
	update : *node* × *bool* → *ê*	(u)
	destroy : *node* → *ê*	(d)

Fig. 4. Example of an event signature

In the following we abbreviate the operation names as indicated on the right hand side above. To give an example for an event algebra $M_{E\Sigma}$ we require that the attribute part of $M_{E\Sigma}$ is isomorphic to the attribute algebra from Example 6, i.e., $U_{E\Sigma\to A\Sigma}(M_{E\Sigma}) = M_{A\Sigma}$. This event algebra $M_{E\Sigma}$ is intended to be an algebra describing possible events occurring in the attribute algebra of Example 6.
The more interesting part of $M_{E\Sigma}$ is the interpretation of $\hat{e}$. Intuitively, this event algebra requires three events to happen, namely three updates for the "proper" objects or more formally $M_{\hat{e}} = \{u(i,t), u(l(i),f), u(r(i),f), \bot\}$. The operations are defined as follows: $u_{M_{E\Sigma}}(i,t) = u(i,t)$, $u_{M_{E\Sigma}}(l(i),f) = u(l(i),f)$, $u_{M_{E\Sigma}}(r(i),f) = u(r(i),f)$; all other applications of event symbols yield $\bot$. For instance, events which are in this situation not allowed in the life cycles (like $c(i)$) or events not changing an attribute (like $u(i,f)$) evaluate to bottom: $c_{M_{E\Sigma}}(i) = \bot$ and $u_{M_{E\Sigma}}(i,f) = \bot$. Thus, the exception value $\bot$ indicates that an event does not happen.
In this example (and in the ones to follow) we assume the events in the interpretation of $\hat{e}$ to be freely generated over an adequate attribute algebra. But this is not a general restriction.

The overall syntactic situation is depicted in Fig. 5. The signatures $D\Sigma$, $A\Sigma$, and $E\Sigma$ are all signatures in the classical sense. Thus, object signatures with event symbols have been reduced to classical signatures.
We now come to our central definition, namely the definition of a model for an object signature. Because in such models different objects co-exist and communicate with each other, we call such models object communities.

Definition 9. Let an object signature $O\Sigma$ over $D\Sigma$ together with the induced attribute signature $A\Sigma$ and event signature $E\Sigma$ be given. An $O\Sigma$**-model** $M_{O\Sigma}$, i.e., an **object community**, is given by a relation

$$M_{O\Sigma} \subseteq ALG_{A\Sigma} \times ALG_{E\Sigma} \times ALG_{A\Sigma}.$$

The data part of triples $\langle A_L, \hat{A}, A_R \rangle$ in $M_{O\Sigma}$ is required to coincide with the fixed data algebra DA, i.e., $U_{A\Sigma\to D\Sigma}(A_L) = U_{E\Sigma\to D\Sigma}(\hat{A}) = U_{A\Sigma\to D\Sigma}(A_R) = DA$.

Intuitively, triples $\langle A_L, \hat{A}, A_R \rangle$ in $M_{O\Sigma}$ express that there is a state transition from attribute algebra A_L to attribute algebra A_R via the occurrence of the

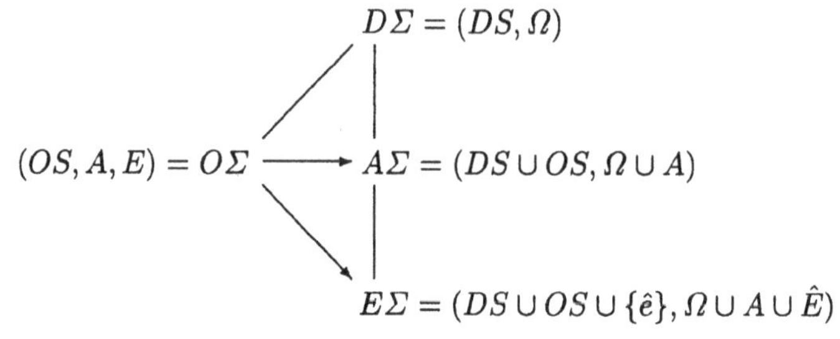

Fig. 5. Signatures for object communities

events in $\hat{A}$. Of course, triples $\langle A_L, \hat{A}, A_R \rangle$ in $M_{O\Sigma}$ can also be regarded as one algebra whose signature is the disjoint union of $A\Sigma$, $E\Sigma$, and $A\Sigma$.

Example 10 (Object community). In Fig. 6 we have sketched part of an object community for our running example. Each arrow stands for a triple $\langle A_L, \hat{A}, A_R \rangle$. Event algebras are depicted next to arrows by giving only the elements of $\hat{e}$ different from $\perp$. Let us explain some details a bit more. (1) The transition along $\{cR(i), c(r(i))\}$ stands for the event $cR(i)$ occurring in i and the create event $c(r(i))$ occurring in $r(i)$. (2) The transition along $\{d(l(i)), d(r(i))\}$ stands for the simultaneous occurrence of two delete events in the respective objects. Of course much more transitions than the depicted ones are possible.
A general remark on the usefulness of the algebraic properties of our approach might be in order here. In this example, we have decided that $cR(i)$ and $c(r(i))$ denote different elements in an event algebra. But our approach also allows to model the interaction rule more directly by giving an event algebra $M_{E\Sigma}$ for the transition where both $cR(i)$ and $c(r(i)$ evaluate to the same element, for instance to a quotient element: $cR_{M_{E\Sigma}}(i) = c_{M_{E\Sigma}}(r(i)) = \{cR(i), c(r(i))\}$. This reflects the fact that the occurrence of the two events is considered as an atomic unit from a conceptional point of view. It possible only by taking a general algebraic structure into consideration.
For the transition $\langle A_L, \hat{A}, A_R \rangle$ belonging to $\{u(i,t), u(l(i), f), u(r(i), f)\}$ it was the case that $U_{E\Sigma \to A\Sigma}(\hat{A}) = A_L$ was true. But in general, we cannot require that the $A\Sigma$-part of $\hat{A}$ coincides with A_L or A_R because in one transition some objects may vanish while others newly show up. Thus, it seems most likely that $\hat{A}$ includes all objects in A_L and A_R. Therefore, it makes sense to require that $\hat{A}_{node} = A_{L,node} \cup A_{R,node}$ holds. One can generalize this remark and could further restrict the definition of an object community $M_{O\Sigma}$ in the sense that $\hat{A}_{os} = A_{L,os} \cup A_{R,os}$ must be true for all triples in $M_{O\Sigma}$.

3 Algebraic Semantics of TROLL *light*

Our TROLL *light* example template does not mention all possibilities of the language. In general, templates show the structure given in Fig. 7.

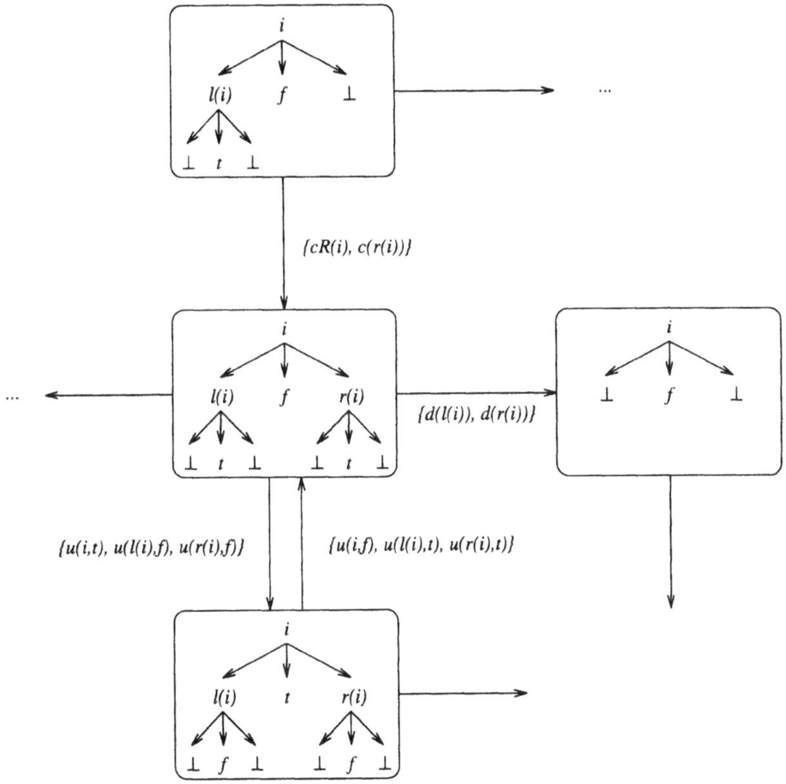

Fig. 6. Part of an example for a simple object community

```
TEMPLATE name of the template
  DATA TYPES    data types used in current template
  TEMPLATES     other templates used in current template
  ATTRIBUTES    slots for attributes
  SUBOBJECTS    slots for subobjects
  EVENTS        event generators
  CONSTRAINTS   restricting conditions on object states
  DERIVATION    rules for derived attributes
  VALUATION     effect of event occurrences on attributes
  INTERACTION   synchronization of events in different objects
  BEHAVIOR      description of object behavior by a CSP-like process
END TEMPLATE
```

Fig. 7. General structure of TROLL *light* templates

The TROLL *light* **ATTRIBUTES** and **SUBOBJECTS** determine the object signature and the TROLL *light* **EVENTS** the event signature. Thus, we have discussed the signature part, and that means we have finished the **DATA TYPES**, **TEMPLATES**, **ATTRIBUTES**, **SUBOBJECTS**, and **EVENTS** sections. We now consider the remaining sections corresponding to axioms over the object signature. For the following definitions let an object signature $O\Sigma$ and an object community $M_{O\Sigma}$ over $O\Sigma$ be given.

Definition 11. A **constraint** φ is a formula restricting the class of possible attribute algebras $ALG_{A\Sigma}$. A constraint is **valid** in $M_{O\Sigma}$ iff for all triples $\langle A_L, \hat{A}, A_R\rangle$ in $M_{O\Sigma}$ φ holds in A_L and A_R.
We do not require that φ holds in the intermediate algebra $U_{E\Sigma \to A\Sigma}(\hat{A})$. The details of the logic for the formulation of constraints — a variation of first-order predicate calculus tailored for information system purposes — can be found in [HG94a].

Example 12 (Constraint). As an example for our `Node` template consider the constraint that, if the subobjects exist, then the `Content` attribute values of the subobjects are not allowed to coincide.

```
(DEF(Left) AND DEF(Right)) => (Content(Left)<>Content(Right))
```

Definition 13. A **derivation rule** is of the form $\alpha = t_\alpha$ where α is an attribute and t_α is a term with the same sort as the attribute. A derivation rule is **valid** in $M_{O\Sigma}$ iff for all triples $\langle A_L, \hat{A}, A_R\rangle$ in $M_{O\Sigma}$ attribute α evaluates in A_L and A_R to the value of t_α.

Example 14 (Derivation rule). As an example for a `Node` template derivation rule consider an attribute `Count:nat` which should give for a node object the number of direct and indirect subobjects including the node object itself.

```
Count =
  ( IF DEF(Left)  THEN Count(Left)  ELSE 0 FI ) +
  ( IF DEF(Right) THEN Count(Right) ELSE 0 FI ) + 1
```

The above derivation rule is an example for a recursively defined derived attribute. Nevertheless, in this case the evaluation is well-defined because no cycles can be introduced with subobject relationships. But we will come to this point later in Example 26 after we have discussed the special interpretation of subobject symbols.

Definition 15. A **valuation rule** is of the form $\{\varphi\}[t_{\hat{e}}]\alpha = t_\alpha$, where φ is a formula, $t_{\hat{e}}$ is an event term, α is an attribute, and t_α is a term with the same sort as the attribute α. A valuation rule is **valid** in $M_{O\Sigma}$ iff for all triples $\langle A_L, \hat{A}, A_R\rangle$ in $M_{O\Sigma}$ the following is true: If the formula φ holds in A_L and the event $t_{\hat{e}}$ occurs in[3] $\hat{A}$, then the attribute α evalutes in A_R to the value which t_α had in A_L.

[3] We say an event e occurs in $\hat{A}$ if e evaluates to something different from $\perp$ in $\hat{A}$.

Example 16 (Valuation rule). Examples for valuation rules appeared in the introductory TROLL *light* template. For instance, the rule for the event `create` sets the `Content` attribute to `true`. Missing formulas φ are assumed to be *true*.

Definition 17. An **interaction rule** is of the form $\{\varphi\}\ t_{\hat{e}} >> t'_{\hat{e}}$ where φ is a formula, and $t_{\hat{e}}$ and $t'_{\hat{e}}$ are event terms. An interaction rule is **valid** in $M_{O\Sigma}$ iff for all triples $\langle A_L, \hat{A}, A_R\rangle$ in $M_{O\Sigma}$ the following holds: If φ is true in A_L and $t_{\hat{e}}$ occurs in $\hat{A}$, then $t'_{\hat{e}}$ must also occur in $\hat{A}$.

Example 18 (Interaction rule). Examples for interaction rules showed up in our running TROLL *light* example. For instance, the first interaction rule demanded, that whenever the `createLeft` event in the current object occurs, the `create` event must occur for the left subobject as well. Missing formulas φ are again assumed to be *true*.
The running example shows only interaction rules where birth events are involved. In principle, however, event calling between arbitrary events is possible.

A TROLL *light* object is always in one of a fixed set of process states. Therefore we have to extend for each template T the object signature by a special sort $processStateSort_T$ and a special attribute $processState_T : os_T \rightarrow processStateSort_T$ reflecting this current process state (os_T is the object sort induced by template T). Roughly speaking, the values this attribute can take are the process names mentioned in the template. Furthermore, the event symbols have to be splitted into *birth*, normal *life*, and *death* events according to the given TROLL *light* specification.

Definition 19. A **behavior definition** for a template T consists of a set of process definitions of the following form:
$\Pi_0 = (\{\varphi_1\}t_{\hat{e}_1} \rightarrow \Pi_1 \mid \{\varphi_2\}t_{\hat{e}_2} \rightarrow \Pi_2 \mid \ldots \mid \{\varphi_n\}t_{\hat{e}_n} \rightarrow \Pi_n)$
Here the Π_i's are process names, the φ_i's formulas, and the $t_{\hat{e}_i}$'s event terms. A behavior definition for template T is **valid** in $M_{O\Sigma}$ iff for all triples $\langle A_L, \hat{A}, A_R\rangle$ in $M_{O\Sigma}$ the following holds: If an event e of template T occurs in $\hat{A}$ for an object o of object sort os_T, then there is a process definition and an index j such that $t_{\hat{e}_j}$ evaluates in $\hat{A}$ to e, φ_j is true in A_L, $processState_T(o) = \Pi_0$ in A_L, and $processState_T(o) = \Pi_j$ in A_R. Furthermore, a birth event b for an object o is only allowed to occur in a transition $\langle A_L, \hat{A}, A_R\rangle$ if $o \notin A_L$, b occurs in $\hat{A}$, and $o \in A_R$ holds. A death event d for o is only allowed to occur if $o \in A_L$, d occurs in $\hat{A}$, $o \notin A_R$, and $o' \notin A_R$ holds for all subobjects[4] o' of o.

Example 20 (Behavior definition). The `BEHAVIOR` section of the running example required that a node's life starts with the `create` event. Afterwards `createLeft`, `createRight`, and `update` events follow as long as (in particular) interaction rules are obeyed. So, for example, a `createLeft` event is only allowed if the left subobject accepts the `create` event in its life cycle. The `destroy` event is only allowed to occur when there are no subobjects. Let us finally consider in Fig. 8 how the running example looks like if we present it in the syntax according to the previous definitions.

[4] The notion of subobject is made precise in Requirement 25.

$$
\begin{array}{ll}
\textit{valuation} & \{true\}\ [create(Self)]\ Content(Self) = true \\
 & \{true\}\ [update(Self, B)]\ Content(Self) = B \\
\textit{interaction} & \{true\}\ createLeft(Self)\ >>\ create(Left(Self)) \\
 & \{true\}\ createRight(Self)\ >>\ create(Right(Self)) \\
\textit{behavior} & Node = (\{true\}\ create(Self) \rightarrow NodeLife\ ) \\
 & NodeLife = (\ \{true\}\ createLeft(Self) \rightarrow NodeLife\ | \\
 & \qquad \{true\}\ createRight(Self) \rightarrow NodeLife\ | \\
 & \qquad \{true\}\ update(Self, B) \rightarrow NodeLife\ | \\
 & \qquad \{\neg Def(Left(Self)) \wedge \neg Def(Right(Self))\} \\
 & \qquad\ \ destroy(Self) \rightarrow Node\ )
\end{array}
$$

Fig. 8. TROLL *light* example in abstract syntax

The behavior part is graphically represented in Fig. 9. In order to refer to the current object which is to be defined we introduced the special constant *Self*. In the BEHAVIOR section, the concrete syntax of TROLL *light* is a little bit more general in allowing sequences of formulas and event terms separated by arrrows. However, by employing more process names, all TROLL *light* behavior patterns can be brought into the above form.

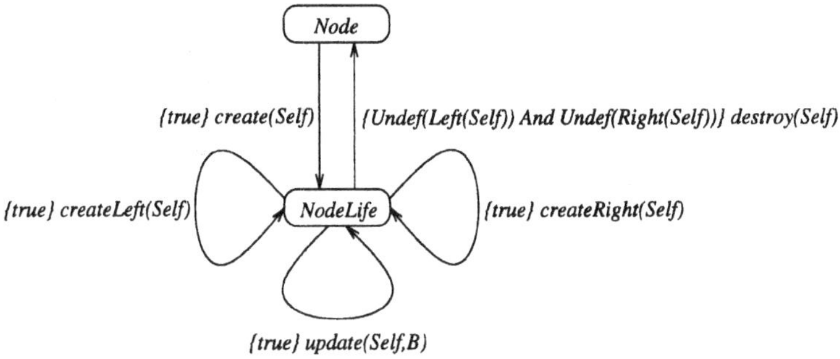

Fig. 9. Graphical representation of object behavior

In Fig. 10 we review the ingredients of the axioms and show their effect on object communities: Constraints and derivation rules have influence on A_L and A_R, interaction rules touch A_L and $\hat{A}$, and valuation rules and behavior definitions concern A_L, $\hat{A}$, and A_R. The above five kinds of axioms restricting object communities are special for TROLL *light* because at the beginning of the project we regarded these forms as a compromise between expresiveness and feasibility of implementation. Of course, many other choices are possible.

We now come to an important point with regard to the semantics of TROLL *light*, namely the distinction between attribute and subobject symbols which syntactically look the same. The main point is that subobject symbols are used to generate object identities. For a given collection of TROLL *light* templates, one template must be chosen as the schema template. Furthermore,

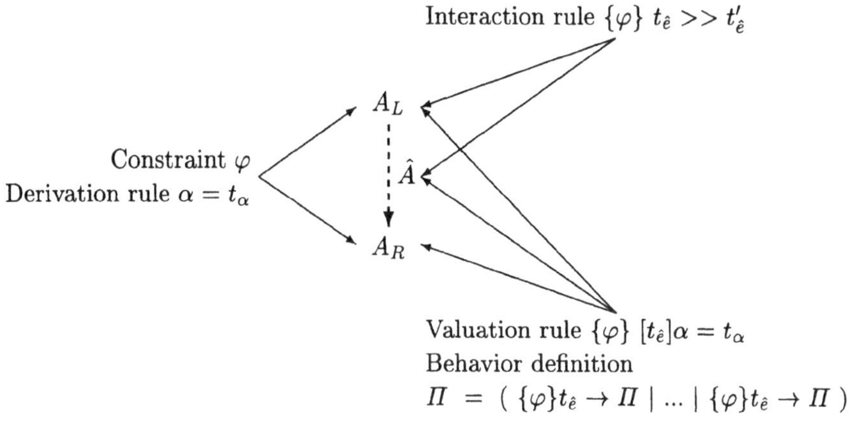

Fig. 10. Overview on axioms and their effect on object communities

there is one schema object belonging to the schema template which exists per se. All other objects are generated by finite birth event calling as direct or indirect subobjects of this schema object. This means that in each state only a finite number of objects can exist. Speaking in more technical terms, this is realized as follows.

Definition 21. Let a TROLL *light* specification and its induced object signature $O\Sigma$ and attribute signature $A\Sigma$ be given. The subset of the attribute symbols corresponding to the TROLL *light* subobject symbols is called the **subobject signature** $S\Sigma$.

Example 22 (Subobject signature). In our running example, the two symbols $left$ and $right$ constitute the subobject signature.

Definition 23. Let a subobject signature $S\Sigma$ and one distinguished schema template be given. The **object identities** are given by the term algebra generated by the subobject signature and by one distinguished constant i denoting the schema object and belonging to the object sort induced by the schema template: $T_{S\Sigma}(i)$. The notation i stands for "initially[5] existing object".

Example 24 (Object identities). In our running example we have the following object identities: $\{\ i,\ left(i),\ right(i),\ left(left(i)),\ right(left(i)),\ ...\ \}$.

Requirement 25 (Interpretation of object sorts and $\hat{e}$). The construction for object identities has severe consequences for TROLL *light* object communities. It restricts the interpretation for object sorts in the following way. If we have a triple $\langle A_L, \hat{A}, A_R\rangle$ in $M_{O\Sigma}$, then[6] $A_{L,os}, A_{R,os} \subseteq_{finite} T_{S\Sigma,os}(i)^{\perp}$ for $os \in OS$

[5] Initially is not meant in the category theory sense of the word.
[6] If X is a set, then $X^{\perp}$ stands for $X \cup \{\perp\}$.

and $\hat{A}_s \subseteq_{finite} T_{E\Sigma,s}(i)^{\perp}$ for $s \in OS \cup \{\hat{e}\}$. Thus, in each state there is only a finite number of objects, and each transition is caused by a finite number of events. Moreover, the interpretation of subobject symbols as attributes in A_L, $\hat{A}$, and A_R must coincide with the interpretation in $T_{S\Sigma,os}(i)$ resp. $T_{E\Sigma,s}(i)$ except for the special treatment of $\perp$. Additionally, all objects in A_L, $\hat{A}$, and A_R must be reachable from i via subobject connections. In consequence, the objects build a strict subobject hierarchy with i at its top. These requirements are already fulfilled, for instance, in the attribute algebra described in Example 6 and in the event algebra mentioned in Example 8.

Example 26 (Definedness of attribute `Count`*).* We now can explain why the attribute `Count` in Example 14 is well-defined: The `Node` objects in our running example build a strict hierarchy. Therefore, every `Count` computation terminates after a finite number of recursively triggered `Count` computations.

Requirement 27 (One event per object). In order to make things easier for the implementation of the TROLL *light* animator [HG94b] we have required that at most one event can occur in one object during one transition. But this is not a general requirement one has to make.

Requirement 28 (Frame rule). In the semantics of TROLL *light* we have also an implicit frame rule concerning the valuation rules: If we have a transition $\langle A_L, \hat{A}, A_R\rangle$ in $M_{O\Sigma}$, then changes of attribute values are implied by valuation rules triggered by events occurring in $\hat{A}$, and there are no other changes of attribute values. More formally, we require for $\langle A_L, \hat{A}, A_R\rangle$ in $M_{O\Sigma}$ the following to be true[7].

$$[\![\alpha(x)]\!]_{A_R} = \begin{cases} [\![t_\alpha]\!]_{A_L} & \text{if there is a valuation rule } \{\varphi\}[t_{\hat{e}}]\alpha = t_\alpha \text{ such} \\ & \text{that } \varphi \text{ holds in } A_L \text{ and } t_{\hat{e}} \text{ occurs in } \hat{A} \\ [\![\alpha(x)]\!]_{A_L} & \text{otherwise} \end{cases}$$

TROLL *light* does not have a loose semantics in the sense that a specification is associated with a class of models, but the semantics of a TROLL *light* text is one distinguished object community.

Definition 29. Let an object signature $O\Sigma$, and sets of constraints, valuation, derivation, interaction rules, and behavior definitions, i.e., a TROLL *light* specification, be given. The **specified object community** is the minimal[8] object community which (1) satisfies the given axioms, (2) obeys the Requirements 25, 27, and 28, and (3) is generated by (3.a) starting in an empty attribute algebra and performing a birth event for the schema object i and by (3.b) successively generating all other attribute algebras by performing all possible finite sets of events.

[7] The notation $[\![t]\!]_A$ stands for the value of t in the algebra A.

[8] Minimal is meant in the sense of set theory. We have worked out a notion of object community morphism, and our semantics for TROLL *light* is an initial semantics in an appropriate category. These details, however, are beyond the scope of this paper.

In general, the model class associated with a TROLL *light* specification may be empty. This is because we allow (some variant of) first-order predicate logic to be used for constraints, pre-conditions in behavior patterns, etc. Therefore it is possible to specify contradictions.

Example 30 (Semantics of the running TROLL light example). The previously explained object community in Example 10 was already the object community which we associate with our running example.

4 Relation to Other Approaches

Due to space limitations, a detailed comparison between our and other approaches is beyond the scope of this paper. We can only briefly comment on existing work. Our proposal is along the informal line presented in [EO94]. There, a four-level proposal for dynamic abstract data type is presented. Their level one (value type specification) corresponds to our data signatures and data algebras, their level two (instant structure specification) to our attribute signatures and attribute algebras, and their level three (dynamic operations specification) to our event signatures and event algebras. Their level four (higher level dynamic specification) would correspond to parametrized object signatures and specifications.

Another recent proposal combining algebraic specifications and object-oriented ideas can be found in [AZ94]. But, in contrast to [AZ94] we do not have events returning values. Instead, we have the possiblity of querying the system states in an SQL-like style [HG94a]. A predecessor of [AZ94] was the entity algebra approach introduced in [Reg91].

Algebraic specifications with implicit state are proposed in [DG94]. Their extension of PLUSS looks very close to TROLL *light*. There are also proposals around to embed object-oriented ideas into conventional algebraic specifications, for instance [GM87, Bre91, GD94]. Another line of research are extensions of the Berlin module approach [EW85] into the direction of object-oriented programming [GR91, PPP94] concentrating on the relationship between algebraic data types and classes in the sense of object-oriented programming. In [Rei94] a semantics for objects is given in terms of pure category theory. Close to our approach are also the transformation rule approach [BHK84] and the evolving algebras [Gur88] and their applications [GKS91]. Last but not least, within the IS-CORE working group a plenty of logic-based approaches like [FM92, SSC92, EDS93] are around. In contrast to them, we here put emphasis on pure model-theoretic aspects.

5 Conclusion and Future Work

We shortly introduced the specification language TROLL *light* and mentioned its development environment. We have pointed out a standard semantics for

TROLL *light* in pure algebraic terms obtaining a relative simple model for an object community.

We hope, this simplicity may open research directions for other important issues like parametrization, modularization, or implementation of object communities. In particular, we want to study the relation of our approach to the level four (higher level dynamic specification) of the informal proposal made in [EO94]. Another exciting question is what other types of axioms are helpful in specifying structure and behavior of object communities.

Acknowledgements

The authors have benefitted from comments of the referees and various COMPASS people. TROLL *light* was developed in cooperation with (former) Braunschweig collegues.

References

[AAR94] R. Achuthan, V.S. Alagar, and T. Radhakrishnan. An Object-Oriented Framework for Specifying Reactive Systems. In V.S. Alagar and R. Missaoui, editors, *Proc. Colloquium on Object Orientation in Databases and Software Engineering (COODBSE'94)*, pages 18–30. Université du Quebéc à Montréal, 1994.

[AZ94] E. Astesiano and E. Zucca. D-Oids: A Model for Dynamic Data-Types. *Mathematical Structures in Computer Science*, 1994.

[BBE+90] G. v. Bochmann, M. Barbeau, M. Erradi, L. Lecomte, P. Mondain-Monval, and N. Williams. Mondel: An Object-Oriented Specification Language. Département d'Informatique et de Recherche Opérationnelle, Publication 748, Université de Montréal, 1990.

[BHK84] J.A. Bergstra, J. Heering, and J.W. Klop. Object-Oriented Algebraic Specification: Proposal for a Notation and 12 Examples. Technical Report CS-R8411, CWI, Department of Computer Science, Amsterdam, 1984.

[Bre91] R. Breu. *Algebraic Specification Techniques in Object Oriented Programming Environments.* Springer, Berlin, LNCS 562, 1991.

[CGH92] S. Conrad, M. Gogolla, and R. Herzig. TROLL *light*: A Core Language for Specifying Objects. Informatik-Bericht 92-02, TU Braunschweig, 1992.

[CJO94] S. Clerici, R. Jimenez, and F. Orejas. Semantic Constructions in the Specification Language GLIDER. In H. Ehrig and F. Orejas, editors, *Recent Trends in Data Type Specification (WADT'92)*, pages 144–157. Springer, Berlin, LNCS 785, 1994.

[DG94] P. Dauchy and M.-C. Gaudel. Algebraic Specifications with Implicit State. Technical Report 887, Université de Paris-Sud, 1994.

[DO91] O.-J. Dahl and O. Owe. Formal Development with ABEL. Technical Report 159, University of Oslo, 1991.

[EDS93] H.-D. Ehrich, G. Denker, and A. Sernadas. Constructing Systems as Object Communities. In M.-C. Gaudel and J.-P. Jouannaud, editors, *Proc. Theory and Practice of Software Development (TAPSOFT'93)*, pages 453–467. Springer, Berlin, LNCS 668, 1993.

[EM85] H. Ehrig and B. Mahr. *Fundamentals of Algebraic Specification 1: Equations and Initial Semantics.* Springer, Berlin, 1985.

[EM90] H. Ehrig and B. Mahr. *Fundamentals of Algebraic Specification 2: Modules and Constraints.* Springer, Berlin, 1990.

[EO94] H. Ehrig and F. Orejas. Dynamic Abstract Data Types: An Informal Proposal. *EATCS Bulletin*, 53:162–169, 1994.

[EW85] H. Ehrig and H. Weber. Algebraic Specification of Modules. In E.J. Neuhold and G. Chroust, editors, *Formal Models in Programming – Proc. of the IFIP TC2 Working Conf. on the Role of Abstract Models in Information Processing*, pages 231–258. North-Holland, Amsterdam, 1985.

[FM92] J. Fiadeiro and T. Maibaum. Temporal Theories as Modularisation Units for Concurrent System Specification. *Formal Aspects of Computing*, 4(3):239–272, 1992.

[Gab93] P. Gabriel. The Object-Based Specification Language *Π*: Concepts, Syntax, and Semantics. In M. Bidoit and C. Choppy, editors, *Recent Trends in Data Type Specification (WADT'91)*, pages 254–270. Springer, LNCS 655, 1993.

[GCH93] M. Gogolla, S. Conrad, and R. Herzig. Sketching Concepts and Computational Model of TROLL *light*. In A. Miola, editor, *Proc. 3rd Int. Conf. Design and Implementation of Symbolic Computation Systems (DISCO'93)*, pages 17–32. Springer, Berlin, LNCS 722, 1993.

[GD94] J.A. Goguen and R. Diaconescu. Towards an Algebraic Semantics for the Object Paradigm. In H. Ehrig and F. Orejas, editors, *Recent Trends in Data Type Specification (WADT'92)*, pages 1–29. Springer, LNCS 785, 1994.

[GHC+94] M. Gogolla, R. Herzig, S. Conrad, G. Denker, and N. Vlachantonis. Integrating the ER Approach in an OO Environment. In R. Elmasri, V. Kouramajian, and B. Thalheim, editors, *Proc. 12th Int. Conf. on the Entity-Relationship Approach (ER'93)*, pages 376–389. Springer, Berlin, LNCS 823, 1994.

[GKS91] G. Gottlob, G. Kappel, and M. Schrefl. Semantics of Object-Oriented Data Models – The Evolving Algebra Approach. In J.W. Schmidt and A.A. Stogny, editors, *Proc. 1st Int. East-West Database Workshop*, pages 144–160. Springer, Berlin, LNCS 504, 1991.

[GM87] J.A. Goguen and J. Meseguer. Unifying Functional, Object-Oriented and Relational Programming with Logical Semantics. In B. Shriver and P. Wegner, editors, *Research Directions in Object-Oriented Programming*, pages 417–477. MIT Press, 1987.

[Gog89] M. Gogolla. Algebraization and Integrity Constraints for an Extended Entity-Relationship Approach. In J. Diaz and F. Orejas, editors, *Proc. Theory and Practice of Software Development (TAPSOFT'89)*, pages 259–274. Springer, Berlin, LNCS 351, 1989.

[GR91] M. Grosse-Rhode. Towards Object-Oriented Algebraic Specifications. In H. Ehrig, K.P. Jantke, F. Orejas, and H. Reichel, editors, *Recent Trends in Data Type Specification (WADT'90)*, pages 98–116. Springer, Berlin, LNCS 534, 1991.

[Gur88] Y. Gurevich. Logic and the Challenge of Computer Science. In E. Börger, editor, *Trends in Theoretical Computer Science*, pages 1–57. Computer Science Press, Rockville (MD), 1988.

[GVH+94] M. Gogolla, N. Vlachantonis, R. Herzig, G. Denker, S. Conrad, and H.-D. Ehrich. The KORSO Approach to the Development of Reliable Information Systems. Technical Report 94-06, TU Braunschweig, 1994.

[HCG94] R. Herzig, S. Conrad, and M. Gogolla. Compositional Description of Object Communities with TROLL *light*. In C. Chrisment, editor, *Proc. Basque Int. Workshop on Information Technology (BIWIT'94)*, pages 183–194. Cépaduès-Éditions, Toulouse, 1994.

[Hen88] M. Hennessy. *Algebraic Theory of Processes*. MIT Press, Cambridge (MA), 1988.

[HG94a] R. Herzig and M. Gogolla. A SQL-like Query Calculus for Object-Oriented Database Systems. In E. Bertino and S. Urban, editors, *Proc. Int. Symp. on Object-Oriented Methodologies and Systems (ISOOMS'94)*, pages 20–39. Springer, Berlin, LNCS 858, 1994.

[HG94b] R. Herzig and M. Gogolla. An Animator for the Object Specification Language TROLL *light*. In V.S. Alagar and R. Missaoui, editors, *Proc. Colloquium on Object Orientation in Databases and Software Engineering (COODBSE'94)*, pages 4–17. Université du Quebéc à Montréal, 1994.

[HK87] R. Hull and R. King. Semantic Database Modelling: Survey, Applications, and Research Issues. *ACM Computing Surveys*, 19(3):201–260, 1987.

[Hoa85] C.A.R. Hoare. *Communicating Sequential Processes*. Prentice-Hall, Englewood Cliffs (NJ), 1985.

[JSHS91] R. Jungclaus, G. Saake, T. Hartmann, and C. Sernadas. Object-Oriented Specification of Information Systems: The TROLL Language. Informatik-Bericht 91–04, Technische Universität Braunschweig, 1991.

[Mil89] R. Milner. *Communication and Concurrency*. Prentice-Hall, Englewood Cliffs (NJ), 1989.

[PM88] J. Peckham and F. Maryanski. Semantic Data Models. *ACM Computing Surveys*, 20(3):153–189, 1988.

[PPP94] F. Parisi-Presicce and A. Pierantonio. Structured Inheritance for Algebraic Class Specifications. In H. Ehrig and F. Orejas, editors, *Recent Trends in Data Type Specification (WADT'92)*, pages 295–309. Springer, Berlin, LNCS 785, 1994.

[Reg91] G. Reggio. Entities: An Institution for Dynamic Systems. In H. Ehrig, K.P. Jantke, F. Orejas, and H. Reichel, editors, *Recent Trends in Data Type Specification (WADT'90)*, pages 246–265. Springer, LNCS 534, 1991.

[Rei94] H. Reichel. An Approach to Object Semantics Based on Terminal Co-Algebras. *Mathematical Structures in Computer Science*, 1994.

[SSC92] A. Sernadas, C. Sernadas, and J.F. Costa. Object Specification Logic. Internal Report, INESC, University of Lisbon, 1992. To appear in Journal of Logic and Computation.

[SSE87] A. Sernadas, C. Sernadas, and H.-D. Ehrich. Object-Oriented Specification of Databases: An Algebraic Approach. In P.M. Stocker and W. Kent, editors, *Proc. 13th Int. Conf. on Very Large Data Bases (VLDB'87)*, pages 107–116. Morgan-Kaufmann, Palo Alto, 1987.

[Wie91] R. Wieringa. Equational Specification of Dynamic Objects. In R.A. Meersman, W. Kent, and S. Khosla, editors, *Object-Oriented Databases: Analysis, Design & Construction (DS-4), Proc. IFIP WG 2.6 Working Conference, Windermere (UK) 1990*, pages 415–438. North-Holland, 1991.

[Wir90] M. Wirsing. Algebraic Specification. In J. Van Leeuwen, editor, *Handbook of Theoretical Computer Science, Vol. B*, pages 677–788. North-Holland, Amsterdam, 1990.

Defining Equations in Terminal Coalgebras *

Ulrich Hensel and Horst Reichel

Institut für Theoretische Informatik
Technische Universität Dresden
Mommsenstraße 13, D–01069 Dresden
Germany

Abstract. Defining equations on constructors of abstract data types (with initial semantics) are used to express that different combinations of constructors generate equal values. In this paper we will study the role of equations on the destructors of terminal coalgebras for the specification of behavior classes. It turns out that equations on the destructors may be used to constrain the behavior by defining subcoalgebras of terminal coalgebras. Defining equations on destructors may be used to formalize safety properties, i.e. properties that have to be invariant with respect to changes of states.

1 Introduction

In [Rei94] we suggested terminal coalgebras as a formal basis for the implementation independent specification of behavior classes. In this introduction we will shortly discuss the suitability of coalgebras which in our approach appear in addition to algebras within specifications. There are different approaches that use algebras to represent both states of dynamic systems and sets of values, see for instance [Gur91], [DG94], and [Ehr94].

We have got the feeling that in algebraic specifications always both algebras and coalgebras are around. To make this clear we recall that for an endofunctor

$$T : Set \to Set$$

a T–algebra $A = (A; \alpha : T(A) \to A)$ is given by a carrier set A (we hope that we do not cause confusion if we denote the algebra and its carrier by the same letter) and by a mapping $\alpha : T(A) \to A$ representing all defining operations. Dually a T–coalgebra $B = (B; \beta : B \to T(B))$ is given by a carrier set again but by a mapping $\beta : B \to T(B)$.

Let us consider the endofunctor

$$T_P : Set \to Set$$

defined by

$$\begin{array}{rll} T_P(M) = 1 + P \times M & \text{for each set } M, \\ T_P(f) = id_1 + id_P \times f & \text{for each mapping } f : A \to B \end{array} \qquad (1)$$

* This work has been partially supported by ESPRIT - BRA WG n. 6112 COMPASS.

where P is an arbitrary but fixed set and $1 = \{()\}$ denotes the one–element set consisting of the zero–tuple $()$.

A T_P–algebra $(A; \alpha : T_P(A) \to A)$ is given by one constant operation $\alpha_0 :\to A$ and by a heterogeneous operation $\alpha_1 : P \times A \to A$ whereas a T_P-coalgebra $(B; \beta : B \to T_P(B))$ is given by one partial mapping $\beta_0 : B \overset{par}{\to} 1$ and by another partial mapping $\beta_1 : B \overset{par}{\to} P \times B$ which corresponds to two partial mappings $\beta_{10} : B \overset{par}{\to} P$, $\beta_{11} : B \overset{par}{\to} B$. A T_P-coalgebra $(B; \beta : B \to T_P(B))$ may be interpreted as a possibly terminating automata with a state set B, where $b \in B$ is a terminal state iff $\beta_0(b) = ()$, with an output function $\beta_{10} : B \overset{par}{\to} P$ and with a state transition function $\beta_{11} : B \overset{par}{\to} B$.

The next point we want to recall is that a solution of the recursive type equation

$$M = 1 + P \times M \tag{2}$$

is any set M together with a bijection $\varphi : M \to 1 + P \times M$. Thus, any solution of the recursive type equation represents both a T_P-coalgebra $(M; \varphi : M \to 1 + P \times M)$ and a T_P-algebra $(M; \varphi^{-1} : 1 + P \times M \to M)$.

The recursive type equation above is an example which has more than one solution. Distinguished solutions one obtains if one takes the initial T_P–algebra on the one hand and the terminal T_P–coalgebra on the other hand. The initial algebra solution corresponds to the least solution and the terminal coalgebra solution corresponds to the greatest solution of the recursive type equation (2).

The initial algebra $L(P)$ is given by the set of all finite lists of elements of P with *nil* and *cons* as the two operations. The corresponding coalgebra view at $L(P)$ is given by the following mappings: $\beta_{0,L(P)}(l) = ()$ iff $l = nil$ for each $l \in L(P)$, $\beta_{10,L(P)}(cons(x,l)) = x$ and $\beta_{11,L(P)}(cons(x,l)) = l$ for each $x \in P$ and $l \in L(P)$.

The terminal coalgebra $B(P)$ is given by

$$B(P) = L(P) \cup \{f : Nat \to P\}$$

with $\beta_{0,B(P)}(l) = ()$ iff $l = nil$ for all $l \in B(P)$, $\beta_{10,B(P)}(cons(x,l)) = x$ and $\beta_{11,B(P)}(cons(x,l)) = l$ for each $x \in P$ and $l \in L(P)$ and $\beta_{10,B(P)}(f) = f(0)$ for each $f \in B(P)\backslash L(P)$, $\beta_{11,B(P)}(f) = f'$ with $f'(n) = f(n+1)$ for each $n \in Nat$ and each $f \in B(P)\backslash L(P)$. Thus, $B(P)$ consists of all automata functions of all T_P–automata , respectively T_P–coalgebras. The corresponding algebra view at $B(P)$ is given by *nil* as constant operation and *cons* for finite and infinite list, whereas the *cons*–operation in the terminology of T_P–automata corresponds to the *action prefixing* operation known from Milners CCS calculus.

The coalgebra view at initial algebras is strongly related to the representation of data types within the π–calculus , see [Mil93]. This calculus knows only processes and represents data types by means of processes. The coalgebra view at initial algebras opens a natural way for the representation of data types by processes.

In the previous example the coalgebra view at the initial algebra as well as the algebra view at the terminal coalgebra induce a unique homomorphic embedding of the least solution into the greatest solution of the recursive type equation. By a general result of Barr, see [Bar93], in the given case the greatest solution is the Cauchy completion of the least one.

By a slight modification of the previous example the least solution will no more generate the greatest solution by means of Cauchy completion. We take the endofunctor

$$T'_P : Set \to Set, \quad M \mapsto P \times M.$$

In this case the initial T'_P–algebra becomes empty and the terminal T'_P–coalgebra is given by all infinite streams of elements of P. This is an example where the initial algebra is of no interest but the terminal coalgebra is still an interesting construction.

By the examples above we want to illustrate that both views the *algebra view* and the *coalgebra view* are equally relevant within specifications.

We suggest to use within system specifications initial algebras to represent data types and terminal coalgebras to represent the behavior of processes and to describe the composition of behaviors. States of components of dynamic systems should be represented by elements of suitable terminal coalgebras. Thus, if the value aspect is dominating the initial algebra view is appropriate and if the state aspect is dominating the terminal coalgebra view is appropriate.

Since the algebra view at specifications is thoroughly investigated we concentrate in this paper on the coalgebra view and especially on the use of defining equations on destructors of terminal coalgebras.

2 Equational Specifications with Terminal Coalgebras

Before we discuss in detail the equational specification of behavior classes we will make more visible the relations between the used framework of T–algebras and T–coalgebras.

T–algebras are a slight modification of functorial representations of algebras as initiated by F.W. Lawvere in his famous paper *Functorial Semantics of Algebraic Theories*, see [Law63] or [Poi92]. In this approach an algebraic theory is represented by a category closed under finite products and algebras are finite product preserving functors from the theory into another category usually the category of sets. Homomorphisms are represented by natural transformations.

In the framework of T–algebras the defining operations, usually described by a signature, are unified to one defining operation by structuring the domain of the unique operation as a sum of finite products in the one–sorted case. In the many–sorted case we have for each sort the corresponding sum of products unifying all those operations into one which yields values of the corresponding sort.

This implies that each type $T : Set \to Set$ may be associated with a corresponding theory representing the weakest type theory needed to describe the domain construction of the unique defining operation. For algebraic structures with finitely many defining operations the weakest type theory needed presents finite products. An explicit description of that type theory is given in [Poi92] by the π–calculus.[2] The associated algebraic theory as category consist of all derived operations (terms) and all equations between derived operations. This theory is usually constructed in two steps. In the first step an algebraic theory is constructed which represents all the derived operations. By constructing a quotient category of the first one the defining equations are taken into account.

If we consider the type functor

$$T_P : Set \to Set, \quad M \mapsto 1 + P \times M,$$

then the associated algebraic theory is the weakest category with finite products and coproducts (sums) generated by two objects B, P and one morphism

$$op : 1 + P \times B \to B.$$

The T_P–algebras are then product and coproduct preserving functors from the associated algebraic theory into the category of sets with an arbitrary but fixed interpretation of the object P. The traditional two defining operations appear now as derived operations $in_l; op, in_r; op$ resulting from composing the canonic injections $in_l : 1 \to 1+P \times B$, $in_r : P \times B \to 1+P \times B$ with the unique defining operation $op : 1 + P \times B \to B$.

In a categorically dual approach the associated *coalgebraic theory* becomes the weakest category with finite products and coproducts generated by two objects B, P and one morphism

$$dop : B \to 1 + P \times B.$$

The morphisms of this category represent the *derived dual operations*, since in this example there are no defining equations.

This example makes visible a fist serious difference between algebraic theories and coalgebraic theories. Whereas the algebraic theory could also be given as the weakest category closed under finite products and generated by two objects B, P and two morphisms $nil : 1 \to B$, $cons : P \times B \to B$ in the associated coalgebraic theory both products and coproducts are necessary.

The dualization of traditional algebraic types, where the domain of the unique defining operation is a coproduct of finite products would lead to types of coalgebras where the codomain of the unique defining dual operation is a product of finite coproducts. Unfortunately this setting does not cover all intended applications. The example above for instance does not fit into that type of coalgebras.

Using terminal coalgebras for the specification of behavior classes leads to different calculi representing the associated coalgebraic theories. This means that not only one equational calculus can be developed for the equational specification of behavior classes.

If terminal coalgebras are used to describe the behavior of nondeterministic labeled transition systems an essential different equational calculus has to be developed. In that case the finitary power set type is used in the description of the codomain of the dual operation. This type would not be used within coalgebraic theories in case of behavior classes of deterministic processes.

[2] Note that this calculus shares only a common name with the π–calculus mentioned above.

2.1 An Example of a Coalgebraic Theory - the $C\Pi\Sigma$–calculus

In the following we present the $C\Pi\Sigma$– calculus which may be used to represent coalgebraic theories using products and coproducts. $C\Pi\Sigma$ is used as an acronym for ***categories with finite products and finite sums.*** This calculus will be given by means of deduction rules with can be used to derive

- objects (types) of the coalgebraic theory (as a category),
- morphisms (derived dual operations),
- equations.

The first group of derivation rules ensures that a *coalgebraic theory is at least a category*

$$\frac{A : obj}{id_A : A \to A}\ cat1$$

$$\frac{f : A \to C \quad g : C \to B}{f;g : A \to B}\ cat2$$

$$\frac{f : A \to B}{id_A; f = f}\ cat3$$

$$\frac{f : A \to B}{f = f; id_B}\ cat4$$

$$\frac{f : A \to B \quad g : B \to C \quad h : C \to D}{f;(g;h) = (f;g);h}\ cat5$$

The second group of derivation rules represents *equational deduction:*

$$\frac{f : A \to B}{f = f}\ eq1 \qquad \frac{f = g}{g = f}\ eq2 \qquad \frac{f = g \quad g = h}{f = h}\ eq3$$

$$\frac{f : A \to B \quad g : A \to B \quad h : B \to C \quad i : B \to C \quad f = g \quad h = i}{f;h = g;i}\ eq4$$

The next group of derivation rules, omitted here, makes a coalgebraic theory to a category with finite products and coproducts where $1 \in Obj$ denotes the empty product, $0 \in Obj$ denotes the empty coproduct, $!^A : A \to 1$, $?_A : 0 \to A$ denote the corresponding unique homomorphisms, and where $\langle f, g\rangle : C \to A \times B, \{f, g\} : A + B \to C$ denote the pairing and the case–construction respectively. We have not joint a rule that makes a coalgebraic theory to a distributive category, since distributivity will not be of importance for the following considerations.

A specific coalgebraic theory is the initial model defined by

1. all those objects,
2. all those morphisms, and
3. all those equations

that can be derived from some ***basic assumptions*** by means of the rules described above.

The example mainly used in this paper results from the following basic assumptions

$$\frac{}{B : obj}\ ass1 \quad \frac{}{P : obj}\ ass2 \quad \frac{}{dop : B \rightarrow 1 + (P \times B)}\ ass3$$

In this specific coalgebraic theory we call the object B in the domain of the defining dual operation *dop* the ***state object*** and the object P the ***parameter object***.

Since this specification does not contain any defining equations within the basic assumption, all equations that can be derived are ***structural equations***, which means, equations expressing general properties of the types and the derived operations within the coalgebraic theory. Structural equations do not express properties that are satisfied by some coalgebras and dissatisfied by the others.

To get closer to usual functional notation we introduce the following abbreviations:

$$\begin{aligned} f \times g &= (p_l^{AC}; f, p_r^{AC}; g) : A \times C \rightarrow B \times D \\ f + g &= \{f; in_l^{BD}, g; in_r^{BD}\} : A + C \rightarrow B + D \end{aligned} \tag{3}$$

where $f : A \rightarrow B$, $g : C \rightarrow D$.

With this notation we can give one example of a ***derived dual operation:***

$$dop; (id_1 + (id_P \times dop)) : B \rightarrow 1 + P \times (1 + P \times B))$$

representing the twofold application of the defining dual operation *dop*.

2.2 Validity of Equations

Let $T_{1+P\times B}$ denote the category representing the coalgebraic theory freely generated by the defining assumptions and the rule system of the previous section. A $T_{1+P\times B}$–model is then a product and coproduct preserving functor

$$M : T_{1+P\times B} \rightarrow Set.$$

Each $T_{1+P\times B}$–model M is up to natural isomorphism uniquely determined by the two sets $M(P)$, $M(B)$ and the defining dual operation $M(dop) : M(B) \rightarrow \{()\} + M(P) \times M(B)$.

The notion of a $T_{1+P\times B}$–model differs from the notion of a T_P–coalgebra as used above in so far as the interpretation of P is fixed for T_P–coalgebras and it is not constraint for $T_{1+P\times B}$–models. But each T_P-coalgebra is also a $T_{1+P\times B}$–model and vice versa with varying interpretation of P.

A homomorphism between $T_{1+P\times B}$–models is a natural transformation between the corresponding functors which means that

$$\varphi : M_1 \to M_2$$

is given by two mappings

$$\varphi_P : M_1(P) \to M_2(P),\ \varphi_B : M_1(B) \to M_2(B)$$

such that for each $b \in M_1(B)$ the equation

$$(id_1 + \varphi_P \times \varphi_B)(M_1(dop)(b)) = M_2(dop)(\varphi_B(b))$$

holds. Homomorphisms between T_P–coalgebras result from $T_{1+P\times B}$–homomorphisms by fixing $\varphi_P = id_P$ for the fixed interpretation P of the object $P \in T_{1+P\times B}$ (where we used the same symbol for the interpretation of the object and the object). Thus, for each $T_{1+P\times B}$–model M we can determine a homomorphism φ^M which is given by the unique homomorphism φ^M_B from the T_P–coalgebra $(M(B), M(dop))$ to the terminal T_P–coalgebra and by $\varphi^M_P = id_P$.

Fixing the interpretation of some parts of an algebraic or a coalgebraic theory in the way described above is a rather ad hoc approach. A more systematic approach results if one describes the constraints for the semantic interpretation within the theory itself. We will illustrate this way by constraining the interpretation of the sort P within $T_{1+P\times B}$ to natural numbers. This can be done by adding the following rules:

$$\frac{}{zero : 1 \to P}\ nat1 \qquad \frac{}{succ : P \to P}\ nat2$$

$$\frac{f : 1 \to A \quad g : A \to A}{ind_{f,g} : P \to A}\ nat3$$

$$\frac{f : 1 \to A \quad g : A \to A}{zero; ind_{f,g} = f}\ nat4 \qquad \frac{f : 1 \to A \quad g : A \to A}{succ; ind_{f,g} = ind_{f,g}; g}\ nat5$$

$$\frac{h : P \to A \quad zero; h = f \quad succ; h = h; g}{h = ind_{f,g}}\ nat6$$

If $T_{1+Nat\times B}$ denotes the coalgebraic theory which is freely generated by the basic assumptions, then a $T_{1+Nat\times B}$–model M is uniquely determined by the interpretations $M(B)$, $M(dop)$, since up to isomorphism $M(P)$ becomes the set of natural numbers.

A practically more interesting system of basic assumption would result if the rules [$nat3$], ..., [$nat6$] would be replaced by the following rules

$$\frac{f : C \times 1 \to A \quad g : A \to A}{ind_{f,g} : C \times P \to A}\ nat3$$

$$\frac{f : C \times 1 \to A \quad g : A \to A}{(id_C \times zero); ind_{f,g} = f}\ nat4 \qquad \frac{f : C \times 1 \to A \quad g : A \to A}{(id_C \times succ); ind_{f,g} = ind_{f,g}; g}\ nat5$$

$$\frac{h : C \times P \to A \quad (id_C \times zero); h = f \quad (id_C \times succ); h = h; g}{h = ind_{f,g}} \; nat6$$

since the previous system does for instance not allow to define inductively the addition of natural numbers.

In this way we are not able to describe each fixed semantic interpretation $M(P)$ of P but all those ones where $M(P)$ can be specified as an initial algebra. For all applications this is sufficient.

Definition 1. Let T denote any coalgebraic theory.

1. An equation is a pair of morphisms t_1, t_2 in T with common domain and codomain, written
$$t_1 =_{A,B} t_2,$$
if $t_1, t_2 : A \to B$.
2. An equation $t_1 =_{A,B} t_2$ is valid in a model $M : T \to Set$ written
$$M \models t_1 =_{A,B} t_2,$$
if $M(t_1) = M(t_2)$.
3. An equation $t_1 =_{A,B} t_2$ is behaviorally valid in a model $M : T \to Set$, written
$$M \models_{beh} t_1 =_{A,B} t_2$$
if
$$\varphi_B^M(M(t_1)(x)) = \varphi_B^M(M(t_2)(x))$$
for each $x \in M(A)$ holds, where $\varphi^M : M \to Ter_M$ denotes the homomorphism which is generated by the unique coalgebra–homomorphism from M considered as a T–coalgebra to the corresponding terminal T–coalgebra.

If one wants to constrain the behavior of automatas by using defining equations it suffices to take only equations into account which domain equals to a state object. We call this type of equations *state equations*.

The following example should illustrate how the validity of equations can distinguish different behaviors. Let us consider the coalgebraic theory $T_{1+Nat \times B}$ and the state equation

$$dop; (! + p_1^{NatB}; dop); (! + (! + p_1^{NatB})) =_{B,1+(1+B)} in_r^{1B}; in_r^{1(1+B)} \tag{4}$$

which is clarified by the following diagram:

$$\begin{array}{ccccc}
B & \xrightarrow{dop} & 1 + Nat \times B & \xrightarrow{(! + p_1^{NatB}; dop)} & 1 + (1 + Nat \times B) \\
{\scriptstyle in_r^{1B}} \downarrow & & & & \downarrow {\scriptstyle (! + (! + p_1^{NatB}))} \\
1 + B & & \xrightarrow[in_r^{1(1+B)}]{} & & 1 + (1 + B)
\end{array}$$

In more conventional notation this equation says

$$dop_B(dop_B(b)) = b$$

where $dop_B : B \rightarrow B$ denotes the state component of the defining dual operation.

In contrast to structural equation now there are both models satisfying and models dissatisfying equation (4).

For instance, the $T_{1+Nat\times B}$–model M_1 with $M_1(Nat) = \mathbb{N}$, $M_1(B) = \mathbb{N}$, and $[M_1(dop)](n) = (n, n+1)$ does obviously not satisfy the equation (4), however, M_2 with $M_2(Nat) = \mathbb{N}$, $M_2(B) = \{0, 1\}$ and

$$[M_2(dop)](x) = \begin{cases} (0,1) & : \quad x = 0 \\ (1,0) & : \quad x = 1 \end{cases}$$

does.

In the $T_{1+Nat\times B}$–model M_3 with $M_3(Nat) = \mathbb{N}$, $M_3(B) = \mathbb{N}$ and with $[M_3(dop)](n) = (mod2(n), n+1)$ for all $n \in \mathbb{N}$ the equation (4) is not valid, however, it is behaviorally valid since the map $\varphi^{M_3}_{1+(1+B)}$ is uniquely determined by $\varphi^{M_3}_B$ and $\varphi^{M_3}_B((succ; succ)(x))$ maps to the same automata function as $\varphi^{M_3}_B(x)$.

The simple cyclic property of equation (4) can not be satisfied by any process that may terminate. In case of termination there would be a state send to the unique element of 1 by the defining dual operation. This state is a counterexample for the required cyclic property.

Finally we discuss for reasons of illustration the case of deterministic sequential automata with fixed input and output alphabet. Let us consider the case where both the input and the output alphabet is given by the set of natural numbers. The corresponding coalgebraic theory is freely generated by a rule system specifying categories with finite products and with a natural number object and by the following basic assumptions:

$$\frac{}{P : obj}\ aut1 \qquad \frac{}{B : obj}\ aut2$$

$$\frac{}{out : B \rightarrow P}\ aut3 \qquad \frac{x : 1 \rightarrow P}{next_x : B \rightarrow B}\ aut4$$

If T_{Aut} denotes the coalgebraic theory freely generated by the described rule set, T_{Aut}–models are finite product preserving functors $M : T_{Aut} \rightarrow Set$ that map the object P up to isomorphism onto the set of natural numbers $\mathbb{N}$. Thus, each T_{Aut}–model is uniquely determined by $M(B), M(out) : M(B) \rightarrow \mathbb{N}$, and $M(next_x) : M(B) \rightarrow M(B)$ for each $x \in \mathbb{N} = M(P)$.

If one introduces a further object P' and a further rule set which specifies initially another data type, then one obtains deterministic sequential automata with different input and output alphabet provided the rule [aut3] is modified to

$$\frac{}{out : B \rightarrow P'}\ aut3'.$$

In this case there is no difference between the concepts of an algebraic theory and a coalgebraic theory because all operations (or dual operations) are unary.

Since there are countably many defining dual operations we would need infinite products to unify these dual operations into a single one (or we would need an infinite coproduct to unify all these operations into a single one). By means of rule [*aut*4] we are able to avoid infinite products.

Let $\mathbf{E}$ denote a set of equations within a coalgebraic theory T. Then

$$Mod(T, \mathbf{E})$$

denotes the class of all T–models that satisfy each equation out of $\mathbf{E}$ and

$$Mod_{beh}(T, \mathbf{E})$$

denotes the class of all T–models that behaviorally satisfy each equation out of $\mathbf{E}$.

Theorem 2. *If there exists a terminal T–model and $\boldsymbol{E}$ is a set of state equations, then there are terminal objects in both categories $Mod(T, \boldsymbol{E})$ and $Mod_{beh}(T, \boldsymbol{E})$ and these terminal objects coincide.*

Proof of theorem. Let Ter denote the terminal object in the category of T–models and let Ter_E be the T–model which is given by

1. $Ter_E(B) = \{\mu_B^M(m) | M \in Mod(T, \mathbf{E}), m \in M(B)\}$ where $B \in obj(T)$ id a state object and $\mu^M : M \to Ter$ denotes the unique homomorphism from the T–model M to the terminal T–model Ter,
2. $Ter_E(P) = Ter(P)$ where P is a parameter object and
3. $Ter_E(dop) = Ter(dop)$ where dop is a defining dual operation of T.

At first we prove that Ter_E is a T–submodel of Ter. Let $dop : B \to X$ denote any defining dual operation of T and $dop_B : B \overset{par}{\to} B$ a corresponding partial mapping. By assumption $\mu_B^M(m) \in Ter_E(A)$ holds for $m \in M(B)$ and $M \in Mod(T, \mathbf{E})$ and therefore

$$Ter_E(dop)(\mu_B^M(m)) = Ter(dop)(\mu_B^M(m)) = \mu_X^M(M(dop)(m))$$

holds, since $\mu^M : M \to Ter$ is a natural transformation. If we consider the partial defining dual operation dop_B then follows

$$Ter_E(dop_B)(\mu_B^M(m)) = \mu_B^M(M(dop_B)(m)) \in Ter_E(B)$$

since $M(dop_B)(m) \in M(B)$. This proves that $Ter_E(B)$ is closed under application of defining dual operations.

Furthermore we have to prove that the equations out of E are valid in Ter_E. Each equation is by assumption a state equation of the form $t_1 =_{B,X} t_2$ where X is an arbitrary object of the coalgebraic theory. The natural transformation μ^M provides that the squares (1) and (2) of the following diagram commute:

$$\begin{array}{ccccc}
Ter_E(B) & \xleftarrow{\mu_B^M} & M(B) & \xrightarrow{\mu_B^M} & Ter_E(B) \\
\Big\downarrow Ter_E(t_0) & (1)\; M(t_0) & \Big\downarrow\Big\downarrow & M(t_1)\; (2) & \Big\downarrow Ter(t_1) \\
Ter_E(X) & \xleftarrow[\mu_X^M]{} & M(X) & \xrightarrow[\mu_X^M]{} & Ter_E(X)
\end{array}$$

If M satisfies the equation then $M(t_1) = M(t_2)$ and

$$Ter_E(t_1)(\mu_B^M(m)) = Ter_E(t_2)(\mu_B^M(m))$$

hold which establishes the validity of the equation for all elements of $Ter_E(B)$.

It remains to show that the T-model Ter_E is terminal in $Mod_{beh}(T, \mathbf{E})$. Since $Mod(T, \mathbf{E})$ is a subcategory of $Mod_{beh}(T, \mathbf{E})$, this would prove the theorem. Let M be any T-model in $Mod_{beh}(T, \mathbf{E})$ and $ker(\varphi^M)$ the congruence generated by the homomorphism φ^M which is given by the corresponding unique coalgebra-homomorphism to the terminal T-coalgebra. The quotient T-model $M/ker(\varphi^M)$ is then in $Mod(T, \mathbf{E})$, since elements in M are behaviorally equivalent if they are identified by φ^M.

This implies that the unique homomorphism

$$\mu^{M/ker(\varphi^M)} : M/ker(\varphi^M) \rightarrow Ter$$

maps the quotient model to Ter_E. The unique homomorphism $\mu^M : M \rightarrow Ter$ also maps M to Ter_E, since μ^M equals to the composition $nat_M; \mu^{M/ker(\varphi^M)}$ where $nat_M : M \rightarrow M/ker(\varphi^M)$ is the epimorphism uniquely generated by the factorization of M.

Thus, for each T-model M in $Mod_{beh}(T, \mathbf{E})$ there is a unique homomorphism to Ter_E.

Note that in contrast to the construction of the initial algebra by factoring with the congruence hull of a set of equations the terminal T-model is given as a T-submodel of Ter.

Corollary 3. *An equationally defined terminal coalgebra is the collection of the behaviors of all coalgebras satisfying the defining equations.*

2.3 Equationally Constraint Behaviors

If a terminal T-coalgebra represents all possible behaviors of T-coalgebras then each subset of the terminal T-coalgebra represents an abstract property of behaviors. In this way each T-subcoalgebra represents a property which is invariant with respect to all defining dual operation, which means that those properties are invariant against all state changes. Those properties may be seen as safety properties because they represent properties that hold in any state. Usually safety properties are described in such a way that some wanted property is always satisfied or that an undesired event will never happen. We will call each property that forms a T-subcoalgebra of the terminal T-coalgebra a *safety property.*

Corollary 4. *Each abstract property of behaviors that can be expressed equationally is a safety property.*

This corollary is an immediate consequence of our formalization of the corresponding concepts.

On the other hand, there are safety properties that can not be specified by a finite or recursively enumerable set of equations. One of the anonymous referees pointed out that this follows from cardinality considerations. There are uncountably many $T_{1+Nat\times B}$-subcoalgebras of the terminal $T_{1+Nat\times B}$-coalgebras. For each infinite stream the set of streams generated by successive applications of dops forms a subcoalgebra and there are obviously uncountably many subcoalgebras of this form.

Acknowledgements

We wish to thank two anonymous referees, who provided valuable comments. The categorical diagrams were drawn with the macro package by Paul Taylor.

References

[Bar93] Barr,M.: Terminal coalgebras in well-founded set theory. Theoretical Computer Science 114 (1993), 299–315.

[DG94] Dauchy,P., Gaudel, M.C.: Algebraic Specifications with Implicit State. Techn. Report, n 887 (1994) Univ. Paris-Sud.

[Ehr94] Ehrig, H.: Dynamic Abstract Data Types, An Informal Proposal. Bull. EATCS 53 (1994).

[GU71] Gabriel, P., Ulmer,F.: Lokal präsentierbare Kategorien. Springer Lect. Notes Math. 221 (1971): 1 - 200.

[Gur91] Gurevitch, Y.: Evolving Algebras, A Tutorial Introduction. Bull. EATCS 43 (1991), pp.264–284.

[Law63] Lawvere,F.W.:Functorial Semantics of Algebraic Theories. Proc. Nat. Acad. Sci. USA, 1963

[Mil93] Milner,R.: The Polyadic π-Calculus, A Tutorial. In: Bauer, F.L.,Brauer,W., Schwichtenberg,H. (eds): Logic and Algebra of Specification, NATO ASI Series, Series F : Computer and Systems Science, Vol. 94, Springer–Verlag, 1993.

[Poi92] Poigné,A.: Basic Category Theory. In: Abramsky,S., Gabbay,Dov M., Maibaum, T.S.E. (eds): Handbook of Logic in Computer Science, Vol. 1, Oxford Science Publications, Clarendon Press, Oxford, 1992.

[Rei87] Reichel, H.: Initial Computability, Algebraic Specifications, and Partial Algebras. Oxford Science Publications, 1987.

[Rei94] Reichel,H.: An Approach to Object Semantics based on Terminal Co-algebras. Mathematical Structures in Computer Science (in print)

Sort Inheritance for Order-Sorted Equational Presentations

Claus Hintermeier, Claude Kirchner, Hélène Kirchner

CRIN-CNRS & INRIA-Lorraine
BP239, 54506 Vandœuvre-lès-Nancy Cedex
France
E-mail: hinterme@loria.fr, ckirchne@loria.fr, hkirchne@loria.fr

Abstract. In an algebraic framework, where equational, membership and existence formulas can be expressed, decorated terms and rewriting provide operational semantics and decision procedures for these formulas. We focus in this work on testing sort inheritance, an undecidable property of specifications, needed for unification in this context. A test and three specific processes, based on completion of a set of rewrite rules, are proposed to check sort inheritance. They depend on the kinds of membership formulas $(t : A)$ allowed in the specifications: flat and linear, shallow and general terms t are studied.

1 Introduction

The operationalisation of order-sorted frameworks ([Obe62, SS87, SNGM89, GM92]) led to several problems in the past, due to the purely syntactic treatment of membership formulas $(t : A)$, also called term declarations. Assuming them as parsing-oriented declarations, a first pitfall is that equality in the quotient algebra is no more a congruence in general: consider for example two sorts A and B, with $A \leq B$, two constants $(a : A)$ and $(b : B)$, a unary operator $f : A \mapsto A$, and the equality $a = b$. Although $f(a) = f(b)$ is expected, $f(b)$ is not well-formed if parsing is performed using only the membership formulas $(a : A)$, $(b : B)$ and $(f(x) : A)$ for any variable x of sort A, corresponding to the operator declarations.

One possible solution to this problem is to impose sort-decreasingness and confluence of the rules associated with the equalities in a specification (see [GM92, GKK90]). However, there are examples, where sort-decreasingness is an uncomfortable restriction: for instance a definition of the square function on integers is given with two sorts Nat and Int with $Nat \leq Int$, operators $0 : \mapsto Nat$, $* : Int, Int \mapsto Int$, $sq : Int \mapsto Nat$, and for any variable $x :: Int$, $sq(x) = x * x$. However orienting this last equality is problematic since the rule $sq(x) \rightarrow x * x$ is not sort-decreasing.

Even with confluent and sort-decreasing rules, syntactic sorts are restrictive, since terms, that are not syntactically well-formed, can evaluate to a well-formed one: a well-known example is the stack of naturals, with sorts Nat (naturals), St (stacks) and $NeSt$ (non-empty stacks), such that $NeSt \leq St$, operators

$nil\ :\mapsto St$, $push\ :\ Nat, St \mapsto NeSt$, $pop\ :\ NeSt \mapsto St$, $top\ :\ NeSt \mapsto Nat$, variables $x :: Nat$, $z :: St$, and two rewrite rules $top(push(x,z)) \to x$ and $pop(push(x,z)) \to z$.
The term $top(pop(push(2, push(1, nil))))$ is not syntactically well-formed but clearly is semantically meaningful, since it evaluates to 1.

A solution for this problem were retracts, proposed in [GJM85, GM92]. Another solution consists in the semantic interpretation of membership formulas, i.e. equal terms belong by definition to the same sorts. Assuming sort-decreasingness, the term to be reduced is meaningful if and only if its normal form is well-formed [Wer93]. This approach also solves the congruence problem.

In order to further increase expressivity of order-sorted specifications, it makes sense to allow term declarations of the form $(t : A)$, that generalise flat and linear declarations, such as $(f(x) : B)$ for any $(x :: A)$ to declare an operator $f\ :\ A \mapsto B$. Non-linear term declarations are useful for instance in a specification involving again naturals and integers and the declarations $Nat \leq Int$, $0\ :\mapsto Nat$, $suc\ :\ Nat \mapsto Nat$, $opp\ :\ Int \mapsto Int$, $*\ :\ Int, Int \mapsto Int$. Now, $(x * x : Nat)$ for any $x :: Int$ is a flat but non-linear membership formula.

Therefore, we adopt an algebraic framework called G-algebra, where membership formulas and equalities interact to compute semantic sorts of terms. However deduction in this context needs a unification which is undecidable in general, due to semantic membership and general term declarations.

In [HKK94a, HKK94b], we proposed an extended term structure, called decorated terms, where each node contains the set of sorts already proved for the corresponding subterm. Rewriting is defined on these terms and a completion process is proposed, based on the hypothesis that the axiomatisation is modularised in three parts: (i) equalities $(t = t')$, (ii) term declarations $(t : A)$ and (iii) sort inclusions $(A \leq B)$. (i) and (ii) are handled via rewrite rules (decorated and decoration rules) and are thus modified and enriched during completion. On the contrary, (iii) is stable during the *whole* completion. In particular, matchers and unifiers are computed using as usual the term structure but also the sort information given in decorations and in the *fixed* sort structure. Since matching and unification use only the sort information available in the decorated term at unification or matching time, they are correct but non complete in general for the peak reduction involved in the completion process. This completeness property will be achieved only at the end of the completion process provided it does not fail. In order to get an algorithm that computes a complete set of unifiers on decorated terms, it is necessary that the sort information given in part (iii) contains enough information to have the following property, called sort inheritance: if a term t can be proved to be of sorts A_i, $i \in [1..n]$, then there must exist a sort C with $C \leq A_i$ for all $i \in [1..n]$. Sort inheritance is in general undecidable. In [HKK94a], the completion process is performed assuming sort inheritance. When a fair completion does not fail, the resulting set of rewrite rules provides a way to prove not only equational theorems of the form $(t = t')$ but also membership theorems $(t : A)$ and existence theorems $(EX\ t)$ (cf. [Sco77]).

Thus sort inheritance is a crucial property in this framework. We propose in this paper a test of sort inheritance based on the computation of top critical pairs between decoration rules generated during completion. It the test succeeds, it provides a counter-example for sort inheritance. Conversely, if the test never succeeds during completion, the specification is proved sort inheriting in three different situations: the first one is the case of flat and linear term declarations. This is the simplest case that corresponds to usual operator declarations. In that case, the test for sort inheritance can be postponed at the end of the completion process. The second case is when term declarations are shallow (i.e. have no variable at depth more than one). Then simplification and critical pair computation must be adapted to simultaneously reduce identical subterms at the same depth. Eventually, for general term declarations, all identical subterms have to be reduced in one step during simplification and a specific completion strategy has to be designed. This last case also forbids inter-reduction using decorated rewrite rules, which may cause divergence of the process in many cases.

This paper focusses on checking sort inheritance and is built as follows. The algebraic framework is stated in Section 2 and Section 3 explains the assumptions for the used sort structure. Then, in Section 4, the notions of decorated terms and rewriting with decorated and decoration rewrite rules are briefly recalled, with a completeness theorem stating the equivalence of replacement of equal by equal on decorated terms with deduction in G-algebra. Section 5 briefly gives the results of [HKK94a]. Section 6 provides the test for detecting non sort inheritance and successively considers the case of flat and linear term declarations, shallow declarations, and any kind of term declarations. In the conclusion, our approach is briefly compared with other related works. The full version of this paper [HKK94b] includes all proofs, examples and extended discussions of the concepts introduced here.

2 G-Algebra

A main feature of G-algebra is that function and term declarations, usually seen as part of the (static) signature in classical approaches, become formulas and are involved in proofs at the same level as equalities.

Our notations are consistent with [SNGM89, DJ90]. All notions concerning terms are defined in the same way as for classical terms.

Let $\Sigma = (\mathcal{S}, \mathcal{F})$ be a signature, providing a set of sorts $\mathcal{S}$ and of function symbols $\mathcal{F}$. $\mathcal{S}$ always contains the universal sort symbol Ω. The set of terms $\mathcal{T}(\Sigma, \mathcal{X})$ is defined as in the unsorted case, but each variable $x \in \mathcal{X}$ belongs to a unique sort, say A, denoted by $sort(x)$. This is written $(x :: A)$. With $A \in \mathcal{S}$ and $t, t' \in \mathcal{T}(\Sigma, \mathcal{X})$, existence formulas $(\mathit{EX}\ t)$, membership formulas $(t : A)$ and equalities $(t = t')$ are all implicitly closed by universal quantification.

Presentations $\mathcal{P}$ are sets of formulas. A pair $(signature, presentation)$ is called specification. A Σ-algebra $\mathcal{A}$ is given by a domain $|\mathcal{A}|$ and interpretations for each symbol in $\mathcal{S}$ and $\mathcal{F}$: each $A \in \mathcal{S}$ is interpreted as a non-empty set $A^{\mathcal{A}}$, $\Omega^{\mathcal{A}}$ as $|\mathcal{A}|$, and each $f \in \mathcal{F}$ as a partial function $f^{\mathcal{A}} : |\mathcal{A}|^{arity(f)} \rightarrow |\mathcal{A}|$. A variable assignment α is a mapping from $\mathcal{X}$ to $\Omega^{\mathcal{A}}$ with $\alpha(x) \in A^{\mathcal{A}}$ whenever

$sort(x) = A$ (for all $x \in \mathcal{X}$). A model of $\mathcal{P}$ is a Σ-algebra s.t. for all variable assignments α, for all $(\mathit{EX}\ t) \in \mathcal{P}$, $\alpha^*(t) \in \Omega^{\mathcal{A}}$, for all $(t : A) \in \mathcal{P}$, $\alpha^*(t) \in A^{\mathcal{A}}$ and for all $(t = t') \in \mathcal{P}$, $\alpha^*(t) = \alpha^*(t')$, where α^* is the unique homomorphic extension of α on terms. Homomorphisms are identical to those of [SNGM89]. If some formula ϕ is true in all models of $\mathcal{P}$, we write $\mathcal{P} \models \phi$.

In [Még90] (see also [HKK94a]), a sound and complete set of deduction rules is proposed, giving a relation $\vdash$ of deductibility, s.t. $\vdash$ and $\models$ coincide. The involved substitutions σ are supposed to be *conform* with the current presentation, i.e. $(x \mapsto t) \in \sigma$ and $(x :: A) \in \mathcal{P}$ implies $\mathcal{P} \vdash (t : A)$.

Specifications with inhabited sorts (i.e. for each $A \in \mathcal{S}$, there is some $t \in \mathcal{T}(\Sigma)$, s.t. $\mathcal{P} \models (t : A)$) have an initial Σ-model whose domain is $\{t \in \mathcal{T}(\Sigma) \mid \mathcal{P} \vdash \mathit{EX}\ t\}$. The congruence $\equiv$ defined on $\mathcal{T}(\Sigma)$ as $\{(t,t') \mid \mathcal{P} \vdash \mathit{EX}\ t, \mathit{EX}\ t', t = t'\}$ is s.t. the quotient $\mathcal{T}(\Sigma)_{/\equiv}$ is initial in the class of models of $\mathcal{P}$.

The main difference w.r.t. purely syntactic approaches, like [GM92], relies on the typing notion. Instead of syntactic typing, where the judgement whether some t in $\mathcal{T}(\Sigma, \mathcal{X})$ belongs to a sort $A \in \mathcal{S}$ only depends on the term declarations in $\mathcal{P}$, in our approach (as in [WD89, Com92, Wit92, Wer93]), such a judgement also depends on equalities. This actually corresponds to the intuition that equal terms belong to the same sorts and is reflected by the semantic sort rule in the deduction system of G-algebra [Még90]:

$$\boxed{t : A, t = s \quad \Rightarrow \quad s : A}$$

Let us come back to the stack of naturals example, expressed in G-algebra:

$$\mathcal{P} = \left\{ \begin{array}{l|l} x :: Nat, z :: St & y :: NeSt, y : St \\ nil : St & push(x,z) : NeSt \\ pop(y) : St & top(y) : Nat \\ top(push(x,z)) = x & pop(push(x,z)) = z \end{array} \right\}$$

First remark that $(y :: NeSt), (y : St)$ is the G-algebra way to express $NeSt \leq St$. Then $\mathcal{P} \models pop(pop(push(y, push(x, nil)))) : St$ and $\mathcal{P} \not\models pop(pop(push(x, nil))) : St$. Note also, that the first membership formula is not syntactically well-formed, although the term makes sense in any model of $\mathcal{P}$.

3 The Sort Structure

In order to effectively compute in G-algebra, we have to overcome the difficulty of semantic sorts. Indeed, defining a semantic sort ordering $\leq_{\mathcal{S}}^{sem}$ in $\mathcal{P}$ as the transitive and reflexive closure of the relation: $A \leq_{\mathcal{S}}^{sem} B$ if $(x :: A) \in \mathcal{P}$ implies $\mathcal{P} \vdash (x : B)$, results in undecidability of the subsort relation. Consequently, we need to work with an approximation. We use a syntactic relation, defined as the transitive and reflexive closure of $A \leq_{\mathcal{S}}^{syn} B$ if $\{x :: A,\ x : B\} \subseteq \mathcal{P}$. Therefore, expressing a subsort relation $A \leq_{\mathcal{S}}^{syn} B$ in our framework is equivalent to give a variable definition $(x :: A)$ and a corresponding term declaration $(x : B)$.

In ordered sort structures, incomparable sorts $A_1, \ldots, A_n$ without common subsort are considered to have no term in common. If there are common subsorts

$B_1, \ldots B_m$, usually as in [GM92], only terms in these common subsorts are considered to be simultaneously in $A_1, \ldots, A_n$. This is guaranteed by a restriction called regularity, saying that each term must have a unique least sort. Regularity ensures decidability of unification and therefore feasibility of completion.

Our approach introduces new sorts in order to cope also with terms in all A_i, $i \in [1..n]$, but not in the B_j's, $j \in [1..m]$. Hence, the next step is to find a replacement for regularity, adapted to the extended sort structure, that ensures decidability of unification. We call a specification $(\Sigma, \mathcal{P})$ *sort inheriting* (SI for short) w.r.t. a subsort ordering $\leq$, if for any term $t \in \mathcal{T}(\Sigma, \mathcal{X}), \forall T \subseteq \mathcal{S}$:

$$(\forall A \in T, \mathcal{P} \vdash t : A) \Rightarrow (\exists C \in \mathcal{S}, \forall A \in T, C \leq A)$$

Fortunately, sort inheritance w.r.t. $\leq_{\mathcal{S}}^{syn}$ is stricter than $\leq_{\mathcal{S}}^{sem}$. Hence, it is sufficient to test SI w.r.t. $\leq_{\mathcal{S}}^{syn}$, the decidable relation. This motivates to write SI without precising the used relation, which implicitly means SI w.r.t. $\leq_{\mathcal{S}}^{syn}$. Sort inheritance is undecidable in general, but a constructive test computing terms that destroy SI is developed in Section 6. Simple restrictions such as syntactic regularity and sort-decreasingness of [SNGM89, GKK90, Wal92] are sufficient to ensure SI.

We assume in the following that:

- (1) all sorts are non-empty,
- (2) $<_{\mathcal{S}}^{syn}$, the strict part of $\leq_{\mathcal{S}}^{syn}$, does not contain cycles,
- (3) the specification has bounded membership, i.e. $\{A \mid \mathcal{P} \vdash t : A\}$ is finite for all $t \in \mathcal{T}(\Sigma, \mathcal{X})$,
- (4) the set $mlb(S)$ of maximal elements of the set of lower bounds of any subset of sorts $S \subseteq \mathcal{S}$ is computable.

In our framework, since emptiness of sorts is related to equality, it is undecidable, but can be enforced by a decidable syntactic non-emptiness condition. In signatures with finite $\mathcal{S}$, as in G-algebra, (2) is decidable, (3) is trivial and (4) is satisfied. However, in polymorphic signatures more sophisticated properties have to be introduced (see [Smo89]).

To express unifiers of two variables using SI instead of regularity, an extended sort structure $(\mathcal{S}_\Diamond, \leq_{\mathcal{S}_\Diamond}^{syn})$ is needed. For a finite subset S of $\mathcal{S}$ s.t. $mlb(S) \neq \emptyset$ and all $A \in S$ are incomparable, the sort $\langle S \rangle$ may be understood as the intersection of all sorts A in S. Instead of $\langle \{A, \ldots\} \rangle$, we simply write $\langle A, \ldots \rangle$ and $\langle A \rangle$ is written A. $\mathcal{S}_\Diamond$ denotes the set of all $\langle S \rangle$. The sort ordering $\leq_{\mathcal{S}}^{syn}$ is conservatively extended to a new subsort relation $\leq_{\mathcal{S}_\Diamond}^{syn}$ defined by:

$$\langle S \rangle \leq_{\mathcal{S}_\Diamond}^{syn} \langle S' \rangle \text{ if } \forall B \in S', \exists A \in S, \text{ s.t. } A \leq_{\mathcal{S}}^{syn} B.$$

Example 1. Let $\mathcal{S} = \{Zero,\ P,\ N,\ Int\}$, s.t. $Zero \leq_{\mathcal{S}}^{syn} P$, $Zero \leq_{\mathcal{S}}^{syn} N$, $P \leq_{\mathcal{S}}^{syn} Int$, $N \leq_{\mathcal{S}}^{syn} Int$. Then $\mathcal{S}_\Diamond = \{Zero,\ \langle P, N \rangle,\ P,\ N,\ Int\}$. Now, $\langle P, N \rangle \leq_{\mathcal{S}_\Diamond}^{syn} N$, since $N \leq_{\mathcal{S}}^{syn} N$. Analogously, $\langle P, N \rangle \leq_{\mathcal{S}_\Diamond}^{syn} P$. Furthermore, $Zero \leq_{\mathcal{S}_\Diamond}^{syn} \langle P, N \rangle$, since $Zero \leq_{\mathcal{S}}^{syn} P$ and $Zero \leq_{\mathcal{S}}^{syn} N$. Finally, $N \leq_{\mathcal{S}_\Diamond}^{syn} Int$ and $P \leq_{\mathcal{S}_\Diamond}^{syn} Int$ hold as before. Remark that interpreting $\langle P, N \rangle$ intuitively as intersection of P and N results in the same subsort relation.

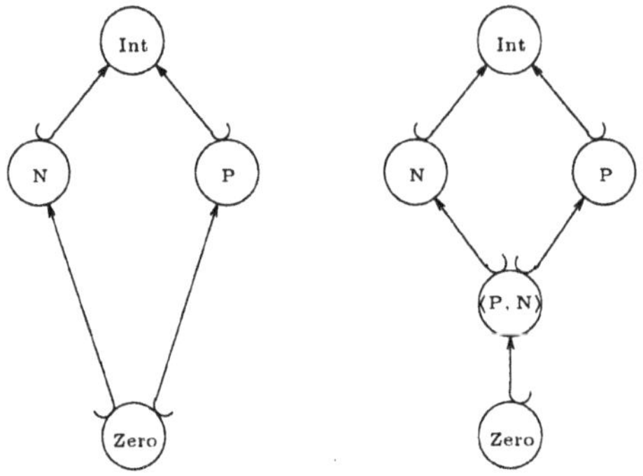

In what follows, we assume $(\Sigma, \mathcal{P})$ to be a fixed specification leading to an extended sort set $\mathcal{S}_\Diamond$ with a subsort relation $\leq_{\mathcal{S}_\Diamond}^{syn}$.

4 Decorated Terms, Rewriting and Presentations

Semantic sorts lead to difficulties when parsing terms. Clearly, as long as there is no decision procedure for typing in some presentation $\mathcal{P}$, we need to restrict the sorts of terms to those which are currently proved. Hence, we extend the term structure with typing information in each node.

Terms and Substitutions. Let $\mathcal{X}_\Diamond$ be a $\mathcal{S}_\Diamond$-sorted variable set and $\mathbf{V}$ a set of set-variables disjoint from $\mathcal{X}_\Diamond$. A decorated term is either a decorated variable $x^{:\{\langle A \rangle\}}$, where $(x :: A) \in \mathcal{X}_\Diamond$, or of the form $f(t_1{}^{:S_1}, \ldots, t_n{}^{:S_n})^{:S}$, where $t_1{}^{:S_1}, \ldots, t_n{}^{:S_n}$ are decorated terms, $f \in \mathcal{F}$ with $arity(f) = n$. Subsets S, S_i of $\mathcal{S}_\Diamond$, for $i \in [1..n]$, are called decorations. t_{nd} stands for $t^{:S}$ without decorations.

A decorated term $t^{:S}$ is said valid in a presentation $\mathcal{P}$ if all its subterms $u^{:U}$ satisfy $\forall \langle \ldots, A, \ldots \rangle \in U,\ \mathcal{P} \vdash (\alpha(u_{nd}) : A)$ for all $\mathcal{T}(\Sigma, \mathcal{X})$-instances α of u_{nd}. $\mathcal{T}_d(\mathcal{S}_\Diamond, \mathcal{F}, \mathcal{X}_\Diamond)$ or just $\mathcal{T}_d$ is the set of decorated $(\Sigma, \mathcal{X}_\Diamond)$-terms, $\mathcal{VT}_d$ the set of valid terms in $\mathcal{T}_d$. $t^{:\downarrow\emptyset}$ represents t with empty decorations everywhere, except at positions with variables, where $x^{:S}$ becomes $x^{:\{sort(x)\}}$. Syntactic equality over decorated terms is denoted by $=_d$.

To get decidable notions of matching and unification, we need to express SI on decorated terms as a property on their decorations only. Obviously, we have to avoid arbitrary decorations, since they can be interpreted incorrectly as membership formulas. Hence, it only makes sense to define SI on valid terms. Furthermore, a decidable test of SI can only be assured on subsets of $\mathcal{VT}_d$. Therefore, we need a property for arbitrary subsets $\mathcal{T}$ of $\mathcal{VT}_d$. So, a specification $(\Sigma, \mathcal{P})$ is $\mathcal{T}$-SI, if:

$$\forall t^{:T} \in \mathcal{T}\ :\ (\exists C \in \mathcal{S}, \forall A \in T\ :\ C \leq_{\mathcal{S}_\Diamond}^{syn} A).$$

This means that we have added a sort $\langle S \rangle$ with $S = min(\{B \mid \langle \ldots, B, \ldots \rangle \in T\})$ to $\mathcal{S}_\Diamond$ w.r.t. $\mathcal{S}$, i.e. intuitively for the intersection of all sorts from $\mathcal{S}$ occurring in the decoration T. Hence, every term in $\mathcal{T}$ is *covered* by some unique, minimal sort, just as this is the case with regularity. The difference is that SI is defined after an extension of the sort structure and furthermore SI is relative to a set of valid decorated terms. Remark that the extension of the sort structure depends only on the subsort relation $\leq_S^{syn}$ and not on membership formulas, which are a priori undecidable.

Decorated substitutions are a subset of $\mathcal{P}$-conform substitutions. We restrict the used membership theory once more to the information already existing in the term nodes, modulo a SI closure that computes minimal sorts and performs transitive closure on them w.r.t. $\leq_{\mathcal{S}_\Diamond}^{syn}$. The SI closure $\widehat{S}$ of S is defined as:

$$\widehat{S} = \{D \in \mathcal{S}_\Diamond \mid \exists \langle T_1 \rangle, \ldots, \langle T_n \rangle \in S \; : \; \langle min(\bigcup_{i \in [1..n]} T_i) \rangle \leq_{\mathcal{S}_\Diamond}^{syn} D\}$$

Example 2. Let $\mathcal{S} = \{A, B, C, D\}$ with $D \leq_S^{syn} B, D \leq_S^{syn} C$ and therefore $\mathcal{S}_\Diamond = \{A, B, C, D, \langle B, C \rangle\}$ with $D \leq_{\mathcal{S}_\Diamond}^{syn} \langle B, C \rangle$, $\langle B, C \rangle \leq_{\mathcal{S}_\Diamond}^{syn} B$ and $\langle B, C \rangle \leq_{\mathcal{S}_\Diamond}^{syn} C$.

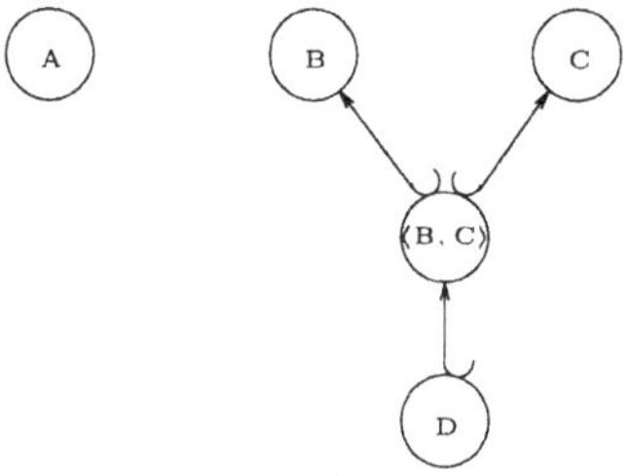

Let now $S_1 = \{A\}$, $S_2 = \{D\}$, $S_3 = \{B, C\}$ and $S_4 = \{A, B, C\}$ be subsets of $\mathcal{S}_\Diamond$. Then $\widehat{S_1} = \{A\}$, $\widehat{S_2} = \{B, C, D, \langle B, C \rangle\}$, $\widehat{S_3} = \{B, C, \langle B, C \rangle\}$ and $\widehat{S_4} = \{A, B, C, \langle B, C \rangle\}$.

$S \lesssim S'$ abbreviates $\widehat{S} \subseteq \widehat{S'}$, $S \approx S'$ means $S \lesssim S'$ and $S' \lesssim S$. The SI closure $\widehat{t^{:S}}$ of $t^{:S}$ is obtained by recursively applying $\widehat{\ }$ to its decorations. $\widehat{t^{:S}} = \widehat{t'^{:S'}}$ is written $t^{:S} \cong_d t'^{:S'}$ and means syntactic equality up to the SI closure of decorations at each node.

A decorated substitution σ is a mapping from decorated variables in $\mathcal{X}_\Diamond$ to valid decorated terms, such that if $\sigma(x^{:S}) =_d t^{:T}$ with $t^{:T} \neq_d x^{:S}$ and $(x :: A) \in \mathcal{P}$, then $A \in \widehat{T}$. Remark that $A \approx S$, since x is a decorated variable. We represent σ by its graph $\bigcup_{i \in [1..n]} \{x_i^{:S_i} \mapsto t_i^{:T_i}\}$ and $\mathcal{D}om(\sigma) = \{x_i \mid i \in [1..n]\}$.

Decorated term subsumption, matching and unification can be defined as for classical terms [JK91], using decorated substitutions and terms instead of the classical ones together with $\cong_d$ as term equality. The exact definitions can be found in [HKK94b] together with a matching and unification algorithm.

Rewriting. A decorated equality is a pair of decorated terms, denoted by $(p^{:S} = q^{:S'})$, $p^{:S}, q^{:S'} \in \mathcal{T}_d$. A decorated rewrite rule is an ordered pair of decorated terms, written $(p^{:S} \to q^{:S'})$, s.t. $p^{:S}, q^{:S'} \in \mathcal{T}_d$ and $\mathcal{V}ar(p^{:S}) \supseteq \mathcal{V}ar(q^{:S'})$. Applying equalities and decorated rewrite rules on valid terms is defined analogously to undecorated equalities and rewrite rules (as e.g. in [DJ90]), except that the equality symbol (=) and substitutions have to be replaced by decorated equality modulo SI ($\cong_d$) and decorated substitutions.

A decorated one-step equality application in E is written $t^{:S} \longleftrightarrow_E^{\omega,\sigma,\phi} t'^{:S'}$, where $\phi \in E$, $\omega \in \mathcal{O}cc(t^{:S})$ and σ is a decorated substitution. Decorated rewriting is analogously denoted by $t^{:S} \rightarrowtail_R^{\omega,\sigma,\phi} t'^{:S'}$, where $\phi \in R$ and ω, σ are as before. If the used rule/equality, substitution or occurrence is not needed in the current context, we may simply omit it in our notation.

Example 3. Let $top(push(x^{:\{Nat\}}, z^{:\{St\}})^{:\{NeSt\}})^{:\{Nat\}} \to x^{:\{Nat\}}$ be a decorated rewrite rule in R. Then $top(push(0^{:\{Nat\}}, nil^{:\{St\}})^{:\emptyset})^{:\emptyset}$ cannot be rewritten, but $top(push(0^{:\{Nat\}}, nil^{:\{St\}})^{:\{NeSt\}})^{:\{Nat\}} \rightarrowtail_R 0^{:\{Nat\}}$.

Another kind of rules is introduced, whose purpose is to increase decorations. Let s be in **V**. A decoration rewrite rule is of the form ($l^{:s} \to l^{:s \cup S_l}$ if $S_l \not\subseteq s$), where $l^{:\emptyset} \in \mathcal{T}_d$ and $S_l \subseteq \mathcal{S}_\Diamond$.

The valid decorated term $t^{:T}$ rewrites in D to $t'^{:T'}$, written $t^{:T} \rightarrowtail_D^{\omega,\sigma,\phi} t'^{:T'}$, if $\phi = (l^{:s} \to l^{:s \cup S_l}$ if $S_l \not\subseteq s) \in D$, $t^{:T}|_\omega =_d u^{:U}$, σ is a decorated match from $l^{:U}$ to $u^{:U}$, $S_l \not\subseteq U$ and $t'^{:T'} =_d t^{:T}[\sigma(l^{:U})^{:U \cup S_l}]_\omega$.

Decorated and decoration rewriting are stable by context and substitution. Furthermore, they preserve validity of terms. To prove termination, the classical notion of reduction ordering can easily be extended on decorated terms (see [HKK94b] for details). A decorated or decoration rewrite step is denoted by $\rightarrowtail_{R \cup D}$, an application of $\rightarrowtail_D$ or $\longleftrightarrow_E$ is denoted by $\longleftrightarrow_{D \cup E}$. A star over a relation denotes its reflexive and transitive closure.

Example 4. Let ($0^{:s} \to 0^{:s \cup \{Nat\}}$ if $\{Nat\} \not\subseteq s$) be a decoration rewrite rule. Then $0^{:\{Int\}} \rightarrowtail_D 0^{:\{Nat,Int\}}$. Remark that $\{Nat, Int\} \approx \{Nat\}$ if $Nat \leq^{syn}_{\mathcal{S}_\Diamond} Int$.

Decorated Presentations. In order to replace $\vdash$-derivations in the G-algebra deduction system [Még90] by $\longleftrightarrow_{D,E,R}$-steps, we have to extract a set of decorated equalities $E_\mathcal{P}$ and a set of decoration rules $D_\mathcal{P}$ from $\mathcal{P}$. Therefore, we take for each subterm u of a term appearing in a formula in $\mathcal{P}$ a decoration rewrite rule ($(u^{:\downarrow\emptyset})^{:s} \to (u^{:\downarrow\emptyset})^{:s \cup \{\Omega\}}$ if $\{\Omega\} \not\subseteq s$). For all $(u : A)$ in $\mathcal{P}$, s.t. $u \notin \mathcal{X}$, we add ($(u^{:\downarrow\emptyset})^{:s} \to (u^{:\downarrow\emptyset})^{:s \cup \{A\}}$ if $\{A\} \not\subseteq s$). The resulting set of decoration rewrite rules is called $D_\mathcal{P}$. Analogously, $E_\mathcal{P}$ is defined as the set of decorated equalities $(p^{:\downarrow\emptyset} = q^{:\downarrow\emptyset})$, for each equality $(p = q)$ in $\mathcal{P}$. Now, we can state:

Theorem 1. *[HKK94b] Let t, t' be two terms, $\mathcal{P}$ be a Σ-presentation. Let A be a sort and U be a set of sorts. Then:*

$(\mathcal{P} \vdash t = t') \Leftrightarrow \exists t_0, A$ *s.t.* $t^{:\downarrow\emptyset} \overset{*}{\longleftrightarrow}_{D_\mathcal{P} \cup E_\mathcal{P}} t_0^{:\{A\} \cup U} \overset{*}{\longleftrightarrow}_{D_\mathcal{P} \cup E_\mathcal{P}} t'^{:\downarrow\emptyset}$.

$(\mathcal{P} \vdash t : A) \Leftrightarrow \exists t', A' \leq^{syn}_{\mathcal{S}_\Diamond} A$ *s.t.* $t^{:\downarrow\emptyset} \overset{*}{\longleftrightarrow}_{D_\mathcal{P} \cup E_\mathcal{P}} t'^{:\{A'\} \cup U}$.

$(\mathcal{P} \vdash EX\ t) \Leftrightarrow \exists t'$ *s.t.* $t^{:\downarrow\emptyset} \overset{*}{\longleftrightarrow}_{D_\mathcal{P} \cup E_\mathcal{P}} t'^{:\{A\} \cup U}$.

5 Completion

In order to further motivate the need for SI, let us briefly recall the completion process in which it appears as an essential requirement. A completion procedure is described in [HKK94a] by a set $\mathcal{OSC}$ of rules that transforms triples

$P = (D, E, R)$, called decorated presentations, starting from $P_0 = (D_{\mathcal{P}}, E_{\mathcal{P}}, \emptyset)$. $D_\infty, E_\infty, R_\infty$ denote the sets of persisting rules and equalities in a derivation using $\mathcal{OSC}$. The purpose of completion is to generate a resulting decorated presentation, given by $(D_\infty, E_\infty, R_\infty)$ where $E_\infty = \emptyset$, that satisfies the following properties for $D_\infty \cup R_\infty$:

- Church-Rosser property:
  $\mathcal{P} \vdash (t = t') \Leftrightarrow \exists t'', A, S : t^{:\downarrow\emptyset} \overset{*}{\rightarrowtail}_{R_\infty \cup D_\infty} t''^{:\{A\} \cup S} \overset{*}{\leftarrowtail}_{R_\infty \cup D_\infty} t'^{:\downarrow\emptyset}$,
- Type completeness:
  $\mathcal{P} \vdash (t : A) \Leftrightarrow \exists t', S, A' \leq_{S_\Diamond}^{syn} A : t^{:\downarrow\emptyset} \overset{*}{\rightarrowtail}_{R_\infty \cup D_\infty} t'^{:\{A'\} \cup S}$,
- Existential completeness:
  $\mathcal{P} \vdash (\mathcal{EX}\ t) \Leftrightarrow \exists t', A, S : t^{:\downarrow\emptyset} \overset{*}{\rightarrowtail}_{R_\infty \cup D_\infty} t'^{:\{A\} \cup S}$,

The completion procedure essentially computes critical pairs between the two kinds of decoration/decorated rewrite rules, in order to handle critical interactions between membership formulas and rewrite rules in a convenient way. Simplification of critical pairs and inter-reduction of rules using decoration and decorated rules are allowed as in usual completion. The difference relies in the orientation process that always produces rewrite rules that increase the sort information at the replacement position, but in addition may introduce new membership formulas via decoration rewrite rules. The two orientation rules are given in Figure 1 and use an ordering $>_d$ on decorated terms defined in [HKK94b].

1. **Orient_SD**

$$\frac{D, E \cup \{p^{:S} = q^{:S'}\}, R}{D, E, R \cup \{p^{:S} \to q^{:S'}\}} \quad \text{if } p^{:S} >_d q^{:S'} \text{ and } S \subsetneq S'$$

2. **Orient_NSD**

$$\frac{D, E \cup \{p^{:S} = q^{:S'}\}, R}{D \cup \{(q^{:s} \to q^{:s \cup S \setminus S'} \text{ if } S \setminus S' \not\subseteq s)\}, E, R \cup \{p^{:S} \to q^{:S \cup S'}\}}$$
if $p^{:S} >_d q^{:S \cup S'}$ and $S \not\subseteq S'$
and if $q \in \mathcal{X}_\Diamond$ with $q :: A$ then $\{A\} \approx S \cup S'$

Fig. 1. Orientation rules for decorated equations.

Assuming a sort inheriting initial presentation, the main result for the completion process is stated in the next theorem.

Theorem 2. *[HKK94b] Let $\mathcal{P}$ be SI and $P_\infty = (D_\infty, E_\infty, R_\infty)$ obtained with $\mathcal{OSC}$ from $(D_{\mathcal{P}}, E_{\mathcal{P}}, \emptyset)$ s.t. $E_\infty = \emptyset$ and all critical pairs of $D_\infty \cup R_\infty$ have been computed. Then $D_\infty \cup R_\infty$ is terminating, Church-Rosser, type complete and existentially complete on $\mathcal{VT}_d$.*

In the orientation rules given in Figure 1, decorated equations of the form $(p^{:S} = x^{:S'})$ s.t. $S \cup S' \not\approx sort(x)$ are not oriented, and thus the condition $E_\infty = \emptyset$

of Theorem 2 may not be fulfilled. We add a failure rule detecting this case:

Detect_Subsort

$$\frac{D, E \cup \{p^{:S\cup\{B\}} = (x :: A)^{:S'}\}, R}{\bot,\bot,\bot} \text{ if } x \in \mathcal{X}_\Diamond \text{ and } x :: A \in \mathcal{P} \text{ and not } A \leq^{syn}_{S_\Diamond} B$$

With this additional failure rule, we can improve Theorem 2 with another result more precisely stated in [HKK94a]: starting from a sort inheriting presentation, when completion succeeds (i.e. terminates after computing all the critical pairs and without any application of the **Detect_Subsort** rule), then $\leq^{syn}_S = \leq^{sem}_S$. When **Detect_Subsort** is applicable, then $\leq^{syn}_S \neq \leq^{sem}_S$. This means in particular that the unification algorithm used in the completion does not always compute a complete set of unifiers in the initial presentation. However when **Detect_Subsort** applies, it provides us with the information that $\mathcal{P} \vdash (x : B)$. Adding this term declaration to the presentation yields a conservative extension of the initial presentation $\mathcal{P}$. Consequently, the completion can be restarted, but now using more information, since $\leq^{syn}_S$ has then been increased.

6 Testing Sort Inheritance

Since all results of the last section depend on the sort inheritance of $\mathcal{P}$, we are now left with the problem of designing a test for this undecidable property. We propose in this section a test that is applied in three kinds of completion processes according to the form of term declarations. In all three cases, the completion process including the test allows checking sort inheritance of the initial presentation.

The test for detecting non sort inheritance is realized by the **Detect_NonSI** rule given below.

Detect_NonSI

$$\frac{D \cup_{i\in[0..n]} \{(p_i{}^{:s} \to p_i{}^{:s\cup S_i} \text{ if } S_i \not\subseteq s)\}, E, R}{\bot,\bot,\bot}$$

$$\text{if } (\exists\psi, \forall i \in [1..n], \psi(p_0{}^{:\emptyset}) \cong_d \psi(p_i{}^{:\emptyset})) \text{ and } (\exists S \subseteq \bigcup_{i\in[0..n]} S_i, \nexists C \leq^{syn}_{S_\Diamond} S)$$

Clearly, if **Detect_NonSI** applies, then $\mathcal{P}$ is not SI. If $P_\infty = (\bot,\bot,\bot)$, then we can add $(\psi(p^{:\emptyset})_{nd} : C)$, since this is a conservative extension of the initial presentation $\mathcal{P}$. As in the case of **Detect_Subsort**, the completion can then be restarted.

Moreover, this test characterises SI on the set of decorated terms called D-typable, i.e. reachable with D from terms with empty decorations, provided confluence of D:

Proposition 3. *In a decorated presentation $P = (D, E, R)$, let us consider the set $\mathcal{T}_D = \{t \mid \exists t' \in \mathcal{T}_d^{:\downarrow\emptyset} : t' \overset{*}{\longleftrightarrow}_D t\}$. Let us assume that D is confluent on $\mathcal{T}_D$. Then, the* **Detect_NonSI**-*rule succeeds on D iff P is not $\mathcal{T}_D$-SI.*

The main difficulty is to extend this result from $\mathcal{T}_D$ to the set of all valid decorated terms. This extension relies on the following facts.
(1) The proof of Theorem 1 reveals that for each G-algebra proof, there is a proof using $\overset{*}{\longleftrightarrow}_{D_\mathcal{P} \cup E_\mathcal{P}}$, s.t. all decorated terms $t^{:S}$ in the latter have a typing proof $(t^{:S})^{:\downarrow\emptyset} \overset{*}{\longleftrightarrow}_{D_\mathcal{P}} t^{:S}$.
(2) If we check that the set of all typable terms does not contain any counter-example for SI, then the unification algorithm computes all critical pairs needed for peak reduction.
(3) Typability can be preserved until P_∞, if proof reductions and completion strategies are adapted to the form of term declarations.

The main problems are hence first to find a proof transformation that preserves typability of terms and second to ensure that the set of typable terms at each step of the completion does not contain a counter-example for SI.

Under these conditions, if completion does not fail, $\mathcal{P}$ is SI: indeed if $t^{:S}$ is a counter-example for SI of $\mathcal{P}$, there must exist (cf. Theorem 1) a proof

$$\Psi \; : \; (t^{:\downarrow\emptyset} \overset{*}{\longleftrightarrow}_{P_0} t_1{}^{:S_1} \overset{*}{\longleftrightarrow}_{P_0} t^{:\downarrow\emptyset} \overset{*}{\longleftrightarrow}_{P_0} \dots \overset{*}{\longleftrightarrow}_{P_0} t_n{}^{:S_n} \overset{*}{\longleftrightarrow}_{P_0} t^{:\downarrow\emptyset})$$

such that $S \subseteq \cup_{i\in[1..n]} S_i$. By proof reduction, we get a rewrite proof: $\Psi' \; : \; (t^{:\downarrow\emptyset} \overset{*}{\rightarrowtail}_{D_\infty \cup R_\infty} t'^{:S'})$ with $\cup_{i\in[1..n]} S_i \subseteq S'$ and $t'^{:S'}$ is also a counterexample for SI. Since typability is preserved, $t'^{:S'}$ has yet a typing proof using D_∞ $(t'^{:\downarrow\emptyset} \overset{*}{\longleftrightarrow}_{D_\infty} t'^{:S'})$, so **Detect_NonSI** must apply to D_∞.

6.1 Flat and Linear Term Declarations

Let us call $\mathcal{SSC}$ the set of completion rules $\mathcal{OSC}$ with the two additional failure rules **Detect_Subsort** and **Detect_NonSI**.

The case of flat and linear term declarations is the most simple one. We can even postpone the relatively expensive application of the **Detect_nonSI** rule to the final decorated presentation, provided we ensure that if we simplify decoration rewrite rules with decorated rewrite rules, then the latter are decoration preserving, i.e. of the form $\phi \; : \; l^{:S} \to r^{:S}$. In this case, we call also the completion derivation decoration preserving.

Theorem 4. *[HKK94b] Let $P_\infty \neq (\perp, \perp, \perp)$ be obtained with $\mathcal{SSC}$ from $(D_\mathcal{P}, E_\mathcal{P}, \emptyset)$. Let us assume furthermore that all terms in D_∞ are flat and linear, $E_\infty = \emptyset$, all critical pairs of $D_\infty \cup R_\infty$ have been computed and the completion derivation is decoration preserving. Then the initial presentation $\mathcal{P}$ is SI on $\mathcal{VT}_d$ and $D_\infty \cup R_\infty$ is Church-Rosser, type and existentially complete.*

Intuitively, if all terms in D_∞ are flat and linear and $P_\infty \neq (\perp, \perp, \perp)$, the rewrite proofs with $D_\infty \cup R_\infty$ and all terms in proofs in intermediate decorated presentation P_k only contain D_∞-typable terms, so $\mathcal{T}_{D_\infty}$-SI is equivalent to $\mathcal{VT}_d$-SI. Therefore, it is sufficient to test SI on D_∞.

6.2 Shallow Term Declarations

A similar result to Theorem 4 for flat, possibly non-linear term declarations can be proved. It covers the class of presentations with shallow term declarations $(t : A)$, where all $x \in \mathcal{V}ar(t)$ occur either at the top or at depth one in t. These presentations can be conservatively transformed into presentations with flat, possibly non-linear term declarations.

Dropping the linearity condition forces us to simultaneously reduce identical subterms at the same depth, and to prohibit decoration rewrite rule simplification with decorated rewrite rules. Let $t^{:S}, t'^{:S'} \in \mathcal{T}_d(\mathcal{S}_\diamond, \mathcal{F}, \mathcal{X}_\diamond)$, $\phi \in R$ and k be a natural number. Then $t^{:S}$ *layer rewrites* to $t'^{:S'}$, written $t^{:S} \rightleftarrows_R^{\phi,\sigma,k} t'^{:S'}$, if there exists a maximal set O of positions ω in t s.t.$\forall\omega \in O$, $|\omega| = k$ and t concurrently rewrites at positions in O with the same rule ϕ and substitution σ.

Example 5. Let $\phi = (opp(opp(x^{:\{Nat\}})^{:\{Int\}})^{:\{Int\}} \to x^{:\{Nat\}}) \in R$ be a decorated rewrite rule. Consider the decorated following terms:

$$t_1 = (opp(opp(0^{:\{Nat\}})^{:\{Int\}})^{:\{Int\}} * opp(opp(0^{:\{Nat\}})^{:\{Int\}})^{:\{Int\}})^{:\{Int\}}$$
$$t_2 = (opp(opp(s(0^{:\{Nat\}})^{:\{Nat\}})^{:\{Int\}})^{:\{Int\}} * opp(opp(0^{:\{Nat\}})^{:\{Int\}})^{:\{Int\}})^{:\{Int\}}$$
$$t_3 = (opp(opp(0^{:\{Nat\}})^{:\{Int\}})^{:\{Int\}} * s(opp(opp(0^{:\{Nat\}})^{:\{Int\}})^{:\{Int\}})^{:\{Int\}})^{:\{Int\}}$$

Let $\sigma = \{x^{:\{Nat\}} \mapsto 0^{:\{Nat\}}\}$. Then

$$t_1 \rightleftarrows_R^{\phi,\sigma,1} (0^{:\{Nat\}} * 0^{:\{Nat\}})^{:\{Int\}}$$
$$t_2 \rightleftarrows_R^{\phi,\sigma,1} (opp(opp(s(0^{:\{Nat\}})^{:\{Nat\}})^{:\{Int\}})^{:\{Int\}} * 0^{:\{Nat\}})^{:\{Int\}}$$
$$t_3 \rightleftarrows_R^{\phi,\sigma,1} (0^{:\{Nat\}} * s(opp(opp(0^{:\{Nat\}})^{:\{Int\}})^{:\{Int\}})^{:\{Int\}})^{:\{Int\}}$$

Remark that in t_2, the left subterm of $*$ does not match σ and in t_3, there are two identical redexes, but at different depth.

Let us call $\mathcal{LSC}$ the set of completion rules similar to $\mathcal{SSC}$, except that layer rewriting is used instead of standard decorated rewriting defined in section 4, which also changes the definition of critical pairs (see [HKK94b]), now called *layer critical pairs.*

Theorem 5. *[HKK94b] Let $P_\infty \neq (\perp, \perp, \perp)$ be obtained with $\mathcal{LSC}$ from $(D_\mathcal{P}, E_\mathcal{P}, \emptyset)$. Let us assume furthermore that $E_\infty = \emptyset$, all layer critical pairs of $D_\infty \cup R_\infty$ have been computed, and all terms in all generated decoration rules are flat. Then the initial presentation $\mathcal{P}$ is SI on $\mathcal{VT}_d$ and $D_\infty \cup R_\infty$ is Church-Rosser, type and existentially complete.*

Once more, one can prove that it is sufficient to test SI in D_∞. The following example illustrates the use of this proposition and provides a comparison with [Wer93]. Remark that $\rightleftarrows_R$ and $\rightarrowtail_R$ coincide here, whenever $\rightleftarrows_R$ is used.

Example 6. $\mathcal{P} = \{x :: N,\ y :: Z,\ z :: Z,\ x : Z,\ 0 : N,\ suc(x) : N,\ opp(y) : Z,\ sq(y) : N,\ sqrt(x) : N,\ |y| : N,\ y * z : Z,\ |x| = x,\ sq(y) = y * y,\ opp(y) * opp(y) = y * y\}$ The initial decoration rules are:

$$\begin{array}{rll} 0^{:s} & \rightarrow 0^{:s\cup\{N\}} & \text{if } \{N\} \not\subseteq s \\ suc(x^{:\{N\}})^{:s} & \rightarrow suc(x^{:\{N\}})^{:s\cup\{N\}} & \text{if } \{N\} \not\subseteq s' \\ opp(y^{:\{Z\}})^{:s} & \rightarrow opp(y^{:\{Z\}})^{:s\cup\{Z\}} & \text{if } \{Z\} \not\subseteq s \\ sq(y^{:\{Z\}})^{:s} & \rightarrow sq(y^{:\{Z\}})^{:s\cup\{N\}} & \text{if } \{N\} \not\subseteq s \\ sqrt(x^{:\{N\}})^{:s} & \rightarrow sqrt(x^{:\{N\}})^{:s\cup\{N\}} & \text{if } \{N\} \not\subseteq s \\ |y^{:\{Z\}}|^{:s} & \rightarrow |y^{:\{Z\}}|^{:s\cup\{N\}} & \text{if } \{N\} \not\subseteq s \\ (y^{:\{Z\}} * z^{:\{Z\}})^{:s} & \rightarrow (y^{:\{Z\}} * z^{:\{Z\}})^{:s\cup\{Z\}} & \text{if } \{Z\} \not\subseteq s \end{array}$$

The initial decorated equalities:

$$\begin{array}{rl} |x^{:\{N\}}|^{:\emptyset} & = x^{:\{N\}} \\ sq(y^{:\{Z\}})^{:\emptyset} & = (y^{:\{Z\}} * y^{:\{Z\}})^{:\emptyset} \\ (opp(y^{:\{Z\}})^{:\emptyset} * opp(y^{:\{Z\}})^{:\emptyset})^{:\emptyset} & = (y^{:\{Z\}} * y^{:\{Z\}})^{:\emptyset} \end{array}$$

After simplification with decoration rewrite rules, we get:

$$\begin{array}{rl} |x^{:\{N\}}|^{:\{N\}} & = x^{:\{N\}} \\ sq(y^{:\{Z\}})^{:\{N\}} & = (y^{:\{Z\}} * y^{:\{Z\}})^{:\{Z\}} \\ (opp(y^{:\{Z\}})^{:\{Z\}} * opp(y^{:\{Z\}})^{:\{Z\}})^{:\{Z\}} & = (y^{:\{Z\}} * y^{:\{Z\}})^{:\{Z\}} \end{array}$$

Now, decorating and orienting the equalities yields:

$$\begin{array}{rll} |x^{:\{N\}}|^{:\{N\}} & \rightarrow x^{:\{N\}} & \\ sq(y^{:\{Z\}})^{:\{N\}} & \rightarrow (y^{:\{Z\}} * y^{:\{Z\}})^{:\{N,Z\}} & \\ (y^{:\{Z\}} * y^{:\{Z\}})^{:s} & \rightarrow (y^{:\{Z\}} * y^{:\{Z\}})^{:s\cup\{N\}} & \text{if } \{N\} \not\subseteq s \\ (opp(y^{:\{Z\}})^{:\{Z\}} * opp(y^{:\{Z\}})^{:\{Z\}})^{:\{Z\}} & \rightarrow (y^{:\{Z\}} * y^{:\{Z\}})^{:\{N,Z\}} & \end{array}$$

This is already the final presentation, since no more completion rule is applicable.

The equality $sqrt(sq(y)) = sqrt(sq(opp(y)))$ can be proved as follows:

$$\begin{array}{rl} sqrt(sq(y))^{:\downarrow\emptyset} \downarrow_{D\cup R} & =_d sqrt((y^{:\{Z\}} * y^{:\{Z\}})^{:\{N,Z\}})^{:\{N\}} \\ & =_d sqrt(sq(opp(y)))^{:\downarrow\emptyset} \downarrow_{D\cup R}. \end{array}$$

6.3 Arbitrary Term Declarations

Further extension for non-linear arbitrary term declarations needs a different proof reduction [HKK94b] and a rewrite relation in which all identical redexes are reduced simultaneously. A decorated term $t^{:S}$ *rewrites in a maximally subterm sharing way* into $t'^{:S'}$ using a decorated rewrite rule $\phi : l^{:S_l} \rightarrow r^{:S_r}$ and a decorated substitution σ if there exists a maximal set of positions $O = \{\omega \in \mathcal{O}cc(t^{:S}) \mid t^{:S}|_\omega \cong_d \sigma(l^{:S_l})\}$ s.t. t concurrently rewrites at all positions in O. This is written $t^{:S} \twoheadrightarrow^{\sigma,\phi}_R t'^{:S'}$. Clearly, this changes once again the definition of critical pairs.

Example 7. Consider once more ϕ, t_1, t_2, t_3 and σ from example 5. Then

$$t_1 \rightarrowtail\!\!\!\rightarrow_R^{\sigma,\phi} (0^{:\{Nat\}} * 0^{:\{Nat\}})^{:\{Int\}}$$
$$t_2 \rightarrowtail\!\!\!\rightarrow_R^{\sigma,\phi} (opp(opp(s(0^{:\{Nat\}})^{:\{Nat\}})^{:\{Int\}})^{:\{Int\}} * 0^{:\{Nat\}})^{:\{Int\}}$$
$$t_3 \rightarrowtail\!\!\!\rightarrow_R^{\sigma,\phi} (0^{:\{Nat\}} * s(0^{:\{Nat\}})^{:\{Int\}})^{:\{Int\}}$$

Remark that in t_2, again the left subterm of $*$ does not match σ, but in t_3, the two identical redexes are reduced simultaneously this time.

The set of completion rules called $\mathcal{MSSC}$ is obtained from $\mathcal{SSC}$ by dropping any simplification by decorated rewrite rules and using adequate critical pairs, called $\mathcal{MSS}$-critical pairs. The completion rules have to be applied with a strategy that essentially gives a higher priority to computation of critical pairs between decoration rewrite rules (see [HKK94b]).

Theorem 6. *Let $P_\infty \neq (\bot, \bot, \bot)$ be obtained with $\mathcal{MSSC}$ from $(D_\mathcal{P}, E_\mathcal{P}, \emptyset)$ s.t. the strategy restrictions are fulfilled. Let us assume furthermore that $E_\infty = \emptyset$ and all $\mathcal{MSS}$-critical pairs of $D_\infty \cup R_\infty$ have been computed. Then the initial presentation $\mathcal{P}$ is SI on $\mathcal{VT}_d$ and $D_\infty \cup R_\infty$ is Church-Rosser, type and existentially complete.*

Remark that under the conditions of this theorem, $\mathcal{P}$ is SI and hence full $\mathcal{OSC}$ from [HKK94a] can be applied to continue completion, i.e. essentially interreduce the rules in $D_\infty \cup R_\infty$. Note that every $\rightrightarrows_R^{\phi,\sigma,k}$ and $\rightarrowtail\!\!\!\rightarrow_R^{\sigma,\phi}$ step can be replaced by a sequence of $\rightarrowtail_R^{\sigma,\phi,\omega}$ steps, i.e. all proofs using the former relations can be transformed into ones using $\rightarrowtail_R^{\sigma,\phi,\omega}$ only.

In order to illustrate the difficulties arising with non-flat, non-linear term declarations, consider the following example:

Example 8. Let $nil \rightarrow List$ and $cons : NatList \rightarrow List$ be the usual operator declarations for lists of natural numbers. Now, if we want to distinguish lists, where two identical numbers follow each other (let us call them ML, for multi-lists), we need to say something like, $cons(x, cons(x, l)) : ML$, where x is of sort Nat and l of sort $List$.

Remark that ML should now be declared as subsort of $List$, i.e. $ML \leq_S^{syn} List$. The non-linear, non-flat term declaration becomes in the decorated term framework the following self-overlapping decoration rewrite rule ϕ:

$$cons(x^{:\{Nat\}}, cons(x^{:\{Nat\}}, l^{:\{List\}})^{:\{List\}})^{:s}$$
$$\rightarrow cons(x^{:\{Nat\}}, cons(x^{:\{Nat\}}, l^{:\{List\}})^{:\{List\}})^{:s \cup \{ML\}} \text{ if } \{ML\} \not\subseteq s$$

Now, overlapping ϕ at position 2 with itself or the result of the overlap can be repeated ad infinitum, resulting in a non-terminating completion of the set of decoration rewrite rules. Hence, the SI test is not complete either, since we cannot guarantee confluence. This situation may be encountered with practically relevant examples – for instance multisets realized as ordered lists.

The way out of this dilemma seems to be the use of more sophisticated decoration rewrite rules, like the following ϕ':

$$\begin{aligned} & cons(x^{:\{Nat\}}, cons(x^{:\{Nat\}}, l^{:\{List\}})^{:\{ML\}})^{:s} \\ & \quad \rightarrow cons(x^{:\{Nat\}}, cons(x^{:\{Nat\}}, l^{:\{List\}})^{:\{ML\}})^{:s \cup \{ML\}} \text{ if } \{ML\} \not\subseteq s \end{aligned}$$

Remark that the only difference to ϕ consists in the decoration at position 2, which became ML instead of $List$. Using ϕ and ϕ' does not prevent ϕ from being self-overlapping but makes the result of the overlap being subsumed by ϕ'. Hence, the completion of ϕ and ϕ' only terminates.

ϕ' does not correspond to any formula in G-algebra. However, allowing for conditional rules for membership formulas, similar to the sort constraints in [GJM85], gives an extension of G-algebra where ϕ' is translated into the following formula:

$$cons(x, cons(x, l)) : ML \quad \textbf{if} \quad cons(x, l) : ML$$

We extended G-algebras lately to an equational Horn clause logics, called G^n-logics [HKM94], where sets of nesting depth up to n can be specified. Sets of depth 1 correspond with sorts. G^n-logics share the useful properties of existence of a sound and complete deduction system and initial models with G-algebras. We hope to extend the results given in this paper to a fragment of G^n-logics covering the problems illustrated by the last example.

7 Related Work and Conclusion

Completion procedures for order-sorted algebraic specifications have already been proposed, but either fail by non-sort decreasingness or do not handle term declarations and semantic sorts. The completion using "syntactic sorts" [GKK90] is subsumed by our completion, i.e. for every completion in that framework, we can do a similar one using our decorated completion.

The tree automata approach of [Com92] produces rewrite rule schemas using second order variables instead of critical pairs between decoration rewrite rules and decorated rewrite rules. In [HKK94b], we give an example for a specification, that can be completed in a finite number of steps using our approach, but which does not terminate with the approach described in [Com92].

Another related approach is the signature extension method [CH91], which introduces new function symbols in order to solve the problem of equalities that cannot be oriented into sort-decreasing rules. However, this technique does not seem to be well-adapted to functional programming, since evaluation may result in a term involving a new function symbol that has no interpretation in the initial specification.

The T-contact method ([Wer93]) uses variable overlaps in order to cope with non-sort-decreasing rules. This results in a high number of new equations and may cause the completion to diverge.

The works of L. With (see [Wit92]) or Watson and Dick [WD89]) are very close to our approach, but do not really contain solutions concerning the undecidability problems for unification. More detailed comparisons with all these approaches can be found in [HKK94b]. We currently investigate relations with unified algebras [Mos89] or many-sorted algebras with semantic sorts and sort operations [Mei92].

To summarize, the main contribution of this paper relies in the elaboration of a test for sort inheritance in presentations with term declarations. Even when term declarations are not explicitely used in specifications, they may occur as a consequence of equality orientation when the semantic sort approach is adopted (see Example 6) and it is thus crucial to handle them in completion.

Decorations have been successfully used to formalize typing and to compute with semantic sorts. While keeping the interesting notion of sorts as constraints, they provide an adequate tool for testing sort inheritance.

Acknowledgements: We thank Uwe Waldmann and Andreas Werner for their comments on earlier drafts of this work. This work is partially supported by the Esprit Basic Research working group 6112, COMPASS.

References

[CH91] H. Chen and J. Hsiang. Order-sorted equational specification and completion. Technical report, State University of New York at Stony Brook, November 1991.

[Com92] H. Comon. Completion of rewrite systems with membership constraints. In W. Kuich, editor, *Proceedings of ICALP 92*, volume 623 of *Lecture Notes in Computer Science*. Springer-Verlag, 1992.

[DJ90] N. Dershowitz and J.-P. Jouannaud. Rewrite Systems. In J. van Leeuwen, editor, *Handbook of Theoretical Computer Science*, chapter 6, pages 244–320. Elsevier Science Publishers B. V. (North-Holland), 1990.

[GJM85] J. A. Goguen, J.-P. Jouannaud, and J. Meseguer. Operational semantics for order-sorted algebra. In W. Brauer, editor, *Proceeding of the 12th International Colloquium on Automata, Languages and Programming, Nafplion (Greece)*, volume 194 of *Lecture Notes in Computer Science*, pages 221–231. Springer-Verlag, 1985.

[GKK90] I. Gnaedig, C. Kirchner, and H. Kirchner. Equational completion in order-sorted algebras. *Theoretical Computer Science*, 72:169–202, 1990.

[GM92] J. A. Goguen and J. Meseguer. Order-sorted algebra I: equational deduction for multiple inheritance, overloading, exceptions and partial operations. *Theoretical Computer Science*, 2(105):217–273, 1992.

[HKK94a] C. Hintermeier, C. Kirchner, and H. Kirchner. Dynamically-typed computations for order-sorted equational presentations –extended abstract–. In S. Abiteboul and E. Shamir, editors, *Proc. 21st International Colloquium on Automata, Languages, and Programming*, volume 820 of *Lecture Notes in Computer Science*, pages 450–461. Springer-Verlag, 1994.

[HKK94b] C. Hintermeier, C. Kirchner, and H. Kirchner. Dynamically-typed computations for order-sorted equational presentations. research report 2208, INRIA, Inria Lorraine, March 1994. 114 p., also as CRIN report 93-R-309.

[HKM94] C. Hintermeier, H. Kirchner, and P. Mosses. R^n- and G^n-logics. Technical report, Centre de Recherche en Informatique de Nancy, 1994.

[JK91] J.-P. Jouannaud and C. Kirchner. Solving equations in abstract algebras: a rule-based survey of unification. In J.-L. Lassez and G. Plotkin, editors, *Computational Logic. Essays in honor of Alan Robinson*, chapter 8, pages 257–321. The MIT press, Cambridge (MA, USA), 1991.

[Még90] A. Mégrelis. *Algèbre galactique — Un procédé de calcul formel, relatif aux semi-fonctions, à l'inclusion et à l'égalité.* Thèse de Doctorat d'Université, Université de Nancy 1, 1990.

[Mei92] K. Meinke. Algebraic semantics of rewriting terms and types. In M. Rusinowitch and J. Rémy, editors, *Proceedings 3rd International Workshop on Conditional Term Rewriting Systems, Pont-à-Mousson (France)*, volume 656 of *Lecture Notes in Computer Science*, pages 1–20. Springer-Verlag, 1992.

[Mos89] P. D. Mosses. Unified algebras and institutions. In *Proceedings 4th IEEE Symposium on Logic in Computer Science, Pacific Grove*, pages 304–312, 1989.

[Obe62] A. Oberschelp. Untersuchungen zur mehrsortigen Quantorenlogik. *Math. Annalen*, 145(1):297–333, 1962.

[Sco77] D. Scott. Identity and existence in intuitionistic logic. In M. P. Fourman and C. J. Mulvey, editors, *Applications of Sheaves*, volume 753 of *Lecture Notes in Mathematics*, pages 660–696. Springer-Verlag, 1977.

[Smo89] G. Smolka. *Logic Programming over Polymorphically Order-Sorted Types.* PhD thesis, FB Informatik, Universität Kaiserslautern, Germany, 1989.

[SNGM89] G. Smolka, W. Nutt, J. A. Goguen, and J. Meseguer. Order-sorted equational computation. In H. Aït-Kaci and M. Nivat, editors, *Resolution of Equations in Algebraic Structures, Volume 2: Rewriting Techniques*, pages 297–367. Academic Press, 1989.

[SS87] M. Schmidt-Schauß. *Computational Aspects of an Order-Sorted Logic with Term Declarations.* PhD thesis, Universität Kaiserslautern (Germany), 1987.

[Wal92] U. Waldmann. Semantics of order-sorted specifications. *Theoretical Computer Science*, 94(1):1–33, 1992.

[WD89] P. Watson and J. Dick. Least sorts in order-sorted term rewriting. Technical report, Royal Holloway and Bedford New College, University of London, 1989.

[Wer93] A. Werner. A semantic approach to order-sorted rewriting. In C. Kirchner, editor, *Proceedings 5th Conference on Rewriting Techniques and Applications, Montreal (Canada)*, volume 690 of *Lecture Notes in Computer Science*, pages 47–61. Springer-Verlag, 1993.

[Wit92] L. With. Completeness and confluence of order-sorted term rewriting. In M. Rusinowitch and J.-L. Rémy, editors, *Proceedings 3rd International Workshop on Conditional Term Rewriting Systems, Pont-à-Mousson (France)*, number 656 in Lecture Notes in Computer Science, pages 393–407. Springer-Verlag, July 1992.

Axiomatic Specification of Large Information Systems: Experiences and Consequences

Heinrich Hussmann [1]

Siemens AG, Public Communication Networks Group
Hofmannstr. 51, 81359 München, Germany [2]

Abstract. This paper reports on a case study where formal (axiomatic) techniques were applied to the functional specification of a large medical information system. In order to cope with the size of the specification and with the process of requirements engineering, a combination of semi-formal (mainly diagrammatic) and purely formal notations were used. For the semi-formal notations, a translation into axiomatic specifications was defined such that the whole specification is still on the formal level. In this paper, a short overview of the case study is given together with a critical evaluation. Two problematic issues are pointed out regarding the results of the case study, and proposals for a further improvement are made. The systematic usage of a hybrid approach mixing semi-formal and formal notation is strongly recommended for the precise specification of large application systems.

1 Introduction

1.1 Why Yet Another Case Study?

Research in formal methods of software specification and development always was accompanied by experiments in applying the methods to realistic examples. A collection of case studies is given in [6], more recent surveys are [2, 5]. Unfortunately, most of the reported case studies refer to relatively small systems; for instance the largest code size mentioned in [5] is 10 KLOC[3], which was achievable only with very extensive manpower effort. So serious doubts remain whether formal methods are scalable to very large application cases. This scalability problem seems to be connected with a missing integration of formal methods with the techniques used nowadays in industry for managing the development of large systems. In particular, the systematic analysis of system requirements usually involves techniques which are quite different from formal notation; so a smooth transition into formal design

---

1 The work reported here was carried out when the author was at the Institut für Informatik, Technische Universität München. It was sponsored by the German Ministry of Research and Technology (BMFT) as part of the compound project KORSO.

2 Email address: hussmann@oenzl.siemens.de

3 KLOC = Thousand lines of code

specification is needed. This position is supported by the following statement, taken from [5]: "There is a clear need for improved integration of formal methods with other Software Engineering practices. [...] Successful integration is important to the long-term success of formal methods."

Recently, several approaches are discussed which try to integrate formal methods with traditional Software Engineering methods, most of them oriented towards Entity-Relationship modelling or Structured Analysis. An overview is given in [15], an example of an ambitious project in this area is SAZ (SSADM plus Z [14]). However, only little experience is available how these integrated approaches work in larger case studies.

So the main aim of the case study reported here was to try out an approach integrating formal and semi-formal methods for a large application. The example was chosen is such a way that it shows many of the problems appearing in a particular kind of large systems (information systems).

1.2 HDMS-A: A Medical Information System

This paper reports on a case study where formal (axiomatic) techniques were applied to the functional specification of a large medical information system. The application which was specified in this experiment is an abstract version of an integrated medical information system for a specialised hospital.

The "Deutsches Herz-Zentrum Berlin" (literally translated: German Heart Center Berlin) is a hospital which is specialised into the diagnosis and therapy of cardiac diseases. This area of medicine involves extensive use of modern technology like cardiac catheterization or automated blood analysis procedures. It is the aim of the HDMS project (Heterogeneous Distributed Data Management System) to provide an integrated computer-supported access to all the medical and administrative data for the patients in this clinic. This is a practical project which mainly adresses the problems caused by interfacing quite heterogeneous hardware and software systems, including the deployment of a broadband communication network for medical data.

Independently of these more realisation-oriented aspects, the organisation of the medical and administrative work in the hospital was analysed within the HDMS project, in order to describe the necessary functionality of the integrated information system. The HDMS-A case study (where the suffix "-A" means "abstract version") concentrates on this aspect; it covers pure functionality without reference to implementation decisions. For the case study reported here, a subset of the needed functionality was selected and specified in detail. This subset covers typical representatives for the most important functions to be supported by the information system, but it has reduced the amount of the material such that it could be dealt with in an academic research project. HDMS-A covers the following four functional areas in the hospital:

- Reception: Check-in and check-out of patients
- Ward: Daily routine of patient care (medication, blood samples etc.)
- Laboratory: Automated analysis of blood samples
- Cardiac Catheterization, as an example for a complex medical treatment.

1.3 KORSO: A Formal Methods Project

The project KORSO (1990-1994) was a compound research project in which 13 German universities and one industrial partner (Siemens Central Research) were involved. Its aim was to investigate the applicability of formal methods to realistic software development problems. The scope of the project includes specification languages, software development methodology as well as improvement of automated support tools. Obviously, a significant part of the effort in this project went into case studies. HDMS-A was one of the largest case studies carried out within KORSO. Its purpose was to investigate the transfer of formal (axiomatic) development methods towards large application cases; other supplementary case studies were dedicated to smaller but algorithmically more complex examples.

1.4 The HDMS-A Case Study

In the HDMS-A case study, 11 different organisations were involved[4]. Within HDMS-A, several different aspects were studied by the various partners, as summarized in [4]. This paper reports only on the part of the case study where an abstract specification of the functionality of the system was given, based on quite informal requirements descriptions.

The resulting specification is a document of approximately 50 pages [16] which is accompanied by a set of papers explaining the approach which was taken [7, 8, 11]. However, the process of development of this document was an incremental one. Starting from informal descriptions supplied by the collegues in Berlin, the rest of the group tried to give a formal abstract specification. This effort led to various important questions which were to be answered on the informal level, for instance by asking specialists familiar with the clinic. After several revisions of the informal requirements descriptions as well as the formal specification, finally a stable state of all these documents was reached. So in summary, only a relatively small effort went into formal specification, and much work was invested into informal investigations. This observation illustrates a fact which, unfortunately, is not yet a common understanding of all people working with formal methods: As soon as the application reaches a significant size, formal methods can no longer be seen as a replacement for the techniques known from classical Software Engineering. Instead, a way has to be found for *synergistic use* of established Software Engineering techniques and formal methods.

2 Formality Applied to Functional Specification

2.1 Formal vs. Semi-Formal Specification

Generally, there is a well-known trade-off between formal specification of the functionality of a system and the more traditional approaches, which we will call here "semi-formal". A formal method is usually based on mathematics, as the language SPECTRUM [3] which was used in HDMS-A. Such specifications have a very precise semantics; so in theory they do not necessarily require any additional explanations in natural language. Semi-formal approaches also use a fixed syntactical framework, but

---

[4] Technische Universität Berlin, Universität Bremen, Technische Universität Braunschweig, Universität Karlsruhe, Forschungszentrum Informatik Karlsruhe, Ludwig-Maximilians-Universität München, Universität Oldenburg, Universität des Saarlandes Saarbrücken, Siemens AG München, Universität Ulm

usually with a less rigorous definition. The semi-formal documents (in most cases, diagrams and tables) are meaningful only if accompanied by explanatory text in plain prose.

Formal methods (as the method around the axiomatic specification language SPECTRUM) ensure a high level of semantic precision. The disadvantage is here that these precise descriptions are very difficult to understand even for well-trained readers. So in practical applications, also the formal approach to specification relies on textual explanations to achieve an understandable style of specification. In particular during the very early stages of a specification where concepts are sketched only roughly, without going into technical detail, formal specifications are not yet helpful.

The advantage of the semi-formal methods is that they cover a tentative level of thinking which is necessary anyway in the development of a system, whether the aim is a formal specification or not. In any case, clear textual explanations, a clear terminology and illustrative pictorial sketches are of great help in the development of a system specification. Moreover, many of the semi-formal approaches come complete with extensive methodical guidance, which has been distilled out of hundreds of large development projects. However, a semi-formal method cannot prohibit the danger of misinterpretation and ambiguity which is inherent to any natural language.

So it is a quite obvious idea to combine the advantages of semi-formal and formal approaches into a hybrid approach. This idea has been investigated already by a number of authors for several combinations of approaches. The original contribution of HDMS-A is in this context that the introduction of semi-formal notation was driven by practical needs when dealing with a large example.

2.2 Hybrid Formal / Semi-Formal Specification

For the formal methods specialists involved in HDMS-A, it was a somehow surprising experience that the specification turned out as a *large task composed of many almost trivial pieces*. For instance, the information held in the medical data base is rich in detail and in volume; the logical structure, however, follows a simple record-like schema. Similarly hundreds of access and update functions to the data base exist in a pure algebraic view, which again follow a generic schema. So for the HDMS-A specification, we did not only combine formal and semi-formal notation by putting it together in one document, but we have constructed a much more intense relationship between the two kinds of notations. The semi-formal notations are understood as *abbreviations for schematic parts of a formal specification.*

The HDMS-A approach uses a selection of semi-formal notations for which a schematic *translation* into pure axiomatic SPECTRUM specifications could be given. If this translation is applied consequently, the semi-formal specifications even get the quality of formal specifications, where repeated schematic parts have been condensed into "macros". But please note that the hybrid approach allows the specifier to use semi-formal notations also in a preliminary stage, without the detailed translation in mind, and therefore enables a smooth transition between semi-formal and formal levels of thinking about the system to be realized.

The semi-formal notations which were used in the HDMS-A case study were:

- Entity-Relationship Diagrams [7] and
- Data Flow Diagrams [11].

This decision has enabled us to follow closely the methodical guidance offered by so-called "Essential Systems Analysis" [10], to obtain a specification of true functionality, which abstracts from all implementation details.

3 The KORSO Specification of HDMS-A

3.1 Entity-Relationship Model

For a large information system like HDMS-A, the set of data held in the system always has the form of a collection of linked records. For the representation of such a data structure, more specialised representations are much more adequate than the universal mechanism of abstract data types. The most frequently used representation is here the Entity-Relationship (ER) diagram. The data model of an information system is similar to an instantiation of a special abstract data type scheme which provides the notation used in ER diagrams. The ER diagram is supplemented by a more detailed description of the internal structure of the records (attributes). Due to space limitations, we omit this aspect here, and just mention that attributes and keys are handled in the same style as the ER diagram itself.

In HDMS-A, a precise definition of the meaning of an ER diagram was given by a schematic translation into an axiomatic specification, as described in [7]. So the ER diagram for HDMS-A can be viewed as an abbreviation for a relatively large axiomatic specification. The specification document of HDMS-A itself does contain only the ER diagram and not the corresponding formal specification, since the inclusion of this lengthy formal text would not improve the understandability of the specification. To give an impression of the size of the case study, figure 1 shows the full ER diagram for the HDMS-A case study.

The schematic translation of the ER diagram of figure 1 into the axiomatic specification language SPECTRUM introduces:

- A data base sort `Db`;
- A sort for each entity in the diagram, for instance, `Patient` and `Stay`;
- For each entity in the diagram, algebraic operations to put records into the data base and to remove them, for instance for the entity "Patient":
  `put_Patient: Patient × Db → Db;`
- For each entity in the diagram, algebraic operations to test the presence of records in the data base and to retrieve them, for instance for the entity "Lab-Order":
  `get_LabOrder: OrderNo × Db → Db;`
  As it can be seen from this example, the selection of a record requires some identifying attribute values (key) to be known. This information appears as a parameter in the function signature (here: OrderNo), and is derived from the attribute descriptions of the entities (which are not discussed here).
- For each relationship between entities in the diagram, algebraic operations to establish and remove such a link, for instance for the relationship "spends":
  `establish_spends: Db × Patient × Stay → Db;`
- For each relationship between entities in the diagram, an algebraic operation to test the presence of such a link between two given entity instances, for instance for the relationship "leads_to" between "Lab-Order" and "Blood-Count":
  `leads_to: Db → LabOrder × BloodCount → Bool;`

Moreover, the special marks which are found at the endpoints of a relationship (crow's foot and dashed lines) are translated into algebraically formulated integrity conditions for the data base, concerning the maximal and minimal number of records which can involve themselves into a certain relationship.

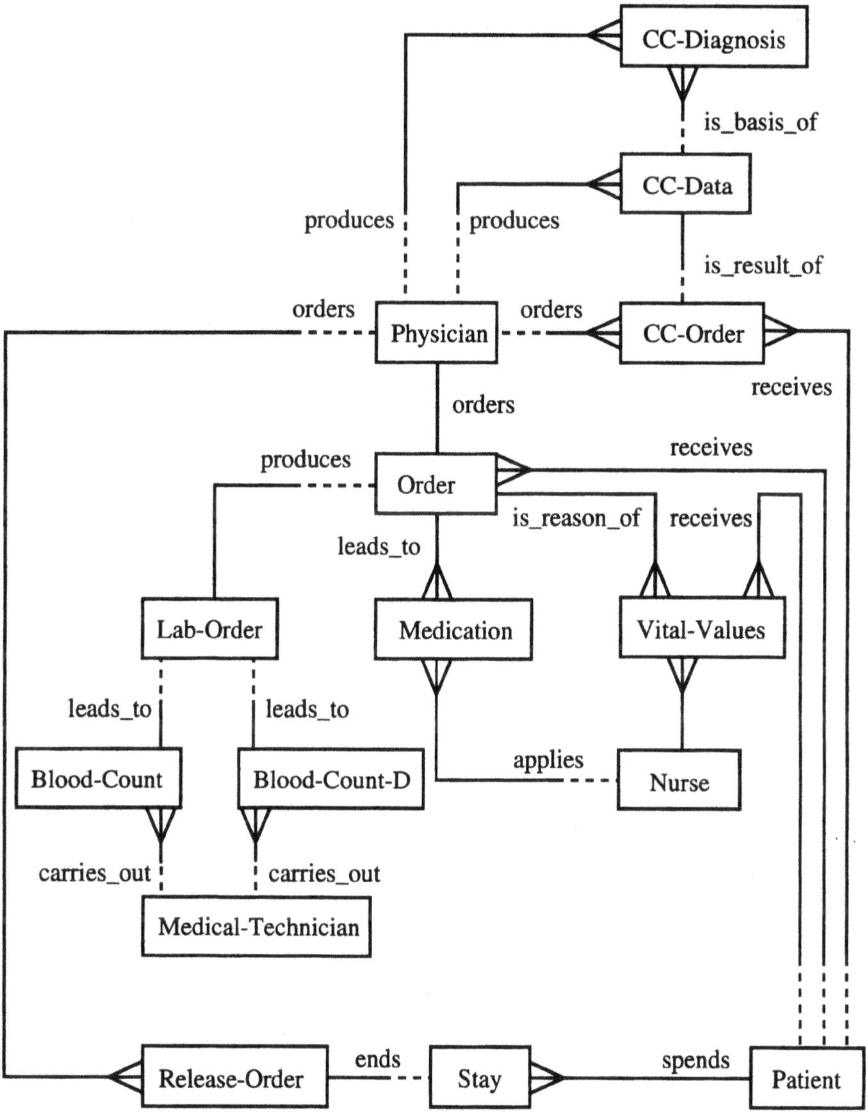

Fig. 1. HDMS-A Entity-Relationship Diagram

The SPECTRUM signature which is derived by this translation from the ER diagram forms the basis for all further specification of the HDMS-A system. The further specification covers mainly the dynamic aspects of the system (see sections 3.2 and 3.3). But also the static data structure can be specified more precisely, using the translated ER diagram as a basis. For instance, a few more complex integrity conditions for the data base of HDMS-A should be defined in plain axiomatic SPECTRUM. These are conditions which are not expressible within an ER diagram.

An example for such a SPECTRUM integrity condition is the following condition, which can be easily formulated as a formal predicate on the data base sort:

> "For each 'Patient', there is at most one connected 'Stay' which is not yet terminated by a 'Release-Order'."

In the HDMS-A case study, this condition (as several similar ones) is expressed by a SPECTRUM predicate on data base states. The full power of first-order logic is available here, and the formulation can rely on the sorts and functions available from the translation of the ER diagram.

3.2 Data Flow Modelling

The dynamic aspects of the system are described in the HDMS-A specification by a combination of semi-formal notation (data flow diagrams) and formal notation (axiomatic specifications in SPECTRUM). In contrast to the static aspects, the formal part of the specification is much more dominant here, but the data flow diagrams provide a simple pictorial introduction to the detailed specification of system dynamics.

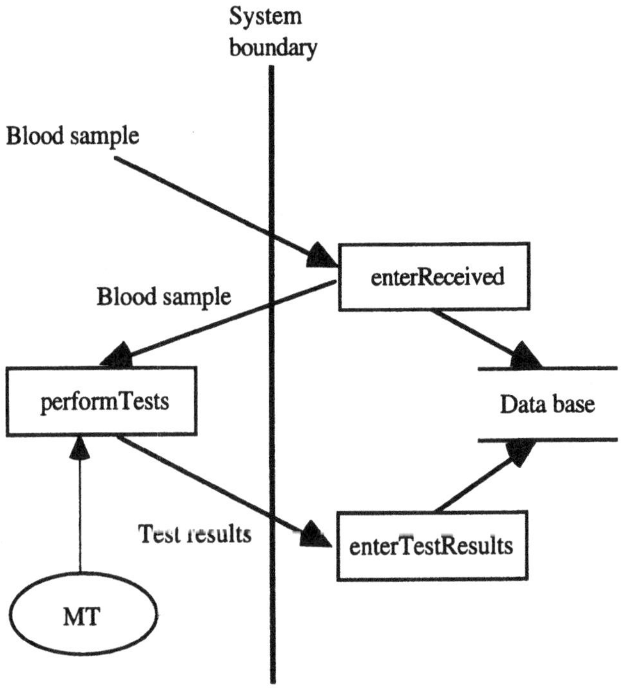

Fig. 2. Sample Data Flow Diagram

As a simple example for a data flow diagram, figure 2 shows a part of the functionality of the laboratory, where blood samples are tested for chemical and biological parameter values. This is an interesting example, since this functionality involves a mixture of system-internal and system-external activities. Please note that figure 2 is only an excerpt (about one third) of the respective diagram in the HDMS-A specification. Moreover, the specification contains seven other data flow diagrams of about the same size.

The data flow diagram of figure 2 shows three different aspects of system functionality:

- Everything which is placed outside (left) of the "system boundary" is carried out by humans or by equipment external to the system. Here the tests on the blood samples are carried out by some functional block which is external to the system. The person operating the equipment (a medical technician, abbreviated by MT) is also indicated here.

- The input and output of the functional blocks is shown by the arrows. Arrows crossing the system border denote input and output of the system, arrows to or from the data base symbol indicate update and read operations on the data base.

- Finally, some order of execution is implied, as an incoming blood sample triggers a chain of activities: Its receipt in the laboratory is registered, the blood tests are performed and the resulting data is recorded in the data base.

Please note that the data flow diagram does not yet tell us anything about the detailed content of any of the functional blocks it shows. It is possible to refine a box into a collection of further boxes, stopping at some level of refinement. If a box in the data flow diagram represents some system-internal computation and is no longer refined into other boxes, it is called an *elementary transaction*. The semantics of elementary transactions is left to the formal specification level (see section 3.3 below). However, the information which chain of activities is triggered by an incoming sample is described by the diagram so precisely that it can be translated into a formal specification.

In [11, 12] it is explained in detail how a data flow diagram can be interpreted as a network of communicating agents, and how SPECTRUM's facilities to define stream-processing functions can be used to specify precisely the communication behaviour of such a network. We do not go into the details of this translation here, since this would require relatively complex technical background information.

3.3 Specification of Elementary Transactions

The detailed semantics of the elementary transactions which appear in the data flow diagrams for HDMS-A are specified in plain SPECTRUM. Each elementary transaction corresponds to a single algebraic operation declared in the specification, the semantics of which may be given through several axioms. This specification is based on the semi-formal documents in the following way:

- From the ER diagram, the derived sorts and functions are used in the formal specification of elementary transactions.

- From the data flow diagram, the signature (the parameter line) of the elementary transaction is derived.

As an example, consider the elementary transaction "enterTestResults" from figure 2. The data flow diagram shows that this transaction updates the data base, therefore the data base sort `Db` appears as an input parameter and as a result value in the signature of the corresponding algebraic operation. Additional input parameters cover the test results, as also shown in the diagram, and additional information to uniquely identify the blood sample (laboratory order number) and to identify the medical technician who has carried out the test (MT identifier). The signature is therefore:

```
enterTestResults: Db × OrderNo × MTId × TestResults → Db;
```

In the HDMS-A example, it has turned out that most of the elementary transactions are adequately specified by exactly two axioms. The first axiom specifies the definedness of the result depending on the input parameters (since SPECTRUM operations generally are partial), the second axiom gives an explicit definition of the result value. For the example transaction, the definedness axioms reads as follows, where the δ-sign is a universal definedness test (predefined in SPECTRUM):

```
δ (enterTestResults(db, no, mtid, res)) ⇔
    δ (get_LabOrder(no, db)) ∧
    δ (get_MedicalTechnician(mitid, db))∧
    (¬∃v. (leads_to db (get_LabOrder(no, db), v)));
```

This definedness condition ensures that the laboratory order and the MT identifier are valid and that the data base does not yet contain results for this laboratory order. As indicated above, the functions `get_LabOrder` and `get_MedicalTechnician` are implicitly defined by the ER diagram, as well as the predicate `leads_to`, which tests for the presence of a relationship link in the data base.

The result values for the transaction are defined by the following axiom:

```
δ (enterTestResults(db, no, mtid, res)) ⇒
    let bc = create_BloodCount(no, res, time(db))
    and a = get_LabOrder(no, db)
    and mt = get_MedicalTechician(mtid, db)
    and db' = put_BloodCount(bc, db)
    in
    enterTestResults(db, no, mtid, res) =
            establish_leads_to(
            establish_carries_out(db', bc, mt), a, bc)
    endlet;
```

This axiom provides an explicit step-by-step explanation of the elementary transaction: A new data record for the results of the test is created (which is called a "blood count" for historical reasons), the data records for the laboratory order and the MT identification are retrieved from the data base. Afterwards, the new data record is entered into the database and linked with the laboratory order and the MT.

This style of specifying the functionality is well suitable for relatively large information systems, as can be seen from the HDMS-A experiment. However, also a number of problematic issues also can be observed. Therefore the rest of this paper is devoted towards a critical evaluation of the specification style which was used in HDMS-A.

4 First Criticism: Explicitness

4.1 Explicitness vs. Abstractness

A closer look on the formal specification of elementary transactions shows that the steps to be performed in such a transaction and even their order are defined quite *explicitly*. In fact, axioms like those given above can be seen as *programs* on a rather abstract level which could be executed by an appropriate software tool. This is in some sense a contradiction to the aims of algebraic specification (and formal specification in general) which claim to describe functionality on a quite abstract level. Compared with, for instance, an SQL program performing the same functionality, the algebraic specification does not provide a significant gain in abstractness.

The quite explicit style of definition has been chosen mainly due to one problem, which is so general that it appears also in several other approaches to formal specification of large systems. In an interesting paper, Borgida, Mylopoulos and Reiter [1] have given a detailed treatment of this question: How to specify that "nothing else changes".

4.2 The Closure Problem

At a first look, one could find it quite easy to give a formal *and* descriptive specification of an elementary transaction like "enterTestResults" from above. For instance, such a specification could just state:

- That there is a new "Blood-Count" record in the data base after the transaction which was not present before.
- That there are new links between this record and some existing records (laboratory order, MT), which were not present before.

However, there remains the problem to state that these are *all* the updates to the database. Without a statement of "nothing else changes", it would be perfectly admitted to remove for instance some patient record from the data base which is not involved in the current transaction at all!

In [1] it is mentioned that this class of problem appears in several areas of computer science, since it is related to the simple fact that most description mechanisms rely on logical monotony. Typical variants of the "nothing else changes"-problem are the incorporation of negation into logic programming (negation as failure) and the frame problem in artificial intelligence.

So the challenge is to find some level of description which is as precise as the formal description from section 3.3 (including "nothing else changes"), but which is more abstract. The next section tries to sketch a proposal fulfilling these requirements.

4.3 Proposal: Matrix Techniques

In several semi-formal specification frameworks (for instance in SSADM or in James Martin's Information Engineering), extensive use of *matrices* is made in order to provide an overview of all the elementary transactions in a system and their scope with respect to the data model. Figure 3 shows an example for this style of description, adapted to the "enterTestResults" example. The columns in this matrix are labelled by so-called *targets*. In simple cases, a target is identical with an entity name. However, if several records of the same entity are updated by the same elementary transaction, an additional qualification may be necessary to distinguish these different targets. For our example, it is sufficient to use entity names for the targets. The rows of the matrix are labelled with names of elementary transactions.

The entries in the matrix are simple codes indicating whether the respective target remains unchanged (no entry) or otherwise specifiying the kind of update which takes place. The updates are classified here as one out of "created", "modified" or "deleted". From such a matrix, a formal specification can be derived in a schematic way which restricts the maximal extent of updates by an elementary transaction. This specification then takes over the duty of specifying the cases where "nothing else changes", and the formal specification of the elementary specifications themselves is free to be formulated in a more descriptive style.

Targets / Elem. transactions	...	LabOrder	...	BloodCount
...				
enter TestResults		modified		created
...				

Fig. 3. Example Transaction/Target Matrix

Due to space restrictions, the details of such a matrix technique cannot be worked out here in detail. However, the approach has been applied successfully to specifications in the framework of SSADM, as it is documented in [9].

Obviously, this kind of approach is not restricted to the level of creation, modification and removal of whole records from the database. The same style of description can also be applied to more detailed levels, for instance to the attributes of a given record or the links in which a record participates. This means the introduction of more matrices into the specification document. These matrices are more easy to read than the compact formal specifications which are used in the current HDMS-A specification; and they enable more simplicity and more abstractness in the formal specification texts which accompany the matrices.

It is an interesting observation that the abstractness of a hybrid formal / semi-formal specification can be improved by enlarging the semi-formal portion of it. This is due to the fact that a closure principle is for good reasons part of the informal concepts for the specification of information systems. Therefore, it also makes sense to give a precise formal semantics for this principle only once and generically for all specifications using the hybrid method.

5 Second Criticism: Semantic Complexity

5.1 Semantic Complexity of Data Flow Modelling

In a second aspect, the specification style which is used in HDMS-A is viable, but not yet perfect. It has turned out that the formal semantics for data flow diagrams (which interprets them as networks of communicating agents) is relatively complex and difficult to understand for non-specialists. In the HDMS-A approach, the role of data flow diagrams is a twofold one:

- On one hand, the data flow diagrams give an overview of the elementary transactions and form the basis for the signature in the detailed specification. The discussion of data flow diagrams in this paper has followed this aspect of data flow diagrams.

- On the other hand, if the data flow diagrams are viewed as a model of a distributed system, they entail specific orders of execution which have to be supported for the elementary transactions. For instance, some data item may be communicated from elementary transaction A (where it is output) into elementary transaction B (where it is input). In this case, the transaction B has to accept everything which is a legal output of A. The detailed formal specifications have to be checked whether they mirror this relationship between A and B.

On the basis of the HDMS-A specification, these semantic consistency tests between data flow diagrams and formal specifications of elementary transactions are possible. Several examples for such proofs have been carried out by a specialist in the formal modelling of data flow diagrams. However, in the current stage of development the semantics is too sophisticated for being used, for instance, in an industrial context.

5.2 Distributed vs. Centralized Formal Models

The problems concerning the semantic complexity of data flow diagrams are not restricted to the HDMS-A approach. In fact, most of the documented approaches to integrate formal and semi-formal specification techniques are devoted to the topic of semantics for data flow diagrams (see [15] for an overview). Several variants of the dynamic semantics of data flow diagrams have been developed, which essentially demonstrates that data flow diagrams do not have a unique and clear semantics at all. See [13] for an interesting discussion of this topic.

In a more global perspective, it seems questionable whether data flow diagrams are the right approach to specify the dynamics of a system. In particular in the specification of an information system, it is not adequate to view the information system itself as a distributed system. The whole information system should, for the sake of abstractness, be viewed as a single process composed of various functional units. The only aspect of distribution and communication which is present also in an abstract specification of functionality is between the system and *external entities* (like users and external equipment). For most of these external entities, it is not realistic to specify their behaviour in such a level of detail that mathematics can be applied.

5.3 Proposal: Restricted Use of Data Flow Diagrams

So one experience out of the HDMS-A case study is (at least in the personal view of the author), that the role of data flow diagrams in system specification should be revised. The restricted use of data flow diagrams which was used in this paper (as an overview picture, and as a representation of the signature of elementary transactions) seems adequate and usable. However, this means that data flow diagrams are restricted to a specification of *static* aspects of the system, and they are no longer related to system dynamics. This is also more adequate for the term "data flow" diagram, which has been explicitly coined as a counterpart of control flow.

The practical consequence of such a restricted use of data flow diagrams is that only some aspects of a data flow diagram are given a formal semantics. These are, for a given elementary transaction:

- The structure of the data items on incoming and outgoing arrows.
- The fact, whether there are arrows to and from the data base symbol.

These pieces of information can be used for determining the signature of the elementary transaction, as it was explained in section 3.3. However, the fact that a data flow directly connects two elementary transactions, as indicated in figure 4, cannot be reflected in any particular way in such a simple formal semantics. The best solution probably is to rule out such arrows at all.

Fig. 4. Data Flow between Elementary Transactions

In an approach as it is proposed in this section, there is some need for another semi-formal notation for system dynamics. It is the opinion of the author that the state-transition diagrams and entity life-cycle models, which are used in modern object-oriented specification frameworks can be effectively integrated into a combined formal / semi-formal specification methods. For the "Entity Life Histories" of SSADM, this is demonstrated in [9].

6 Conclusion and Perspectives

In this paper, experiences have been reported from an attempt to specify an information system of an almost realistic scale in a hybrid formal / semi-formal way. The starting point for the experiment was that a naive application of formal (algebraic) specification to a large information system is not practicable. A combination with more specialised notations which have been developed in the area of semi-formal Software Engineering was seen as necessary.

The HDMS-A case study has demonstrated that such a combination can be designed on top of the existing state of the art in semi-formal and formal specification languages, in particular in the area of axiomatic specification. The approach which was used in HDMS-A seems to be scalable even for very large information systems.

The case study has also shown that a significant amount of research and development effort is still needed in order to achieve a well-balanced combination of semi-formal and formal notations, together with methodical guidance and good tool-support. It has been demonstrated that the HDMS-A approach should be be improved in several respects. A particularly interesting observation is that the specification as a whole seems to become better structured and more readable if the semi-formal portion

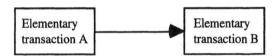

is enlarged in comparison to the current approach. In this sense, the HDMS-A approach still seems to rely too much on formal notation.

Generally, research into practically viable combinations of semi-formal and formal notations can achieve a significant step forward for formal methods, since this may remove the last obstacle for a broader application of formal methods in industrial practice. On the other hand, also the area of classical software engineering methods can benefit from this kind of work, since solid theoretical foundations are urgently needed in the current practice of describing and defining semi-formal specification frameworks.

Acknowledgement. The work reported here was carried out jointly by the author and the following persons: Felix Cornelius (TU Berlin), Rudi Hettler (TU München), Michael Löwe (TU Berlin), Friederike Nickl (LMU München), Stephan Merz (LMU München), Oscar Slotosch (TU München).

References

1. Borgida, A.; J. Mylopoulos, R. Reiter, "...And nothing else changes": The frame problem in procedure specifications. In: 15th International Conference on Software Engineering, Proceedings, IEEE, 1993, pp. 303-314.

2. Bowen, J.; Stavridou, V., The industrial take-up of formal methods in safety-critical and other areas: A perspective. In: F. C. P. Woodcock, P. G. Larsen (eds), FME' 93, Lecture Notes in Computer Science Vol. 670, Springer 1993, pp. 183-195.

3. Broy, M.; C. Facchi, R. Grosu, R. Hettler, H. Hußmann, D. Nazareth, F. Regensburger, O. Slotosch, K. Stølen, The requirement and design specification language SPECTRUM, An informal introduction. Technical reports TUM I9311 and I9312, Technische Universität München 1993.

4. Cornelius, F.; H. Hussmann, M. Löwe, The KORSO case study for Software Engineering with formal methods: A medical information system. In: M. Broy, S. Jähnichen (eds.), KORSO – Correct software by formal methods. To appear 1995.

5. Craigen, D.; S. Gerhart, T. Ralston, Formal methods reality check: Industrial usage. In: F. C. P. Woodcock, P. G. Larsen (eds), FME' 93, Lecture Notes in Computer Science Vol. 670, Springer 1993, pp. 250-267.

6. Hayes, I. (ed.), Specification case studies. Prentice-Hall 1987.

7. Hettler, R., On the translation of E/R schemata to SPECTRUM (in German). Technical report TUM-I9333, Technische Universität München, 1993.

8. Hussmann, H., On the Formal Description of Functional Requirements for an Information System (in German). Technical report TUM-I9332, Technische Universität München 1993.

9. Hussmann, H., Formal Foundations for SSADM. Habilitation Thesis, Technische Universität München 1994.

10. McMenamin, S.; J. Palmer, Essential systems analysis. Prentice-Hall 1984.

11. Nickl, F., Specification of System Dynamics by Data Flow Modelling and Stream-Processing Functions (in German). Technical report TUM-I9334, Technische Universität München 1993.

12. Nickl, F.; M. Wirsing, A formal approach to requirements engineering. In: D. Bjørner et al. (eds.), Proc. International Symposium on Formal Methods in Programming and their Applications, Lecture Notes in Computer Science Vol. 735, Springer 1993, pp. 312-334.

13. Petersohn, C.; C. Huizing, J. Peleska, W.-P. de Roever, Formal semantics for Ward & Mellor's Transformation Schemas. In: D. Till (ed.), Proc. of the Sixth Refinement Workshop of the BCS FACS Group. Springer 1994.

14. Polack, F.; M. Whiston, K. Mander, The SAZ project: Integrating SSADM and Z. In: F. C. P. Woodcock, P. G. Larsen (eds), FME ' 93, Lecture Notes in Computer Science Vol. 670, Springer 1993, pp. 541-557.

15. Semmens, L. T.; R. B. France, T. W. G. Docker, Integrated structured analysis and formal specification techniques. *The Computer Journal* **35** (1992) 600-610.

16. Slotosch, O.; F. Nickl, S. Merz, H. Hussmann, R. Hettler, The Functional Essence of HDMS-A (in German). Technical report TUM-I9335, Technische Universität München 1993.

An Object-Oriented Airport: Specification and Refinement in Maude

Ulrike Lechner[1], Christian Lengauer[1] and Martin Wirsing[2]

[1] Fakultät für Mathematik und Informatik, Universität Passau, D–94030 Passau, Germany, email: {lechner,lengauer}@fmi.uni-passau.de
[2] Institut für Informatik, Ludwig-Maximilians-Universität, D–80802 München, Germany, email: wirsing@informatik.uni-muenchen.de

Abstract. An object-oriented model of an airport has been developed to assess the parallel object-oriented specification language Maude. The model includes airplanes, gates, baggage handling, ground control and tower and has been implemented on the OBJ3 system, which serves as a rudimentary interpreter for Maude. We discuss two ways of specifying objects and present two notions of behavioral refinement in Maude.

1 Introduction

Maude [15, 16, 18] is a language for object-oriented specification. Its semantics is based on concurrent rewriting and can be viewed as a natural extension of the semantics of the OBJ3 rewriting system [9]. Our example is based on a case study at the University of Passau [21], whose goal was the development of a detailed model of an airport in order to gain experience in modeling with Maude and develop techniques for object-oriented specification. As far as possible, the model was implemented and validated in OBJ3. We present a refinement from an abstract to a concrete specification in Maude and propose two different notions of refinement: behavioral transition refinement and behavioral simulation refinement.

2 Overview of Maude

We concentrate on the object-oriented part of Maude and on its module concept. For a more detailed description, see [15, 16, 18].

In Maude, a *class* is declared by an identifier and a list of attributes and their types. `OId` is the type of Maude identifiers reserved for all object identifiers.

The object-oriented concept in Maude is the *object module*. The declaration of an object module (keyword `omod`) consists of an import list (`protecting`, `extending` or `using`), a number of class declarations (`class`), message declarations (`msg`), variable declarations (`var`), rewrite rules (`rl`) and, possibly, equations (`eq`).

A *message* is a term that consists of the message's name, the identifiers of the objects the message is addressed to and, possibly, parameters (in mixfix notation).

A Maude program makes computational progress by rewriting its global state, its *configuration*. (In the rest of this paper, we use the term "state" only in the airport world that we are modeling.) A configuration is a multiset, or bag, of objects and messages. A rewrite step transforms a configuration into a subsequent configuration.

Objects are declared together with in rules for rewriting the configuration. An *object* is represented by a term—more precisely by a tuple—comprising a unique object identifier, an identifier for the class the object belongs to and a set of attributes with their values. E.g., the term `< P : Plane | Delay: D >` represents an object with object identifier `P` belonging to class `Plane`. The attribute `Delay` has value `D`.

The following specification of class `Plane` plays a central role in our case study:

```
omod M-PLANE is
   protecting "some modules where basic types are declared" .
   class Plane |
       FlightNo   : Nat,     Destination: OId,
       PlaneType  : String,  Runway     : Nat,
       TOLControl : OId,     Tower      : OId,
       Departure  : Time,    Arrival    : Time, Delay: Time .
   msg to _ NewDelay _ : OId Time -> Msg .
   msg to _ NewArrivalTime of _ is _ : OId OId Time -> Msg .

   var P T : OId .
   var A D N : Time .

   rl (to P NewDelay N)
       < P : Plane | Arrival: A, Delay: D, Tower: T >
   =>  < P : Plane | Delay: D + N >
      (to T NewArrivalTime of P is (A + D + N) ) .
endom
```

Class `Plane` has several attributes. The attributes `Destination`, `TOLControl` (take-off-and-landing control) and `Tower` are used to store identifiers of objects to which a plane sends messages. The attributes `FlightNo`, `Runway`, `Departure`, `Arrival` and `Delay` contain the data of the current flight of the plane. Objects of class `Plane` accept one message: `(to P NewDelay N)` indicates that a new delay of duration `N` has occurred in the schedule of plane `P`. Sending the message triggers a state change of plane `P` and initiates a message to the tower `T` to indicate that the plane has a new arrival time. The arrival time is computed from the scheduled arrival time `A`, the delay `D` and the new delay `N`. The rewrite rule is applicable in configurations which contain a message and a plane with matching object identifier.

Note that, in the rewrite rule, only those attributes are mentioned whose values are changed or needed for some computation. For example, the attributes `FlightNo`, `Destination`, `PlaneType`, `Runway`, `TOLControl` and `Departure` of class `Plane` are not mentioned. The value of the attribute `Tower` is needed as an address for the initiated message. Additionally, we are allowed to omit attributes whose values remain unchanged at the right-hand side of rewrite rules, e.g., the attribute `Arrival`.

One distinguishing feature of Maude is that it supports two structuring mechanisms: class inheritance and module inheritance.

Class inheritance is subtyping. The declaration `subclass FlyingPl < Plane` states that class `FlyingPl` (assumed to be previously declared) is a subclass of `Plane`; then, `FlyingPl` inherits all attributes from `Plane`, and all rules that are applicable to an object of class `Plane` are also applicable to objects of class `FlyingPl`.

Module inheritance is the concept of importing code pieces into a module. Maude has three ways of importing modules, denoted by the keywords **`protecting`**, **`extending`** and **`using`**. **`protecting`** prohibits all changes of the sorts of the imported module ("no junk, no confusion" [15]), **`extending`** allows adding new constants to the declared sorts and **`using`** (by f) allows arbitrary changes and extensions of the defined sorts according to a stated signature morphism f.

The semantics of Maude is based on concurrent term rewriting. We present the four rewriting rules for the unsorted case of unconditional rewrite rules. For a more detailed description, see [13]. A specification in Maude is a rewrite system $R = (\Sigma, E, L, T)$, where $\Sigma = (S, C, \leq, F, M)$ is a signature (consisting of sort names, class declarations, subsort ordering, function symbols and message names), E a set of equations, L a set of labels of rewrite rules and T a set of rewrite rules for state transitions. The rewrite rules in T model transitions between configurations, i.e., between equivalence classes $[t]$ of terms, here equivalence classes modulo the set of equations E.

$T(\Sigma, X)$ denotes the set of all terms over the signature Σ with free variables X. $T^E(\Sigma, X)$ is the same set partitioned into equivalence classes by the equations in E.

$R \vdash [t] \rightarrow [t']$ denotes that $[t]$ can be rewritten to $[t']$ by finitely many applications of the rules in R and the four rules of the rewriting calculus below.

Maude's semantics has a static and a dynamic part. The static part, the semantics of the function symbols and the objects and their classes, is defined by the signature Σ and the set E of equations of the rewrite system. The dynamic part is defined by the set of rules T for concurrent rewriting of configurations.

There are four rewrite rules of the rewriting calculus:

Reflexivity. For each $[t] \in T^E(\Sigma, X)$:

$$\frac{}{[t] \rightarrow [t]}$$

Transitivity.

$$\frac{[t_1] \rightarrow [t_2], [t_2] \rightarrow [t_3]}{[t_1] \rightarrow [t_3]}$$

Congruence. For each $(f : s_1 \times \ldots \times s_n \rightarrow s) \in F$

$$\frac{[t_1] \rightarrow [t'_1] \ \ldots \ [t_n] \rightarrow [t'_n]}{[f(t_1, \ldots, t_n)] \rightarrow [f(t'_1, \ldots, t'_n)]}$$

Replacement. For each rewrite rule $r : [t(x_1, \ldots, x_n)] \rightarrow [t'(x_1, \ldots, x_n)]$ in T:

$$\frac{[w_1] \rightarrow [w'_1] \ \ldots \ [w_n] \rightarrow [w'_n]}{[t(\overline{w}/\overline{x})] \rightarrow [t'(\overline{w}'/\overline{x})]}$$

The congruence and the replacement rule allow simultaneous rewrites. Rewrite rules can only be applied concurrently when their redexes are disjoint.

3 Modeling States

The state of an object plays a decisive role in the way the object reacts to a message sent to it—most fundamentally, whether it reacts at all! In the literature, a popular example for an object whose behavior differs depending on the internal state is a buffer that accepts a "get" message only if it is not empty [12, 16]. We use planes to illustrate how the states and behaviors of objects might be represented and how their representation interacts with inheritance (Sect. 3) and with the refinement of specifications (Sect. 4).

The behavior of a plane depends on two properties: its type and its state. There are two plane types: cargo planes and passenger planes. We use five different kinds of states to model the behavior of a plane. Passenger and cargo planes behave differently on the ground but identically from take-off to landing. That is, the tower and the take-off-and-landing (TOL) control treat all planes equally. We model four different kinds of states of a (cargo or passenger) plane that are relevant for the tower: Takeoff, Starting (waiting for clearance; this kind of state will be used in Sect. 4), Takeoff, Flying and Landing. One further kind of state is of relevance for the ground control and has different meanings for cargo and passenger planes, respectively: OnGround. Fig. 1 depicts a plane's behavior in terms of state transitions.

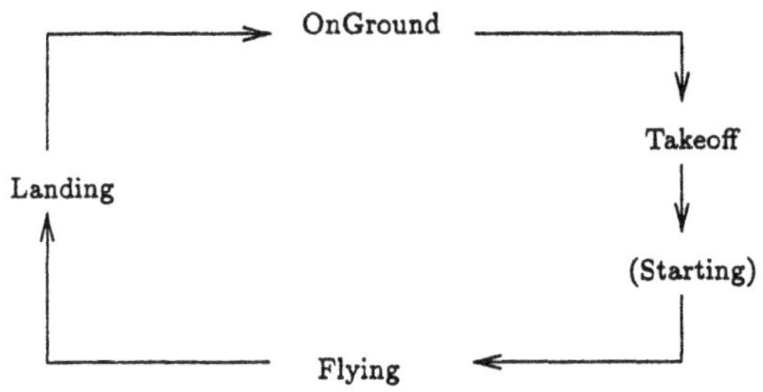

Fig. 1. The states of a plane

We consider two different ways of modeling states. In one model, states are represented by attributes; this model can be adopted similarly in other specification languages. In the other model, states are represented by classes; we argue that this model is more object-oriented—and typical for Maude because it makes better use of Maude's concept of class inheritance and Maude's convenient provisions for letting an object change its class membership.

Both models represent the same behavior of planes with respect to airport institutions like the tower and the ground control.

In the following sections, we illustrate both models on the transition from Flying to Landing.

3.1 States as Attributes

In conventional object-oriented programming languages, the state of an object is often modeled by a (hidden) attribute, or attributes. We use boolean attributes, i.e., we install one "flag" for each state. Assume we have declared two subclasses of `Plane`: `CargoPl` and `PassengerPl`. Among others, a plane has the two attributes

`Flying` and `Landing`. Then, e.g., the transition from the state that represents a plane in flight to the state that represent the landing of that plane can be defined by the following, self-explanatory rewrite rule:

```
rl (landing P)
    < P : Plane | Flying: true, Landing: false, Runway: X, Tower: T >
=>  < P : Plane | Flying: false, Landing: true >
   (to T from P landing on X) .
```

The advantage of this solution is that the rule is applicable to planes belonging to both subclasses `CargoPl` and `PassengerPl`.

The disadvantage is that the different kinds of states of an object are modeled in the same way as other properties of the object: by attributes. We believe that, because of their central role and, potentially, high number, states deserve a special treatment. Explicit state changes by attribute redefinition seems cumbersome and error-prone.

Furthermore, adding a new kind of state in the states-as-attributes model does not observe the principle that previously written code and its properties should not change in an extension.

3.2 States as Classes

One can also model state change by making the object change class. This model requires (at least) one class per state.

There are several kinds of classes: classes that determine the plane type (`CargoPl` or `PassengerPl`), classes that determine the state of the plane (`OnGroundPl`...) and classes that contain the actual planes and inherit type and state.

The advantages of the states-as-classes model are:

- The messages that are applicable only in a certain state can be defined in the scope of the class that models the state. The result is a more modular and more transparent module structure.
- The specification of the data and of the dynamic behavior are quite independent from each other. A refinement of the dynamic structure often induces a refinement of the data by new attributes and new classes (see Sect. 4). The fine-grained class structure of states as classes increases the safety of the specification (see Sect. 6), and it is supported by behavioral refinement (see Sect. 5).

Let us sketch the class structure and the corresponding module structure of our plane model. Fig. 2 depicts the class hierarchy for one concrete class `FlyingCargoPl`.

In the following, we sketch how we build up the class and module hierarchy. Each class is wrapped inside a module. For the declaration of the class plane, see Sect. 2.

All subclasses of `Plane` inherit the attributes of `Plane`. The two kinds of planes have different attributes, e.g., the class `CargoPl` has one additional attribute, `Weight`, the maximal weight it is allowed to transport.

A module `MK-CARGOPLANE` imports all modules in which the whole class hierarchy for cargo planes is set up. This class hierarchy is reproduced for passenger planes. The module concept of Maude facilitates duplication of the entire class hierarchy with a

```
class FlyingPl .
subclass FlyingPl < Plane .

class CargoPl | Weight: Int .
subclass CargoPl < Plane .

class FlyingCargoPl .
subclass FlyingCargoPl < CargoPl FlyingPl .
```

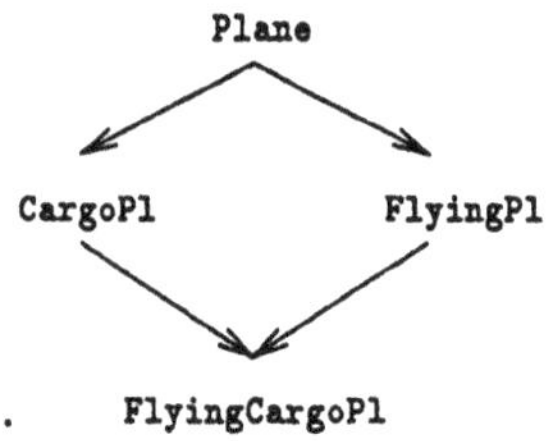

Fig. 2. The class hierarchy for a flying cargo plane

single signature morphism. This morphism is applied to the encapsulating module **MK-CARGOPLANE**. Additionally, the attribute **Weight** is renamed to **#Passengers**, the maximal number of passengers.

```
omod MK-PASSPLANE is
using MK-CARGOPLANE *(class CargoPl to PassengerPl,
                      class FlyingCargoPl to FlyingPassPl,
                      "more renamings of classes"
                      att Weight to #Passengers) .
```

Up to now, we have developed a class hierarchy without any messages or rewrite rules. Let us discuss how message declarations and rewrite rules fit into the class concept with multiple inheritance and states as classes.

The states-as-classes model has one drawback in the specification of the rewrite rules. [16] discusses inheritance of rewrite rules for objects that do not change class. The following rewrite rule is problematic because the resulting class **LandingPl** is not declared properly:

```
rl (landing P)
    < P : FlyingPl  | Runway: X, Tower: T >
=>  < P : LandingPl >
   (to T from P landing on X) .
```

In the denotational semantics of Maude [9, 15], the class hierarchy of planes corresponds to a hierarchy of sets. To make a special point, we have added an additional refinement of passenger planes in which we specify the company producing the plane:

$$\begin{aligned} \texttt{Plane} &\supset \texttt{FlyingPl, LandingPl, PassengerPl} \\ \texttt{PassengerPl} &\supseteq \texttt{Boeing, Airbus} \\ \texttt{FlyingPassPl} &= \texttt{FlyingPl} \cap \texttt{PassengerPl} \end{aligned}$$

Assuming the parameters of a message are fixed, rewrite rules induce mappings between these sets, e.g., the rule **landing** between the sets **FlyingPl** and **LandingPl**.

The denotational semantics of Maude permits object P to change in any way consistent with the rule, as long as it does not violate the requirements on objects of class `FlyingPl` and `LandingPl`. This becomes a problem when different subclasses are characterized by the same attributes.

In our example, passenger and cargo planes (both subclasses of `Plane`) do have different attributes and, thus, can be distinguished, but Boeing and Airbus planes (both passenger planes) cannot be distinguished. Consider the rule `landing`. It specifies a transition of one object from class `FlyingPl` to class `LandingPl` without specifying the subclass of `LandingPl` that the object should belong to. Given that the object is a passenger plane, it is perfectly consistent with the rule that it change its type from `Boeing` to `Airbus`, say, since both types are indistinguishable in the rule.

This problem can be avoided in two different ways. One alternative is to use a different object model in which, instead of a single class identifier, a set or a record of class identifiers specifies the state transitions more precisely. The rule `landing` would specify that the class `PlaneType` remains the same, while the class representing the state changes:

```
... < P : {PlState: FlyingPl , Type: PlaneType} >
=>  < P : {PlState: LandingPl, Type: PlaneType} > ...
```

Another alternative is to add explicit subtyping to Maude and specify the change of the class explicitly:

```
rl (landing P)
    < P : C | Runway: X, Tower: T >
=>  < P : C' >
    (to T from P landing on X)  if C < FlyingPl and C' < LandingPl and
          (forall D : (C < D  and not(D <= FlyingPl)) implies C' < D) .
```

For an implementation, this extension is a serious step. However, the implementation of Maude in OBJ3 already goes part of the way by providing class variables for subsort polymorphism. Both solutions reduce the number of classes needed because they do not refer to the concrete class, e.g., `FlyingCargoPl`, but to its superclasses. In the rest of the paper, we assume that a rewrite rule specifying a state transition changes only the class mentioned in the rule and leaves other superclasses the objects belong to unchanged.

4 From Synchronous to Asynchronous Communication

Maude supports two different ways of communication: synchronous and asynchronous communication. A communication is called *synchronous* when a rewrite step involves more than one object on the left-hand side; an *asynchronous* communication is defined by a rewrite rule with only one object (but possibly several messages) at the left-hand side [15, 18].

We investigate the model of the take-off of a plane in either communication style. The synchronous model describes the change of the states of the objects. The asynchronous model specifies, additionally, the implementation of the communication protocol. Thus, the asynchronous model can be viewed as a refinement of the synchronous model. We present formal definitions of refinement in Sect. 5.

One important difference between the two styles of communication is the degree of parallelism (our metric is the number of replacement rules applicable in parallel [16]). An object is only allowed to be involved in one rewrite rule per rewrite step, even if its state is not changed. Thus, objects that are involved in many communications reduce the concurrency in a specification.

We illustrate the take-off of a plane on a runway. A plane that is ready for take-off sends a request to the TOL control. The TOL control is responsible for the scheduling, the tower for the use of the two (independent) runways. A plane is cleared for take-off when it is next in line according to the schedule and a runway is free. Take-off is modeled by change of the plane's state to Flying. A plane is identified by the plane number (the object identifier) and the flight number because it is possible for one plane to make several flights from one airport in one day.

4.1 Synchronous Communication

In a synchronous communication, we can represent the entire take-off procedure by a single rewrite rule:

```
rl (takeoff?(P, S, T))
    < P : TakeoffPl   | FlightNo: No, Runway: X, Destination: D >
    < S : TOLControl  | Schedule: [(P,No),RestSchedule] >
    < T : Tower       | FreeRunways: X FreeSet >
=>  < P : FlyingPl >
    < S : TOLControl  | Schedule: RestSchedule >
    < T : Tower       | FreeRunways: X FreeSet >
   (toDestination D flying (P,No)) .
```

This is not a faithful model of an airport because data are exchanged without communication—not explicitly via messages as in the "real world". Moreover, the tower and the TOL control are unable to deal with other planes simultaneously when handling a take-off.

4.2 Asynchronous Communication

In our asynchronous model, the single transition of the synchronous model is divided into a number of rewrite steps, each involving only one object. Thus, the model reflects not only the state change of the plane, the TOL control and the tower but also the communication protocol that leads to this change.

A new plane state, Starting, ensures that, during the time interval in which the plane is waiting for permission to take off, no other action can be taken that is possible in the states Takeoff or Flying. This new state simplifies the correctness proof of the refinement—the extension of the synchronous model—because none of the rules that are applicable in the states of the abstract specification is applicable in the new state Starting.

A request to the TOL control for clearance for take-off (right-hand side of the rule) is accompanied with all relevant flight data:

```
rl (takeoff?(P,S,T))
    < P : TakeoffPl | FlightNo: No, Runway: X, TOLControl: S >
=>  < P : StartingPl >
   (toTOLControl S clearance? (P,No) on X) .
```

The TOL control checks that the plane is scheduled as the next plane to take off and sends an inquiry concerning the state of the runway to the tower:

```
rl (toTOLControl S clearance? (P,No) on X)
    < S : TOLControl | Schedule: [(P,No),RestSchedule], Tower: T >
=>  < S : TOLControl >
   (toTower T clearance? (P,No) on X) .
```

If the requested runway is free, the tower stores the data of the flight in a list and informs the plane that it is cleared:

```
rl (toTower T clearance? (P,No) on X)
    < T : Tower | FreeRunways: X FreeSet, OnRunway: OnRunwaySet >
=>  < T : Tower | FreeRunways: FreeSet,
                  OnRunway: (X,(P,No)) OnRunwaySet >
   (to P cleared at X) .
```

The plane, in state Takeoff, takes off when receiving the message **cleared**. The take-off is modeled by messages from the plane to itself and to the TOL control:

```
rl (to P cleared at X)
    < P : StartingPl | Runway: X, TOLControl: S >
=>  < P : StartingPl >
   (toTOLControl S takeoffack of P at X) (airborne P) .
```

Message **airborne** triggers a state transition from Starting to Flying. Also, the plane sends a message to the tower that the runway is free and a request to the target airport D to send the new object identifiers of, e.g., the TOL control and the tower:

```
rl (airborne P)
    < P : StartingPl | FlightNo: No, Runway: X,
                       Destination: D, Tower: T >
=>  < P : FlyingPl >
   (toTower       T  (P,No) airborne at X)
   (toDestination D  flying (P,No)) .
```

TOL control and tower of the source airport react to the messages of the plane:

```
rl (toTOLControl S takeoffack of P at X)
    < S : TOLControl | Schedule: [(P,No),RestSchedule] >
=>  < S : TOLControl | Schedule: RestSchedule > .

rl (toTower T (P,No) airborne at X)
    < T : Tower | FreeRunways: FreeSet,
                  OnRunway: (X,(P,No)) OnRunwaySet >
=>  < T : Tower | FreeRunways: X FreeSet, OnRunway: OnRunwaySet > .
```

In both models, synchronous and asynchronous, a take-off results in the same state: the plane is in state Flying, the flight is removed from the list of planes waiting for take-off and the runway is free.

The increase in parallelism we obtain in the asynchronous model is that two planes may take off or land independently on the two runways and that the tower can answer other communication requests, e.g., for the control of planes waiting and circling in the air. The asynchronous model is more realistic because the communication is explicit and only one object is involved in one rewrite step and, thus, both tower and TOL control can handle several planes at a time.

5 Behavioral Refinement of Specifications

In this section, we present some ideas on how to refine specifications written in Maude. Consider the refinement of a synchronous by an asynchronous specification in the previous section. The refined specification contains a new class, i.e., a new intermediate state, new messages that model the asynchronous exchange of data and new intermediate state transitions.

We abstract from the way a state transition is deduced from rewrite rules and consider only the existence of a state transition. We regard a rewrite system (Σ, E, L, T) as an algebraic specification with an additional relation $\rightarrow$. In this paper, we restrict ourselves to the syntactic characterization of refinement. We will develop the corresponding semantic notions in future work.

A refinement is a relation between two specifications. We refer to them as the abstract and the concrete specification. In our setting, both specifications are written in Maude.

Our work on refinement is based on the loose approach of Wirsing [24]. In this approach, the semantics of a specification is the set of all algebras that satisfy the equations and contain the state transition relation. Refinement can be characterized by implication: all equations and state transitions derivable in the abstract specification have to be derivable in the concrete specification as well.

$T_s(\Sigma)$ is the set of all ground terms of sort s over the signature Σ. One constant for sorts we use is "Conf", an abbreviation of the sort `Configuration`, the sort of the configurations of a rewrite system.

Note that $\Sigma \subseteq \Sigma'$ if and only if $(S \subseteq S') \wedge (C \subseteq C') \wedge (\leq \subseteq \leq') \wedge (F \subseteq F') \wedge (M \subseteq M')$.

Definition 1 (Refinement). A rewrite system R is *refined* by a rewrite system R', written $R \rightsquigarrow R'$ iff

$$\begin{aligned} & \Sigma \subseteq \Sigma' && (1) \\ \wedge\ & (\forall\, t_1, t_2 \in T(\Sigma) : R \vdash t_1 = t_2 \ \Rightarrow\ R' \vdash t_1 = t_2) && (2) \\ \wedge\ & (\forall\, c, c' \in T_{\mathrm{Conf}}(\Sigma) : R \vdash c \rightarrow c' \ \Rightarrow\ R' \vdash c \rightarrow c') && (3) \end{aligned}$$

The step from synchrony to asynchrony in Sect. 4 involves a refinement of the object model, the communication and the order in which the objects reach their common final configuration. Since we use the loose approach, we are allowed to refine an abstract state transition specified by a single application of some rewrite rule to a concrete state transition specified by multiple applications of rewrite rules—as long as every abstract state transition is represented by a (sequence of) concrete state transitions.

The observable part of a specification consists of the primitive sorts, classes and messages that we would like to observe.

Definition 2 (Observable part). The *observable part Obs* of a rewrite system R with $\Sigma = (S, C, \leq, F, M)$ is a triple (S', C', M') such that $S' \subseteq S$, $M' \subseteq M$ and $(\texttt{c'}\,|\,\texttt{atts'}) \in C' \Rightarrow (\exists\, \texttt{atts} : ((\texttt{c'}\,|\,\texttt{atts}) \in C \wedge \texttt{atts'} \subseteq \texttt{atts}))$.

We presume that all sorts of observable attributes and the class identifiers are observable.

We write `<o:c|a1:v1,...,an:vn>` $\in C'$, where `o` is an object of class `(c|a1:s1,..., an:sn)`$\in C'$, and `(m(p1,...,pn))`$\in M'$, where `m` is a message built using `(m:s1...sn -> Msg)`$\in M'$.

Subclasses do not inherit observability properties from their superclasses: the attributes that we observe in a class are not necessarily observed in all subclasses or all superclasses.

Note that the configurations are terms of the sort `Configuration`, which consists of both observable and unobservable messages and objects. In order to be able to observe part of a configuration, we define an observation function obs_R on the configurations of rewrite system R that projects the observable part $Obs = (S', C', M')$. We call the images of the observation function *observations*. Let us state the definition and then explain it.

We write $\cup$ for the multiset union of configurations and ϵ for the empty configuration.

Definition 3 (Observation function). The observation function obs_R of a rewrite system R for an observable part Obs is defined by:

$$\text{obs}_R : \texttt{Configuration} \rightarrow \texttt{Set of Configuration}$$

$$\text{obs}_R(\epsilon) = \{\epsilon\} \tag{1}$$

$$\text{obs}_R(\texttt{c1} \cup \texttt{c2}) = \{a \cup b \mid a \in \text{obs}_R(\texttt{c1}) \wedge b \in \text{obs}_R(\texttt{c2})\} \tag{2}$$

$$\text{obs}_R(\texttt{<o:c|atts>}) = \begin{cases} \{\texttt{<o:c'|atts'>} \mid \texttt{<o:c'|atts'>} \in C' \wedge \texttt{c} \leq \texttt{c'}\} \\ \qquad\qquad \text{if } (\exists\, \texttt{c'} \in C' : \texttt{c} \leq \texttt{c'}) \\ \{\epsilon\} \qquad \text{otherwise} \end{cases} \tag{3}$$

$$\text{obs}_R(\texttt{(message)}) = \begin{cases} \{\texttt{(message)}\} & \text{if } \texttt{(message)} \in M' \\ \{\epsilon\} & \text{if } \texttt{(message)} \notin M' \end{cases} \tag{4}$$

Each observation of a configuration is a set of observable parts. Each object may be observable in a number of superclasses, and its observations may differ depending on which superclass observes it. Thus, the range of the observation function is a set of configurations. Remember, that a configuration is itself a multiset of messages and objects.

The observations in the abstract specification form a subset of the observations in the concrete specification because a refinement into new subclasses may generate new subtype dependences between observable classes. This may lead to added observations (see our example in Sect. 6).

Our concept of an observable part refines the concept of an observable part defined for algebraic specifications in [3, 4, 20, 24] and the concept of a visible action in process algebras in [19]. Our extension covers the addition of attributes and messages and the refinement of the class hierarchy and of communication protocols.

In the following, we make two suggestions for relating the behavior of an abstract specification to a concrete specification: behavioral transition refinement and behavioral simulation refinement. The refinement of the static part of the language is the same for both refinement relations. See Sect. 6 for a discussion and a comparison of the two refinement relations.

Definition 4 (Behavioral transition refinement). A rewrite system R' is a *behavioral transition refinement* of a rewrite system R with respect to an observable part *Obs*, written $R \leadsto^{\mathrm{tr}}_{Obs} R'$, iff

$$\begin{aligned}
&\Sigma \subseteq \Sigma' && (1)\\
\wedge\ &(\forall\, s \in Obs,\ t_1, t_2 \in T_s(\Sigma) : R \vdash t_1 = t_2 \Rightarrow\ R' \vdash t_1 = t_2) && (2)\\
\wedge\ &(\forall\, c, c' \in T_{\mathrm{Conf}}(\Sigma) : && (3)\\
&\quad (\exists\, d, d' \in T_{\mathrm{Conf}}(\Sigma') : \mathrm{obs}_R(c) \subseteq \mathrm{obs}_{R'}(d)\ \wedge\ \mathrm{obs}_R(c') \subseteq \mathrm{obs}_{R'}(d')\ \wedge\\
&\quad\ (R \vdash c \to c'\ \Rightarrow\ R' \vdash d \to d')))
\end{aligned}$$

We call this relation transition refinement because it relates a transition in the abstract specification to a transition in the concrete specification. This relation takes neither traces, i.e., sequences of transitions nor choices into account. Thus, one configuration can be refined into several configurations that are not connected appropriately by transitions: each concrete configuration may have fewer successor configurations than the abstract one, or transitions between the concrete configurations may be missing. This relation is, in some sense, the weakest possible relation between two specifications. In process theory, a relation that ensures that the behavior of the concrete specification has at least the same traces and the same choices is called a simulation. We have a similar refinement relation here.

Definition 5 (Behavioral simulation refinement). A rewrite system R' is a *behavioral simulation refinement* of a rewrite system R' with respect to an observable part *Obs*, written $R \leadsto^{\precsim}_{Obs} R'$, iff (1) and (2) of Def. 4 hold and, in addition,

$$\begin{aligned}
&(\exists \precsim\ \subseteq T_{\mathrm{Conf}}(\Sigma) \times T_{\mathrm{Conf}}(\Sigma') : (c \precsim d\ \Rightarrow && (3)\\
&\quad (\forall\, c' \in T_{\mathrm{Conf}}(\Sigma) : R \vdash c \to c' \Rightarrow (\exists\, d' \in T_{\mathrm{Conf}}(\Sigma') : R' \vdash d \to d' \wedge c' \precsim d')))\\
&\quad \wedge\ (\forall\, c \in T_{\mathrm{Conf}}(\Sigma) : (\exists\, d \in T_{\mathrm{Conf}}(\Sigma') : c \precsim d))\\
&\quad \wedge\ (c \precsim d\ \Rightarrow\ \mathrm{obs}_R(c) \subseteq \mathrm{obs}_{R'}(d)))
\end{aligned}$$

In the refinement step in Sect. 4, the observable part consists of the classes with the attributes and the messages that appear in the abstract specification. Not observable are the class that models the intermediate state Starting, the attributes necessary to store object identifiers and the messages necessary for implementing the asynchronous communication.

The observation functions are the identity for the abstract (synchronous) specification and the corresponding projection in the concrete (asynchronous) specification.

The only non-trivial state transition defined in our abstract specification is derivable for observably equal configurations in the concrete specification. Thus, the concrete specification is both a behavioral transition refinement and a behavioral simulation refinement of the abstract specification. Our approach ensures only that the state transitions in the abstract specifications exist in the concrete specification; it permits additional transitions in the concrete specification. We have to ensure that the action refinement is safe, i.e., that it does not enable a take-off if either the state of TOL control and tower are inappropriate or the plane is not ready for take-off. Due to the addition of class `Starting` in the states-as-classes approach, none of the rewrite rules applicable in the states Takeoff or Flying are applicable in the state Starting, i.e., while the plane is waiting for clearance. The TOL control and the tower can decide by the values of the attributes and the communication protocol to give clearance only when the schedule permits it and the runway is free and to give only one plane at a time access to a runway.

One can distinguish two notions of refinement:

(1) The refinement by which a program is derived from a final specification. Here, it is paramount that one does not introduce behaviors in the refinement process which are not permitted in the specification.
(2) The refinement by which a specification is finalized via "requirements engineering". Here, one may want to add behaviors during the refinement process, but one must make sure that the final specification permits only desired behaviors.

In this paper, we follow the philosophy of (2).

6 Behavioral Transition vs. Behavioral Simulation Refinement

Let us illustrate that both notions of behavioral refinement presented in the previous section—transition and simulation refinement—have reasonable applications. We expect the concrete specification to be at least as powerful as the abstract specification, i.e., to offer all choices and all transitions that exist at the abstract level. From this point of view, behavioral simulation refinement is the better choice.

Here is an example for a behavioral transition refinement which demonstrates that simulation refinement can be too strong and that behavioral transition refinement can be a good choice as well. We omit the Maude code; we illustrate the state transitions graphically in Fig. 3 instead.

Let us consider a new state, Loading, for planes on the ground. This state differs for passenger and cargo planes. A passenger plane loads passengers, a cargo plane cargo. All loading planes have the additional attributes `cargo` and `pass`. An attribute is `true` if the corresponding entity has been loaded and `false` otherwise. The process of loading is modeled by two different messages, `(to P load cargo)` and `(to P`

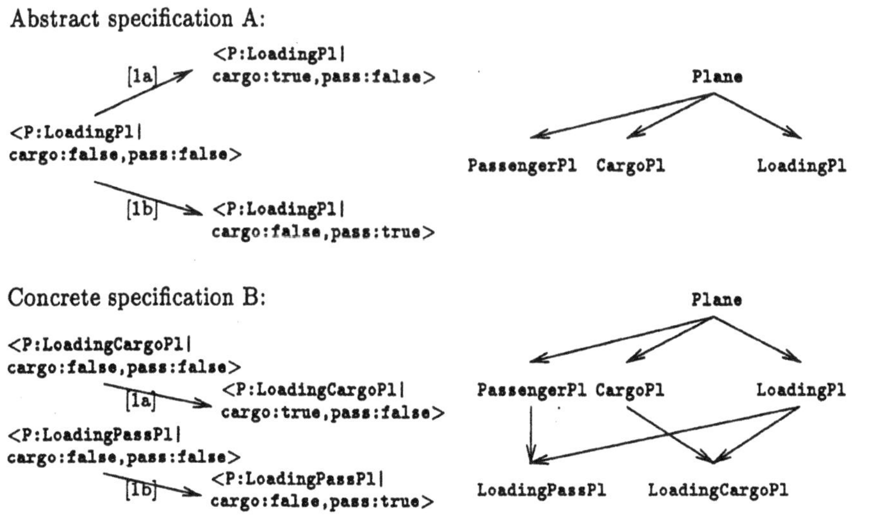

Fig. 3. State transitions and class hierarchy of the abstract and the concrete specification

`load passengers`). These messages are sent from the ground control to the plane to be loaded.

In the abstract specification, a class, `LoadingPl`, represents a plane that is ready to load cargo or passengers. Both cargo and passenger planes accept both requests, although one of them contradicts the value of attribute `PlaneType`.

Let us refine this specification by introducing two subclasses, `LoadingCargoPl` and `LoadingPassPl`. Both subclasses accept only the message compatible with the plane's type. This refinement increases safety because the plane can reject messages of the ground control that are not compatible with its type.

Of our specification, we would like to observe the class `LoadingPl` with its two attributes and the two messages. We would also like to make some observations of class `Plane` and classes `PassengerPl` and `CargoPl`. The observational part of the specifications consists of:

S' = "all primitive sorts"
C' = { (`Plane | FlightNo: Nat, Destination: OId`),
(`PassengerPl | #Passengers: Nat`), (`CargoPl | Weight: Nat`),
(`LoadingPl | cargo: Bool, pass: Bool`) }
M' = { `to _ load cargo : OId -> Msg`,
`to _ load passengers : OId -> Msg` }

Let us consider the configuration D (the variable `ATTS` subsumes attributes of `P` not needed in this example):

D = `< P : LoadingPl | cargo: false, pass: false,`
`PlaneType: Passenger, Destination: D,`

```
                    FlightNo: N, #Passengers: 100, ATTS >
      (to P load passengers)
```

In the abstract specification, the plane is observable in two classes, **LoadingPl** and **Plane**. Our observation is a set of two configurations that are different projections of D:

$\mathrm{obs}_A(D) =$

```
{ < P : LoadingPl | cargo: false, pass: false > (to P load passengers),
  < P : Plane | FlightNo: N, Destination: D > (to P load passengers) }
```

In the concrete specification, the smallest sort of plane P is **LoadingPassPl** (where the attribute **cargo** is false). Configuration D', the refinement of configuration D which we observe in the concrete specification, differs from configuration D in one point: the class the plane belongs to is **LoadingPassPl**, not **LoadingPl**. By (3) of Def. 3, the plane is observable in one more class, **PassengerPl**. Thus, our observation of configuration D' is:

$\mathrm{obs}_B(D') = \mathrm{obs}_A(D) \cup$

```
{ < P : PassengerPl | #Passengers: 100 > (to P load passengers) }
```

The refinement is a behavioral transition refinement. Every state transition in the abstract specification is implemented by a corresponding state transition in the concrete specification. In Fig. 3, corresponding state transitions are labeled identically.

The refinement is not a behavioral simulation refinement. In the abstract specification, a plane in state Loading, with both attributes false (as in configuration D), can accept two different messages. In the concrete specification, there are two different states in each of which only one message can be accepted.

7 Related work

Several papers of Meseguer et al. cited earlier point out that synchronous and asynchronous specifications represent different levels of abstraction. In [11], an asynchronous implementation of a synchronous specification of a spreadsheet is presented and the related issues of the transformation from synchrony to asynchrony, and of deadlock and fairness are discussed. Meseguer refers to a categorical semantics of Maude and relates the rewriting logic to other logical frameworks [17]. In [14], a rewrite relation similar to our configuration transition relation is defined and a mechanism for an implementation relation between rewrite theories expressed in terms of their associated (2-)Lawvere categories is presented.

A different approach to integrating the specification of static data types and of dynamic process behavior, more closely related to the traditional approach of algebraic specification, is SMoLCS [1, 2]. The models in SMoLCS are *dynamic algebras*, which are algebras with relations. A hierarchy of labeled transition systems specifies data types and sequential behavior, communication, parallelization and abstraction. In [5], temporal logic and the SMoLCS approach are used in the specification of a distributed program semantics.

In [6, 7, 8], *action reification* describes the process of implementing an action of an object at a high level of abstraction by a number of actions of objects at a lower level of abstraction. The specification language is Troll [10], and the formal basis for the refinement of the actions is event structures. Action refinement for event structures is described in [22, 23]. A logical framework for the algebraic specification of classes at different levels of granularity is proposed in [8].

8 Conclusion

In future work, we plan to develop model-theoretic definitions of our refinement notions. In order to apply the loose approach in a more reasonable setting, we shall also admit concepts that Maude does not provide like a way of disallowing state transitions. Furthermore, we plan to admit observation functions that allow us to make substantial changes to objects and messages in the process of refinement.

Acknowledgements

We are indebted to José Meseguer for clarifying and explaining several issues and, especially, for pointing out the idea of the representation of states by sets of classes. Thanks to Friederike Nickl for carefully reading a preliminary version and to Rolf Hennicker for helpful discussions. Thanks also to the anonymous referees for their helpful comments. This work is part of the DFG project Osidris.

References

1. E. Astesiano and G. Reggio. An outline of the SMoLCS approach. In *Mathematical Model for the Semantics of Parallelism*, Lecture Notes in Computer Science 280. Springer-Verlag, 1986.
2. E. Astesiano and G. Reggio. Direct semantics of concurrent languages in the SMoLCS approach. *IBM Journal of Research and Development*, 31(5):512–534, 1987.
3. M. Bidoit and R. Hennicker. A general framework for modular implementations of modular system specifications. In M.-C. Gaudel and J.-P. Jouannaud, editors, *TAPSOFT '93: Theory and Practice of Software Development*, Lecture Notes in Computer Science 668, pages 199–214. Springer-Verlag, 1993.
4. M. Bidoit, R. Hennicker, and M. Wirsing. Characterizing behavioural and abstractor semantics. In D. Sannella, editor, *Programming Languages and Systems - ESOP '94*, Lecture Notes in Computer Science 788, pages 105–119. Springer-Verlag, 1994. Long version: Behavioural and Abstractor Specifications. Technical Report 9414, Institut für Informatik, Ludwig-Maximilians-Universität München.
5. G. Costa and G. Reggio. Abstract dynamic data types: a temporal logic approach. In A. Tarlecki, editor, *Mathematical Foundations of Computer Science (MFCS '91)*, Lecture Notes in Computer Science 520, pages 103–112. Springer-Verlag, 1991.
6. G. Denker and H.-D. Ehrich. Action reification in object oriented specifications. In *Proc. ISCORE Workshop Amsterdam*. Vrije Universiteit Amsterdam, 1994. To appear.
7. H.-D. Ehrich, G. Denker, and A. Sernadas. Constructing systems as object communities. In M.-C. Gaudel and J.-P. Jouannaud, editors, *Theory and Practice of Software Development (TAPSOFT '93)*, Lecture Notes in Computer Science 668, pages 453–467. Springer-Verlag, 1993.

8. J.L. Fiadeiro and T. Maibaum. Sometimes "tomorrow" is "sometime" - action refinement in a temporal logic of objects. In D. M. Gabbay and H. J. Ohlbach, editors, *Temporal Logic (ICTL '94)*, Lecture Notes in Artificial Intelligence 827, pages 48–66. Springer-Verlag, 1994.
9. J. A. Goguen and J. Meseguer. Order-sorted algebra I: Equational deduction for multiple inheritance, overloading, exceptions and partial operations. *Theoretical Computer Science*, 105:217–273, 1992.
10. R. Jungclaus, G. Saake, T. Hartmann, and C. Sernadas. Object-oriented specification of information systems: The TROLL language. Technical Report Version 0.01, Report 91-04, December 1991.
11. P. Lincoln, N. Martí-Oliet, and J. Meseguer. Specification, transformation, and programming of concurrent systems in rewriting logic. In G. Blelloch, K. M. Chandy, and S. Jagannathan, editors, *Proc. DIMACS Workshop on Specification of Parallel Algorithms*, DIMACS Series in Discrete Mathematics and Theoretical Computer Science. American Mathematical Society, May 1994.
12. D. R. Maeng, J. W. Cho, and K. Ryu. Concurrency and inheritance in actor-based object-oriented languages. *Systems Software*, 20:53–67, 1993.
13. J. Meseguer. A logical theory of concurrent objects. *ACM SIGPLAN Notices*, 25(10):101–115, Oct 1990.
14. J. Meseguer. Rewriting as a unified model of concurrency. Technical Report SRI-CSL-90-02R, SRI International, February 1990.
15. J. Meseguer. A logical theory of concurrent objects and its realization in the Maude language. Technical Report SRI-CSL-92-08, SRI International, July 1992.
16. J. Meseguer. Solving the inheritance anomaly in concurrent object-oriented programming. In O. Nierstrasz, editor, *ECOOP '93 - Object-Oriented Programming*, Lecture Notes in Computer Science 707, pages 220–246. Springer-Verlag, 1993.
17. J. Meseguer and N. Martí-Oliet. From abstract data types to logical frameworks. In this volume.
18. J. Meseguer and T. Winkler. Parallel programming in Maude. In J.-P. Banâtre and D. Le Métayer, editors, *Research Directions in High-Level Parallel Programming Languages*, Lecture Notes in Computer Science 574, pages 253–293. Springer-Verlag, 1992.
19. R. Milner. *Communication and Concurrency.* Series in Computer Science. Prentice/Hall, Int., 1989.
20. F. Orejas, M. Navarro, and A. Sanchez. Implementation and behavioural equivalence: A survey. In M. Bidoit and C. Choppy, editors, *Recent Trends in Data Type Specifications*, Lecture Notes in Computer Science 655, pages 93–125. Springer-Verlag, 1993.
21. B. Salmansberger. Objektorientierte Spezifikation von verteilten Systemen in Maude am Beispiel eines Flughafens. Diplomarbeit, Fakultät für Mathematik und Informatik, Universität Passau, 1993.
22. R. J. van Glabbeek and U. Goltz. Equivalence notion for concurrent systems and refinement for actions. In A. Kreczmar and G. Mirkowska, editors, *Mathematical Foundations of Computer Science (MFCS '89)*, Lecture Notes in Computer Science 379, pages 237–248. Springer-Verlag, 1989.
23. R. J. van Glabbeek and U. Goltz. Refinement of actions in causality based models. In J. W. de Bakker, W.-P. de Roever, and G. Rozenberg, editors, *Stepwise Refinement of Distributed Systems*, Lecture Notes in Computer Science 430, pages 267–300. Springer-Verlag, 1990.
24. M. Wirsing. Algebraic specification. In J. V. Leeuwen, editor, *Handbook of Theoretical Computer Science*, volume B, pages 675–788. Elsevier (North-Holland), 1990.

Topological Methods for Algebraic Specification

Karl Meinke

Department of Computer Science
University College of Swansea
Swansea SA2 8PP
Great Britain

July 1994

ABSTRACT. We introduce an algebraic construction for the Hausdorff extension $H(A)$ of a many–sorted universal algebra A with respect to a family T of Hausdorff topologies on the carrier sets of A. This construction can be combined with other algebraic constructions, such as the initial model construction, to provide methods for the algebraic specification of uncountable algebras, e.g. algebras of reals, function spaces and streams.

0. INTRODUCTION.

Topology is often regarded as being complementary to algebra in its scope. The idea that these two subjects might therefore be usefully combined is not new. Nineteenth century mathematics saw the introduction of groups of continuous transformations in the work of S. Lie. The theories of topological groups, rings, fields and vector spaces have since been extensively developed, a recent survey is Warner [1989].

Universal algebra provides the mathematical foundation for the theory of abstract data types and algebraic specification methods. Therefore it is not surprising to find that *topological universal algebra* can also contribute in this area. The theory of topological universal algebra was introduced in von Dantzig [1933] and Birkhoff [1935] and has been further developed in for example Markov [1945], Pontrjagin [1954], Malcev [1957], Taylor [1977] and Arkhangel'skii [1987]. In this paper we present a general study of the topological construction of *closure*, applied to universal algebras.

Topological closure allows us to extend the carrier set of an algebra A by adding all limit points of A in a topology T on a set B which contains A. We may think of these limit points as "ideal elements" which can be used to solve certain types of equations over the signature of A. For example, let $\mathbf{Q}$ be the ring of rationals and $\mathbf{R}$ be the set of real numbers and let E be the usual Euclidean metric topology on $\mathbf{R}$. The closure of the carrier set of $\mathbf{Q}$ in E is $\mathbf{R}$ itself. (In this case we say that the subset $\mathbf{Q}$ is *dense* in E.)

Now one can consider extending each operation f_A of the algebra A to the limit points in B. If we can find an extension $\hat{f}$ for each f_A which is continuous with respect to the topology T (or the appropriate subspace topology if A is not dense in B), then these extensions, together with the original constants of A and the closure $Cl(A)$ of the carrier of A, form a *closed continuous extension* $\hat{A}$ of A. We will show, using basic topology, that if T is Hausdorff then $\hat{A}$ is the *unique* closed continuous extension of A. Thus, when T is Hausdorff, we term the unique closed continuous extension $H(A)$ of A, if it exists, the *Hausdorff extension* of A.

In the case of the ring $\mathbf{Q}$ of rationals, recalling that every metric space is Hausdorff, the Hausdorff extension $H(\mathbf{Q})$ with respect to E exists, namely the ring $\mathbf{R}$ of real numbers. Observe that in this case $H(\mathbf{Q})$ satisfies the ring axioms, which are equational. Inside the ring $\mathbf{R}$ we may also solve equations such as

$$x \cdot x = 2.$$

A fundamental property of *every* Hausdorff extension, that we will establish by means of an algebraic construction of $H(A)$, is that the equations valid in A and $H(A)$ are the same. In particular, if A arises in the context of data type theory as some data type which is a model of an equational specification (Σ, E) then $H(A)$ is a model of the same specification.

We view the construction of Hausdorff extensions as a useful additional method in the area of algebraic specification. Computations in certain specialist fields such as numerical analysis, hardware design, neural networks and dynamical systems, control systems theory and mathematical logic make use of uncountable algebras as *idealised specifications*. Such specifications are *approximated* to some degree of accuracy by actual implementations. Examples include algebras based on:

(i) real or complex valued functions on $\mathbf{R}$ and $\mathbf{C}$,

(ii) transformations on discrete, dense and continuous stream spaces

$$[\mathbf{N} \to \mathbf{A}], \quad [\mathbf{Q}^+ \to \mathbf{A}], \quad [\mathbf{R}^+ \to \mathbf{A}],$$

(iii) operators on function spaces $[\mathbf{R}^m \to \mathbf{R}^n]$, $[\mathbf{C}^m \to \mathbf{C}^n]$,

(iv) higher-order functions.

Clearly, by cardinality constraints, such algebras cannot be given a countable algebraic specification using any of the familiar term model constructions such as first-order initial semantics (ADJ [1975]), first-order final semantics (Wand [1981]) or higher-order initial semantics (Möller [1987], Meinke [1992]). However, given an appropriate separable topological space, (i.e. a space with a countable dense subspace) we may be able to give a recursive (or even finite!) equational specification of a countable dense subalgebra and then construct the (uncountable) Hausdorff extension of a countable term model.

In this paper we introduce a construction for the Hausdorff extension (when it exists) of a (many-sorted) universal algebra with respect to an arbitrary (many-sorted) Hausdorff space. We consider sufficient conditions which guarantee existence for various topologies. We show how the construction can be refined in the case that the given topology satisfies stronger separation or countability axioms. An extended version of this paper will appear elsewhere, in which we will illustrate the Hausdorff extension construction by applying it to a case study of second-order algebras including algebras of infinite streams.

The structure of the paper is as follows. In Section 1 we briefly review elementary concepts and results from universal algebra and topology. In Section 2 we introduce the Hausdorff extension construction in the context of closed continuous extensions over arbitrary topological spaces. We consider the existence, uniqueness and construction of Hausdorff extensions. We also consider refinements of the construction in the presence of strong separation and countability conditions.

We have attempted to make the paper mostly self contained although the reader will benefit from some prior knowledge of universal algebra and topology. For further information and background results in these areas we suggest Kelley [1955] for topology and Cohn [1981] for universal algebra. Surveys of these two subjects oriented towards computer science are Smyth [1993] for topology and Meinke and Tucker [1993] for universal algebra. A recent survey of algebraic specification techniques is Wirsing [1990].

1. UNIVERSAL ALGEBRA AND TOPOLOGY.

In this section we review some basic definitions, constructions and results of universal algebra, topology and topological universal algebra.

We begin by fixing our notation for many-sorted universal algebra.

1.1. Definition. A *many-sorted signature* is a pair $(S,\ \Sigma)$ consisting of:

(i) A non-empty set S. An element $s \in S$ is termed a *sort* and S is termed a *sort set.*

(ii) An $S^* \times S$-indexed family

$$\Sigma = \langle\ \Sigma_{w,s}\ \mid\ w \in S^*,\ s \in S\ \rangle$$

of sets of constant and operation symbols. For the empty word $\lambda \in S^*$ and any sort $s \in S$, an element

$$c \in \Sigma_{\lambda,s}$$

is termed a *constant symbol* of sort s. For each non-empty word $w = s(1)\ldots s(n) \in S^+$ and any sort $s \in S$, an element

$$f \in \Sigma_{w,s}$$

is termed an *operation* or *function symbol* of *domain type* w, *codomain type* s and *arity* n. When no ambiguity arises we may use Σ as the name of the signature $(S,\ \Sigma)$ and refer to Σ as an *S-sorted signature.* □

1.2. Definition. Let Σ be an S-sorted signature. An (S-sorted) *Σ algebra* is a pair $(A,\ \Sigma^A)$ consisting of:

(i) An S-indexed family

$$A = \langle\ A_s\ \mid\ s \in S\ \rangle$$

of non–empty sets. For each sort $s \in S$, the set A_s is termed the *carrier* of sort s.

(ii) An $S^* \times S$–indexed family

$$\Sigma^A = \langle\, \Sigma^A_{w,s} \mid w \in S^*,\, s \in S \,\rangle$$

of sets of constants and operations. For $\lambda \in S^*$ and any sort $s \in S$,

$$\Sigma_{\lambda,s} = \langle\, c_A \mid c \in \Sigma_{\lambda,s} \,\rangle,$$

where $c_A \in A_s$ is termed a constant of sort $s \in S$ which interprets the constant symbol $c \in \Sigma_{\lambda,s}$. For each non–empty word $w = s(1)\ldots s(n) \in S^+$ and $s \in S$,

$$\Sigma^A_{w,s} = \langle\, f_A \mid f \in \Sigma_{w,s} \,\rangle,$$

where $f_A : A^w \to A_s$ is a total function with domain $A^w = A_{s(1)} \times \ldots \times A_{s(n)}$, codomain A_s and arity n, which interprets the function symbol $f \in \Sigma_{w,s}$. When no ambiguity arises we may use A as the name of the Σ algebra $(A,\, \Sigma^A)$. □

If $A = \langle\, A_s \mid s \in S \,\rangle$ and $B = \langle\, B_s \mid s \in S \,\rangle$ are S-indexed families of sets then the basic set theoretic operations extend pointwise to A and B. Thus we let $A \subseteq B$ denote pointwise inclusion, $A_s \subseteq B_s$ for each $s \in S$. Similarly $A \cap B$, $A \cup B$ and $A = B$ will denote pointwise intersection, union and equality. We use $f : A \to B$ to denote an S indexed family of mappings $\langle\, f_s : A_s \to B_s \mid s \in S \,\rangle$. We let $f(A)$ denote the family $\langle\, f(A)_s = f_s(A_s) \mid s \in S \,\rangle$.

Henceforth we will assume the reader is familiar with the basic definitions and results of universal algebra including the notions of Σ subalgebra, Σ congruence and quotient Σ algebra, Σ homomorphism, isomorphism and embedding, Σ equation and equational class or variety of Σ algebras. A special case of the direct product, the *direct power*, will be used extensively in section 2. We recall this construction here.

1.3. Definition. Let Σ be an S-sorted signature, let A be a Σ algebra and let I be any non-empty set. The *direct power* A^I of A is the Σ algebra with carrier sets

$$A^I_s = [I \to A_s]$$

for each $s \in S$, (i.e. A^I_s is the set of all total functions from I to A_s, or I-indexed vectors from A_s). For each sort $s \in S$ and each constant symbol $c \in \Sigma_{\lambda,\,s}$ we define

$$c_{A^I}(i) = c_A$$

for each $i \in I$. For each $w = s(1)\ldots s(n) \in S^+$, each $s \in S$, each operation symbol $f \in \Sigma_{w,\,s}$ and any $a_j \in A^I_{s(j)}$ for $1 \leq j \leq n$ we define

$$f_{A^I}(a_1,\, \ldots,\, a_n)(i) = f_A(\, a_1(i),\, \ldots,\, a_n(i)\,)$$

for each $i \in I$.

We define the S-indexed family $\delta : A \to A^I$ of *diagonal mappings* by

$$\delta_s(a)(i) = a$$

for each sort $s \in S$ and each $a \in A_s$. □

It is easily shown that the family $\delta : A \to A^I$ of diagonal mappings is a Σ embedding of A in A^I. Next we introduce a notation for many–sorted topological spaces.

1.4. Definition. Let S be a non-empty set. By an *S-indexed family* (A, T) *of topological spaces* we mean a family

$$(A, T) = (\langle A_s \mid s \in S \rangle, \langle T_s \mid s \in S \rangle)$$

where for each $s \in S$, A_s is a set and T_s is a topology on A_s, i.e. a collection of subsets of A_s satisfying:

(i) if $F \subseteq T_s$ then $\cup F \in T_s$,

(ii) if $U, U' \in T_s$ then $U \cap U' \in T_s$,

(iii) $\emptyset \in T_s$ and $A_s \in T_s$.

The members of T_s are termed *open sets* on A_s. For any $s \in S$ and $a \in A_s$ an open set $U \in T_s$ such that $a \in U$ is termed a *neighbourhood* of a. We let $Nbd_A(a)$ denote the set of all neighbourhoods of a in A. Given an S-indexed family of subsets $B \subseteq A$, for any $s \in S$ an element $a \in A_s$ is said to be *adherent* to B if, and only if, for every neighbourhood $U \in Nbd_A(a)$, we have $U \cap B_s \neq \emptyset$. The set of all points $a \in A_s$ adherent to B_s is termed the *closure* of B_s. We let $Cl(B_s)$ denote the closure of B_s and $Cl(B)$ denotes the family $\langle\, Cl(B)_s = Cl(B_s) \mid s \in S \rangle$. The subset B_s is said to *closed* if, and only if, $B_s = Cl(B_s)$, and B_s is said to be *dense* in T_s if, and only if, $Cl(B_s) = A_s$.

For any $w = s(1) \ldots s(n) \in S^+$ we let T^w denote the product topology on the cartesian product $A^w = A_{s(1)} \times \ldots \times A_{s(n)}$ with subbasic open sets

$$\langle U \rangle = \{\ (a_1, \ldots, a_n) \in A^w \mid a_i \in U\ \}$$

for each open $U \in T_{s(i)}$ and each $1 \leq i \leq n$. We let $\langle U_1, \ldots, U_n \rangle$ denote the finite intersection $\langle U_1 \rangle \cap \ldots \cap \langle U_n \rangle$. For any n-tuple $(a_1, \ldots, a_n) \in A^w$ we let $Nbd_A(a_1, \ldots, a_n)$ denote the set of all neighbourhoods of $(a_1, \ldots, a_n)$ in T^w.

For any $s \in S$ and function $f : A^w \to A_s$, f is said to be *continuous* with respect to T if, and only if, for each open set $U \in T_s$,

$$f^{-1}(U) \in T^w,$$

i.e. inverse images of open sets are open.

Let A be an S–sorted Σ algebra and T be an S–indexed family of topological spaces over the carrier sets of A. Then the pair (A, T) is a *topological* Σ *algebra* if, and only if, for each $w \in S^+$, $s \in S$ and $f \in \Sigma_{w,s}$, the operation $f_A : A^w \to A_s$ is continuous with respect to T. We let $TopAlg(\Sigma)$ denote the class of all topological Σ algebras. □

Most definitions and properties from topology can be extended pointwise from a topological space to an S–indexed family of topological spaces. For example in Section 2 we require the notions of *subspace* and *Hausdorff space*. We make these concepts precise in the many-sorted case.

1.5. Definition. Let (A, T) and (B, T') be S–indexed families of topological spaces.

(i) We say that (A, T) is a *subspace* of (B, T') if, and only if, $A \subseteq B$ and

$$T_s = \{ \ U \cap A_s \ \mid U \in T_s' \ \}.$$

(ii) We say that (A, T) is a *Hausdorff space* if, and only if, for each sort $s \in S$ the topology T_s is Hausdorff, i.e. for any pair of elements $a, a' \in A_s$, if $a \neq a'$ then there exist neighbourhoods $U \in Nbd_A(a)$ and $V \in Nbd_A(a')$ such that

$$U \cap V = \emptyset.$$

□

Clearly if (A, T) is Hausdorff and (B, T') is a subspace of (A, T) then (B, T') is Hausdorff.

The notion of *convergence* is central to topology. A concise way to describe convergence properties is by using *filterbases.* (Another more algebraic approach is to use *nets*. We introduce this latter approach in section 2.)

1.6. Definition. Let A be a non–empty set. A *filterbase* F on A is a non–empty family of subsets of A such that:

(i) for each $X \in F$, $X \neq \emptyset$,

(ii) for any $X_1, X_2 \in F$ there exists $X_3 \in F$ such that $X_3 \subseteq X_1 \cap X_2$.

A filterbase F on A is a basis for a filter $\hat{F}$ on A by taking

$$\hat{F} = \{ \ Y \subseteq A \mid Y \supseteq X \text{ for some } X \in F \ \}.$$

By abuse of notation, if $A' \subseteq A$ is any dense subset we let $A' \cap F$ denote the collection of sets

$$A' \cap F = \{ \ A' \cap X \mid X \in F \ \}.$$

Then $A' \cap F$ is also a filterbase. If B is any non–empty set and $f : A \to B$ is any map then the image of F under f,

$$f(F) = \{ \ f(X) \mid X \in F \ \}$$

is a filterbase on B. If T is a topology on A and $a \in A$ then the set $Nbd_A(a)$ of all neighbourhoods of a is a filterbase on A termed the *neighbourhood filterbase* of a.

Given a topology T on A, a filterbase F on A *converges* to an element $a \in A$ (with respect to T) if, and only if, for each neighbourhood $U \in Nbd_A(a)$ there exists $X \in F$ such that $X \subseteq U$. □

2. HAUSDORFF EXTENSIONS.

In this section we consider the existence, uniqueness and construction of closed continuous extensions of a many-sorted algebra A with respect a family T of topological spaces. For reasons already indicated in the introduction, we will concentrate on the important special case where T is a family of Hausdorff spaces.

2.1. Closed Continuous Extensions in Topological Spaces.

Let Σ be an S-sorted signature and let A be a Σ algebra. In the context of algebraic specification A will typically arise as some model of an axiomatic specification (Σ, Φ), where Φ is some set of logical formulas (for example equations) over Σ. Let (B, T) be an S-indexed family of topological spaces such that $A \subseteq B$. For each sort $s \in S$, we may form the topological closure $Cl(A_s)$ of the carrier set A_s in T_s. The subset $Cl(A_s) \subseteq B_s$ may be given the subspace topology induced on T_s. Now $A_s \subseteq Cl(A_s)$ and if A_s is not closed in T_s then $A_s \subset Cl(A_s)$. This topological construction on the carrier sets of the algebra A adds the adherent elements of B_s to A_s as new data elements. These elements can be regarded as limit points of sequences (or more generally nets) of elements of A_s. The problem arises to construct a Σ algebra C which is a *closed continuous extension* of A in the sense that C extends A, for each sort $s \in S$ the carrier set C_s is the closure $Cl(A_s)$ of A_s in T_s, and each operation f_C of C is continuous. We make these concepts precise as follows.

2.1.1. Definition. Let Σ be an S-sorted signature, let A and C be Σ algebras and let (B, T) be an S-indexed family of topological spaces such that $A \subseteq B$. We say that C is a *closed continuous extension* of A with respect to (B, T), if, and only if:

(i) C extends A,

(ii) for each sort $s \in S$, $C_s = Cl(A_s)$, and

(iii) for each $w \in S^+$, $s \in S$ and operation symbol $f \in \Sigma_{w,s}$, the operation

$$f_C : C^w \to C_s$$

is continuous in the induced subspace topology (C, T') on T. □

Since it can be easily answered using elementary results from topology, we next address the question of uniqueness of closed continuous extensions.

2.2. Uniqueness of Hausdorff Extensions.

Given an S-sorted signature Σ, a Σ algebra A and an S-indexed family (B, T) of topological spaces such that $A \subseteq B$ we consider the following

Uniqueness Problem. *Find sufficient conditions on the family T of topologies such that a closed continuous extension of A, if it exists, is unique.*

In general there may exist many different closed continuous extensions of A with respect to (B, T). However, a solution to the uniqueness problem can be easily obtained from elementary topology. We consider the situation in which T

is a family of Hausdorff topologies. Then a simple consequence of the Hausdorff separation axiom ensures that a closed continuous extension of A with respect to (B, T) (if it exists) is unique. The basic fact we use is the following.

2.2.1. Proposition. *If T is a family of Hausdorff topologies and A is a dense in T then for any $w \in S^+$, any $s \in S$ and any continuous functions $f, g : B^w \to B_s$,*

$$f = g \quad \Leftrightarrow f|_A = g|_A,$$

where $f|_A$ and $g|_A$ are the restrictions to A of f and g respectively.

Proof. $\Rightarrow$ Trivial since $f|_A$ and $g|_A$ are restrictions.

$\Leftarrow$ We prove the contrapositive. Suppose $f \neq g$. Then for some $\bar{b} \in B^w$,

$$f(\bar{b}) \neq g(\bar{b}).$$

Let $b = f(\bar{b})$ and $b' = g(\bar{b})$ then $b \neq b'$. Since T_s is Hausdorff there exist disjoint neighbourhoods $U_b \in Nbd_B(b)$ and $U_{b'} \in Nbd_B(b')$. Since f and g are continuous then $f^{-1}(U_b)$ and $g^{-1}(U_{b'})$ are open. Then $f^{-1}(U_b)$ contains a non–empty basic open set $U \subseteq B^w$ and $g^{-1}(U_{b'})$ contains a non–empty basic open set $U' \subseteq B^w$. Since A_s is dense in T_s for each $s \in S$ then

$$U \cap A^w \neq \emptyset, \quad U' \cap A^w \neq \emptyset.$$

Let $\bar{a} \in U \cap A^w$ and $\overline{a'} \in U' \cap A^w$. Then

$$f|_A(\bar{a}) \in U_b \cap A_s, \quad g|_A(\overline{a'}) \in U_{b'} \cap A_s.$$

But U_b and $U_{b'}$ are disjoint so

$$f|_A(\bar{a}) \neq g|_A(\overline{a'}).$$

Hence $f|_A \neq g|_A$. □

2.2.2. Corollary. *Let C_1 and C_2 be Σ algebras. If (B, T) is Hausdorff and C_1 and C_2 are closed continuous extensions of A with respect to (B, T) then $C_1 = C_2$.*

Proof. Immediate from Proposition 2.2.1. □

Corollary 2.2.2 motivates the following special case of a closed continuous extension that will be studied in the sequel.

2.2.3. Definition. Let Σ be an S-sorted signature, let A be a Σ algebra and let (B, T) be an S-indexed family of Hausdorff spaces such that $A \subseteq B$. The unique closed continuous extension of A with respect to (B, T), if it exists, is termed the *Hausdorff extension* of A. We let $H(A)$ denote the Hausdorff extension of A.

In the next two subsections we concern ourselves first with the question of construction and then with the question of existence of Hausdorff extensions:

2.3. Algebraic Construction of Hausdorff Extensions.
Given an S-sorted signature Σ, a Σ algebra A and an S-indexed family (B, T) of Hausdorff spaces such that $A \subseteq B$ we consider the following

Construction Problem. *Assuming that the Hausdorff extension $H(A)$ of A exists, give an explicit algebraic construction of $H(A)$ from A and (B, T).*

The construction problem for $H(A)$ is fundamental since an explicit algebraic construction is required to determine the validity or satisfiability of logical formulas with respect to $H(A)$. In particular, for applications to algebraic specification, if A is a model of some axiomatic specification Φ then we wish to know whether $H(A)$ is also a model of Φ.

We shall present a general solution to the construction problem for Hausdorff extensions. Our construction is applicable to any many-sorted algebra A and any family (B, T) of Hausdorff spaces. It generalises the well known completion of the ring of rational numbers to the ring of real numbers using Cauchy sequences. Furthermore, this construction can be used to identify conditions on A and (B, T) which are sufficient to ensure that $H(A)$ exists. Thus the results of this section will be applied in the next subsection where we consider the existence problem for Hausdorff extensions.

To give a general solution to the construction problem we may assume that the Hausdorff extension $H(A)$ of A exists. We then begin by considering the algebraic relationships that must hold between A and $H(A)$.

First recall the basic topological concepts of nets and their convergence.

2.3.1. Definition. Let $(I, \leq)$ be any directed poset. An element $a \in A_s^I$ from the direct power A^I is termed a *net*. For any $s \in S$ and $a \in A_s^I$ and $b \in B_s$ we say that *a has limit b* or *a converges to b* if, and only if, for each neighbourhood $U \in Nbd_B(b)$ there exists $i \in I$ such that for all $j \geq i$,

$$a(j) \in U.$$

By the definition of topological closure, if a converges to b then $b \in Cl(A_s)$.

We say that a is *convergent* if, and only if, for some $b \in B_s$, a has limit b. We say that a is *uniquely convergent* if, and only if, for any b, $b' \in B_s$ if a converges to b and a converges to b' then $b = b'$.

We define the S-indexed family $A^* = A^{*(I)}$ of sets of convergent nets by

$$A_s^* = \{ \ a \in A_s^I \mid a \textit{ is convergent } \}$$

for each sort $s \in S$. □

A well known property of the Hausdorff separation axiom is that this axiom is necessary and sufficient to ensure uniqueness of convergence for all nets. Thus we have:

2.3.2. Lemma. *For any directed poset $(I, \leq)$ and any $s \in S$, each element $a \in A_s^*$ is uniquely convergent.*

Proof. See for example Kelley [1955]. □

Let us consider a fixed but arbitrarily chosen directed poset $(I, \leq)$. Now by Lemma 2.3.2 we can uniquely map every convergent net $a \in A^*_s$ to its limit, which is an element of $Cl(A_s)$, as follows.

2.3.3. Definition. Define the S-indexed family $lim : A^* \rightarrow Cl(A)$ of *limit mappings* by

$$lim_s(a) = b \;\Leftrightarrow\; a \textit{ converges to } b$$

for each $s \in S$ and each $a \in A^*_s$ and $b \in Cl(A_s)$. By Lemma 2.3.2, lim is well defined.

The family lim induces an S-indexed family $\equiv^{lim}$ of equivalence relations on A^* defined by

$$a \equiv^{lim}_s a' \;\Leftrightarrow\; lim_s(a) = lim_s(a')$$

for each $s \in S$ and $a, a' \in A^*_s$. □

The limit mappings on A^* have the following basic property.

2.3.4. Lemma. *For any $w = s(1) \ldots s(n) \in S^+$, $s \in S$ any function symbol $f \in \Sigma_{w,s}$, and for any convergent nets $a_j \in A^*_{s(j)}$ for $1 \leq j \leq n$,*

$$f_{A^I}(a_1, \ldots, a_n) \textit{ converges to } f_{H(A)}(\, lim_{s(1)}(a_1), \ldots, lim_{s(n)}(a_n)\,).$$

Proof. Since $H(A)$ is a closed continuous extension of A then $f_{H(A)}$ is continuous. Consider any convergent nets $a_j \in A^*_{s(j)}$ for $1 \leq j \leq n$ and let $b = f_{H(A)}(\, lim_{s(1)}(a_1), \ldots, lim_{s(n)}(a_n)\,)$. Consider any neighbourhood $U \in Nbd_{Cl(A)}(b)$. Since $f_{H(A)}$ is continuous, $f^{-1}_{H(A)}(U) \in T^w_{Cl(A)}$ is open in the subspace topology $T_{Cl(A)}$ on $Cl(A)$. Since U is a neighbourhood of b then $(\, lim_{s(1)}(a_1), \ldots, lim_{s(n)}(a_n)\,) \in f^{-1}_{H(A)}(U)$. So for some basic open $U' \subseteq f^{-1}_{H(A)}(U)$ in the subspace topology where $U' = U'_1 \times \ldots \times U'_n$

$$(\, lim_{s(1)}(a_1), \ldots, lim_{s(n)}(a_n)\,) \in U'.$$

Now for each $1 \leq j \leq n$, a_j is convergent, so there exists $k_j \in I$ such that for all $i \geq k_j$,

$$a_j(i) \in U'_j.$$

Let k be an upper bound of $k_1, \ldots, k_n$ then for all $i \geq k$

$$(\, a_1(i), \ldots, a_n(i)\,) \in U'.$$

Thus for all $i \geq k$,

$$f_{A^I}(a_1, \ldots, a_n)(i) = f_A(\, a_1(i), \ldots, a_n(i)\,)$$

$$= f_{H(A)}(\, a_1(i), \ldots, a_n(i)\,) \in U.$$

Since U was arbitrarily chosen then $f_{A^I}(a_1, \ldots, a_n)$ converges to

$$f_{H(A)}(\, lim_{s(1)}(a_1), \ldots, lim_{s(n)}(a_n)\,).$$

□

Lemma 2.3.4 leads to the following relationships between algebras. First, the S-indexed family A^* of sets of convergent nets is closed under the operations of the direct power A^I. So we have:

2.3.5. Corollary. *The family A^* is the carrier family of a subalgebra of A^I and the family $\delta : A \to A^I$ of diagonal maps is a Σ embedding of A in A^*.*

Proof. We need only show that the family of sets A^* contains each constant of A^I and is closed under the operations of A^I.

Consider any $s \in S$ and constant symbol $c \in \Sigma_{\lambda,s}$. Then c_{A^I} is convergent with limit c_A and thus $c_{A^I} \in A^*_s$.

Consider any $w = s(1)\ldots s(n) \in S^+$, any $s \in S$, any function symbol $f \in \Sigma_{w,s}$ and any convergent nets $a_j \in A^*_{s(j)}$ for $1 \leq j \leq n$. By Lemma 2.3.4,

$$f_{A^I}(a_1, \ldots, a_n) \in A^*_s,$$

i.e. A^* is closed under f_{A^I}.

To show that $\delta : A \to A^I$ is a Σ embedding of A in A^*, since δ is a Σ embedding of A in A^I and $A^* \leq A^I$ by above, it suffices to show that $\delta(A) \subseteq A^*$. So consider any $s \in S$ and $a \in A_s$. For all $i \in I$, $\delta_s(a)(i) = a$ and so $\delta_s(a)$ converges to a. Thus $\delta_s(a) \in A^*_s$. □

Secondly, the family *lim* of limit maps is a homomorphism from the algebra A^* to the Hausdorff extension $H(A)$.

2.3.6. Proposition. *The S-indexed family $lim : A^* \to Cl(A)$ of limit mappings is a Σ homomorphism from A^* to $H(A)$.*

Proof. Consider any $s \in S$ and constant symbol $c \in \Sigma_{\lambda,s}$. Then

$$lim_s(c_{A^*}) = lim_s(c_{A^I})$$

since $A^* \leq A^I$,

$$= c_A = c_{H(A)}$$

since $A < H(A)$.

Consider any $w = s(1)\ldots s(n) \in S^+$, $s \in S$, any function symbol $f \in \Sigma_{w,s}$, any convergent $a_j \in A^*_{s(j)}$ for $1 \leq j \leq n$ and the operation f_{A^*}. Then

$$lim_s(\, f_{A^*}(a_1, \ldots, a_n)\,) = lim_s(\, f_{A^I}(a_1, \ldots, a_n))$$

since $A^* \leq A^I$

$$= f_{H(A)}(\, lim_{s(1)}(a_1), \ldots, lim_{s(n)}(a_n)\,)$$

by Lemma 2.3.4. □

Thus we may form the homomorphic image $lim(A^*)$ of A^* which stands in the following relationship to A and the Hausdorff extension $H(A)$.

2.3.7. Continuous Extension Theorem.

$$A \leq lim(A^*) \leq H(A).$$

Proof. Since $lim : A^* \rightarrow H(A)$ is a Σ homomorphism by Proposition 2.3.6 then

$$lim(A^*) \leq H(A).$$

To show that $A \leq lim(A^*)$ note that $A \leq H(A)$ by definition of $H(A)$ and $lim(A^*) \leq H(A)$ by above. So it suffices to show that $A \subseteq lim(A^*)$. Consider any $s \in S$ and $a \in A_s$ and the diagonal map $\delta_s : A_s \rightarrow A_s^I$. By Corollary 2.3.5, $\delta_s(a) \in A_s^*$ and so $lim_s(\delta_s(a)) \in lim(A^*)_s$. But $lim_s(\delta_s(a)) = a$ and so $a \in lim(A^*)_s$. □

Now since $lim(A^*) \leq H(A)$ we may naturally ask: when is $lim(A^*) = H(A)$? In this case we have an algebraic construction of the Hausdorff extension $H(A)$ as required. For a particular adherent element $b \in Cl(A_s)$, if a net converging to b can be constructed over the directed poset $(I, \leq)$ then $b \in lim(A^*)_s$. Recall that the set $Nbd_B(b)$ of all neighbourhoods of b in T_s can be partially ordered by $U \succeq U' \Leftrightarrow U \subseteq U'$. Then $(Nbd_B(b), \succeq)$ is a directed poset termed the *neighbourhood poset* of b. A sufficient condition on $(I, \leq)$ such that $b \in lim(A^*)_s$ can be given in terms of the neighbourhood poset $(Nbd_B(b), \succeq)$. Recall that if $(I, \leq)$ and $(I', \leq)$ are posets then an *embedding retraction pair* of monotonic maps is a pair

$$e : (I, \leq) \rightarrow (I', \leq'), \quad r : (I', \leq') \rightarrow (I, \leq)$$

satisfying

$$r(e(i)) = i \tag{i}$$

for all $i \in I$, and

$$i \leq j \;\Rightarrow\; e(i) \leq e(j), \quad i' \leq j' \;\Rightarrow\; r(i') \leq r(j') \tag{ii}$$

for all $i, j \in I$ and $i', j' \in I'$.

2.3.8. Adherence Lemma. *For any $s \in S$ and $b \in Cl(A_s)$, if there exists an embedding retraction pair of monotonic maps*

$$e : (\, Nbd_B(b), \preceq\,) \rightarrow (I, \leq)$$

$$r : (I, \leq) \rightarrow (\, Nbd_B(b), \preceq\,),$$

then $b \in lim(A^*)_s$.

Proof. Let e and r be an embedding retraction pair of monotonic maps. We must show that for some $a \in A_s^*$, $lim_s(a) = b$. Define a by

$$a(i) = a_{r(i)}$$

for each $i \in I$, where $a_{r(i)} \in r(i) \cap A_s$. Since $b \in Cl(A_s)$ then $a_{r(i)}$ exists for each $i \in I$. Now $lim_s(a) = b$, for consider any $U \in Nbd_B(b)$ and $e(U) \in I$ and any $j \geq e(U)$. Since r is monotonic and r and e form an embedding retraction pair then $r(j) \succeq r(e(U)) = U$. By definition

$$a(j) \in r(j) \cap A_s.$$

But $r(j) \succeq U$ so $r(j) \subseteq U$ and so $a(j) \in U$. Since j was arbitrarily chosen then for all $j \geq e(U)$, $a(j) \in U$. Since U was arbitrarily chosen then a converges to b. So $a \in A_s^*$ and $lim_s(a) = b$. □

Lemma 2.3.8 suggests that we construct a single directed poset in which the neighbourhood poset of every adherent point can be embedded.

2.3.9. Definition. Let $\coprod_{s \in S} Cl(A_s)$ denote the disjoint sum (coproduct) of the sets $Cl(A_s)$. Define the poset

$$(I(A), \leq^A) = \prod_{(s,\, b) \in \coprod_{s \in S} Cl(A_s)} (\, Nbd_B(b), \preceq).$$

Clearly the direct product of a family of directed posets is again directed. □

Thus $(I(A), \leq^A)$ is the direct product of the neighbourhood posets of all elements of all sets $Cl(A_s)$. Then $(I(A), \leq^A)$ has the following strong embedding property with respect to its coordinate posets.

2.3.10. Proposition. *For any $n \geq 1$, any $s(1), \ldots, s(n) \in S$ and any $b_j \in Cl(A_{s(j)})$ for $1 \leq j \leq n$ there exists an embedding retraction pair of monotonic maps*

$$e : (\, Nbd_B(b_1), \preceq) \times \ldots \times (\, Nbd_B(b_n), \preceq) \rightarrow (I(A), \leq^A)$$

$$r : (I(A), \leq^A) \rightarrow (\, Nbd_B(b_1), \preceq) \times \ldots \times (\, Nbd_B(b_n), \preceq)$$

Proof. Define the embedding e by

$$e(U_1, \ldots, U_n)(s, b) = \begin{cases} U_j, & \text{if } (s, b) = (s(j), b_j); \\ B_s, & \text{otherwise,} \end{cases}$$

for any $U_j \in Nbd_B(b_j)$ for $1 \leq j \leq n$, any $s \in S$ and $b \in Cl(A_s)$. Define the retraction r by

$$r(i) = (\, i(s(1), b_1), \ldots, i(s(n), b_n)\,)$$

for each $i \in I(A)$. Clearly e and r are monotonic, e is injective and for any $U_j \in Nbd_B(b_j)$ for $1 \leq j \leq n$,

$$r(e(U_1, \ldots U_n)) = (U_1, \ldots U_n).$$

□

Thus we have the following explicit algebraic construction of the Hausdorff extension $H(A)$ from A and T.

2.3.11. Construction Theorem. *Let* $(I, \leq) = (I(A), \leq^A)$ *and let* $A^* \leq A^{I(A)}$ *be the subalgebra of convergent nets. Then* $lim(A^*)$ *is the Hausdorff extension* $H(A)$ *of* A.

Proof. Follows immediately from Theorem 2.3.7, Lemma 2.3.8 and Proposition 2.3.10. □

An important property of every Hausdorff extension $H(A)$ is determined by the form of this construction for $H(A)$: the equational theories of A and $H(A)$ are the same.

2.3.12. Conservative Extension Theorem. *For any equation* $e \in Eqn(\Sigma, X)$,

$$A \models e \;\Leftrightarrow\; H(A) \models e.$$

Proof. By Theorem 2.3.11, $H(A) = lim(A^*)$ where $I = I(A)$.

$\Rightarrow$ Suppose $A \models e$. Since A^I is a direct power of A then $A^I \models e$. By Corollary 2.3.5, $A^* \leq A^I$ so $A^* \models e$. By Proposition 2.3.6, $lim(A^*)$ is a homomorphic image of A^* and so $lim(A^*) \models e$. Thus $H(A) \models e$.

$\Leftarrow$ Suppose $H(A) \models e$, then $lim(A^*) \models e$. By Theorem 2.3.7, $A \leq lim(A^*)$ and so $A \models e$. □

Theorem 2.3.12 is of fundamental importance from the point of view of algebraic specification. If A is a model of an equational specification E (for example an initial model, final model or higher-order initial model) then so is $H(A)$.

It is natural to consider whether our construction of $H(A)$ can be simplified in the presence of stronger topological axioms. In particular, when can we replace an arbitrary directed poset with the usual linear ordering $\leq$ on $\mathbf{N}$ and consider convergent sequences rather than arbitrary convergent nets? (Recall for example the Cauchy completion of the ring of rationals to the ring of reals.)

2.3.13. Definition. Let $(\mathbf{N}, \leq)$ be the poset of natural numbers with the usual linear ordering $\leq$. A convergent net $a \in A_s^{\mathbf{N}}$ is termed a *convergent sequence*. □

Recall the first axiom of countability for a topological space.

2.3.14. Definition. An S-indexed family (B, T) of topological spaces is 1° *countable* if, and only if, for each $s \in S$ the topology T_s is 1° countable, i.e. for each $b \in B_s$ there exists a countable family

$$\langle\, U_n(b) \in Nbd_B(b) \mid n \in \mathbf{N} \,\rangle$$

of neighbourhoods of b such that for any neighbourhood $U \in Nbd_B(b)$ of b,

$$U_n(b) \subseteq U$$

for some $n \in \mathbf{N}$. □

If (B, T) is 1° countable then we may replace the directed poset $(I(A), \leq^A)$ by $(\mathbf{N}, \leq^{\mathbf{N}})$ in the construction of the Hausdorff extension $H(A)$.

2.3.15. Theorem. *Let $(I, \leq) = (\mathbf{N}, \leq)$. If (B, T) is 1° countable then $H(A) = lim(A^*)$.*

Proof. By Theorem 2.3.7, $lim(A^*) \leq H(A)$ so we need only show that $Cl(A) \subseteq lim(A^*)$. Consider any sort $s \in S$ and any $b \in Cl(A_s)$. Since T_s is 1° countable there exists a countable family

$$\langle U_n(b) \in Nbd_B(b) \mid n \in \mathbf{N} \rangle$$

of neighbourhoods of b such that for any neighbourhood $U \in Nbd_B(b)$, $U_n(b) \subseteq U$ for some $n \in \mathbf{N}$.

Define the family $\langle U'_n(b) \subseteq B_s \mid n \in \mathbf{N} \rangle$ of sets inductively by

$$U'_0(b) = U_0(b)$$

and for any $n \in \mathbf{N}$,

$$U'_{n+1}(b) = U'_n(b) \cap U_{n+1}(b).$$

It is easily shown by induction on n that for all $n \in \mathbf{N}$,

$$U'_n(b) \in Nbd_B(b) \tag{1}$$

$$U'_{n+1}(b) \subseteq U'_n(b) \tag{2}$$

and

$$U'_n(b) \subseteq U_n(b). \tag{3}$$

We show that for some convergent sequence $a \in A_s^{\mathbf{N}}$, $lim_s(a) = b$. Define a by

$$a(n) = a_n$$

for each $n \in \mathbf{N}$, where $a_n \in U'_n(b) \cap A_s$. Since $b \in Cl(A_s)$ then by (1) above a_n exists for each $n \in \mathbf{N}$. Now consider any neighbourhood $U \in Nbd_B(b)$. For some $n \in \mathbf{N}$, $U_n(b) \subseteq U$ so for such n by (2) and (3) above, $U'_m(b) \subseteq U$ for all $m \geq n$. Thus $a(m) \in U$ for all $m \geq n$. So a converges to b, i.e. $lim_s(a) = b$. □

2.4. Existence of Hausdorff Extensions.

In the previous subsection we assumed the existence of the Hausdorff extension $H(A)$ of A and used this fact to derive an explicit algebraic construction of this extension. But how can we tell whether $H(A)$ exists in the first place? We shall consider the following

Existence Problem. *Given an S-sorted signature Σ, a Σ algebra A and an S-indexed family (B, T) of Hausdorff spaces such that $A \subseteq B$, find sufficient conditions on A and (B, T) such that the Hausdorff extension $H(A)$ exists.*

Our approach to this problem will be to analyse the construction of section 2.3 and determine general conditions sufficient to allow this construction to be carried out. We note however that given more detailed information about the algebraic structure of A and the nature of T we may be able to derive much stronger results than those presented in this section. For example it is a non-trivial result of topological group theory (see for example Warner [1989]) that if G is a group and (B, T) is a Hausdorff space such that $G \subseteq B$ and G is continous in the subspace topology on T then there exists a group $\hat{G}$ which is a closed continous extension of G in (B, T). The group $\hat{G}$ is usually termed the *bilinear completion* of G rather than the Hausdorff extension.

We begin with the following elementary fact, which is based on simply checking the feasibility of each step of the construction introduced in 2.3.

2.4.1. Proposition. *Let* $(I, \leq) = (I(A), \leq^A)$. *If:*

(i) A^* *is a subalgebra of* A^I, *and*

(ii) $\equiv^{lim}$ *is a congruence on* A^*, *and*

(iii) $A^*/\equiv^{lim}$ *is continuous with respect to the induced topology* $T_{A^*/\equiv^{lim}}$

then the Hausdorff extension $H(A)$ *of* A *exists and*

$$H(A) \cong A^*/\equiv^{lim} .$$

Proof. Assume (i), (ii) and (iii) hold. Define the S-indexed family $\psi : A^*/\equiv^{lim} \rightarrow B$ of mappings by

$$\psi_s(a/\equiv^{lim}) = lim_s(a)$$

for each sort $s \in S$ and each $a \in A^*_s$. Now define the Σ algebra $H(A)$ as follows. For each $s \in S$, define

$$H(A)_s = \psi_s(\,(A^*/\equiv^{lim})_s\,).$$

For each $s \in S$ and constant symbol $c \in \Sigma_{\lambda,\,s}$, define

$$c_{H(A)} = lim_s(c_{A^*}).$$

For any $w = s(1)\dots s(n) \in S^+$, any $s \in S$, any $f \in \Sigma_{w,s}$ and any $a_j \in A^*_{s(j)}$ for $1 \leq j \leq n$, define

$$f_{H(A)}(\,\psi_{s(1)}(a_1/\equiv^{lim}),\,\dots,\,\psi_{s(n)}(a_n/\equiv^{lim})\,) = \psi_s(\,f_{A^*}(a_1,\,\dots,\,a_n)/\equiv^{lim}\,).$$

Clearly $H(A)$ is well defined as a Σ algebra and $\psi : A^*/\equiv^{lim}\rightarrow H(A)$ is a Σ isomorphism. We show that $H(A)$ is a closed continuous extension of A. Recall Definition 2.1.1.

(i) To show that $H(A)$ extends A consider any sort $s \in S$ and any constant symbol $c \in \Sigma_{\lambda,\,s}$. Then

$$c_{H(A)} = lim_s(c_{A^*}) = c_A.$$

Consider any $w = s(1)\ldots s(n) \in S^+$, any sort $s \in S$, any function symbol $f \in \Sigma_{w,\,s}$ and any $a_j \in A_{s(j)}$ for $1 \leq j \leq n$. Then

$$f_{H(A)}(a_1,\,\ldots,\,a_n)$$

$$= f_{H(A)}(\ \psi_{s(1)}(\delta_{s(1)}(a_1)/ \equiv^{lim}),\,\ldots,\,\psi_{s(n)}(\delta_{s(n)}(a_n)/ \equiv^{lim})\ )$$

$$= \psi_s(\ f_{A^*}(\,\delta_{s(1)}(a_1),\,\ldots,\,\delta_{s(n)}(a_n)\,)/ \equiv^{lim}\ )$$

by definition of $f_{H(A)}$

$$= lim_s(\ f_{A^*}(\,\delta_{s(1)}(a_1),\,\ldots,\,\delta_{s(n)}(a_n)\,)\ )$$

by definition of ψ

$$= lim_s(\ \delta_s(\ f_A(a_1,\,\ldots,\,a_n)\ )\ )$$

by Corollary 2.3.5

$$= f_A(a_1,\,\ldots,\,a_n).$$

Thus $H(A)$ is an extension of A.

(ii) By the definition of ψ, for any sort $s \in S$,

$$H(A)_s = \psi_s(\,(A^*/\equiv^{lim})_s\,) = lim(A^*)_s.$$

Since $I = I(A)$ then by Lemma 2.3.8 and Proposition 2.3.10, $H(A)_s = Cl(A_s)$.

(iii) For each sort $s \in S$ let $T_s^{H(A)}$ be the subspace topology on $H(A)_s$ and define the induced topology $T_s^{A^*/\equiv^{lim}}$ on $(A^*/\equiv^{lim})_s$ by

$$U \in T_s^{A^*/\equiv^{lim}} \quad \Leftrightarrow \quad \psi_s(U) \in T_s^{H(A)}$$

for each $U \subseteq (A^*/\equiv^{lim})_s$. Then

$$\psi : (A^*/\equiv^{lim},\, T^{A^*/\equiv^{lim}}) \rightarrow (H(A),\, T^{H(A)})$$

is a homeomorphism. Since ψ is both a homeomorphism and a Σ isomorphism and $A^*/\equiv^{lim}$ is continuous then so is $H(A)$.

So by (i), (ii) and (iii), $H(A)$ is a closed continuous extension of A. □

Condition (iii) of Proposition 2.4.1 is not very satisfactory since it indicates that even if A is continuous with respect to the subspace topology on T and the algebra $A^*/\equiv^{lim}$ is well defined, the latter may fail to be continuous. However, if we assume slightly stronger separation properties on T then this possibility cannot arise. Recall the separation axiom of regularity.

2.4.2. Definition. An S-indexed family $(B,\,T)$ of topological spaces is *regular* if, and only if, for each sort $s \in S$ the topology T_s is regular, i.e. for any $b \in B_s$ and closed set $U \in T_s$ not containing b there exist open sets $V,\,V' \in T_s$ with $b \in V$, $U \subseteq V'$ and

$$V \cap V' = \emptyset.$$

□

Clearly every regular space is Hausdorff. Regular spaces include for example all metric spaces. Recall that if $T_{s(1)}, \ldots, T_{s(n)}$ are regular topologies on the sets $B_{s(1)}, \ldots, B_{s(n)}$ then the product topology T^w on the cartesian product A^w is regular. Regular spaces have the following important property.

2.4.3. Theorem. *Let (X, T) be a topological space, let (Y, T') be a regular space, let $D \subseteq X$ be dense in T and let $f : D \to Y$ be a continuous map. Then f has a continuous extension $\hat{f} : X \to Y$ if, and only if, the filterbase $f(D \cap Nbd_X(x))$ converges for each $x \in X$. If $\hat{f}$ exists then it is unique.*

Proof. See for example Dugundji [1966]. □

To apply Theorem 2.4.3 to Proposition 2.4.1 we relate convergence on nets to convergence on filterbases.

2.4.4. Lemma. *Let $(I, \leq) = (I(A), \leq^A)$ and suppose A is dense in T. For any $w = s(1)\ldots s(n) \in S^+$, any $s \in S$, any operation symbol $f \in \Sigma_{w,s}$, any $b_j \in B_{s(j)}$ for $1 \leq j \leq n$, and any $b \in B_s$, if*

$$f_{A^I}(a_1, \ldots, a_n) \text{ converges to } b$$

for all $a_j \in A^I_{s(j)}$ converging to b_j for $1 \leq j \leq n$ then

$$f_A(A^w \cap Nbd_B(b_1, \ldots b_n)) \text{ converges to } b.$$

Proof. We prove the contrapositive. Suppose $f_A(A^w \cap Nbd_B(b_1, \ldots, b_n))$ does not converge to b. Then for some $V \in Nbd_B(b)$ there is no $U \in Nbd_B(b_1, \ldots, b_n)$ such that

$$f_A(A^w \cap U) \subseteq V.$$

For each $U \in Nbd_B(b_1, \ldots, b_n)$ let $(a_1^U, \ldots, a_n^U) \in A^w \cap U$ be an n-tuple satisfying

$$f_A(a_1^U, \ldots, a_n^U) \notin V.$$

By density of A in T, for each $1 \leq j \leq n$, $b_j \in Cl(A_{s(j)})$, and since $I = I(A)$ then by Proposition 2.3.10 there exists an embedding retraction pair

$$e : (Nbd_B(b_1), \preceq) \times \ldots \times (Nbd_B(b_n), \preceq) \to (I, \leq)$$

$$r : (I, \leq) \to (Nbd_B(b_1), \preceq) \times \ldots \times (Nbd_B(b_n), \preceq).$$

For each $1 \leq j \leq n$, define $a_j \in A^I_{s(j)}$ by

$$a_j(i) = a_j^{r(i)}$$

for each $i \in I$. Consider any $1 \leq j \leq n$ and $U^j \in Nbd_B(b_j)$ and

$$U = B_{s(1)} \times \ldots \times B_{s(j-1)} \times U^j \times B_{s(j+1)} \times \ldots \times B_{s(n)}$$

For any $i \geq e(U)$ we have $r(i) \succeq r(e(U)) = U$. So $r(i)_j \succeq U^j$ and hence $r(i)_j \subseteq U^j$. But

$$a_j(i) = a_j^{r(i)} \in r(i)_j.$$

So for all $i \geq e(U)$, $a_j(i) \in U^j$. Since j and U^j were arbitrarily chosen then a_j converges to b_j for each $1 \leq j \leq n$. Now consider $f_{A^I}(a_1, \ldots, a_n)$. For all $i \in I$,

$$\begin{aligned} f_{A^I}(a_1, \ldots, a_n)(i) &= f_A(a_1(i), \ldots, a_n(i)) \\ &= f_A(a_1^{r(i)}, \ldots, a_n^{r(i)}) \notin V. \end{aligned}$$

So $f_{A^I}(a_1, \ldots, a_n)$ does not converge to b. □

2.4.5. Corollary. *Let $(I, \leq) = (I(A), \leq^A)$ and suppose A is dense in T. If:*

(i) A^* is a subalgebra of A^I, and

(ii) $\equiv^{lim}$ is a congruence on A^*

then for each $w = s(1)\ldots s(n) \in S^+$, each $s \in S$, each operation symbol $f \in \Sigma_{w,s}$ and for any $b_j \in B_{s(j)}$, for $1 \leq j \leq n$,

$$f_A(A^w \cap Nbd_B(b_1, \ldots, b_n))$$

converges.

Proof. Suppose A is dense in T and assume (i) and (ii) hold. Consider any $w = s(1)\ldots s(n) \in S^+$, any $s \in S$ any operation symbol $f \in \Sigma_{w,s}$ and any $b_j \in B_{s(j)}$ for $1 \leq j \leq n$. Since A is dense in T then $b_j \in Cl(A_{s(j)})$ for each $1 \leq j \leq n$. Since $I = I(A)$, by Lemma 2.3.8 and Proposition 2.3.10, for each $1 \leq j \leq n$ there exists $a_j \in A^*_{s(j)}$ such that a_j converges to b_j. By (i) for some $b \in B_s$, $f_{A^I}(a_1, \ldots, a_n)$ converges to b.

Now consider any other $a'_j \in A^*_{s(j)}$ converging to b_j for $1 \leq j \leq n$. Then $a_j \equiv^{lim}_{s(j)} a'_j$ for $1 \leq j \leq n$ and so by (ii)

$$f_{A^I}(a_1, \ldots, a_n) \equiv^{lim}_s f_{A^I}(a'_1, \ldots, a'_n).$$

Thus $f_{A^I}(a'_1, \ldots, a'_n)$ converges to b.

Therefore for all $a_j \in A^I_{s(j)}$ converging to b_j, for $1 \leq j \leq n$, $f_{A^I}(a_1, \ldots, a_n)$ converges to b. So by Lemma 2.4.4,

$$f_A(A^w \cap Nbd_B(b_1, \ldots, b_n))$$

converges to b. □

Combining Corollary 2.4.5 and Theorem 2.4.3 we can refine Proposition 2.4.1 to the following.

2.4.6. Theorem. *Let $(I, \leq) = (I(A), \leq^A)$ and suppose (B, T) is a family of regular spaces. If:*

(i) A is continuous with respect to the subspace topology, and

(ii) A^* *is a subalgebra of* A^I, *and*

(iii) $\equiv^{lim}$ *is a congruence on* A^*

then the Hausdorff extension $H(A)$ *of* A *exists and*

$$H(A) \cong A^* / \equiv^{lim} .$$

Proof. Suppose (B, T) is regular and assume (i), (ii) and (iii) hold. Consider any $w = s(1) \ldots s(n) \in S^+$, any $s \in S$ and any function symbol $f \in \Sigma_{w,s}$. By (ii), (iii) and Corollary 2.4.5 for any $b_j \in Cl(A_{s(j)})$ for $1 \leq j \leq n$ the filterbase $f_A(A^w \cap Nbd_B(b_1, \ldots, b_n))$ converges. By (i) f_A is continuous so by Theorem 2.4.3, f_A has an extension

$$\hat{f} : Cl(A_{s(1)}) \times \ldots \times Cl(A_{s(n)}) \rightarrow Cl(A_s)$$

which is continuous with respect to the subspace topology.

We construct the Hausdorff extension $H(A)$ of A as follows. For each sort $s \in S$ define the carrier set $H(A)_s = Cl(A_s)$. For each $s \in S$ and constant symbol $c \in \Sigma_{\lambda, s}$ define

$$c_{H(A)} = c_A .$$

For each $w \in S^+$, $s \in S$ and operation symbol $f \in \Sigma_{w,s}$ define

$$f_{H(A)} = \hat{f} .$$

Clearly $H(A)$ is the Hausdorff extension of A.

Since $I = I(A)$, by Theorem 2.3.11, $lim(A^*)_s = Cl(A_s) = H(A)_s$ for each $s \in S$. So by Proposition 2.3.6, $lim : A \rightarrow H(A)$ is an epimorphism with kernel $\equiv^{lim}$. Then by the First Homomorphism Theorem $A^* / \equiv^{lim} \cong lim(A^*) \cong H(A)$. □

Acknowledgements.

We gratefully acknowledge the financial support of the Deutscher Akademischer Austauschdienst. This research was carried out during an extended visit by the author to the Technical University of Munich, we wish to express our gratitude to Manfred Broy for making this visit possible.

REFERENCES.

A.V. Arkhangel'skii [1981], Classes of topological groups, Uspekhi. Matem. Nauk. 36 (1981), No 1, 127–146.

G. Birkhoff [1935], On the structure of abstract algebras, Proc. Camb. Philos. Soc. 31 (1935), 433–454.

P.M. Cohn [1981], Universal Algebra, second edition, D. Reidel, Dordrecht, 1981.

D. von Dantzig [1933], Zur topologischen Algebra, Math. Ann. 107 (1933), 587–626.

J. Dugundji [1966], Topology, Allyn and Bacon Inc, Boston, 1966.
H. Ehrig et al [1988], H. Ehrig, F. Parisi-Presicce, P. Boehm, C. Rieckhoff, C. Dimitrovici and M. Grosse-Rhode, Algebraic data type and process specifications based on projection spaces, 23–43 in: D. Sanella and A. Tarlecki (eds), Recent Trends in Data Type Specification, LNCS 332, Springer, Berlin, 1988.
ADJ [1975], J.A. Goguen, J. Thatcher, E. Wagner and J.B. Wright, Abstract data types as initial algebras and the correctness of data representations, in: A. Klinger (ed), Computer Graphics, Pattern Recognition and Data Structure, 89–93, IEEE 1975.
J.L. Kelley [1955], General Topology, Van Nostrand, Princeton, 1955.
A.I. Mal'cev [1957], Free topological algebras, Izv. Acad. Nauk. SSSR 21 (1957) 171–198. English translation: Trans. Amer. Math. Soc. (2) 17 (1961).
A.A. Markov [1945], On free topological groups, Izv. Acad. Nauk. SSSR 9 (1945), 3–64. English translation: Trans Amer. Math. Soc. 8 (1962), 195–272.
K. Meinke, Universal algebra in higher types, Theoretical Computer Science 100 (1992), 385–417.
K. Meinke and J.V. Tucker [1993], Universal Algebra, 189–411 in: S. Abramsky, D. Gabbay and T.S.E. Maibaum (eds), Handbook of Logic in Computer Science, Oxford University Press, Oxford, 1993.
B. Möller [1987], Higher-order algebraic specification, Habilitationsschrift, Fakultät Mathematik und Informatik, TU München, 1987.
L.S. Pontrjagin [1954], Topological Groups, second edition, Princeton University Press, Princeton, 1954.
M. Smyth [1993], Topology, 642–761 in: S. Abramsky, D. Gabbay and T.S.E. Maibaum (eds), Handbook of Logic in Computer Science, Oxford University Press, Oxford, 1993.
V. Stoltenberg–Hansen and J.V. Tucker [1991], Algebraic equations and fixed–point equations in inverse limits, Theoretical Computer Science, 87 (1991), 1–24.
W. Taylor [1977], Varieties of topological algebras, J. Austral. Math. Soc. 23A (1977), 207–241.
M. Wand [1981], Final algebra semantics and data type extensions, J. Comput. System Sci. 19 (1981) 27–44.
S. Warner [1989], Topological Fields, Mathematics Studies, Vol 157, North Holland, Amsterdam, 1989.
M. Wirsing [1990], Algebraic Specification, 675–788 in: J. van Leeuwen (ed), Handbook of Theoretical Computer Science, Volume B, Formal Models and Semantics, Elsevier, Amsterdam, 1990.

A Hierarchy of Institutions Separated by Properties of Parameterized Abstract Data Types

Till Mossakowski

University of Bremen, Department of Computer Science
P.O.Box 33 04 40, D-28334 Bremen
Phone: +49-421-218-2935, E-mail: e13p@alf.zfn.uni-bremen.de

1 Introduction

Specification languages are based upon logical frameworks, which include models, theories, satisfaction and so on. We only list some of the logical frameworks studied in the literature: equational logic [12, 8], conditional equational logic [22], Horn Clause Theories (with relations) [11, 17] and partial algebraic systems with conditional axioms [4], see also [18]. To have comparable settings, we additionally equip all these logical frameworks with (restricted) partiality and relations.

We use Burstall's and Goguen's notion of institution [10] to speak about logical frameworks formally. To compare institutions, we introduce a notion of weak subinstitution, based upon Meseguer's notions [14].

Our aim is twofold:

1. to examine the relations and equivalences between the above institutions and
2. to differentiate among them in an objective way by looking at characteristic properties of institutions. There are (at least) three kinds of properties which are potentially useful here:
   (a) The institutions cited above differ in categorical properties of their model categories. This gives us a hierarchy. But how relevant is this to writing and using specifications?
   (b) Considering initial semantics does not help — the hierarchy collapses.
   (c) When turning to parameterized abstract data types, the situation changes. We consider PADTs to be functors which are specifiable using import, body and export specifications in the sense of [9]. Technically, these are free functors followed by forgetful functors.

Our main theorem separates the institutions using algebraic properties of these specifiable functors. We get a strict hierarchy of institutions. This hierarchy is also set up in a companion paper [16] using recursion theoretical methods. Here, we get simplified proofs by directly using the usual construction of free PADTs.

Besides, we illustrate the usefulness of the hierarchy theorem by locating a sample PADT (bounded stacks) in the hierarchy. In general, given a sample PADT, the algebraic properties help to find out the lowest position (= most restricted institution) in the hierarchy usable to specify it. This is important because the available tools may become weaker, if we choose a too general institution.

The paper is organized as follows: Section 2 recalls some institutions and the notion of PADT. In section 3, the notion of weak subinstitution is introduced and the institutions are ordered in a hierarchy. In section 4, we prove properties of PADTs showing this hierarchy to be proper. Being such prepared, in section 5, we locate a sample PADT within the hierarchy. In section 6, we interpret the technical results.

2 Preliminaries

2.1 Specification Frames and Institutions

Specification frames by Ehrig, Jimenez and Orejas [7] formalize abstract unstructured theories and models of theories: A *specification frame* $F = (\underline{Th}^F, \underline{Mod}^F)$ consists of

1. a category $\underline{Th}^F$ of theories
2. a functor $\underline{Mod}^F : (\underline{Th}^F)^{op} \longrightarrow \underline{\mathcal{CAT}}$[1] giving the category of *models* of a given theory

We omit the index F when it is clear form the context and write $M'|_\sigma$ (the *σ-reduct* of M' under σ) for $\underline{Mod}(\sigma)(M')$. M' is called an *expansion* of $M'|_\sigma$.

Goguen's and Burstall's notion of institutions (see [10]) additionally includes sentences and satisfaction: An *institution* $I = (\underline{Sign}^I, sen^I, \underline{Mod}^I, \models^I)$ consists of

1. a category $\underline{Sign}^I$ of *signatures*,
2. a functor $sen^I : \underline{Sign}^I \longrightarrow \underline{Set}$ giving the set of *sentences* over a given signature,
3. a functor $\underline{Mod}^I : (\underline{Sign}^I)^{op} \longrightarrow \underline{\mathcal{CAT}}$ giving the category of *models* of a given signature,
4. a satisfaction relation $\models^I_\Sigma \subseteq |\underline{Mod}^I(\Sigma)| \times sen^I(\Sigma)$ for each $\Sigma \in \underline{Sign}^I$

such that for each morphism $\sigma: \Sigma \longrightarrow \Sigma'$ in $\underline{Sign}^I$ the *Satisfaction Condition*

$$M' \models^I_{\Sigma'} \sigma\varphi \iff M'|_\sigma \models^I_\Sigma \varphi$$

holds for each model $M' \in |\underline{Mod}^I(\Sigma')|$ and each sentence $\varphi \in sen^I(\Sigma)$.

[1] $\underline{\mathcal{CAT}}$ is the quasicategory of all categories, see [1].

We omit the index I if its clear from context and write $\sigma\varphi$ for $sen(\sigma)(\varphi)$.

An institution $I = (\underline{Sign}, sen, \underline{Mod}, \models)$ induces the category of *theories with axiom-preserving theory morphisms* $\underline{Th_0}$. Objects are theories $T = (\Sigma, \Gamma)$, where $\Sigma \in |\underline{Sign}|$ and $\Gamma \subseteq sen(\Sigma)$. Morphisms $\sigma: (\Sigma, \Gamma) \longrightarrow (\Sigma', \Gamma')$ in $\underline{Th_0}$ are signature morphisms $\sigma: \Sigma \longrightarrow \Sigma'$ such that $\sigma(\Gamma) \subseteq \Gamma'$, that is, axioms are mapped to axioms. There is a forgetful functor $sign: \underline{Th_0} \longrightarrow \underline{Sign}$ which simply projects to the first component. $ax(\Sigma, \Gamma) = \Gamma$ extracts the axiom component. $\underline{Mod}$ can be extended to $\underline{Th_0}$, this gives us a specification frame $\underline{Th_0}(I)$.

A specification frame or an institution has *(finitely) composable theories*, if $\underline{Th}$ resp. $\underline{Th_0}$ is (finitely) cocomplete and $\underline{Mod}$ maps (finite) colimits to limits in $\underline{\mathcal{CAT}}$.

2.2 Relational Partial Conditional Existence-Equation Logic and Some Restrictions

We now recall the institution $\mathcal{RPCEL}$ (for: Relational Partial Conditional Existence-Equation Logic) of partial algebraic systems with conditional existence equations (see [4, 16]).

Signatures $\Sigma = (S, OP, POP, REL)$ consist of (finite sets) of sort symbols $s \in S$, total operation symbols $op: s_1, \ldots, s_n \longrightarrow s \in OP$, partial operation symbols $pop: s_1, \ldots, s_n \longrightarrow s \in POP$, and relation symbols $R : s_1, \ldots, s_n \in REL$. Signature morphisms map symbols of the appropriate kind to each other, respecting the sorting. A Σ-model (or Σ-algebra) A consists of a family $| A | = (A_s)_{s \in S}$ of carrier sets, a family $(op_A: A_{\overline{s}} \longrightarrow A_s)_{op:\overline{s} \longrightarrow s \in OP}$ of total operations, a family $(pop_A\colon \text{dom}\ pop_A \longrightarrow A_s)_{pop:\overline{s} \longrightarrow s \in POP}$, where dom $pop_A \subseteq A_{\overline{s}}$ is the domain of pop_A, and a family $(R_A \subseteq A_{\overline{s}})_{R:\overline{s} \in REL}$ of relations[2].

A Σ-homomorphism $h: A \longrightarrow B$ is a family $h = (h_s: A_s \longrightarrow B_s)_{s \in S}$ of total functions, such that

- $h_s(op_A(\overline{a})) = op_B(h_{\overline{s}}(\overline{a}))$ for any $op: \overline{s} \longrightarrow s \in OP$ and any $\overline{a} \in A_{\overline{s}}$,
- $\overline{a} \in \text{dom}\, pop_A$ and $pop_A(\overline{a}) = a$ implies $h_{\overline{s}}(\overline{a}) \in \text{dom}\, pop_B$ and $pop_B(h_{\overline{s}}(\overline{a})) = h_s(a)$ for $pop: \overline{s} \longrightarrow s \in POP, a \in A_s, \overline{a} \in A_{\overline{s}}$ and
- $\overline{a} \in R_A$ implies $h_{\overline{s}}(\overline{a}) \in R_B$ for $R : \overline{s} \in REL$ and $\overline{a} \in A_{\overline{s}}$

If $\Sigma = (S, OP, POP, REL)$, $\sigma: \Sigma \longrightarrow \Sigma'$ is a signature morphism and $A' \in |\underline{Mod}\, \Sigma'|$, then $A' |_\sigma$ is the Σ-algebra A with $A_s := A'_{\sigma(s)}$ $(s \in S)$, $op_A := (\sigma(op))_{A'}$ $(op \in OP)$ and so on. Similarly for homomorphisms.

A sentence over a signature $\Sigma = (S, OP, POP, REL)$ is a conditional formula

$$(X: e_1 \wedge \ldots \wedge e_n \longrightarrow e)$$

where X is an S-sorted system of variables and the atomic formulas e and e_i are of two kinds: Either $t_1 \stackrel{e}{=} t_2$, where t_1, t_2 are terms with same sort (from the

[2] We abbreviate $s_1, \ldots, s_n$ by $\overline{s}$, $A_{s_1} \times \cdots \times A_{s_n}$ by $A_{\overline{s}}$. $h_{\overline{s}}(\overline{a})$ abbreviates $h_1(a_1), \ldots, h_n(a_n)$ and so on.

term algebra with variables $T_\Sigma(X)_s$ using total and partial operation symbols. See, e.g., [8]). Or $R(t_1, \dots, t_n)$, where $R : \overline{s} \in REL$ and t_i is a term of sort s_i (from $T_\Sigma(X)_{s_i}$). Sentence translation is defined inductively, where X is mapped to $\sigma(X)$ with $\sigma(X)_{s'} = \bigcup_{\sigma(s)=s'} X_s$.

Finally, satisfaction is defined as follows: $A \models_\Sigma (X: e_1 \wedge \ldots \wedge e_n \longrightarrow e)$ if and only if all valuations $\nu: X \longrightarrow A$ which satisfy the premises satisfy the conclusion as well. Satisfaction of atomic formulas is defined as

$$\nu \models t_1 \overset{e}{=} t_2 \iff \nu^\#(t_1) \text{ and } \nu^\#(t_2) \text{ are both defined and equal}$$

$$\nu \models R(\overline{t}) \iff \nu^\#(\overline{t}) \text{ is defined and } \in R_A$$

where $\nu^\#$ is the partial homomorphic extension of ν from X to dom $\nu^\# \subseteq T_\Sigma(X)$ (see [18]).

For sets of variables, we use the following notation: $X = \{ x : s_1; y : s_2 \}$ means that $X_{s_1} = \{ x \}$, $X_{s_2} = \{ y \}$ and $X_s = \emptyset$ otherwise.

A Σ-homomorphism $h: A \longrightarrow B$ is called *full*, if for all $pop: \overline{s} \longrightarrow s \in POP$ and for all $R : \overline{s} \in REL$:

$$h_{\overline{s}} \times h_s[graph(pop_A)] = graph(pop_B) \cap h_{\overline{s}} \times h_s[A_{\overline{s}} \times A_s] \text{ and } h_{\overline{s}}[R_A] = R_B \cap h_{\overline{s}}[A_{\overline{s}}]$$

A *congruence* $\equiv$ on a Σ-algebra A is an S-relation $(\equiv_s \subseteq A_s \times A_s)_{s \in S}$ which is reflexive, symmetric, transitive and compatible with the operations. The latter means that for $op: \overline{s} \longrightarrow s \in OP, \overline{a}, \overline{a}' \in A_{\overline{s}}$ resp. for $op: \overline{s} \longrightarrow s \in POP, \overline{a}, \overline{a}' \in$ dom op_A we have

$$\text{If } (\overline{a}, \overline{a}') \in \equiv_{\overline{s}}, \text{ then } (op_A(\overline{a}), op_A(\overline{a}')) \in \equiv_s$$

The congruence *generated* by an S-relation $R \subseteq A \times A$ is the least congruence containing R. It is denoted by $< R >$. Given a Σ-homomorphism $h: A \longrightarrow B$, its *kernel* $\ker h$ with

$$(\ker h)_s := \{ (a, a') \mid a, a' \in A_s, h_s(a) = h_s(a') \}$$

is a congruence.

Given a family of morphisms $(A \xrightarrow{h_i} B_i)_{i=1,\dots,n}$, let $< h_1, \dots, h_n >: A \longrightarrow B_1 \times \dots \times B_n$ denote the unique morphism h with $A \xrightarrow{h} B_1 \times \dots \times B_n \xrightarrow{\pi_i} B_i = A \xrightarrow{h_i} B_i$ for $i = 1, \dots, n$.

We now gain a variety of institutions by restricting $\mathcal{RPCEL}$.

institution	relations	partiality	axioms involving relations	axioms involving partiality	axioms involving only total operations
$\mathcal{RPCEL}$	x	x	conditional	conditional	conditional
$\mathcal{PCEL}$	–	x	–	conditional	conditional
$\mathcal{FPHCL}$	x	x	cond. flat	conditional flat	conditional
$\mathcal{HCL}$	x	–	conditional	–	conditional
$\mathcal{FPCEL}$	x	x	unconditional	unconditional flat	conditional
$\mathcal{CEL}$	–	–	–	–	conditional
$\mathcal{FPEL}$	x	x	unconditional	unconditional flat	unconditional
$\mathcal{EL}$	–	–	–	–	unconditional

"Flat" partiality means that atomic formulas in axioms are of type

$$pop(\bar{t}) \stackrel{e}{=} t_0 \quad \text{or} \quad R(\bar{t})$$

where $\bar{t}$ and t_0 consist of total operation symbols only. That is, there is no nested partiality and no partiality combined with relations.

Now $\mathcal{PCEL}$ (Partial Conditional Existence-Equation Logic), $\mathcal{HCL}$ (Horn Clause Logic), $\mathcal{CEL}$ (Conditional Equational Logic) and $\mathcal{EL}$ (Equational Logic) are well-known institutions [5, 8, 11, 17, 18]. $\mathcal{RPCEL}$, $\mathcal{FPHCL}$ (Horn Clause Logic with Flat Partiality) and $\mathcal{FPCEL}$ (Conditional Equational Logic with Flat Partiality) are extensions of $\mathcal{PCEL}$, $\mathcal{HCL}$ and $\mathcal{CEL}$, respectively, which are shown below to add no expressive power, but which make the institutions easier to compare: $\mathcal{RPCEL}$, $\mathcal{FPHCL}$, $\mathcal{FPCEL}$ and $\mathcal{FPEL}$ (Equational Logic with Flat Partiality) all include relations and partial operations.

2.3 Parameterized Abstract Data Types (PADTs)

PADTs are useful for designing modular specifications. Specification with hidden machinery here means specification of modules with import, export and body parts in the sense of Ehrig and Mahr [9]. The body ADT is constructed freely over the parameter ADT, and the export interface is a view which forgets all irrelevant details ("hidden parts") of the body ADT.

A *parameterized theory* is a theory morphism $T \xrightarrow{\theta} T1$. A $T \xrightarrow{\theta} T1$-*parameterized abstract data type* is a pair (η, F), with $F\colon \underline{Mod}T \longrightarrow \underline{Mod}T1$ a functor and $\eta\colon Id_{\underline{Mod}T} \longrightarrow \underline{Mod}\theta \circ F$ a natural transformation.

Canonical PADTs are obtained by free constructions: A $T \xrightarrow{\theta} T1$-PADT (η, F) is called *free*, if F is left adjoint to $\underline{Mod}\theta$ with unit η, that is, for each $T1$-model B and each T-morphism $h\colon A \longrightarrow B|_\theta$, there exists a unique $T1$-morphism $h^\#\colon F\,A \longrightarrow B$ such that $h^\#|_\theta \circ \eta_A = h$.

Fact 1. *In $\mathcal{RPCEL}$ and all its restrictions, for each parameterized theory $T \xrightarrow{\theta} T1$, a free PADT exists. We denote it by (η^θ, F^θ).*

Proof. This follows from a general theorem of Tarlecki [20]. Since we need a definite construction later on, we follow Reichel's book ([18], 3.2, 3.3.1 and 3.5.6.) and [8]. $F^\theta\,A$ can be constructed as follows: Let $T1 = (\Sigma1, \Gamma1)$, $\Sigma1(A)$

be $\Sigma 1$ augmented by constants $c^a : \theta\, s$ for $a \in A_s$, and let $\Gamma 1(A)$ be $\Gamma 1$ plus $(\emptyset : \theta\, op(c^{\bar a}) \stackrel{e}{=} c^{op_A(\bar a)})$ for $\bar a \in$ dom op_A and $(\emptyset : \theta\, R(c^{\bar a}))$ for $\bar a \in R_A$. We write $T_{\Sigma 1}(A)$ for $T_{\Sigma 1(A)}|_{\Sigma 1 \hookrightarrow \Sigma 1(A)}$. Putting $T1(A) = (\Sigma 1(A), \Gamma 1(A))$, let $H_{T1}(A) \subseteq T_{\Sigma 1}(A)$ be the algebra of all terms for which $T1(A) \models (\emptyset : t \stackrel{e}{=} t)$ with usual term algebra operations and relations $R_{H_{T1}(A)} = \{ \bar t \mid T1(A) \models (\emptyset : R(\bar t)) \}$. Then there is a quotient (i.e. a full surjection) $H_{T1}(A) \xrightarrow{q_A} F^\theta A$ with kernel $\ker q_A = \{ (t_1, t_2) \mid T1(A) \models (\emptyset : t_1 \stackrel{e}{=} t_2) \}$. □

3 Relating Different Institutions

3.1 Subinstitutions and Equivalent Expressiveness of Institutions

To formalize equivalence of expressiveness, we first need a notion of map between specification frames and institutions.

A map of specification frames $\mu : F \longrightarrow F'$ consists of

1. a functor $\Phi : \underline{Th}^F \longrightarrow \underline{Th}^{F'}$ and
2. a natural transformation $\beta : \underline{Mod}^{F'} \circ \Phi \longrightarrow \underline{Mod}^F$

Meseguer [14] defines *maps of institutions.* For our purposes, Meseguer's *simple* maps of institutions suffice. See [6] for a detailed comparison with other formalisms.

Given institutions I and J, a *simple map of institutions* [14] $\mu = (\Phi, \alpha, \beta) : I \longrightarrow J$ consists of

- a map of specification frames $(\Phi, \beta) : \underline{Th_0}(I) \longrightarrow \underline{Th_0}(J)$ and
- a natural transformation $\alpha : sen^I \longrightarrow sen^J \circ \Phi$

such that Φ is the α-extension to theories[3] of some functor $\Phi : \underline{Sign}^I \longrightarrow \underline{Th_0}^J$ and the following property is satisfied:

$$M' \models^J_{sign(\Phi(\Sigma))} \alpha_\Sigma(\varphi) \iff \beta_{(\Sigma,\emptyset)}(M') \models^I_\Sigma \varphi \qquad (1)$$

Concerning the natural transformation of models, we need only define it on signatures. The extension to theories can then be done using (1).

An *embedding of specification frames* is a map of specification frames $\mu = (\Phi, \beta) : F \longrightarrow F'$ with Φ an embedding and β a natural equivalence. If there is such a map, F is called *subframe* of F'.

An *embedding of institutions* is a simple map of institutions $\mu = (\Phi, \alpha, \beta) : I \longrightarrow J$, with (Φ, β) an embedding of specification frames and α pointwise injective. If there is such a map, I is called *subinstitution* of J.

[3] the α-extension to theories of Φ maps (Σ, Γ) to $(sign\, \Phi\, \Sigma, ax\, \Phi\, \Sigma \cup \alpha_\Sigma(\Gamma))$

If we embed specification frames or institutions having finitely composable theories, we require additionally that Φ preserves finite colimits.

Definition 2 [13]. We call two institutions *equivalent in expressiveness*, if there are embeddings in both directions. □

It is easy to show that institution independent specification language constructs [19] are then preserved in both directions.

By the above defining table, the embeddings indicated by vertical and left to right horizontal arrows in the following diagram are obvious:

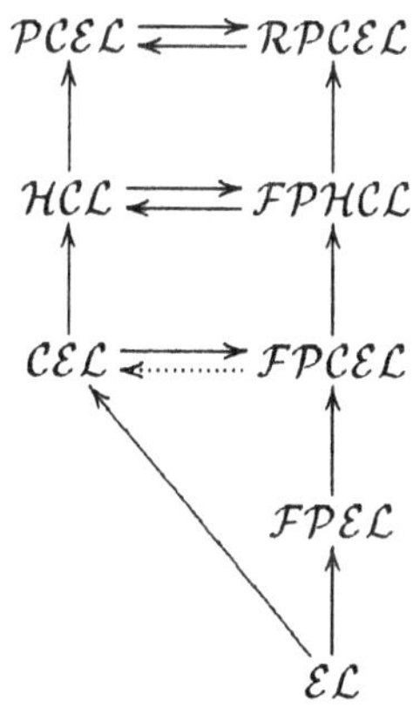

Considering the horizontal right to left arrows, the embedding μ^{graph} from [13], representing partial operations by their graphs, can easily be extended to an embedding $\mu^{graph}: \mathcal{FPHCL} \longrightarrow \mathcal{HCL}$. Likewise, the embedding $\mu^{chardom}$ from [13], representing relations by domains of partial operations, can easily be extended to an embedding $\mu^{chardom}: \mathcal{RPCEL} \longrightarrow \mathcal{PCEL}$. It remains to examine whether the dotted arrow exists.

3.2 Weak subinstitutions and weakly equivalent expressiveness

In some cases, we want to define a map of institutions but cannot translate sentences to sentences. Instead we need to talk about the existence of some operation with certain properties, and take this as translation of a sentence. In the case that this operation is always unique, we do not alter the model categories if we allow to talk about such existence.

More generally, enrich an institution I which has finitely composable theories to the institution $\exists!(I)$. $\exists!(I)$ has the same signatures and models as I, only sentences and satisfaction differ. They are formed similar to Tarlecki's abstract quantifiers over an arbitrary institution [21]. We allow Σ-sentences to guess if there is a T-expansion of a model (which has to be unique):

- $sen^{\exists!(I)}\,\Sigma = sen^{I}\,\Sigma \;\cup \{\exists!\Sigma \xrightarrow{\theta} T \mid$ there is at most one T-expansion of each Σ-model$\}$

- $(sen^{\exists!(I)}\sigma)(\exists!\Sigma \xrightarrow{\theta} T) = \exists!\Sigma' \xrightarrow{\theta'} T'$ where $\Sigma' \xrightarrow{\theta'} T'$ comes from the pushout[4]

$$\begin{array}{ccc} \Sigma & \xrightarrow{\theta} & T \\ \downarrow{\sigma} & & \downarrow{\sigma'} \\ \Sigma' & \xrightarrow{\theta'} & T' \end{array}$$

- $M \models_{\Sigma}^{\exists!(I)} \exists!\Sigma \xrightarrow{\theta} T$ iff there exists a θ-expansion of M (note that by the above condition, there exists at most one θ-expansion of M).

This notion makes sense, since I and $\exists!(I)$ are close together, at least a the model theoretic side. I is trivially a subinstitution of $\exists!(I)$. Now $\exists!(I)$ is generally no subinstitution, but at least a subframe of I, that is, there is an embedding of specification frames $\nu^I: \underline{Th_0}(\exists!(I)) \longrightarrow \underline{Th_0}(I)$ defined by

- $\Phi: \underline{Th_0}^{\exists!(I)} \longrightarrow \underline{Th_0}^I$ maps a theory (Σ, Γ) to T'', where $\Sigma \xrightarrow{\theta'} T'$ is the multiple pushout of the source consisting of all arrows $\exists!\Sigma \xrightarrow{\rho} T$ in Γ, and T'' is T' plus the θ'-translation of the I-sentences in Γ.
- $\beta_{(\Sigma,\Gamma)}: \underline{Mod}^I \circ \Phi^{op}(\Sigma,\Gamma) \longrightarrow \underline{Mod}^{\exists!(I)}(\Sigma,\Gamma)$ maps a T''-model M'' to $M''|_\theta$, where $\Sigma \xrightarrow{\theta} T'' = \Sigma \xrightarrow{\theta'} T' \hookrightarrow T''$ is defined as above. Now for $\exists!\Sigma \xrightarrow{\rho} T \in \Gamma$, by the above multiple pushout construction, there is some $\rho': T \longrightarrow T''$ with $\Sigma \xrightarrow{\rho} T \xrightarrow{\rho'} T'' = \Sigma \xrightarrow{\theta} T''$. Thus $M''|_{\rho'}$ is a ρ-expansion of $M''|_\theta$, so $M''|_\theta$ satisfies $\exists!\Sigma \xrightarrow{\rho} T$.
Conversely, $\beta^{-1}_{(\Sigma,\Gamma)}$ maps M to the amalgamation of $(M^\rho)_{\exists!\Sigma \xrightarrow{\rho} T \in \Gamma}$ with M^ρ the unique ρ-expansion of M. For cocontinous $\underline{Mod}$, this amalgamation is defined by Baumeister [3]. Thus β is a natural isomorphism.

In particular, model categories of theories in I and $\exists!(I)$ coincide.

Now a *weak map* (*weak embedding*) of I to J is a map (embedding) of I to $\exists!(J)$. Two institutions are called *weakly equivalent expressive*, if there are weak embeddings in both directions.

With the notion of weak equivalence, the realm of institutions can be ordered much better. For example, there are at least seven institutions used in the literature which are weakly equivalent to $\mathcal{RPCEL}$ (see [15], where also further details are provided). Here, we want to show weak equivalence of $\mathcal{FPCEL}$ and $\mathcal{CEL}$.

Define $\mu^{rs}: \mathcal{FPCEL} \longrightarrow \exists!(\mathcal{CEL})$ by

- $\Phi^{rs}(S, OP, POP, REL)$ is the theory with
  - sort set S plus
    - s^R for each $R \in REL$
    - s^{pop} for each $pop \in POP$

[4] Pushouts are generally only unique up to isomorphism. For simplicity, we assume that $\underline{Sign}$ is replaced by a skeleton (see [1, 4.12]). Then isomorphic signatures and theories are identical.

- with total operations OP plus
  - $\pi_i^R : s^R \longrightarrow s_i$ for $R : s_1 \ \ldots \ s_n \in REL$, $i = 1, \ldots, n$
  - $\pi_i^{pop} : s^{pop} \longrightarrow s_i$ for $pop : s_1 \ \ldots \ s_n \longrightarrow s_0 \in POP$, $i = 0, \ldots, n$
- and the following axioms
  - $x, y : s^{pop} \ \bigwedge_{i=0,\ldots,n} \pi_i^{pop}(x) = \pi_i^{pop}(y) \longrightarrow x = y$
    for $pop : s_1 \ \ldots \ s_n \longrightarrow s_0 \in POP$
  - $x, y : s^R \ \bigwedge_{i=1,\ldots,n} \pi_i^R(x) = \pi_i^R(y) \longrightarrow x = y$
    for $R : s_1 \ \ldots \ s_n \in REL$
  - $x, y : s^{pop} \ \bigwedge_{i=1,\ldots,n} \pi_i^{pop}(x) = \pi_i^{pop}(y) \longrightarrow \pi_0^{pop}(x) = \pi_0^{pop}(y)$

  The first axiom states that the π_i^{pop} are "together injective", that is, $< \pi_1^{pop}, \ldots, \pi_n^{pop}, \pi_0^{pop} >$ is injective. The second axiom states the same for relations. The third axiom states that the relation encoded by s^{pop} and the π_i^{pop} is actually the graph of a partial function.

- $\Phi^{rs}(\sigma)$ maps $op \in OP$ to $\sigma(op)$, s^{pop} to $s^{\sigma(pop)}$ and so on.
- To translate an axiom $\varphi = (X : pop(t_1, \ldots, t_n) \stackrel{e}{=} t_0)$ with $X = \{ x_1 : s_1, \ldots, x_m : s_m \}$, introduce an operation

$$op^{\varphi} : s_1 \ \ldots \ s_m \longrightarrow s^{pop}$$

  which maps a valuation ν of X to the corresponding element $(\nu^{\#}(t_1), \ldots, \nu^{\#}(t_n), \nu^{\#}(t_0))$ of the graph of pop. This correspondence is expressed by the axioms

$$(X : \pi_i^{pop}(op^{\varphi}(x_1, \ldots, x_m) = t_i)) \quad (i = 0, \ldots, n)$$

  Now $\alpha_{\Sigma}^{rs}(\varphi)$ is $\exists! \Sigma' \hookrightarrow T$, where $\Sigma' = sign \, \Phi \, \Sigma$ and T is the extension of Σ' outlined above. Since the π_i^{pop} are "together injective", op^{φ} is defined uniquely, so $\exists! \Sigma' \hookrightarrow T$ is a legitimate axiom.
- Axioms of form $(X : R(t_1, \ldots, t_n))$ are translated similarly. α_{Σ}^{rs} is the identity on (conditional) equations
- $\beta^{rs}_{(S,OP,POP,REL)}$ takes a Σ'-model M' and replaces for each relation symbol $R : s_1 \ldots s_n \in REL$ the components s^R and $\pi_i^R : s^R \longrightarrow s_i$ $(i = 1, \ldots, n)$ by the relation $< \pi^R_{1,M'}, \ldots, \pi^R_{n,M'} > [M'_{s^R}]$. Similarly, s^{pop} and π_i^{pop} are replaced by the partial operation with graph $< \pi^{pop}_{1,M'}, \ldots, \pi^{pop}_{n,M'}, \pi^{pop}_{0,M'} > [M'_{s^{pop}}]$. Homomorphisms are left unchanged (except that the components for the s^R and s^{pop} fall away).

  Vice versa, ${\beta^{rs}_{(S,OP,POP,REL)}}^{-1}$ takes a Σ-model M and replaces for each relation symbol $R : \overline{s} \in REL$ the relation $R_M \subseteq M_{\overline{s}}$ by the carrier set $M'_{s^R} := R_M$ and the projections $\pi^R_{i,M'} = R_M \hookrightarrow M'_{s_1} \times \cdots \times M'_{s_n} \xrightarrow{\pi_i} M'_{s_i}$. Similarly for (graphs of) partial operations. Homomorphisms are extended by components for s^R and s^{pop} by a restriction.

Note that Φ embeds $\mathcal{CEL}$ identically, so it is isomorphism-dense. This implies preservation of colimits (see [1, 13.11]). Condition (1) can be verified as well and so μ^{rs} is a weak embedding indicated by a dotted arrow in the above diagram. □

Note that, up to weak equivalence, we now have total ordering on the institutions. To illustrate how μ^{rs} works, we give an example. Consider the following $\mathcal{FPCEL}$-theory which views graphs as relations:

GRAPH_AS_REL =
  sorts *nodes*
  rels $R : nodes\ nodes$

Now Φ^{rs}(**GRAPH_AS_REL**) is (up to renaming) the following theory:

GRAPH_AS_EGDE_SET =
  sorts *nodes*, *edges*
  total opns *source*, *target*: $edges \longrightarrow nodes$
  axioms $x, y : edges\ source(x) = source(y) \wedge target(x) = target(y) \longrightarrow x = y$

The axiom states that there are no multiple edges. Now the reflexivity axiom $x : s\ R(x, x)$ is mapped to

DIAGONAL = **GRAPH_AS_EGDE_SET** +
  total opns *diagonal*: $nodes \longrightarrow edges$
  axioms $x : nodes\ source(diagonal(x)) = x$
  $x : nodes\ target(diagonal(x)) = x$

4 Hierarchy Theorems

After having established a total ordering on expressiveness equivalence classes of institutions, in this section, we examine the hierarchy $\mathcal{EL}$, $\mathcal{FPEL}$, $\mathcal{FPCEL}$, $\mathcal{FPHCL}$, $\mathcal{RPCEL}$ (that is, one representative per equivalence class). We prove properties of the institutions which can be used to separate the levels of the hierarchy from each other. We start with properties of model categories, then look at initial semantics and finally at parameterized abstract data types.

4.1 A Model Theoretic Hierarchy Theorem

Theorem 3. *The five institutions we consider form a proper hierarchy:*

Institution	*Properties of model categories*	*Separating example*
$\mathcal{EL}$	*has effective congruence relations*	
$\mathcal{FPEL}$	*subobjects commute with coequalizers*	*binary relations*
$\mathcal{FPCEL}$	*∃ dense set of regular projectives*	*injective functions*
$\mathcal{FPHCL}$	*∃ generating set of regular projectives*	*transitive binary relations*
$\mathcal{RPCEL}$	*locally finitely presentable*	*transitive multigraphs*

Proof. By section 3.2, model categories in $\mathcal{FPCEL}$, $\mathcal{FPHCL}$ and $\mathcal{RPCEL}$ are isomorphic to model categories in $\mathcal{CEL}$, $\mathcal{HCL}$ and $\mathcal{PCEL}$, respectively. The categorical properties of the latter and of $\mathcal{EL}$ are proved in [2], where also the corresponding counter-examples are given. Due to lack of space, we omit the proof for $\mathcal{FPEL}$. □

Now one seldom encounters a specification problem like: I want to specify this abstract category, with which formalism can I do it? Even if loose semantics is considered, for a given problem, different model categories may be acceptable, for example because only generated (in some sense) models matter. Can the hierarchy be separated on a more concrete level?

4.2 Initial Semantics

A more common specification problem is the question whether some given PADT is specifiable with initial semantics.

Theorem 4. *Concerning initial semantics, the hierarchy collapses almost totally: In $\mathcal{FPEL}$, $\mathcal{FPCEL}$, $\mathcal{FPHCL}$ and $\mathcal{RPCEL}$ (resp. $\mathcal{EL}$), the ADTs specifiable initially using hidden machinery coincide with the semi-computable ADTs (resp. total semi-computable ADTs).*

Proof. See [16]. □

4.3 A hierarchy theorem using parameterized ADTs

Another common specification problem is the question if some PADT can be specified with hidden machinery, i.e. whether it is expressible as composite of a free and a forgetful functor:

$$\begin{array}{ccc} \underline{Mod}(import) & \xrightarrow{\quad F \quad} & \underline{Mod}(export) \\ & {\scriptstyle free}\searrow \qquad \nearrow{\scriptstyle forgetful} & \\ & \underline{Mod}(body) & \end{array}$$

The following theorem was proved in [16] with recursion theoretic methods. We now prove it more directly, using the construction of PADTs in fact 1.

Theorem 5. *With respect to specifiable PADTs, our hierarchy has the following properties:*

Institution	*Properties of specifiable functors F*	*Separating example*
$\mathcal{EL}$	*F h is full*	
$\mathcal{FPEL}$	*F preserves kernels*	*Making a relation reflexive*
$\mathcal{FPCEL}$	*F preserves full surjective homomorphisms*	*Factorization of a function over the image*
$\mathcal{FPHCL}$	*F preserves surjective homomorphisms*	*Making a binary relation transitive*
$\mathcal{RPCEL}$		*Generating the paths in a multigraph*

Preservation of kernels means the following. Let A^2 be the product of A with itself, with projections $\pi_1, \pi_2 \colon A^2 \longrightarrow A$. Let $\Pi \colon F\,A^2 \longrightarrow (F\,A)^2 := < F\,\pi_1, F\,\pi_2 >$.

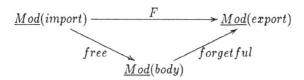

Let m be the inclusion of $\ker h$ *into* A^2 *(thus* $\ker h$ *can be interpreted as a T-algebra). Then*

$$< \Pi \circ F\, m[F\, \ker h] >= \ker F\, h \cap \Pi[F\, A^2]$$

where $< \_ >$ *denotes congruence generation.*

Proof. (1) $\mathcal{FPHCL}$
Since forgetful functors obviously preserve surjectivity, w. l. o. g. we can assume that F is a free $T \xrightarrow{\theta} T1$-PADT in $\mathcal{FPHCL}$. Let $h: A \longrightarrow B$ be a surjective T-homomorphism. We want to show that $F\, h$ is surjective as well.

This is done in two steps. First we represent the free construction as a quotient of a term algebra $T_{\Sigma 1}(A)$ over the parameter A. Then $F\, h$ acts as inductive extension of h to terms, which is denoted by $T_{\Sigma 1}(h)$, with $\Sigma 1 = sign\, T1$. In a second step, we "factor out" the parameter A by representing a term from $T_{\Sigma 1}(A)$ by a term from the term algebra $T_{\Sigma 1}(Y)$ over a fixed variable set Y, together with a valuation $\nu: Y \longrightarrow A$, which is used to replace the leaves of the term. With this representation, $T_{\Sigma 1}(h)$ acts by composing a valuation with h, and this is surjective because h is surjective.

More formally, let $\Sigma 1$ be the signature of $\Phi^{graph}\, T1$ and let F' be the free $\Phi^{graph}\, T \xrightarrow{\Phi^{graph}\, \theta} \Phi^{graph}\, T1$-PADT. Since $\Sigma 1$ contains only total operation symbols, the construction of fact 1 has the property that $H_{T1}(A) = T_{\Sigma 1}(A)$. Thus there is a quotient $T_{\Sigma 1}({\beta_T^{graph}}^{-1} A) \xrightarrow{q_A} F'\, {\beta_T^{graph}}^{-1} A$. Because β_T^{graph} and β_{T1}^{graph} are the identity on carrier sets, we can represent $\mid F\, A \mid$ as quotient (full surjection) $\mid T_{\Sigma 1}(A) \mid \xrightarrow{q_A} \mid F\, A \mid$. Similarly, we get a quotient $\mid T_{\Sigma 1}(B) \mid \xrightarrow{q_B} \mid F\, B \mid$.

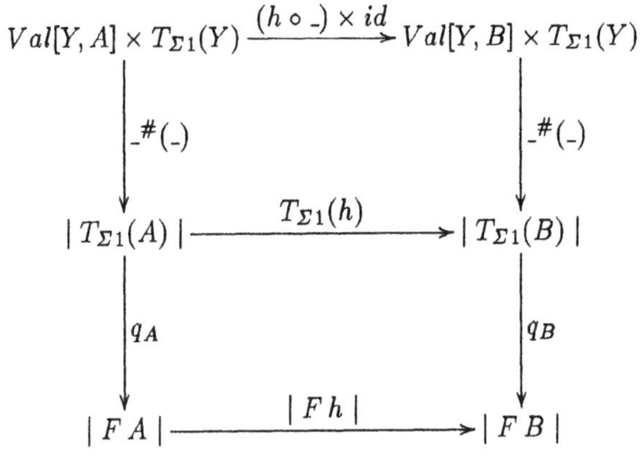

Since the lower rectangle commutes, surjectivity of $F\, h$ now follows from surjectivity of $T_{\Sigma 1}(h)$. To show the latter, fix some infinite S-sorted variable system Y, where S are the sorts of T. We represent $\mid T_{\Sigma 1}(A) \mid$ by $Val[Y, A] \times T_{\Sigma 1}(Y)$. A pair $(\nu: Y \longrightarrow A, t)$ is mapped to $\nu^{\#}(t) \in \mid T_{\Sigma 1}(A) \mid$. Since each term in $\mid T_{\Sigma 1}(A) \mid$ only uses finitely many elements of A, this assignment is surjective. A similar representation holds for B. By commutativity of the upper diagram, surjectivity of $T_{\Sigma 1}(h)$ now follows from surjectivity of $(h \circ \_) \times id$. To prove the latter, let $\nu: Y \longrightarrow B$ some valuation. By surjectivity of h, there is some factorization $Y \xrightarrow{\nu} B = Y \xrightarrow{\lambda} A \xrightarrow{h} B$. Thus, $h \circ \_$ is surjective.

(2) $\mathcal{FPCEL}$

By observing that $\beta^{rs^{-1}}$ exactly maps full surjective homomorphisms to surjective homomorphisms, we can use (1). More exactly, full surjectivity of $h: A \longrightarrow B$ means surjectivity and

$$h[graph(pop_A)] = graph(pop_B) \quad (pop: \overline{s} \longrightarrow s \in POP)$$
$$h[R_A] = R_B \quad (R : \overline{s} \in REL)$$

These two are equivalent to surjectivity of $(\beta^{rs}{}_T^{-1}\, h)_{s^{pop}}$ $(pop \in POP)$ and $(\beta^{rs}{}_T^{-1}\, h)_{s^R}$ $(R \in REL)$, respectively.

Assume that F is a free $T \xrightarrow{\theta} T1$-PADT (now in $\mathcal{FPCEL}$) and $h: A \longrightarrow B$ is a full surjective homomorphism. By the above equivalence, $\beta_T^{rs^{-1}}\, h$ is surjective as well. Let F' be the free $\Phi^{rs}\, T \xrightarrow{\Phi^{rs}\theta} \Phi^{rs}\, T1$-PADT. By (1), we have that $F'\, \beta_T^{rs^{-1}}\, h \cong \beta_{T1}^{rs^{-1}}\, F\, h$ is surjective. By the above equivalence, $F\, h$ is full and surjective.

(3) $\mathcal{FPEL}$

With a similar argument as in (1), we can use μ^{graph} to restrict ourselves to $\mathcal{REL}$. Now

$$\begin{array}{ccc} T_{\Sigma 1}(A) & \xrightarrow{T_{\Sigma 1}(h)} & T_{\Sigma 1}(B) \\ \downarrow{\scriptstyle q_A} & & \downarrow{\scriptstyle q_B} \\ F\,A & \xrightarrow{F\,h} & F\,B \end{array}$$

commutes in $\underline{Mod}^{\mathcal{REL}}\, sign\, T1$. Then we have

Lemma 6. *For surjective T-homomorphisms h,*

$$\ker(q_B \circ T_{\Sigma 1}(h)) = < \ker q_A \cup \ker T_{\Sigma 1}(h) >$$

Proof. "$\supseteq$": This follows from

$$\ker q_A \subseteq \ker(F\,h \circ q_A) = \ker(q_B \circ T_{\Sigma 1}(h)) \text{ and}$$

$$\ker T_{\Sigma 1}(h) \subseteq \ker(q_B \circ T_{\Sigma 1}(h))$$

"$\subseteq$": In $\mathcal{EL}$ and also in $\mathcal{REL}$, we have that logical consequence is expressible by congruence generation, see [8]. The equation for $\ker q_A$ from fact 1 can thus be rewritten as

$$\ker q_A = < \{ (\nu^\#(t_1), \nu^\#(t_2)) \mid \nu: X \longrightarrow T_{\Sigma 1}(A), (X : t_1 = t_2) \in \Gamma 1(A) \} >$$

Thus $(t_1, t_2) \in \ker(q_B \circ T_{\Sigma 1}(h))$ implies $(T_{\Sigma 1}(h)(t_1), T_{\Sigma 1}(h)(t_2)) \in \ker q_B$, which implies that there is some $\nu: X \longrightarrow T_{\Sigma 1}(B)$ and some $(X : u_1 = u_2) \in \Gamma 1(B)$ with $\nu^\#(u_1) = T_{\Sigma 1}(h)(t_1)$ and $\nu^\#(u_2) = T_{\Sigma 1}(h)(t_2)$. By surjectivity of h (and thus, by (1), of $T_{\Sigma 1}(h)$), we can factor $X \xrightarrow{\nu} T_{\Sigma 1}(B)$ as $X \xrightarrow{\lambda} T_{\Sigma 1}(A) \xrightarrow{T_{\Sigma 1}(h)}$

$T_{\Sigma 1}(B)$, so that $\nu^\# = T_{\Sigma 1}(h) \circ \lambda^\#$. Fix $(X : v_1 = v_2) \in \Gamma 1(A)$ with $u_i = T_{\Sigma 1}(h)(v_i)$ $(i = 1, 2)$. Now $T_{\Sigma 1}(h)(t_i) = \nu^\#(u_i) = T_{\Sigma 1}(h)(\lambda^\#(v_i))$ $(i = 1, 2)$.

Thus $(t_1, \lambda^\#(v_1)) \in \ker T_{\Sigma 1}(h), (\lambda^\#(v_1), \lambda^\#(v_2)) \in \ker q_A$ and $(\lambda^\#(v_2), t_2) \in \ker T_{\Sigma 1}(h)$, so altogether $(t_1, t_2) \in < \ker q_A \cup \ker T_{\Sigma 1}(h) >$. □

Lemma 6 is now the key for relating free construction and term algebra in the proof of

$$< \Pi \circ F\, m[F \ker h] >= \ker F\, h \cap \Pi[F\, A^2]$$

The details are similar to the proof in [16].

(4) $\mathcal{EL}$
In $\mathcal{EL}$, all homomorphisms are full (this is in fact a property of the model classes).

The counter-examples are worked out in [16]. □

5 Locating Bounded Stacks in the Hierarchy

Consider the following requirement:

BOUNDED_ELEM = NAT + BOOL +
sorts *elem*
total opns *inbound*: $nat \longrightarrow bool$
axioms $inbound(succ(n)) = true \longrightarrow inbound(n) = true$
$inbound(n) = false \longrightarrow inbound(succ(n)) = false$

BOUNDED_STACK = BOUNDED_ELEM +
sorts *stack*
total opns $mt : stack$
partial opns $push$: $elem\ stack \longrightarrow stack$
pop: $stack \longrightarrow stack$
top: $stack \longrightarrow stack$

Let C be the subcategory of $\underline{Mod}^{\mathcal{FPCEL}}$ **BOUNDED_ELEM** which contains all models with **NAT**-reduct isomorphic to the natural numbers and **BOOL**-reduct isomorphic to the standard booleans. Our aim is to specify the persistent functor **BSTACK**: $C \longrightarrow \underline{Mod}^{\mathcal{FPCEL}}$ **BOUNDED_STACK** such that **BSTACK**$(A)_{stack}$ contains all stacks over A_{elem} with heights n for which $inbound_A(succ_A^n(0_A)) = true_A$, with *pop*, *push* and *top* the usual (partial!) stack operations.

Now in $\mathcal{PCEL}$, this is easy:

BOUNDED_STACK_BODY1 = BOUNDED_STACK +
total opns *height*: $stack \longrightarrow nat$
axioms $height(mt) = 0$
$inbound(height(s)) = true \longleftrightarrow push(m, s) \stackrel{e}{=} push(m, s)$
$push(m, s) \stackrel{e}{=} push(m, s) \longrightarrow height(push(m, s)) \stackrel{e}{=} succ(height(s))$
$push(m, s) \stackrel{e}{=} push(m, s) \longrightarrow pop(push(m, s)) \stackrel{e}{=} s$
$push(m, s) \stackrel{e}{=} push(m, s) \longrightarrow top(push(m, s)) \stackrel{e}{=} m$

The free **BOUNDED_ELEM**$\hookrightarrow$**BOUNDED_STACK_BODY1**-functor composed with the forgetful functor from $\underline{Mod}$**BOUNDED_STACK_BODY1** to $\underline{Mod}$**BOUNDED_STACK**, when restricted to C, is equal to **BSTACK**. The free functor does not preserve surjectivity (consider homomorphisms into the terminal model) and is thus not specifiable in $\mathcal{FPHCL}$ by theorem 5.

So we have to look for a different way to specify **BSTACK** in $\mathcal{FPHCL}$. Instead of generating bounded stacks by a partial operation (which is impossible in $\mathcal{FPHCL}$), we generate them by a total operation, factor out those stacks which are too high and then specify the partial push as a derived operation.

BOUNDED_STACK_BODY2 = **BOUNDED_STACK** +
total opns $push1\colon elem\ stack \longrightarrow stack$
$height\colon stack \longrightarrow nat$
axioms $height(mt) = 0$
$inbound(height(s)) = true \longrightarrow height(push1(m,s)) = succ(height(s))$
$inbound(height(s)) = false \longrightarrow push1(m,s) = s$
$inbound(height(s)) = true \longrightarrow push(m,s) \stackrel{e}{=} push1(m,s)$
$inbound(height(s)) = true \longrightarrow pop(push1(m,s)) \stackrel{e}{=} s$
$inbound(height(s)) = true \longrightarrow top(push1(m,s)) \stackrel{e}{=} m$

What about $\mathcal{FPCEL}$? Consider the **BOUNDED_ELEM**-algebras $A = (\mathbb{N}, \{false, true\}, \{*\}, inbound_A)$ with $inbound_A(n) = false$ and $B = (\mathbb{N}, \{false, true\}, \{*\}, inbound_B)$ with $inbound_B(n) = true$. Let $A \xrightarrow{h} 1$ and $B \xrightarrow{k} 1$ be the unique homomorphisms into the terminal object. They are full and surjective. Since **BSTACK** B are unbounded stacks over $\{*\}$, $push_{\mathbf{BSTACK}\,B}(*, mt_{\mathbf{BSTACK}\,B})$ is defined. Therefore $push_{\mathbf{BSTACK}\,1}(\mathbf{BSTACK}\,k(*), \mathbf{BSTACK}\,k(mt_{\mathbf{BSTACK}\,B})) = push_{\mathbf{BSTACK}\,1}(*, mt_{\mathbf{BSTACK}\,1})$ is defined as well.

On the other hand, **BSTACK** A has a totally undefined *push*. In particular, $push_{\mathbf{BSTACK}\,A}(*, mt_{\mathbf{BSTACK}\,A})$ is undefined, but

$$push_{\mathbf{BSTACK}\,1}(*, mt_{\mathbf{BSTACK}\,1})$$
$$= push_{\mathbf{BSTACK}\,1}(\mathbf{BSTACK}\,h(*), \mathbf{BSTACK}\,h(mt_{\mathbf{BSTACK}\,A}))$$

is defined. This means that **BSTACK** h cannot be full. This implies **BSTACK** does not preserve full surjectivity, and by theorem 5, **BSTACK** cannot be specified in $\mathcal{FPCEL}$!

6 Conclusion

We have proved a hierarchy theorem concerning widely-used institutions, ranging from equational logic ($\mathcal{EL}$) to Relational Partial Conditional Existence-Equation Logic ($\mathcal{RPCEL}$). While the institutions do not differ with respect to initial semantics, they do differ in their properties of model categories. But our hierarchy theorem proving properties of PADTs, which are important for modular specification, seems to be more applicable to specification problems.

We argue that differences in the hierarchy are *not* caused by the availability of partiality and/or relations. This is shown by introducing institutions having those features which are (weakly) equivalent in expressiveness to the widely-used institutions which not (all) have these features. The real cause of the differences is the degree of conditionality in the axioms we may use.

In the most expressive institutions $\mathcal{RPCEL}$ and $\mathcal{PCEL}$, we have *conditional generation of data*. This corresponds to availability of conditional axioms with conclusion $pop(\bar{t}) \stackrel{e}{=} pop(\bar{t})$, i.e. a conclusion which may generate data in the free construction. On the other hand, in $\mathcal{FPHCL}$ and $\mathcal{HCL}$, we only have unconditional generation of data in the free construction. This corresponds to the property of PADTs to preserve surjective homomorphisms.

But in $\mathcal{FPHCL}$ and $\mathcal{HCL}$, we can *conditionally generate relation or partial operation graph members* using conclusions of the form $R(\bar{t})$ or $pop(\bar{t}) \stackrel{e}{=} t_0$. On the other hand, in $\mathcal{FPCEL}$ and $\mathcal{CEL}$, this is not possible, and PADTs here preserve full surjective homomorphisms.

Now in $\mathcal{FPCEL}$ and $\mathcal{CEL}$, we have the same thing with *conditional generation of kernel members*, which is not possible in $\mathcal{FPEL}$ and $\mathcal{EL}$, where kernels are preserved by PADTs.

We demonstrate the usefulness of the hierarchy theorem by locating the PADT of bounded stacks within the hierarchy.

It would be interesting to have purely categorical separating properties of PADTs as well, because they would be institution independent. The properties of model categories have a flair similar to the interpretation above, but it seems to be difficult to formulate corresponding properties of specifiable functors: as composites of free an forgetful functors, they lack most categorical preservation and reflection properties. Thus there is further work to be done in order to bridge the gap between institution independent properties and useful characteristic properties of particular institutions.

References

[1] J. Adámek, H. Herrlich, and G. Strecker. *Abstract and Concrete Categories*. Wiley, New York, 1990.

[2] J. Adámek and J. Rosický. *Locally presentable and accessible categories*. Cambrigde University Press, 1994.

[3] H. Baumeister. Unifying initial and loose semantics of parameterized specifications in an arbitrary institution. In S. Abramsky and T.S.E. Maibaum, editors, *TAPSOFT 91 Vol. 1: CAAP 91*, volume 493 of *Lecture Notes in Computer Science*, pages 103–120. Springer Verlag, 1991.

[4] P. Burmeister. Partial algebras — survey of a unifying approach towards a two-valued model theory for partial algebras. *Algebra Universalis*, 15:306–358, 1982.

[5] P. Burmeister. *A model theoretic approach to partial algebras*. Akademie Verlag, Berlin, 1986.

[6] M. Cerioli. *Relationships between Logical Formalisms.* PhD thesis, TD-4/93, Università di Pisa-Genova-Udine, 1993.

[7] H. Ehrig, R. M. Jimenez, and F. Orejas. Compositionality results for different types of parameterization and parameter passing in specification languages. In M.-C. Gaudel and J.-P. Jouannaud, editors, *TAPSOFT 93*, volume 668 of *Lecture Notes in Computer Science*, pages 31–45. Springer Verlag, 1993.

[8] H. Ehrig and B. Mahr. *Fundamentals of Algebraic Specification 1.* Springer Verlag, Heidelberg, 1985.

[9] H. Ehrig and B. Mahr. *Fundamentals of Algebraic Specification 2.* Springer Verlag, Heidelberg, 1990.

[10] J. A. Goguen and R. M. Burstall. Institutions: Abstract model theory for specification and programming. *Journal of the Association for Computing Machinery*, 39:95–146, 1992. Predecessor in: Lecture Notes in Computer Science 164(1984):221–256.

[11] J. A. Goguen and J. Meseguer. Eqlog: Equality, types, and generic modules for logic programming. In D. DeGroot and G. Lindstrom, editors, *Logic Programming. Functions, Relations and Equations*, pages 295–363. Prentice-Hall, Englewood Cliffs, New Jersey, 1986.

[12] J. A. Goguen, J. W. Thatcher, and E. G. Wagner. An initial algebra approach to the specification, correctness and implementation of abstract data types. In R. Yeh, editor, *Current Trends in Programming Methodology*, volume 4, pages 80–144. Prentice Hall, 1978.

[13] H.-J. Kreowski and T. Mossakowski. Equivalence and difference of institutions: Simulating horn clause logic with based algebras. *Mathematical Structures in Computer Science*, to appear.

[14] J. Meseguer. General logics. In *Logic Colloquium 87*, pages 275–329. North Holland, 1989.

[15] T. Mossakowski. Equivalences among various logical frameworks of partial algebras. Submitted to LICS 95.

[16] T. Mossakowski. Parameterized recursion theory – a tool for the systematic classification of specification methods. Submitted to Theoretical Computer Science.

[17] P. Padawitz. *Computing in Horn Clause Theories.* Springer Verlag, Heidelberg, 1988.

[18] H. Reichel. *Initial Computability, Algebraic Specifications and Partial Algebras.* Oxford Science Publications, 1987.

[19] D. Sannella and A. Tarlecki. Specifications in an arbitrary institution. *Information and Computation*, 76:165–210, 1988.

[20] A. Tarlecki. On the existence of free models in abstract algebraic institutions. *Theoretical Computer Science*, 37:269–304, 1985.

[21] A. Tarlecki. Quasi-varieties in abstract algebraic institutions. *Journal of Computer and System Sciences*, 33:333–360, 1986.

[22] J. W. Thatcher, E. G. Wagner, and J. B. Wright. Specification of abstract data types using conditional axioms. Technical Report RC 6214, IBM Yorktown Heigths, 1981.

Dynamical Behavior of Object Systems*

Francesco Parisi–Presicce[1] and Alfonso Pierantonio[2]

[1] Dip. Scienze dell'Informazione
Università di Roma La Sapienza
I–00198 Roma, Italy
[2] Fachbereich Informatik
Technische Universität Berlin
D–10587 Berlin, Germany

Abstract. A semantic framework for modeling the dynamics of object systems is proposed, based on algebraic methods and formulated categorically. The static properties of objects are described by algebraic specifications which could be given as the public interfaces of class specifications. Objects are persistent entities which survive method executions allowing the model to distinguish between object identity and object values. Configurations of objects are modeled by many–sorted algebras and each configuration represents a community of objects (possibly related) with a given state. Configurations can evolve through state changes modeled via non homomorphic algebra transformations. The configurations and the evolutions form a category which represents an object transition system. The structure of the object transition system may reflect the architecture of the interconnections of the software system components (classes).

1 Introduction

In the last fifteen years the object oriented paradigm has received widespread acceptance in the context of software production. One of the main reasons is the more natural modeling of real life problems by means of objects and their creation, transformation and destruction. Another advantage of this methodology is the possibility of reusing and maintaining software systems with less effort than traditional methodologies. There have been many attempts recently at formalizing the main properties of the object oriented paradigm. Some of them (such as [4, 5, 18] for example) use algebraic methods to describe notions such as class, encapsulation, inheritance and subtyping. Categorical techniques have been very useful for the treatment of abstract data types, in the last twenty years, as they are based on a well–developed semantical theory, and have proved to be more than adequate to describe functional (static) properties of data. The algebraic framework so far has been inadequate in describing the dynamical properties of objects and their state transformations as well as more complex notions typical of the object oriented paradigm such as object identity and persistency of objects. The identity of objects allows to distinguish

* The work has been partially supported by the European Community under ESPRIT BRWG 6112 COMPASS and under the program Human Capital and Mobility, contract ERBCHBICT930300

between two instances of the same abstraction which return the same values for a given set of observations (for example, two distinguished lists which contain exactly the same elements in the same order). The notion of persistency allows to relate the states of an object before and after the execution of a method (for example, the object representing a list *evolves*, after the execution of a method which adds an element, into the object whose associated value is the longer list). The identities can be used to handle persistency.

There have been some attempts at transfering algebraic frameworks and techniques to the object oriented paradigm. The idea of using algebras to model states has been proposed in [13] although in the context of giving an operational semantics to programming languages. Modifications of algebras model changes of states in [5] where classical algebraic specification are extended in order to model implicit states and not to distinguish between stored values and computed values. In [2] the well-known algebraic approach for modeling static data structures is extended to a mathematical setting called *d-oid* which consists of a set of algebras (instant structures) and a set of transformations (dynamic operations). The notion of tracking map is used to model persistency and is the basis for the identity of objects.

In our framework, an object consists of an identity, an encapsulated structure and behavior [3]. Objects with similar structure and behavior are called instances of a class, which contains the descriptions of the visible behavior and of the hidden structure of these objects. The behavior and the values of the objects are given by an algebraic specification (if specified by class specification [19] it is the instance export interface) and a model of this specification gives all the possible values of the instances. An object community is an algebra in which the existing objects (determined by the evolution of the system) are associated to their values. In this paper, only abstract objects (identity and behavior) are treated explicitly since the structure of an object is viewed as an implicit state in the sense of [5]. Since the interest is on reasoning about objects, a detailed description of the structure is deferred to subsequent papers. The identity is also treated at an abstract level, without referring to any specific mechanism to retrieve the identity of an object (such as addresses or key attributes).

Three of the four levels proposed in [10] can be found in our model. The algebra of values constitutes the first level, the community of objects (instances) forms the second level; while the third level consists of the dynamic operations which transform states and which are specified in the instance interface.

The next section introduces the specification of the configurations, used to describe the association of values to objects. Section 3 defines the category of the transition system, derived from the value specification, whose morphisms model state changes. Furthermore the semantics of methods is given via morphisms in the object transition system. The last section contains some comparisons with other works and some concluding remarks.

2 Configuration Specifications

The subject of this section is the configuration specifications needed to describe what the state of an object community looks like. In order to present the mathematical setting we need some preliminary notation. We briefly review some basic notions of algebraic specifications; details can be found in [8].

A *signature* Σ is a pair (S, OP) where S is a set of *sorts* and OP a set of *constants* and *function symbols*. By a Σ-*algebra* $A = (S_A, OP_A)$ on a signature $\Sigma = (S, OP)$ we mean a family $S_A = (A_s)_{s \in S}$ of sets and a set $OP_A = (N_A)_{N \in OP}$ of operations. The category of all Σ-algebras is denoted by $Alg(\Sigma)$.
A *signature morphism* $h : \Sigma_1 = (S_1, OP_1) \longrightarrow \Sigma_2 = (S_2, OP_2)$ is a pair of consistent functions $(h^S : S_1 \longrightarrow S_2, h^{OP} : OP_1 \longrightarrow OP_2)$. Every signature morphism $h : \Sigma_1 \longrightarrow \Sigma_2$ induces a *forgetful functor* $V_h : Alg(\Sigma_2) \longrightarrow Alg(\Sigma_1)$.
By an *algebraic specification* SPEC $= (\Sigma, E)$ we intend a pair consisting of a signature Σ and a set E of (positive conditional) equations. If $\text{SPEC}_1 = (\Sigma_1, E_1)$ and $\text{SPEC}_2 = (\Sigma_2, E_2)$ are two algebraic specifications, a *specification morphism* $f : \text{SPEC}_1 \longrightarrow \text{SPEC}_2$ is a signature morphism $f : \Sigma_1 \longrightarrow \Sigma_2$ such that the translation $f^{\#}(E_1)$ of the equations of SPEC_1 is contained in E_2. The algebraic specifications and the specification morphisms form the category CATSPEC of algebraic specifications [8]. Each object community is modelled as an algebra and object evolution as functions from algebra to algebra which do not preserve all the structure and thus are not morphisms. To handle evolutions, we need the notion of families associated with a specification SPEC.

Definition 1. The category of *families* of a specification SPEC $= (S, OP, E)$, denoted **Fam**(SPEC), has SPEC–algebras as objects, and as morphisms

$$\mathbf{Mor}(A, B) = \{h | h : V_i(A) \longrightarrow V_i(B) \in Alg(S)\}$$

where $A, B \in Alg(\text{SPEC})$ and $V_i : Alg(\text{SPEC}) \longrightarrow Alg(S)$ is the forgetful functor associated with the specification morphism $i : S \longrightarrow \text{SPEC}$ inclusion of the sorts S into SPEC. Composition of morphisms and the identity morphisms are as in $Alg(S)$. (This clearly forms a category).

Note 2. If SPEC $= (S, \phi, \phi)$ then **Fam**(SPEC) corresponds to $Alg(S)$ where S is the specification consisting of the sorts of SPEC only.

As already mentioned, we intend to use the notion of many–sorted algebra in order to model the state of a complex system consisting of (possibly interacting) objects. The abstract behavior of such objects is given by an ordinary algebraic specification, called *base specification*, which describes those properties which are common to all the instances and which can be referred to as the declarative semantics of the systems. It is reasonable to expect that the behavior of the objects depends strictly on the static part. The base specification is interpreted as the specification of values and a model of such a specification is therefore a *value algebra* where the elements of the carrier sets are the values which can be assumed by the instances of the data types described in the specification, while the functions determine how to pass from a value to another. At a given time, each object has a current state value which is an element of the value algebra model for the base specification.

The basic idea is to extend the semantical framework of the usual many–sorted algebras in order to cover more complex concepts such as *persistency* and *object identity*. The former is the property of an object to survive the execution of a method (this is usually addressed as short-term persistency in contrast with the long-term of the data base systems). The latter is the property which allows to distinguish between two objects existing at the same time. It is widely believed that objects are capsules with structure, behavior, and identity (see for instance [3]). Since we want to treat objects with an implicit state in the sense of [5] only behavior and identity are considered. More generally, we intend to define an *object transition system* (briefly OTS) in which every state is represented by a many-sorted algebra called *instant structure* in the terminology of [2]. Each state encodes some information such as the existing objects, all the values such objects can have, and a family of actual state functions which provide for each object its current value. The value part of the instant structures is fixed and corresponds to the value algebra.

The instant structures contain more information than the value algebra and we introduce the *configuration specifications* in order to describe them. Configuration specifications needed to represent both objects and their values are canonical extension of the base specifications. Given a base specification $\mathrm{SPEC}^v = (S^v, OP^v, E^v)$ we construct in a canonical way another specification SIG^φ in which the sorts in the base specification are duplicated in object sorts and value sorts and state function symbols are added. Given a base specification $\mathrm{SPEC}^v = (S^v, OP^v, E^v)$, let $S^\Omega = S^v$ be a copy of the set of sorts of SPEC^v and for each $s^v \in S^v$, let s^Ω denote its copy in S^Ω. While each $s^v \in S^v$ is intended to denote the corresponding carrier of values of the SPEC^v-algebra, each s^Ω denotes the (changing) set of objects whose values are in A^v_s. The association object-value is given, for each $s^v \in S^v$, by the interpretation of $\varphi_s\colon s^\Omega \longrightarrow s^v$. Let then SIG^φ be the specification whose signature has the disjoint union of S^v and S^Ω as sorts and $\{ \varphi_s\colon s^\Omega \longrightarrow s^v : s^v \in S^v \}$ as operator symbols. Let $i_1 : S^v \longrightarrow SPEC^v$, $i_2 : S^v \longrightarrow \mathrm{SIG}^\varphi$ and $i_3 : S^\Omega \longrightarrow \mathrm{SIG}^\varphi$ be the obvious inclusion specification morphisms. The configuration specification SPEC^φ is then obtained as the pushout object of the specificatins SPEC^v and SIG^φ with respect to S^v, i.e.

$$\mathrm{SPEC}^\varphi = \mathrm{SPEC}^v +_{S^v} \mathrm{SIG}^\varphi$$

as in the commutative diagram in fig. 1.

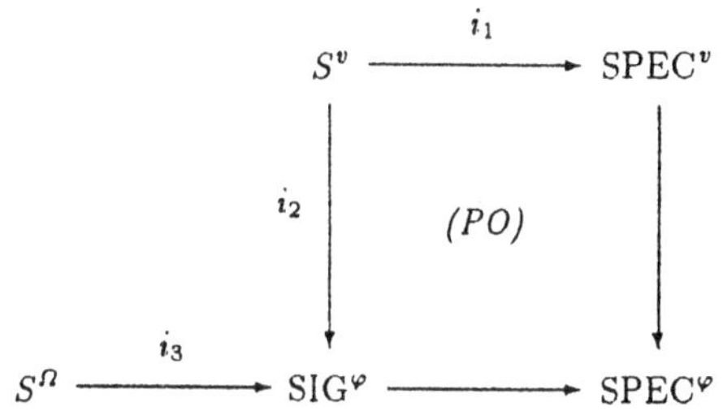

Fig. 1. The configuration specification diagram

Example 1. Consider a base specification $\mathrm{SPEC}^{v}(\mathbf{str})$ with **str** the sort of interest, in which *strings of naturals* are described as follows

$\mathrm{SPEC}^{v}(\mathbf{str})$ =

<u>sorts</u>	string, nat
<u>opns</u>	0: nat
	succ: nat ⟶ nat
	nil: string
	make: nat ⟶ string
	conc: string string ⟶ string
	cons: string nat ⟶ string
<u>eqns</u>	conc(nil,x) = x = conc(x,nil)
	cons(x,n) = conc(make(n),x)
	conc(conc(x,y),z) = conc(x,conc(y,z))

The specification $\mathrm{SIG}^{\varphi}(\mathbf{str})$ is defined canonically as follows

$\mathrm{SIG}^{\varphi}(\mathbf{str}) = S^{v}(\mathbf{str}) + S^{\Omega}(\mathbf{str}) +$

<u>opns</u>	$\varphi_{\mathrm{string}}: \mathrm{string}^{\Omega} \longrightarrow \mathrm{string}^{v}$
	$\varphi_{\mathrm{nat}}: \mathrm{nat}^{\Omega} \longrightarrow \mathrm{nat}^{v}$

where

$$S^{v}(\mathbf{str}) = \underline{\mathrm{sorts}} \quad \mathrm{string}^{v}, \mathrm{nat}^{v}$$

$$S^{\Omega}(\mathbf{str}) = \underline{\mathrm{sorts}} \quad \mathrm{string}^{\Omega}, \mathrm{nat}^{\Omega}$$

The configuration specification $\mathrm{SPEC}^{\varphi}(\mathbf{str})$ is then obtained as the pushout object of $\mathrm{SPEC}^{v}(\mathbf{str})$ and $\mathrm{SIG}^{\varphi}(\mathbf{str})$ with respect to $S^{v}(\mathbf{str})$

$\mathrm{SPEC}^{\varphi}(\mathbf{str}) = \mathrm{SPEC}^{v}(\mathbf{str}) +_{S^{v}(\mathbf{str})} \mathrm{SIG}^{\varphi}(\mathbf{str}) =$

<u>sorts</u>	$\mathrm{string}^{v}, \mathrm{nat}^{v}, \mathrm{string}^{\Omega}, \mathrm{nat}^{\Omega}$
<u>opns</u>	$0: \mathrm{nat}^{v}$
	$\mathrm{succ}: \mathrm{nat}^{v} \longrightarrow \mathrm{nat}^{v}$
	$\mathrm{nil}: \mathrm{string}^{v}$
	$\mathrm{make}: \mathrm{nat}^{v} \longrightarrow \mathrm{string}^{v}$
	$\mathrm{conc}: \mathrm{string}^{v}\ \mathrm{string}^{v} \longrightarrow \mathrm{string}^{v}$
	$\mathrm{cons}: \mathrm{string}^{v}\ \mathrm{nat}^{v} \longrightarrow \mathrm{string}^{v}$
	$\varphi_{\mathrm{nat}}: \mathrm{nat}^{\Omega} \longrightarrow \mathrm{nat}^{v}$
	$\varphi_{\mathrm{string}}: \mathrm{string}^{\Omega} \longrightarrow \mathrm{string}^{v}$
<u>eqns</u>	conc(nil,x) = x = conc(x,nil)
	cons(x,n) = conc(make(n),x)
	conc(conc(x,y),z) = conc(x,conc(y,z))

Since the value algebra is fixed, each transformation from state to state (each configuration morphism) must be the identity on this algebra, while it may change the *object* algebra (i.e., the set of existing objects) and the interpretation of φ_S for some s as it maps, for example, an existing object to its new value. A transformation of configurations therefore cannot be a SPEC^{φ}-morphism since the SIG^{φ}-structure is not preserved. This is the main motivation for introducing the notion of families of a specification **Fam**(SPEC) at the beginning of this section. In fact, the states of the OTS are those algebras in the category of families of the configuration specification which preserve the value algebra as shown in the next section.

Definition 3. Given $\mathrm{SPEC}_1 = (S_1, OP_1, E_1)$, $\mathrm{SPEC}_2 = (S_2, OP_2, E_2)$, $i_1 : S_1 \hookrightarrow \mathrm{SPEC}_1$, $i_2 : S_2 \hookrightarrow \mathrm{SPEC}_2$ and a specification morphism $f : \mathrm{SPEC}_1 \longrightarrow \mathrm{SPEC}_2$, the forgetful functor over the families

$$U_f : \mathbf{Fam}(\mathrm{SPEC}_2) \longrightarrow \mathbf{Fam}(\mathrm{SPEC}_1)$$

is defined for all SPEC_2-algebras (objects of $\mathbf{Fam}(\mathrm{SPEC}_2)$) A_2 by

$$U_f(A_2) = V_f(A_2)$$

where $V_f : Alg(\mathrm{SPEC}_2) \longrightarrow Alg(\mathrm{SPEC}_1)$ is the usual forgetful functor and for all $h : V_{i_2}(B_1) \longrightarrow V_{i_2}(B_2) \in \mathbf{Fam}(\mathrm{SPEC}_2)$

$$U_f(h : V_{i_2}(B_1) \longrightarrow V_{i_2}(B_2)) = U_f(h) : V_{i_2 \circ f^S}(B_1) \longrightarrow V_{i_2 \circ f^S}(B_2)$$

where f^S is the sort component of the morphism f.

As for the categories of algebras we can reformulate the Amalgamation Lemma [8]

Theorem 4 Amalgamation Lemma. *Given a pushout diagram as in fig. 2 the amalgamated sum has the following properties*

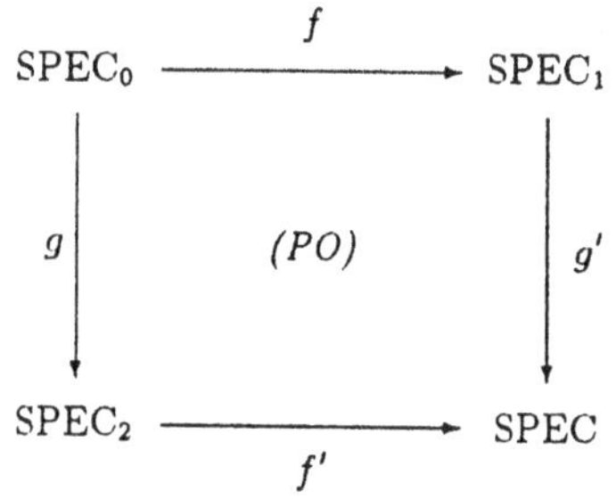

Fig. 2. Pushout diagram

1. *Given algebras* $A_j \in \mathbf{Fam}(\mathrm{SPEC}_j)$, $j \in \{0,1,2\}$ *with* $U_f(A_1) = A_0 = U_g(A_2)$, *the amalgamated sum* $A_1 +_{A_0} A_2$ *is the unique* **Fam***(SPEC)-algebra A satisfying*

$$U_{g'}(A) = A_1 \text{ and } U_{f'}(A) = A_2$$

Conversely, each $A \in \mathbf{Fam}(\mathrm{SPEC})$ *has a unique representation*

$$A_1 +_{A_0} A_2$$

where $A_1 = U_{g'}(A)$, $A_2 = U_{f'}(A)$, *and* $A_0 = U_g(A_2) = U_f(A_1)$.

2. *Given morphisms* $h_j : V_{i_j}(A_j) \longrightarrow V_{i_j}(B_j)$, $j \in \{0,1,2\}$ *with* $U_f(h_1) = A_0 = U_g(h_2)$, *the amalgamated sum* $h_1 +_{h_0} h_2$ *is the unique* **Fam***(SPEC) morphism h satisfying*

$$U_{g'}(h) = h_1 \text{ and } U_{f'}(h) = h_2$$

Conversely, each $h \in \mathbf{Fam}(\mathrm{SPEC})$ *has a unique representation*

$$h_1 +_{h_0} h_2$$

where $h_1 = U_{g'}(h)$, $h_2 = U_{f'}(h)$, *and* $h_0 = U_g(h_2) = U_f(h_1)$.

Another interesting result is that the algebraic specification endowed with the families constitutes a specification frame ([6])

Theorem 5. *The indexed category (CATSPEC,***Fam***) where CATSPEC is the category of algebraic specifications and* **Fam** : $\mathrm{CATSPEC}^{\mathrm{OP}} \longrightarrow \mathrm{CATCAT}$ *is a functor that associates to every specification SPEC the category of families* **Fam***(SPEC) and to every specification morphism* $f : SPEC_1 \longrightarrow SPEC_2$ *a functor*

$$U_f : \mathbf{Fam}(\mathrm{SPEC}_2) \longrightarrow \mathbf{Fam}(\mathrm{SPEC}_1)$$

is a specification frame.

Proof idea. It suffices to check that CATSPEC is close under pushouts, that **Fam** transforms pushouts in CATSPEC into pullbacks in CATCAT and that CATSPEC has initial object ϕSPEC and $\mathbf{Fam}(\phi\mathrm{SPEC}) = \mathbf{1}$, the category consisting of exactly one object and one morphism.

The base specification is usually the outcome of a design process and therefore usually a structured specification. The structuring mechanisms are mainly based on colimits, e.g. parameter passing and composition of module specifications ([9]); actualization, combination, and inheritance in our class specification model ([19, 20]); parameter passing in the OBJ language. We call generically such mechanisms *design*. The canonical extension of the base specification preserves the design.

Theorem 6. *The transformation from the base specification* SPEC^{υ} *into the intermediate specification* SIG^{φ} *and into the configuration specification* SPEC^{φ} *are endofunctors in CATSPEC denoted by*

$$\mathrm{SPEC}^{\varphi} : \mathrm{CATSPEC} \longrightarrow \mathrm{CATSPEC} \text{ and } \mathrm{SIG}^{\varphi} : \mathrm{CATSPEC} \longrightarrow \mathrm{CATSPEC}.$$

The canonical construction of SIG^{φ} and $SPEC^{\varphi}$ preserves the design of the base specification SPEC. In particular, if

SPEC is obtained as the colimit object of $F : I \longrightarrow CATSPEC$, then the corresponding configuration specification can be constructed by taking the appropriate colimit of the canonical construction of the components. In particular, we have the following result which states the compatibility of the structuring mechanisms with the configuration functor.

Theorem 7. $(SPEC_1 +_{SPEC_0} SPEC_2)^{\varphi} = SPEC_1^{\varphi} +_{SPEC_0^{\varphi}} SPEC_2^{\varphi}$

Proof idea. Choose

$$I = \begin{array}{c} 0 \rightarrow 1 \\ \downarrow \\ 2 \end{array} \quad \text{and} \quad J = \begin{array}{cc} S^{v} & \rightarrow \mathrm{SPEC}^{v} \\ \downarrow & \\ S^{\Omega} & \rightarrow \mathrm{SIG}^{\varphi} \end{array}$$

and let $D : I \times J \longrightarrow$CATSPEC be given by
$D(i, \mathrm{SPEC}^{v}) = SPEC_i$ etc. in the obvious way. Then
$Colim_I(Colim_J D(i,j) = SPEC_1^{\varphi} +_{SPEC_0^{\varphi}} SPEC_2^{\varphi}$
$Colim_J(Colim_I D(i,j)) = (SPEC_1 +_{SPEC_0} SPEC_2)^{\varphi}$
Now the result follows by applying the Commutation of Colimits [14].

Corollary 8. *The configuration extension functor* SPEC^{φ} *is compatible with the design.*

3 Object Transition Systems

The main aim of this work is the definition of a transition system as the operational semantics of a community of objects whose states are modeled by many–sorted algebras and whose transitions are non–homomorphic transformations of such algebras. The transition systems formulated as a category, denoted by **Trans**, where the categorical objects represent the states of the transition system, and the morphisms the evolutions of the system due to the execution of methods over objects.

Given a base specification SPEC, the transition system is defined by fixing a particular value algebra, i.e. by taking a specific model A for the base specification in Alg(SPEC). Each choice gives raise to a different transition system. Such a value algebra is referred to as the *world of values* over which the state of the objects ranges. Formally

Definition 9 Object transition system. The category of an object transition system with respect to a base specification SPEC over a value algebra A, denoted by **Trans**(A), has as objects

$$\underline{\mathbf{Obj}} = \{B | B \in \mathbf{Fam}(\mathrm{SIG}^{\varphi}) \text{ and } U_{i_2}(B) = V_{i_1}(A))\} \tag{1}$$

where $i_1 : S^{v} \hookrightarrow \mathrm{SPEC}^{v}$ and $i_2 : S^{v} \hookrightarrow \mathrm{SIG}^{\varphi}$ (see diagram in fig. 1) and as morphisms

$$\underline{\mathbf{Mor}}(B, C) = \Big\{(h, (f^{o})_{o \in U_{i_3}(B)}) | h \in \underline{\mathbf{Fam}}(B, C) \text{ s.t.}$$

$$U_{i_2}(h) = \mathrm{id}_{V_{i_1}(A)} \tag{2}$$

$$U_{i_2}(h) = \mathrm{id}_{U_{i_2}(B)} \tag{3}$$

$$(f^o : U_{i_2}(B) \longrightarrow U_{i_2}(C))_{o \in U_{i_3}(B)} \text{ and} \tag{4}$$

$$\varphi_s^C(h(o)) = f_s^o(\varphi_s^B(o))\} \tag{5}$$

Given two morphisms

$$m_1 = (h, (f^o)_{o \in U_{i_3}(B)}) : B \longrightarrow C \text{ and } m_2 = (k, (g^{o'})_{o' \in U_{i_3}(C)}) : C \longrightarrow D$$

the composition $m_2 \circ m_1 : B \longrightarrow D$ is the morphism given by

$$\left(k \circ h, g^{U_{i_3}(h)(o)} \circ f^o\right)$$

Note 10. Since $Alg(S) = \mathbf{Fam}(S)$ (1) is well-defined. Condition (5) is called *quasi-homomorphic condition.*

Interpretation. The objects of the category $\mathbf{Trans}(A)$ model the states of the transition system. Each state contains the existing objects, the values corresponding to the value algebra, and the state functions. The morphisms are pairs of mappings: the first component maps objects in a state to objects into a subsequent state and it is used mainly for bookeeping of the objects (creation and disposal); the second component is used to model the changes over the state of the objects and in particular used to modify the state function of an object which is subject to some changes due to the execution of a method.

Remark.
1. The intention is to use the morphisms as the interpretation of method executions. Not all the morphisms from B to C model a state transformation determined by a method specified in the base specification SPEC, but only those generated, by composition, by functions of the form $\lambda x.m^A(x, a_1, \ldots, a_n)$ for method symbols $m : ss_1 \cdots s_n \longrightarrow s$ in SPEC. The elements $a1, \ldots, a_n$ are actual parameter of the method. The subcategory of $\mathbf{Trans}(A)$ with the same objects and this kind of morphisms is denoted by $\mathbf{GTrans}(A)$.
2. By varying the constraint on the morphisms from B to C (e.g. removing condition (5) or ignoring the component (4)) we obtain a category $\mathbf{CatTrans}(A)$ of "loose"transition systems corresponding to the same algebra of values A. The whole category could be taken as the loose semantcs of the dynamical behavior of the instances determined by the base specification. The transition system $\mathbf{Trans}(A)$ is a specific choice within this category of transition systems: further restrictions (to be discussed in a subsequent paper) will define the initial object in the category $\mathbf{CatTrans}(A)$.

Example 2. Given the base specification $\mathrm{SPEC}^v(\mathbf{str})$ and the configuration specification $\mathrm{SPEC}^\varphi(\mathbf{str})$ in Ex. 1 consider the following states S_1 and S_2

$$S_1 = \begin{pmatrix} \varphi_{\text{string}} & \varphi_{\text{nat}} \\ o_1 \longmapsto 01 & n_1 \longmapsto 0 \\ o_2 \longmapsto 011 & n_2 \longmapsto 1 \\ & n_3 \longmapsto 1 \end{pmatrix} \quad \text{and} \quad S_2 = \begin{pmatrix} \varphi_{\text{string}} & \varphi_{\text{nat}} \\ o_1 \longmapsto 101 & n_1 \longmapsto 0 \\ o_2 \longmapsto 011 & n_2 \longmapsto 1 \\ & n_3 \longmapsto 0 \end{pmatrix}$$

Let $m : S_1 \longrightarrow S_2$ be a morphism which transforms the state S_1 into the state S_2 and it is defined as follows

$$m = \left(h, (f^o)_{o \in S_1^\Omega}\right)$$

($S_1^\Omega = V_{i_3}(S_1)$, i.e. is the set of all existing objects) where h is the identity over S_1 since no objects have been created or disposed, and

$$\begin{array}{rll} f^{o_1}_{\mathrm{str}} : A_{\mathrm{str}} \longrightarrow A_{\mathrm{str}} & \forall s \in A_{\mathrm{str}}, f^{o_1}_{\mathrm{str}}(s) = 1 \cdot s \\ f^{o_2}_{\mathrm{str}} : A_{\mathrm{str}} \longrightarrow A_{\mathrm{str}} & f^{o_2}_{\mathrm{str}} = \mathrm{id}_{A_{\mathrm{str}}} \\ f^{n_1}_{\mathrm{nat}}, f^{n_2}_{\mathrm{nat}} : A_{\mathrm{nat}} \longrightarrow A_{\mathrm{nat}} & f^{n_1}_{\mathrm{nat}} = f^{n_2}_{\mathrm{nat}} = \mathrm{id}_{A_{\mathrm{nat}}} \\ f^{n_3}_{\mathrm{nat}} : A_{\mathrm{nat}} \longrightarrow A_{\mathrm{nat}} & \forall n \in A_{\mathrm{nat}}, f^{n_3}_{\mathrm{nat}}(n) = (n+1) \bmod 2 \end{array}$$

the conditions (2-5) holds, in particular for the quasi-homomorphic condition over the object o_1 we have

$$\begin{aligned} \varphi^{S_2}_{\mathrm{str}}(h(o_1)) &= \varphi^{S_2}_{\mathrm{str}}(o_1) \\ &= 101 \\ &= f^{o_1}_{\mathrm{str}}(01) \\ &= f^{o_1}_{\mathrm{str}}(\varphi^{S_1}_{\mathrm{str}}(01)) \end{aligned}$$

Example 3. The morphism m just introduced can be decomposed into

$$m_1 = \left(l, (s^o)_{o \in S_1^\Omega}\right) : S_1 \longrightarrow S \quad \text{and} \quad m_2 = \left(k, (t^{o'})_{o' \in S_2^\Omega}\right) : S \longrightarrow S_2$$

where

$$S = \begin{pmatrix} \varphi_{\mathrm{string}} & \varphi_{\mathrm{nat}} \\ o_1 \longmapsto 101 & n_1 \longmapsto 0 \\ o_2 \longmapsto 011 & n_2 \longmapsto 1 \\ & n_3 \longmapsto 1 \end{pmatrix}$$

Note that as $\varphi^{S}_{\mathrm{str}} = \varphi^{S_2}_{\mathrm{str}}$ and $\varphi^{S}_{\mathrm{nat}} = \varphi^{S_2}_{\mathrm{nat}}$. The mappings l and k are the indentity over the corresponding object parts, whereas

$$\begin{array}{rl} s^{o_1}_{\mathrm{str}} : A_{\mathrm{str}} \longrightarrow A_{\mathrm{str}} & \forall x \in A_{\mathrm{str}}, s^{o_1}_{\mathrm{str}}(x) = 1 \cdot x \\ s^{o_2}_{\mathrm{str}} : A_{\mathrm{str}} \longrightarrow A_{\mathrm{str}} & s^{o_2}_{\mathrm{str}} = \mathrm{id}_{A_{\mathrm{str}}} \\ s^{n_1}_{\mathrm{nat}}, s^{n_2}_{\mathrm{nat}}, s^{n_3}_{\mathrm{nat}} : A_{\mathrm{nat}} \longrightarrow A_{\mathrm{nat}} & f^{n_1}_{\mathrm{nat}} = f^{n_2}_{\mathrm{nat}} = f^{n_3}_{\mathrm{nat}} = \mathrm{id}_{A_{\mathrm{nat}}} \end{array}$$

and

$$\begin{array}{rl} t^{o_1}_{\mathrm{str}}, t^{o_2}_{\mathrm{str}} : A_{\mathrm{str}} \longrightarrow A_{\mathrm{str}} & t^{o_1}_{\mathrm{str}} = t^{o_2}_{\mathrm{str}} = \mathrm{id}_{A_{\mathrm{str}}} \\ t^{n_1}_{\mathrm{nat}}, t^{n_2}_{\mathrm{nat}} : A_{\mathrm{nat}} \longrightarrow A_{\mathrm{nat}} & t^{n_1}_{\mathrm{nat}} = t^{n_2}_{\mathrm{nat}} = \mathrm{id}_{A_{\mathrm{nat}}} \\ t^{n_3}_{\mathrm{nat}} : A_{\mathrm{nat}} \longrightarrow A_{\mathrm{nat}} & \forall n \in A_{\mathrm{nat}}, t^{n_3}_{\mathrm{nat}}(n) = (n+1) \bmod 2 \end{array}$$

Referring to remark (1) after def. 9 it is easy to see that the string component of the values part $(s^o)_{o \in S_1^\Omega}$ of the morphism $m_1 : S_1 \longrightarrow S$ consists of the interpretation $\lambda x.\mathrm{cons}^A(x, 1)$ of the operation *cons:string nat⟶string* in the base specification $\mathrm{SPEC}^v(\mathbf{str})$ with parameter $1 \in A_{\mathrm{nat}}$ applied to the object o_1 and the identity applied to all the other objects.

As expected

Theorem 11. **Trans**(A) *forms a category.*

Proof idea. It suffices to verify that the associativity of the composition follows from the associativity of the composition in **Fam**$(SPEC)$ and that the quasi-homomorphic property holds, i.e. given $m_1 = (h, (f^o)_{o \in B^\Omega})$ and $m_2 = (k, (g^{o'})_{o' \in C^\Omega})$ such that

$$\varphi^C(h(o)) = f^o(\varphi^B(o)) \text{ for all } o \in B^\Omega$$
$$\varphi^D(k(o')) = g^{o'}(\varphi^C(o')) \text{ for all } o' \in C^\Omega$$

then

$$\begin{aligned}\varphi^D(k(h(0))) &= g^{h(o)}(\varphi^C(h(o)))\\ &= g^{h(o)}(f^o(\varphi^B(o)))\end{aligned}$$

Theorem 12. *The category* **Trans**(A) *is not closed under pushouts.*

Proof idea. The following two morphisms do not have a pushout

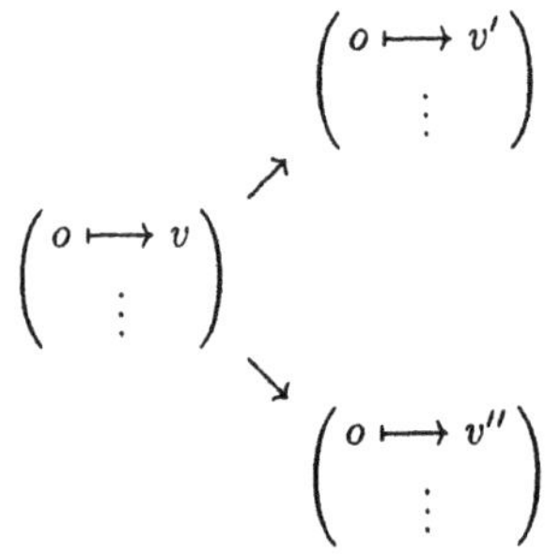

Theorem 13. *Two morphisms in* **Trans**(A) *have a pushout whenever the morphisms model changes over different objects.*

Such theorem states the fact that pushouts exist if the evolutions refer to different objects and the changes they imply can be carried out independently and even simuntaneously.

Example 4. Given S_1 as in Ex. 2 and S as in Ex. 3, define

$$S' = \begin{pmatrix} \varphi_{\text{string}} & \varphi_{\text{nat}} \\ o_1 \longmapsto 01 & n_1 \longmapsto 0 \\ o_2 \longmapsto 011 & n_2 \longmapsto 1 \\ & n_3 \longmapsto 0 \end{pmatrix}$$

and $p_1 = (\text{id}, (g^o)_{o \in S_1^\Omega}) : S_1 \longrightarrow S'$ where the first component is the identity over the object part, while the second component is the component g of m_2 in Ex. 3. The pushout object is exactly the state S_2 in Ex. 2. There is no pushout of the morphism m_1 (which changes the value associated to the object o_1 to the string 101) and the morphism $q1 : S_1 \longrightarrow S''$ (which does not create or delete objects and associates to o_1 the string 1101).

The following result concerns the relationship between two different transition systems defined for the same value specification but over two different value algebras which are in turn related via a homomorphism

Theorem 14. *There is a unique way to extend a homomorphism* $p : A1 \longrightarrow A2 \in$ Alg(SPEC) *to a functor* F_p : **GTrans**$(A1) \longrightarrow$**GTrans**$(A2)$

Proof idea. Given $p : A1 \longrightarrow A2 \in Alg$(SPEC) and

$$\underline{\mathbf{Obj}}(\mathbf{GTrans}(A1)) = \{B1 | B1 \in \mathbf{Fam}(\mathrm{SIG}^{\varphi}) \text{ and } U_{i_2}(B_1) = V_{i_1}(A1)\}$$

define F_p on <u>objects</u> as $F_p(B1) = B2 \in$ **GTrans**$(A2)$ where

$$\begin{aligned} U_{i_3}(B2) &= U_{i_3}(B1) \\ U_{i_2}(B2) &= V_{i_1}(A1) \\ \varphi^{B2} &= p \circ \varphi^{B1} \end{aligned}$$

and on <u>morphisms</u> as

$$F_p\left((h, (f^o)_{o \in B1^{\Omega}}) : B1 \longrightarrow C1\right) = (k, (g^{o'})_{o' \in B2^{\Omega}}) : B2 \longrightarrow C2$$

where $U_{i_3}(k) = U_{i_3}(h)$, i.e. the object part changes according to h, and $U_{i_2}(k) = id_{U_{i_2}(B2)}$, i.e. the value part remains the same. Since $B_2^{\Omega} = U_{i_3}(B2) = U_{i_3}(B1) = B_1^{\Omega}$ the families of mappings $(f^o)_{o \in B1^{\Omega}}$ and $(g^{o'})_{o' \in B2^{\Omega}}$ have the same index set. By assumption

$$f^o = \lambda x.m^{B1^v}(x, a_1, \ldots, a_n) \tag{6}$$

$(B1^v = U_{i_2}(B1))$ for some $m : ss_1 \cdots s_n \longrightarrow s$ (see remark (1) after def. 9) and $a_i \in B1^v_{s_i}, i \in \{1, \ldots, n\}$. For $a' = p(a) \in p(A1^v)$ define $g^o(a') = p(f^o(a))$ and for $a' \in A2^v - p(A1^v)$ define $g^o(a') = a'$. Since p is an homorphism from $A1$ to $A2$, g is well-defined.

Each homomorphism between value algebras determines a morphism between the corresponding transition system. The transition systems in turn form a category related to a specific base category. By varying the base specification, a number of categories of transition systems is obtainable. Formally

Theorem 15. *The objects* **GTrans**(A) *for* $A \in$ Alg(SPEC) *and the functors* F_p *as in Th. 14 form a category called* GTRANS(SPEC).

Theorem 16. *The association of* A *to* **GTrans**(A) *and of* p *to* F_p *as in Th. 14 defines a functor* **GTrans** : Alg(SPEC)$\longrightarrow$GTRANS(SPEC).

Definition 17. The category of generated transition systems, denoted by CAT-GTRANS, has as objects GTRANS(SPEC) for all SPEC $\in$ CATSPEC. There exists a morphism from GTRANS($SPEC_2$) to GTRANS($SPEC_1$) if and only if there exixts a morphism $f : SPEC_1 \longrightarrow SPEC_2$. Given $f : SPEC_1 \longrightarrow SPEC_2$ denote by GTRANS(f) : GTRANS($SPEC_2$)$\longrightarrow$GTRANS($SPEC_1$) the morphism in CATSPEC defined as follows:

- on objects, it maps **GTrans**(A_2), for all $A_2 \in Alg(SPEC_2)$, to **GTrans**$(V_f(A_2))$

- on morphisms, it associates F_p : **GTrans**$(A_2)\longrightarrow$**GTrans**(A_1), defined by $p: A_2\longrightarrow B_2$ in $Alg(\text{SPEC}_2)$, to $F_{V_f(p)}$: **GTrans**$(V_f(A_2))\longrightarrow$**GTrans**$(V_f(B_2))$.

Theorem 18. *The functor* GTRANS : CATSPEC$\longrightarrow$CATGTRANS *which maps* SPEC *to* GTRANS(SPEC) *and* f : SPEC$_1\longrightarrow$SPEC$_2$ *to* GTRANS(f) : GTRANS(SPEC$_2$)$\longrightarrow$GTRANS(SPEC$_1$) *is a controvariant functor.*

Corollary 19. *The category* CATSPEC *along with model functor* GTRANS *defines a specification frame.*

Theorem 20. *The category* CATTRANS *is closed under finite colimits.*

Theorem 21. *The model functor* GTRANS *preserves colimits.*

Proof idea. Use the commutativity of colimits over a cartesian product.

Corollary 22. *The category* GTRANS(SPEC$_1$ $+_{\text{SPEC}_0}$ SPEC$_2$) *is equivalent to*

$$\text{GTRANS}(\text{SPEC}_1) +_{\text{GTRANS}(\text{SPEC}_0)} \text{GTRANS}(\text{SPEC}_2)$$

4 Concluding Remarks

This paper presents a categorical framework of a model for state changes in object communities. Each configuration consists of a value part (a static model of an algebraic specification in the classical sense), an object part (which contains the identities of all the objects created but not destroyed during the evolution of the system) and a state function (which relates each existing object to its current value). Configuration specifications can be constructed in a functorial way from the value specification so that its structure is preserved (Compatibility Theorem). An Object Transition System is defined from the configuration specifications: the different configurations and the morphisms between them modeling method executions form a category.

Objects with an implicit state can be dynamically created and deleted whereas in [5] the size of the implicit state is statically determined. Furthermore, the state observations change via elementary modifiers, while in our approach state observations of a single object change after method executions. We present the possibility of deriving the dynamic behavior from a fully specified static part, whereas the *d-oids* have only a semantical nature. The approach presented here has an explicit treatment of identities although an identification mechanism is not chosen. The first component of the morphisms in the category **Trans**(A) could be used to simulate the identity bookkeeping mechanism called *tracking map* in [2]. The specification of parallel state dependent systems in [12] has also a statically determined size of the state. The state changes are modeled by dynamic operations explicitly specified in an imperative manner. The identification is performed in a way similar to our approach, while the underlying static framework is based on partial algebras.

For simplicity of presentation, we have not considered the very important problem of structured objects. Our framework can easily be extended be adding to the trivial specification S^{Ω} a specification of the operators and relations which define the structure of the objects.

References

1. America,P.: *Designing an Object-Oriented Programming Language with Behavioral Subtyping.* Proc. REX/FOO L, Springer Lect.Notes in Comp.Sci. 489, 1990, pp. 60-90
2. Astesiano,E., Zucca,E.: *D–oids: A Model for Dynamic Data Types.* Special Issue of MSCS, to appear 1994
3. Booch,G.: *Object Oriented Design with Applications.* Benjamin Cummings, 1991
4. Breu,R.: *Algebraic Specification Techniques in Object Oriented Programming Environments.* Springer Lect.Notes in Comp.Sci. 561, 1991
5. Dauchy,P., Gaudel,M.C.: *Algebraic Specification with Implicit State.* Techn. Report, Univ. Paris–Sud, 1994
6. Ehrig,H., Baldamus,M., Orejas,F.: *New Concepts for Amalgamation and Extension in the Framework of the Specification Logic.* TUB Technical Report, 1991
7. Ehrig,H., Jimenez,R.M., Orejas,F.: *Compositionality Result for different Types of Parameterization and Parameter Passing in Specification Languages.* Proc. TapSoft 1993, Springer Lect.Notes in Comp.Sci. 668, pp.38-45
8. Ehrig,H., Mahr,B.: *Fundamentals of Algebraic Specification 1. Equations and Initial Semantics.* EATCS Monograph in Computer Science, Vol.6, Springer Verlag, 1985
9. Ehrig,H., Mahr,B.: *Fundamentals of Algebraic Specification 2. Module Specifications and Constraints.* EATCS Monograph in Computer Science, Vol.21, Springer Verlag, 1990
10. Ehrig,H., Orejas,F.: *Dynamic Abstract Data Types: An Informal Proposal.* Bull. EATCS 53, June 1994
11. Goguen,J., Diaconescu,D.: *Towards an Algebraic Semantics for the Object Paradigm.* Proc. 10th WADT, Springer Lect.Notes in Comp.Sci., 1994
12. Große–Rhode,M.: *Specification of Parallel State Dependent Systems.* TU Berlin, 1994, in preparation
13. Gurevitch,Y.: *Evolving Algebras, A Tutorial Introduction.* Bull. EATCS 43, 1991, pp.264–284
14. Herrlich,H., Strecker,G.E.: *Category Theory.* Allyn and Bacon Inc., Boston, 1993
15. Khoshafian,S., Copeland,G.: *Object Identity.* Proc. OOPSLA 1986, ACM Press, 1986, pp. 406–416
16. Meyer,B.: *Genericity versus Inheritance.* Proc. OOPSLA 1986, ACM Press, 1986, pp. 391–405
17. Meyer,B.: *Object-Oriented Software Construction.* Prentice-Hall, 1988
18. Parisi–Presicce,F., Pierantonio, A.: *An Algebraic Approach to Inheritance and Subtyping.* Proc. ESEC 1991, Springer Lect.Notes in Comp.Sci. 550, 1991, pp. 364–379
19. Parisi–Presicce,F., Pierantonio, A.: *An Algebraic Theory of Class Specification.* ACM Transaction on Software Engineering and Methodology, accepted for publication 1994
20. Parisi–Presicce,F., Pierantonio, A.: *Reusing Object Oriented Design: An Algebraic Approach.* Proc. International Symposium on Object–Oriented Methodologies and Systems, Springer Lect.Notes in Comp.Sci.858, 1994
21. Snyder,A.: *Encapsulation and Inheritance in Object–Oriented Programming Languages.* Proc. OOPSLA 1986, ACM Press, 1986, pp. 38–45
22. Weber,H., Ehrig,H.: *Specification of Concurrently Executable Modules and Distributed Modular Systems.* Proc. Workshop Future Trends of Distr. Comp. Systems in the 1990's, Hong Kong, 1988, pp. 202–215
23. Wegner,P.: *Dimensions of Object–Based Language Design.* Proc. OOPSLA 1987, ACM Press, 1987, pp. 168–182. Also as special issue of SIGPLAN No. 22, 12, Dec 1987

A Theory-based Topological Notion of Institution*

Amílcar Sernadas[1], Cristina Sernadas[1], José Manuel Valença[2]

[1] Instituto Superior Técnico, Lisboa, Portugal
[2] Universidade do Minho, Braga, Portugal,

Abstract. By adopting theories as primitive components of a logic and recognizing that formulae are just presentation details we arrive at the concept of topological institution. In a topological institution, we have, for each signature, a frame of theories, a set of interpretation structures and a satisfaction relation. More precisely, we have, for each signature, a topological system. We show how to extract a topological institution from a given institution and establish an adjunction. Illustrations are given within the context of equational logic. We study the compositionality of theories. Formulae are recovered when we establish a general technique for presenting topological institutions. Topological institutions with finitely observable theories are shown to be useful in temporal monitoring applications where we would like to be able to characterize the properties of the system that can be monitored. Namely, an invariant property ($\mathbf{G}\varphi$) cannot be monitored because it cannot be positively established in finite time. On the contrary, a reactivity property ($\mathbf{F}\varphi$) can be positively established in finite time.

1 Introduction

Institutions [4, 5], π-institutions [3, 2] and entailment systems [9] are abstractions that subsume the informal notion of logic system with its varying alphabets. Institutions are semantically based, contrarily to π-institutions and entailment systems. In all cases the central notion of theory is not primitive. Formulae and their models or formulae and consequence relations are taken as the starting point.

However, the (categorial) framework of institutions has proved to be quite useful in software specification and in knowledge representation precisely because it provides the means for composing and structuring theories (and their presentations). In both domains of application we need to be able to describe and reason about "properties" of the system at hand. To this end, a bijection is assumed between theories and properties. Clearly, formulae are used just for presenting properties. Thus, *the central concept is the theory, not the formula.* And indeed all interesting institutional developments deal with theories.

Therefore, one may wonder why the theory is not the primitive concept in institutions. We could easily envisage an alternative structure built around theories (properties) instead of formulae (presentations of properties). Such a structure should

* This work was partly supported by CEC under ESPRIT-III BRA WG 6071 IS-CORE (Information Systems - COrrectness and REusability) and BRA WG 6112 COMPASS (COMPrehensive Algebraic approach to System Specification and development) and by ESDI under research contract OBLOG (OBject LOGic).

include signatures (alphabets) plus theories and their semantics. The introduction of this concept is the main goal of the paper.

The basic problem is to find a suitable formula-independent notion of theory. Furthermore, we must also decide upon a suitable structure for the theories over a given signature. Just a set seems to be too little since we do have operations on theories. Maybe a complete lattice, recognizing that we have all joins (and meets) of theories over a given signature. But as we shall see, this would be too much and, on computability grounds, we adopt instead the (weaker) frame structure.

Indeed, a parallel development within the broad area of domain theory provides the starting point: the notion of topological system proposed in [14]. Vickers arrived at this concept by further exploring the consequences of Smyth's dogma: *open sets are semidecidable properties* [13]. Topological systems subsume both topological spaces and locales. A topological system includes a frame of "opens", a set of "points" and a "satisfaction" relation between points and opens. Topological system morphisms satisfy the constraint $x \Vdash_D \Omega h(a')$ iff $\mathrm{pt}\, h(x) \Vdash_{D'} a'$ that is strongly reminiscent of the satisfaction condition of institutions.

If we identify the "opens" with formulae we are dealing with geometric logic, as discussed in [14, 15]. But there is an obvious alternative that we explore in this paper: if we restrict our attention to "semidecidable properties" then theories are the opens! Therefore, by working with topological systems we find a structure where we can deal with theories that are not necessarily built from formulae. That is, we are able to deal in this way with *theories as first class citizens.*

Finitary topological institutions promise to be useful in monitoring and querying. We examine herein how to set up a weak version of a temporal logic suitable for monitoring. In database monitoring applications [8] we would like to be able to characterize the properties of the system that can be monitored. Namely, an invariant property ($\mathbf{G}\varphi$) cannot be monitored because it cannot be positively established in finite time. On the contrary, a reactivity property ($\mathbf{F}\varphi$) can be positively established in finite time. Herein, we set up the envisaged logic as a finitary topological institution.

After introducing the concept of topological institution in Section 2 we characterize the relationship between theories and models and we proceed to recover the results on colimits of theories. In Section 3 we start by showing how to extract a topological institution out of an institution and establish an adjunction between the categories of topological institutions and institutions. In Section 4 we consider how to present topological institutions and show how deductive systems can be used to this end. We also examine possible applications of topological institutions with finitely observable theories, namely to temporal monitoring. The proofs omitted herein and further material can be found in [12].

2 Topological institutions

2.1 Topological systems

The interested reader should consult [6, 14] for a full development of the theory of frames, locales and topological spaces. Herein we follow the approach in [14], namely with respect to the introduction of the notion of topological system and starting from there. The main component of a topological system is its frame of "opens". Hence it is worthwhile to recall that a *frame* is a poset $F = \langle |F|, \leq_F \rangle$ such that each subset $S \subseteq |F|$ has a join $\bigvee S$, and binary meets distribute over joins: $a \wedge \bigvee S = \bigvee \{a \wedge s : s \in S\}$. In the sequel we use the two-element frame **2** with elements **t** and **f** such that $\mathbf{f} \leq_{\mathbf{2}} \mathbf{t}$. A *frame morphism* $h : F \to F'$ is a map from $|F|$ into $|F'|$ preserving all joins and finite meets (thus, a monotone map). Frames and their morphisms constitute a category that we denote by *Fr*. We are now ready to bring in the notion proposed by Vickers:

Definition 1. A *topological system* D is a triple $\langle \mathrm{pt}\, D, \Omega\, D, \Vdash_D \rangle$ where:

- $\mathrm{pt}\, D$ is a set;
- $\Omega\, D$ is a frame;
- $\Vdash_D \subseteq \mathrm{pt}\, D \times \Omega\, D$ such that[3]:
  - for any $S \subseteq \Omega\, D$, $x \Vdash_D \bigvee S$ iff $x \Vdash_D a$ for some $a \in S$;
  - for any finite $S \subseteq \Omega\, D$, $x \Vdash_D \bigwedge S$ iff $x \Vdash_D a$ for every $a \in S$.

The elements of $\mathrm{pt}\, D$ are called *points*. The elements of $\Omega\, D$ are called *opens*. The relation $\Vdash_D$ is named *satisfaction relation*. Note that the last property on $\Vdash$ leads to monotonicity: if $x \Vdash_D a$ and $a \leq_{\Omega\, D} b$ then $x \Vdash_D b$.

Definition 2. A *topological system morphism* $h : D \to D'$ is a pair $\langle \mathrm{pt}\, h, \Omega\, h \rangle$ where:

- $\mathrm{pt}\, h : \mathrm{pt}\, D \to \mathrm{pt}\, D'$ is a map;
- $\Omega\, h : \Omega\, D' \to \Omega\, D$ is a frame morphism such that $x \Vdash_D \Omega\, h(a')$ iff $\mathrm{pt}\, h(x) \Vdash_{D'} a'$ for every $x \in \mathrm{pt}\, D$ and $a' \in \Omega\, D'$.

By looking at points as "models" and at opens as "formulae", the condition will remind the reader familiar with the notion of institution [4, 5] of the satisfaction condition. Topological systems and their morphisms constitute a category that we denote by TSy. Topological systems with frame F establish a full subcategory TSy_F of TSy.

We now proceed to identify topological spaces among topological systems, following the idea in [14]. A topological space is a special topological system where the opens are subsets of points. And there is a canonical construction for building a topological space out of any given topological system. As we shall see, this construction helps in the characterization of the relationship between properties and models.

A *topological space* X is a topological system $\langle \mathrm{pt}\, X \Omega\, X, \Vdash_X \rangle$ such that there is an inclusion frame morphism $\Omega\, X \hookrightarrow \wp \mathrm{pt}\, X$[4], and $\Vdash_X$ is set membership ($x \Vdash_X a$ iff $x \in a$). Topological spaces constitute a full subcategory of TSy that we denote by TSp[5]. Note that for a topological space morphism $h : X \to X'$ we have that $\Omega\, h = (\mathrm{pt}\, h)^{-1}$. We denote by $IncSp$ the inclusion functor $TSp \hookrightarrow TSy$.

[3] We write $x \Vdash_D a$ instead of $\langle x, a \rangle \in \Vdash_D$ saying that x *satisfies* a.

[4] That is, unions of opens are open and finite intersections of opens are open. Clearly, an infinite meet of opens (still open) may not coincide with the corresponding intersection.

[5] The category TSp is isomorphic to the traditional category Top of topological spaces and continuous maps not presented as special cases of topological systems and their morphisms.

Definition 3. A topological system is said to be *spatial* iff it is isomorphic to a topological space.

Definition 4. Let D be a topological system and $a \in \Omega D$. The *extension* of a is the set $ext(a) = \{x \in \mathrm{pt}\, D : x \Vdash_D a\}$.

Clearly, if we consider points to be interpretation structures and opens to be properties then the extension of a is the set of models of a.

Definition 5. Given a topological system D we define its *spatialization* Spat$D$ as the topological space such that:

- pt Spat$D$ = pt D;
- $\Omega\, \mathrm{Spat}D = \langle \{ext(a) : a \in \Omega\, D\}, \subseteq \rangle$.

It is easy to verify that we do obtain a frame with the inclusion ordering on the extensions. Moreover, we have soundness: if $a \leq_{\Omega\, D} a'$ then $ext(a) \subseteq ext(a')$.

Definition 6. Given a topological system D, its *TSp-coreflection* is the topological system morphism $e : \mathrm{Spat}D \rightarrow D$ defined as follows:

- $\mathrm{pt}\, e(x) = x$;
- $\Omega\, e(a) = ext(a)$.

This terminology is justified by the following result [12]:

Theorem 7. TSp is a coreflective subcategory of TSy.

It follows that a topological system D is spatial iff its *TSp-coreflection* is iso iff for every $a, a' \in \Omega\, D$ if $ext(a) \subseteq ext(a')$ then $a \leq_{\Omega\, D} a'$. That is, we have completeness iff the topological system is spatial. Using the universal property of the coreflections, it is straightforward to verify that the spatialization construction extends to a functor *Spat* : $TSy \rightarrow TSp$. Furthermore, *Spat* is right adjoint to *IncSp*.

2.2 Basic concept and theories

As envisaged, we want for each signature a topological system with the theories, the interpretation structures and the satisfaction relation for that signature. Therefore:

Definition 8. A *topological institution* T is a pair $\langle \mathrm{sg}T, \mathrm{sy}T \rangle$ where

- sg$T$ is a category (of signatures);
- sy$T$: sg$T \rightarrow TSy^{op}$ is a functor.

The opens in $\Omega\, \mathrm{sy}T(\Sigma)$ are called *theories over the signature* Σ, the points in pt sy$T(\Sigma)$ are called *interpretation structures* over Σ and $\Vdash_{\mathrm{sy}T(\Sigma)}$ the *satisfaction relation* over Σ. In the sequel T will always denote a topological institution.

Definition 9. A topological institution T is *spatial* iff, for each signature Σ, the topological system sy$T(\Sigma)$ is spatial.

Definition 10. A *topological institution morphism* $\tau : T \to T'$ is a pair $\langle \mathrm{sg}\tau, \mathrm{sy}\tau \rangle$ where

- $\mathrm{sg}\tau : \mathrm{sg}T \to \mathrm{sg}T'$ is functor;
- $\mathrm{sy}\tau : \mathrm{sy}T \to \mathrm{sg}\tau; \mathrm{sy}T'$ is a natural transformation.

Topological institutions and their morphisms constitute a category: TIn. It is interesting to explore the spatialization construction for topological institutions, but we refrain herein to establish the resulting coreflection.

Definition 11. The *model topological institution* $\mathrm{Mod}T$ induced by T is as follows:

- $\mathrm{sgMod}T = \mathrm{sg}T$;
- $\mathrm{syMod}T$ is such that:
  - $\mathrm{syMod}T(\Sigma) = \mathrm{Spatsy}T(\Sigma)$;
  - $\mathrm{syMod}T(\sigma) : \mathrm{syMod}T(\Sigma') \to \mathrm{syMod}T(\Sigma)$ is the unique morphism in TSy such that $e'; \mathrm{sy}T(\sigma) = \mathrm{syMod}T(\sigma); e$ where e and e' are the TSp-coreflection morphisms for $\mathrm{sy}T_\Sigma$ and $\mathrm{sy}T_{\Sigma'}$ respectively.

Note that the morphism $\mathrm{syMod}T(\sigma)$ is unique because of the universal property of the coreflection e. Each theory th of $\mathrm{sy}T(\Sigma)$ is replaced in $\mathrm{syMod}T(\Sigma)$ by the set of interpretation structures $ext(th)$ that satisfy th. Therefore, if T is spatial then we have for each Σ: $th \leq_{\mathrm{sy}T(\Sigma)} th'$ iff $ext(th) \subseteq ext(th')$.

We now look at the "flat" category of theories in T. As expected, we recover the result that (finite) colimits of signatures can be lifted to (finite) colimits of theories.

Definition 12. A *theory* is a pair $th = \langle \Sigma, a \rangle$ where $\Sigma \in |\mathrm{sg}T|$ and $a \in \Omega\,\mathrm{sy}T(\Sigma)$.

Definition 13. Let $th = \langle \Sigma, a \rangle$ and $th' = \langle \Sigma', a' \rangle$ be theories. A *morphism* from th into th' is a signature morphism $\sigma : \Sigma \to \Sigma'$ such that $a' \leq_{\Omega\,\mathrm{syT}(\Sigma')} \Omega\,\mathrm{sy}T(\sigma)(a)$.

Theories and theory morphisms constitute a category: Th_T. Furthermore, assuming that $Sg : Th_T \to \mathrm{sg}T$ is the functor mapping theories and theory morphisms into their signatures and signature morphisms, $\langle Th_T, Sg \rangle$ is a concrete category over $\mathrm{sg}T$. It is straightforward to establish [12]:

Theorem 14. If sgT *has finite colimits so does* Th_T.

We consider for instance how coproducts are lifted. Let $th = \langle \Sigma, a \rangle$ and $th' = \langle \Sigma', a' \rangle$ be theories and $\langle \Sigma + \Sigma', inj_\Sigma, inj_{\Sigma'} \rangle$ be "the" coproduct in $\mathrm{sg}T$ of Σ and Σ'. Then, the triple $\langle th + th', inj_\Sigma, inj_{\Sigma'} \rangle$ where $th + th' = \langle \Sigma + \Sigma', \Omega\,\mathrm{syT}(inj_\Sigma)(a) \wedge \Omega\,\mathrm{syT}(inj_{\Sigma'})(a') \rangle$ is "the" coproduct in Th_T of th and th'.

3 Institutions versus topological institutions

Before we can show how to extract a topological institution from any given institution, we need to see how to complete a meet-semilattice, while respecting (some of) the existing joins, in order to obtain a frame, using Johnstone's technique of coverages [6].

3.1 Ideal completion

We proceed to review Johnstone's technique, characterizing the envisaged universal property (of the canonical construction) as a reflection. To this end, we introduce the category of sites and its subcategory of frame sites.

Definition 15. A *site* Y is a pair $\langle \text{ms}Y, \text{cv}Y \rangle$ where:

- $\text{ms}Y$ is a meet-semilattice, that is, a poset $\langle |\text{ms}Y|, \leq_{\text{ms}Y} \rangle$ such that every finite subset $S \subseteq |\text{ms}Y|$ has a meet;
- $\text{cv}Y$ is *coverage* on $\text{ms}Y$, that is, a map $\text{cv}Y : |\text{ms}Y| \to \wp\wp|\text{ms}Y|$ such that:
  - $\text{cv}Y(a) \subseteq \wp{\downarrow}(a)$[6];
  - for every $a' \leq a$, if $S \in \text{cv}Y(a)$ then $\{s \wedge a' : s \in S\} \in \text{cv}Y(a')$.

Definition 16. A *site morphism* $h : Y \to Y'$ is a meet-semilattice morphism from $\text{ms}Y$ into $\text{ms}Y'$[7] such that if $S \in \text{cv}Y(a)$ then $h(S) \in \text{cv}Y'(h(a))$.

Sites and their morphisms constitute a category that we denote by *Sit*. Some sites correspond to frames as we proceed to explain.

Definition 17. A *frame site* is a site $Y = \langle \text{ms}Y, \text{cv}Y \rangle$ such that $\text{ms}Y$ is a frame, and $S \in \text{cv}Y(a)$ iff $a = \bigvee S$.

We denote by *FrSit* the full subcategory of *Sit* whose objects are the frame sites. We denote by *IncFr* the inclusion functor *FrSit* $\hookrightarrow$ *Sit*. Clearly, the category *FrSit* is isomorphic to *Fr*. We now show how to extract a canonical frame site from any given site by ideal completion.

Definition 18. A *Y-ideal* is a lower closed[8] subset I of $|\text{ms}Y|$ such that, for every $a \in |\text{ms}Y|$ and $S \in \text{cv}Y(a)$, if $S \subseteq I$ then $a \in I$.

Definition 19. Given a site Y, the pair $\text{Idl}Y = \langle \{I : I \text{ is a } Y\text{-ideal}\}, \subseteq \rangle$ is a frame called the *ideal completion* of Y.

We denote by $\text{SIdl}Y$ the corresponding frame site.

Definition 20. Given a site Y, its *FrSit-reflection* is the site morphism $q : Y \to \text{SIdl}Y$ induced by the map from $|\text{ms}Y|$ into $|\text{msSIdl}Y|$ defined as follows:

- $q(a) = \bigcap\{I \in |\text{msSIdl}Y| : a \in I\}$.

It is necessary to verify that the indicated map does induce a site morphism. That is to say, it should preserve finite meets and the coverage[9]. The reflection name is justified by the following result [12]:

Theorem 21. FrSit is a reflective subcategory of Sit.

Using the universal property of reflections, it is straightforward to verify that the ideal completion construction extends to a functor *Idl* : *Sit* $\to$ *FrSit*. Furthermore, *Idl* is left adjoint to *IncFr*.

---

[6] ${\downarrow}(a)$ denotes as usual the set $\{a' : a' \leq a\}$

[7] A map from $|\text{ms}Y|$ into $|\text{ms}Y'|$ preserving finite meets.

[8] If $a' \leq a$ and $a \in I$ then $a' \in I$.

[9] It should transform covers to joins.

3.2 Institutions induce topological institutions

Given a signature Σ in some institution, the idea is to establish a topological system where the opens are the theories over Σ, the points are the interpretation structures over Σ and the satisfaction relation is as given for Σ. However, this naive workplan has to be refined, mainly because satisfaction does not always respect joins of theories as required in topological systems. In the sequel I will always denote an elementary institution $\langle Sig_I, Sen_I, Int_I, \Vdash_I \rangle$[10].

If $\Phi \subseteq Sen_I(\Sigma)$ and $\psi \in Sen_I(\Sigma)$ then we say that Φ *semantically entails* ψ, written $\Phi \vDash_{I_\Sigma} \psi$, iff, for every $x \in Int_I(\Sigma)$, if $x \Vdash_{I_\Sigma} \varphi$ for every $\varphi \in \Phi$ then $x \Vdash_{I_\Sigma} \psi$. We denote by $\Phi^{\vDash_{I_\Sigma}}$ the set $\{\psi \in Sen_I(\Sigma) : \Phi \vDash_{I_\Sigma} \psi\}$ of formulae semantically entailed by Φ. We denote the class of all theories by $|Th_I|$ and, for each signature Σ, the class of all theories over Σ by $|Th_{I_\Sigma}|$. We say that $x \in Int(\Sigma)$ satisfies a theory $th = \langle \Sigma, \Phi \rangle$, indicated by $x \Vdash_{I_\Sigma} th$ or $x \Vdash_{I_\Sigma} \Phi$, iff $x \Vdash_{I_\Sigma} \varphi$ for all $\varphi \in \Phi$. Clearly:

Proposition 22. *Consider the binary relation $\leq_{I_\Sigma}$ in $|Th_{I_\Sigma}|$ such that $\langle \Sigma, \Phi_1 \rangle \leq_{I_\Sigma} \langle \Sigma, \Phi_2 \rangle$ iff $\Phi_1 \vDash_{I_\Sigma} \Phi_2$. The pair $Th^{op}_{I_\Sigma} = \langle |Th_{I_\Sigma}|, \leq_{I_\Sigma} \rangle$ is a complete lattice.*

For each $S \subseteq |Th_{I_\Sigma}|$, $\bigvee S = \bigcap S$ and $\bigwedge S = (\bigcup S)^{\vDash_{I_\Sigma}}$. The bottom theory is $\langle \Sigma, Sen_I(\Sigma) \rangle$ and the top theory is $\langle \Sigma, \emptyset^{\vDash_{I_\Sigma}} \rangle$. We use the *op* notation since $th_1 \leq_{I_\Sigma} th_2$ iff the set of formulae of th_2 is included in the set of formulae of th_1.

Note that, in general $\langle Int_I(\Sigma), Th^{op}_{I_\Sigma}, \Vdash_{I_\Sigma} \rangle$ is not a topological system. Indeed, we do not know if we do have a frame (distributivity?) and whether every join is respected by the satisfaction relation: $x \Vdash_{I_\Sigma} \bigvee S$ iff $x \Vdash_{I_\Sigma} s$ for some $s \in S$. Therefore, we proceed to complete (using the coverage technique) the meet-semilattice of theories while preserving only the joins that are respected by the satisfaction relation. Afterwards, we extend the satisfaction relation to the new theories.

Definition 23. A set $S \subseteq |Th^{op}_{I_\Sigma}|$ is said to be *join-acceptable* by $\Vdash_{I_\Sigma}$ iff the following condition holds: $x \Vdash_{I_\Sigma} \bigvee S$ iff $x \Vdash_{I_\Sigma} th$ for some $th \in S$.

Example 1. Let EqI be the equational elementary institution. A non-empty $S \subseteq |Th^{op}_{EqI_\Sigma}|$ is join-acceptable iff S has a maximum theory.

The following result [12] shows how to set up a site with the theories of the institution at hand:

Proposition 24. *Let $\mathrm{cv}_{I_\Sigma} : Th^{op}_{I_\Sigma} \to \wp\wp Th^{op}_{I_\Sigma}$ be as follows: for each theory th, $S \in \mathrm{cv}_{I_\Sigma}(th)$ iff $\bigvee S = th$ and S is join-acceptable. Then, the pair $Y_{I_\Sigma} = \langle Th^{op}_{I_\Sigma}, \mathrm{cv}_{I_\Sigma} \rangle$ is a site and the FrSit-reflection $q_{I_\Sigma} : Y_{I_\Sigma} \to SIdlY_{I_\Sigma}$ is injective.*

Example 2. In the simple case of EqI, for each theory $\langle \Sigma, E \rangle$ we have:

- $\mathrm{cv}_{EqI_\Sigma}(\langle \Sigma, E \rangle) = \{S \subseteq |Th^{op}_{EqI_\Sigma}| : max(S) = \langle \Sigma, E \rangle\}$;
- $q_{EqI_\Sigma}(\langle \Sigma, E \rangle) = \{\langle \Sigma, E' \rangle \in |Th^{op}_{EqI_\Sigma}| : E' \vDash_{EqI_\Sigma} E\}$

For more complex examples see [12] namely the case of propositional logic.

[10] By "elementary" (or pre-institution as it is called in [10]) we mean that the functor Int_I goes into Set^{op}.

Definition 25. The *frame of theories* induced by a given elementary institution I is $\overline{Th}^{op}_{I_\Sigma} = IdlY_{I_\Sigma}$.

Example 3. In $\overline{Th}^{op}_{EqI_\Sigma}$ we find a new theory for each set $S \subseteq |Th^{op}_{EqI_\Sigma}|$ that is not join-acceptable. For instance, consider the set $\{\langle\Sigma, E_1\rangle, \langle\Sigma, E_2\rangle\}$ of equational theories such that $E_1 \not\models_{EqI_\Sigma} E_2$ and $E_2 \not\models_{EqI_\Sigma} E_1$. Then, we get the new theory $\bigvee\{q_{EqI_\Sigma}(\langle\Sigma, E_1\rangle), q_{EqI_\Sigma}(\langle\Sigma, E_2\rangle)\}$ in $\overline{Th}^{op}_{EqI_\Sigma}$ that appears below the theory $q_{EqI_\Sigma}(\langle\Sigma, E_1 \cap E_2\rangle)$.

In short, in order to set up a topological system for each signature of an institution, we start by identifying the join-acceptable sets of theories. These sets are then reflected in the coverage used for the ideal completion of the meet-semilattice of theories. It remains to be seen that it is possible to extend the satisfaction relation to the new theories while ensuring that all joins are respected by satisfaction.

But before we proceed with this extension note that the ideal completion adds only the necessary joins besides the acceptable ones: "no junk". Also, all existing theories are preserved as different from each other: "no confusion".

Lemma 26. *For each $\Sigma \in |Sig_I|$ and $x \in Int_I(\Sigma)$ let $sat^x_{I_\Sigma} : Th^{op}_{I_\Sigma} \to 2$ be the meet-semilattice morphism defined as follows: $sat^x_{I_\Sigma} = \lambda th.$ if $x \Vdash_{I_\Sigma} th$ then **t** else **f**. Let S2 be the frame site corresponding to the frame 2. Then, $sat^x_{I_\Sigma} : Y_{I_\Sigma} \to$ S2 is a site morphism.*

Proposition 27. *Let $\overline{sat}^x_{I_\Sigma} : \overline{Th}^{op}_{I_\Sigma} \to$ S2 be the unique frame (site) morphism such that $q_{I_\Sigma}; \overline{sat}^x_{I_\Sigma} = sat^x_{I_\Sigma}$. For each $ith \in |\overline{Th}^{op}_{I_\Sigma}|$ let $x \Vdash_{I_\Sigma} ith$ iff $\overline{sat}^x_{I_\Sigma}(ith) = \mathsf{t}$. Then, the triple $D_{I_\Sigma} = \langle Int_I(\Sigma), \overline{Th}^{op}_{I_\Sigma}, \Vdash_{I_\Sigma}\rangle$ is a spatial topological system.*

Proof. Assume without loss of generality that $ith = \bigvee q_{I_\Sigma}(S)$. Then $x \Vdash_{I_\Sigma} ith$ iff $\overline{sat}^x_{I_\Sigma}(ith) = \mathsf{t}$ iff $\bigvee_{s\in S} \overline{sat}^x_{I_\Sigma}(q_{I_\Sigma}(s)) = \mathsf{t}$ iff $\overline{sat}^x_{I_\Sigma}(q_{I_\Sigma}(s)) = \mathsf{t}$ for some $s \in S$ iff $x \Vdash_{I_\Sigma} q_{I_\Sigma}(s)$ for some $s \in S$. A similar reasoning applies to finite meets.

Let $ith \models_{I_\Sigma} ith'$ iff for every $x \in Int_I(\Sigma)$ if $x \Vdash_{I_\Sigma} ith$ then $x \Vdash_{I_\Sigma} ith'$ (or in other words $ext(ith) \subseteq ext(ith')$). Assume without loss of generality that $ith = \bigvee\{q_{I_\Sigma}(s) : s \in S\}$ and $ith' = \bigvee\{q_{I_\Sigma}(s') : s' \in S'\}$. For every $x \in Int_I(\Sigma)$ if $\overline{sat}^x_{I_\Sigma}(q_{I_\Sigma}(s)) = \mathsf{t}$ then $\overline{sat}^x_{I_\Sigma}(q_{I_\Sigma}(s')) = \mathsf{t}$ for some $s' \in S'$. Moreover, for every $x \in Int_I(\Sigma)$ if $sat^x_{I_\Sigma}(s) = \mathsf{t}$ then $sat^x_{I_\Sigma}(s') = \mathsf{t}$ for some $s' \in S'$. Hence $s \models_{I_\Sigma} \bigvee S'$ for every $s \in S$ and so $\bigvee S \leq_{I_\Sigma} \bigvee S'$. For every $r' \subset q_{I_\Sigma}(\bigvee S')$ we have $r' \subseteq ith'$ and so, in particular, $q_{I_\Sigma}(s) \subseteq ith'$ for every $s \in S$. Moreover, $ith \subseteq ith'$. □

The spatiality of the resulting topological system (for each signature) is only to be expected since theories are semantically defined in institutions. In order to obtain the induced topological institution, it remains to check that each signature morphism produces a topological system morphism (the proofs that can be found in [12]).

Lemma 28. *For each signature morphism $\sigma : \Sigma \to \Sigma'$, let $\Omega h_{I_\sigma} : |Y_{I_\Sigma}| \to |Y_{I_{\Sigma'}}|$ be such that $\Omega h_{I_\sigma}(\langle\Sigma, \Phi\rangle) = \langle\Sigma', \{Sen_I(\sigma)(\varphi) : \varphi \in \Phi\}^{\models_{I_{\Sigma'}}}\rangle$. Then, $\Omega h_{I_\sigma} : Y_{I_\Sigma} \to Y_{I_{\Sigma'}}$ is a site morphism.*

Proposition 29. *Let* $\overline{\Omega h_{I_\sigma}} : \overline{Th}^{op}_{I_\Sigma} \to \overline{Th}^{op}_{I_{\Sigma'}}$ *be the unique frame (site) morphism such that* $q_{I_\Sigma}; \overline{\Omega h_{I_\sigma}} = \Omega h_{I_\sigma}; q_{I_{\Sigma'}}$. *Let* $\mathrm{pt}\, h_{I_\sigma} : Int_I(\Sigma') \to Int_I(\Sigma)$ *be such that* $\mathrm{pt}\, h_{I_\sigma}(x') = Int_I(\sigma)(x')$. *Then the pair* $h_{I_\sigma} = \langle \mathrm{pt}\, h_{I_\sigma}, \overline{\Omega h_{I_\sigma}} \rangle : D_{I_{\Sigma'}} \to D_{I_\Sigma}$ *is a topological system morphism.*

Theorem 30. *Every institution* I *induces the topological institution* $Top(I)$ *such that:*

- $\mathrm{sg}Top(I) = Sig_I$;
- $\mathrm{sy}Top(I)(\Sigma) = D_{I_\Sigma}$;
- $\mathrm{sy}Top(I)(\sigma) = h_{I_\sigma}$.

We denote by EqT the topological institution $Top(EqI)$.

3.3 Adjunction

We conclude this section by showing that the map $I \mapsto Top(I)$ can be extended to a functor with a left adjoint. We adopt the definition of institution morphism given in [5] and denote the category of institutions by In.

Note that for every institution morphism $m : I \to I'$ and signature Σ in Sig_I, the map $m_{\alpha_\Sigma} : Sen_{I'}(m_s(\Sigma)) \to Sen_I(\Sigma)$ can be extended to $m_{\alpha_\Sigma} : Th_{I'_{m_s(\Sigma)}} \to Th_{I_\Sigma}$ as follows: $m_{\alpha_\Sigma}(\langle m_s(\Sigma), \Phi' \rangle) = \langle \Sigma, \{m_{\alpha_\Sigma}(\varphi') : \varphi' \in \Phi'\}^{\models_{I_\Sigma}} \rangle$. Furthermore, consider the site $Y_{I_\Sigma} = \langle Th^{op}_{I_\Sigma}, cv_{I_\Sigma} \rangle$ where $cv_{I_\Sigma}(m_{\alpha_\Sigma}(th')) = \{m_{\alpha_\Sigma}(S') : S' \in cv_{I'_{m_s(\Sigma)}}(th')\}$. Then, m_{α_Σ} is a site morphism.

Lemma 31. *Every institution morphism* $m : I \to I'$ *induces a topological institution morphism* $Top(m) : Top(I) \to Top(I')$ *defined as follows:*

- $\mathrm{sg}Top(m) = m_s$;
- $\mathrm{pt}\ \mathrm{sy}Top(m)_\Sigma = m_{\beta_\Sigma}$;
- $\Omega\, \mathrm{sy}Top(m)_\Sigma$ *is the unique* $\overline{m}_{\alpha_\Sigma}$ *such that* $q_{I'_{\mathrm{sg}Top(\Sigma)}}; \overline{m}_{\alpha_\Sigma} = m_{\alpha_\Sigma}; q_{I_\Sigma}$.

So in order to get a topological institution out of an institution we have to set up the frame of theories, by selecting the appropriate coverage and then making the ideal completion as we did in subsection 3.2, and then to extend the satisfaction relation to this frame. We have thus established the envisaged functor $Top : In \to TIn$. Conversely:

Lemma 32. *Every topological institution* T *induces the institution* $Geo(T)$ *such that:*

- $Sig_{Geo(T)} = \mathrm{sg}T$;
- $Sen_{Geo(T)}(\Sigma) = |\Omega\, \mathrm{sy}T(\Sigma)|$ *and* $Sen_{Geo(T)}(\sigma) = \Omega\, \mathrm{sy}T(\sigma)$;
- $Int_{Geo(T)}(\Sigma) = \mathrm{pt}\ \mathrm{sy}T(\Sigma)$ *and* $Int_{Geo(T)}(\sigma) = \mathrm{pt}\ \mathrm{sy}T(\sigma)$;
- $\Vdash_{Geo(T)} = \Vdash_T$.

The main step for getting an institution out of a topological institution is to recognize that each open will be a formula. All the other components are then straightforward.

Lemma 33. *Every topological institution morphism $\tau : T \rightarrow T'$ induces an institution morphism $Geo(\tau) : Geo(T) \rightarrow Geo(T')$ defined as follows:*

- $Geo(\tau)_s = \mathrm{sg}\tau$;
- $Geo(\tau)_{\alpha_\Sigma} = \Omega\,\mathrm{sy}\tau_\Sigma$;
- $Geo(\tau)_{\beta_\Sigma} = \mathrm{pt}\ \mathrm{sy}\tau_\Sigma$.

We have thus established the functor $Geo : TIn \rightarrow In$. Finally:

Theorem 34. *Geo is left adjoint to Top.*

Proof. The counit $\epsilon : Top; Geo \rightarrow id_{In}$ is as follows: for each institution I, $\epsilon_{I_s} = id_{Sig_I}$; $\epsilon_{I_{\alpha_\Sigma}}(\varphi) = q_{I_\Sigma}(\langle \Sigma, \{\varphi\}^{\models_{I_\Sigma}} \rangle)$; $\epsilon_{I_\beta} = id_{Int_I}$. Indeed, given a topological institution T and an institution morphism $m : Geo(T) \rightarrow I$, we show that there is a unique topological institution morphism $\tau : T \rightarrow Top(I)$ such that $Geo(\tau); \epsilon_I = m$. (1) Consider the map $h_\Sigma : |Th^{op}_{Geo(T)_\Sigma}| \rightarrow |\Omega\,\mathrm{sy}T(\Sigma)|$ such that $h_\Sigma(\langle \Sigma, A \rangle) = \bigwedge A$. We show that h_Σ is a site morphism. We have that h_Σ is a meet-semilattice morphism. We verify that h_Σ preserves the coverage. Let $m_{\alpha_\Sigma}(S) \in cv_{Geo(T)_\Sigma}(m_{\alpha_\Sigma}(th))$. Then, $m_{\alpha_\Sigma}(s) \leq_{Th^{op}_{Geo(T)_\Sigma}} m_{\alpha_\Sigma}(th)$ for every $s \in S$. Therefore, the set of formulae of $m_{\alpha_\Sigma}(th)$ is included in the set of formulae of $m_{\alpha_\Sigma}(s)$ for every $s \in S$. Hence, $h_\Sigma(m_{\alpha_\Sigma}(s)) \leq_{\Omega\,\mathrm{sy}T(\Sigma)} h_\Sigma(m_{\alpha_\Sigma}(th))$ for every $s \in S$ and so $m_{\alpha_\Sigma}(th)$ is an upper bound of $m_{\alpha_\Sigma}(S)$. Assume that there is $a' \in \Omega\,\mathrm{sy}T(\Sigma)$ such that $h_\Sigma(m_{\alpha_\Sigma}(s)) \leq_{\Omega\,\mathrm{sy}T(\Sigma)} a'$ for every $s \in S$ and $a' \leq_{\Omega\,\mathrm{sy}T(\Sigma)} h_\Sigma(m_{\alpha_\Sigma}(th))$. Assume that $x \Vdash_{Geo(T)_\Sigma} m_{\alpha_\Sigma}(s)$. Then, $x \Vdash_{\mathrm{sy}T(\Sigma)} h_\Sigma(m_{\alpha_\Sigma}(s))$, $x \Vdash_{\mathrm{sy}T(\Sigma)} a'$ and so $x \Vdash_{Geo(T)_\Sigma} \langle \Sigma, \{a'\}^{\models_{Geo(T)_\Sigma}} \rangle$. Hence, $m_{\alpha_\Sigma}(s) \leq_{Geo(T)_\Sigma} \langle \Sigma, \{a'\}^{\models_{Geo(T)_\Sigma}} \rangle$. Similarly, $\langle \Sigma, \{a'\}^{\models_{Geo(T)_\Sigma}} \rangle \leq_{Geo(T)_\Sigma} m_{\alpha_\Sigma}(th)$. So $m_{\alpha_\Sigma}(th)$ would not be the join of $m_{\alpha_\Sigma}(S)$. Therefore, h_Σ is a site morphism.

(2) Consider the pair $\mathrm{sy}\tau_\Sigma = \langle m_{\beta_\Sigma}, \Omega\,\mathrm{sy}\tau_\Sigma \rangle$ where $\Omega\,\mathrm{sy}\tau_\Sigma$ is the unique frame (site) morphism such that $q_{I_{m_s(\Sigma)}}; \Omega\,\mathrm{sy}\tau_\Sigma = m_{\alpha_\Sigma}; h_\Sigma$. We show that $\mathrm{sy}\tau_\Sigma$ is a topological system morphism: $x \Vdash_{\mathrm{sy}T(\Sigma)} \bigvee \Omega\,\mathrm{sy}\tau_\Sigma(q_{I_{m_s(\Sigma)}}(S))$ iff $x \Vdash_{\mathrm{sy}T(\Sigma)} h_\Sigma(m_{\alpha_\Sigma}(s))$ for some $s \in S$ iff $x \Vdash_{\mathrm{sy}T(\Sigma)} \bigwedge\{a : a \in m_{\alpha_\Sigma}(s)\}$ for some $s \in S$ iff $x \Vdash_{Geo(T)_\Sigma} \langle \Sigma, \{m_{\alpha_\Sigma}(\varphi) : \varphi \in s\}^{\models_{Geo(T)_\Sigma}} \rangle$ for some $s \in S$ iff $m_{\beta_\Sigma}(x) \Vdash_{I_{m_s(\Sigma)}} s$ for some $s \in S$ iff $m_{\beta_\Sigma}(x) \Vdash_{\mathrm{sy}Top(I)_{m_s(\Sigma)}} q_{I_{m_s(\Sigma)}}(s)$ for some $s \in S$ iff $m_{\beta_\Sigma}(x) \Vdash_{\mathrm{sy}Top(I)_{m_s(\Sigma)}} \bigvee q_{I_{m_s(\Sigma)}}(S)$.

(3) We show that $Geo(\tau); \epsilon_I = m$. Let $A = \{m_{\alpha_\Sigma}(\psi) : \psi \in \{\varphi\}^{\models_{I_{m_s(\Sigma)}}}\}^{\models_{Geo(T)_\Sigma}}$. Then we have: $Geo(\tau)_{\alpha_\Sigma}(\epsilon_{I_{\alpha_{m_s(\Sigma)}}}(\varphi)) = Geo(\tau)_{\alpha_\Sigma}(q_{I_{m_s(\Sigma)}}(\langle m_s(\Sigma), \{\varphi\}^{\models_{I_{m_s(\Sigma)}}} \rangle)) = h_\Sigma(\langle \Sigma, A \rangle) = \bigwedge A = m_{\alpha_\Sigma}(\varphi)$. The equality of the other components is immediate. And it is straightforward to check that τ is the unique morphism fulfilling this condition. □

The sentence counterpart of the institution morphism ϵ_Σ for signature Σ assigns to each formula, for that signature, the ideal for the theory presented by that formula. The other components are just identities.

4 Presenting topological institutions

Although topological institutions provide the right level of abstraction for working with theories and their models, we do need a mechanism for presenting the envisaged frame of theories. As expected such a mechanism may involve formulae, axioms and inference rules. Actually, we introduce the notion of topological institution presentation directly based on the notion of frame presentation. And only afterwards we recognize how deductive systems can be used for presenting topological institutions.

4.1 Frame presentations

Frames can be presented as (uni-sorted) algebras as long as we accept operations of unbounded arity. But with such operations the general method of finding an initial model by setting up the algebra of congruence classes of terms fails because the class of all freely generated terms is a proper class. Fortunately, in the specific case of frames there is a solution using the coverage technique already described: first generate a meet-semilattice using the traditional congruence method; then find the suitable coverage and produce by ideal completion the envisaged frame; the resulting frame is canonical in the sense of having the universal property of a reflection. Besides reviewing the method as explained in [14], we introduce the notion of frame presentation morphism and show how it extends uniquely to a frame (site) morphism.

Definition 35. A *frame presentation* is a pair $pres = \langle \Sigma_{pres}, Req_{pres} \rangle$ where:

- the signature Σ_{pres} contains the following operation symbols:
  - t of arity 0,
  - $\wedge$ of arity 2,
  - $\bigvee$ of unbounded arity,
  - g of arity 0, for each $g \in G_{pres}$ (the set of proper symbols known as *generators*);
- Req_{pres} is a set (of equational *proper requirements*) such that:
  - each $e \in Req_{pres}$ is a pair $\langle e_1, e_2 \rangle$ where both e_1 and e_2 are of the form: $\bigvee\{\wedge_{i=1}^{n_k} g_{k_i} : k \in K\}$ where K is a set of indexes.

Each requirement $\langle e_1, e_2 \rangle$ is to be understood as stating that the left element e_1 is equal to the right element e_2. Note that any requirement of the form $y \leq z$ can be rewritten as $\langle y \wedge z, y \rangle$.

Definition 36. A frame presentation $pres = \langle \Sigma_{pres}, Req_{pres} \rangle$ is said to be *simple* iff in each requirement $\langle e_1, e_2 \rangle \in Req_{pres}$ the member e_2 is a generator.

Without loss of generality we may assume that we work only with simple frame presentations. Indeed, any frame presentation can be reduced to a simple frame presentation by enriching the set of generators with an additional element $z_{\langle e_1, e_2 \rangle}$ for each offending requirement $\langle e_1, e_2 \rangle$ and replacing it by the two following requirements: $\langle e_1, z_{\langle e_1, e_2 \rangle} \rangle$ and $\langle e_2, z_{\langle e_1, e_2 \rangle} \rangle$. From any frame presentation *pres*, we extract a meet-semilattice finitary equational presentation $mpres = \langle \Sigma_{mpres}, Req_{mpres} \rangle$, where Σ_{mpres} is Σ_{pres} minus $\bigvee$ and Req_{mpres} contains:

- the $\wedge$-laws: commutativity, associativity, idempotence and t-neutrality;
- the proper requirements: $g \wedge (\wedge_{i=1}^{n_k} g_{k_i}) = \wedge_{i=1}^{n_k} g_{k_i}$ for each $k \in K$ such that $\langle \bigvee\{\wedge_{i=1}^{n_k} g_{k_i} : k \in K\}, g \rangle$ is in Req_{pres}.

Definition 37. The meet-semilattice M_{pres} presented by *pres* is induced by the Σ_{mpres}-algebra T_{mpres} with $a \leq a'$ iff $a \wedge a' = a$.

The existence of the initial model T_{mpres} of m*pres* is a well known result of universal algebra extensively used in algebraic specification of abstract data types [1].

Definition 38. The map $\mathrm{pcv}_{pres} : |M_{pres}| \to \wp\wp|M_{pres}|$, called in the sequel the *precoverage* induced by *pres*, is established as follows. For each $a \in |M_{pres}|$, $\mathrm{pcv}_{pres}(a)$ is the least set satisfying $\{\wedge_{i=1}^{n_k} g_{k_i} : k \in K\} \in \mathrm{pcv}_{pres}(a)$ whenever $\langle \bigvee\{\wedge_{i=1}^{n_k} g_{k_i} : k \in K\}, a\rangle \in Req_{pres}$.

Theorem 39. The precoverage pcv_{pres} generates a coverage cv_{pres} on $|M_{pres}|$ as follows: for each $a \in |M_{pres}|$, $\mathrm{cv}_{pres}(a)$ is the least set satisfying $\{a' \wedge s : s \in S\} \in \mathrm{cv}_{pres}(a')$ whenever $a' \leq a$ and $S \in \mathrm{pcv}_{pres}(a)$. Therefore, $Y_{pres} = \langle M_{pres}, \mathrm{cv}_{pres}\rangle$ is a site.

Definition 40. The *frame presented* by *pres* is $F_{pres} = \mathrm{Idl}\langle M_{pres}, \mathrm{cv}_{pres}\rangle$.

We denote by FS_{pres} the frame site corresponding to the frame F_{pres} and by q_{pres} the $FrSit$-reflection for the site $\langle M_{pres}, \mathrm{cv}_{pres}\rangle$.

Definition 41. *A frame presentation morphism $h : pres \to pres'$ is a map $h : G_{pres} \to G_{pres'}$ such that if $\langle \bigvee\{\wedge_{i=1}^{n_k} g_{k_i} : k \in K\}, g\rangle \in Req_{pres}$ then $\langle \bigvee\{\wedge_{i=1}^{n_k} h(g_{k_i}) : k \in K\}, h(g)\rangle \in Req_{pres'}$.*

Frame presentations and their morphisms constitute a category: FrP. As expected, frame presentation morphisms induce morphisms between the presented frames [12]:

Theorem 42. A frame presentation morphism $h : pres \to pres'$ induces the site morphism $h^* : Y_{pres} \to Y_{pres'}$ defined as follows: $h^*([\bigwedge_{i=1}^{n} g_i]) = [\bigwedge_{i=1}^{n} h(g_i)]$. Then $\overline{h}^* : F_{pres} \to F_{pres'}$ is the unique frame (site) morphism such that $q_{pres}; \overline{h}^* = h^*; q_{pres'}$.

4.2 Deductive systems present topological institutions

Definition 43. A *topological institution presentation* U is a pair $\langle \mathrm{sg}U, \mathrm{fp}U\rangle$ where

- $\mathrm{sg}U$ is a category (of signatures);
- $\mathrm{fp}U : \mathrm{sg}U \to FrP$ is a functor.

Definition 44. A topological institution T is said to *comply* with a topological institution presentation U iff

- $\mathrm{sg}T = \mathrm{sg}U$;
- for each signature Σ, $\mathrm{sy}T(\Sigma) \in |TSy_{F_{\mathrm{fp}U(\Sigma)}}|$;
- for each signature morphism $\sigma : \Sigma \to \Sigma'$, $\Omega\,\mathrm{sy}T(\sigma) = \overline{\mathrm{fp}U(\sigma)}^*$.

Definition 45. A *deductive system* Δ is a quadruple $\langle \mathrm{sg}\Delta, \mathrm{sen}\Delta, \mathrm{ax}\Delta, \mathrm{ru}\Delta \rangle$ where

- $\mathrm{sg}\Delta$ is a category (of signatures);
- $\mathrm{sen}\Delta : \mathrm{sg}\Delta \to \mathit{Set}$ is a functor (the formula functor);
- $\mathrm{ax}\Delta = \{\mathrm{ax}\Delta_\Sigma\}_{\Sigma \in |\mathrm{sg}\Delta|}$ where:
  - $\mathrm{ax}\Delta_\Sigma \subseteq \mathrm{sen}\Delta(\Sigma)$;
  - $\mathrm{sen}\Delta(\sigma)(\alpha) \in \mathrm{ax}\Delta_{\Sigma'}$ for each $\sigma : \Sigma \to \Sigma'$ and $\alpha \in \mathrm{ax}\Delta_\Sigma$;
- $\mathrm{ru}\Delta = \{\mathrm{ru}\Delta_\Sigma\}_{\Sigma \in |\mathrm{sg}\Delta|}$ where[11]:
  - $\mathrm{ru}\Delta_\Sigma \subseteq \wp^f \mathrm{sen}\Delta(\Sigma) \times \mathrm{sen}\Delta(\Sigma)$;
  - $\langle \{\mathrm{sen}\Delta(\sigma)(\varphi) : \varphi \in p_\rho\}, \mathrm{sen}\Delta(\sigma)(c_\rho) \rangle \in \mathrm{ru}\Delta_{\Sigma'}$ for each $\sigma : \Sigma \to \Sigma'$ and $\rho = \langle p_\rho, c_\rho \rangle \in \mathrm{ru}\Delta_\Sigma$.

The elements in $\mathrm{ax}\Delta_\Sigma$ are called *axioms* over Σ and the elements in $\mathrm{ru}\Delta_\Sigma$ are called *inference rules* over Σ. For each $\rho \in \mathrm{ru}\Delta_\Sigma$ we say the elements in p_ρ are *premises* and that c_ρ is the *conclusion*.

Theorem 46. *Every deductive system Δ induces a topological institution presentation U_Δ as follows:*

- $\mathrm{sg}U_\Delta = \mathrm{sg}\Delta$;
- *for each signature Σ, $\mathrm{fp}U_\Delta(\Sigma)$ is the frame presentation $pres_{\Delta,\Sigma}$ such that*
  - $G_{pres_{\Delta,\Sigma}} = \mathrm{sen}\Delta(\Sigma)$;
  - $Req_{pres_{\Delta,\Sigma}}$ *contains:*
    - $\langle \alpha \wedge \varphi, \varphi \rangle$ *for each* $\alpha \in \mathrm{ax}\Delta_\Sigma, \varphi \in \mathrm{sen}\Delta(\Sigma)$;
    - $\langle (\wedge_{\varphi \in p_\rho} \varphi) \wedge c_\rho, (\wedge_{\varphi \in p_\rho} \varphi) \rangle$ *for each* $\rho \in \mathrm{ru}\Delta_\Sigma$;
- *for each signature morphism $\sigma : \Sigma \to \Sigma'$, $\mathrm{fp}U_\Delta(\sigma) = \mathrm{sen}\Delta(\sigma)$.*

In $M_{pres_{\Delta,\Sigma}}$ we have:

- $[\alpha] = [\alpha']$ for every $\alpha, \alpha' \in \mathrm{ax}\Delta_\Sigma$ meaning that the theories generated by the axioms are the same;
- $[(\wedge_{\varphi \in p_\rho} \varphi) \wedge c_\rho] = [(\wedge_{\varphi \in p_\rho} \varphi)]$ which leads to $[c_\rho] \subseteq [(\wedge_{\varphi \in p_\rho} \varphi)]$ meaning that the theory generated by the conclusion of an inference rule must be included in the theory generated by the premises of that rule.

We consider now an example of a "finitary" topological institution. This terminology arises from the fact that every theory is finitely observable provided that the generator theories are finitely observable.

Example 4. In the equational case, assume that we adopt the deductive system in [1], which we call $Eq\Delta$. Then, we would have the following requirements inter alia assuming a given equational signature Σ:

- $e = (t = t) \wedge e$ where e is any equation and t is any term;
- $(t = t') \wedge (o(t) = o(t')) = (t = t')$ where t, t' are terms of the same sort, say s and o is an operation symbol with argument sort s.

Therefore, in $M_{pres_{Eq\Delta,\Sigma}}$ we have:

[11] We denote by $\wp^f \mathrm{sen}\Delta(\Sigma)$ the set of all finite subsets of $\mathrm{sen}\Delta(\Sigma)$.

- $[e] = [(t = t) \wedge e]$ which leads to $[t = t] \subseteq [e]$ meaning that the theory generated by $(t = t)$ is included in the theory generated by e;
- $[(t = t') \wedge (o(t) = o(t'))] = [(t = t')]$ which leads to $[(o(t) = o(t'))] \subseteq [t = t']$ meaning that the theory generated by $(o(t) = o(t'))$ is included in the theory generated by $(t = t')$.

We denote by EqT^f the topological institution complying with the presentation $U_{EqΔ}$, and such that:

- pt sy$EqT^f(\Sigma)$ is the class of Σ-algebras;
- for each signature $\Sigma \in |\text{sg}EqT^f|$, the satisfaction relation $\Vdash_{\text{pt sy}EqT^f(\Sigma)}$ is as follows:

$$x \Vdash_{\text{pt sy}EqT^f(\Sigma)} ith \text{ iff } \overline{sat}_{\text{pt sy}EqT^f(\Sigma)}(ith) = \mathbf{t}$$

where $\overline{sat}_{\text{pt sy}EqT^f(\Sigma)}$ the unique frame (site) morphism extending the site morphism

$$sat_{\text{pt sy}EqT^f(\Sigma)} : Y_{\text{fp}U_{Eq\Delta}} \to S2$$

such that

$$sat_{\text{pt sy}EqT^f(\Sigma)} = \lambda th. \text{ if } x \Vdash_{\Sigma} th \text{ then } \mathbf{t} \text{ else } \mathbf{f}.$$

We should stress that when we extend the satisfaction to theories in the resulting frame (as we did in the example above) we make sure that satisfaction does respect joins while still respecting finite meets. However, in general, infinite meets will not be respected by the extended satisfaction.

4.3 Applications

Finitary topological institutions promise to be useful in monitoring and querying. We examine herein how to set up a weak version of a temporal logic suitable for monitoring. In database monitoring applications [8] we would like to be able to characterize the properties of the system that can be monitored. Namely, an invariant property $(\mathbf{G}\varphi)$ cannot be monitored because it cannot be positively established in finite time. On the contrary, a reactivity property $(\mathbf{F}\varphi)$ can be positively established in finite time.

Therefore, we set up the envisaged logic as a finitary topological institution as follows. We first adopt a propositional deductive system enriched with the next operator $\mathbf{X}$. To this end, we enrich the language (if φ is a formula so is $(\mathbf{X}\varphi)$) and accept the necessary axioms on $\mathbf{X}$ (such as $((\mathbf{X}(\varphi \Rightarrow \varphi')) \Rightarrow ((\mathbf{X}\varphi) \Rightarrow (\mathbf{X}\varphi'))))$. Let us call this deductive system $TM\Delta$. Then, we generate the topological institution presentation $U_{TM\Delta}$. Finally, we choose the (finitary) topological institution TMT complying with $U_{TM\Delta}$ as follows. For each Σ, pt sy$TMT(\Sigma)$ is the set of sequences $\lambda : \mathbb{N} \to \wp\Sigma$. Satisfaction is defined on the generator theories as expected. First we define satisfaction by a sequence at a point:

- $\lambda \Vdash_n p$ iff $p \in \lambda(n)$;
- $\lambda \Vdash_n (\varphi \Rightarrow \varphi')$ iff $\lambda \Vdash_n \varphi'$ or $\lambda \nVdash_n \varphi$;
- $\lambda \Vdash_n (\neg\varphi)$ iff $\lambda \nVdash_n \varphi$;
- $\lambda \Vdash_n (\mathbf{X}\varphi)$ iff $\lambda \Vdash_{n+1} \varphi$.

Then, we have $\lambda \Vdash \varphi$ iff $\lambda \Vdash_0 \varphi$. It is straightforward to verify the compliance with $U_{TM\Delta}$. Finally, satisfaction is extended to all theories by universal construction as we did in Example 5 above.

Recall that each generator theory is presented by a single formula of the proposed language (using only propositional symbols and connectives as well as the next operator). Clearly, all generator theories can be monitored in the sense that they can be positively observed in finite time.

Therefore, it is easy to see that *all* theories of the proposed topological institution can be monitored. Indeed, arbitrary joins can be monitored. For instance, the reactivity property $(\mathbf{F}\varphi)$ is represented by the theory $\bigvee\{[(\mathbf{X}^n\varphi)] : n \in \mathbb{N}\}$. And its semantics is as envisaged. On the other hand, we cannot find in the proposed topological institution a theory corresponding to an invariant property such as $(\mathbf{G}\varphi)$ since the theory $\bigwedge\{[(\mathbf{X}^n\varphi)] : n \in \mathbb{N}\}$ does not have the same semantics. But we can find theories corresponding to bounded invariant properties (invariants up to a certain finite time).

In short, a temporal property can be monitored iff we can find a theory of *TMT* with the same semantics.

5 Conclusion and Outlook

The concept of institution as proposed by Goguen and Burstall in [4, 5] is now widely accepted. But, by recognizing that theories are the key components of institutions and that formulae are just presentation details, we arrived at the new concept of topological institution: a signature-indexed family of topological systems. Topological systems as proposed by Vickers in [14] provided the starting point. We believe that this is indeed the "natural" notion of institution to be built around theories. Indeed, the obvious alternative of, given an institution I, replacing the functor *Sen* by a functor Th' mapping each signature to the complete lattice of theories over that signature leads to a concept with undesirable properties. Namely, the satisfaction relations (suitably extended to theories as usual) do not respect in general the joins. Furthermore, if this requirement is forced by canonical addition of more theories (using the coverage technique), then meets will not be respected in general by satisfaction. Only finite meets are guaranteed to be respected. That is, by forcing we arrive at a frame structure.

On the way to the envisaged concept, we showed how to extract a topological institution out of a given institution, using the completion technique proposed by Johnstone in [6]. Already in the setting of a topological institution, we recovered the results on composition of theories and provided a characterization of the relationship between theories and models. We also established an adjunction between topological institutions and institutions. We are now investigating the existence of an adjunction when considering the more general notion of institution morphism presented in [9]. Although theories are the key components and not formulae, we may need to work with the latter for presenting the former. To this end, we introduced a general technique for presenting topological institutions adopting an algebraic view on deductive systems. We applied this technique for setting up logics with finitely observable theories and examined their usefulness in monitoring appplications. Other applications of topological concepts in the area of behavior specification are already reported in the literature. See for instance [7]. It remains to bring in the institutional approach that may help with compositionality.

The main limitation of this paper concerns the fact that we disregarded homomorphisms between interpretation structures. That is, we work only with "elementary" institutions where the codomain of the semantic functor is Set^{op}. However, it is clear what should be done towards endowing topological institutions with a category of points (instead of a simple set of points) for each signature. We leave for future work this extension, as well as initiality and liberality issues. It is clear that the concept of "determinate" theory will play an important role. The "dual" view of considering suitable sets of models as opens and taking formulae as points is another interesting topic for future work. We already explored this dual view in the context of a temporal logic institution in order to provide a categorial semantics of object behavior [11].

Acknowledgments

The authors are grateful to Mark Ryan for many stimulating discussions about the impact of this work within the propositional setting, to Udo Lipeck for debating about possible applications, to Joseph Goguen for a lively discussion on the role of theories, and to Steven Vickers for criticizing an early version of the full report.

References

1. H. Ehrig and B. Mahr. *Fundamentals of Algebraic Specification I: Equations and Initial Semantics.* Springer-Verlag, 1985.
2. J. Fiadeiro and A. Sernadas. Structuring theories on consequence. In D. Sannella and A. Tarlecki, editors, *Recent Trends in Data Type Specification*, pages 44–72. Springer-Verlag, 1988.
3. J. Fiadeiro, A. Sernadas, and C. Sernadas. Knowledge bases as structured theories. In K. V. Nori, editor, *Foundations of Software Technology and Theoretical Computer Science*, pages 469–486. Springer-Verlag, 1987.
4. J. Goguen and R. Burstall. Introducing institutions. In E. Clarke and D. Kozen, editors, *Proceedings of the Logics of Programming Workshop*, pages 221–256. Springer-Verlag, 1984.
5. J. Goguen and R. Burstall. Institutions: Abstract model theory for specification and programming. *Journal of the ACM*, 39(1):95–146, 1992.
6. P. Johnstone. *Stone Spaces.* Cambridge University Press, 1982.
7. M. Kwiatkowska. On topological characterization of behavioural properties. In G. Reed, A. Roscoe, and R. Wachter, editors, *Topology and Category Theory in Computer Science*, pages 153–177. Oxford University Press, 1991.
8. U. Lipeck and G. Saake. Monitoring dynamic integrity constraints based on temporal logic. *Information Systems*, 12:255–269, 1987.
9. J. Meseguer. General logics. In H.-D. Ebbinghaus et al, editor, *Proceedings of the Logic Colloquium, 1987.* North-Holland, 1989.
10. A. Salibra and G. Scollo. A soft starway to institutions. In M. Bidoit and C. Choppy, editors, *Recent Trends in Data Type Specification*, pages 310–329. Springer-Verlag, 1993.

11. A. Sernadas and C. Sernadas. Denotational semantics of object specification within an arbitrary temporal logic institution. Research report, Section of Computer Science, Department of Mathematics, Instituto Superior Técnico, 1096 Lisboa, Portugal, 1993. Presented at IS-CORE Workshop 93 - Submitted for publication.
12. A. Sernadas, C. Sernadas, and J. Valença. A topological view on institutions. Research report, Section of Computer Science, Department of Mathematics, Instituto Superior Técnico, 1096 Lisboa, Portugal, 1994. Available on the ftp server yoda.inesc.pt (146.193.1.5).
13. M. Smyth. Powerdomains and predicate transformers: A topological view. In J. Diaz, editor, *Automata, Languages and Programming*, pages 662–675. Springer-Verlag, 1983.
14. S. Vickers. *Topology Via Logic*. Cambridge University Press, 1989.
15. S. Vickers. Geometric logic in computer science. In G. Burn, S. Gay, and M. Ryan, editors, *Theory and Formal Methods 1993*, pages 37–54. Springer-Verlag, 1993.

Typing Abstract Data Types

Judith Underwood*

Department of Computer Science, University of Edinburgh, The King's Buildings, Edinburgh EH9 3JZ, Scotland

Abstract. The purpose of this paper is threefold. First, we describe some basic ideas of constructive type theory, with emphasis on their value for specification. Second, we demonstrate the use of type theory as a specification language. This is done by means of a detailed example, namely, the specification of an abstract data type (ADT) for multisets. (This example is a refinement of the multiset example in [3].) Finally, we describe how a theorem proving environment built on type theory can be used to aid in implementation of the ADT.

1 Introduction

This paper describes an approach to the specification and implementation of abstract data types using type theory. A rich language of types is used to express the desired properties of an implementation of an abstract data type in such a way that correctness is enforced by the type discipline. The use of constructive type theory allows the formal development of an implementation by means of an automated proof assistant.

One goal of this paper is to introduce ideas from type theory to the algebraic specification community. To this end, we begin with an introduction to the basic ideas of constructive type theory. We then illustrate the use of these ideas by means of a detailed example, namely, the specification of an abstract data type for multisets. In the course of the presentation of this example, we shall see how the issues of observational equivalence and parameterization of specifications can be treated in a type theoretic context. Finally, we describe how an implementation of the ADT can be developed in a theorem proving environment based on type theory.

The particular type theory we use is that of Nuprl [4]. In this paper, we will highlight aspects of Nuprl's type theory (not necessarily unique to Nuprl) which we consider useful for the purposes of specification. The implementation comes from the fact that Nuprl has a *constructive* type theory; a proof in Nuprl describes a program. Many other proof systems have been developed on type theoretic foundations [22, 14, 6, 18, 13, 15], and other proof systems [9, 16, 17] can support reasoning in this style. Nuprl's type theory is related to that of Martin-Löf [14].

* This research was supported by EPSRC grant GR/H73103.

This paper presents a few aspects of the work in [2], which is a development of idéas in [3]. The original motivation for this work was in the context of using constructive metamathematics to assist in developing tools for theorem provers [5]. Given a metatheorem which states that provability of certain classes of formulas is decidable, a constructive proof of this theorem leads to an implementation of a decision procedure for these formulas. If a theorem proving system is powerful enough to describe its own formulas and proofs, then such a metatheorem may be proven within the system itself. With the addition of a mechanism such as Nuprl's reflection rule [1] for mapping the internal descriptions of formulas and proofs to actual formulas and proofs, we can use the theorem proving system to soundly extend its own store of decision procedures.

This plan is carried out in [2], by the author along with Aitken and Constable. In that paper, we used abstract data types to describe the logic for which we produce a decision procedure. Here, we present one of those datatypes (for multisets) in detail and describe its use and implementation. The ADT is a refinement of one defined in [3]; a number of details have been filled in and clarifications made.

This paper differs from earlier treatments in a number of ways. (In addition to those works already mentioned, the paper of Luo [12], which uses a different type theory, has many of the same goals.) First, we chose to specify the ADT of multisets in a very flexible way. In particular, we include an induction operator, i.e. a general purpose operator for defining functions and predicates on multisets by induction. The fact that models of this specification are (isomorphic to) nontrivial quotients of the term algebra creates special problems for the specification and use of the induction operator. Furthermore, we treat in more detail the issues involved in the development of an implementation. As a part of this treatment, we present a technique for increasing the efficiency of the implementation of the induction operator by using general recursion in a principled way.

One particular difference between the type theory used in this paper and that used by Luo is in the treatment of equality. Equality in Nuprl is *extensional* – functions are equal if they give equal output on equal inputs. We believe this approach is more natural for specification than the intensional equality used in Luo's ECC.

2 Introduction to Type Theory

In this paper, we are interested in using type theory to specify abstract data types. However, it is easier to understand the power of type theory if we consider it in a broader framework; namely, as a foundation for constructive mathematics.

The general principles underlying the constructive approach to type theory are "propositions as types" and "proofs as programs". We assume the existence of some basic mathematical objects, represent these objects as terms, and describe them by giving them types. These fundamental types are called *ground* types. We may also assume we have some axioms about the properties of the elements of these types.

In order to reason about the fundamental types and their elements, we must have a language which describes how more complex formulas can be constructed from ground types, and a logic which describes the valid inferences we can make from the axioms. In a constructive type theory, the formulas are themselves types, and a logical inference is valid only when it can be expressed computationally. In this way, the logic represents a programming language, and a type corresponds to a theorem only when there is a program of that type.

For example, consider the theory of arithmetic over the natural numbers. We can express this by designating a ground type N as that of the natural numbers, and supplying axioms about the behaviour of elements of N, for example, the Peano axioms. Recall that the terms in N are defined by

$$0 \in N$$
$$x \in N \rightarrow s(x) \in N$$

where s denotes the successor function.

Some of the axioms for arithmetic are:

$$x + 0 = x$$
$$x + s(y) = s(x + y)$$

Axioms similar to those for $+$ may be added for any primitive recursive function. In addition, we have an axiom schema for induction which allows us to prove properties of all elements of N:

$$A(0) \wedge \forall x.(A(x) \rightarrow A(s(x))) \rightarrow \forall x.A(x)$$

Other formulas may be built from the type N using the usual logical connectives: $\wedge$ (and), $\vee$ (or), $\neg$ (not), $\rightarrow$ (implies), $\forall$ (for all), and $\exists$ (there exists). However, in the inference system, these connectives are interpreted constructively. This means that a proof of a formula is an explicit construction of an element of the type which the formula represents.

As an example, consider implication. If A and B are types, the type $A \rightarrow B$ is the type of functions from A to B. A constructive proof of the formula $A \rightarrow B$ is a function mapping proofs of A to proofs of B; so, the formula $A \rightarrow B$ is provable if there is a function of type $A \rightarrow B$.

As another example, consider disjunction. The type $A \vee B$ is a disjoint union type, and an inhabitant of $A \vee B$ is either an element of A or an element of B. Furthermore, an element of $A \vee B$ is tagged, so that we can decide which of A or B it inhabits. Note that this is a dramatically different approach than that taken in classical logic, where $A \rightarrow B$ is identical to $\neg A \vee B$. No such identity holds when $A \rightarrow B$ is interpreted as a function type and $\neg A \vee B$ is interpreted as a disjoint union. (The type $\neg A$ is considered shorthand for $A \rightarrow Void$, where $Void$ is an empty type.)

Quantifiers also have computational significance. In order to prove $\exists x : A.P(x)$ constructively, we must provide a particular a of type A paired with a proof that $P(a)$ holds. It is insufficient to merely show that assuming that there is no such a leads to a contradiction; such a line of reasoning does not *construct* the a which we want. Similarly, the type $\forall x{:}A.\exists y{:}B.P(x,y)$ is provable when we can provide a function mapping elements a of A to elements b of B paired with elements of $P(a,b)$. This idea will be explained in more detail in the next section, along with the means by which a type may depend on an element of another type.

Returning to the axioms given above for arithmetic, we find that the axioms of arithmetic fall into two general categories. The logical axioms have computational content; the equational ones do not. The only non-equational axiom we have given is the induction schema. Its computational representation is a function which takes two arguments: an element of $A(0)$ (representing a proof that $A(0)$ holds) and a function from $x : N$ which returns a function from $A(x)$ to $A(s(x))$. Given these arguments, the function returns a function from N to A. We call such a function an induction operator, which can be used for defining functions by induction on the natural numbers. (We use the term induction instead of recursion in this case because recursion, in general, may be unbounded. The induction operator can only define functions by primitive recursion, though in a higher-order system this does not mean the only functions definable are primitive recursive.)

Some other type theoretic approaches to specification (e.g. [12]) distinguish between types and propositions. Types correspond to the logical axioms, and their proofs have computational content. Propositions represent the equational axioms, and their proofs need not be computationally meaningful at all. In Nuprl, no distinction is made between propositions and types; to supply evidence for noncomputational axioms, they are considered to represent a type with a single element which we will call *yes*. As an example of the treatment , the theorem $\forall x : N.\exists y{:}N.y = x+s(0)$ has computational content which we write as $\lambda x.\langle s(x), yes$. Given x in N, we show there exists a y such that $y = x + s(0)$ by calculating such a y, namely $s(x)$. The proof that $s(x) = x + s(0)$ has no computational content, so it is written as *yes*, denoting that it has been proven. (In the actual Nuprl system, the *yes* token is called *axiom*.)

In summary, describing mathematics in a constructive type theory allows us to formally relate proofs and programs. Given a constructive proof of a formula, we may automatically extract a program of the type corresponding to the formula, representing the computational content of the proof. In other words, if we consider the formula as a specification, we can generate a program meeting the specification from a proof of the formula.

Given this general approach, there are still many options available in the design of such a constructive type theory. Some of these relate to aspects of the logic corresponding to the types; others involve the associated computation system. For sufficiently strong type theories (in particular, any which can describe first order arithmetic), provability is undecidable by Gödel's theorem. Because of this, in implemented systems proof search is generally interactive, with the user of the system applying rules either directly or through tactics which apply a sequence of rules. Besides Nuprl, such systems include [6, 10, 18, 13, 15].

2.1 Useful Types and Type Constructors

Here we describe some desirable properties for a type system if it is to be used in the context of specification. We present a number of different types and type constructors, along with an explanation of their computational significance. All of these types are present in Nuprl.

Built in types. For a type system to be usable as a specification language for programs, we would like it to supply a reasonable number of built in ground types and type constructors, along with tools for reasoning about them. In this paper, we assume we have a ground type *bool* for Boolean values, the built in type N, and a built in type constructor *list*, which, given a type A, describes the type of lists of elements of A. We assume that among the axioms for *list* types is an induction principle, so that in the computation system, we have a corresponding induction operator.

Dependent product types. The dependent product type is the type theoretic representation of existential quantification. If A and B are types, then $x\!:\!A \times B$ is a type. If x is free in B, then B represents a family of types parameterized by elements of A. An element of $x\!:\!A \times B$ is a pair $\langle a, b\rangle$, where $a \in A$ and $b \in B[a/x]$. Note that this is evidence for the logical assertion $\exists x\!:\!A.B$. Note also that if x is not actually free in B, this is just a Cartesian product type. In this case, we may just write $A \times B$, omitting the variable binding. (The dependent product type is sometimes denoted $\Sigma x\!:\!A.B$; when this is the case, it is referred to as a Σ type or a dependent sum, taking the view that it is an abbreviation for the infinite disjoint union of all $B[x]$ as x ranges over A.) This type will be most useful when x ranges over types rather than elements of a type.

Dependent function types. The dependent function type is the type theoretic representation of universal quantification. If A and B are types, then $x\!:\!A \rightarrow B$ is a type. Elements of this type are functions which, given an argument $a \in A$, return an element of $B[a/x]$. An example is a function which, given a natural number n, returns the n-tuple $\langle 1, \ldots, n\rangle$. Thus, the type of the result of function application can depend on the argument to the function. Note that such a function is evidence for the logical assertion $\forall x : A.B$. If the variable x does not actually appear in B, this is a simple function type, and may be written $A \rightarrow B$. In the remainder of this paper, we may use both $\forall x : A.B$ and $x\!:\!A \rightarrow B$ notations, depending on whether we wish to emphasize the logical or the computational aspect of the type. (The dependent function type is sometimes denoted $\Pi x\!:\!A.B$, and referred to as a Π type or a dependent product. This terminology arises from the classical view of functions as sets of pairs of elements from the domain and range.)

Universe types. To express types parameterized by other types, we would like to have a "type of types" over which the parameter can range. In Nuprl, this is achieved by the use of universe types. Nuprl includes a hierarchy of universe types (to prevent foundational problems with the type of all types), so that types built from ground types only are in universe type U_1, and U_{k+1} includes types built from types in U_k plus the type U_k itself. Where it is not necessary to specify the precise universe level, we use U_i. Note that the presence of both type universes and dependent types allows a form of quantification over types (limited by the universe hierarchy), resulting in types parameterized by other types. This idea will prove very useful for introducing abstractness in a specification.

Set types. It is often convenient to describe an object as an element of a certain type satisfying some extra conditions. To describe this, we use a *set* (sometimes called *subset*) type. The type of all elements of T satisfying property P is denoted $\{t:T \mid P(t)\}$. This could be called a subtype; however, that word has somewhat different connotations in type theory.

The types and type constructors listed above provide a very flexible and powerful language for specification. The use of dependent types together with universes allows higher order types and reasoning. For example, functions may take types as arguments and return types as values. This technique can be used to represent parameterized specifications. We will return to this idea once we have seen how dependent types are used in the example in the next section.

There are a few aspects of Nuprl's type theory which distinguish it from others (e.g. ECC [11]). One such feature lies in its treatment of equality. All types come equipped with an equality predicate and rules for reasoning about equality in the type. The notation $a = a' \in T$ is used for assertions about equality to specify the type involved. The notation $a \in T$ is shorthand for $a = a \in T$, which simply asserts a is of type T. For the typing assumptions of variables, we use the notation $x : T$.

An important point about Nuprl's equality (in contrast to that used by ECC) is that it is extensional; that is, functions are equal if they produce the same output on equal inputs. Extensional equality is well suited to the purpose of implementation of specifications, since specifications are concerned with the *behaviour* of functions rather than the details of their implementation. Furthermore, given an implementation of a specification in this kind of theory, we can replace a function with another function equal to it in its type and be assured that all the properties required of it still hold.

3 Multisets: An Example

We now show how to use the machinery of type theory to describe an abstract data type. A *multiset* over a type A is a collection of elements of A in which a given element may appear multiple times, but in which there is no ordering of the elements. We will give an abstract data type for finite multisets over A. There are a number of things we require from the ADT. First, it should be parameterized by the type A, so that it can be used to implement multisets over a number of different types. Second, we need a carrier set of multisets, and tools for constructing multisets. Third, in order to provide a general mechanism for defining functions on multisets, we provide a multiset induction operator, i.e. a tool for defining functions and predicates by induction. This is a departure from the usual algebraic specification for multisets; we use this operator to avoid having to specify in advance exactly which functions on multisets we will want. This flexibility comes at the price of increased complexity of the specification, since the specification of an induction operator is the induction principle for multisets and this specification requires higher-order logic. Furthermore, since multisets are not a simple term algebra, specifying the behaviour of the induction operator is not straightforward. Finally, we need axioms which ensure that all the operators defined in the ADT have the properties we want them to have.

One of these properties is functionality, in the sense that any function defined on multisets must map equal multisets to equal values. This is not trivial, because equality on multisets may not be the same as equality in the type used to implement multisets. This is the well-known issue of *behavioural equivalence* [7, 8, 21, 19]; namely, ensuring that there is no way to tell that the type used to implement multisets is not a true multiset type. We do this by defining equality on multisets explicitly as part of the ADT, and ensuring that the types of the multiset operations are such that the defined equality is respected.

We now describe in more detail the specification of the ADT. In order to parameterize the multiset data type by the type of elements A, we must have a "type of types" over which A can range. This is precisely what we have called a "universe type". For increased flexibility, we also take a parameter which is an equality decider on A, rather than assuming we wish to use the built in equality associated with A. This allows us to define multisets of multisets. For simplicity of notation, we define, for any type S,

$$EqDecider(S) \equiv \{f : S \to S \to bool \mid \lambda x, y. f(x)(y) \text{ is an equivalence on } S\}$$

(It is straightforward to describe the conditions for f to be an equivalence relation.) So, in addition to the type A, we take a parameter Aeq of type $EqDecider(A)$.

Given these parameters, we describe the abstract data type of multisets over A. This is written as a product of the types of various elements of the ADT: the carrier set, the construction and induction operators, and the axioms. We begin by using a universe type as the type of the carrier set M of multisets. Using a dependent product type, we describe the rest of the types in the product in terms of the types A and M. So, given M as the type of multisets, the type of multiset equality Eq is $EqDecider(M)$. This is intended to represent abstract multiset equality; we will ensure it does so by specifying an axiom for its behaviour later.

The construction operators we use are a nullary operator $Empty$, representing the empty multiset, and a function $Add(a, m)$, which adds the element a of type A to the multiset m. We wish to ensure that Add is functional with respect to Eq. We define $AddType$ to be

$$
\begin{aligned}
AddType \equiv \ \{f : A \to M \to M \\
& \mid \forall a, a' : A, m, m' : M. \\
& \quad Aeq(a)(a') = true \Rightarrow Eq(m)(m') = true \\
& \quad\quad \Rightarrow Eq\big(f(a)(m), f(a')(m')\big) = true \\
\}
\end{aligned}
$$

This definition merely formalizes the requirement that functions map equal elements of A (equal under Aeq) and equal elements of M (equal under Eq) to equal elements of M. Although we have curried the arguments to Add in specifying its type, we will use the notation $Add(a, m)$ to avoid proliferation of parentheses.

We now consider the type of the multiset induction operator $MInd$. The idea is that this represents the computational content of the multiset induction principle. Given a type constructor P parameterized by multisets, the induction principle gives us a means by which to produce an element of the type $P(x)$ for any multiset x. To do so, we must provide an object of type $P(Empty)$, where $Empty$ is the empty multiset. We must also provide a function f that maps a multiset m, an element a, and an object of type $P(m)$, to an object of type $P(Add(a, m))$. The intuition is that we begin with the object of type $P(Empty)$, and use f repeatedly, once for each element of x, to build up an object of type $P(x)$.

There are a number of requirements on the type of the multiset induction operator. Specifically, these are requirements on the types of the arguments to the operator; when these are satisfied (along with axioms introduced later for the behaviour of $MInd$), functions defined by induction will be guaranteed to be functional with respect to the equality defined on multisets. To express the restrictions on types more concisely, we introduce some notation.

For any type constructor $T(a, m)$ parameterized by an element a of A and a multiset m, we define $a : A \mapsto m : M \mapsto T(a, m)$ to be the type of functions that map an element a of A and a multiset m to $T(a, m)$, and that are functional in the appropriate fashion.

$$
\begin{aligned}
a : A \mapsto m : M \mapsto T(a, m) \equiv \ \{f : (a : A \to m : M \to T(a, m)) \\
& \mid \forall a, a' : A, m, m' : M. \\
& \quad Aeq(a)(a') = true \Rightarrow Eq(m)(m') = true \\
& \quad\quad \Rightarrow \big(f(a)(m) = f(a')(m') \in T(a, m)\big) \\
\}
\end{aligned}
$$

We specialize this notation to include

$$M \mapsto T \equiv \{f : M \to T \mid \forall m, m' : Eq(m)(m') = true \Rightarrow f(m) = f(m') \in T\}.$$

As before, this describes, for any type T, the type $M \mapsto T$ which contains all the functions from M to T that are functional with respect to the equivalence relation induced by Eq.

With this notation, we may describe the type of $MInd$. First, the type constructor P must be functional with respect to multiset equality. So, the type of P is $M \mapsto U_i$. Recall that this means $P(m)$ is a *type*; the induction operator $MInd$ is used to produce members of that type.

The next argument to $MInd$ is the value of the function being defined on the empty multiset; therefore, the type of this argument is $P(Empty)$. After this, we have a function f which, given an element a of type A and a multiset m of type M, produces a function from $P(m)$ to $P(Add(a,m))$ which describes how to compute an element in $P(Add(a,m))$ from a,m, and an element of $P(m)$. Since we require f to be functional with respect to the defined equalities on types A and M, the type of f is partly described by $a\!:\!A \mapsto m\!:\!M \mapsto (P(m) \rightarrow P(Add(a,m)))$. However, we have an additional restriction on f, namely that the function it produces (i.e. the element of $P(m) \rightarrow P(Add(a,m))$) be insensitive to the order in which m is constructed. We can describe this in the type of f by using the set type to restrict f to those elements f of $a\!:\!A \mapsto m\!:\!M \mapsto (P(m) \rightarrow P(Add(a,m)))$ which have this property. We examine the need for this restriction further in the next section. Formally, we define

$$
\begin{aligned}
&FInd(A, Aeq, M, Eq, Add, P) \equiv \\
&\quad \{f\!:\!(a\!:\!A \mapsto m\!:\!M \mapsto (P(m) \rightarrow P(Add(a,m)))) \mid \\
&\qquad \forall a, b\!:\!A, m\!:\!M, p\!:\!P(m). \\
&\qquad\quad f(a)(Add(b,m))(f(b)(m)(p)) = f(b)(Add(a,m))(f(a)(m)(p)) \\
&\qquad\qquad \in P(Add(a, Add(b,m)))\}.
\end{aligned}
$$

We shall abbreviate $FInd(A, Aeq, M, Eq, Add, P)$ as $FInd(\ldots)$.

The result of applying the $MInd$ operator to arguments P, $e : P(Empty)$, and $f : FInd(\ldots)$ is a function from $m : M$ to $P(m)$. Thus, the final type of $MInd$ is

$$P\!:\!(M \mapsto U_i) \rightarrow e\!:\!P(Empty) \rightarrow f\!:\!FInd(\ldots) \rightarrow m\!:\!M \rightarrow P(m).$$

The axioms which describe the desired behaviour of the operators on multisets are also expressed as types, although we are only concerned that these types be inhabited. There are four axioms. The first is a restriction on the Add operator, requiring it to produce equal multisets regardless of the order of the addition of elements. It is sufficient to require that for any pair of elements a and a' and multiset m, the result of adding a and then a' to m is equal to the result of adding a' and then a. This is expressed as the axiom:

$$Axiom1 \equiv \forall a, a'\!:\!A, m\!:\!M. Eq(Add(a, Add(a', m)))(Add(a', Add(a,m))) = true.$$

Rather than introducing this as an axiom, we could have included this as part of the type of Add.

The other axioms are guarantees on the behaviour of $MInd$.

$$
\begin{aligned}
&Axiom2 \equiv\\
&\quad \forall P: M \mapsto U_i, e: P(Empty), f: FInd(\ldots), m, m': M.\\
&\qquad Eq(m)(m') = true \Rightarrow MInd(P)(e)(f)(m) = MInd(P)(e)(f)(m') \in P(m)\\
&Axiom3 \equiv\\
&\quad \forall P: M \mapsto U_i, e: P(Empty), f: FInd(\ldots).\\
&\qquad MInd(P)(e)(f)(Empty) = e \in P(Empty)\\
&Axiom4 \equiv\\
&\quad \forall P: M \mapsto U_i, e: P(Empty), f: FInd(\ldots), a: A, m: M.\\
&\qquad MInd(P)(e)(f)(Add(a,m)) = f(a)(m)(MInd(P)(e)(f)(m))\\
&\qquad\quad \in P(Add(a,m))
\end{aligned}
$$

The first of these axioms ensures that functions on multisets defined by induction are actually functions, i.e. they respect multiset equality. This seems obvious, but it does not follow from the type of $MInd$ alone, since the type in this case does not carry any restrictions on the behaviour of $MInd$. The remaining two axioms are similar, in that they guarantee that the functions produced by $MInd$ actually do what we expect them to do, given the arguments to $MInd$; the value of the function on $Empty$ is the value given to $MInd$, and the value of the inductive case is computed by f.

The result is the definition:

$$
\begin{aligned}
&MULTISET \equiv\\
&\qquad A: U_i\\
&\quad \rightarrow Aeq: EqDecider(A)\\
&\quad \rightarrow M: U_i\\
&\qquad \times\ Eq: EqDecider(M)\\
&\qquad \times\ Empty: M\\
&\qquad \times\ Add: AddType\\
&\qquad \times\ MInd: P: (M \mapsto U_i) \rightarrow e: P(Empty) \rightarrow f: FInd(\ldots) \rightarrow m: M \rightarrow P(m)\\
&\qquad \times\ Axiom1\\
&\qquad \times\ Axiom2\\
&\qquad \times\ Axiom3\\
&\qquad \times\ Axiom4
\end{aligned}
$$

An interesting aspect of this description of multisets is that the types of the operators and the axioms which describe their behaviour are expressed in the same language. However, we have provided this specification with some structure by separating the "local" requirements for the behaviour of operators (expressed in their types) from the "interactive" behaviour (expressed in the axioms). Clearly there is not a strict distinction between these two ideas; the first axiom could have been expressed instead as a restriction on the type of the *Add* operator. However, such separation can be conceptually helpful, as in the separation between the type of the $MInd$ operator and the list of its properties.

Before we examine the use of the ADT of multisets, a couple of points should be noted. First, the treatment of parameterization should be highlighted. Dependent types have been used to describe parameterization of the ADT by the choice of the carrier type for multisets. In fact, it appears that dependent types can be used to describe the two kinds of parameterization distinguished in [20], namely, the specification of a parameterized object and the parameterization of the specification itself. As written, the multiset ADT specification is of the first kind; any implementation must describe the other components of the specification *uniformly* with respect to the choice of a carrier type. This is because we have used a dependent function type. However, if we had instead used a dependent product type to describe the dependency of the implementation on the choice of a carrier type, we would have avoided the need for a uniform implementation.

Second, and more generally, the definition of the ADT seems very complex compared with an algebraic approach. This is due to two factors. First is the decision to include an induction operator; the specification of such a general operator is more complex than that of a simple function in any system. Second, because we have explicitly specified our intended equality on multisets, we must ensure in the specification that other parts of the ADT respect that equality. In an algebraic approach, this issue is separated from the specification and must be dealt with by reasoning about the behaviour of an implementation or a model. Since the type theoretic treatment effectively includes such reasoning, it is more complex.

3.1 Examples of the use of the ADT.

Perhaps the most unusual aspect of this ADT is the $MInd$ operator. Because of this, and because of the complexity of its type, it may be illuminating to examine some examples of its use.

First, we define a function $Size$ which computes the size of a multiset. The type of this function is $M \rightarrow N$. The first argument (P) to $MInd$ is a function describing how the type of the result of $MInd$ depends on the argument m in M it is given. Since in this case the type of the result does not depend on m, the first argument to $MInd$ is simply $\lambda x : M.N$. Since this function does not depend on the element m it is given, it is clearly in $M \mapsto U_i$.

The value of $Size$ on the empty multiset is zero, so this is the second argument to $MInd$.

The third argument to $MInd$ is a function f from arguments a of type A, m of type M, and p of type N to N, which describes how to compute $Size(Add(a, m))$ from a, m, and p, the value of $Size(m)$. This function is simply $\lambda a.\lambda m.\lambda p.p + 1$. It is clear that this function respects the equalities on A and M. Furthermore, it is easy to see that

$$f(a)(Add(b, m))(f(b)(m)(p)) = f(b)(Add(a, m))(f(a)(m)(p))$$

since both sides evaluate to $p + 2$.

Applying $MInd$ to these arguments, we can now define

$$Size = MInd(\lambda x.N, 0, \lambda a.\lambda m.\lambda p.p + 1).$$

Note that this is of type $m : M \rightarrow P(m)$, or, given $P = \lambda x.N$, simply $M \rightarrow N$, as desired.

Suppose we wanted to define a function from multisets to lists. According to our understanding of the restrictions on the types involved, this should be very difficult, since the functions defined by induction must map equal multisets to arguments equal in the result type, in this case, lists. A straightforward mapping of $Add(a_1, \ldots (Add(a_n, Empty)))$ to $(a_1, \ldots, a_n)$ should not be definable by multiset induction.

To see that it is not definable, let us attempt to define it and see where the attempt fails. The type of the resulting function is simply $M \rightarrow A\ list$, so the first argument to $MInd$ will be $\lambda x.A\ list$. The value of the map on the empty multiset should be *nil*, the empty list, so this is the second argument.

The third argument to $MInd$ is a function describing how to build a list for $Add(a, m)$ from a, m, and the list resulting from m. Our candidate for this function is $\lambda a.\lambda m.\lambda p.cons(a, p)$. This function respects equality on both A and M (the latter because the result does not depend on m directly), but it fails the extra condition that

$$f(a)(Add(b, m))(f(b)(m)(p)) = f(b)(Add(a, m))(f(a)(m)(p)).$$

4 Implementation

In this section, we demonstrate the use of Nuprl as a tool for implementing an ADT and proving that the implementation is correct. We show how the multiset example of the previous section can be implemented using Nuprl's built in list type, how the resulting implementation may be used, and how the implementation can be made more efficient without sacrificing correctness.

Recall that an implementation of the multiset ADT is a function which, given a type A and Aeq (the equality on A) returns a tuple consisting of a type M representing the carrier set for multisets of elements of A, an equivalence relation Eq on that type, a distinguished element $Empty$ of M representing the empty multiset, an operator Add for adding elements to a multiset, and a multiset induction operator $MInd$, along with evidence that the axioms listed in the previous section hold for the types and operators supplied.

Given the types A and Aeq, we choose the Nuprl type $A\ list$ as the carrier set. We must supply an equivalence relation Eq, distinct from list equality, which identifies lists which differ only in the order of their elements. Otherwise, this instantiation is straightforward. The empty multiset is implemented as the empty list; multiset element addition is implemented using *cons*; multiset induction is implemented by list induction.

List induction in Nuprl is performed by a built-in induction form *list_ind*. A function f from type $A\ list$ to T is defined by

$$\lambda l.list\_ind(l, b, \lambda h \lambda t \lambda v.e)$$

where l is the argument to the function, $b : T$ is the value of the function on the empty list, and e is an expression describing how to construct the value of $f(cons(h, t))$ given h, t, and $v = f(t)$ (i.e. v is the value of the function on the tail of the list). The *list_ind* form is evaluated by "unrolling" the induction, so that

$$list\_ind(nil, b, \lambda h \lambda t \lambda v.e) \longrightarrow b$$
$$list\_ind(cons(a, l), b, \lambda h \lambda t \lambda v.e) \longrightarrow e[a/h, l/t, list\_ind(l, b, \lambda h \lambda t \lambda v.e)/v]$$

Given these choices for the implementation of the components of the ADT, evidence for the various axioms is most easily constructed by proving them true in Nuprl for the list type and its operations. This is fairly straightforward, since we have proof rules describing the type and its operators. The evidence for these axioms has no computational content, so we do not express it in detail.

The implementation is then:

$$\begin{array}{l} Multiset \equiv \lambda A.\lambda Aeq.\langle \\ \quad A\ list \\ \quad \lambda x.\lambda y.is\_permutation(x, y, Aeq) \\ \quad nil, \\ \quad \lambda a.\lambda m.cons(a, m), \\ \quad \lambda P.\lambda hb.\lambda hi.\lambda m.list\_ind(m, hb, \lambda u \lambda v \lambda w.hi(u)(v)(w)), \\ \quad \lambda a.\lambda b.\lambda m.(evidence\ for\ axiom\ 1) \\ \quad \lambda P.\lambda hb.\lambda hi.\lambda m.\lambda n.\lambda x.(evidence\ for\ axiom\ 2) \\ \quad \lambda P.\lambda hb.\lambda hi.(evidence\ for\ axiom\ 3) \\ \quad \lambda P.\lambda hb.\lambda hi.\lambda a.\lambda m.axiom(evidence\ for\ axiom\ 4) \\ \rangle \end{array}$$

Here, $is\_permutation(x, a, Aeq)$ returns the boolean true value if x and y are permutations of each other, and returns false otherwise. The function Aeq is used to decide equality between elements of x and y. The implementation of *is_permutation* is a straightforward application of Nuprl's *list_ind* operator.

Another implementation possible in Nuprl is through Nuprl's quotient types. We can define the type of multisets by taking the quotient of $A\ list$ by the equivalence relation $is\_permutation(x, y, Aeq)$. The notation for this is $(x, y) : A\ list//is\_permutation(x, y, Aeq)$. The leading (x, y) serves as a binding operator for the variables representing the arguments to *is_permutation*. Elements of $(x, y) : A\ list//is\_permutation(x, y, Aeq)$ are elements of $A\ list$, and two elements t and t' are equal in the type if $is\_permutation(t, t', Aeq)$ holds. So, Eq is the standard equality on this type. With this implementation, the conditions ensuring that the various operators on multisets are functional become trivial. Multiset induction can still be implemented by list induction.

4.1 Efficient Induction

In the implementation given above, we use the built in *list_ind* induction form to implement multiset induction. While this is correct, it can be inefficient; evaluation of a function f defined by $list\_ind(l, b, \lambda h \lambda t \lambda v.e)$ requires that, on each unwinding of the definition, we evaluate the head h and tail t of the list, when we may not use this information at all. For example, if we merely wish to count the number of items in the list, e is merely $v + 1$, and we use neither h nor t. Furthermore, if we wish to compute the value of of f by dividing the list into two parts and evaluating the function on each part, we cannot express this naturally in terms of h, t, and v. The induction operator follows strictly the form of the inductive definition of lists, and when a function is more naturally defined by another induction, *list_ind* can be cumbersome and inefficient.

Because of this, we may wish to replace the induction form with a more flexible and more efficient recursive operator. To do this, we prove a more general induction principle for well founded orderings defined by a measure on lists.

The induction lemma we prove is

$$\begin{array}{l} \forall A{:}U_i. \\ \ \forall P{:}A\ list.{\rightarrow}U_i. \\ \ \ \forall f{:}A\ list{\rightarrow}N(\forall l{:}A\ list. \\ \ \ \ (\forall l'{:}\{l'{:}A\ list|f(l') < f(l)\}.P(l')){\Rightarrow}P(l)) \\ \ \ \ \ {\Rightarrow}(\forall l{:}A\ list.P(l)) \end{array}$$

The use of the set type $\{l' : A\ list|f(l') < f(l)\}$ guarantees that the computational content of the proof that the inductive measure of l' is less than the measure of l is not used in the extraction. The set type effectively prevents this by hiding the proof that $f(l') < f(l)$. This means that the numerical induction measures need not be explicitly calculated at run time as long as they were shown to have been reduced when this lemma was used. In other words, the proof that the measure is reduced is required once, while the program is being developed; the induction measure need not be checked at each stage of the evaluation.

The induction principle above may be proved in Nuprl by supplying an explicit witness for its truth. In this case, the witness is

$$\lambda A.\lambda P.\lambda f.\lambda g.(Y\lambda h.\lambda x.(gxh))$$

where $Y = \lambda f.(\lambda x.f(x(x)))(\lambda x.f(x(x)))$ is the usual fixpoint combinator. This term is shown to be an inhabitant of the appropriate type using Nuprl's computation rules, which allow the Y combinator to be "unrolled" in order to use the inductive hypothesis.

The result of this is a more flexible and efficient induction operator for lists, which can also be used for multiset induction. The only significant change in the use of this operator is that one must explicitly supply the inductive measure as a function to natural numbers, and show that it is reduced at each stage. The tradeoff here is then between complexity of the proof using this induction and the efficiency of the algorithm extracted from the proof.

5 Conclusions

We have seen how constructive type theory can be used to specify an abstract data type and guide its implementation. The advantages of this approach lie in the expressiveness of type theory as a specification language and in its close relationship to implementation. This expressiveness includes a uniform language for types and statements about behaviour, as well as a representation of parameterization and higher order logic. Flexibility extends to the specification of an induction operator, which allows users of the ADT to write their own functions. Finally, an automated proof assistant for constructive type theory can be used to guide the implementation of the ADT and verify its correctness.

Thanks to Don Sannella for helpful comments, and Bill Aitken and Bob Constable for previous collaboration.

References

1. W. Aitken. *Metaprogramming in Nuprl Using Reflection.* PhD thesis, Computer Science Department, Cornell University, Ithaca, NY, 1994.
2. William Aitken, Robert Constable, and Judith Underwood. Metalogical frameworks II: Using reflected decision procedures. unpublished manuscript.
3. D. Basin and R. Constable. Metalogical frameworks. In G. Huet and G. Plotkin, editors, *Logical Environments*, chapter 1, pages 1–29. Cambridge University Press, Great Britain, 1993.
4. R. L. Constable et al. *Implementing Mathematics with the Nuprl Development System.* Prentice-Hall, NJ, 1986.
5. R. L. Constable and D. J. Howe. Implementing metamathematics as an approach to automatic theorem proving. In R.B. Banerji, editor, *Formal Techniques in Artificial Intelligence: A Source Book*, pages 45–76. Elsevier Science Publishers (North-Holland), 1990.
6. T. Coquand and G. Huet. The Calculus of Constructions. *Information and Computation*, 76:95–120, 1988.
7. V. Giarratana, F. Gimona, and U. Montanari. Observability concepts in abstract data type specification. In *Proc. 1976 Symposium on Mathematical Foundations of Computer Science*, pages 567–578. Springer LNCS 45, 1976.
8. J. Goguen and J. Meseguer. Universal realization, persistent interconnection and implementation of abstract modules. In *Proc. 9th Intl. Colloquium on Automata, Languages, and Programming*, pages 265–281. Springer LNCS 140, 1982.
9. M. Gordon. HOL: A machine oriented formalization of higher order logic. Technical Report 68, Cambridge University, 1985.
10. Christian Horn. The nurprl proof development system. Technical report, University of Edinburgh, 1988. The Edinburgh version of Nurprl has been renamed Oyster.
11. Z. Luo. ECC: An extended calculus of constructions. In *Proceedings of the Fourth Annual Symposium on Logic in Computer Science.* IEEE, 1989.
12. Z. Luo. Program specification and data refinement in type theory. In *Proceedings of the Fourth International Joint Conference on the Theory and Practice of Software Development (TAPSOFT)*, 1991.
13. Zhaohui Luo. *Computation and Reasoning: A Type Theory for Computer Science.* Oxford University Press, 1994.
14. P. Martin-Löf. Constructive mathematics and computer programming. In *Sixth International Congress for Logic, Methodology, and Philosophy of Science*, pages 153–75. North-Holland, Amsterdam, 1982.

15. Bengt Nordström. The ALF proof editor. In *TYPES'93: Proceedings of the Fourth Annual Workshop of the EU Esprit Basic Research Action "Types for Proofs and Programs"*, number 806 in Lecture Notes in Computer Science. Springer-Verlag, 1993.
16. S. Owre, J.M. Rushby, and N. Shankar. PVS: An integrated approach to specification and verification. Preprint, January, 1992.
17. L.C. Paulson. A formulation of the simple theory of types (for Isabelle). In P. Martin-Löf and G. Mints, editors, *Proc. of the Int. Conference on Computer Logic, Lecture Notes in Computer Science, Vol. 417*, pages 246–274. Springer-Verlag, New York, December, 1988.
18. R. Pollack. *The Theory of Lego*. PhD thesis, University of Edinburgh, 1994. Forthcoming as a technical report.
19. D. Sannella and A. Tarlecki. On observational equivalence and algebraic specification. *Journal of Computer and System Sciences*, 34:150–178, 1987.
20. D. Sannella and A. Tarlecki. Toward formal development of programs from algebraic specifications: model theoretic foundations. In *Proc. 19th Intl. Colloquium on Automata, Languages, and Programming*, pages 656–671. Springer LNCS 623, 1992.
21. Donald Sannella, Stefan Sokolowski, and Andrzej Tarlecki. Toward formal development of programs from algebraic specifications: parameterisation revisited. *Acta Informatica*, 29:689–739, 1992.
22. D.T. van Daalen. *The Language Theory of AUTOMATH*. PhD thesis, Technical University of Eindhoven, Eindhoven, Netherlands, 1980.

Multialgebras, Power Algebras and Complete Calculi of Identities and Inclusions*

Michal Walicki and Sigurd Meldal
Department of Informatics, University of Bergen
HiB, N–5020 Bergen, Norway
{michal,sigurd}@ii.uib.no

Abstract: After motivating the introduction of nondeterministic operators into algebraic specifications, a language $\mathcal{L}$ with two primitive predicates, *identity* and *inclusion*, for specifying nondeterministic operations is introduced. It is given a *multialgebraic* semantics which captures the *singular* (call-time-choice) strategy of passing nondeterministic parameters. A calculus NEQ, with restricted substitutivity rules, is introduced. NEQ is sound and complete wrt. the multialgebraic semantics.

A language $\mathcal{L}^*$ is obtained by a slight modification of $\mathcal{L}$ admitting *plural* (run-time-choice) parameters. The multialgebraic semantics is not sufficient for modeling such parameters and it is generalized to *power algebras*. Augmenting NEQ with one rule for unrestricted substitutivity for the plural variables yields NEQ* which is sound and complete wrt. to the power algebra semantics.

1. Introduction

A major motivating force behind research into abstract data types and algebraic specifications is the realization that software in general and types in particular should be descibed ("specified") in an abstract manner. The objective is to give specifications at some level of abstraction: on the one hand leaving open decisions regarding further refinement and on the other allowing for substitutivity of modules as long as they satisfy a particular specificaiton.

We argue that the use of nondeterministic operators is an appropriate and useful abstraction tool, and more: nondeterminism is a *natural* abstraction concept whenever there is a hidden state or other components of a system description which are, methodologically, conceptually or technically, inaccessible at a particular level of abstraction.

Having established our motivation for using nondeterministic operators, we discuss the distinction between two modes of parameter passing – "call by value" and "call by name." In deterministic programming this distinction is well known. The former corresponds to the situation where the actual parameters to function calls are evaluated and passed as values. The latter allows parameters which are function expressions, passed by a kind of Algol copy rule [23], and which are evaluated whenever a need for their value arises. Thus call-by-name will terminate in many cases when the value of a function may be determined without looking at (some of) the actual parameters, i.e., even if these parameters are undefined. Call-by-value will, in such cases,

* This work has been partially supported by the Architectural Abstraction project under NFR (Norway), by CEC under ESPRIT–II Basic Reearch Working Group No. 6112 COMPASS, by the US DARPA under ONR contract N00014-92-J-1928, N00014-93-1-1335 and by the US Air Force Office of Scientific Research under Grant AFOSR-91-0354.

lead to an undefined result of the call. Nevertheless, the call-by-value semantics is usually preferred in the actual programming languages since it results in clearer and more tractable programs.

The nondeterministic counterparts of these two notions[1] are what we call *singular* (also called *call-time-choice* and corresponding to call-by-value) and *plural* (*run-time-choice* corresponding to call-by-name) parameter passing [2, 7, 24]. In the context where one allows nondeterministic parameters the difference between the two semantics becomes quite obvious even without looking at their termination properties. Let us suppose that we have defined an operation $g(x)$ as "***if*** x=0 ***then*** 0 ***elseif*** x=1 ***then*** 1 ***else*** 2", and that we have a nondeterministic choice operation "$\sqcup$._: Set(S)$\rightarrow$ S" returning an arbitrary element from the argument set. The singular interpretation of g($\sqcup$.{0,1}) will yield either 0 or 1, i.e., the result set of g($\sqcup$.{0,1}) is {0,1}. The plural interpretation will give {0,1,2} as the set of possible results. (In a deterministic environment both semantics would yield the same results for this example.)

Another important difference concerns reasoning in the presence of nondeterministic operations, in particular, the substitutivity property. The inside-out substitution (corresponding, roughly speaking, to singular parameters) is not associative in the nondeterministic context [3, 4], and complicates the reasoning system by requiring specific restrictions on the substitution rules [12, 25]. Plural parameters, on the other hand, admit unrestricted substitution rules and, although semantically more complex, lead to simpler reasoning systems [25].

The above observations, together with the fact that the distinction has not received a thorough algebraic treatment,[2] motivate our investigation.

Multialgebras, used to model *singular* parameters, are algebras where operations are interpeted as set-valued functions and composition is defined by pointwise extension. This reflects the fact that, when the argument to an operation is a "set" (i.e., a nondeterministic expression), the choice of denotation for the expression (i.e. which element is to be used) is made at call-time, before passing the argument to the body of the operation. To model *plural* arguments, one has to generalize this construction and allow passing "whole sets" as arguments. This is achieved by using power algebras – algebras with carriers being (subsets of) power sets, and with operations mapping sets to sets (which in this setting are just the elements of the carriers).

In section 2 we give a general motivation for introducing nondeterministic operators as specification tools. In section 3 we define the language for specifying nondeterministic operators and its multialgebraic semantics which allow us to present, in section 4, two examples illustrating the usefulness of nondeterminism in achieving appropriate levels of abstraction. In section 5 we introduce a sound and complete calculus and discuss some of its features. Then we present an *algebraic* perspective on the distinction between the singular and plural passing of nondeterministic parameters. In section 6 the multialgebraic semantics for singular parameters is generalized to *power algebras* capable of modelling plural parameters. The corresponding sound and complete extension of the calculus is discussed in section 7. A comparison of both semantics in section 8 is guided by the similarity of the respective calculi. We indicate the

[1] We are not focusing here on the related distinctions (such as eager vs. lazy, IO vs. OI evaluation), discussion of which is beyond the scope of this paper.

[2] Unified algebras [19, 20] of P.D.Mosses, and rewriting logic [17, 16] of J. Meseguer handle both kinds of parameters. However, they do it in a highly non-standard, albeit elegant, way. We feel that multi- and power algebras stay closer to the traditional algebraic framework.

increased complexity of the power algebra semantics reflecting the problems with intuitive understanding of plural arguments. We also point out that plural variables can be used meaningfully to increase expressibility of the specification formalism even if all operations have only singular arguments.

The main (completeness) proofs are quite long and involved. The space limitation does not allow us to include them here, but all the proofs may be found in [26].

2. Nondeterministic Operators as Specification Tools

There are essentially two reasons why one might want to include the concept of nondeterminism in the traditional algebraic specification methods:

(1) *Real* nondeterminism.
The system being specified really is nondeterministic – its behavior is not fully predictable, nor fully reproducible.

(2) *Representational* nondeterminism.
The behavior of the system being specified may be fully predictable in its final implementation (i.e. deterministic), but it may not be so at the level of abstraction of the specification.

Though many think of representational nondeterminism as identical to underspecification, they turn out to be technically and conceptually quite distinct (as we shall see shortly).

Whether the world *really* is nondeterministic or not we leave to the physicists and philosophers to ponder. A computer system *in isolation* certainly is deterministic: When started from a particular state (given in full detail) twice, both executions will demonstrate identical behavior. Possible sources of perceived nondeterminism lie only in the unpredictability of the environment such as hardware failures or human factors. Considering all such factors as parts of the total state given in full detail may obviate the perceived nondeterminism, but leads to undesirable complexity and is possible only in principle.

The primary argument in favor of accepting nondeterministic operators is instrumental, and identical to the credo of the abstract data type community: One should specify a system *only in such detail that any implementation satisfying the specification also satisfies the user, and no more.* It turns out that nondeterministic operators ease the process of specifying systems by allowing one to disregard irrelevant aspects – be they the external influences or implementation details – and thus reducing the danger of overspecification resulting from technical rather than methodical reasons.

For purposes of discussion it may be convenient to further identify three variants of representational nondeterminism: (1) abstraction from hidden state, (2) abstraction from time, and (3) abstraction from external entities. Though dealt with uniformly within our framework, these have often been considered distinct. In particular, the introduction of nondeterminism as a result of abstraction from *time* is usually taken as a given in the process algebra community without thereby necessesarily accepting abstraction over *state* as requiring nondeterminsm for specification purposes.

How does this use of nondeterminism differ from the usual notion of underspecification? Consider for a moment a choice function $\sqcup$ from sets of integers to integers, returning one of the elements of the set:

For instance, $\sqcup.\{0,1\}$ may return either of the values 0 and 1. If $\sqcup$ were just an underspecified function, then we would have that $\sqcup.\{0,1\}=\sqcup.\{1,0\}$, since the arguments of the function are equal (though not syntactically identical) in the two terms.

In practical terms, this would require the choice operator always to return the same value when applied to a particular set. I.e., ⊔.{0,1} is always 0, or always 1.

However, this kind of underspecification does not allow for abstraction from (conceptually) invisible entities that might influence the choice (such as a hidden state, timing or interaction with a human being). E.g., if set values were implemented as unordered sequences with new elements always added to the front of the sequence, this underspecified description of the choice function would disallow using a simple implementation of choice as the head-function, since such an implementation would sometimes return the value 0, sometimes the value 1, when applied to the set {0,1}, depending on which of the two elements were added first. If we were to treat ⊔ as a nondeterministic operator, on the other hand, then such a straightforward implementation (though deterministic) would be quite acceptable (both formally and according to the usual intuition about the requirements of an operator picking some element from a set).

Similarly, if the implementation of the choice function asked a human operator to pick an element then one would encounter the same difficulty: The behavior of human beings may be deterministic, but even were that the case their inner state determining that behavior is not available for inspection. A specification needs to abstract away from that inner state, and nondeterminism is the right concept for doing that.

And similarly again, if the choice depended upon timing properties (e.g. the set was distributed among a number of processors, and the choice function simply queried them all, returning the first (in terms of time) value returned to it by one of these processors) the abstraction away from timing properties would introduce a seeming nondeterminism.

In order to make further examples more understandable, we have to introduce a formal language for specifying (possibly nondeterministic) operators and its semantics.

3. The Language $\mathcal{L}$ and the Multialgebra Semantics

A specification is a pair (Σ, Π), where the *signature* Σ is a pair of a sets (S, F) of sorts S and operation symbols F (with argument and result sorts in S). There exists a denumerable set V of variables for every sort. For any syntactic entity (term, formula, set of formulae) χ, $V[\chi]$ will denote the set of variables in χ.

The set of terms over the signature Σ and a variable set X is denoted $W_{\Sigma,X}$. We always assume that the set of ground terms of every sort S, S^{W_Σ}, is not empty.[1]

Π is a set of *sequents* of atomic formulae written as $a_1,...,a_n \mapsto e_1,...,e_m$. The left hand side of $\mapsto$ is called the *antecedent* and the right hand side the *consequent*, and both are to be understood as sets of atomic formulae (i.e., the ordering and multiplicity of the atomic formulae do not matter). In general, we allow either antecedent or consequent to be empty, in which case $\emptyset$ is usually dropped in the notation. A sequent with exactly one formula in the consequent (m=1) is called a *Horn formula*, and a Horn formula with empty antecedent (n=0) is a *simple formula* (or a *simple sequent*).

An atomic formula is either an *equation*, t=s, or an *inclusion*, $t \prec s$, of terms t,

[1] We do not address the problem of empty sorts here and will present calculi which work under the assumption that sorts are not empty. We use signatures with at least one constant for every sort but other ways of approaching this problem [5, 6, 11] seem to be compatible with our framework.

$s \in W_{\Sigma,X}$. All variables occurring in a sequent are implicitly universally quantified over the whole sequent. For a specification $SP=(\Sigma, \Pi)$, $\mathcal{L}(SP)$ is the restriction of $\mathcal{L}$ to $W_{\Sigma,V}$.

The semantics of $\mathcal{L}$ specifications uses multistructures. Our definitions are very similar to those used by other authors [9, 12, 13, 21] except for the notion of equality. Also, we provide the means to interpret the occurrences of terms in $\mathcal{L}$ as *applications* of (possibly nondeterministic) operations rather than, as it is usually the case, as the sets of possible results.

Definition 3.1 (Multistructures). Let SP be an $\mathcal{L}$ specification. M is an SP-*multistructure* if

1. its carrier $|M|$ is an S-sorted set and
2. for every $f: S_1 \times ... \times S_n \rightarrow S$ in **F** there is a corresponding function $f^M: S_1^M \times ... \times S_n^M \rightarrow \mathcal{P}^+(S^M)$.

□

where $\mathcal{P}^+$ denotes the power set with the empty set excluded. We let *MStr(SP)* denote the class of SP-multistructures. It has the distinguished term structure:

Definition 3.2 (Term multistructure). The *term multistructure* W_Σ for a specification $SP=(\Sigma,\Pi)$ is defined as:

1. for each $S \in \mathbf{S}$, S^{W_Σ} is the set of ground terms of sort S,
2. for each $f: S_1 \times ... \times S_n \rightarrow S$ in **F**, $t_i \in S_i^{W_\Sigma}$: $f^{W_\Sigma}(t_1 ... t_n) = \{f(t_1 ... t_n)\}$

□

It is a known fact that, in the general case, one cannot guarantee the existence of initial multimodels. Hußmann [12] has shown that even if we restrict $\mathcal{L}$ to simple formulae such multimodels may not exist. Therefore we admit general, and not only Horn, formulae in the specifications and will consider the whole class of multimodels of a specification.[1] The significance of the term multistructure is then summarized in

Lemma 3.3. If M is an SP-multistructure then for every set X of variables and assignment $\beta: X \rightarrow |M|$, there exists a unique function $\beta[\_]$: $W_{\Sigma,X} \rightarrow \mathcal{P}^+(|M|)$ such that:

$$\beta[x] = \{\beta(x)\},\ \beta[c] = c^M \text{ and } \beta[f(t_1 ... t_n)] = \{f^M(t1 ... tn) \mid ti \in \beta[t_i]\}$$

□

Application of multialgebraic operations to sets is defined by pointwise extension. Consequently, all operations in multistructures are $\subseteq$-monotonic, i.e., $\beta[s] \subseteq \beta[t] \Rightarrow \beta[f(s)] \subseteq \beta[f(t)]$.

Definition 3.4. An SP-multistructure M *satisfies* an $\mathcal{L}$(SP) sequent

$$\pi: t_i = s_i, ..., t_j \prec s_j \mapsto p_n = r_n, ... p_m \prec r_m\ ,$$

written $M \models \pi$, iff for every assignment $\beta : X \rightarrow |M|$ we have

---

[1] For a discussion of initiality the reader is referred to [12, 25]. All the results reported in this paper remain valid for the specification language restricted to Horn formulae.

$$\beta[t_i]\equiv\beta[s_i] \wedge \ldots \wedge \beta[t_j]\subseteq\beta[s_j] \Rightarrow \beta[p_n]\equiv\beta[r_n] \vee \ldots \vee \beta[p_m]\subseteq\beta[r_m]$$

where $A\equiv B$ iff A and B are the same 1-element set.

An SP-*multimodel* is an SP-multistructure which satisfies all the axioms of SP. *MMod(SP)* denotes the class of multimodels of SP.

⊡

As a consequence of this definition, = is not an equivalence relation (it is not reflexive). $\mapsto t{=}t$ holds in a multialgebra M only if t^M has exactly one element, i.e., if the term t is deterministic. Of course, the set equality of two terms is expressible as two inclusions: $\mapsto s{\prec}t$ and $\mapsto t{\prec}s$.

Note that all variables are used singularly, i.e., they range over individuals (1-element sets) and not over arbitrary sets. In particular, assignments in lemma 3.3 and definition 3.4 assign to each variable a 1-element set. This fact is utilized to distinguish between the *result set* of an operation (which is represented by the corresponding term) and the result returned by a *particular application* of the operation as the following example illustrates.

Example 3.5.

The axiom $\mapsto x\sqcup y{=}x,\ x\sqcup y{=}y$ would make the binary choice operation $\_\sqcup\_$: $S\times S\to S$ deterministic (though underspecified). It says that (for any value of x,y), the set $x\sqcup y$ is either the same as the 1-element set x or y. In order to make $\sqcup$ a nondeterministic choice we have to say that *any application* of $x\sqcup y$ returns either x or y. This is expressed by the axiom: $z{\prec}x\sqcup y \mapsto z{=}x,\ z{=}y$.

⊡

4. Two Examples

Consider the problem of generating a depth-first traversal tree of nodes reachable from a particular node in a directed graph. The algorithm is found in standard algorithms textbooks (e.g. [15]), and is often given imperatively along the following lines (G is the graph, v is the start node, T is traversal tree being created and edges are ordered pairs of nodes):

Example 4.1.a

```
DFS(G,v) =
      begin T := Ø;
            trav(G,v,T);
            return T;
      end;
trav(G,v,T) =
      begin mark v;
            for all edges (v,x) do
              if x is unmarked then trav(G,x,T); T := T∪(v,x); endif ;
            endloop;
      end;
```

⊡

Now, consider an equational definition of DFS as a deterministic function. Let the function $n(\_,\_)$: Graph × Node → Set(Node) return the set of neighbors of a node in a given graph.

Example 4.1.b

$G, v, T, S, x \in V$:

$$\mapsto \mathrm{DFS}(G,v) = trav(G,v,\emptyset)$$

$$n(G,v)=\emptyset \mapsto trav(G,v,T) = T$$

$$\left.\begin{array}{l} n(G,v) = add(S,x), \\ x \in T = True \end{array}\right\} \mapsto trav(G,v,T) = trav(G\backslash\{(v,x)\},\ v,\ T)$$

$$\left.\begin{array}{l} n(G,v) = add(S,x), \\ x \in T = False \end{array}\right\} \mapsto trav(G,v,T) = trav(G\backslash\{(v,x)\},\ v,\ trav(G\backslash\{(v,x)\},\ x,\ T\cup\{(v,x)\}))$$

⊡

(The element tests check whether a node is in the tree (i.e., marked) already.) This definition looks plausible only as long as we do not inspect the Set sort. Adding elements to a set should be commutative – we have that

$$\mapsto add(add(S,x),y) = add(add(S,y),x)$$

But then we also obtain

$$\mapsto trav(\ add(add(G,(v,a)),(v,b)),\ v,\ \emptyset) = trav(\ add(add(G,(v,b)),(v,a)),\ v,\ \emptyset)$$

In other words, for the graph

G = 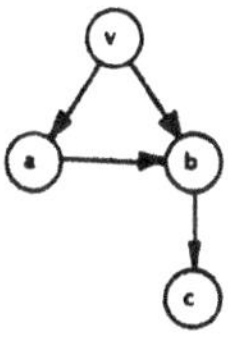 we get the DFS-tree equality: 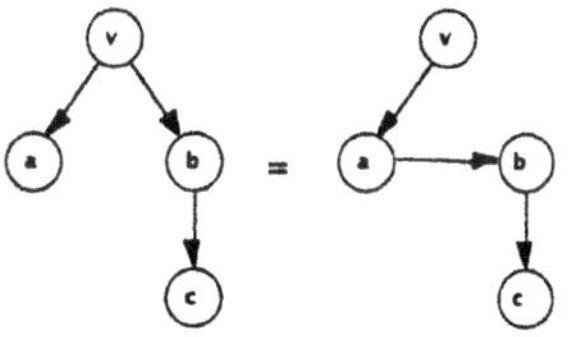

which was not at all the intention – it collapses distinct tree values.

The problem is that the internal structure of the set value (in this case, the definition of DFS in terms of adding elements to the set) intrudes into the specification, quite contrary to the central tenet of abstract specifications.

An abstract definition of the DFS operator could be

Example 4.1.c

$G, v, T, S, x, y \in V$:

$$\mapsto \mathrm{DFS}(G,v) \prec trav(G,v,\emptyset)$$

$$n(G,v)=\emptyset \mapsto trav(G,v,T) = T$$

$$\left.\begin{array}{l} n(G,v) = add(S,y), \\ x \prec \sqcup.n(G,v), \\ x \in T = True \end{array}\right\} \mapsto trav(G,v,T) \prec trav(G\backslash\{(v,x)\},\ v,\ T)$$

$$\left.\begin{array}{l} n(G,v) = add(S,y), \\ x \prec \sqcup.n(G,v), \\ x \in T = False \end{array}\right\} \mapsto trav(G,v,T) \prec trav(G\backslash\{(v,x)\},\ v,\ trav(G\backslash\{(v,x)\},\ x,\ T\cup\{(v,x)\}))$$

⊡

Though the specification still makes use of the structure of the set-generator functions, this no longer intrudes into the valuation of the function itself beyond ensuring a distinction between empty neighbor-sets and non-empty such. The variable x denotes the result of an arbitrary choice among these neighbors. The resultant definition defines the function without being concerned with (or specifying) the internal, representational structure of the graph. We no longer collapse "distinct" trees, instead we only get the following (and plausible) result; that DFS-traversal will generate one of two trees:

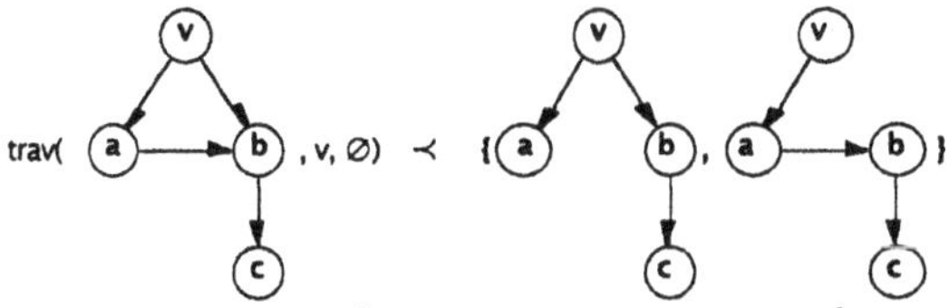

In general, iterating over sets or other structures is a natural operation, even when there is no intrinsic total order on the elements of such a structure. Such iteration is often deterministic, but representation-dependent, and if the iteration operation is *specified* as deterministic then we get an overspecification. The possibility to ignore the representation-dependent structure of the specified data is one of the fundamental requirements for a specification formalism.

The last small example illustrates another aspect of the abstraction potential inherent in nondeterminism.

Abstracting over *time* is such a natural thing to do that many consider timing dependencies as representing *real* nondeterminism. However, time is just another component of state, and abstraction over time could therefore be handled similarly to abstraction over state in general. As an example of how time can be removed from consideration in a specification, consider the specification of a merge function m. Its arguments are two streams of data, and the result a new stream which is a merger of the two (here the metric aspects of time have been removed, leaving time only in a vestigial form as a total order for each of the input- and output-streams, ignoring even the relative ordering of elements in distinct streams) (e.g. in [10, 18] and related works).

Let M be a function with only one input stream, but constructed from m with the output stream fed back as one of the input streams of m (see figure).

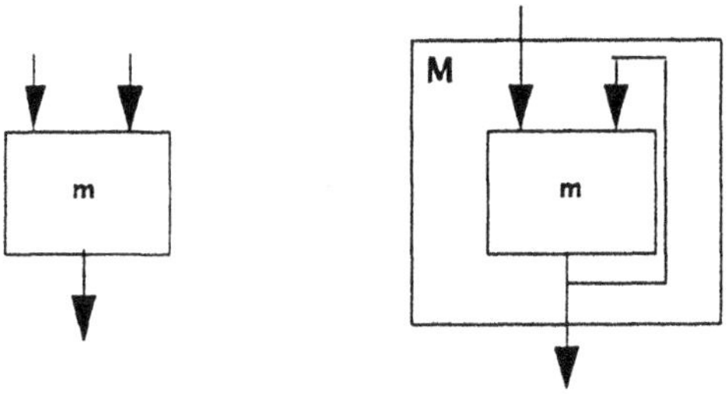

A specification of these two functions could be (where ^ is the concatenation operator on streams and ε is an empty stream):

Example 4.2

$q, p, x, y, r \in V$:

$$
\begin{aligned}
& \mapsto m(\varepsilon,q) = q \\
& \mapsto m(q,\varepsilon) = q \\
r \prec m(x\^{}q, y\^{}p) & \mapsto r \prec x\^{}m(q, y\^{}p),\ r \prec y\^{}m(x\^{}q, p) \\
& \mapsto M(\varepsilon) = \varepsilon \\
r \prec M(x\^{}q) & \mapsto r \prec x\^{}m(q, r)
\end{aligned}
$$

⊡

As we can see, m is deterministic when there is only one non-empty input stream. Buf if there are two, then the first element of the result stream (r) is the first element of *one or the other* of the two input streams. When we construct the feedback function M then any nonempty input stream results in an infinite output stream, but the composition of the output is not determined – that would reflect the timing property of the function evaluation and of the input, which we have abstracted. Again, the abstraction shows up as nondeterminism.

It may be an interesting excercise for the reader to convince himself that the above specification yields the intended meaning for the M operator and does not lead to the classical merge-anomalies [11, 14]. The example is discussed in more detail in [25].

Finally, we can mention that the close relation between nondeterministic terms and sets makes it possible to use the former to define and handle subsorting directly at the term level. This is the basic intuition behind the framework of unified algebras [19, 20] and can also be done within the formalism we have introduced here.

5. The Calculus NEQ

The last axiom in the merge example 4.2 uses the variable r to specify the desired properties of *each possible* result produced by the M operator. It says that any such r is obtained by taking the first element x of the input sequence and then merging the rest of the input sequence with r *itself*. This is different from the axiom obtained by replacing the occurrences of r with $M(x\hat{}q)$: $\mapsto M(x\hat{}q) \prec x\hat{}m(q,M(x\hat{}q))$ which, plausible as it may seem, creates the usual merge-anomalies.

This illustrates the inherent problem of reasoning with nondeterminism, namely, unsoundness of unrestricted substitution of terms for variables. In our formalism we handle this problem by turning = into a partial equivalence realtion and allowing substitution of a term t for a variable only if $\mapsto t{=}t$ is derivable (rule SB). The rules of the calculus NEQ are:

R1: $\mapsto x{=}x \qquad x \in V$

R2: $$\frac{\Gamma^x_t \mapsto \Delta^x_t \quad ; \quad \Gamma' \mapsto s{=}t, \Delta'}{\Gamma^x_s, \Gamma' \mapsto \Delta^x_s, \Delta'}$$

R3: $$\frac{\Gamma \mapsto \Delta^x_t \quad ; \quad \Gamma' \mapsto s{\prec}t, \Delta'}{\Gamma, \Gamma' \mapsto \Delta^x_s, \Delta'}$$ x not in a RHS[1] of $\prec$

R4: $e \mapsto e$

R5: $$\frac{\Gamma \mapsto \Delta, e \quad ; \quad \Gamma', e \mapsto \Delta'}{\Gamma, \Gamma' \mapsto \Delta, \Delta'}$$ (CUT)

R6: a) $$\frac{\Gamma \mapsto \Delta}{\Gamma \mapsto \Delta, e}$$ b) $$\frac{\Gamma \mapsto \Delta}{\Gamma, e \mapsto \Delta}$$ (WEAK)

[1] RHS, resp. LHS, stand for right, resp. left, hand side.

R7: a) $\dfrac{\Gamma, x \prec t \mapsto \Delta}{\Gamma^x_t \mapsto \Delta^x_t}$ b) $\dfrac{\Gamma, x \prec t, y \prec r \mapsto \Delta}{\Gamma, y \prec r^x_t \mapsto \Delta}$ (ELIM)

a) $x \in V \backslash V[t]$
at most one x in $\Gamma \mapsto \Delta$
x in Γ isn't in RHS of $\prec$

b) $x \in V \backslash V[t]$, $y \in V$
no x in $\Gamma \mapsto \Delta$
at most one x in r
x and y are distinct variables

χ^a_b denotes χ with b substituted for a. The rule R1 expresses the fact that only variables are guaranteed to be deterministic. The restriction on R3 prevents one, for instance, from drawing the unsound conclusion $s \prec p$ from the premises $s \prec t$ and $p \prec t$.

The R7 rules allow one to eliminate a redundant binding $x \prec t$ replacing x by t. Since x refers to one and the same value, such a replacement requires that there be at most one occurrence of x. Otherwise we could, for instance, derive $t{=}t$ (for *arbitrary* t) from $x \prec t \mapsto x = x$ by a single application of R7a.

A similar problem would occur if we removed the second or third restriction from R7b. The other restrictions are of purely technical character. Allowing x to occur in t would, for instance, lead to the unsound deduction (using R7a): $\dfrac{x \prec t(x), x = 1}{t(x) = 1}$

The last restriction in R7a excludes the special case which is related to the singular semantics and is treated by R7b.

As an example of the semantic import of thes rules we give a few derived rules:

NE: $\dfrac{x \prec t \mapsto}{\mapsto}$ Restrictions as for R7a (Terms represent non-empty sets)

SI: $\dfrac{x \prec t, s \prec r \mapsto \; ; \; \mapsto s = s}{s \prec r^x_t \mapsto}$ Restrictions as for R7b (Arguments are singular)

This rule can be rephrased as $\dfrac{\forall x(x \in t \Rightarrow s \notin r(x))}{s \notin r(t)}$ which, read contravariantly, says: if s is in the result set of $r(t)$ then there exists an individual $x \in t$ such that s is in the result set $r(x)$, i.e., the argument t to r is singular.

SB: $\dfrac{\Gamma \mapsto \Delta \qquad \Gamma' \mapsto t{=}t, \Delta'}{\Gamma^x_t, \Gamma' \mapsto \Delta^x_t, \Delta'}$ (Variables are replacable by deterministic terms)

The main theorem states soundness and completeness of NEQ wrt. the multialgebraic semantics:

Theorem 5.1. For every specification SP=(Σ,Π), sequent $\pi \in \mathcal{L}(SP)$

$$\mathrm{MMod}(SP) \models \pi \text{ iff } \Pi \vdash_{NEQ} \pi$$

⊡

6. Power Algebras

Singular arguments have the usual algebraic property that they refer to a unique value. This corresponds to evaluation at the moment of substitution and passing the result to the following computation. Plural arguments, on the other hand, are best understood as textual parameters. They are not passed as a single value but the expression receiving them is first expanded and evaluation takes place only when the expansion is completed.

To capture this possibility we have to extend the multialgebra semantics to power algebras where operations map sets to sets. We will allow both singular and plural parameter passing in anyone specification. The corresponding semantic distinction will be between the power set functions which are merely $\subseteq$-monotonic and those which also are $\cup$-additive.

In the language we merely introduce a notational device for distinguishing the singular and plural arguments. We allow annotating the sorts in the profiles of the operation by a superscript, as in S^+, to indicate that an argument is plural. Furthermore, we partition the set of variables into two disjoint subsets of singular, X, and plural, X^+, variables. x and x^+ are to be understood as distinct symbols. We will say that an operation f is *singular in the* i^{th} *argument* iff the ith argument (in its signature) is singular. The specification language extended with such annotations of the signatures will be referred to as $\mathcal{L}^+$. By a *singular specification* we will mean one where all arguments to all operations are singular.

Definition 6.1. Let each S_i be the power set of some underlying set $\underline{S}_i$, i.e., $S_i = \mathcal{P}^+(\underline{S}_i)$. A function f: $S_1 \times \ldots \times S_n \to S$ is $\cup$*-additive* in the ith argument iff for all $x_i \in S_i$ and all $x_k \in S_k$ (for $k \neq i$) : $f(x_1 \ldots x_i \ldots x_n) = \bigcup \{ f(x_1 \ldots \{x\} \ldots x_n) \mid x \in x_i \}$.
⊡

Definition 6.2. Let Σ be a $\mathcal{L}^+$-signature. A is a Σ*-powerstructure*, $A \in PStr(\Sigma)$, iff A is a (deterministic) structure such that:
1. for every $S \in S$, the carrier $S^A \subseteq \mathcal{P}^+(\underline{S})$, for some underlying set $\underline{S}$,
2. for every f: $S_1 \times \ldots \times S_n \to S$ in Σ, f^A is a $\subseteq$-monotonic function $S_1^A \times \ldots \times S_n^A \to S^A$ such that, if the ith argument of f is singular then f^A is additive in the ith argument.

⊡

Note the unorthodox point in definition 6.2 – we do not require the carrier of a power structure to be the whole power set but allow it to be a *subset* of some power set. All finite subsets are needed, for instance, if one assumes a primitive nondeterministic choice with predefined semantics of set union. We do not assume anything of the kind and expect that quite many meaningful specifications may do very well without all possible subsets. In addition, using full power sets as carriers would always yield unreachable structures whenever the underlying set is infinite.

Given an f:$S \times S^+ \to T$, we will say that an actual argument at the first position has a *singular occurrence*. E.g., in $f(t,t)$, the first t has a singular, and the second one a plural occurrence. More precisely:

Definition 6.3. α has a *singular occurrence* in a term t iff one of the following holds ($\doteq$ denotes syntactical identity):
1. $t \doteq \alpha$
2. $t \doteq f(\ldots,\alpha,\ldots)$ and f is singular in the argument corresponding to α,
3. $t \doteq f(t_1,\ldots,t_n)$ and α has a singular occurence in one of t_i.

⊡

The first point is included for the technical reasons – the definition will be used to specify additional restrictions on the application of some reasoning rules. To define satisfiability of formulae by a power structure we only need to extend the definition of an assignment

Definition 6.4. Let X be a set of singular and X^+ a set of plural variables. By an *assignment* into a power structure A we mean a function $\beta: X \cup X^+ \to |A|$ such that, for all $x \in X$, $|\beta(x)| = 1$.
$\boxdot$

If β is as in this definition, then every term $t(x,x^+) \in W_{\Sigma,X,X^+}$ has a unique set interpretation $\beta[t(x,x^+)]$ in A defined as $t^A(\beta(x),\beta(x^+))$. Satisfiability of sequents over $\mathcal{L}^+(\Sigma,X,X^+)$ by a power structure is then defined exactly as before (def. 3.4) and the class of power models of a specification SP is denoted PMod(SP).

Since functions from A to $\mathcal{P}^+(B)$ are isomorphic to $\cup$-additive functions from $\mathcal{P}^+(A)$ to $\mathcal{P}^+(B)$, $[A \to \mathcal{P}^+(B)] \simeq [\mathcal{P}^+(A) \to_{\cup} \mathcal{P}^+(B)]$, we may consider every multistructure A to be a power structure A^+ by taking $|A^+| = \mathcal{P}^+(A)$ and extending all operations in A pointwise. We then have the obvious

Lemma 6.5. Let SP be a singular specification, $A \in$MStr(SP), and π be a sequent in $\mathcal{L}$(SP). Then $A \models \pi$ iff $A^+ \models \pi$, and so $A \in$MMod(SP) iff $A^+ \in$PMod(SP).
$\boxdot$

7. The Calculus NEQ$^+$ for Join Semantics

We let $V[t]$ be the set of singular and $V^+[t]$ the set of plural variables in t. Rules R1-R7 are as in NEQ (except for a new restriction in R7) but now all terms t_i belong to W_{Σ,X,X^+}. In particular, any t_i may be a plural variable.

R1: $\quad \mapsto x{=}x \qquad\qquad x \in V$

R2: $$\frac{\Gamma^x_t \mapsto \Delta^x_t \quad ; \quad \Gamma' \mapsto s{=}t, \Delta'}{\Gamma^x_s, \Gamma' \mapsto \Delta^x_s, \Delta'}$$

R3: $$\frac{\Gamma \mapsto \Delta^x_t \quad ; \quad \Gamma' \mapsto s{\prec}t, \Delta'}{\Gamma, \Gamma' \mapsto \Delta^x_s, \Delta'} \qquad x \text{ not in a RHS of } \prec$$

R4: $\quad e \mapsto e$

R5: $$\frac{\Gamma \mapsto \Delta, e \quad ; \quad \Gamma', e \mapsto \Delta'}{\Gamma, \Gamma' \mapsto \Delta, \Delta'} \qquad \text{(CUT)}$$

R6: a) $$\frac{\Gamma \mapsto \Delta}{\Gamma \mapsto \Delta, e}$$ b) $$\frac{\Gamma \mapsto \Delta}{\Gamma, e \mapsto \Delta}$$ (WEAK)

R7: a) $\dfrac{\Gamma, x \prec t \mapsto \Delta}{\Gamma^x_t \mapsto \Delta^x_t}$ b) $\dfrac{\Gamma, x \prec t, y \prec r \mapsto \Delta}{\Gamma, y \prec r^x_t \mapsto \Delta}$ (ELIM)

a) $x \in V \backslash V[t]$
at most one x in $\Gamma \mapsto \Delta$
x in Γ isn't in RHS of $\prec$
the occurrence of x is *singular*

b) $x \in V \backslash V[t]$, $y \in V$
no x in $\Gamma \mapsto \Delta$
at most one x in r
the occurrence of x in r is *singular*
x and y are distinct variables

R8: $\dfrac{\Gamma \mapsto \Delta}{\Gamma^{x^+}_t \mapsto \Delta^{x^+}_t}$ (SUBP)

We used R7b from NEQ to derive SI, which expressed singularity of all arguments. Therefore, in NEQ$^+$ we need an additional restriction to make sure that the substitution for x takes place only at the arguments which are singular. The derived rules MO, NE, SB are the same as for NEQ, but SI is now restricted to the singular occurrences of x.

The new rule R8 expresses the semantics of plural variables. It allows us to substitute an arbitrary term t for a plural variable x^+. Taking t to be a singular variable x, we can thus exchange plural variables in a provable sequent π with singular ones. The opposite is, in general, not possible because rule R1 applies only to singular variables. Thus a plural variable x^+ will satisfy $\mapsto x^+ \prec x^+$, but this is not sufficient for performing a substitution for a singular variable according to SB.

The result corresponding to theorem 5.1 is:

Theorem 7.1. For any $\mathcal{L}^+$-specification SP and $\mathcal{L}^+$(SP) sequent π:

$$\text{PMod(SP)} \models \pi \text{ iff } \Pi \vdash_{\text{NEQ}^+} \pi$$

□

8. Singular vs. Plural, Arguments vs. Variables

NEQ$^+$ has the additional rule R8 which could suggest that more formulae are derivable with it than with NEQ. This would go counter lemma 6.5 and the intuition that power models form a more general class than multimodels. There is no contradiction, however, because what actually limits the number of derivations in NEQ$^+$ is the additional restriction on the rules R7. For instance, having operations g:S→ T, and f:S$^+$→T, we may in both calculi prove:

$$\frac{x \prec t, y \prec g(x) \mapsto}{y \prec g(t) \mapsto} \text{ R7b}$$

Replacing g with f in the assumption would disallow the analogous conclusion in NEQ$^+$.

Rule R8, admitting instantiation of plural variables, is useful only if the axioms of the specification contain such variables. Axioms with plural variables can also be viewed as axiom schemata for axioms without such variables. From the logical point of view, axiom $\mapsto f(x^+) \prec r(x^+, x^+)$ leads to the same formulae (without plural variables) as the set of axioms $\{ \mapsto f(t) \prec r(t,t) \mid t \in W_{\Sigma,X} \}$.

Thus we can see that rule R7$^+$ is concerned with plural *arguments*, while rule R8 with plural *variables*. In fact, introducing plural arguments does not force one to use plural variables and, on the other hand, axioms containing plural variables can be used even if all operations are singular. We may set up the relations between the use of singular/plural variables/arguments and the associated sound and complete reasoning systems in the following way ($R7^+$ denotes R7 with the restrictions from NEQ^+):

arguments \ variables	singular	plural
singular	1 NEQ	2 NEQ,$R7^+$
plural	3 NEQ,R8	4 NEQ^+

If a specification contains only singular variables, then NEQ is sufficient for proving all its consequences if all operations are singular (1) – if some arguments are plural (2) then we have to use the more restricted version $R7^+$. Obviously, we have that $2 \subseteq 1$ and $4 \subseteq 3$.

If all operations are singular then we may still use plural variables in the formulae and need to extend NEQ with the rule R8 (3). In this case, we have to consider multialgebras as power algebras with all operations being additive (according to lemma 6.5), in order to obtain a proper notion of assignment to the plural variables. In fact, this is the alternative we would prefer in general, unless one is explicitly interested in the specification of plural arguments. We feel that this combination of the singular semantics of parameter passing with the use of plural variables gives us both simplicity of multialgebras (as compared to power algebras) and the increased expressive power in writing specification as illustrated by the following example.

Example 8.1.

Consider the following (singular) specification of binary choice $\_\sqcup\_ : S\times S \rightarrow S$ as the join operator:

$$\mapsto x^+ \prec x^+ \sqcup y^+$$
$$\mapsto y^+ \prec x^+ \sqcup y^+$$
$$x^+ \prec z^+, y^+ \prec z^+ \mapsto x^+ \sqcup y^+ \prec z^+$$

An analogous attempt to specify join with singular variables only would fail, because the last axiom would then be $x \prec z, y \prec z \mapsto x \sqcup y \prec z$ which is equivalent to $\mapsto z \sqcup z = z$. This observation indicates that plural variables may be an alternative to disjunctions which had to be used for the specification of choice in example 3.5.

□

9. Conclusions and Further Work.

We have introduced a formalism for specification of (possibly) nondeterministic operations and defined multialgebra and power algebra semantics for the singular, respectively, plural parameters. The main result of the paper are the two reasoning systems which are sound and complete for the respective semantics.

The comparison of the two semantics led us to point out that the singular/plural distinction has two, relatively independent, facets. On the one hand, it may be taken as a purely semantic distinction concerning the mechanism of parameter passing. On the other hand, plural variables may be used as a merely syntactic device to increase expressiveness of the specification language, which does not force one to accept the plural semantics of parameter passing.

We have considered only flat specifications and consequently the current results must be seen only as the first step toward a full specification formalism which would be applicable in software develompment practice. The work on structural specification with nondeterminism is in progress and we can only indicate some main points. The central idea is the one emphasized in this and other papers [7, 22, 25, 27]: *non-determinism is a natural abstraction tool* and this fact may prove valuable when considering the implementation and composition of specifications.

Specification-building operations such as **enrich** (+), **derive**, (**reduct**) and hence **export** and **rename** should extend smoothly to the nondeterministic context.

Quotient needs a slight generalisation since we have only partial equivalence and not congruence. Releasing the congruency claim w.r.t. nondeterminisitc operations may seem a blasphemy to the mathematical practice, but it turns out to be a crucial move in achieving a sound data refinement in a nondeterminisitic setting. Our current experiences and [22] show that some problematic cases may be elegantly handled using our nondeterministic framework. Consider for instance the implementation of abstract sets with a (non- or underdetermined) choice operator. A natural and simple implementation would represent sets as sequences with the "head" operation implementing choice. Accepting this as a correct implementaiton would traditionally require the notion of *behavioral equivalence.* In such cases, the abstract character of nondeterministic operations may be used successfully as an alternative to the behavioural abstraction. Whether this is a viable way for a wider range of applications and whether this will allow one to limit the need for behavioral abstraction remains to be seen.

As we have observed, initial multialgebras do not exist even in very elementary cases. Since initiality and quotient are special cases of free extensions, one shouldn't expect much of the **extend-freely** operation. Reachable extensions seem still possible but one will face several choices of the notion of reachability [25].

References

1. Brock, J.D., Ackermann, W.B., "Scenarios: A model of non-determinate computation", in *Formalization of Programming Concepts*, LNCS, vol. 107, Springer, 1981.
2. Clinger, W., "Nondeterministic call by need is neither lazy nor by name", *Proc. ACM Symp. LISP and Functional Programming*, 226-234, 1982.
3. Engelfriet, J., Schmidt, E.M., "IO and OI. 1", *Journal of Computer and System Sciences*, vol. 15, 328-353, 1977
4. Engelfriet, J., Schmidt, E.M., "IO and OI. 2", *Journal of Computer and System Sciences*, vol. 16, 67-99, 1978.
5. Goguen, J.A., Meseguer, J., "Completeness of Many-Sorted Equational Logic", *SIGPLAN Notices*, vol. 16, no. 7, 1981.
6. Goguen, J.A., Meseguer, J., "Remarks on Remarks on Many-Sorted Equational Logic", *SIGPLAN Notices*, vol. 22, no. 4, 41-48, April 1987.
7. Hayes, I., Jones, C., "Specifications are not (necessarily) executable", in *Software Engineering Journal*, 4(6): 330-338. 1989.
8. Hennessy, M.C.B., "The semantics of call-by-value and call-by-name in a nondeterministic environment", *SIAM J. Comput.*, vol. 9, no. 1, 1980.
9. Hesselink, W.H., "A Mathematical Approach to Nondeterminism in Data Types", *ACM: Transactions on Programming Languages and Systems*, vol. 10, 1988.

10. Hoare, C.A.R., *Communicating Sequential Processes*, Prentice-Hall International Ltd., 1985.
11. Huet, G., Oppen, D., "Equations and Rewrite Rules: A Survey", in *Formal Language Theory: Perspectives and Open Problems*, Academic Press, 1980.
12. Hußmann, H., *Nondeterminism in Algebraic Specifications and Algebraic Programs*, Birkhäuser, 1993.
13. Kapur, D., *Towards a theory of abstract data types*, Ph.D. thesis, Laboratory for CS, MIT, 1980.
14. Keller, R.M., "Denotational models for parallel programs with indeterminate operators", in *Formal Descriptions of Programming Concepts*, North-Holland, Amsterdam, 1978.
15. Manber, U., *Introduction to Algorithms*, Addison-Wesley, 1989.
16. Meseguer, J., "Conditional rewriting logic as a unified model of concurrency", *TCS*, no. 96, 73-155, 1992.
17. Meseguer, J., "Conditional Rewriting Logic: Deduction, Models and Concurrency", in Proceedings of *CTRS'90,* LNCS vol. 516, 1990.
18. Milner, R., *Communication and Concurrency*, Prentice Hall International, 1989.
19. Mosses, P.D., "Unified Algebras and Action Semantics", in *STACS'89*, LNCS, vol. 349, Springer, 1989.
20. Mosses, P.D., "Unified Algebras and Institutions", in *Proceedings of LICS'89, Fourth Annual Symposium on Logic in Computer Science,* 1989.
21. Nipkow, T., "Non-deterministic Data Types: Models and Implementations", *Acta Informatica*, vol. 22, 629–661, 1986.
22. Qian, X., Goldberg, A., "Referential Opacity in Nondeterministic Data Refinement", in *ACM LoPLAS*, vol.2, no.1-4, 1993.
23. Schwartz, R.L., "An axiomatic treatment of ALGOL 68 routines", in Proceedings of *Sixth Colloquium on Automata, Languages and Programming,* vol. 71, Springer, 1979.
24. Søndergaard, H., Sestoft, P., *Non-Determinacy and Its Semantics*, Tech. Rep. 86/12, Datalogisk Institut, Københavns Universitet, January 1987.
25. Walicki, M., *Algebraic Specifications of Nondeterminism*, Ph.D. thesis, University of Bergen, Department of Informatics, 1993.
26. Walicki, M., *Singular and Plural Nondeterministic Parameters: Multialgebras, Power Algebras and Complete Reasoning Systems*, Tech. Rep. 96, Department of Informatics, University of Bergen, 1994.
27. Ward, N., *"A Refinement Calculus for Nondeterminisitc Expressions"*, PhD Thesis, Dept.. of Computer Science, The University of Queensland, submitted February 1994.

Institutional Frames*

Uwe Wolter

Technische Universität Berlin, FB Informatik
Sekr. 6-1, Franklinstr. 28/29, D-10587 Berlin

E-mail: wolter@cs.tu-berlin.de

Abstract. The concept of "institution" [GB84, GB92] has been proven to be appropriate to describe and classify a wide range of specification formalisms or logical systems respectively. But considering the relations between logical systems we are faced with many different kinds of relevant examples leading to an inflation of definitions of maps between institutions [Cer93, CM93, KM93, Mes89, SS92].
The present paper is devoted to overcome this divergence of definitions. Using the results in [TBG91] we analyze the concepts "institution" and "entailment system" [Mes89]. As a result we propose the concepts "institutional frame" and "institutional map" providing a new perspective on logical systems. Thereby we describe logical systems on the conceptual level of signatures, specifications, and subcategories of models respectively.
Finally we sketch how the introduced concepts can provide new insights into the nature of examples discussed in the literature.

1 Introduction

The present paper has its roots in a number of problems we tackled within the german project "KORSO - Korrekte Software". One of the main objectives of this project was a framework and a methodology for supporting the development of correct software by means of the application of semantically well-founded specification techniques and languages.

Our major concerns within KORSO were firstly the semantical foundation of the general purpose specification language SPECTRUM and secondly the realization of case studies. In both directions of research the following situations showed to be typical for the use of specification techniques and languages in software development:

- For the specification of a small local part of a problem it is convenient to use a small and adequate specification language with a restricted expressiveness but with a well-understood semantics at hand or at least in mind. After solving the local parts of the problem we are forced to embed or to integrate, in a semantically compatible way, all the different local solutions into a general solution within a big and complex specification framework, e.g. SPECTRUM.

* This work has been partly supported by the German Ministry of Research and Technology (BMFT) as part of the project "KORSO – Korrekte Software".

- We have to specify different aspects of one and the same problem in parallel. We have to treat algebraic and operational aspects as well as aspects of dataflow, safety and concurrency. For each of these aspects we have appropriate but quite different specification techniques which cannot or shall not be agglomerated to one oversized specification language. In this situation we have to ensure that all the different views to one and the same problem are semantically compatible on the overlapping parts of the specification languages in question.
- We have to implement specifications by programs, i.e. we have to transform specifications in a specification language and their model theoretic semantics into programs in a programming language and their operational semantics. Thereby results concerning correctness and compositionality should be preserved by this transformation.

Looking at these situations it becomes quite obvious that the application of formal methods in software development requires a conceptual and theoretical framework which enables us to describe, to relate, and moreover to combine the logical systems underlying the different specification and programming languages. Especially we have to describe transitions from one specification formalism to other specification formalisms and we have to prove relevant properties of these transitions.

For a unified description of logical systems the concept of institution, developed in [GB84, GB92], has been proven to be appropriate. On the basis of this concept we give for instance in [WKWC94] a unified formal description of four logical systems used for specification purposes.

But concerning the relations between logical systems the situation is really unsatisfactory. Motivated by different kinds of examples there is a lot of definitions what a map between institutions should be (see [Cer93, CM93, KM93, Mes89, SS92]). But unfortunately none of these concepts was suited for the description of the maps between the logical systems, we had to deal with in the project. This was the starting point for our analysis of the concepts "institution", "entailment system" [Mes89], and of some of the corresponding concepts of maps. The crucial observation is that in many cases we are not able to relate institutions by a pointwise assignment from sentence to sentence and from model to model respectively. In many cases we can relate institutions only on the level of specifications, i.e. of sets of sentences, and on the level of subcategories of models respectively. Therefore we decided to introduce the concepts "institutional frame" and "institutional map" providing a new perspective on logical systems which is located on this level of abstraction.

By means of these concepts we were able to describe the relations between logical systems, we had to deal with in the project (see [WDC+94]). Further these new concepts provide new insights into the nature of examples discussed in the literature. Moreover we hope that the present paper provides a basis for an integration of all the different concepts of maps between institutions proposed in the literature. Finally it should be mentioned that our concepts cover naturally the extension of satisfaction from models to morphisms.

2 Institutions

In this section we reconstruct some definitions and results from [GB84, GB92].

Definition 1 (Institution). An *institution* is a quadruple $\mathcal{I} = (SIGN, Sen, Mod, \models)$ with $SIGN$ a category whose objects are called *signatures*, $Sen : SIGN \to SET$ a functor associating to each signature Σ a set of *sentences*, $Mod : SIGN \to CAT^{op}$ a functor associating to each signature a corresponding category of models, and $\models$ a function associating to each signature Σ a binary relation $\models_\Sigma \subseteq |Mod(\Sigma)| \times Sen(\Sigma)$ called *satisfaction relation*, where $|Mod(\Sigma)|$ denotes the set of all objects in the category $Mod(\Sigma)$, in such a way that for each morphism $\phi : \Sigma_1 \to \Sigma_2$ in $SIGN$ the *satisfaction condition*

$$M_2 \models_{\Sigma_2} Sen(\phi)(\varphi_1) \iff Mod(\phi)(M_2) \models_{\Sigma_1} \varphi_1,$$

holds for any $M_2 \in |Mod(\Sigma_2)|$ and any $\varphi_1 \in Sen(\Sigma_1)$

The following pictures may help in visualizing these relationships:

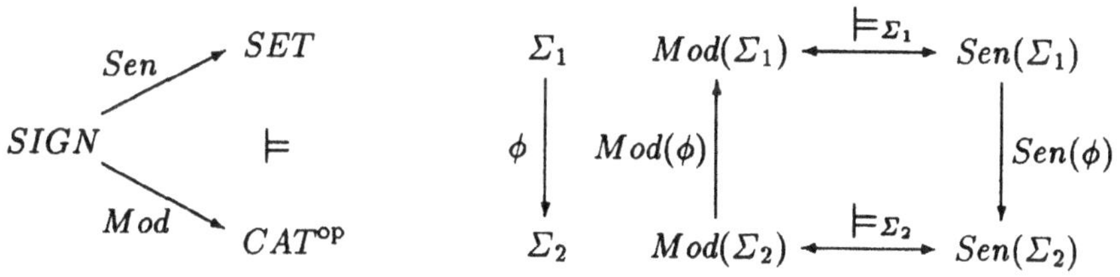

Given a set of Σ-sentences, i.e. a specification $\Gamma \subseteq Sen(\Sigma)$, we define the category $mod(\Sigma)(\Gamma)$ as the full subcategory of $Mod(\Sigma)$ determined by those models $M \in Mod(\Sigma)$ that satisfy all the sentences in Γ, i.e. we have

$$|mod(\Sigma)(\Gamma)| = \{M \in |Mod(\Sigma)| \mid \forall \varphi \in \Gamma : M \models_\Sigma \varphi\}. \tag{1}$$

Analogously we define for a subcategory $\mathcal{M} \subseteq Mod(\Sigma)$ of Σ-models the specification $th(\Sigma)(\mathcal{M}) \subseteq Sen(\Sigma)$ given by those sentences $\varphi \in Sen(\Sigma)$ which are satisfied by all models in $\mathcal{M}$, i.e. we set

$$th(\Sigma)(\mathcal{M}) = \{\varphi \in Sen(\Sigma) \mid \forall M \in |\mathcal{M}| : M \models_\Sigma \varphi\}. \tag{2}$$

Obviously $mod(\Sigma)$ and $th(\Sigma)$ determine mappings between Σ-specifications and subcategories of Σ-models and vice versa. The next definition provides the correct domains and codomains of these mappings.

Definition 2 (Specifications and Subcategories). Given a signature $\Sigma \in |SIGN|$ we define the category $Spec(\Sigma)$ of all Σ-specifications as follows:

- *objects:* are all specifications $\Gamma \subseteq Sen(\Sigma)$,
- *morphisms:* are all inverse inclusions $\Gamma_1 \supseteq \Gamma_2$,
- *composition:* is given by the composition of inclusions.

Analogously we define the category $Sub(\Sigma)$ of all subcategories of Σ-models:

- *objects:* are all subcategories $\mathcal{M} \subseteq Mod(\Sigma)$,
- *morphisms:* are all inclusion functors $\mathcal{M}_1 \subseteq \mathcal{M}_2$,
- *composition:* is given by the composition of inclusion functors.

Note, that $Spec(\Sigma)$ and $Sub(\Sigma)$ are so-called *preorder categories*, i.e. there is at most one morphism from one object to another object in these categories. Now we give a categorical formulation of the properties of the Galois correspondence connected with the satisfaction relation $\models_\Sigma$.

Proposition 3 (Galois Correspondence). *Given a signature $\Sigma \in |SIGN|$ the equations (1) and (2) define functors*

$$mod(\Sigma) : Spec(\Sigma) \to Sub(\Sigma) \quad \text{and} \quad th(\Sigma) : Sub(\Sigma) \to Spec(\Sigma)$$

such that $th(\Sigma)$ is left-adjoint to $mod(\Sigma)$ i.e. for any specifications Γ, Γ_1, $\Gamma_2 \in |Spec(\Sigma)|$ and any subcategories $\mathcal{M}$, $\mathcal{M}_1$, $\mathcal{M}_2 \in |Sub(\Sigma)|$ we have:

- $mod(\Sigma)$ functor: $\Gamma_1 \supseteq \Gamma_2$ *implies* $mod(\Sigma)(\Gamma_1) \subseteq mod(\Sigma)(\Gamma_2)$,
- $th(\Sigma)$ functor: $\mathcal{M}_1 \subseteq \mathcal{M}_2$ *implies* $th(\Sigma)(\mathcal{M}_1) \supseteq th(\Sigma)(\mathcal{M}_2)$,
- unit: $\mathcal{M} \subseteq mod(\Sigma)(th(\Sigma)(\mathcal{M}))$,
- counit: $th(\Sigma)(mod(\Sigma)(\Gamma)) \supseteq \Gamma$,
- adjointness: $\mathcal{M} \subseteq mod(\Sigma)(\Gamma)$ *iff* $th(\Sigma)(\mathcal{M}) \supseteq \Gamma$,

Proposition 3 shows how the satisfaction relation can be equivalently described by two functors on the conceptual level of specifications and of subcategories of models. Now we want to formulate the satisfaction condition on this level of abstraction. For the next proposition we have to bear in mind that the preimage $F^{-1}(\mathcal{B}_0)$ of a subcategory $\mathcal{B}_0 \subseteq \mathcal{B}$ w.r.t. a functor $F : \mathcal{A} \to \mathcal{B}$ yields a subcategory of $\mathcal{A}$.

Proposition 4 (Satisfaction Condition). *For any morphism $\phi : \Sigma_1 \to \Sigma_2$ in $SIGN$ the following condition is equivalent to the satisfaction condition:*

1. $Mod(\phi)^{-1}(mod(\Sigma_1)(\Gamma_1)) = mod(\Sigma_2)(Sen(\phi)(\Gamma_1))$ *for any* $\Gamma_1 \in |Spec(\Sigma_1)|$.

Moreover we have an inclusion which can be proper:

2. $th(\Sigma_2)(Mod(\phi)^{-1}(\mathcal{M}_1)) \supseteq Sen(\phi)(th(\Sigma_1)(\mathcal{M}_1))$ *for any* $\mathcal{M}_1 \in |Sub(\Sigma_1)|$.

3 Entailment Systems

The concept of "entailment system" introduced in [Mes89] reflects those properties of the entailment relation $\Gamma \vdash \varphi$ which are independent from the particular rules used to generate the relation $\vdash$.

Definition 5 (Entailment System). An entailment system is a triple $\mathcal{E} = (SIGN, Sen, \vdash)$ with $SIGN$ a category of *signatures*, $Sen : SIGN \to SET$ a functor, and $\vdash$ a function associating to each signature Σ a binary relation $\vdash_\Sigma \subseteq \wp(Sen(\Sigma)) \times Sen(\Sigma)$ called *entailment relation* such that the following properties are satisfied:

1. *reflexivity:* for any $\varphi \in Sen(\Sigma)$, $\{\varphi\} \vdash_\Sigma \varphi$;
2. *monotonicity:* if $\Gamma_1 \vdash_\Sigma \varphi$ and $\Gamma_2 \supseteq \Gamma_1$ then $\Gamma_2 \vdash_\Sigma \varphi$;
3. *transitivity:* if $\Gamma \vdash_\Sigma \varphi_i$, for $i \in I$, and $\Gamma \cup \{\varphi_i \mid i \in I\} \vdash_\Sigma \psi$, then $\Gamma \vdash_\Sigma \psi$;
4. $\vdash$*-translation:* if $\Gamma_1 \vdash_{\Sigma_1} \varphi_1$, then for any $\phi : \Sigma_1 \to \Sigma_2$ in $SIGN$, $Sen(\phi)(\Gamma_1) \vdash_{\Sigma_2} Sen(\phi)(\varphi_1)$.

The entailment relation $\vdash_\Sigma$ between sets of Σ-sentences and single Σ-sentences can be straightforwardly extended to an equivalent entailment relation between Σ-specifications. For any specification Σ in $SIGN$ we define a corresponding *extended entailment relation*

$$\vdash^{\wp}_\Sigma \subseteq \wp(Sen(\Sigma)) \times \wp(Sen(\Sigma)) = |Spec(\Sigma)| \times |Spec(\Sigma)|$$

where we set for any Σ-specifications $\Gamma_1, \Gamma_2 \in Spec(\Sigma)$:

$$\Gamma_1 \vdash^{\wp}_\Sigma \Gamma_2 \quad \text{iff} \quad \forall\, \varphi_2 \in \Gamma_2 : \Gamma_1 \vdash_\Sigma \varphi_2 \tag{3}$$

Lemma 6. *Given a specification $\Sigma \in |SIGN|$ the entailment relation $\vdash_\Sigma$ has the properties (1)-(4) of definition 5 if and only if the extended entailment relation $\vdash^{\wp}_\Sigma$ satisfies the following properties for any $\Gamma_1, \Gamma_2, \Gamma_3 \in Spec(\Sigma)$:*

1. projection: $\Gamma_1 \cup \Gamma_2 \vdash^{\wp}_\Sigma \Gamma_2$, *i.e. especially $\Gamma_1 \supseteq \Gamma_2$ implies $\Gamma_1 \vdash^{\wp}_\Sigma \Gamma_2$;*
2. product property: *if $\Gamma_1 \vdash^{\wp}_\Sigma \Gamma_2$ and $\Gamma_1 \vdash^{\wp}_\Sigma \Gamma_3$, then $\Gamma_1 \vdash^{\wp}_\Sigma \Gamma_2 \cup \Gamma_3$;*
3. compositionality: *if $\Gamma_1 \vdash^{\wp}_\Sigma \Gamma_2$ and $\Gamma_2 \vdash^{\wp}_\Sigma \Gamma_3$, then $\Gamma_1 \vdash^{\wp}_\Sigma \Gamma_3$;*
4. functor property: *if $\Gamma_1 \vdash^{\wp}_{\Sigma_1} \Gamma_2$, then for any $\phi : \Sigma_1 \to \Sigma_2$ in $SIGN$, $Sen(\phi)(\Gamma_1) \vdash^{\wp}_{\Sigma_2} Sen(\phi)(\Gamma_2)$.*

Note, that for $\Gamma_1 = \emptyset$ the projection property provides the identity property, i.e. $\Gamma \vdash^{\wp}_\Sigma \Gamma$ for any $\Gamma \in Spec(\Sigma)$. Lemma 6 makes clear that the extended entailment relation $\vdash^{\wp}_\Sigma$ determines a preorder category $Ent(\Sigma)$.

Definition 7 (Extended Entailment). Given a signature $\Sigma \in |SIGN|$ we define the category $Ent(\Sigma)$ of all Σ-specifications with entailment as follows:

- *objects:* are all specifications $\Gamma \in |Spec(\Sigma)|$,
- *morphisms:* are all extended entailment relations $\Gamma_1 \vdash^{\wp}_\Sigma \Gamma_2$,
- *composition:* is given by the compositionality property in lemma 6.

The *projection* property in lemma 6 proves that $Ent(\Sigma)$ is an extension of the category $Spec(\Sigma)$, i.e. for any signature Σ we obtain an embedding functor

$$in(\Sigma) : Spec(\Sigma) \to Ent(\Sigma) \quad \text{with} \quad in(\Sigma)(\Gamma) = \Gamma. \tag{4}$$

If we consider the set of sentences provable from a specification Γ we obtain a so-called *closure* functor from $Ent(\Sigma)$ to $Spec(\Sigma)$, i.e. we set

$$cl(\Sigma)(\Gamma) = \{\varphi \in Sen(\Sigma) \mid \Gamma \vdash_\Sigma \varphi\}. \tag{5}$$

Proposition 8 (Closure). *Given a signature $\Sigma \in |SIGN|$ the equations (4) and (5) define functors*

$$in(\Sigma) : Spec(\Sigma) \to Ent(\Sigma) \quad \text{and} \quad cl(\Sigma) : Ent(\Sigma) \to Spec(\Sigma)$$

such that $cl(\Sigma)$ is left-adjoint to $in(\Sigma)$, i.e. for any specifications Γ, Γ_1, $\Gamma_2 \in |Spec(\Sigma)| = |Ent(\Sigma)|$ we have:

- $in(\Sigma)$ functor: $\Gamma_1 \supseteq \Gamma_2$ *implies* $\Gamma_1 \vdash^{\wp}_{\Sigma} \Gamma_2$,
- $cl(\Sigma)$ functor: $\Gamma_1 \vdash^{\wp}_{\Sigma} \Gamma_2$ *implies* $cl(\Sigma)(\Gamma_1) \supseteq cl(\Sigma)(\Gamma_2)$,
- unit: $\Gamma \vdash^{\wp}_{\Sigma} cl(\Sigma)(\Gamma)$ *in* $Ent(\Sigma)$,
- counit: $cl(\Sigma)(\Gamma) \supseteq \Gamma$ *in* $Spec(\Sigma)$,
- adjointness: $\Gamma_1 \vdash^{\wp}_{\Sigma} \Gamma_2$ *iff* $cl(\Sigma)(\Gamma_1) \supseteq \Gamma_2$.

In the next steps we exploit the functor property in lemma 6 to gain a final elegant categorical presentation of the concept "entailment system".

Proposition 9 (Entailment Functor). *The mappings Spec: $|SIGN| \to |CAT|$ and Ent: $|SIGN| \to |CAT|$ given by definition 2 and definition 7 respectively can be extended to functors $Spec : SIGN \to CAT$ and $Ent : SIGN \to CAT$ if we set for any $\phi : \Sigma_1 \to \Sigma_2$ in SIGN and for any $\Gamma_1 \in |Spec(\Sigma_1)|$:*

$$Spec(\phi)(\Gamma_1) = Ent(\phi)(\Gamma_1) = Sen(\phi)(\Gamma_1)$$

Note that we can describe *Spec* by a composition $Spec = \wp \circ Sen$ if $\wp : SET \to CAT$ is assumed to be the power set functor assigning to any set A the preorder $(\wp(A), \supseteq)$ considered as a category and assigning to any map $f; A \to B$ the corresponding extension $f : \wp(A) \to \wp(B)$ to sets.

Theorem 10 (Entailment Categorically). *A triple $\mathcal{E} = (SIGN, Sen, \vdash)$ is an entailment system iff the 5-tuple $\mathcal{EC} = (SIGN, Spec, Ent, in, cl)$ satisfies the following conditions:*

1. *$Spec : SIGN \to CAT$ and $Ent : SIGN \to CAT$ are functors.*
2. *The inclusion functors $in(\Sigma) : Spec(\Sigma) \to Ent(\Sigma)$, $\Sigma \in |SIGN|$ form a natural transformation $in : Spec \Rightarrow Ent : SIGN \to CAT$ with functors $cl(\Sigma) : Ent(\Sigma) \to Spec(\Sigma)$ left-adjoint to $in(\Sigma)$ for each $\Sigma \in |SIGN|$.*

Using the concepts in [TBG91] theorem 10 can be summed up in the slogan

An entailment system is an indexed functor with a left-adjoint locally.

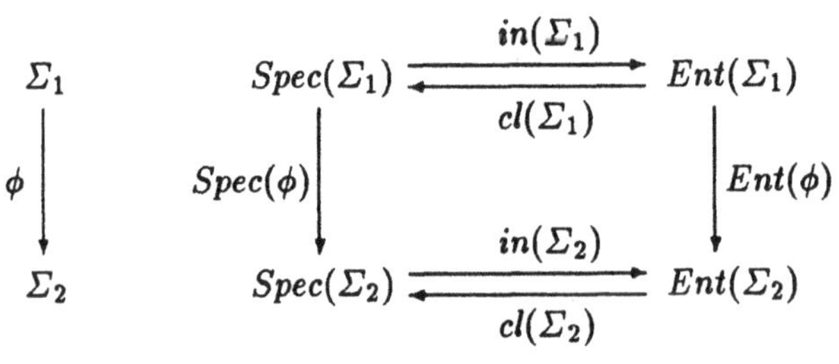

The functors $cl(\Sigma)$ don't form a natural transformation $cl : Ent \Rightarrow Spec$. We only have for any $\phi : \Sigma_1 \to \Sigma_2$ in $SIGN$ and any Γ_1 in $Ent(\Sigma_1)$ an inclusion

$$cl(\Sigma_2)\big(Ent(\phi)(\Gamma_1)\big) \supseteq Spec(\phi)\big(cl(\Sigma_1)(\Gamma_1)\big). \tag{6}$$

It is easy to see that these inclusions can be interpreted as a natural transformation

$$\mu(\phi) : cl(\Sigma_2) \circ Ent(\phi) \Longrightarrow Spec(\phi) \circ cl(\Sigma_1) : Ent(\Sigma_1) \to Spec(\Sigma_2). \tag{7}$$

Further this system of natural transformations has the necessary property that the functors $cl(\Sigma) : Ent(\Sigma) \to Spec(\Sigma)$, form a lax natural transformation in the sense of definition 18 in the appendix (recall that $SIGN = (SIGN^{op})^{op}$)

$$cl : Ent \rightrightarrows Spec : SIGN \to CAT \tag{8}$$

In [Wol95] we will prove that this fact is generally a consequence of the property "locally left-adjoint".

Meseguer uses the category TH of theories to describe maps between entailment systems. TH has as objects (Σ, Γ) with Σ a signature and $\Gamma \subseteq Sen(\Sigma)$ and as morphisms, $\phi{:}(\Sigma_1, \Gamma_1) \to (\Sigma_2, \Gamma_2)$, signature morphisms $\phi : \Sigma_1 \to \Sigma_2$ such that $\Gamma_2 \supseteq Sen(\phi)(\Gamma_1)$. It is easy to verify that TH can be obtained by the flattening of $Spec : (SIGN^{op})^{op} \to CAT$ (see definition 17 and equation 17)

$$TH = Flat(Spec)^{op} \quad \text{with} \quad Sign = Proj^{op}_{Spec} : TH \to SIGN. \tag{9}$$

A map from an entailment system $\mathcal{E}_1 = (SIGN_1, Sen_1, \vdash^1)$ to an entailment system $\mathcal{E}_2 = (SIGN_2, Sen_2, \vdash^2)$ in the sense of Meseguer is firstly given by two functors $\Phi : SIGN_1 \to SIGN_2$ and $\theta{:}TH_1 \to TH_2$ such that $Sign_2 \circ \theta = \Phi \circ Sign_1$. Using theorem 20 and proposition 21 in appendix it can be proved that this is equivalent to the existence of a lax natural transformation

$$\gamma : Spec_1 \rightrightarrows Spec_2 \circ \Phi : SIGN_1 \to CAT \ \text{ with } \theta = Flat(\gamma). \tag{10}$$

It is worth to mention that the functor property of $\gamma(\Sigma) : Spec_1(\Sigma) \to Spec_2(\Phi(\Sigma))$ entails $\gamma(\Sigma)(\Gamma) \supseteq \gamma(\Sigma)(\emptyset)$ for any Γ in $Spec_1(\Sigma)$, i.e. $\gamma(\Sigma)(\emptyset)$ can be seen as the specification obtained by the translation of Σ.

Secondly Meseguer assumes a natural transformation $\alpha^\diamond : Sen_1 \Rightarrow Sen_2 \circ \Phi : SIGN_1 \to SET$ such that the corresponding natural transformation on specifications

$$\alpha = \wp \circ \alpha^\diamond : Spec_1 \Rightarrow Spec_2 \circ \Phi : SIGN_1 \to SET$$

satisfies for any signature Σ in $SIGN_1$ and any specification Γ in $Spec_1(\Sigma)$

$$cl(\Sigma)\big(\gamma(\Sigma)(\Gamma)\big) = cl(\Sigma)\big(\gamma(\Sigma)(\emptyset) \cup \alpha(\Sigma)(\Gamma)\big), \tag{11}$$

i.e. equivalently $\gamma(\Sigma)(\Gamma) \vdash^2_{\Phi(\Sigma)} \alpha(\Sigma)(\Gamma)$ and $\gamma(\Sigma)(\emptyset) \cup \alpha(\Sigma)(\Gamma) \vdash^2_{\Phi(\Sigma)} \gamma(\Sigma)(\Gamma)$. Finally Meseguer requires for any Σ in $SIGN_1$ and any Γ_1 and Γ_2 in $Spec_1(\Sigma)$:

$$\Gamma_1 \vdash^1_\Sigma \Gamma_2 \quad \text{implies} \quad \alpha(\Sigma)(\Gamma_1) \cup \gamma(\Sigma)(\emptyset) \vdash^2_{\Phi(\Sigma)} \alpha(\Sigma)(\Gamma_2). \tag{12}$$

Supposing property 11 this is equivalent to

$$\Gamma_1 \vdash^1_\Sigma \Gamma_2 \quad \text{implies} \quad \gamma(\Sigma)(\Gamma_1) \vdash^2_{\Phi(\Sigma)} \gamma(\Sigma)(\Gamma_2). \tag{13}$$

But this means that for any Σ in $SIGN_1$ the functor $\gamma(\Sigma) : Spec_1(\Sigma) \to Spec_2(\Phi(\Sigma))$ is required to define also a functor $\gamma^\vdash(\Sigma) : Ent_1(\Sigma) \to Ent_2(\Phi(\Sigma))$ where all these functors form a lax natural transformation

$$\gamma^\vdash : Ent_1 \rightrightarrows Ent_2 \circ \Phi : SIGN_1 \to CAT \quad \text{with} \quad (in_2 \circ \Phi) \bullet \gamma = \gamma^\vdash \bullet in_1. \tag{14}$$

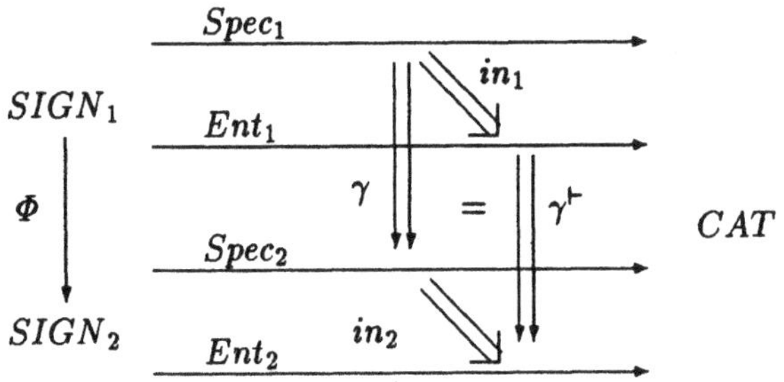

In such a way the concept of maps in [Mes89] can be devided into two independent components. Firstly we have a transition γ on the level of specifications. Secondly it is assumed that this transition can be represented up to isomorphim by a translation of signatures to specifications plus a pointwise translation α of sentences.

As a result of our analysis it seems appropriate to introduce the following general concept of mapping entailment systems. This general concept also covers the translation of sentences into sets of sentences, a situation we are faced with for instance if we have to relate different entailment systems for partial algebras.

Definition 11 (Institutional Map of Entailment Systems). Given entailment systems $\mathcal{E}_1 = (SIGN_1, Sen_1, \vdash^1)$ and $\mathcal{E}_2 = (SIGN_2, Sen_2, \vdash^2)$, an *institutional map of entailment systems* $(\Phi, \gamma){:}\mathcal{E}_1 \to \mathcal{E}_2$ consists of a functor $\Phi : SIGN_1 \to SIGN_2$ and a lax natural transformation $\gamma : Spec_1 \rightrightarrows Spec_2 \circ \Phi$ such that there exists a unique lax natural transformation $\gamma^\vdash : Ent_1 \rightrightarrows Ent_2 \circ \Phi$ with $(in_2 \circ \Phi) \bullet \gamma = \gamma^\vdash \bullet in_1$.

We call (Φ, γ) *natural* if γ is a natural transformation. We call (Φ, γ) *plain* if there exists a natural transformation $\alpha : Sen_1 \Rightarrow Sen_2 \circ \Phi$ with $\gamma = \wp \circ \alpha$.

4 Institutional Frames

Using the results and insights gained for entailment systems we carry on with our analysis of the concept of "institution". Condition (1) in proposition 4 suggests the following extension of *Sub* to a functor.

Proposition 12 (Subcategory Functor). *The mapping Sub given by definition 2 can be extended to a functor* $Sub : SIGN \to CAT$ *if we set for any* $\phi : \Sigma_1 \to \Sigma_2$ *in SIGN and for any* $\mathcal{M}_1 \in |Sub(\Sigma_1)|$:

$$Sub(\phi)(\mathcal{M}_1) = Mod(\phi)^{-1}(\mathcal{M}_1)$$

Note that $Sub = \mathfrak{S} \circ Mod$ where $\mathfrak{S} : CAT^{op} \to CAT$ is the contravariant subcategory functor. Proposition 3 and condition (1) in proposition 4 make "*mod*" to a natural transformation with a left-adjoint locally.

Proposition 13. *The functors* $mod(\Sigma) : Spec(\Sigma) \to Sub(\Sigma)$, $\Sigma \in |SIGN|$ *form a natural transformation*

$$mod : Spec \Rightarrow Sub : SIGN \to CAT$$

with functors $th(\Sigma) : Sub(\Sigma) \to Spec(\Sigma)$ *left-adjoint to* $mod(\Sigma)$ *for each* $\Sigma \in |SIGN|$.

Analogously to the closure "*cl*" for entailment systems the inclusions in condition (2) of proposition 4 ensure that the functors $th(\Sigma) : Sub(\Sigma) \to Spec(\Sigma)$ form a lax natural transformation

$$th : Sub \rightrightarrows Spec : SIGN \to CAT. \qquad (15)$$

Now we summarize our investigations by introducing the concept of "institutional frame".

Definition 14 (Institutional Frame). The *institutional frame*, associated to an institution $\mathcal{I} = (SIGN, Sen, Mod, \models)$, is the 5-tuple

$$\mathcal{IF} = (SIGN, Spec, Sub, mod, th)$$

with $SIGN$ the category of signatures, $Spec : SIGN \to CAT$ the functor associating to each signature Σ the category of Σ-specifications, $Sub : SIGN \to CAT$ the functor associating to each signature Σ the category of subcategories of Σ-models, and $mod : Spec \Rightarrow Sub$ the natural transformation determined by $\models$ which has a locally left-adjoint lax natural transformation $th : Sub \rightrightarrows Spec$.

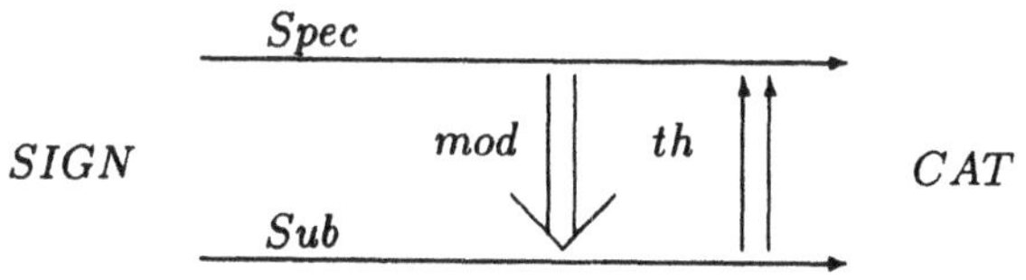

Obviously the concept of "institutional frame" could be defined without refering to institutions. But for the present paper we have decided for the restricted version.

Any institutional frame yields immediately the categorical presentation of an entailment system. For any signature Σ in $SIGN$ we obtain an extended entailment relation $\models_\Sigma$ if we set for any Γ_1 and Γ_2 in $Spec(\Sigma)$:

$$\Gamma_1 \models_\Sigma \Gamma_2 \quad \text{iff} \quad mod(\Sigma)(\Gamma_1) \models_\Sigma mod(\Sigma)(\Gamma_2). \qquad (16)$$

It is easy to see that this defines an entailment category $Ent^{\models}(\Sigma)$ for any Σ in $SIGN$ and that these categories provide a functor $Ent^{\models} : SIGN \to CAT$. Further equation 16 ensures that the maps $mod(\Sigma) : |Spec(\Sigma)| \to |Sub(\Sigma)|$ can be interpreted as functors $mod(\Sigma)^{\models} : Ent^{\models}(\Sigma) \to Sub(\Sigma)$.

Proposition 15 (Induced Entailment System). *An institutional frame $\mathcal{IF}$ = $(SIGN, Spec, Sub, mod, th)$ defines an entailment functor $Ent^{\models} : SIGN \to CAT$ such that the natural transformation $mod : Spec \Rightarrow Sub$ can be decomposed into a natural inclusion $in : Spec \Rightarrow Ent^{\models}$ and a natural transformation $mod : Ent^{\models} \Rightarrow Sub$ such that $mod = mod^{\models} \circ in$.*

Moreover the 5-tuple $\mathcal{EC} = (SIGN, Spec, Ent^{\models}, in, cl)$ with $cl = mod^{\models} \circ th$ defines an entailment system.

For the definition of maps of institutions Meseguer uses the so-called extended model functor $Mod : TH^{op} \to CAT$ associating to each theory (Σ, Γ) in TH the category $mod(\Sigma)(\Gamma)$ and to each morphism $\phi : (\Sigma_1, \Gamma_1) \to (\Sigma_2, \Gamma_2)$ in TH the restriction $Mod(\phi) : mod(\Sigma_2)(\Gamma_2) \to mod(\Sigma_1)(\Gamma_1)$ of the functor $Mod(\phi) : Mod(\Sigma_2) \to Mod(\Sigma_1)$ where $\Gamma_2 \supseteq Sen(\phi)(\Gamma_1)$ together with the satisfaction condition ensures the definedness of this restriction.

We can describe this extended model functor, also called the "specification frame" associated to the institution $\mathcal{I}$, in the following way. Flattening of $mod : Spec \Rightarrow Sub$ provides a functor $Flat(mod) : TH^{op} \to Flat(Sub)$ since $Flat(Spec) = TH^{op}$. Thereby $Flat(mod)$ associates to each theory (Σ, Γ) the pair $(\Sigma, mod(\Sigma)(\Gamma))$ and to each morphism $\phi : (\Sigma_1, \Gamma_1) \to (\Sigma_2, \Gamma_2)$, i.e. to each pair $(\phi : \Sigma_1 \to \Sigma_2, \Gamma_2 \supseteq Sen(\phi)(\Gamma_1))$, the pair $(\phi : \Sigma_1 \to \Sigma_2, mod(\Sigma_2)(\Gamma_2) \subseteq Mod^{-1}(mod(\Sigma_1)(\Gamma_1))$.

Next we can define a functor $Em : Flat(Sub) \to CAT$ which associates to each object $(\Sigma, \mathcal{M})$ in $Flat(Sub)$ the category $\mathcal{M}$ and to each morphism

$$(\phi : \Sigma_1 \to \Sigma_2, \mathcal{M}_2 \subseteq Mod^{-1}(\mathcal{M}_1)) : (\Sigma_1, \mathcal{M}_1) \longrightarrow (\Sigma_2, \mathcal{M}_2)$$

the restricted functor $Mod(\phi) : \mathcal{M}_2 \to \mathcal{M}_1$. Finally we obtain $Mod = Em \circ Flat(mod)$ for the extended model functor $Mod : TH^{op} \to CAT$.

The crucial point is that we lose the component "*th*" if we restrict ourselves on the use of Mod. But in our framework we want to keep the functor which is left-adjoint to $Flat(mod)$ and which is provided by the flattening of "*th*", i.e. the functor $Flat(th) : Flat(Spec) \to TH^{op}$ (see [TBG91]).

Analogously to entailment systems it should be possible to show that the concept of maps of institutions in [Mes89] can be devided into two independent components each of it a map of institutional frames.

Definition 16 (Map of Institutional Frames). Given institutional frames $\mathcal{IF}_1 = (SIGN_1, Spec_1, Sub_1, mod_1, th_1)$ and $\mathcal{IF}_2 = (SIGN_2, Spec_2, Sub_2, mod_2, th_2)$, a *map of institutional frames* $(\Phi, \gamma, \beta): \mathcal{IF}_1 \to \mathcal{IF}_2$ consists of a functor $\Phi : SIGN_1 \to SIGN_2$, a lax natural transformation $\gamma : Spec_1 \rightrightarrows Spec_2 \circ \Phi$, and a lax natural transformation $\beta : Sub_1 \rightrightarrows Sub_2 \circ \Phi$ such that $\beta \circ mod_1 = mod_2 \circ \gamma$.

We call (Φ, γ, β) ***natural*** if γ and β are natural transformations. We call (Φ, γ, β) ***plain*** if there exist natural transformations $\alpha : Sen_1 \Rightarrow Sen_2 \circ \Phi$ and $\beta_{pl} : Mod_1 \Rightarrow Mod_2 \circ \Phi$ with $\gamma = \wp \circ \alpha$ and $\beta = \mathfrak{S} \circ \beta_{pl}$ respectively.

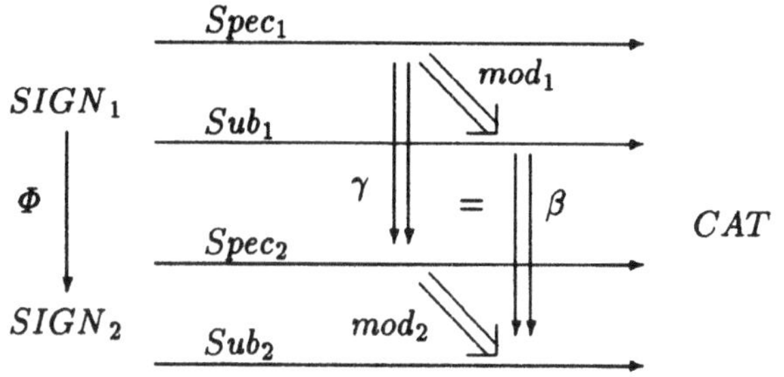

There are some indications that in general the equality $\beta \circ mod_1 = mod_2 \circ \gamma$ should be weakened to a so-called indexed natural transformation. But this will be a point of future research (see [Wol95]).

We believe that the introduced concepts provide a good basis for the study of relations between logical systems. But we are only at the beginning of this research. Especially we hope that the well-developed results in [Cer93, CM93, Mes89] carry over to our framework.

5 One Example

In this final section we want to illustrate the application of our concepts. Because of the limited space we concentrate on one of the motivating examples in [Mes89]. We investigate the relationships between unsorted equational logic and many-sorted equational logic.

Let $\mathcal{I}_{UEQ}$ be the institution of unsorted equational logic for total algebras and let $\mathcal{I}_{MEQ}$ be the institution of many-sorted equational logic for total algebras. Obviously the transition from unsortedness to one-sortedness provides a functor $\Phi_1 : SIGN_{UEQ} \to SIGN_{MEQ}$ with $\Phi_1(\Sigma) = (\{*\}, \mathcal{OP})$ for any unsorted signature $\Sigma = (\mathcal{OP})$ in $SIGN_{UEQ}$. Moreover there are for any Σ in $SIGN_{UEQ}$ isomorphisms $\gamma_1(\Sigma) : Spec_{UEQ}(\Sigma) \to Spec_{MEQ}(\Phi_1(\Sigma))$ and $\beta_1(\Sigma) : Sub_{UEQ}(\Sigma) \to Sub_{MEQ}(\Phi_1(\Sigma))$, i.e. we have natural isomorphisms

$$\gamma_1 : Spec_{UEQ} \Rightarrow Spec_{MEQ} \circ \Phi_1 : SIGN_{UEQ} \to CAT \text{ and}$$
$$\beta_1 : Sub_{UEQ} \Rightarrow Sub_{MEQ} \circ \Phi_1 : SIGN_{UEQ} \to CAT$$

such that $\beta_1 \circ mod_{UEQ} = mod_{MEQ} \circ \gamma_1$. In such a way we obtain a trivial map of institutional frames $(\Phi_1, \gamma_1, \beta_1)$: $\mathcal{I}_{UEQ} \to \mathcal{I}_{MEQ}$.

The crucial point is that forgetting sorts provides moreover a functor $\Phi_2 : SIGN_{MEQ} \to SIGN_{UEQ}$ left-adjoint to Φ_1 where $\Phi_2((\mathcal{S}, \mathcal{OP})) = (\mathcal{OP})$ for any signature $\Sigma = (\mathcal{S}, \mathcal{OP})$ in $SIGN_{MEQ}$. The counit is the identity, i.e. $\Phi_2(\Phi_1((\mathcal{OP}))) = (\mathcal{OP})$ for any $\Sigma = (\mathcal{OP})$ in $SIGN_{UEQ}$. The unit is given by the canonical signature morphisms $\eta(\Sigma) : (\mathcal{S}, \mathcal{OP}) \to (\{*\}, \mathcal{OP})$ for any signature $\Sigma = (\mathcal{S}, \mathcal{OP})$ in $SIGN_{MEQ}$. This adjoint situation on signatures defines now straightforwardly a map of institutional frames $(\Phi_2, \gamma_2, \beta_2)$: $\mathcal{I}_{MEQ} \to \mathcal{I}_{UEQ}$ if we set

$$\gamma_2 = (\alpha^{-1} \circ \Phi_2) \bullet (Spec_{MEQ} \circ \eta) : Spec_{MEQ} \Rightarrow Spec_{UEQ} \circ \Phi_2, \text{ and}$$
$$\beta_2 = (\beta^{-1} \circ \Phi_2) \bullet (Sub_{MEQ} \circ \eta) : Sub_{MEQ} \Rightarrow Sub_{UEQ} \circ \Phi_1.$$

In such a way the relation between unsorted and many-sorted equational logic can be classified as an adjoint situation caused by adjoint functors between the corresponding categories of signatures. As a concluding remark we want mention that the motivating example for the concept of "institution morphisms" introduced in [GB84, GB92], namely the extension of equational logic to first order logic, is also characterized by adjoint functors between the corresponding categories of signatures. The interesting point is that in this case the trivial transition, i.e. the transition from an equational specification to a first order specification with an empty predicate component, is the left-adjoint and not the right-adjoint as in the example above.

References

[Cer93] Maura Cerioli. *Relationships between Logical Formalisms.* PhD thesis, Università di Pisa–Genova–Udine, 1993. TD-4/93.

[CM93] M. Cerioli and J. Meseguer. May I Borrow Your Logic? Proc. MFCS'93, LNCS 711, Springer, 1993, pp. 342-351.

[GB84] J. A. Goguen and R. M. Burstall. Introducing institutions. In *Proc. Logics of Programming Workshop, LNCS 164*, pages 221–256. Carnegie–Mellon, Springer, 1984.

[GB92] J. A. Goguen and R. M. Burstall. Institutions: Abstract Model Theory for Specification and Programming. *Journals of the ACM*, 39(1):95–146, January 1992.

[KM93] H.-J. Kreowski and T. Mossakowski. Equivalence and Difference of Intitutions: Simulating Horn Clause Logic With Based Algebras. Technical report, Universität Bremen, 1993, to appear in MSCS.

[Mes89] J. Meseguer. General logics. In H.-D. Ebbinghaus et. al., editor, *Logic colloquium '87*, pages 275–329. Elsevier Science Publishers B. V.,North Holland, 1989.

[SS92] S. Salibra and G. Scollo. A soft stairway to institutions. In *Recent Trends in Data Type Specification*, pages 310–329. Springer, 1992. LNCS 655.

[TBG91] A. Tarlecki, R.M. Burstall, and J.A. Goguen. Some fundamental algebraic tools for the semantics of computation. Part III: Indexed categories. TCS, 1991, pp. 239-264.

[WDC+94] U. Wolter, K. Didrich, F. Cornelius, M. Klar, R. Wess"aly, and H. Ehrig. How to Cope with the Spectrum of SPECTRUM. Technical Report Bericht-Nr. 94-22, TU Berlin, FB Informatik, 1994.

[WKWC94] U. Wolter, M. Klar, R. Wessäly, and F. Cornelius. Four Institutions – A Unified Presentation of Logical Systems for Specification. Technical Report Bericht-Nr. 94-24, TU Berlin, Fachbereich Informatik, 1994.

[Wol95] Uwe Wolter. Institutional frames – a new perspective on logical systems. Technical report, TU Berlin, Fachbereich Informatik, 1995. in preparation.

A Indexed Categories

An *indexed category* C over an index category IND is a functor $C : IND^{op} \to CAT$. For indexed categories we can consider the corresponding flattened categories obtained by the so-called "Grothendieck construction".

Definition 17 (Flattened Category). Given an indexed category $C : IND^{op} \to CAT$ we define the category $Flat(C)$ as follows:

- *objects:* are pairs (i, a) where $i \in |IND|$ and $a \in |C(i)|$.
- *morphisms:* from (i, a) to (j, b) are pairs (σ, f) where $\sigma : i \to j$ is a morphism in IND and $f : a \to C(\sigma)(b)$ is a morphism in $C(i)$.
- *composition:* Given morphisms $(\sigma, f) : (i, a) \to (j, b)$ and $(\rho, g) : (j, b) \to (k, c)$ in $Flat(C)$, let $(\rho, g) \circ (\sigma, f) = (\rho \circ \sigma\, ,\, C(\sigma)(g) \circ f) : (i, a) \longrightarrow (k, c)$.

A flattened category $Flat(C)$ comes with a projection functor

$$Proj_C : Flat(C) \to IND \tag{17}$$

where $Proj_C((i, a)) = i$ for any (i, a) in $Flat(C)$ and $Proj_C((\sigma, f)) = \sigma$ for any (σ, f) in $Flat(C)$. The next definition generalizes as well the concept of "indexed functor" in [TBG91] as the concept of "natural transformation".

Definition 18 (Lax Natural Transformation). A *lax indexed functor* F from one indexed category $C : IND^{op} \to CAT$ to another $D : IND^{op} \to CAT$ is a *lax natural transformation*

$$F : C \rightrightarrows D : IND^{op} \to CAT,$$

that is, for each $i \in |IND|$, there is a functor $F(i) : C(i) \to D(i)$, and for each $\sigma : i \to j$ in IND there is a natural transformation

$$\mu(\sigma) : F(i) \circ C(\sigma) \Rightarrow D(\sigma) \circ F(j) : C(j) \to D(i)$$

such that for any $\sigma : i \to j$ and $\rho : j \to k$ in IND

$$\mu(\rho \circ \sigma) = (D(\sigma) \circ \mu(\rho)) \bullet (\mu(\sigma) \circ C(\rho)).$$

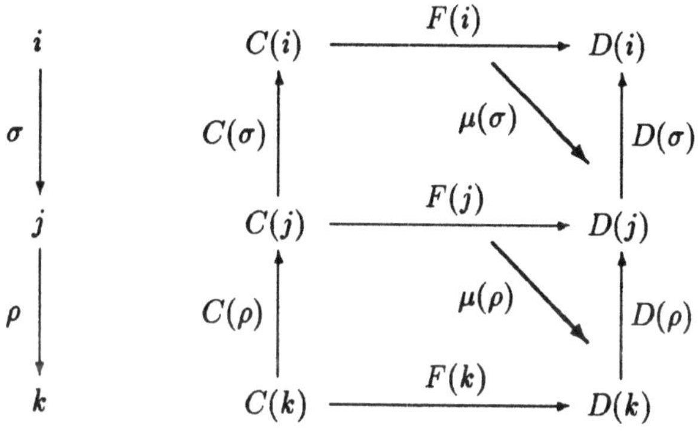

Flattening extends even to lax indexed functors.

Definition 19 (Flattened Lax Functor). Given a lax indexed functor $F : C \rightrightarrows D : IND^{op} \rightarrow CAT$ the flatten functor $Flat(F)$: $Flat(C) \rightarrow Flat(D)$ is defined as follows:

- *objects:* Given $(i, a) \in |Flat(C)|$, let $Flat(F)((i, a)) = (i, F(i)(a))$.
- *morphisms:* Given a morphism $(\sigma, f) : (i, a) \rightarrow (j, b)$ in $Flat(C)$, let $Flat(F)((\sigma, f)) = (\sigma\,,\, \mu(\rho)(b) \circ F(i)(f)) \;:\; (i, F(i)(a)) \longrightarrow (j, F(j)(b))$ in $Flat(D)$, recalling that $\mu(\sigma)(b) : F(i)(C(\sigma)(b)) \rightarrow D(\sigma)(F(j)(b))$.

It is straightforward to show, $Flat(F)$ is a functor. The construction of $Flat(F)$ entails $Proj_D \circ Flat(F) = Proj_C$. In [Wol95] we will prove the following theorem.

Theorem 20 (Flat versus Lax). *For each functor G: $Flat(C) \rightarrow Flat(D)$ with $Proj_D \circ G = Proj_C$ there exists a lax indexed functor $Dec(G) : C \rightrightarrows D : IND^{op} \rightarrow CAT$ with $Flat(Dec(G)) = G$. Moreover $Dec(Flat(F)) = F$ for any lax indexed functor $F : C \rightrightarrows D : IND^{op} \rightarrow CAT$.*

In [Wol95] we also investigate the interaction of flattening and composition.

Proposition 21 (Flattening and Composition). *For any indexed category $C : IND_1^{op} \rightarrow CAT$ and any functor $G : IND_2 \rightarrow IND_1$ the assignments*

$G^{fl}((i_2, a)) = (G(i_2), a)$ *for any* (i_2, a) *in* $Flat(C \circ G)$ *and*

$G^{fl}((\sigma_2, f)) = (G(\sigma_2), f)$ *for any* (σ_2, f) *in* $Flat(C \circ G)$

define a functor $G^{fl} : Flat(C \circ G) \rightarrow Flat(C)$ such that the following diagram is a pullback diagram in CAT.

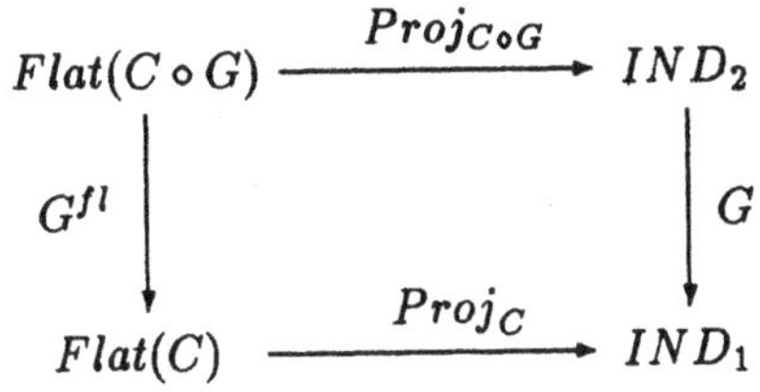

Implementation of data structures in an imperative framework*

Elena Zucca

DISI - Dipartimento di Informatica e Scienze dell'Informazione
Viale Benedetto XV, 3
16132 Genova (Italy)
email: zucca@disi.unige.it

Abstract. We present a formal definition of implementation between concrete structures within the framework of dynamic data-types. The main outcome is an adequate and uniform semantic model for stating when a software module in an imperative or object based language is a correct implementation of a data structure. Moreover, the definition is obtained extending in a natural way the notion used in the static case, showing that our dynamic frameworks are a "sound" generalization of static frameworks.

Introduction

Within a hierarchical approach to the development of software and the proof of its correctness, a basic ingredient is to have a formal notion of data implementation, enabling us to prove that some software module (low-level description) is a correct implementation of some data structure we have in mind (high-level description).
Within a traditional algebraic framework, the usual solution is to formalize both the high-level and the low-level descriptions as (static) data-types (algebras); in this way there is a formal notion of implementation which is the natural translation in algebraic terms of the notion originally developed by Hoare in his pioneering paper ([8]). Roughly speaking, there is a mapping from low-level into high-level values (abstraction map) which is compatible with high-level operations.
Anyway, if we consider software modules in an imperative or object based language (in general, a language supporting a notion of evolving state), then this approach is not completely adequate, as can be seen for instance in a pointer-based implementation: first of all, the mapping from low-level into high-level values is usually state-dependent; second, implementing a data-type means not only to implement operations (functions), but also commands (e.g. a copy procedure implementing assignment is usually needed); finally, requiring only functional properties is not enough (e.g. we could require also that no sharing is introduced, or that no memory is lost). These properties are usually stated as additional requirements outside of the algebraic formalization.
A better solution to the above problems can be found by extending the implementation notion from static data-types to dynamic data-types. A dynamic framework

* Work partially supported by Esprit BRA WG N. 6112 COMPASS, HCM-MEDICIS, and Murst 40% - Modelli della Computazione e dei Linguaggi di Programmazione

is obtained from a static algebraic framework adding a new dimension: the dynamic evolution. More precisely, a dynamic structure (*d-oid*) is characterized by a set of possible configurations (e.g. states in the imperative case), which can be viewed as structures in the underlying static framework, together with a definition of the possible evolutions from a configuration into another (e.g. state transformations in the imperative case).

Within a dynamic framework, both the high- and the low-level descriptions are formalized as dynamic structures and it turns out that it is possible to "lift-up" in a natural way the static implementation notion. Roughly speaking, there is a mapping from low-level configurations into high-level configurations which is compatible with dynamic evolution, and s.t. each low-level configuration implements (in the static sense) the corresponding high-level configuration. In this way all the desired properties can be handled homogeneously, being expressed within a unique implementation notion.

This work is part of ongoing research on the formalization of dynamic data-types. A first extension of the notion of data-type in order to cope with imperative features has been given in [2] using left-right structures, which are models particularly suited for Pascal-like languages; d-oids (described in [3], [4], [5]) are much more general models including left-right structures as a particular case and are suited for modelling imperative and object-based languages, data bases and dynamic systems. In this paper the d-oid approach is described only for what is needed; an extended presentation with examples of applications can be found in [3] and [4].

For what concerns the notion of implementation, the first presentation has been given, as already mentioned, in [8]; the formalization we give in this paper is, in our opinion, the natural rephrasing of that notion in the framework of dynamic data-types. After [8], there have been many papers dealing with that concept; see e.g. [10] and [9] for a survey and a unifying view within the framework of institutions. The implementation we describe here can be considered among the "simulation" implementations, following the classification in [9]; anyway, this comparison makes sense only to a certain extent since we are not dealing here with implementation as a relation between specifications, but as a relation between "concrete" models.

The paper is organized as follows. In sect. 1, we recall the usual notion of data-type implementation (1.1) and give its formalization in a generic algebraic framework (1.2). In sect. 2, we illustrate by an example that this notion is not satisfactory in the case of state-based languages (2.1); hence, we introduce dynamic data-types (2.2) and the related implementation definition (2.3); finally in subsect. 2.4 we show on the example how the problems are solved in the new setting.

1 Implementing static data-types

In this section we briefly recall the usual notion of data-type implementation and give its formalization in a generic algebraic framework.

1.1 What an implementation should be

We illustrate the usual notion of implementation using the standard example of the implementation of stacks (with a maximal size max) by pairs (records) consisting of

an array and a number representing the actual length.
We model these two data-types as partial algebras (as defined, e.g., in [6]). The algebra *Stack* of stacks has signature

sig Σ_{Stack} =
  sorts *elem*, *stack*
  opns
    empty: $\rightarrow$ *stack*, *top*: *stack* $\rightarrow$ *elem*
    push: *stack*, *elem* $\rightarrow$ *stack*, *pop*: *stack* $\rightarrow$ *stack*

and is defined (assuming that *Elem* denotes a given set of elements) by:

$$Stack_{elem} = Elem,\ Stack_{stack} = \{s \mid s \in Elem^{\star}, \mid s \mid \leq max\}$$
$$empty^{Stack} = \Lambda,\ top^{Stack}(e \cdot s) = e,\ top^{Stack}(\Lambda) \text{ undefined}$$
$$pop^{Stack}(e \cdot s) = s,\ pop^{Stack}(\Lambda) \text{ undefined},$$
$$push^{Stack}(s, e) = e \cdot s \text{ if } \mid s \mid < max, \text{ undefined otherwise.}$$

The algebra *Rec* of records has signature

sig Σ_{Rec} =
  sorts *elem*, *rec*, *array*, *index*, *length*
  opns
    zero: $\rightarrow$ *length*
    succ, *pred*: *length* $\rightarrow$ *length*
    $<-,->$: *array*, *length* $\rightarrow$ *rec*
    $-.elems$: *rec* $\rightarrow$ *array*, $-.length$: *rec* $\rightarrow$ *length*
    $\emptyset$: $\rightarrow$ *array*, $-[-]$: *array*, *index* $\rightarrow$ *elem*
    $-[-/-]$: *array*, *elem*, *index* $\rightarrow$ *array*

and is defined by:

$$Rec_{rec} = Rec_{array} \times Rec_{length},\ Rec_{length} = \mathbb{N}$$
$$Rec_{index} = \{1, \ldots, max\},\ Rec_{array} = [\{1, \ldots, max\} \rightarrow Elem],\ Rec_{elem} = Elem$$

and the obvious interpretation of the operations.
Here and in what follows $[A \rightarrow B]$ denotes the set of the partial functions from A into B.
Implementing stacks by records means that, after fixing the correspondence from high-level into low-level sorts (in the example, from *stack* into *rec* and from *elem* into itself), one defines a map (called by Hoare *abstraction function* in [8]) which associates with each record value the stack value it represents, if any. This map, say ϕ, can be defined as follows:

$$\phi(<a,l>) = a[l] \cdot \ldots \cdot a[1], \text{ if } l \leq max \text{ and } a[1], \ldots, a[l] \text{ are defined.}$$

The abstraction map is defined over low-level values which represent some high-level value. In the example, records $<a, l>$ where $l > max$, or some of $a[1]$, ..., $a[l]$ is undefined, do not represent any stack value. Hence low-level values can be distinguished in "sound" and "junk" values w.r.t. their role in the implementation.

The abstraction function is usually not injective, since many low-level values represent the same high-level value (in the example $<a, l>$ and $<a', l>$ represent the same stack if $a[i] = a'[i]$ for each $i = 1, \ldots, l$); however, it must be surjective since each high-level value must be represented.
In order to have an implementation of stacks by records it is moreover necessary to implement the operations, i.e. to define stack operations over records. Formally that corresponds to define a Σ_{Stack}-structure, say Rec^+, whose values are values of *Rec* and whose operations are defined "on top" of the operations in *Rec*, as shown below.

- $empty^{Rec^+} = <\emptyset, zero>$
- $top^{Rec^+}(r) =_\perp r.elems[r.length]$
- $pop^{Rec^+}(r) =_\perp <r.elems, pred(r.length)>$
- $push^{Rec^+}(r, e) =_\perp <r.elems[e/succ(r.length)], succ(r.length)>$

Here and in what follows $e_1 =_\perp e_2$ denotes strong equality, i.e. it means "e_1 and e_2 are either both defined and equal, or both undefined".
The interpretation of the operations in the right-hand-side of the above clauses is intended to be in *Rec*.
In order to have a correct implementation, i.e. one whose "behaviour" is the same of the high-level structure, the implementation of the operations must be compatible with the abstraction function; this means that applying an operation to "sound" values:

1. first, we cannot get a junk value;
2. moreover, what we get is a representation of the correct high-level result (including undefined).

In other words, operations and abstraction function must commute. Formally: the set of the sound values must be closed w.r.t. to the operations, and, for each operation in Σ_{Stack}, say $op: s_1 \ldots s_n \to s$,

$$\phi(op^{Rec^+}(a_1, \ldots, a_n)) =_\perp op^{Stack}(\phi(a_1), \ldots, \phi(a_n))$$

must hold. That can be easily verified for the definitions above.

1.2 A formalization of implementation within static frameworks

We give now a formalization of the notion of implementation of data structures as a relation between two (static) data-types, informally illustrated by the preceding example. We want a definition independent from the particular algebraic framework we choose (e.g. total algebras, partial algebras, order-sorted algebras and so on ...). Hence we unify all these algebraic frameworks under the notion of "static framework" (we will use indeed the name "dynamic framework" later referring to a framework for modelling data structures in a dynamic context). Basically, our static frameworks are particular (model parts of) institutions in which structures are (many-sorted) sets enriched by some mathematical structure. Indeed in this paper we do not deal with specifications, but only with "concrete" structures.
In the sequel, let **Fam**: $\mathbf{Set}^{op} \to \mathbf{Cat}$ be the functor giving, for each set of sorts S, the category of the S-families of sets (formally defined in the Appendix, def. 17).

Definition 1. A static framework is a 4-tuple

$$\mathcal{ST} = <\mathbf{Sig}, \mathbf{Sorts}, \mathbf{Struct}, | - |>$$

where

- **Sig** is a category, whose objects are called *signatures*;
- **Sorts** is a functor, **Sorts**: **Sig** $\rightarrow$ **Set**; for each signature Σ, the elements of **Sorts**(Σ) are called *sorts* of Σ, for each signature morphism σ, **Sorts**(σ) is denoted by σ^{Sorts}, or simply σ when there is no ambiguity;
- **Struct** is a functor, **Struct**: $\mathbf{Sig}^{op} \rightarrow \mathbf{Cat}$; for each signature Σ, objects in **Struct**(Σ) are called *(static) structures over* Σ or Σ*-structures*, and morphisms in **Struct**(Σ) are called Σ*-morphisms*; for each signature morphism σ, the functor **Struct**(σ) is called the σ*-reduct* and denoted by $-|_\sigma$.
- $| - |$ is a natural transformation, $| - |$: **Struct** $\rightarrow$ **Fam** $\circ$ $\mathbf{Sorts}^{op}$; for each signature Σ with sorts S, $| - |_\Sigma$: **Struct**(Σ) $\rightarrow$ **Fam**(S) is a faithful functor; for each object A in **Struct**(Σ), $| A |_\Sigma$ is called the *carrier of* A and denoted simply by A, when there is no ambiguity; for each morphism f in **Struct**(Σ), $| f |_\Sigma$ is denoted simply by f, when there is no ambiguity. □

Accordingly to the terminology of [1], for each signature Σ with sorts S, the pair <**Struct**(Σ), $| - |_\Sigma$> is a concrete category over **Fam**(S). Note that the assumption that $| - |_\Sigma$ is faithful (i.e. all the hom-set restrictions are injective) models the fact that morphisms of static structures are basically maps. Hence we call surjective morphisms the morphisms whose underlying map is surjective, and so on.
Moreover, if $f: A \rightarrow B$ is a Σ-morphism s.t. $| f |$ is an embedding (set inclusion), then we say that f is an embedding Σ-morphism and A is a (Σ-)*substructure of* B, and write $A \subseteq B$.
An implementation relation binds two structures over two different signatures, thus generalizing somehow the morphism notion. As pointed out in [9], there are two different points of view about that. According to the first, implementing a structure H over Σ_H by a structure L over a signature Σ_L (we always use H and L for "high-" and "low"-level, respectively) means defining the operations in Σ_H over elements of L in terms of the operations in Σ_L, in such a way that the obtained structure "behaves" like H. In this sense, an implementation is a *construction* of Σ_H-structures from Σ_L-structures, together with an *abstraction* which relates H with the Σ_H-structure obtained by the construction step. A simpler point of view consists in assuming that the construction step has already taken place, i.e. the operations of Σ_H are present in some sense in Σ_L; in this sense an implementation is just a signature morphism from Σ_H into Σ_L, together with the abstraction step. In the following we consider the second point of view as a particular case of the first.

Definition 2. Let Σ_H, Σ_L be two signatures with sorts S_H, S_L respectively, $\overline{H}$ be a structure over Σ_H, $\overline{L}$ be a structure over Σ_L. Then an *implementation relation* ϕ *from* $\overline{H}$ *into* $\overline{L}$ is a triple $<\phi^{Sorts}, \phi^{Cons}, \phi^{Abs}>$ s.t.

1. ϕ^{Sorts} is a morphism in **Set**, $\phi^{Sorts}: S_H \rightarrow S_L$;
2. ϕ^{Cons} is a functor, ϕ^{Cons}: **Struct**(Σ_L) $\rightarrow$ **Struct**(Σ_H), s.t., for each L structure in **Struct**(Σ_L)

$$| \phi^{Cons}(L) |_{\Sigma_H} \subseteq (| L |_{\Sigma_L})_{|\phi^{Sorts}};$$

3. ϕ^{Abs} is a surjective morphism[2] in $\mathbf{Struct}(\Sigma_H)$, $\phi^{Abs}: \phi^{Cons}(\overline{L}) \to \overline{H}$. □

Intuitively the three components above correspond to the following steps.

1. Each sort in the high-level signature is mapped into a sort in the low-level signature.
2. The high-level operations are defined as derived operations on top of the low-level structure $\overline{L}$, thus making (a subset of) the elements of $\overline{L}$ a Σ_H-structure $\phi^{Cons}(\overline{L})$.
3. The low-level elements are mapped into high-level elements. Note that the informal assumptions 1 and 2 of the preceding subsection are modelled by requiring respectively that $\phi^{Cons}(\overline{L})$ is a Σ_H-structure and that ϕ^{Abs} is a Σ_H-morphism.

In the case in which the high-level operations are already "present" in the low-level structure, the construction step modelled by ϕ^{Cons} consists in taking (a substructure of) the reduct w.r.t. to some signature morphism. Formally, there exists a signature morphism $\sigma: \Sigma_H \to \Sigma_L$ s.t. for each L structure in $\mathbf{Struct}(\Sigma_L)$

$$\phi^{Cons}(L) \subseteq L_{|\sigma}.$$

2 Implementing dynamic data-types

2.1 What is missing

In the preceding section, we have presented from both an informal and a formal point of view the notion of implementation of data structures as a relation between two (static) data-types. We will show now that this approach is not completely adequate for modelling what we require when implementing some data structure in an imperative language (more generally, in a language whose underlying model is based on some notion of evolving state).

To this end, we consider another classical implementation of stacks, which uses linked lists. That means, using a Pascal-like syntax, that the type *stack* is implemented by a pointer type *point* declared as follows:

```
type    point =↑ node
        node =  record
                top : elem;
                rest : point;
        end
```

Assuming the standard definition of a state as a (sort-respecting) partial mapping from left values (locations) into (right) values, values of type *point* are either the

[2] In this paper, we model implementation as a relation from a high-level structure into just one low-level structure. However, that can be naturally generalized to a class of low-level structures, making ϕ^{Abs} a natural transformation instead of one morphism.

special value *nil* or locations of type *node* and values of type *node* are pairs $<e, l>$ where e is a value of type *elem* and l is in turn a value of type *point*. Stack values are represented in this implementation by values of type *point*, i.e. locations of type *node* (or *nil*). More precisely, the stack value represented by a value of type *point* (i.e. the definition of the abstraction function) is as follows (where σ denotes the current state):

$\phi^{Abs}(nil) = \Lambda$
for each $l \in Loc_{node}$,
$(\phi^{Abs})(l) =_{\perp} e \cdot \phi^{Abs}(l')$, if $\sigma(l) = <e, l'>$, undefined otherwise.

This definition shows immediately a first difficulty in applying the schema used for the array implementation; in this case the abstraction function, i.e. the correspondence from low- into high-level values, turns out to be state-dependent (indeed we should have written above ϕ_{σ}^{Abs} instead of ϕ^{Abs}). This happens in all the implementations which use some internal dynamically evolving structure.

More important from the point of view of software development is the fact that, within an imperative context, a module implementing stacks is expected to supply more features than the pure implementation of stack operations. For instance, a user of the module wants to declare and assign variables of type *stack*; hence the module must typically include a "copy" procedure implementing assignment, and a "recursive dispose" procedure. In general, implementing a data structure in an imperative language means implementing not only operations (functions) but also commands/procedures (state transformations).

Analogously, the implementation is often assumed to satisfy more requirements than the pure functional behaviour (i.e. the correct implementation of the operations, expressed by the homomorphism property). For instance, a user of the module usually wants that no undesired sharing (or other side-effects) are introduced by using the functions/procedures exported by the module. Hence, the module could be a "wrong" implementation from the point of view of the user, for the reason that it produces states which are "junk" in some sense, even if in each single state the mapping from pointer values into stack values is a correct implementation. As another example, the user could require that no memory is lost by executing procedures exported by the module (i.e. all the locally allocated memory is deallocated at the end of the procedure execution).

All these kind of requirements are usually stated informally, or in any case as additional requirements outside of the algebraic formalization.

In the following, we present a better solution which allows to express all the desired properties in an homogeneous way, through a unique implementation notion. The starting idea, motivated by all the considerations above, is that a data structure in an imperative context cannot be modelled just by a static data-type. Indeed, introducing a new type, say t, in an imperative program, means not only to have values of type t with operations for handling them, but also enriching the structure of the state, adding left values of type t with related state transformations.

Hence, within languages supporting a notion of evolving state, a better formalization of a data structure is a *dynamic data-type* as defined in the next subsection.

2.2 Dynamic frameworks

A dynamic data-type consists in a set of configurations (states), together with operations which transform a configuration into another (*dynamic operations*). Hence our formal presentation below is structured as follows: we first define configuration sets, then dynamic operations, and finally we give the overall definition.
Our definition of dynamic framework is "parameterized" on a given static framework; that means that each configuration "determines" a structure in the underlying static framework: i.e., a dynamic structure with static signature Σ does not have directly Σ-structures as configurations, but "generalized" Σ-structures (i.e., entities which are "viewed" as Σ-structures). The intuitive motivation is that the dynamic evolution of the system can depend on a structure richer than the "visible" one; for instance, a software module can be seen as a dynamic system in which the signature of each configuration is given by the exported function and variable symbols, but the dynamic evolution (state change due to the execution of procedures) may depend on some additional structure (hidden functions and variables).
A notion of generalized structures which has some similarities with the one we are using has been given in [7] for different aims.
In what follows, we assume a fixed static framework $\mathcal{ST} = <\mathbf{Sig}, \mathbf{Sorts}, \mathbf{Struct}, | - |>$.

Definition 3. For each signature Σ, let $\mathbf{ConfSet}(\Sigma)$ be the category of the *configuration sets* over Σ, defined as follows:

- an object is a map $\mathcal{A}: CS \to \mathbf{Struct}(\Sigma)$ where CS is a set, denoted by $Dom(\mathcal{A})$; we write $A \in \mathcal{A}$ instead of $A \in Dom(\mathcal{A})$; for each $A \in \mathcal{A}$, $\mathcal{A}(A)$ is called the *Σ-view of A (in $\mathcal{A}$)* and denoted by $[A]_{\mathcal{A}}$ or simply $[A]$ when there is no ambiguity;
- a morphism $\phi: \mathcal{A} \to \mathcal{B}$ is a map which associates with each $A \in \mathcal{A}$ a structure $B \in \mathcal{B}$ (denoted by $\phi(A)$) and a Σ-morphism $\phi_A: [A] \to [B]$;
- identity and composition are defined in the obvious way. □

Proposition 4. *Let F be a functor, $F: \mathbf{Struct}(\Sigma_1) \to \mathbf{Struct}(\Sigma_2)$, for some signatures Σ_1, Σ_2. Then F can be naturally extended to configuration sets, getting a functor $F: \mathbf{ConfSet}(\Sigma_1) \to \mathbf{ConfSet}(\Sigma_2)$, as follows:*

- *for each object $\mathcal{A}$, $Dom(F(\mathcal{A})) = Dom(\mathcal{A})$ and, for each $A \in F(\mathcal{A})$,*

$$[A]_{F(\mathcal{A})} = F([A]_{\mathcal{A}});$$

- *for each morphism $\phi: \mathcal{A} \to \mathcal{B}$, $F(\phi): F(\mathcal{A}) \to F(\mathcal{B})$ and, for each $A \in \mathcal{A}$,*

$$(F(\mathcal{A}))(A) = \phi(A),\ (F(\mathcal{A}))_A = F(\phi_A).\ \square$$

Proof. Straightforward. □

Definition 5. The functor $\mathbf{ConfSet}: \mathbf{Sig}^{op} \to \mathbf{Cat}$ is defined as follows:

- for each signature Σ, $\mathbf{ConfSet}(\Sigma)$ is the category of the configuration sets over Σ, defined in def. 3;
- for each signature morphism $\sigma: \Sigma_1 \to \Sigma_2$, $\mathbf{ConfSet}(\sigma)$ (denoted by $-_{|\sigma}$) is the extension (defined in 4) of the functor $-_{|\sigma}: \mathbf{Struct}(\Sigma_2) \to \mathbf{Struct}(\Sigma_1)$. □

Proposition 6. *The above definition is justified.*

Proof. Immediate from prop. 4. □

We write $\mathcal{A} \subseteq \mathcal{B}$ meaning graph inclusion, i.e. $Dom(\mathcal{A}) \subseteq Dom(\mathcal{B})$ and, for each $A \in \mathcal{A}$, $[A]_{\mathcal{A}} = [A]_{\mathcal{B}}$. A morphism $\phi: \mathcal{A} \to \mathcal{B}$ is surjective iff for each $B \in \mathcal{B}$ there exists $A \in \mathcal{A}$ s.t. $\phi(A) = B$ and ϕ_A is surjective.

We define now dynamic operations, i.e. transformations of configurations.

If S is a set, then $[S]$ denotes $S \cup \{\Lambda\}$; we use $[s]$ for ranging over $[S]$, i.e. $[s]$ stands for either an element of S or for the empty string.

Definition 7. A *dynamic signature* is a pair $<\Sigma, DOP>$ where

- Σ is a signature; set $S = \mathbf{Sorts}(\Sigma)$;
- DOP is a $(S^\star \times [S])$-family of symbols called *dynamic operation symbols*; if $dop \in DOP_{s_1 \ldots s_n [,s]}$, then we write $dop: s_1 \ldots s_n \Rightarrow [s]$. □

Definition 8. Dynamic signatures with the obvious componentwise definition of morphisms form a category which we call **DynSig**; moreover, **StatSig**: **DynSig** $\to$ **Sig** is the functor giving the first component of a dynamic signature (called the *static part of* $D\Sigma$). □

If $\mathcal{A}$ is a configuration set over Σ, $w = s_1 \ldots s_n \in \mathbf{Sorts}(\Sigma)^\star$, then we denote by $\mathcal{A}_w$ the set of tuples $<A, a_1, \ldots, a_n>$ s.t. $A \in \mathcal{A}$ and, for each $i = 1, \ldots, n$, $a_i \in [A]_{s_i}$.

Definition 9. Let $D\Sigma = <\Sigma, DOP>$ be a dynamic signature. A *d-oid (dynamic structure) over* $D\Sigma$ is a pair $\mathcal{A} = <|\mathcal{A}|, \{dop^{\mathcal{A}}\}_{dop \in DOP}>$ where:

- $|\mathcal{A}|$ is a configuration set over Σ (denoted simply by $\mathcal{A}$ when there is no ambiguity);
- for each $dop: s_1 \ldots s_n \Rightarrow [s]$, $dop^{\mathcal{A}}: \mathcal{A}_{s_1 \ldots s_n} \to \mathcal{A}_{[s]}$. □

Examples of d-oids will be given in subsect. 2.4 coming back to the implementation of stacks by pointers.

Definition 10. The d-oids over a dynamic signature $D\Sigma$ form a category **Doid**($D\Sigma$) taking as morphisms the morphisms $\phi: \mathcal{A} \to \mathcal{B}$ of underlying configuration sets which are compatible with dynamic operations, i.e. for every $dop: w \Rightarrow [s]$, $<A, \overline{a}> \in \mathcal{A}_w$,

$$\text{if } dop^{\mathcal{A}}(<A, \overline{a}>) = <A'[, a']>,\ \phi(A) = B \text{ and } \phi_A(\overline{a}) = \overline{b},$$
$$\text{then } dop^{\mathcal{B}}(<B, \overline{b}>) = <B'[, b']>,\ \phi(A') = B' \ [\text{and } \phi_{A'}(a') = b'].$$

For each dynamic signature morphism $\sigma: D\Sigma_1 \to D\Sigma_2$ with static part $\sigma: \Sigma_1 \to \Sigma_2$, the *d-oid reduct* functor $-_{|\sigma}$: **Doid**($D\Sigma_2$) $\to$ **Doid**($D\Sigma_1$) is defined enriching the corresponding reduct of configuration sets by the interpretation of the dynamic operations:

$$\text{for each } dop: w \Rightarrow [s] \text{ in } D\Sigma_1, \text{ d-oid } \mathcal{A} \text{ over } D\Sigma_2,\ <A, \overline{a}> \in \mathcal{A}_w,$$
$$dop^{\mathcal{A}_{|\sigma}}(<A, \overline{a}>) = dop^{\mathcal{A}}(<A, \overline{a}>).$$

Altogether, we have defined the d-oid functor **Doid**: **DynSig**^{op} $\to$ **Cat**. □

Proposition 11. *The above definition is justified.*

Proof. A worked proof of the fact that d-oids form a category can be found in [4]. The well-definedness of the d-oid reduct functor follows easily from the well-definedness of the configurations set reduct. □

We give now our definition of dynamic framework (parameterized on a given static framework).

Definition 12. The *dynamic framework based on $\mathcal{ST}$* is the 4-tuple

$$\mathcal{DYN}(\mathcal{ST}) = <\mathbf{DynSig}, \mathbf{StatSig}, \mathbf{Doid}, | - |>$$

where

- **DynSig** is the category of dynamic signatures and $\mathbf{StatSig}: \mathbf{DynSig} \to \mathbf{Sig}$ is the static part functor, both defined in def. 8;
- $\mathbf{Doid}: \mathbf{DynSig}^{op} \to \mathbf{Cat}$ is the d-oid functor defined in def. 10.
- $| - |: \mathbf{Doid} \to \mathbf{ConfSet} \circ \mathbf{StatSig}^{op}$ is the natural transformation giving the configuration set underlying a d-oid. □

Proposition 13. *The above definition is justified.*

Proof. The only point to be still checked is that $| - |$ is a natural transformation, whose proof is straightforward. □

The reader should have noticed that the definition of dynamic framework is formally "analogous" to the definition of a static framework: in other words, dynamic frameworks are the generalization of static frameworks to the case in which the elements of a structure, instead of being "atomic" (elements in a set), are in turn structures. Note moreover that our definition above is parameterized on the static part, but "concrete" for what concerns dynamics (i.e. we have fixed the definition of dynamic operations and their interpretations). Indeed, we have preferred in this paper to fix a definition suitable for the imperative case which is our running example. However, the definition of a dynamic framework could be given in a fully abstract way as we did for the static case.

2.3 A formalization of implementation inside dynamic frameworks

In the following, if $\mathcal{A}$ is a configuration set over Σ, $A \in \mathcal{A}$, then we write $| A |_\Sigma$ instead of $| [A] |_\Sigma$.

Definition 14. Let $D\Sigma_\mathcal{H}$, $D\Sigma_\mathcal{L}$ be two dynamic signatures with static parts $\Sigma_\mathcal{H}$ (with sorts $S_\mathcal{H}$), $\Sigma_\mathcal{L}$ (with sorts $S_\mathcal{L}$) respectively, $\overline{\mathcal{H}}$ be a d-oid over $D\Sigma_\mathcal{H}$, $\overline{\mathcal{L}}$ be a d-oid over $D\Sigma_\mathcal{L}$. Then *an implementation relation from $\overline{\mathcal{H}}$ into $\overline{\mathcal{L}}$* is a 4-tuple $\phi = <\phi^{Sorts}, \phi^{StCons}, \phi^{Cons}, \phi^{Abs}>$ s.t.

1. ϕ^{Sorts} is a morphism in **Set**, $\phi^{Sorts}: S_\mathcal{H} \to S_\mathcal{L}$;
2. ϕ^{StCons} is a functor, $\phi^{StCons}: \mathbf{Struct}(\Sigma_L) \to \mathbf{Struct}(\Sigma_H)$;
3. ϕ^{Cons} is a functor, $\phi^{Cons}: \mathbf{Doid}(D\Sigma_\mathcal{L}) \to \mathbf{Doid}(D\Sigma_\mathcal{H})$, s.t., for each $\mathcal{L}$ d-oid in $\mathbf{Doid}(D\Sigma_\mathcal{L})$

(*) $\mid \phi^{Cons}(\mathcal{L}) \mid_{D\Sigma_{\mathcal{H}}} \subseteq \phi^{StCons}(\mid \mathcal{L} \mid_{D\Sigma_{\mathcal{L}}})$;

4. ϕ^{Abs} is a surjective morphism in $\mathbf{Doid}(D\Sigma_{\mathcal{H}})$, $\phi^{Abs}: \phi^{Cons}(\overline{\mathcal{L}}) \to \overline{\mathcal{H}}$. □

Note that in (*) above we use the extension of ϕ^{StCons} to configuration sets, as defined in prop. 4.

Proposition 15. *If $\phi = <\phi^{Sorts}, \phi^{StCons}, \phi^{Cons}, \phi^{Abs}>$ is an implementation relation from $\overline{\mathcal{H}}$ into $\overline{\mathcal{L}}$, then, for each $L \in \mid \phi^{Cons}(\overline{\mathcal{L}}) \mid_{D\Sigma_{\mathcal{H}}}$,*

if $\phi^{Abs}(L) = H$, $\phi^{Abs}_L: [L]_{\phi^{Cons}(\overline{\mathcal{L}})} \to [H]_{\overline{\mathcal{H}}}$,
then $<\phi^{Sorts}, \phi^{StCons}, \phi^{Abs}_L>$

is an implementation relation from $[H]_{\overline{\mathcal{H}}}$ into $[L]_{\phi^{Cons}(\overline{\mathcal{L}})}$. □

Proof. Straightforward. □

The above proposition expresses the fact that the notion of implementation in the dynamic case is the natural extension of the static version. More precisely, in a correct implementation, configurations in the low-level structure must be implementations of configurations in the high-level structure in the static sense, as expected; anyway, that requirement is not enough (the implication above holds in only one sense), since moreover the mapping from low-level into high-level configurations must respect dynamic operations and be surjective (each high-level configuration must be represented).

As in the static case, we consider the situation in which the high-level operations are already "present" in the low-level structure. This corresponds to the particular case in which the construction step modelled by ϕ^{StCons} and ϕ^{Cons} consists in taking (a substructure of) the reduct w.r.t. to some dynamic signature morphism. Formally, there exists a dynamic signature morphism $\sigma: D\Sigma_{\mathcal{H}} \to D\Sigma_{\mathcal{L}}$ s.t. for each $\mathcal{L}$ d-oid over $D\Sigma_{\mathcal{L}}$,

$$\phi^{Cons}(\mathcal{L}) \subseteq \mathcal{L}_{|\sigma}.$$

2.4 An example: imperative languages

We come back now to the example of stacks implemented by pointers showing how to formalize it as an implementation of dynamic structures. Throughout this subsection, we fix partial algebras (see [6]) as underlying static framework, and write $A \in \mathbf{PAlg}(\Sigma)$ meaning that A is a partial Σ-algebra.

We start from the consideration that if a type, say t, is available in an imperative program, then values of type t and operations for handling them are provided, but also variables of that type. Hence, at the semantic level, we have left-values of type t and a t-component of the state, i.e. a mapping from left into right values of type t, formally modelled by an operation $cont_t: L\text{-}t \to t$ below. Moreover, we have related state transformations, e.g. allocation (adding a new left value to the domain), deallocation (deleting an existing left value from the domain) and updating (adding an association from a left into a right value). Formally, for each set of types T, with associated values $\{ Val_t \}_{t \in T}$:

1. Loc is a T-family s.t., for each $t \in T$, Loc_t is a countably infinite set whose elements are called *left values (locations) of type t*;
2. $\Sigma^T_{State} = <\{t, L\text{-}t \mid t \in T\}, \{cont_t: L\text{-}t \to t \mid t \in T\}>$;
3. $State^T = \{A \mid A \in \mathbf{PAlg}(\Sigma^T_{State});\ \forall t \in T, A_t \subseteq Val_t,\ A_{L\text{-}t}$ finite and $A_{L\text{-}t} \subseteq Loc_t\}$;
4. $DOP^T = \{alloc_t\colon \Rightarrow L\text{-}t,\ dealloc_t\colon L\text{-}t \Rightarrow,\ update_t\colon L\text{-}t, t \Rightarrow \mid t \in T\}$;
5. for each $t \in T$, the interpretation as state transformations of $alloc_t$, $dealloc_t$ and $update_t$ is formally defined in the Appendix, def. 18.

We model now stacks and pointers as d-oids. The d-oid $\mathcal{S}$ of stacks has dynamic signature

> **dynsig** $D\Sigma_S =$
> **static part** $\Sigma_S =$ **enrich** $\Sigma^{\{stack,elem\}}_{State}$ **by**
> **opns**
> $top\colon stack \to elem$
> **dynopns**
> $DOP^{\{stack,elem\}} \cup \{push\colon L\text{-}stack, elem \Rightarrow,\ pop\colon L\text{-}stack \Rightarrow\}$

and is defined (assuming $Val_{elem} = Elem$, $Val_{stack} = Elem^\star$) by:

- $Dom(\mid \mathcal{S} \mid) = \{S \mid S \in \mathbf{PAlg}(\Sigma_S), S_{\mid \Sigma^{\{stack,elem\}}_{State}} \in State^{\{stack,elem\}}$, $top^S(e \cdot s) = e, top^S(\Lambda)$ undefined$\}$;
- for each $S \in \mid \mathcal{S} \mid$, $[S]_{\mathcal{S}} = S$;
- for each $S \in \mid \mathcal{S} \mid$, $l \in S_{L\text{-}stack}$, $e \in S_{elem}$,
  $push(S, l, e) =_\perp update_{stack}(S, l, e \cdot s)$, if $s = cont^S(l)$, undefined otherwise;
  $pop(S, l) =_\perp update_{stack}(S, l, s)$ if $e \cdot s = cont^S(l)$, undefined otherwise.
- the interpretation of the dynamic operations in $DOP^{\{stack,elem\}}$ is as in 5 above.

The d-oid above can be viewed as the semantic counterpart of a software module exporting two type *stack* and *elem*, a function *top* of type *elem* with a value parameter
of type *stack* and two procedures *push*, *pop* with a parameter of type *stack* by reference.
The d-oid $\mathcal{P}$ of pointers has signature

> **dynsig** $D\Sigma_{\mathcal{P}} =$
> **static part** $\Sigma_{\mathcal{P}} =$ **enrich** $\Sigma^{\{point,node,elem\}}_{State}$ **by**
> **opns**
> $<-,->\colon elem, point \to node$
> $-.top\colon node \to elem,\ -.rest\colon node \to point$
> **dynopns** $DOP^{\{point,node,elem\}}$

and is defined (assuming $Val_{point} = Loc_{node} \cup \{nil\}$, $Val_{node} = Elem \times Loc_{node}$) by:

- $Dom(\mid \mathcal{P} \mid) = \{P \mid P \in \mathbf{PAlg}(\Sigma_{\mathcal{P}}), P_{\mid \Sigma^{\{point,node,elem\}}_{State}} \in State^{\{point,node,elem\}}$ and $<-,->$, $-.top$, $-.rest$ have the usual interpretation$\}$;
- for each $P \in \mid \mathcal{P} \mid$, $[P]_{\mathcal{P}} = P$;

- the interpretation of the dynamic operations in $DOP^{\{point,node,elem\}}$ is as in 5 above.

We give now the formal definition of the implementation $\overline{\phi}$ from $\mathcal{S}$ into $\mathcal{P}$.

Implementation of sorts

$\overline{\phi}^{Sorts}(stack) = point$, $\overline{\phi}^{Sorts}(elem) = elem$,
$\overline{\phi}^{Sorts}(L\text{-}stack) = L\text{-}point$, $\overline{\phi}^{Sorts}(L\text{-}elem) = L\text{-}elem$.

Implementation of static operations

For each $P \in \mathbf{PAlg}(\Sigma_{\mathcal{P}})$, we define $(\Phi_P)_{stack}: P_{point} \to Val^{\star}$ as follows:

$$(\Phi_P)_{stack}(l) =_{\perp} \text{ if } l = nil \text{ then } \Lambda \text{ else } e \cdot (\Phi_P)_{stack}(l') \text{ where } <e, l'> = cont^P_{node}(l).$$

Then, $\overline{\phi}^{StCons}(P) = P^+$ is the $\Sigma_{\mathcal{S}}$-algebra defined by

$P^+_{stack} = \{l \mid l \in P_{point}, (\Phi_P)_{stack}(l) \text{ is defined}\}$,
$P^+_{L\text{-}stack} = P_{L\text{-}point}$, $P^+_{elem} = P_{elem}$, $P^+_{L\text{-}elem} = P_{L\text{-}elem}$,
for each $l \in P^+_{stack}$,
$cont^{P^+}_{stack}(l) =_{\perp} cont_{point}(l)$, $top^{P^+}(l) =_{\perp} cont_{node}(l).top$

Implementation of dynamic operations

For each d-oid $\mathcal{P}$ over $D\Sigma_{\mathcal{P}}$, $\overline{\phi}^{Cons}(\mathcal{P}) = \mathcal{P}^+$ is the d-oid over $D\Sigma_{\mathcal{S}}$ defined by

- $Dom(\mid \mathcal{P}^+ \mid_{D\Sigma_{\mathcal{S}}}) = \{P \in \mid \mathcal{P} \mid_{D\Sigma_{\mathcal{P}}} \mid NoSh(P)\}$
  where $NoSh(P) = \forall l_1, l_2 \in P_{L\text{-}point}, cont^P(l_1) = cont^P(l_2)$ implies $l_1 = l_2$ ($NoSh$ stands for "no sharing");
- for each $P \in \mid \mathcal{P}^+ \mid$, $[P]_{\mathcal{P}^+} = \overline{\phi}^{StCons}([P]_{\mathcal{P}})$;
- $push^{\mathcal{P}^+}$, $pop^{\mathcal{P}^+}$, $alloc^{\mathcal{P}^+}$, $dealloc^{\mathcal{P}^+}$ and $update^{\mathcal{P}^+}$ are defined "on top" of the static and dynamic operations in $\mathcal{P}$ (the definition is given in the Appendix, def. 19).

Abstraction function

For each $P \in \mathbf{PAlg}(\Sigma_{\mathcal{P}})$, set $(\Phi_P)_{elem} = id_{P_{elem}}$, $(\Phi_P)_{L\text{-}elem} = id_{P_{L\text{-}elem}}$, $(\Phi_P)_{L\text{-}stack} = \eta|_{P_{L\text{-}point}}$ where η is a bijection from Loc_{point} into Loc_{stack}.

Then we define, for each $P \in \mid \mathcal{P}^+ \mid$, $\overline{\phi}^{Abs}(P) = S$ where S is the $\Sigma_{\mathcal{S}}$-algebra uniquely determined by $\mid S \mid = \Phi_P(P)$, $\mid \overline{\phi}^{Abs}_P \mid = \Phi_P$.

Proposition 16. *The 4-tuple* $\overline{\phi} = <\overline{\phi}^{Sorts}, \overline{\phi}^{StCons}, \overline{\phi}^{Cons}, \overline{\phi}^{Abs}>$ *defined above is an implementation from* $\mathcal{S}$ *into* $\mathcal{P}$.

Proof. (Outline) The proof consists in checking that:

1. for each low-level configuration P, if $\overline{\phi}^{Abs}(P) = S$, then $<\overline{\phi}^{Sorts}, \overline{\phi}^{StCons}, \overline{\phi}^{Abs}_P>$ is an implementation relation from $[S]_{\mathcal{S}}$ into $[P]_{\mathcal{P}^+}$; that requires to check that the implementation of each static operation in P^+ commutes with $\overline{\phi}^{Abs}_P$;

2. the implementation of each dynamic operation in $\mathcal{P}^+$ commutes with $\overline{\phi}^{Abs}$;
3. $\overline{\phi}^{Abs}$ is a surjective d-oid morphism: for each low-level configuration P, $\overline{\phi}_P^{Abs}$ is surjective by construction; it remains to check that $\overline{\phi}^{Abs}$ is surjective as mapping from low- into high-level configurations, i.e. that each high-level configuration can be obtained in the implementation; that can be easily checked by structural induction on high-level configurations. □

We describe now briefly how the problems mentioned in subsect. 2.1 are solved within this approach.
First of all, the fact that the correspondence form low- into high-level values is "state-dependent" finds now its formal counterpart in the fact that the "abstraction function" becomes a d-oid morphism, hence a mapping from low-level configurations into high-level configurations together with, for each low-level configuration, a mapping from its values into the values of the corresponding high-level configuration.
The fact that implementing a data structure in an imperative context means also to implement command/procedures (state transformations) is modelled in a natural way passing from static to dynamic data-types: dynamic operations (state transformations) are now part of the overall structure in the same way of static operations.
Analogously, that "lifting-up" from static to dynamic structures allows to handle in an homogeneous way "global" assumptions on the implementation (like requiring no side-effects). Indeed, as the implementation of a static operation is correct iff applying the operation to "sound" values gives a sound value again, and moreover the right one (part 1 of proof of prop. 16); thus now the implementation of a dynamic operation is correct iff applying the dynamic operation to a sound configuration gives a sound configuration again, and moreover the right one (part 2 of proof of prop. 16).

3 Conclusion

We have shown how to give a formal definition of implementation within the framework of dynamic data-types (already presented in [3], [4], [5]).
The outcome of this work is, in our opinion, twofold. First, an implementation relation from a dynamic structure into another, as defined in this paper, gives an adequate and uniform semantic model of the implementation of a data structure by a software module in an imperative or object based language. Moreover, the definition of implementation in a dynamic framework is given "on top" of the definition of implementation in an underlying static framework, hence can be viewed as the natural extension of the usual static notion. This is a contribute in showing that dynamic frameworks are a "sound" generalization of static frameworks, in the sense that important concepts and properties are preserved (see, e.g., [5] for the definition in the dynamic case of term structures with unique evaluation properties).
In this paper, we only deal with concrete models. Hence, of course, the next step to be done is to add the specification aspects. That means taking, instead of a static framework as defined here, a static institution (including a language of static formulas, i.e. formulas which are evaluated in a given configuration) and defining the corresponding dynamic institution (including dynamic formulas) with the related

notion of implementation (being now a relation between two specifications instead of two models).

Acknowledgment. I wish to thank my colleagues E. Astesiano for our common work on dynamic data-types, G. Costa for reading a draft version of this paper and M. Cerioli for many helpful discussions about the implementation concept.

References

1. J. Adámek, H. Herrlich, and G. Strecker. *Abstract and Concrete Categories.* Pure and Applied Mathematics. Wiley Interscience, New York, 1990.
2. E. Astesiano, G. Reggio, and E.Zucca. Stores as homomorphisms and their transformations. In A. M. Borzyszkowsky and S. Sokolowsky, editors, *Proc. Mathematical Foundations of Computer Science 1993*, number 711 in Lecture Notes in Computer Science, pages 242–251. Springer Verlag, Berlin, 1993.
3. E. Astesiano and E. Zucca. A semantic model for dynamic systems. In U.W. Lipeck and B. Thalheim, editors, *Modelling Database Dynamics, Volkse 1992*, Workshops in Computing, pages 63–83. Springer Verlag, Berlin, 1993.
4. E. Astesiano and E. Zucca. D-oids: a model for dynamic data-types. *Mathematical Structures in Computer Science*, 1994. To appear.
5. E. Astesiano and E. Zucca. A free construction of dynamic terms. Technical report, DISI, 1994. Submitted for publication.
6. M. Broy and M. Wirsing. Partial abstract types. *Acta Informatica*, (18), 1982.
7. M. Cerioli and G. Reggio. Institutions for very abstract specifications. In *Recent Trends in Data Type Specification*, number 785 in Lecture Notes in Computer Science, pages 113–127. Springer Verlag, Berlin, 1993.
8. C.A.R. Hoare. Proof of correctness of data representation. *Acta Informatica*, 1:271–281, 1972.
9. F. Orejas, M. Navarro, and A. Sánchez. Implementation and behavioural equivalence: A survey. In M. Bidoit and C. Choppy, editors, *Recent Trends in Data Type Specification*, number 655 in Lecture Notes in Computer Science, pages 93–125. Springer Verlag, Berlin, 1993.
10. D. Sannella and A. Tarlecki. Towards formal development of programs from algebraic specifications: Implementations revisited. *Acta Informatica*, 25:233–281, 1988.

4 Appendix

Definition 17. The functor $\mathbf{Fam}: \mathbf{Set}^{op} \to \mathbf{Cat}$ is defined as follows:

- for each object S in **Set**, $\mathbf{Fam}(S)$ is the category whose objects are S-families of sets and whose morphisms are S-families of (partial) maps;
- for each map $\sigma: S \to S'$,
  - for each object A' in $\mathbf{Fam}(S')$, $\mathbf{Fam}(\sigma)(A')$, shortly denoted by $A'_{|\sigma}$, is the S-family defined by $A'_{|\sigma_s} = A'_{\sigma(s)}$, for each $s \in S$;
  - for each morphism $f': A' \to B'$ in $\mathbf{Fam}(S')$, $\mathbf{Fam}(\sigma)(f')$, shortly denoted by $f'_{|\sigma}$, is defined by: $f'_{|\sigma}: A'_{|\sigma} \to B'_{|\sigma}$, $(f'_{|\sigma})_s(a) =_{\perp} f_{\sigma(s)}(a)$, $\forall a \in A'_{|\sigma}$. □

Definition 18. For each $t \in T$, let new_t be a map which associates with each finite subset L of Loc_t a left value in $Loc_t \setminus L$. Then, for each $A \in State^T$, $l \in A_{L\text{-}t}$, $v \in A_t$,

- $alloc_t(A) = <A + new_t(A_{L\text{-}t}), new_t(A_{L\text{-}t})>$, where $A + l$ is the algebra equal to A except that $(A + l)_{L\text{-}t} = A_{L\text{-}t} \cup \{l\}$;
- $dealloc_t(A, l) = A \setminus \{l\}$ where $A \setminus \{l\}$ is the algebra equal to A except that $(A \setminus \{l\})_{L\text{-}t} = A_{L\text{-}t} \setminus \{l\}$;
- $update_t(A, l, v) = A[v/l]$ where $A[v/l]$ is the algebra equal to A except that $cont^{A[v/l]}(l) = v$. □

Definition 19. For each $P \in | \mathcal{P}^+ |$, $l \in P_{L\text{-}point}$, $e \in P_{elem}$:

- $push^{\mathcal{P}^+}(l, e) =_\perp$ **let** $n = alloc_{node}$ **in**
  $update_{node}(n, <e, cont_{point}(l)>); update_{point}(l, n)$
- $pop^{\mathcal{P}^+}(l) =_\perp$ **let** $n = cont_{point}(l)$ **in**
  let $n' = cont_{node}(n).rest$ **in**
  $dealloc(n); update_{point}(l, n')$
- $alloc^{\mathcal{P}^+}_{stack} =_\perp alloc_{point}$, $dealloc^{\mathcal{P}^+}_{stack}(l) =_\perp dealloc_{point}(l)$,
- $update^{\mathcal{P}^+}_{stack}(l, n) =_\perp$ **let** $n' = copy(n)$ **in** $update_{point}(l, n')$ where
  $copy: point \Rightarrow point$
  $copy(n) =$ **if** $n = nil$ **then** nil **else let** $n' = alloc_{node}$ **in**
  let $r = cont_{node}(n)$ **in**
  $update_{node}(n', <r.top, copy(r.rest)>)$. □

In the above definition we used the following conventions for improving readability:

- the parameter P is omitted everywhere;
- $dop_1(\overline{x}_1); dop_2(\overline{x}_2)$ stands for $dop_2(<dop_1(<P, \overline{x}_1>), \overline{x}_2>)$;
- **let** $x = dop_1(\overline{x}_1)$ **in** $dop_2(\overline{x}_2)$ stands for

$$\textbf{let } <P', x> = dop_1(<P, \overline{x}_1>) \textbf{ in } dop_2(<P', \overline{x}_2>)$$

For a full presentation of a language of dynamic expressions based on d-oids see [5].

What is an Abstract Data Type, after all?

Martin Gogolla[1] and Maura Cerioli[2]

[1] Fachbereich Mathematik und Informatik, Bremen University
D-28334 Bremen, Germany
[2] DISI, Universita di Genova
I-16132 Genova, Italy

adt94@disi.unige.it

Abstract. We look back on ten Workshops on Abstract Data Types. Organizers and publications, a list of authors referencing their talks and papers on the workshops, and a workshop bibliography are presented.

1 Organizers and Publications of the Workshops

1st Workshop on Abstract Data Types (1982)

Organization:	*Hans-Dieter Ehrich, Udo Walter Lipeck* in Langscheid, Sorpesee (BRD) from 22.03.82 to 26.03.82
Handout:	Internal Report, University of Dortmund [EL82]
Proceedings:	— no proceedings internationally published —

2nd Workshop on Abstract Data Types (1983)

Organization:	*Manfred Broy, Martin Wirsing* in Passau (BRD) from 16.05.83 to 20.05.83
Handout:	Internal Report, University of Passau [BW83b]
Proceedings:	— no proceedings internationally published —

3rd Workshop on Abstract Data Types (1984)

Organization:	*Hans-Joerg Kreowski, Anne Wilharm* in Bremen (BRD) from 13.11.84 to 16.11.84
Handout:	Universität Bremen, Informatik-Bericht Nr. 9/84 [KW84]
Proceedings:	Recent Trends in Data Type Specification, Springer, Berlin, Informatik Fachberichte Nr. 116, Hans-Jörg Kreowski (Ed.) [Kre85]

4th Workshop on Abstract Data Types (1986)

Organization: *Klaus Drosten, Hans-Dieter Ehrich, Martin Gogolla, Udo Walter Lipeck* in Warberg (BRD) from 20.05.86 to 23.05.86
Handout: Technische Universität Braunschweig, Informatik-Bericht Nr. 86-09 [DEGL86]
Proceedings: — no proceedings internationally published —

5th Workshop on Abstract Data Types (1987)

Organization: *Don Sannella* in Edinburgh (Scotland) from 01.09.87 to 04.09.87
Handout: University of Edinburgh, Department of Computer Science, Report No. ECS-LFCS-87-41 [San87]
Proceedings: Recent Trends in Data Type Specification, Springer, Berlin, LNCS 332, Don Sannella, Andrzej Tarlecki (Eds.) [ST88b]

6th Workshop on Abstract Data Types (1988)

Organization: *Hartmut Ehrig* in Berlin (BRD) from 29.08.88 to 02.09.88
Handout: Internal Report, University of Berlin [Ehr88]
Proceedings: — no proceedings internationally published —

7th Workshop on Abstract Data Types (1990)

Organization: *Klaus-Peter Jantke, Horst Reichel* in Wusterhausen, Dosse (DDR) from 17.04.90 to 20.04.90
Handout: Internal Report, University of Leipzig [JR90]
Proceedings: Recent Trends in Data Type Specification, Springer, Berlin, LNCS 534, Hartmut Ehrig, Klaus-Peter Jantke, Fernando Orejas, Horst Reichel (Eds.) [EJOR91]

8th Workshop on Abstract Data Types (1991)

Organization: *Michel Bidoit, Christine Choppy* in Dourdan (France) from 26.08.91 to 30.08.91
Handout: Internal Report, University of Paris [BC91]
Proceedings: Recent Trends in Data Type Specification, Springer, Berlin, LNCS 655, Michel Bidoit, Christine Choppy (Eds.) [BC93]

9th Workshop on Abstract Data Types (1992)

Organization:	*Fernando Orejas* in Caldes de Malavella (Spain) from 26.10.92 to 30.10.92
Handout:	Internal Report, University of Barcelona [Ore92]
Proceedings:	Recent Trends in Data Type Specification, Springer, Berlin, LNCS 785, Hartmut Ehrig, Fernando Orejas (Ed.) [EO94]

10th Workshop on Abstract Data Types (1994)

Organization:	*Egidio Astesiano, Maura Cerioli, Gianna Reggio* in Santa Margherita Ligure (Italy) from 30.05.94 to 03.06.94
Handout:	Internal Report, University of Genova [ACR94]
Proceedings:	Recent Trends in Data Type Specification, Springer, Berlin, LNCS, Egidio Astesiano, Gianna Reggio, Andrzej Tarlecki (Ed.) [ART95]

2 The Contributors

Jaume Agusti: [LA92].
Valentin Antimirov: [Ant92].
Grigoris Antoniou: [Ant90].
David Aspinall: [Asp94].
Egidio Astesiano: [AC88], [AGR88], [AR91], [AC91], [AZ92], [RACF94].
Leo Bachmair: [BGW91], [BGS94].
Han Baeumer: [Bae92].
Michael Baldamus: [EBO91].
Guntis Barzdins: [Bar90].
E. Battiston: [BCM90].
Bernhard Bauer: [BH91].
Hubert Baumeister: [Bau92].
Catriel Beeri: [Bee94].
Christoph Beierle: [BV82], [BV83], [BV84], [Bei86].
Jan Bergstra: [Ber82].
Gilles Bernot: [Ber86a], [Ber86b], [Ber87], [BG91], [DB94a], [DGB94].
Didier Bert: [Ber94], [BE94].
Yves Bertrand: [DB94b].
Mohamed Bettaz: [Bet88], [Bet90], [BM91], [BR92], [BM94a].
Michel Bidoit: [Bid83], [BCV84], [Bid86], [Bid87], [Bid88], [BCC90], [Bid92], [HBW94], [BH94].
P. Blauth-Menezes: [BM94b].
Paul Boehm: [Boe86], [EPPB+87].
Michel Bosco: [Bos91].
Pere Botella: [Bot86], [COB88].
Adel Bouhoula: [Bou94].
Michael Breu: [Bre87], [Bre91].
Ruth Breu: [Bre92].
Manfred Broy: [BW83a], [Bro94].
Peter Brueck: [Bru86].
Xavier Burgues: [BG87].
Rod Burstall: [Bur87].
F. Capy: [BCC90].
Maura Cerioli: [AC88], [AC91], [CR92], [Cer94], [GC94].
Boutheina Chetali: [CL94].
Christine Choppy: [BCV84], [Cho86], [Cho87], [BCC90], [Cho92].
Fiorella De Cindio: [BCM90], [Cin94].
Ingo Classen: [Cla88], [CG91].
Kieran Clenaghan: [Cle88], [Cle91].
Silvia Ines Clerici: [Cle87], [COB88], [CO90], [CJO92].
Derek Coleman: [Col87].
Stefan Conrad: [Con92].
Felix Cornelius: [Cor94].
Jose Felix Costa: [FCSM91], [SCS92], [CM94], [FC94].
Ernani Crivelli: [RACF94].
Erwan David: [DB94a].
Grit Denker: [DG92], [Den94].
Anne Deo: [DGB94].
Razvan Diaconescu: [Dia91], [GD92], [Dia94].
Niek Van Diepen: [Die91].
Christian Dimitrovici: [EPPB+87], [Dim88], [DH90].
W. Dosch: [MD84].
Klaus Drosten: [Dro83], [DE84], [Dro86].
Jean-Francois Dufourd: [DB94b].
Dominique Duval: [DR94].
Peter Dybjer: [Dyb83].
Rachid Echahed: [BE94].
Hans-Dieter Ehrich: [Ehr82b], [Ehr82a], [LE83], [DE84], [Ehr84], [Ehr86a], [ESS88], [EGS91], [ES94].
Hartmut Ehrig: [Ehr82c], [Ehr82d], [EFH83], [EW84], [EFH84], [Ehr86b], [EPPB+87], [FEHL88], [EPP90], [EBO91], [EPP91], [EJO92], [EPR92], [OPE94], [ELO94].
Gregor Engels: [EG82].
Jordi Farres-Casals: [FC88], [FC91].
Joachim Faulhaber: [Fau94].
Yulin Feng: [Fen90].
M. Fernandez: [FJ94].

References

[AC88] Egidio Astesiano and Maura Cerioli. Models and Logical Deduction in Partial Higher-Order Conditional Specifications. In [Ehr88], 1988.

[AC91] Egidio Astesiano and Maura Cerioli. Relationships between Logical Frameworks. In [BC93], pp. 126-143, 1991.

[ACR94] Egidio Astesiano, Maura Cerioli, and Gianna Reggio, editors. *Participants' Handout of the 10th Workshop on Abstract Data Type.* University of Genova, Department of Computer Science, 1994. Internal Report.

[AGR88] Egidio Astesiano, Alessandro Giovini, and Gianna Reggio. Data in a Concurrent Environment. In [Ehr88], 1988.

[Ant90] Grigoris Antoniou. On the Correctness of Modular Systems. In [JR90], 1990.

[Ant92] Valentin Antimirov. Term Rewriting in Unified Algebras: An Order-Sorted Approach. In [Ore92], 1992.

[AR91] Egidio Astesiano and Gianna Reggio. Algebraic Specification of Concurrency. In [BC93], pp. 1-39, 1991.

[ART95] Egidio Astesiano, Gianna Reggio, and Andrzej Tarlecki, editors. *Recent Trends in Data Type Specification.* Springer, Berlin, 1995. LNCS.

[Asp94] David Aspinall. Types, Subtypes and ASL+. This volume, pp. 116-131, 1994.

[AZ92] Egidio Astesiano and Elena Zucca. Towards a Theory of Dynamic Data Types. In [Ore92], 1992.

[Bae92] Han Baeumer. Relation Algebraic Specifications and Proofs in the Theory of Reduction Systems. In [Ore92], 1992.

[Bar90] Guntis Barzdins. ADT Implementation and Completion by Induction from Examples. In [EJOR91], pp. 1-10, 1990.

[Bau92] Hubert Baumeister. Parameter Passing in the Typed Lambda Calculus Approach to Parameterized Specifications. In [Ore92], 1992.

[BC91] Michel Bidoit and Christine Choppy, editors. *Participants' Handout of the 8th Workshop on Abstract Data Type.* University of Paris, Department of Computer Science, 1991. Internal Report.

[BC93] Michel Bidoit and Christine Choppy, editors. *Recent Trends in Data Type Specification.* Springer, Berlin, 1993. LNCS 655.

[BCC90] Michel Bidoit, F. Capy, and Christine Choppy. How to Specify Databases with Constraints using Algebraic Techniques. In [JR90], 1990.

[BCM90] E. Battiston, Fiorella De Cindio, and Giancarlo Mauri. The Specification of Concurrent Systems with OBJSA Nets: From the Language to the Environment. In [JR90], 1990.

[BCV84] Michel Bidoit, Christine Choppy, and F. Voisin. The ASSPEGIQUE Specification Environment - Motivations and Design. In [Kre85], pp. 54-72, 1984.

[BE94] Didier Bert and Rachid Echahed. On the Operational Semantics of the Algebraic and Logic Programming Language LPG. This volume, pp. 132-152, 1994.

[Bee94] Catriel Beeri. Bulk Types and Query Language Design. This volume, pp. 30-47, 1994.

[Bei86] Christoph Beierle. Vertical and Horizontal Compositions of Implementation Specifications. In [DEGL86], 1986.

[Ber82] Jan Bergstra. Specification of Parameterized Data Types. In [EL82], 1982.

[Ber86a] Gilles Bernot. Abstract Implementation with Exception Handling. In [DEGL86], 1986.

[Ber86b] Gilles Bernot. Correctness Proofs for Abstract Implementations. In [DEGL86], 1986.

[Ber87] Gilles Bernot. Good Functors ... are those Preserving Philosophy! In [San87], 1987.

[Ber94] Didier Bert. Structuring Specifications in the Algebraic and Logic Language LPG. In [ACR94], 1994.

[Bet88] Mohamed Bettaz. Implementation of Tools for the Specification and Validation of ADTs: Application to Communication Protocols. In [Ehr88], 1988.

[Bet90] Mohamed Bettaz. An Association of Algebraic Term Nets and Abstract Data Types for Specifying Real Communication Protocols. In [EJOR91], pp. 11-30, 1990.

[BG87] Xavier Burgues and Xavier Franch Gutierrez. Communication between an Abstract Syntax Tree Interpreter and a Term Rewriting System. In [San87], 1987.

[BG91] Gilles Bernot and Pascale Le Gall. Label Algebras: A Systematic Use of Terms. In [BC93], pp. 144-163, 1991.

[BGS94] Leo Bachmair, Harald Ganzinger, and J. Stuber. Combining Algebra and Universal Algebra in First-Order Theorem Proving: The Case of Commutative Rings. This volume, pp. 1-29, 1994.

[BGW91] Leo Bachmair, Harald Ganzinger, and Uwe Waldmann. First-Order Theorem Proving for Hierarchic Specifications. In [BC91], 1991.

[BH91] Bernhard Bauer and Rolf Hennicker. An Interactive System for Algebraic Implementation Proofs. In [BC91], 1991.

[BH94] Michel Bidoit and Rolf Hennicker. Behavioural Theories. This volume, pp. 153-169, 1994.

[Bid83] Michel Bidoit. Algebraic Specification of Exception Handling and Error Recovery in Abstract Data Types. In [BW83b], 1983.

[Bid86] Michel Bidoit. The PLUSS Specification Language. In [DEGL86], 1986.

[Bid87] Michel Bidoit. The Stratified Loose Approach: A Generalization of Initial and Loose Semantics. In [ST88b], pp. 1-22, 1987.

[Bid88] Michel Bidoit. Recent Development of the PLUSS Specification Language. In [Ehr88], 1988.

[Bid92] Michel Bidoit. Behavioural Semantics versus Observational Semantics: Is there any deep Difference? In [Ore92], 1992.

[BM91] Mohamed Bettaz and Mourad Maouche. How to Specify Non-Determinism and True Concurrency with Algebraic Term Nets. In [BC93], pp. 164-180, 1991.

[BM94a] Mohamed Bettaz and Mourad Maouche. On the Specification of Protocol Objects. In [ACR94], 1994.

[BM94b] P. Blauth-Menezes. Vertical Composition of Systems with Respect to the Substitution Operation. In [ACR94], 1994.

[Boe86] Paul Boehm. The ACT System - A Software Environment for ACT ONE Specifications. In [DEGL86], 1986.

[Bos91] Michel Bosco. Basic Research Activities in the Framework of the Research and Development Program in Information Technologies of the CEC-DGXIII. In [BC91], 1991.

[Bot86] Pere Botella. Abstract Data Types, Program Schema, and Programming Environments. In [DEGL86], 1986.

[Bou94] Adel Bouhoula. Sufficient Completeness and Implicit Induction in Parameterized Specifications. In [ACR94], 1994.

[BR92] Mohamed Bettaz and Gianna Reggio. A SMoLCS Based Kit for Defining High-Level Algebraic Petri Nets. In [EO94], pp. 98-112, 1992.

[Bre87] Michael Breu. The Semantics of Generics in PANNDA-S. In [San87], 1987.

[Bre91] Michael Breu. Bounded Implementation of Algebraic Specifications. In [BC93], pp. 181-198, 1991.

[Bre92] Ruth Breu. Two Views of Inheritance. In [Ore92], 1992.

[Bro94] Manfred Broy. Equations for Describing Dynamic Nets of Communicating Systems. This volume, pp. 170-187, 1994.

[Bru86] Peter Brueck. ADT as a Design Concept for CHILL. In [DEGL86], 1986.

[Bur87] Rod Burstall. Might the Church Representation of Data Types be Useful? In [San87], 1987.

[BV82] Christoph Beierle and Angelika Voss. Hierarchical Specification of Parameterized Abstract Data Types by Means of Canonical Term Algebras. In [EL82], 1982.

[BV83] Christoph Beierle and Angelika Voss. A Parameterization Concept for Hierarchies of Specifications. In [BW83b], 1983.

[BV84] Christoph Beierle and Angelika Voss. Implementation Specifications. In [Kre85], pp. 39-53, 1984.

[BW83a] Manfred Broy and Martin Wirsing. Generalized Heterogeneous Algebras. In [BW83b], 1983.

[BW83b] Manfred Broy and Martin Wirsing, editors. *Participants' Handout of the 2nd Workshop on Abstract Data Type.* University of Passau, Department of Computer Science, 1983. Internal Report.

[Cer94] Maura Cerioli. A Lazy Approach to Partial Algebras. This volume, pp. 188-202, 1994.

[CG91] Ingo Classen and Martin Gogolla. Towards a Conceptual Model for the Environment of the Algebraic Specification Language ACT ONE. In [BC91], 1991.

[Cho86] Christine Choppy. Complexity of Abstract Data Types. In [DEGL86], 1986.

[Cho87] Christine Choppy. Formal Specification, Prototyping, and Integration Testing. In [San87], 1987.

[Cho92] Christine Choppy. About the Correctness and Adequacy of PLUSS Specifications. In [EO94], pp. 128-143, 1992.

[Cin94] Fiorella De Cindio. A Distributed System Design Method Based on a Class of Modular Algebraic Nets: The Specification of the Coordinator of an Hydro-Electric System. In [ACR94], 1994.

[CJO92] Silvia Ines Clerici, Rosa Jimenez, and Fernando Orejas. Semantic Constructions in the Specification Language GLIDER. In [EO94], pp. 144-157, 1992.

[CL94] Boutheina Chetali and Pierre Lescanne. Faulty Channels, Correct Protocols: Formal Proofs of Concurrent Programs Using the Larch Prover. In [ACR94], 1994.

[Cla88] Ingo Classen. A Revised Version of ACT ONE. In [Ehr88], 1988.

[Cle87] Silvia Ines Clerici. Building Programs from Generic Specifications. In [San87], 1987.

[Cle88] Kieran Clenaghan. Abstract Architecture of an Interactive Programming System. In [Ehr88], 1988.

[Cle91] Kieran Clenaghan. A Look at Formal Program Development through Z. In [BC91], 1991.

[CM94] Jose Felix Costa and Danilo Montesi. A Model for Concurrent Databases. In [ACR94], 1994.

[CO90] Silvia Ines Clerici and Fernando Orejas. The Specification Language GS-BL. In [EJOR91], pp. 31-51, 1990.

[COB88] Silvia Ines Clerici, Fernando Orejas, and Pere Botella. The Specification Language for the GESTALT Environment. In [Ehr88], 1988.

[Col87] Derek Coleman. AXIS. In [San87], 1987.

[Con92] Stefan Conrad. On Certification of Specifications for TROLL light Objects. In [EO94], pp. 158-172, 1992.

[Cor94] Felix Cornelius. Charity: An Interface between Theory and Practice? In [ACR94], 1994.

[CR92] Maura Cerioli and Gianna Reggio. Institutions for Very Abstract Specifications. In [EO94], pp. 113-127, 1992.

[DB94a] Erwan David and Gilles Bernot. On the Usefulness of Semi-Initiality and Semi-Adjuncts for Institution-Independent Issues. In [ACR94], 1994.

[DB94b] Jean-Francois Dufourd and Yves Bertrand. Algebraic Specification and Interactive Solid Modelling. In [ACR94], 1994.

[DE84] Klaus Drosten and Hans-Dieter Ehrich. Translating Algebraic Specifications to PROLOG Programs. In [KW84], 1984.

[DEGL86] Klaus Drosten, Hans-Dieter Ehrich, Martin Gogolla, and Udo Walter Lipeck, editors. *Participants' Handout of the 4th Workshop on Abstract Data Type*. University of Braunschweig, Department of Computer Science, 1986. Informatik-Bericht Nr. 86-09.

[Den94] Grit Denker. Transactions in Object-Oriented Specifications. This volume, pp. 203-218, 1994.

[DG92] Grit Denker and Martin Gogolla. Translating TROLL light Concepts to Maude. In [EO94], pp. 173-187, 1992.

[DGB94] Anne Deo, Pascale Le Gall, and Gilles Bernot. Semantics for Algebraic Specifications with Iterators. In [ACR94], 1994.

[DH90] Christian Dimitrovici and Ulrich Hummert. Composition of Algebraic High-Level Nets. In [EJOR91], pp. 52-73, 1990.

[Dia91] Razvan Diaconescu. Logical Support to Modularization. In [BC91], 1991.

[Dia94] Razvan Diaconescu. Completeness of Model-Theoretic Paramodulation: A Category-Based Approach. In [ACR94], 1994.

[Die91] Niek Van Diepen. From Specification to Implementation - A Swiss System Study. In [BC91], 1991.

[Dim88] Christian Dimitrovici. Projection Spaces. In [Ehr88], 1988.

[DR94] Dominique Duval and Jean-Claude Reynaud. Sketches and Computation. In [ACR94], 1994.

[Dro83] Klaus Drosten. Executing Specifications using Conditional Axioms. In [BW83b], 1983.

[Dro86] Klaus Drosten. Term Rewriting Systems with Restricted Variables. In [DEGL86], 1986.

[Dyb83] Peter Dybjer. Towards a Unified Theory of Data Types: Some Categorical Aspects. In [BW83b], 1983.

[EBO91] Hartmut Ehrig, Michael Baldamus, and Fernando Orejas. New Concepts of Amalgamation and Extension for a General Theory of Specifications. In [BC93], pp. 199-221, 1991.

[EFH83] Hartmut Ehrig, Werner Fey, and Horst Hansen. ACT ONE - An Algebraic Specification Language with two Levels of Semantics. In [BW83b], 1983.

[EFH84] Hartmut Ehrig, Werner Fey, and Horst Hansen. Towards Abstract User Interfaces for Formal System Specifications. In [Kre85], pp. 73-88, 1984.

[EG82] Gregor Engels and Martin Gogolla. Error Handling in Algebraic Specifications. In [EL82], 1982.

[EGS91] Hans-Dieter Ehrich, Martin Gogolla, and Amilcar Sernadas. Objects and their Specification. In [BC93], pp. 40-65, 1991.

[Ehr82a] Hans-Dieter Ehrich. Algebraic Domain Equations. In [EL82], 1982.

[Ehr82b] Hans-Dieter Ehrich. Operational Aspects of Algebraic Specifications. In [EL82], 1982.

[Ehr82c] Hartmut Ehrig. ACT - Algebraic Specification Technique for the Correct Design of Reliable Software Systems. In [EL82], 1982.

[Ehr82d] Hartmut Ehrig. Parameterized Data Types and Parameter Passing. In [EL82], 1982.

[Ehr84] Hans-Dieter Ehrich. Algebraic (?) Specification of Conceptual Database Schemata. In [Kre85], pp. 22-27, 1984.

[Ehr86a] Hans-Dieter Ehrich. Towards an Algebraic Semantics for Databases. In [DEGL86], 1986.

[Ehr86b] Hartmut Ehrig. Towards an Algebraic Semantics of the ISO Specification Language LOTOS. In [DEGL86], 1986.

[Ehr88] Hartmut Ehrig, editor. *Participants' Handout of the 6th Workshop on Abstract Data Type.* University of Berlin, Department of Computer Science, 1988. Internal Report.

[EJO92] Hartmut Ehrig, Rosa Jimenez, and Fernando Orejas. Compositionality Results for Different Types of Parameterization and Parameter Passing in Specification Languages. In [Ore92], 1992.

[EJOR91] Hartmut Ehrig, Klaus-Peter Jantke, Fernando Orejas, and Horst Reichel, editors. *Recent Trends in Data Type Specification.* Springer, Berlin, 1991. LNCS 534.

[EL82] Hans-Dieter Ehrich and Udo Walter Lipeck, editors. *Participants' Handout of the 1st Workshop on Abstract Data Type.* University of Dortmund, Department of Computer Science, 1982. Internal Report.

[ELO94] Hartmut Ehrig, Michael Loewe, and Fernando Orejas. Dynamic Abstract Data Types Based on Algebraic Graph Transformations. This volume, pp. 236-254, 1994.

[EO94] Hartmut Ehrig and Fernando Orejas, editors. *Recent Trends in Data Type Specification.* Springer, Berlin, 1994. LNCS 785.

[EPP90] Hartmut Ehrig and Francesco Parisi-Presicce. A Match Operation for Rule-Based Modular System Design. In [EJOR91], pp. 74-97, 1990.

[EPP91] Hartmut Ehrig and Francesco Parisi-Presicce. Non-Equivalence of Categories for Equational Algebraic Specifications. In [BC93], pp. 222-235, 1991.

[EPPB⁺87] Hartmut Ehrig, Francesco Parisi-Presicce, Paul Boehm, Catharina Rieckhoff, Christian Dimitrovici, and Martin Grosse-Rhode. Algebraic Data

Type and Process Specifications based on Projection Spaces. In [ST88b], pp. 23-43, 1987.

[EPR92] Hartmut Ehrig, Julia Padberg, and Leila Ribeiro. Algebraic High-Level Nets: Petri Nets Revisited. In [EO94], pp. 188-206, 1992.

[ES94] Hans-Dieter Ehrich and Amilcar Sernadas. Local Specification of Distributed Families of Sequential Objects. This volume, pp. 219-235, 1994.

[ESS88] Hans-Dieter Ehrich, Amilcar Sernadas, and Cristina Sernadas. Objects and Object Types. In [Ehr88], 1988.

[EW84] Hartmut Ehrig and Herbert Weber. Algebraic Specifications of Modules. In [KW84], 1984.

[Fau94] Joachim Faulhaber. Better Software through Formal Methods: Development of a Universal Formatting Tool. In [ACR94], 1994.

[FC88] Jordi Farres-Casals. Proving Constructor Implementations in Two Steps. In [Ehr88], 1988.

[FC91] Jordi Farres-Casals. Treating Abstraction as Hiding. In [BC91], 1991.

[FC94] Jose Fiadeiro and Jose Felix Costa. Institutions for Behaviour Specification. This volume, pp. 273-289, 1994.

[FCSM91] Jose Fiadeiro, Jose Felix Costa, Amilcar Sernadas, and Tom S.E. Maibaum. Process Semantics of Temporal Logic Specifications. In [BC93], pp. 236-253, 1991.

[FEHL88] Werner Fey, Hartmut Ehrig, Horst Hansen, and Michael Loewe. Algebraic Theory of Modular Specification Development. In [Ehr88], 1988.

[Fen90] Yulin Feng. A Temporal Approach to Algebraic Specifications. In [JR90], 1990.

[Fey82] Werner Fey. From Requirements to Design Specification. In [EL82], 1982.

[Fey86] Werner Fey. The Module Specification Language ACT TWO. In [DEGL86], 1986.

[Fey87] Werner Fey. Syntax and Semantics of ACT TWO. In [San87], 1987.

[Fey90] Werner Fey. Algebraic Specification of Modules and Configuration Families. In [JR90], 1990.

[Fey91] Werner Fey. ACT TWO in a Specification Logic. In [BC91], 1991.

[Fey92] Werner Fey. Structured Relationship between Algebraic Module Specifications and Program Modules. In [Ore92], 1992.

[FHLL90] Juergen Fuchs, Annette Hoffmann, Thomas Lehmann, and Jacques Loeckx. The Specification System OBSCURE. In [JR90], 1990.

[FJ94] M. Fernandez and Jean-Pierre Jouannaud. Modular Termination of Term Rewriting Systems Revisited. This volume, pp. 255-272, 1994.

[Fon87] Harald-Reto Fonio. Simulation of Predicate-Event Nets by Term Rewriting and some Related Problems. In [San87], 1987.

[Fon88] Harald-Reto Fonio. Abelian Monoids versus Concurrency - An Algebraic Approach to the Specification of Distributed Systems. In [Ehr88], 1988.

[Fre94] Oyvind B. Fredriksen. From Sets with Structure to Algebras with Structure. In [ACR94], 1994.

[FS87] Jose Fiadeiro and Amilcar Sernadas. Structuring Theories on Consequence. In [ST88b], pp. 44-72, 1987.

[Gab91] Peter Gabriel. The Object-Based Specification Language PI: Concepts, Syntax, and Semantics. In [BC93], pp. 254-270, 1991.

[Gan82] Harald Ganzinger. Parameterized Specifications - Parameterized Passing and Implementation with Respect to Observability. In [EL82], 1982.

[Gan83] Harald Ganzinger. Modular Compiler Descriptions based on Abstract Semantic Data Types. In [BW83b], 1983.

[Gan84] Harald Ganzinger. Modular Logic Programming of Compilers. In [KW84], 1984.

[Gan86] Harald Ganzinger. Knuth-Bendix Completion for Parametric Specifications with Conditional Equations. In [DEGL86], 1986.

[Gan87] Harald Ganzinger. Completion with History-Dependent Complexities for Generated Equations. In [ST88b], pp. 73-91, 1987.

[Gan92] Harald Ganzinger. Solving Set Constraints by Ordered Resolution. In [Ore92], 1992.

[Gau92] Marie-Claude Gaudel. Structuring and Modularizing Algebraic Specifications: Evolutions of the PLUSS Specification Language. In [Ore92], 1992.

[GC94] Martin Gogolla and Maura Cerioli. What is an Abstract Data Type, after all? This volume, pp. 488-512, 1994.

[GD92] Joseph A. Goguen and Razvan Diaconescu. Towards an Algebraic Semantics for the Object Paradigm. In [EO94], pp. 1-29, 1992.

[GH94] Martin Gogolla and Rudolf Herzig. An Algebraic Semantics for the Object Specification Language TROLL light. This volume, pp. 290-306, 1994.

[GM94] Joseph A. Goguen and Grant Malcolm. Correctness of Object Refinement. In [ACR94], 1994.

[Goe83] Richard Goebel. Rewrite Rules with Conditions for Algebraic Specifications. In [BW83b], 1983.

[Gog83] Martin Gogolla. Algebraic Specification of Subsorts. In [BW83b], 1983.

[Gog84] Martin Gogolla. A Final Algebra Semantics for Errors and Exceptions. In [Kre85], pp. 89-103, 1984.

[Gog86] Martin Gogolla. Exception Handling and Subsorts. In [DEGL86], 1986.

[GP83] Ulrich Grude and Peter Padawitz. Initial and Fixpoint Semantics of Algebraic Specifications. In [BW83b], 1983.

[GR90] Martin Grosse-Rhode. Towards Object-Oriented Algebraic Specifications. In [EJOR91], pp. 98-116, 1990.

[GR92] Radu Grosu and Franz Regensburger. The Logical Framework of SPECTRUM. In [Ore92], 1992.

[Gra88] John W. Gray. Executable Specifications for Data Type Constructors. In [Ehr88], 1988.

[Gra90] Bernhard Gramlich. Completion Based Inductive Proving with UNICOM. In [JR90], 1990.

[Gru84] Ulrich Grude. Algebraic Specifications of AG Compilers. In [KW84], 1984.

[GRW92] Martin Grosse-Rhode and Uwe Wolter. Two-Categorical Specification of Partial Algebras. In [EO94], pp. 207-219, 1992.

[Gui83] Gerard Guiho. Multi-Operator Algebras. In [BW83b], 1983.

[Han86] Horst Hansen. From Algebraic Specifications towards Algebraic Programs. In [DEGL86], 1986.

[Han87] Horst Hansen. The ACT System: Experiences and Future Enhancements. In [ST88b], pp. 113-130, 1987.

[Han88] Michael Hanus. Horn Clause Specifications with Polymorphic Types. In [Ehr88], 1988.

[Han92] Michael Hanus. Operational Semantics of Equational Logic Languages. In [Ore92], 1992.

[Har87] Robert Harper. Institutions and the Edinburgh Logical Framework. In [San87], 1987.

[Hav87] Magne Haveraaen. WP Observational Algebra Specification. In [San87], 1987.

[Hav88] Magne Haveraaen. The PAL Module Concept. In [Ehr88], 1988.

[Hav90] Magne Haveraaen. Non-Deterministic Imperative Algebras? In [JR90], 1990.

[Hav91] Magne Haveraaen. An Algebraic Interpretation of Computer Programs. In [BC91], 1991.

[Hax88] Anne Haxthausen. Mutually Recursive Algebraic Domain Equations. In [Ehr88], 1988.

[Hax91] Anne Haxthausen. The RAISE Specification Language and Method. In [BC91], 1991.

[HBW94] Rolf Hennicker, Michel Bidoit, and Martin Wirsing. Characterizing Behavioural and Abstractor Specifications. In [ACR94], 1994.

[Hen86] Rolf Hennicker. An Implementation Concept for Observational Specifications. In [DEGL86], 1986.

[Hen87] Rolf Hennicker. Towards a Kernel Language for Reusable Components. In [San87], 1987.

[Her92] C. Hermida. On Fibred Adjunctions and Completeness for Fibred Categories. In [EO94], pp. 235-251, 1992.

[HHHL92] Andreas Heckler, Rudolf Hettler, Heinrich Hussmann, and Jacques Loeckx. The Specification and Prototyping of a LEX-Like Scanner - A Comparative Case Study in the Languages SPECTRUM and OBSCURE. In [Ore92], 1992.

[Hin92] Claus Hintermeier. Matching and Unification in G-Algebra. In [Ore92], 1992.

[HK88] Dieter Hofbauer and Ralf-Detlef Kutsche. Proving Inductive Theorems in Equational Theories. In [Ehr88], 1988.

[HKK94] Claus Hintermeier, Claude Kirchner, and Helene Kirchner. Sort Inheritance for Order-Sorted Equational Presentations. This volume, pp. 319-335, 1994.

[HKLR83] Klaus-Peter Hasler, Hans-Joerg Kreowski, Michael Loewe, and Michaela Reisin. Suggestions on the Interpretation of Algebraic Specifications. In [BW83b], 1983.

[HKP87] Annegret Habel, Hans-Joerg Kreowski, and Detlef Plump. Jungle Evaluation. In [ST88b], pp. 92-112, 1987.

[HL94] Jean-Michel Hufflen and Nicole Levy. The Algebraic Specification Language GLIDER: A Two-Level Language. In [ACR94], 1994.

[HLR82] Klaus-Peter Hasler, Michael Loewe, and Michaela Reisin. An Interpreter for Algebraic Specifications with User Controlled Termination. In [EL82], 1982.

[HM84] Klaus-Peter Hasler and Jan De Meer. OSI Transport Service Considered as an Abstract Data Type. In [Kre85], pp. 104-118, 1984.

[HMK94] Magne Haveraaen and Hans Munthe-Kaas. SOPHUS: A Tool for Solving Partial Differential Equations. In [ACR94], 1994.

[HMMK92] Magne Haveraaen, Victor Madsen, and Hans Munthe-Kaas. Algebraic Programming Technology for Partial Differential Equations. In [Ore92], 1992.

[HN92] Rolf Hennicker and Friederike Nickl. A Behavioural Algebraic Framework for Modular System Design with Reuse. In [EO94], pp. 220-234, 1992.

[Hoh83] B. Hohlfeld. Implementation of Abstract Data Types in PASCAL Programs. In [BW83b], 1983.

[HR94] U. Hensel and Horst Reichel. Defining Equations in Terminal Co-Algebras. This volume, pp. 307-318, 1994.

[Hui87] Lin Huimin. Relative Completeness in Algebraic Specifications. In [San87], 1987.

[Hus88] Heinrich Hussmann. Prototyping Non-Deterministic Algebraic Specifications using the RAP System. In [Ehr88], 1988.

[Hus92] Heinrich Hussmann. An Informal Introduction to the Axiomatic Specification Language SPECTRUM. In [Ore92], 1992.

[Hus94] Heinrich Hussmann. Axiomatic Specification of Large Information Systems: Experiences and Consequences. This volume, pp. 336-350, 1994.

[HW84] Rolf Hennicker and Martin Wirsing. Observational Specification: A Birkhoff Theorem. In [Kre85], pp. 119-135, 1984.

[Ion94] Dan Ionescu. A Temporal Logic Approach to the Design of Real-Time Programs. In [ACR94], 1994.

[Jan86] Klaus P. Jantke. Recursion-Theoretic Problems in Abstract Data Type Theory. In [DEGL86], 1986.

[Jan88] Klaus P. Jantke. On Solving Divergence in Knuth-Bendix Completion. In [Ehr88], 1988.

[JM88] Dean Jacobs and Bernd Mahr. Concepts of Algebraic Database Programming Languages. In [Ehr88], 1988.

[Jou83] Jean-Pierre Jouannaud. Programming and Checking Data Types with REVE. In [BW83b], 1983.

[Jou91] Jean-Pierre Jouannaud. Recent Results on Term Rewriting. In [BC91], 1991.

[Jou92] Jean-Pierre Jouannaud. Rewriting Techniques for Software Engineering. In [EO94], pp. 30-52, 1992.

[JR90] Klaus-Peter Jantke and Horst Reichel, editors. *Participants' Handout of the 7th Workshop on Abstract Data Type.* University of Leipzig, Department of Computer Science, 1990. Internal Report.

[Kap84] Stephan Kaplan. Fair Conditional Term Rewriting Systems: Unification, Termination, and Confluence. In [Kre85], pp. 136-155, 1984.

[Kap87] Stephan Kaplan. Algebraic Specification of Concurrent Systems: A Proposal. In [San87], 1987.

[Kaz90] Edmund Kazmierczak. Modelling Algebraic Theories in Categories Derived from Lambda Algebras. In [JR90], 1990.

[Kaz91] Edmund Kazmierczak. Towards Institution-Dependent Tools for Extended ML: An Institution for Extended ML. In [BC91], 1991.

[KB84] Bernd Krieg-Brueckner. Transformation of Interface Specifications. In [Kre85], pp. 156-170, 1984.

[KB91] Bernd Krieg-Brueckner. The COMPASS Working Group. In [BC91], 1991.

[Kir92] Helene Kirchner. On Primal Algebras and Deduction with Constraints. In [Ore92], 1992.

[KK91] Claude Kirchner and Helene Kirchner. Order-Sorted Rewriting and Completion in G-Algebra. In [BC91], 1991.

[Kla82] Herbert Klaeren. Parameterized Software Specifications with Inductively Defined Operations. In [EL82], 1982.

[Kla83] Herbert Klaeren. Some Thoughts on Practical Usefulness of Operational and Initial Semantics for Algebraic Software Specifications. In [BW83b], 1983.

[KM92] Hans-Joerg Kreowski and Till Mossakowski. Based Algebras and Horn Clause Theories. In [Ore92], 1992.

[Kna91] Teodor Knapik. Specifications with Observable Formulae and Observational Satisfaction Relation. In [BC93], pp. 271-291, 1991.

[Kna94] Teodor Knapik. Specifying Concurrent and Real-Time Systems in Many-Sorted First-Order Logic. In [ACR94], 1994.

[Kre82] Hans-Joerg Kreowski. An Algebraic Implementation Concept for Abstract Data Types. In [EL82], 1982.

[Kre83] Hans-Joerg Kreowski. Specification of Partial Functions - Only a Tentative Suggestion. In [BW83b], 1983.

[Kre84] Hans-Joerg Kreowski. Nets Meet Algebra. In [KW84], 1984.

[Kre85] Hans-Joerg Kreowski, editor. *Recent Trends in Data Type Specification.* Springer, Berlin, 1985. Informatik Fachberichte 116.

[Kre86] Hans-Joerg Kreowski. Based Algebras. In [DEGL86], 1986.

[Kre88] Hans-Joerg Kreowski. Complexity in Algebraic Specifications: An Upper Bound Result. In [Ehr88], 1988.

[Kre91a] Harro Kremer. Design Criteria for, and Experience with, the Use of ADTs in Large LOTOS Specifications. In [BC91], 1991.

[Kre91b] Hans-Joerg Kreowski. Parameterized Specifications with Polymorphic Naming. In [BC91], 1991.

[Kre94] Hans-Joerg Kreowski. Rewriting and Deduction in a Distributed Specification. In [ACR94], 1994.

[KW84] Hans-Joerg Kreowski and Anne Wilharm, editors. *Participants' Handout of the 3rd Workshop on Abstract Data Type.* University of Bremen, Department of Computer Science, 1984. Informatik-Bericht Nr. 9/84.

[LA92] Jordi Levy and Jaume Agusti. Implementing Inequality and Non-Deterministic Specifications with Bi-Rewriting Systems. In [EO94], pp. 252-267, 1992.

[LE83] Udo Lipeck and Hans-Dieter Ehrich. Algebraic Specifications of Database Constraints. In [BW83b], 1983.

[Leh90] Thomas Lehmann. A Notion of Implementation for the Specification Language OBSCURE. In [EJOR91], pp. 141-165, 1990.

[Ler83] Claus-Werner Lermen. OBSCURE - A Language for Algorithmic Specifications. In [BW83b], 1983.

[Les91] Pierre Lescanne. A Survey of Recent Results on Termination of Rewrite Systems. In [BC91], 1991.

[Lev91] Nicole Levy. Using Operators to Construct a Specification. In [BC91], 1991.

[LH88] Jacques Loeckx and Annette Hoffmann. Verification in OBSCURE. In [Ehr88], 1988.

[Lic83] Franz Lichtenberger. A Remark on two Strategies for Software Development: Hoare-Like Verification and Algebraic Implementation. In [BW83b], 1983.

[Lic84] Franz Lichtenberger. Problem Types, Data Types, Algorithm Types: Some Examples. In [KW84], 1984.

[Lip82] Udo Lipeck. Composition and Implementation of Parameterized Data Types. In [EL82], 1982.

[Lip86] Udo Lipeck. On the Semantics of the Frame Rule. In [DEGL86], 1986.

[Liu92] Junbo Liu. A Semantic Basis of Logic-Independent Transformation. In [EO94], pp. 268-279, 1992.

[LJ90] Steffen Lange and Klaus P. Jantke. Inductive Completion for Transformation of Equational Specifications. In [EJOR91], pp. 117-140, 1990.

[LL84] Claus-Werner Lermen and Jacques Loeckx. OBSCURE, A New Specification Language. In [Kre85], pp. 28-30, 1984.

[LL87] Thomas Lehmann and Jacques Loeckx. The Specification Language of OBSCURE. In [ST88b], pp. 131-153, 1987.

[LL91] Thomas Lehmann and Jacques Loeckx. A Calculus for Specification Languages. In [BC91], 1991.

[LLW94] Ulrike Lechner, Christian Lengauer, and Martin Wirsing. An Object-Oriented Airport: Specification and Refinement in Maude. This volume, pp. 351-367, 1994.

[Loe82] Jacques Loeckx. The Description of Programming Languages and the Verification of their Compilers with the Help of Algorithmic Specifications of Abstract Data Types. In [EL82], 1982.

[Loe83] Jacques Loeckx. Program Verification with fewer Tears. In [BW83b], 1983.

[Loe86] Jacques Loeckx. The Specification Language OBSCURE. In [DEGL86], 1986.

[Loe87] Michael Loewe. Using Graph Reduction as Operational Semantics for Algebraic Specifications. In [San87], 1987.

[Loe90] Michael Loewe. Initial Semantics for Algebraic Specifications with Interface. In [JR90], 1990.

[Lue92] Christoph Lueth. Categorical Compositional Term Rewriting in Structured Algebraic Specifications. In [Ore92], 1992.

[Luf83] Alfred Luft. Scientific-Theoretic Foundations of the Concept of Abstract Data Type. In [BW83b], 1983.

[Luo91] Zhaohui Luo. Program Specification and Data Refinement in Type Theory. In [BC91], 1991.

[LW94] Jacques Loeckx and Markus Wolf. Constructive Specifications are Initial Specifications are Loose Specifications. In [ACR94], 1994.

[Mah84] Bernd Mahr. Three Remarks on the Equational Calculus. In [KW84], 1984.

[Mah86] Bernd Mahr. Term Evaluation in Partial Algebras. In [DEGL86], 1986.

[Mai83] Tom S.E. Maibaum. Structuring of Specifications within a Logical Theory of Data Types. In [BW83b], 1983.

[Mai86] Tom S.E. Maibaum. Modular Construction of Logics for Specification. In [DEGL86], 1986.

[Mai88] Tom S.E. Maibaum. Configuration versus Use: Specification Languages versus Logics. In [Ehr88], 1988.

[Man86] Vincenzo Manca. Specification of Abstract Data Types with Experiments. In [DEGL86], 1986.

[Mau86] Giancarlo Mauri. OBJ-SAN: Towards the Definition of a Class of High-Level Nets using OBJ2. In [DEGL86], 1986.

[May82] Heinrich C. Mayr. ORS Specifications: Ideas, Application Examples, and Experiences. In [EL82], 1982.

[MC91] Mila E. Majster-Cederbaum. On the Relation between CPO-Based and Metric Space-Based Semantics for Communicating Sequential Processes. In [BC91], 1991.

[MD84] Bernhard Moeller and W. Dosch. On the Algebraic Specification of Domains. In [Kre85], pp. 178-195, 1984.

[Mei90] Karl Meinke. Universal Algebra in Higher Types. In [EJOR91], pp. 185-203, 1990.

[Mei92] Karl Meinke. Algebraic Specification of Types and Combinators. In [Ore92], 1992.

[Mei94] Karl Meinke. Topological Methods for Algebraic Specifications. This volume, pp. 368-388, 1994.

[Mig84] Pierangelo Miglioli. Abstract Data Types and Constructivism. In [KW84], 1984.

[MJ94] Anamaria Martins and Paul Jacquet. Generalizing Algebraic Specification Components. In [ACR94], 1994.

[MMO94] Jose Meseguer and N. Marti-Oliet. From Abstract Data Types to Logical Frameworks. This volume, pp. 48-80, 1994.

[Moe83] Bernhard Moeller. Ordered and Continuous Models of Algebraic Types. In [BW83b], 1983.

[Moe86] Bernhard Moeller. Algebraic Specifications with Higher-Order Operations. In [DEGL86], 1986.

[Mos86] Peter D. Mosses. Action Semantics. In [DEGL86], 1986.

[Mos87] Peter D. Mosses. Combining Facets of Actions. In [San87], 1987.

[Mos88] Peter D. Mosses. Unified Algebras. In [Ehr88], 1988.

[Mos91] Peter D. Mosses. The Use of Sorts in Algebraic Specifications. In [BC93], pp. 66-92, 1991.

[Mos92] Peter D. Mosses. Unified Algebras and Abstract Syntax. In [EO94], pp. 280-294, 1992.

[Mos94a] Till Mossakowski. A Hierarchy of Institutions Separated by Properties of Parameterized Abstract Data Types. This volume, pp. 389-405, 1994.

[Mos94b] Peter D. Mosses. Unified Algebras Revisited. In [ACR94], 1994.

[MS84] Tom S.E. Maibaum and Martin Sadler. Axiomatizing Specification Theory. In [Kre85], pp. 171-177, 1984.

[MS87] Vincenzo Manca and Antonino Salibra. Soundness and Completeness of Many-Sorted Birkhoff's Equational Calculus. In [San87], 1987.

[MSS90] Vincenzo Manca, Antonino Salibra, and Giuseppe Scollo. ADT Specification Constructs for Equational Type Logic. In [JR90], 1990.

[MT92] Brian McConnel and John V. Tucker. Direct Limits of Algebras and the Parameterization of Synchronous Concurrent Algorithms. In [Ore92], 1992.

[MTW87] Bernhard Moeller, Andrzej Tarlecki, and Martin Wirsing. Algebraic Specifications of Reachable Higher-Order Algebras. In [ST88b], pp. 154-169, 1987.

[MV90] Gianfranco F. Mascari and Antonio Vincenzi. Model-Theoretic Specifications and Back-and-Forth Equivalences. In [EJOR91], pp. 166-184, 1990.

[MW94] Sigurd Meldal and Michal Walicki. Reasoning with Non-Determinism: Some Examples. In [ACR94], 1994.

[Nic86] Friederike Nickl. On the Solution of Recursive Domain Equations Inside an Algebraic Framework. In [DEGL86], 1986.

[Nic88] Friederike Nickl. Order-Theoretic Specification of Algebras with Non-Monotonic Operations. In [Ehr88], 1988.

[Nip86] Tobias N. Nipkow. Behavioural Implementations of Non-Deterministic Data Types. In [DEGL86], 1986.

[Nip87] Tobias N. Nipkow. Observing Non-Deterministic Data Types. In [ST88b], pp. 170-183, 1987.

[Nis87] Celso Niskier. Using Multiple Views for Software Specifications. In [San87], 1987.

[NO87] Maria Pilar Nivela and Fernando Orejas. Initial Behaviour Semantics for Algebraic Specifications. In [ST88b], pp. 184-207, 1987.

[NO88] Maria Pilar Nivela and Fernando Orejas. A Module Concept within the Initial Behaviour Framework. In [Ehr88], 1988.

[NO90] Robert Nieuwenhuis and Fernando Orejas. Clausal Rewriting: Applications and Implementation. In [EJOR91], pp. 204-219, 1990.

[Nou83a] F. Nourani. Abstract Models for Types, Induction, and Proofs. In [BW83b], 1983.

[Nou83b] F. Nourani. Forcing with Universal Sentences and Genericity of Inductive Closures. In [BW83b], 1983.

[NQ92] Tobias N. Nipkow and Zhenyu Qian. Reduction and Unification in Lambda Calculi with Subtypes. In [Ore92], 1992.

[ON90] Fernando Orejas and Maria Pilar Nivela. Constraints for Behavioural Specifications. In [EJOR91], pp. 220-245, 1990.

[ONS91] Fernando Orejas, M. Navarro, and A. Sanchez. Implementation and Behavioural Equivalence: A Survey. In [BC93], pp. 93-125, 1991.

[OPE94] Fernando Orejas, Elvira Pino, and Hartmut Ehrig. Algebraic Methods in the Compositional Analysis of Logic Programs. In [ACR94], 1994.

[Ore83] Fernando Orejas. Some Results on Finite Specifiability of Parameterized Data Types. In [BW83b], 1983.

[Ore84] Fernando Orejas. Passing Compatibility is almost Persistency. In [Kre85], pp. 196-206, 1984.

[Ore86] Fernando Orejas. A Proof-Theoretic Characterization of Persistency for Parameterized Specifications with Boolean Constraints. In [DEGL86], 1986.

[Ore92] Fernando Orejas, editor. *Participants' Handout of the 9th Workshop on Abstract Data Type.* University of Barcelona, Department of Computer Science, 1992. Internal Report.

[OSN+88] Fernando Orejas, A. Sanchez, M. Navarro, Maria Pilar Nivela, and Ricardo Pena. Term Rewriting Methods for Partial Specifications. In [Ehr88], 1988.

[Owe92] Olaf Owe. Partial Logics Reconsidered: A Conservative Approach. In [Ore92], 1992.

[Owe94] Olaf Owe. On Monotonicity in Process Logic. In [ACR94], 1994.

[Pad82] Peter Padawitz. On the Proof of Completeness and Consistency. In [EL82], 1982.

[Pad84] Peter Padawitz. On Logic Programming with Abstract Data Type. In [KW84], 1984.

[Pad86] Peter Padawitz. The Use of Terminal Semantics for Disproving Inductive Theorems. In [DEGL86], 1986.

[Pad88] Peter Padawitz. Inductive Expansion. In [Ehr88], 1988.

[Pad91] Peter Padawitz. On Refinement Proofs. In [BC91], 1991.

[Pad92] Peter Padawitz. Prototyping Specifications with EXPANDER - State of the Art. In [Ore92], 1992.

[Pad94] Peter Padawitz. Proof by Narrowing. In [ACR94], 1994.

[Par83] Helmut Partsch. Algebraic Specification of a Text Editor. In [BW83b], 1983.

[Pep82] Peter Pepper. On the Algebraic Specification of Programming Languages. In [EL82], 1982.

[Pep83] Peter Pepper. Correctness of Type Transformations. In [BW83b], 1983.

[Pep88] Peter Pepper. An Algebraic View of Local Formalisms. In [Ehr88], 1988.

[Pet84] Heiko Petzsch. Automatic Prototyping of Algebraic Specifications using PROLOG. In [Kre85], pp. 207-223, 1984.

[Ple82] Udo Pletat. Ideas for the Development of Software Systems on the Basis of Algebraic Specifications. In [EL82], 1982.

[Ple86] Udo Pletat. Algebraic Specifications of Abstract Data Types and CCS: An Operational Junction. In [DEGL86], 1986.

[Ple87] Udo Pletat. Abstract Data Types Meet Knowledge Representation for Natural Language Understanding. In [San87], 1987.

[PM83] W. Di Palma and Gianfranco F. Mascari. Abstract Data Types and Categorical Logic. In [BW83b], 1983.

[Poi83] Axel Poigne. Programs over Abstract Data Types. In [BW83b], 1983.

[Poi84] Axel Poigne. Error Handling for Parameterized Data Types. In [Kre85], pp. 224-239, 1984.

[Poi86] Axel Poigne. Error Handling as Type Checking. In [DEGL86], 1986.

[Poi87] Axel Poigne. Partial Algebras, Subsorting, and Dependent Types: Prerequisites of Error Handling in Algebraic Specifications. In [ST88b], pp. 208-234, 1987.

[Poi88] Axel Poigne. Towards a Unified Logic for Specification and Programming. In [Ehr88], 1988.

[Poi91] Axel Poigne. Order-Sorted Algebras Revisited. In [BC91], 1991.

[Poi92] Axel Poigne. Identity and Existence, and Types in Algebra - A Survey of Sorts. In [EO94], pp. 53-78, 1992.

[PPP92] Francesco Parisi-Presicce and Alfonso Pierantonio. Structured Inheritance for Algebraic Class Specifications. In [EO94], pp. 295-309, 1992.

[PPP94a] Francesco Parisi-Presicce and Alfonso Pierantonio. Dynamical Behavior of Object Systems. This volume, pp. 406-419, 1994.

[PPP94b] Alfonso Pierantonio and Francesco Parisi-Presicce. Object Dynamics in Class Based Systems. In [ACR94], 1994.

[Qia88] Zhenyu Qian. Parameterization of Order-Sorted Algebraic Specifications with Built-In Coercers. In [Ehr88], 1988.

[Qui88] Gloria Quintanilla. Prototyping of Z Specifications in ML. In [Ehr88], 1988.

[RACF94] Gianna Reggio, Egidio Astesiano, Ernani Crivelli, and Valeria Filippi. Real Systems may be Effectively Formally Specified. In [ACR94], 1994.

[Rap91] Lucia Rapanotti. About Object-Oriented Nets. In [BC91], 1991.

[Reg90] Gianna Reggio. Entities: An Institution for Dynamic Systems. In [EJOR91], pp. 246-265, 1990.

[Reg91] Gianna Reggio. Event Logic for Specifying Abstract Dynamic Data Types. In [BC93], pp. 292-309, 1991.

[Rei86] Horst Reichel. Computable Functional Enrichments of Parameterized Behavioural Data Types. In [DEGL86], 1986.

[Rei87] Horst Reichel. Operational Semantics of Behavioural Canons based on Narrowing. In [ST88b], pp. 235-248, 1987.

[Rei90a] Horst Reichel. A Two-Category Approach to Critical Pair Completion. In [EJOR91], pp. 266-273, 1990.

[Rei90b] Alestair Reid. Access and Information: A Paradigm for Data Structure Design. In [JR90], 1990.

[Rei92a] Horst Reichel. First-Order Specification of Infinite Objects. In [Ore92], 1992.

[Rei92b] Wolfgang Reif. Reuse of Proofs in Software Verification. In [Ore92], 1992.

[Rem83] Jean-Luc Remy. Specifications of Errors in Data Types using Conditional Axioms. In [BW83b], 1983.

[Rie92] Catharina Rieckhoff. Towards a Theory for the Animation of Algebraic Specification. In [EO94], pp. 310-320, 1992.

[Run86] Colin Runciman. Deriving Functional Programs from Equational Specifications. In [DEGL86], 1986.

[Ryc87] Marek Rycko. Mathematics versus Implementation of Partial Evaluators. In [San87], 1987.

[Sad86] Martin Sadler. A Defense of Proof Theory as the Right Foundations. In [DEGL86], 1986.

[San87] Don Sannella, editor. *Participants' Handout of the 5th Workshop on Abstract Data Type*. University of Edinburgh, Department of Computer Science, 1987. Report No. ECS-LFCS-87-41.

[Sch83] Oliver Schoett. Is Data Abstraction Sound? In [BW83b], 1983.

[Sch84a] Heinz-Wilhelm Schmidt. Abstract Types of Behaviour: Petri Nets and ADT. In [KW84], 1984.

[Sch84b] Oliver Schoett. Distinguishing Strong and Weak Implementations. In [KW84], 1984.

[Sch86] Heinz-Wilhelm Schmidt. Polymorphic Types and Algebraic Specifications. In [DEGL86], 1986.

[Sch87a] Heinz-Wilhelm Schmidt. Predicate-Event Nets for Reasoning about Non-Sequential Behaviour. In [San87], 1987.

[Sch87b] Oliver Schoett. Data Abstraction and the Correctness of Modular Programming. In [San87], 1987.

[Sch90] Oliver Schoett. On the Expressive Power of an Observational First-Order Specification Language for Abstract Data Types. In [JR90], 1990.

[Sch92] Pierre-Yves Schobbens. Second-Order Proof Systems for Algebraic Specification Languages. In [EO94], pp. 321-336, 1992.

[Sco86] Giuseppe Scollo. On Hierarchy, Incompleteness and Exception Handling in Equational Specifications of Abstract Data Types. In [DEGL86], 1986.

[Sco88] Giuseppe Scollo. Typed-Equational Types: Pragmatics. In [Ehr88], 1988.

[Sco92] Giuseppe Scollo. On the Engineering of Logics in Software Engineering. In [Ore92], 1992.

[SCS92] Amilcar Sernadas, Jose Felix Costa, and Cristina Sernadas. An institution of object behaviour. In [EO94], pp. 337-351, 1992.

[Sei92] Richard Seifert. Termination Proofs by Combining Polynomial Interpretation and Recursive Path Ordering. In [Ore92], 1992.

[Shi94] Hui Shi. An Efficient Matching Algoritm for Convergent Rewrite Systems. In [ACR94], 1994.

[SKT94] Don Sannella, Stefan Kahrs, and Andrzej Tarlecki. The Semantics of Extended ML. In [ACR94], 1994.

[Smo86] Gerd Smolka. Polymorphic Order-Sorted Algebra. In [DEGL86], 1986.

[Smo88] Gerd Smolka. Type Logic. In [Ehr88], 1988.

[Sou91] Jeanine Souquieres. A Model for the Expression of the Specification Developments. In [BC91], 1991.

[Spe86] Hansi A. Spec. HANSI Evaluates Algebraic Specifications - You will love it. In [DEGL86], 1986.

[SR94] R. K. Shyamasundar and N. Raja. Type Systems for Mobile Processes. In [ACR94], 1994.

[SS91] Antonino Salibra and Giuseppe Scollo. A Soft Stairway to Institutions. In [BC93], pp. 310-329, 1991.

[SS94] Antonino Salibra and Giuseppe Scollo. Polymorphies = Categories + Algebras. In [ACR94], 1994.

[SSF86] Amilcar Sernadas, Cristina Sernadas, and Jose Fiadeiro. Algebraic Knowledge Representation: The Unification of Procedure, Logic and Structure. In [DEGL86], 1986.

[SSV94] Amilcar Sernadas, Cristina Sernadas, and Jose Manuel Valenca. A Theory-Based Topological Notion of Institution. This volume, pp. 420-436, 1994.

[ST84] Don Sannella and Andrzej Tarlecki. Some Thoughts on Algebraic Specification. In [Kre85], pp. 31-38, 1984.

[ST86] Don Sannella and Andrzej Tarlecki. Extended ML: An Institution-Independent Framework for Formal Program Development. In [DEGL86], 1986.

[ST87] Don Sannella and Andrzej Tarlecki. Implementations Revisited. In [San87], 1987.

[ST88a] Don Sannella and Andrzej Tarlecki. Formal Development of ML Programs: Methodological Aspects. In [Ehr88], 1988.

[ST88b] Don Sannella and Andrzej Tarlecki, editors. *Recent Trends in Data Type Specification*. Springer, Berlin, 1988. LNCS 332.

[ST90a] Don Sannella and Andrzej Tarlecki. A Kernel Specification Formalism with Higher-Order Parameterization. In [EJOR91], pp. 274-296, 1990.

[ST90b] Don Sannella and Andrzej Tarlecki. Extended ML: Past, Present, and Future. In [EJOR91], pp. 297-322, 1990.

[Sta87] Vicki Stavridou. Specification and Verification of Programs using OBJ. In [San87], 1987.

[Str84] Thomas Streicher. Model Theory of Denotational Semantics. In [Kre85], pp. 240-253, 1984.

[SW83] Don Sannella and Martin Wirsing. A Kernel Language for Algebraic Specification and Implementation. In [BW83b], 1983.

[SW90] Thomas Streicher and Martin Wirsing. Dependent Types Considered Necessary for Specification Languages. In [EJOR91], pp. 323-340, 1990.

[SW94] Heinz-Wilhelm Schmidt and Richard Walker. Stable Object-Oriented Interface Constructions. In [ACR94], 1994.

[Tar86] Andrzej Tarlecki. Bits and Pieces of the Theory of Institutions. In [DEGL86], 1986.

[Tar91] Andrzej Tarlecki. Towards Formal Development of Programs from Algebraic Specifications: Where do we stand? In [BC91], 1991.

[Tho86] Muffy Thomas. The Storage and Access Structure of Algebraically Specified Data Types. In [DEGL86], 1986.

[Tho88] Muffy Thomas. Towards a Termination Ordering for Loop Programs. In [Ehr88], 1988.

[TQ88] B.C. Thompson-Quintanilla. Generalized Computable Algebra and Its Application to the Implementation of Abstract Data Types. In [Ehr88], 1988.

[TS94] Andrzej Tarlecki and Marian Srebrny. Tennenbaum's Theorem. In [ACR94], 1994.

[Tse87] T.H. Tse. An Abstract Data Type for Structured System Development Tools. In [San87], 1987.

[Und94] Judith Underwood. Typing Abstract Data Types. This volume, pp. 437-452, 1994.

[Vel83] Paulo Veloso. Problems as Abstract Data Types: Applications to Program Construction. In [BW83b], 1983.

[Vel84] Paulo Veloso. Choosing a Repertoire of Updates. In [KW84], 1984.

[Vra87] Jos L.M. Vrancken. The Algebraic Specification of Semi-Computable Data Types. In [ST88b], pp. 249-259, 1987.

[Vra88] Jos L.M. Vrancken. Parallel Object-Oriented Term Rewriting. In [Ehr88], 1988.

[Wag84] Eric G. Wagner. Categorical Semantics, Or Extending Data Types to Include Memory. In [Kre85], pp. 1-21, 1984.

[Wag87] Eric G. Wagner. Recursive Types and Pointers. In [San87], 1987.

[Wag90] Eric G. Wagner. Generic Types in a Language for Data Directed Design. In [EJOR91], pp. 341-361, 1990.

[Wag91] Eric G. Wagner. Generic Classes in an Object-Based Language. In [BC93], pp. 330-344, 1991.

[Wag92] Eric G. Wagner. Overloading and Inheritance. In [EO94], pp. 79-97, 1992.

[Wag94] Eric G. Wagner. Homomorphic Compilers Utilizing Abstract Data Types. In [ACR94], 1994.

[Whi86] Peter White. Position Paper on Requirement Specification Language Project. In [DEGL86], 1986.

[Wir82] Martin Wirsing. Implementation of Parameterized Hierarchical Specifications. In [EL82], 1982.

[Wir94] Martin Wirsing. Algebraic Specification Languages: An Overview. This volume, pp. 81-115, 1994.

[WM92] Michal Walicki and Sigurd Meldal. Multi-Algebras and Computations: Two Algebraic Semantics of Non-Determinism. In [Ore92], 1992.

[WM94] Michal Walicki and Sigurd Meldal. Multi-Algebras, Power Algebras and Complete Calculi of Identities and Inclusions. This volume, pp. 453-468, 1994.

[Wol88] Dietmar Wolz. Compilation of Algebraic Specifications and Term Rewriting Systems. In [Ehr88], 1988.

[Wol90] Dietmar Wolz. Design of a Compiler for Lazy Pattern Driven Narrowing. In [EJOR91], pp. 362-379, 1990.

[Wol91] Dietmar Wolz. Application of Narrowing for LOTOS Simulation. In [BC91], 1991.

[Wol94] Uwe Wolter. Institutional Frames. This volume, pp. 469-482, 1994.

[WS94] Burkhard Wolff and Hui Shi. A Calculus of Transformations. In [ACR94], 1994.

[WSR88] Eric G. Wagner, F.J. Selker, and J.D. Rutledge. Algebraic Data Types and Object-Oriented Programming. In [Ehr88], 1988.

[Yun86] Wu Yunzeng. On Formalization and Its Related Notions. In [DEGL86], 1986.

[Zuc94] Elena Zucca. Implementation of Data Structures in an Imperative Framework. This volume, pp. 483-487, 1994.

However, the question remains ...

Springer-Verlag and the Environment

We at Springer-Verlag firmly believe that an international science publisher has a special obligation to the environment, and our corporate policies consistently reflect this conviction.

We also expect our business partners – paper mills, printers, packaging manufacturers, etc. – to commit themselves to using environmentally friendly materials and production processes.

The paper in this book is made from low- or no-chlorine pulp and is acid free, in conformance with international standards for paper permanency.

Lecture Notes in Computer Science

For information about Vols. 1–831
please contact your bookseller or Springer-Verlag

Vol. 832: E. Börger, Y. Gurevich, K. Meinke (Eds.), Computer Science Logic. Proceedings, 1993. VIII, 336 pages. 1994.

Vol. 833: D. Driankov, P. W. Eklund, A. Ralescu (Eds.), Fuzzy Logic and Fuzzy Control. Proceedings, 1991. XII, 157 pages. 1994. (Subseries LNAI).

Vol. 834: D.-Z. Du, X.-S. Zhang (Eds.), Algorithms and Computation. Proceedings, 1994. XIII, 687 pages. 1994.

Vol. 835: W. M. Tepfenhart, J. P. Dick, J. F. Sowa (Eds.), Conceptual Structures: Current Practices. Proceedings, 1994. VIII, 331 pages. 1994. (Subseries LNAI).

Vol. 836: B. Jonsson, J. Parrow (Eds.), CONCUR '94: Concurrency Theory. Proceedings, 1994. IX, 529 pages. 1994.

Vol. 837: S. Wess, K.-D. Althoff, M. M. Richter (Eds.), Topics in Case-Based Reasoning. Proceedings, 1993. IX, 471 pages. 1994. (Subseries LNAI).

Vol. 838: C. MacNish, D. Pearce, L. Moniz Pereira (Eds.), Logics in Artificial Intelligence. Proceedings, 1994. IX, 413 pages. 1994. (Subseries LNAI).

Vol. 839: Y. G. Desmedt (Ed.), Advances in Cryptology - CRYPTO '94. Proceedings, 1994. XII, 439 pages. 1994.

Vol. 840: G. Reinelt, The Traveling Salesman. VIII, 223 pages. 1994.

Vol. 841: I. Prívara, B. Rovan, P. Ružička (Eds.), Mathematical Foundations of Computer Science 1994. Proceedings, 1994. X, 628 pages. 1994.

Vol. 842: T. Kloks, Treewidth. IX, 209 pages. 1994.

Vol. 843: A. Szepietowski, Turing Machines with Sublogarithmic Space. VIII, 115 pages. 1994.

Vol. 844: M. Hermenegildo, J. Penjam (Eds.), Programming Language Implementation and Logic Programming. Proceedings, 1994. XII, 469 pages. 1994.

Vol. 845: J.-P. Jouannaud (Ed.), Constraints in Computational Logics. Proceedings, 1994. VIII, 367 pages. 1994.

Vol. 846: D. Shepherd, G. Blair, G. Coulson, N. Davies, F. Garcia (Eds.), Network and Operating System Support for Digital Audio and Video. Proceedings, 1993. VIII, 269 pages. 1994.

Vol. 847: A. L. Ralescu (Ed.) Fuzzy Logic in Artificial Intelligence. Proceedings, 1993. VII, 128 pages. 1994. (Subseries LNAI).

Vol. 848: A. R. Krommer, C. W. Ueberhuber, Numerical Integration on Advanced Computer Systems. XIII, 341 pages. 1994.

Vol. 849: R. W. Hartenstein, M. Z. Servít (Eds.), Field-Programmable Logic. Proceedings, 1994. XI, 434 pages. 1994.

Vol. 850: G. Levi, M. Rodríguez-Artalejo (Eds.), Algebraic and Logic Programming. Proceedings, 1994. VIII, 304 pages. 1994.

Vol. 851: H.-J. Kugler, A. Mullery, N. Niebert (Eds.), Towards a Pan-European Telecommunication Service Infrastructure. Proceedings, 1994. XIII, 582 pages. 1994.

Vol. 852: K. Echtle, D. Hammer, D. Powell (Eds.), Dependable Computing – EDCC-1. Proceedings, 1994. XVII, 618 pages. 1994.

Vol. 853: K. Bolding, L. Snyder (Eds.), Parallel Computer Routing and Communication. Proceedings, 1994. IX, 317 pages. 1994.

Vol. 854: B. Buchberger, J. Volkert (Eds.), Parallel Processing: CONPAR 94 – VAPP VI. Proceedings, 1994. XVI, 893 pages. 1994.

Vol. 855: J. van Leeuwen (Ed.), Algorithms – ESA '94. Proceedings, 1994. X, 510 pages.1994.

Vol. 856: D. Karagiannis (Ed.), Database and Expert Systems Applications. Proceedings, 1994. XVII, 807 pages. 1994.

Vol. 857: G. Tel, P. Vitányi (Eds.), Distributed Algorithms. Proceedings, 1994. X, 370 pages. 1994.

Vol. 858: E. Bertino, S. Urban (Eds.), Object-Oriented Methodologies and Systems. Proceedings, 1994. X, 386 pages. 1994.

Vol. 859: T. F. Melham, J. Camilleri (Eds.), Higher Order Logic Theorem Proving and Its Applications. Proceedings, 1994. IX, 470 pages. 1994.

Vol. 860: W. L. Zagler, G. Busby, R. R. Wagner (Eds.), Computers for Handicapped Persons. Proceedings, 1994. XX, 625 pages. 1994.

Vol: 861: B. Nebel, L. Dreschler-Fischer (Eds.), KI-94: Advances in Artificial Intelligence. Proceedings, 1994. IX, 401 pages. 1994. (Subseries LNAI).

Vol. 862: R. C. Carrasco, J. Oncina (Eds.), Grammatical Inference and Applications. Proceedings, 1994. VIII, 290 pages. 1994. (Subseries LNAI).

Vol. 863: H. Langmaack, W.-P. de Roever, J. Vytopil (Eds.), Formal Techniques in Real-Time and Fault-Tolerant Systems. Proceedings, 1994. XIV, 787 pages. 1994.

Vol. 864: B. Le Charlier (Ed.), Static Analysis. Proceedings, 1994. XII, 465 pages. 1994.

Vol. 865: T. C. Fogarty (Ed.), Evolutionary Computing. Proceedings, 1994. XII, 332 pages. 1994.

Vol. 866: Y. Davidor, H.-P. Schwefel, R. Männer (Eds.), Parallel Problem Solving from Nature - PPSN III. Proceedings, 1994. XV, 642 pages. 1994.

Vol 867: L. Steels, G. Schreiber, W. Van de Velde (Eds.), A Future for Knowledge Acquisition. Proceedings, 1994. XII, 414 pages. 1994. (Subseries LNAI).

Vol. 868: R. Steinmetz (Ed.), Multimedia: Advanced Teleservices and High-Speed Communication Architectures. Proceedings, 1994. IX, 451 pages. 1994.

Vol. 869: Z. W. Raś, Zemankova (Eds.), Methodologies for Intelligent Systems. Proceedings, 1994. X, 613 pages. 1994. (Subseries LNAI).

Vol. 870: J. S. Greenfield, Distributed Programming Paradigms with Cryptography Applications. XI, 182 pages. 1994.

Vol. 871: J. P. Lee, G. G. Grinstein (Eds.), Database Issues for Data Visualization. Proceedings, 1993. XIV, 229 pages. 1994.

Vol. 872: S Arikawa, K. P. Jantke (Eds.), Algorithmic Learning Theory. Proceedings, 1994. XIV, 575 pages. 1994.

Vol. 873: M. Naftalin, T. Denvir, M. Bertran (Eds.), FME '94: Industrial Benefit of Formal Methods. Proceedings, 1994. XI, 723 pages. 1994.

Vol. 874: A. Borning (Ed.), Principles and Practice of Constraint Programming. Proceedings, 1994. IX, 361 pages. 1994.

Vol. 875: D. Gollmann (Ed.), Computer Security – ESORICS 94. Proceedings, 1994. XI, 469 pages. 1994.

Vol. 876: B. Blumenthal, J. Gornostaev, C. Unger (Eds.), Human-Computer Interaction. Proceedings, 1994. IX, 239 pages. 1994.

Vol. 877: L. M. Adleman, M.-D. Huang (Eds.), Algorithmic Number Theory. Proceedings, 1994. IX, 323 pages. 1994.

Vol. 878: T. Ishida; Parallel, Distributed and Multiagent Production Systems. XVII, 166 pages. 1994. (Subseries LNAI).

Vol. 879: J. Dongarra, J. Waśniewski (Eds.), Parallel Scientific Computing. Proceedings, 1994. XI, 566 pages. 1994.

Vol. 880: P. S. Thiagarajan (Ed.), Foundations of Software Technology and Theoretical Computer Science. Proceedings, 1994. XI, 451 pages. 1994.

Vol. 881: P. Loucopoulos (Ed.), Entity-Relationship Approach – ER'94. Proceedings, 1994. XIII, 579 pages. 1994.

Vol. 882: D. Hutchison, A. Danthine, H. Leopold, G. Coulson (Eds.), Multimedia Transport and Teleservices. Proceedings, 1994. XI, 380 pages. 1994.

Vol. 883: L. Fribourg, F. Turini (Eds.), Logic Program Synthesis and Transformation – Meta-Programming in Logic. Proceedings, 1994. IX, 451 pages. 1994.

Vol. 884: J. Nievergelt, T. Roos, H.-J. Schek, P. Widmayer (Eds.), IGIS '94: Geographic Information Systems. Proceedings, 1994. VIII, 292 pages. 1994.

Vol. 885: R. C. Veltkamp, Closed Objects Boundaries from Scattered Points. VIII, 144 pages. 1994.

Vol. 886: M. M. Veloso, Planning and Learning by Analogical Reasoning. XIII, 181 pages. 1994. (Subseries LNAI).

Vol. 887: M. Toussaint (Ed.), Ada in Europe. Proceedings, 1994. XII, 521 pages. 1994.

Vol. 888: S. A. Andersson (Ed.), Analysis of Dynamical and Cognitive Systems. Proceedings, 1993. VII, 260 pages. 1995.

Vol. 889: H. P. Lubich, Towards a CSCW Framework for Scientific Cooperation in Europe. X, 268 pages. 1995.

Vol. 890: M. J. Wooldridge, N. R. Jennings (Eds.), Intelligent Agents. Proceedings, 1994. VIII, 407 pages. 1995. (Subseries LNAI).

Vol. 891: C. Lewerentz, T. Lindner (Eds.), Formal Development of Reactive Systems. XI, 394 pages. 1995.

Vol. 892: K. Pingali, U. Banerjee, D. Gelernter, A. Nicolau, D. Padua (Eds.), Languages and Compilers for Parallel Computing. Proceedings, 1994. XI, 496 pages. 1995.

Vol. 893: G. Gottlob, M. Y. Vardi (Eds.), Database Theory – ICDT '95. Proceedings, 1995. XI, 454 pages. 1995.

Vol. 894: R. Tamassia, I. G. Tollis (Eds.), Graph Drawing. Proceedings, 1994. X, 471 pages. 1995.

Vol. 895: R. L. Ibrahim (Ed.), Software Engineering Education. Proceedings, 1995. XII, 449 pages. 1995.

Vol. 896: R. N. Taylor, J. Coutaz (Eds.), Software Engineering and Human-Computer Interaction. Proceedings, 1994. X, 281 pages. 1995.

Vol. 897: M. Fisher, R. Owens (Eds.), Executable Modal and Temporal Logics. Proceedings, 1993. VII, 180 pages. 1995. (Subseries LNAI).

Vol. 898: P. Steffens (Ed.), Machine Translation and the Lexicon. Proceedings, 1993. X, 251 pages. 1995. (Subseries LNAI).

Vol. 899: W. Banzhaf, F. H. Eeckman (Eds.), Evolution and Biocomputation. VII, 277 pages. 1995.

Vol. 900: E. W. Mayr, C. Puech (Eds.), STACS 95. Proceedings, 1995. XIII, 654 pages. 1995.

Vol. 901: R. Kumar, T. Kropf (Eds.), Theorem Provers in Circuit Design. Proceedings, 1994. VIII, 303 pages. 1995.

Vol. 902: M. Dezani-Ciancaglini, G. Plotkin (Eds.), Typed Lambda Calculi and Applications. Proceedings, 1995. VIII, 443 pages. 1995.

Vol. 903: E. W. Mayr, G. Schmidt, G. Tinhofer (Eds.), Graph-Theoretic Concepts in Computer Science. Proceedings, 1994. IX, 414 pages. 1995.

Vol. 904: P. Vitányi (Ed.), Computational Learning Theory. EuroCOLT'95. Proceedings, 1995. XVII, 415 pages. 1995. (Subseries LNAI).

Vol. 905: N. Ayache (Ed.), Computer Vision, Virtual Reality and Robotics in Medicine. Proceedings, 1995. XIV, 567 pages. 1995.

Vol. 906: E. Astesiano, G. Reggio, A. Tarlecki (Eds.), Recent Trends in Data Type Specification. Proceedings, 1995. VIII, 523 pages. 1995.

Vol. 907: T. Ito, A. Yonezawa (Eds.), Theory and Practice of Parallel Programming. Proceedings, 1995. VIII, 485 pages. 1995.

Vol. 908: J. R. Rao Extensions of the UNITY Methodology: Compositionality, Fairness and Probability in Parallelism. XI, 178 pages. 1995.

Vol. 910: A. Podelski (Ed.), Constraint Programming: Basics and Trends. Proceedings, 1995. XI, 315 pages. 1995.